Women Writers of Traditional China

An Anthology of Poetry and Criticism

EDITED BY
Kang-i Sun Chang and Haun Saussy

Charles Kwong,
ASSOCIATE EDITOR

Anthony C. Yu and Yu-kung Kao,
CONSULTING EDITORS

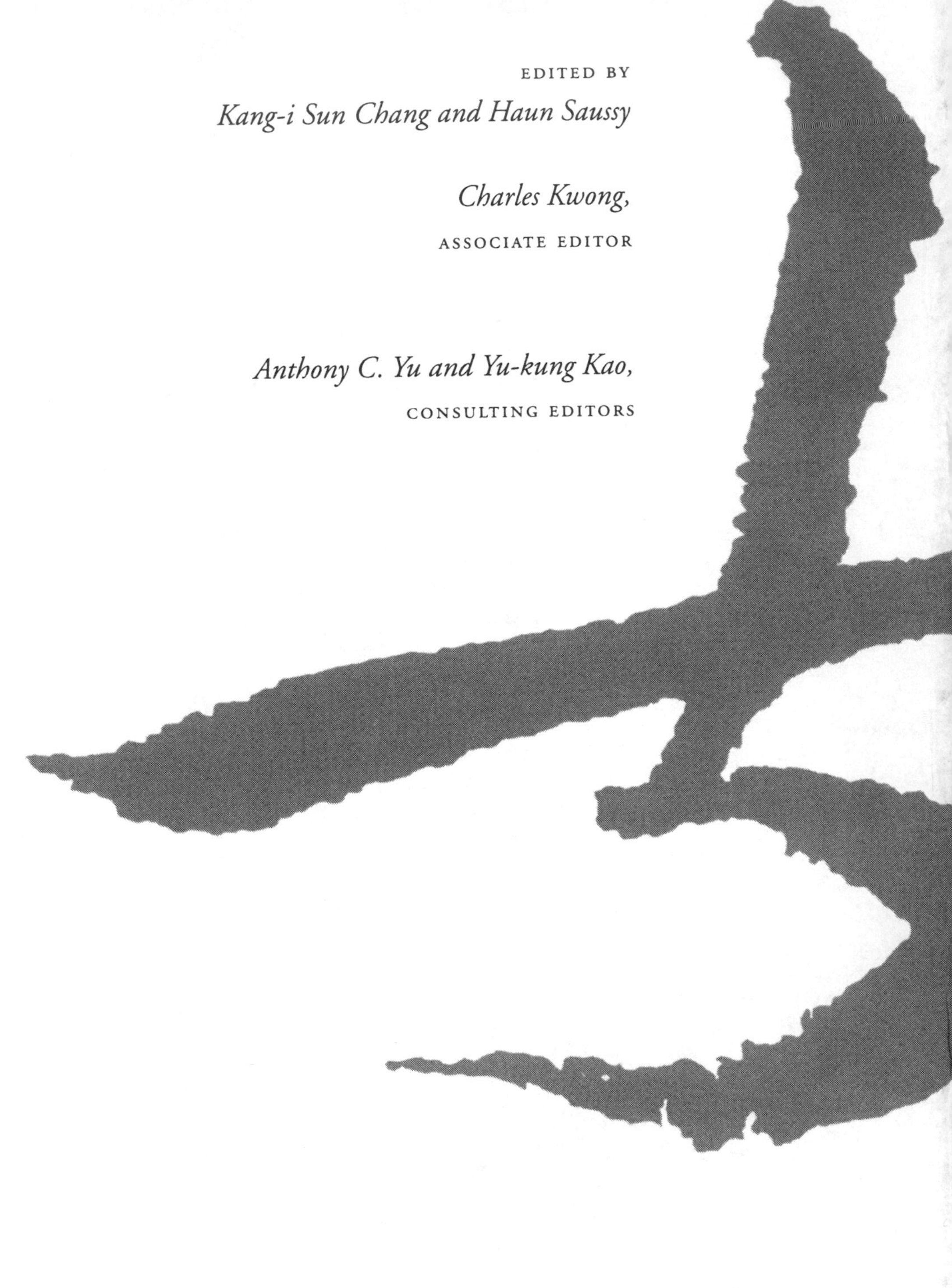

Women Writers of Traditional China

An Anthology of Poetry and Criticism

STANFORD UNIVERSITY PRESS

STANFORD, CALIFORNIA

Stanford University Press, Stanford, California

Printed in the United States of America

CIP data appear at the end of the book

To Hsiao-lan Ch'en and F. W. Mote,
ideal match of "talented woman and learned man,"
and perfect embodiment of the finest in Chinese culture
—*Kang-i Sun Chang*

And to the memory of Lola Norwood Haun
and Mary Quaintance,
talented women whose lives were cut short
—*Haun Saussy*

Preface

For its editors at least, this book is a memorial of the joys and trials of collaboration. Kang-i Sun Chang drew up the original table of contents with the help of the consulting editors, Kao Yu-Kung and Anthony C. Yu, and submitted it to a group of volunteer translators, who responded with suggestions for improving the selection and even resolved some long-standing scholarly confusions. Almost all contributors were able to honor the whole of their original commitment to provide both translations and notes on the selections. Associate editor Charles Kwong and Haun Saussy commented on the first drafts of the translations, annotation, and biographical notes, which were returned to the contributors for revision. The resulting second drafts were then combined into a continuous manuscript by Saussy. In the process redundancies were removed, cross-references inserted, footnotes verified, and a measure of consistency across chapters striven for.

In the long process of assembling this book, we have incurred many obligations. We wish to express our thanks, first of all, to the many contributors who turned their work in on time and patiently endured the process of editing and rewriting, and to Charles Kwong, the associate editor, for his generous help and breadth of knowledge. Consulting editors Kao Yu-kung and Anthony C. Yu have given precious advice. Chang Ch'ung-ho generously contributed her graceful calligraphy. Ellen F. Smith, on behalf of Stanford University Press, spared no efforts to improve the manuscript with her learning, taste, queries, and inventiveness. We thank Professor Shi Zhicun of Shanghai for inspiration, and Ellen Graham of Yale University Press for support in the initial stages of the project. We also recognize our debts to the staffs of the East Asian library collections of Yale, UCLA, and Stanford; to Stanford's Center for East Asian Studies; to the Wu Foundation for conference and planning funds; to Professor Yü Ying-shih, Monica Yü, and Dr. Ching-shing Huang for their aid in gaining support from the Wu Foundation; to Sharon Sanderson for her help in coordinating the work; to Mary Ellen Friends for her assistance with correspondence and preparation of source material; to Chi-hung Yim, Huang Yibing, Edna Tow, James Shou-cheng Yao, and Eileen Chow for help with library research; to Richard Vinograd for art-historical expertise; to Ann Waltner for her many valuable suggestions; and to many friends and colleagues for guidance that they may not have known they were giving.

Our greatest debt, however, is to those women and men who, over the centuries, worked to preserve the traces of a form of writing that had no utility, no career value, and little prestige. Whatever deficiencies the present volume has should not be allowed to obscure their generosity to us all.

K.S.C.

H.S.

Contents

Contributors

Joseph R. Allen
Mark A. Borer
Jennifer Carpenter
Kang-i Sun Chang
Ch'en Hsiao-lan
Li-li Ch'en
Yu-shih Chen
Pei-kai Cheng
Shan Chou
Eileen Cheng-yin Chow
Charles H. Egan
Ronald C. Egan
Eugene Eoyang
Grace S. Fong
Mary Ellen Friends
Nancy J. Hodes
Hu Ying
Carol Rosenthal Kaufmann
David R. Knechtges
Dorothy Ko
Norman Kutcher
Charles Y. Kwong
Frances LaFleur
Jeanne Larsen
Hui-shu Lee
Michael F. Lestz
Dore J. Levy
Wai-yee Li
Shuen-fu Lin
Ch'iu-ti Liu
Wan Liu
Irving Yucheng Lo
Kathryn Lowry
David McCraw
Iona D. Man-cheong
Susan Mann
F. W. Mote
Stephen Owen
Jennifer Purtle
Ren Zipang
Maureen Robertson
Ruth Rogaski
Paul S. Ropp
Paul F. Rouzer
Haun Saussy
William Schultz
Anna Marshall Shields
Cathy Silber

Peter C. Sturman
Chia-lin Pao Tao
Tung Yuan-fang
Paula Varsano
Sophie Volpp
Eliot Weinberger
Stephen West
Ellen Widmer
John Timothy Wixted
Yenna Wu
Michelle Yeh
Anthony C. Yu
Pauline Yu
Judith T. Zeitlin
Zhang Longxi

Editorial Conventions

Format

The writers—or, in some cases, groups of writers—gathered here are presented in numbered sequences, one for poetry and one for criticism. Each individual poem is also numbered; thus, Cai Yan is P.2, and her poem "Eighteen Songs of a Nomad Flute" is P.2.1. Where more than one poet is included in a numbered section, each is assigned a letter; thus Xu Hui is P.8a and Bao Junhui is P.8b. These numbers have been assigned for easy cross-referencing.

Each section begins with a brief biographical note or commentary; notes to these sections appear at the back of the book. Selected texts then follow, each ending with a source note that identifies the Chinese text used for the translation. Annotations and glosses to these texts are provided as notes, keyed to poem line numbers or commentary paragraph numbers, at the end of each selection. Some selections include headnotes or commentary by the author that have come to considered part of the text itself.

The translations follow the line structure of the original Chinese to the extent practicable (see Introduction), and the number of lines is indicated for all poems of eight or more lines. In some cases translators have broken lines to indicate the caesura in the original, and a small number of translations have been rendered quite freely. In these cases, a new line generally begins at the left margin; the first word is always capitalized. "Continued" lines are always indented, with a lowercase first word.

References

In the endnotes and notes to texts, page references are keyed to the editions cited in the Bibliography. For traditional collections in Chinese, however, citations also include, whenever possible, the number of the *juan* referenced, so that readers working from differently paginated editions can still find their way to the source passage. (*Juan*, like chapters, mark divisions of content and are therefore more or less stable among editions of the same work.) The *juan* number is invariably followed by a slash and a page number in one of two formats. Thus, "84/10b" means page 10, verso, of *juan* 84 of a traditionally paginated Chinese book; "16/342" means page 342 of a Chinese book paginated in the Western style, which page occurs in *juan* 16 of the text. (Divisions of content superior to the *juan* are marked by periods when necessary; a glance at the table of contents of the work in question will show what the principle of organization is.)

The volume number of a multivolume work bound in the Western manner is followed by a colon: thus "446: 144" indicates page 144 of volume 446 of a large work or series.

In addition to conventional entries by author's, editor's, or compiler's surname, the Bibliography lists certain standard or well-known works by titles, as they are usually cited (collections such as the *Quan Tang shi*; the Classics; works of reference; and the like). Where appropriate, a cross-reference to the entry by the author or editor of the edition we have used is provided, so that a frequently cited work may be found both by title and by "author."

A Note on Sources

Where the biographical note on a writer mentions a work not included in this Bibliography, the reader can assume that a reference to that work occurs in the sources recorded for the biographical information or for the Chinese originals of the texts translated here. The prefaces of collections of poetry, especially the older ones, often cite critical opinions from works no longer in circulation and, indeed, often provide the only information available on a writer's life. Where no source is specifically cited for a biographical note, the reader can assume that the information comes from the source for the poem texts.

Generally speaking, the researcher into women's literature in premodern China should consult Hu Wenkai, *Zhongguo lidai funü zhuzuo kao* (An inventory of writings by Chinese women, 1957; revised edition, 1985), as the first avenue for locating the biography of a given female author, editions of her writings, and critical testimonia; we found ourselves constantly in Hu's debt. Hu, in turn, built upon the monumental efforts of others. The *Mingyuan shigui*, attributed to Zhong Xing, is an invaluable source for women poets before 1636. Next come Qian Qianyi and Liu Shi, whose *Liechao shiji: Runji* adds names to Zhong's roster and appends critical judgments, often unforgiving;

Wang Duanshu, whose *Mingyuan shiwei* represents many years of editorial labor; Wang Shilu, whose comprehensive *Ranzhi ji* is unfortunately known to us only in fragments; and Xu Naichang, whose several anthologies of Qing verse by men and women print much poetry that is not to be found elsewhere. The modern anthologists Yi Boyin, Zheng Guangyi, and Su Zhecong have also smoothed our path in innumerable ways.

A Note on Names

Chinese surnames (*shi*, referring to one's father's clan) precede the individual's personal name; a woman kept her maiden surname throughout her life.

An individual's personal name, or *ming*, was given by his or her parents; the choice of *ming* was often constrained by family traditions that are helpful evidence of birth-order, generational rank, or kinship.

The *zi* (style name, courtesy name, or literary name) was, in contrast, a name chosen by the individual and appended to his or her writings. To refer to another by his or her literary name is a sign of friendship or esteem.

In addition to *ming* and *zi*, traditional Chinese often possessed further names: the *hao* or sobriquet, often humorous or self-deprecatory; Daoist or Buddhist religious names taken after adopting the monastic way of life; and studio names (usually in the form "X Y *zhai zhuren*," "Master/Mistress of the X Y Studio"). A courtesan might be known by any of these names, as well as by further noms de guerre invented by her admirers.

Many women of premodern China are not known to us by personal name, but only by their surname of origin, or *shi*: thus, one may read of Zhang *shi*, wife of a certain Mr. Li. The accurate but cumbersome English equivalent would be "the woman née Zhang"; here, whenever "Zhang *shi*" is used, it must be with the understanding that "shi" is not in any sense the woman's own name.

A useful source for more information on Chinese names is Charles O. Hucker, *A Dictionary of Official Titles in Imperial China*.

Abbreviations

The following abbreviations are used in the Notes and the Bibliography. Complete bibliographical information for frequently cited sources of and about Chinese poetry can be found in the Bibliography (pp. 851–69). "Series" abbreviations, used in the Bibliography, refer to uniform reprint collections of works of a certain kind or on a certain topic.

Chen Xin	Chen Xin et al., eds., *Lidai funü shici xuan zhu*
CLEJ	Liu Yunfen, ed., *Cuilou erji*
CSJC	*Congshu jicheng* series
GGSC	Cai Dianqi, ed., *Guochao guige shichao*
GGZSJ	Wanyan Yun Zhu, ed., *Guochao guixiu zhengshi ji*
GXCC	Xu Naichang, ed., *Guixiu cichao*
Hu Wenkai	Hu Wenkai, *Zhongguo lidai funü zhuzuo kao*
LCSJ	Qian Qianyi, ed., *Liechao shiji*
LCXZ	Qian Qianyi, ed., *Liechao shiji xiaozhuan*
LR	Liu Shi and Qian Qianyi, eds., *Liechao shiji* [LCSJ]*: Runji*
MYSG	Zhong Xing, attr., *Mingyuan shigui*
MYSW	Wang Duanshu, ed., *Mingyuan shiwei*
QSBC	Shen Deqian, ed., *Qingshi biecai ji*
QSC	*Quan Song ci*
QTS	*Quan Tang shi*
SBBY	*Sibu beiyao* series
SBCK	*Sibu congkan* series
SGCJ	Deng Hanyi, ed., *Shiguan Chuji*
SKQS	*Siku quanshu*
SSJZS	Ruan Yuan, ed., *Shisan jing zhushu*

Su Zhecong	Su Zhecong, ed., *Zhongguo lidai funü zuopin xuan*
Xie Wuliang	Xie Wuliang, *Zhongguo funü wenxue shi*
XTLS	Xu Naichang, ed., *Xiao tan luan shi huike guixiu ci*
Yi Boyin	Yi Boyin, *Lidai nü shici xuan*
YTXY	Xu Ling, comp., *Yutai xinyong*
Zheng Guangyi	Zheng Guangyi, ed., *Zhongguo lidai cainü shige jianshang cidian*

Modern China, with provincial boundaries and major cities.

HEILONGJIANG
Harbin
Changchun
JILIN
NEIMENGU
Shenyang
LIAONING
Sea of Japan
HEPEI
Hohhot
NORTH KOREA
Huang He
(Yellow R.)
Beijing
Great Wall
Tianjin
Gulf of Zhili
ZHILI
Yinchuan
Taiyuan
Shijiazhuang
SOUTH KOREA
JAPAN
NINGXIA
SHANXI
Jinan
SHANDONG
Lanzhou
Yellow Sea
Xi'an
Luoyang
Zhengzhou
JIANGSU
SHAANXI
HENAN
ANHUI
Nanjing
Suzhou
Hefei
Shanghai
HUBEI
Chengdu
Wuhan
Hangzhou
Yangzi R.
ZHEJIANG
East China Sea
Nanchang
HUNAN
Hengyang
JIANGXI
Fuzhou
Guiyang
FUJIAN
GUIZHOU
Taiwan Strait
TAIWAN
GUANGXI
GUANGDONG
Guangzhou
Nanning
VIETNAM
South China Sea
HAINAN
PHILIPPINES

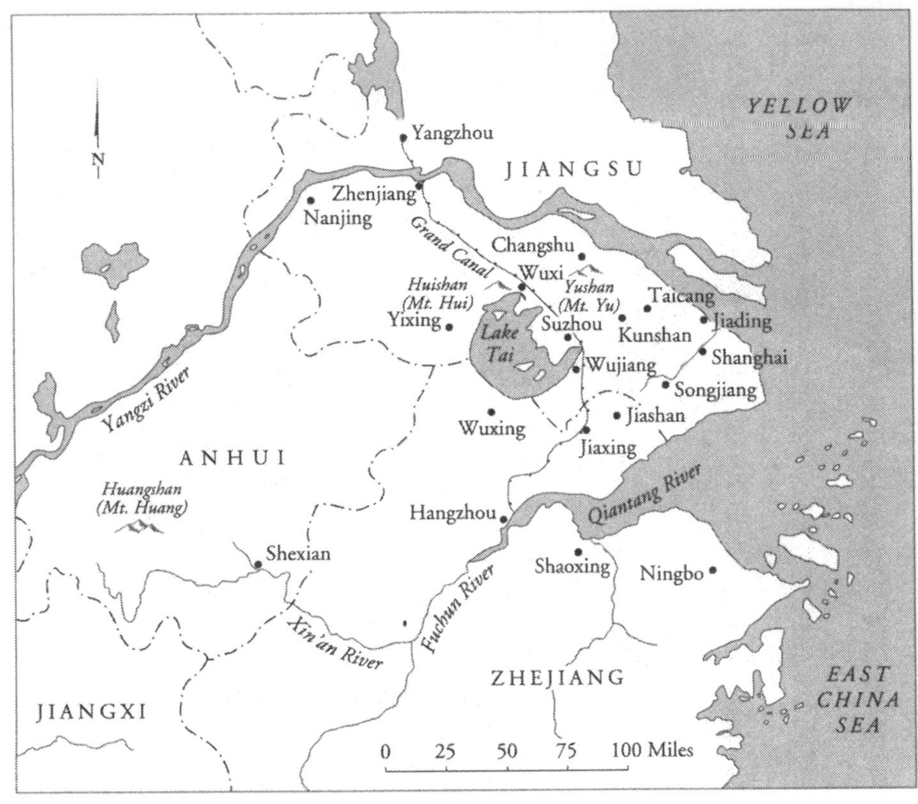

The Hangzhou region in the Ming-Qing period. (From Dorothy Ko, *Teachers of the Inner Chambers: Women and Culture in China, 1573–1722* [Stanford, Calif.: Stanford University Press, 1994], p. xvi.)

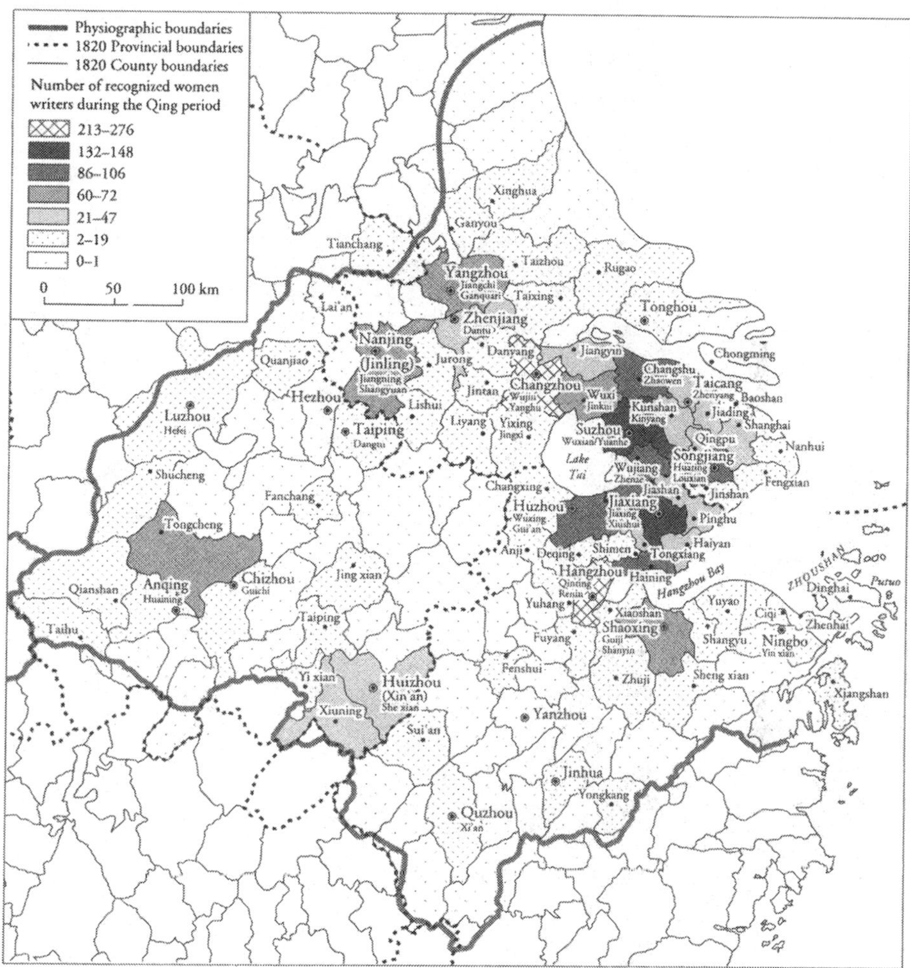

Places of origin of Qing women writers. (From Susan Mann, *Precious Records: Women in China's Long Eighteenth Century* [Stanford, Calif.: Stanford University Press, 1997], p. 6.)

Women Writers of Traditional China

An Anthology of Poetry and Criticism

Introduction
Genealogy and Titles of the Female Poet

Why this anthology? Why "women writers of traditional China"?

An anecdotal answer: In the autumn of 1735, Wang Su, the husband of Mao Xiuhui (P.89), went to Nanjing to take the provincial examination. His position as a student on government fellowship qualified him to compete at this lowest level of the national civil-service recruitment process. Unfortunately, he returned without gaining a place in the next round. (Provincial examinations were held once every three years, and a student who failed repeatedly to go on to the next level might lose his stipend.) To comfort him in his disappointment, Mao Xiuhui wrote three quatrains (see P.89.3), of which the first two (as translated by Paul Ropp) run:

> Newly made up and carefully arranged, she strives for delicacy and grace;
> But another girl, the gaudily painted one, always catches everyone's eye.
> Who notices the one leaning by the tall bamboo in the cold,
> Elegantly standing in the dusk, most solitary and pure?
>
> The poor girl toils on her brocade year after year,
> Lonely and neglected behind the gynacaeum's closed doors.
> But, alas, the evil *zhen* bird has served as go-between;
> Without prospects, she arranges a trousseau facing the autumn wind.

Lines 3 and 4 of Mao's first stanza paraphrase Du Fu's famous poem "The Beauty" ("Jia ren"), a description of a noblewoman beset by disaster. Her father and brothers have died in civil war, her husband has cast her off for a younger woman, and she is reduced to selling her jewelry to stay alive. Du's poem closes with the lines: "Her kingfisher-blue sleeves are thin against the cold, / In the dusk she leans against the tall bamboo." Applied to Mao Xiuhui's husband, the words of the eighth-century poem are obviously consolatory: his hard work and learning have earned him no recognition, set against the flashy writing of less-worthy candidates, but he will have to face his adversity with the steadfastness shown by the abandoned noblewoman. Problems specific to the world of men are clarified by reference to problems specific to women: Mao Xiuhui invites her husband into a space defined as feminine, so that her poem exemplifies a certain kind of "women's poetry."

That is a "women's poetry" for which women writers are (at first glance) not necessary, for Du Fu's poem had already given the scene of the abandoned woman its masculine analogue: according to traditional commentaries, "Jia ren" was "stimulated by something the poet had seen, but carries a suggestion of self-allegory."[1] But the play of gender does not stop with Mao's repetition of Du's transformation of a woman into the metaphorical counterpart of a man. The isolation and "closed doors" of the women's quarters are evoked in phrases that suggest (if we trace them to their literary sources) the willful solitude of reclusive scholars.[2] That somewhat changes the relation between masculine theme and feminine metaphor, making it seem as if female reclusion, an obligatory situation, were equivalent to the chosen retirement of the man for whom public activity no longer means anything. The allusion to the *zhen* bird may transfer the blame for Wang Su's failure onto some badly chosen or untrustworthy intercessor, but it, too, looks back to a moment of gender allegory in earlier literature. The first-person speaker of Qu Yuan's "Li sao" (Encountering sorrow, ca. 300 B.C.E.) enters the poem as one of many ladies vying for the attentions of a male "Fair One" (advisors, that is, trying to capture the trust of their king); afterward, the rejected speaker, now cast as a male, goes in search of a bride, but his matchmaker, the *zhen* bird, is unable to find a suitable alliance. In Mao Xiuhui's poem the *zhen*'s victim is female, the "poor girl" obliged to stitch wedding garments for others but fated never to wear her own. Only through interpretative application does the *zhen* appear as antagonist of the man for whose blocked career the imagined girl stands. Conventional though the parallels are—political service has been represented as a difficult courtship for as long as there has been Chinese poetry—the fact that this poem's author is a woman revives the dead metaphors. Mao Xiuhui invites her husband to look on himself as she might look on an unwanted or unmarriageable girl: the act of sympathy is predicated on an equivalence between marriage and official service—that marriage is the highest calling for women, since they are excluded from holding office—which for the moment overrides the all-important distinction between the two. The web of allusions structuring Mao

Xiuhui's poem stretches from metaphor to literalness, from male to female, from imagination to fact. Had it been written by a man—say, a friend of Wang Su's who might have wanted to suggest, by alluding to Du Fu, that Wang's examination paper had been too good for the judges to appreciate—the tension between metaphor and literalness would not have occurred, and the feminine figures in the poem would simply stand for masculine disappointment.

Mao Xiuhui here stands for a general predicament, that of entering into dialogue as a female writer with a male world. That predicament is what this book is about. Chinese literature can boast of an exceptional number of women writers before the twentieth century, and that, of course, deserves bringing to notice; it is also interesting and important that these women were read, discussed, and ranked by intelligent people of both sexes. Women writers are very much a part of Chinese literature. Though their place has been contested, though they have encountered the usual sorts of peremptory dismissal and trivialization, and though the benefits of a literary reputation typically eluded them, they did participate in that vast conversation. This anthology aims to put before the English-speaking reader some traces of their presence.

Women's writing in China was not a matter of interest for women only. Surely in no other civilization (except perhaps that of Japan) did the concept of a woman author imply so much for the definition of authorship generally. The earliest literary texts in the tradition, the three hundred poems of the ancient *Book of Odes*, which dates from ca. 600 B.C.E., include many compositions framed in a woman's voice, among which a dozen or so were ascribed, from the earliest commentaries onward, to specific women authors. The lived situations of these women became paradigmatic for the Chinese understanding of authorship. The poems in question utter rebukes, protests, appeals. As if having no one else to rely on, these women made their language their defender—and that is precisely the plight of the major male authors of the Chinese tradition. (Indeed, the Du Fu poem to which Mao Xiuhui alluded contains several references to the "women-authored" poems of the *Book of Odes*, which provide him his loci classici for the idea of constancy in adversity.) But the attributions of the *Book of Odes* belong to legend, not to history: unverifiable through contemporary documents, they rest, in any case, on little more than subsequent interpretations. While acknowledging the exemplary force of the *Book of Odes* women as imagined precedents, we begin this book with the first women recorded in both biography and bibliography. The result is still incomplete on both fronts, and better biographies and bibliographies would only be the beginning. A full account of the role of female authors in Chinese literary history—as instigators, as counterexamples, as critics, as salonnières, as transformers of genre, as performers, and in many other capacities—can thus far only be imagined.

But why such an emphasis on women poets? *Why not women* writers? *What is the place of women poets among women writers, or among writers of either sex, that so large an anthology should be devoted to them?*

Women became poets for the same reasons—external reasons at least—that men did. At the juncture of art and life there were, speaking quite broadly, a high road and a low road for women's poetic production. As for the high road, the place of honor accorded to poetry among literary genres is one of the few constants in the long and various Chinese literary tradition. Facility in verse was required of the aspiring scholar-official and joined with the study of the Classics and Histories and the composition of deliberative essays to form the backbone of upper-class education. Even drama could attain the heights of literary culture, provided it was composed in exquisite verse and not planned for actual performance. The writing of fiction was, by contrast, seen as a commercial venture engaged in by men who had failed in their pursuit of an official career or who had stooped to putting their talent at the service of the market. That Chinese literary history should record so many women poets and (before the modern era) virtually no women novelists is partly a sign of the social background of most literate women (they wrote verse because their lives were bound up with those of men who strove to write verse) and partly an effect of the conditions under which an upper-class writer, man or woman, could claim respectability.

The low road leads through other social situations in which women found themselves encouraged to poetic expression. Palace and court life, as well as the protocols of the entertainment quarters, created opportunities for the composition of poetry and rewarded women for learning and wit.

This second social context for women's verbal art created a poetic mode of its own, the genre of song-lyrics, or *ci*. (The particularities of the genre will be discussed in a later section of this introduction and, in further detail, with an inventory of forms, in Appendix A.) Here a word of caution is in order: *ci* are from the beginning associated with women as performers and poetic personae, but the actual authors of *ci* were (insofar as we can be sure) as likely to be male as female.[3] In form, technique, and rhetorical stance, but above all in implicit ethos, there is much to distinguish song-lyrics from the classicizing poetry of literati households. But almost from its origin in the Tang period, *ci* began to make its way into the high literary canon and became acceptable as a medium in which upper-class women, too, might work. The reader of this book can observe the social and artistic ambiguities of *ci*, as well as its transformation, through the compositions of the Song dynasty poets Li Qingzhao (P.17) and Zhu Shuzhen (P.18).

Varying social circumstances thus prepared the way for various types of women poets. Women poets also benefited from the power of example: women of later dynasties could look back to predecessor poets whose fame hinged largely on their being women (Ban *jieyu* [P.1], Cai Yan [P.2], Xie Daoyun [see C.24.1]).[4] A great many poems were made possible by the convention of speaking in the person of one of these women—an indication that their biographical circumstances had taken on the prestige of archetypes; see, for example, Xu Hui's "Regret in Changmen Palace" (P.8a.1).

So poetry conjoined, as no other genre did, the requisites for opening up a women's tradition: a well-marked social function, a group of stylistic and personal models (providing opportunities for creative historical or ethical role-playing), and contexts in which the display of talent was permissible and might eventually become truly public. These conditions were realized differently, of course, for different women. Some women wrote out of isolation and despair, finding in words a mastery that otherwise eluded them (see, for example, Xu Yueying [P.12c], Wang Jiaoluan [P.38]). Others were recruited into the fellowship of poets by family members, friends, or even sympathetic male advocates such as Yuan Mei (see Dai Lanying [P.95], Jiang Zhu [P.111]). Some women dwelt on intimate family matters and cast their poems as addresses to husbands and sons at large in the wide world of men's affairs (see Chai Jingyi [P.75a], Xi Peilan [P.93]). Still others looked on a world men were unable to set to rights and stepped forward, in verse and sometimes in act, to reform it (see Wu Qi [P.72], Qiu Jin [P.126]). There are loyalists, revolutionaries, hermits, concubines,[5] matrons, painters, serving maids, historians, courtesans, farmwives, disappointed lovers, honored grandmothers—each with her own reasons for poetry and her own ways of appropriating the public and obvious conventions of men's verse as well as those, through their unobtrusiveness perhaps best known to practitioners, of women's verse.

What are the hallmarks of women's verse? Is there any definition of women's poetry but the tautological "women's verse is verse written by women"?

The anthology itself is the best argument for the idea that there is such a definition—that by participating in a set of stylistic and rhetorical conventions, writers made themselves into women writers. "In literature if we would not be parvenus we must have a model,"[6] and the awareness of prior models defines women's poetry as such. Chinese poetry is notoriously allusive, a fact that only becomes more obvious when the poetry is translated, requiring that the basis for each allusion be supplied in notes or paraphrases.[7] But allusion is not merely an irritating stylistic tic; it is rather a bid for verbal authority. To repeat an earlier poet's words is to enter sympathetically into that poet's personality. Allusion to an earlier poet, or, more subtly, allusion to the sources to which the earlier poet had alluded, establishes lines of filiation and affiliation. It is a kind of sociability across the centuries, the circulation of tokens and gestures that keeps the tradition alive. Currents and movements within the tradition as a whole become discernible in their patterns of borrowing. It is not enough to write poems about solitary retirement, for example, in order successfully to inscribe oneself within the subtradition of hermit poetry; one must also adopt the commonplaces and kennings of the eremitic canon, most memorably bound together by the already allusive work of Tao Yuanming (365–427).

Similarly, then, women's poetry has its coinage and passwords, shared with the main current of Chinese poetry, yet distinguished by emphasis and topical meaning. The reader of this anthology will discover these patterns of relation, both through careful reading and through the rather clumsy artifice of the cross-references we have provided. The rituals of Double Seventh night, for example, mark a poem as a woman's poem, not only because of the festival's associations with betrothal and women's handiwork, but also because of the chain of women's poems on the subject (though we should not overlook the contributions of men such as Yu Xin [513–81], Li Bai [701–62], and Li Shangyin [813?–58] to this theme). The story of the loyal and long-suffering poet Ban *jieyu* (P.1), dislodged from Emperor Cheng's favor by the dancing-girl Zhao Feiyan, is possessed in common by all Chinese writers, but in the women's tradition it necessarily takes on a different emphasis—especially when it serves to express the discouraging certainty that beauty and seductiveness were more likely to benefit a woman than would literary talent. (The Tang emperor Xuanzong's choice of Yang Guifei—also a dancer—over the more intellectual

Plum-Blossom Consort revived this legendary pattern and creates a new set of allusions.) The fund of allusions with feminine overtones is not, of course, static: particular references have their periods of rise and decline, sometimes in response to historical pressures (observe, for example, the junctures at which the heroic but ineffectual *jingwei* bird, in its Sisyphean effort to fill the sea with pebbles, becomes an obligatory trope).

Without launching on a too-extensive enumeration of the motifs whereby women linked their work with the previous tradition, we may also point out a centripetal tendency taken on by allusions to women's writing: later women persistently read an earlier woman poet's words and images as disguised autobiography, whatever the earlier writer may have had in mind. Thus, the improvisation of the girl Xie Daoyun—likening the falling snow to "willow catkins lifted by the wind"—earned the praise of her scholarly uncle because of its surprising, but apt, combination of spring and winter imagery, yet in later tradition the derived phrase "catkin verses," used as an allusive shorthand for poems by women, suggests the transitoriness and frailty of women's poetic careers. (Xie Daoyun went on to be married to an uncomprehending man.) Associative complexes such as this, in which particular stories or images become emblematic both of their first author and of the fate of female authors generally, demonstrate the efforts of women to maintain a tradition and locate themselves within it.

How have you made your selections? What are the precedents of this book?

This anthology covers the period from the Han dynasty (206 B.C.E.–220 C.E.) to the threshold of the Republican era (1911–). It is intended for the English-speaking general reader of poetry and criticism, while offering the results of a careful scholarly reading of the originals. In presenting close to a hundred and fifty authors whose work ranges over a multitude of genres and styles, it is the first English-language anthology of premodern Chinese women to offer such a degree of breadth and depth. The book's primary purpose is to put before the reader evidence of the talent that has flourished, against all obstacles, among women in premodern China. But it is also our hope that an anthology so designed will spur reflection among specialists and readers of Chinese poetry—that it will inspire new perspectives on both the Chinese poetic tradition and the canon of female poets within that tradition.

An anthologist's first and last job is to account for the choices she has made, choices that she must hope will not please everybody (since the public's dissatisfaction proves that it matters what one has chosen). A glance at the table of contents of this anthology will show a preponderance of selections from the Ming (1368–1644) and Qing (1644–1911) dynasties, and a great number of authors who are hardly household names, even for those acquainted with the literature. That distribution is the result of a deliberate choice. We have examined many anthologies of women poets recently published in China and Taiwan. They usually give pride of place to the handful of generally recognized major women authors from earlier dynasties—Ban *jieyu* (P.1), Xue Tao (P.10), Li Qingzhao (P.17)—and represent the Ming and Qing periods through a small number of poets, each allotted the space of a mere two or three poems. Such an editorial policy, we feel, makes for a misleadingly narrow picture of women's literary position in this later period, and suggests that no woman author apart from the five or six great names deserves other than statistical consideration. But bibliographies and library catalogues attest that the number of women poets recorded in Ming-Qing China is simply unprecedented. This explosion—resulting, to be sure, from a number of factors, including the spread of printing and literacy, long periods of prosperity, and the rise of a large, educated merchant class—deserves to be brought to the general reader's attention as an important event in Chinese cultural history.

It is, moreover, an event planned and executed by the authors themselves. Ming-Qing women differed from their poetic predecessors in their eagerness to preserve their own literary works and to participate, through publication, manuscript circulation, and social networks, in the building of a feminine literary community. Many women who published their work sought consciously not only to acquire a place in the literary canon for their own writings but also to establish retrospectively a tradition of women poets, one which they claimed—though, as we have noted, on rather slender historical evidence—to have existed since the time of the *Book of Odes*. Thus, from the seventeenth century onward, one notices a proliferation of collections and anthologies of poetry by women, ultimately reaching the remarkable total of some three thousand titles (about one-third of which have, unfortunately, been lost). The share of women's writings passed down to us from later imperial China is impressive indeed, and contemporaries plainly recognized women's writing as an important new fact. Regrettably, modern scholars of Chinese literary history, perhaps in an attempt to simplify the complex process of poetic development, have failed to note the critical implications of the numerous anthologies of women's poetry produced in the Ming and Qing. As a consequence, modern anthologies and critical works discount the prominence of late-imperial women writers.

One inescapable reason for the unprecedented numbers of women writers recorded in the Ming-Qing period was the rise of a female readership from the sixteenth century onward, a trend whose origin is to be sought in broader social transformations. Literacy provided women the skills and aspirations necessary for literary creativity. As they grew in numbers and confidence, literate women began to adopt a great variety of poetic genres and to break into print, often with the help of sympathetic male editors and publishers.[8] Women were not alone in benefiting from a broadened literacy. The public exploration of women's writing should be considered in parallel with other cases of Ming interest in diversifying the literary canon—the collecting of peasant songs, for example, or the publication of editions of popular fiction as intensively annotated as if they were classical texts. Philosophical allegiances, such as the application by Wang Yangming and his school of a revised Confucian ethics to everyday life regardless of class boundaries, no doubt also helped to draw the reading public's attention to new kinds of authors. At the risk of a drastic oversimplification, one might say that the rationale for promoting a work to canonical status in traditional China was predominantly cast in moral and instrumental terms. A work deserved to be preserved and imitated if it gave memorable expression to the Way, to the ethical compact that assured the coherence of the individual, the family, and the state. Literature fed into the enterprise of government at several levels—as history, as material for the examinations that directed the recruitment of officials, and as evidence of cultivation; these functions gave literature its weight and purpose. But women neither held office nor took examinations. Their relation to the Way could not be the same as that of literate men. Thus a different canonical rationale would be required to elevate and legitimate the status of female poetry. One argument often presented in vindication of women's poetry states that, since the female substance was composed of the purest cosmic essences (*lingxiu*), a literature that failed to include women's writing would be spiritually impoverished. This view is expressed without reserve in the preface to the anthology *Mingyuan shigui* (MYSG: Selection of poems by famous ladies, ca. 1600; see C.32.1) attributed to Zhong Xing (d. 1625):

> Whether pure as bathing in green waters or dim as dreaming among flowers, women's thoughts and emotions are suddenly strung together by a single thread, and all their rich exuberance comes naturally. . . . Men must

> travel to all the corners of the earth in order to know the world. . . . But women never have to do that. They have country villages right on their pillows and mountain passes in their dreams, all because they are so pure. . . . Alas! How far in their skillfulness men fall behind women!

Another argument is implicitly historical in focus. In contrast to the orthodox view of the poetic canon as extolling works that had run counter to or claimed to correct the prevailing taste of their time—a kind of solitary heroism of literary value—the Ming-Qing anthologists often insisted on the contemporaneity, the topical representativeness, of women's poetry. The previously secondary status of women authors was made into an argument for their importance in the present, for the implicit literary-historical vision of these editors convinced them that an age which prized the female element would be an age unsurpassed for the completeness and variety of its poetry. For example, the woman poet Wang Duanshu (P.69) argued that literature contained a stable and unchanging element—the Classics—and a counterpart to the Classics in a constantly shifting, always contemporary element. She proposed that women's writing be seen as this second body of work, and concluded her preface to the anthology *Mingyuan shiwei* (MYSW: The longitudinal canon of poetry by women of note, 1667; see C.13.1) with the boast that "So truly can these poems be said to be 'of a feather' with the antique *Odes*, they complement their predecessors and form a classic in their own right—a complementary canon [*wei*] answering to the Six Classics. I invite all under the four heavens to see for themselves." In a similar gesture, a man named Zhou Zhibiao published the work of late-Ming female poets in two groups of seven poets each, implicitly ranking these women with the famous "Former Seven Masters" and "Latter Seven Masters" who had so dominated the Ming literary scene (for the preface to this work, composed by Zhi Ruzeng, see C.41.1). Such editorial pronouncements bespeak an intense interest in women's writing in the late Ming and early Qing, an interest voiced by major and minor literary figures of the time. They also suggest the power of the new genre to unsettle familiar assumptions about literary value and permanence. "Unsettling" indeed summarizes the judgment of the critic and philosopher of history Zhang Xuecheng (1738–1801) on the dubious propriety of women choosing publication—and of men sponsoring their enterprise (see C.45.1).

To take the just measure of the development of women's poetry, it is not enough to read the poetry; one must also take into account the prose writings—prefaces, biographies, theoretical tracts—that framed the poetry and attempted to shape women's writing as a distinct category of literature. For this reason, this anthology also contains a section of criticism by and about women writers. Newcomers to the field may wish to start with this section. For—to state the obvious—although the existence of women in traditional China is uncontroversial and although the preservation of works by literate women is valuable and inspiring, the meaning of the category "women's literature" can be developed only through an investigation of the specific contexts in which women were able to set down and circulate their thoughts. Historical and theoretical "framing," as performed in the critical essays included in Part Two, is an important aspect of these writers' context and should not be neglected.

Finally, we offer a very brief introduction to the basics of Chinese poetical forms and practices. From its beginnings Chinese poetry is rhymed. The word that most nearly answers to the English term "poetry," *shi*, has varied in reference over the last twenty-five hundred years, but its core meaning is approximately "compositions with a stable line-length, regularly occurring rhymes, and a stanza or couplet ordering": *shi* is felt to be distinct from *fu* (a composition of unpredetermined length, whose descriptive content and irregular prosody set it apart from song and closer to prose), from *ci* (originally a song form, with lines of unequal length), and from *qu* (aria). *Shi* is the core genre of Chinese poetry, the genre against which others define themselves, and both the term and the basic properties of *shi* reach back to the ancient *Book of Odes* and forward to the present day. The poems of the *Book of Odes* display considerable variety of form, but their most frequent format is a four-verse stanza made of four-syllable lines rhyming *abcb*. In the Han period, this form gained a rival, the *fu*, or rhyme-prose, composed in rambling lines of four to seven characters with the rhyme-words falling at the end of alternate lines: this form was more suited to descriptions and declamations, and its main authors took it in the direction of stylistic display. Like most Chinese poetic genres, the *fu* works by semantic parallelism: verses tend to come paired, and the meaning of one verse is often best clarified by that of the following verse, as in this example from Ban *jieyu* (P.1.2):

> I praised Huang and Ying, wives of the Lord of Yu,
> Extolled Ren and Si, mothers of Zhou.

By the end of the Latter Han, the popular *shi* songs recorded (or more likely recomposed for inclusion) under the title of *yuefu*, or Music Bureau poetry, had taken a new metrical organization. *Yuefu* were originally set to music.

Although the rhyme and stanza patterns were recognizably those of early *shi*, the predominant rhythm was now a five-syllable line (with a caesura between the second and third syllables). Rhyme affected the last syllable of every other line; an unrhymed odd-numbered line and the rhyme-bearing even-numbered line that followed it made up a semantic unit, a couplet, often with some degree of syntactic parallelism (see P.4.2):

> A visitor came from far away,
> He brought me a lacquered singing lute.*
> Its wood displays a "mutual longing" design;
> Its strings diffuse a tone of separateness.*
> All my life I'll keep to this key;
> No season's cold will change my heart.*

(The asterisks mark the rhyme-bearing line-endings.) These characteristics hold true for later *shi* poetry. Seven-character *shi* verse shares with five-character *shi* the same habits of rhyming and couplet organization, except that in every line two syllables are added before the caesura (which now falls between syllables four and five).

Up to ca. 500 C.E. the two aspects of linguistic sound that a poet needed to take into account were the number of syllables in a line (the language being monosyllabic, syllable count was the same thing as character and word count) and the placement of rhyme words. But in the latter part of the period of political fragmentation that fills the centuries between the Han and Tang dynasties, Chinese writers became conscious of the tonal characteristics of their language,[9] and verse form began to stipulate rules of euphony and phonetic patterning. One result of this attention to sound qualities was the "recent-style" or "regulated" verse form of the Tang (*jinti shi*, *lüshi*), in which semantic parallelism between adjacent lines was at times required, at times avoided, and the syllable-tones of adjacent lines were matched throughout for maximum contrast. The result was a verse form in which the pressure of rules was felt in every syllable. Regulated verse occupied an eight-line stanza; related to this was the *jueju* (quatrain), which scholars have long attempted to trace to the shorter *yuefu* or an abbreviation of the *lüshi*. At the same time, poetry in a freer mold, observing the basic conventions as they had existed previous to the Tang, continued to be composed under the name of "ancient-style" verse (*gu shi*).

Beginning in the Tang, also, musical form began to exert a new kind of influence on verse. Melodies from Central Asia, with musical phrases of various length, caught the attention of lyricists who composed for them stanzas of "long and short lines"—the precursors of the poetic genre of *ci* or song-lyrics, one name for which is in fact *changduan ju*, "long and short lines." Lyrics would have to be crafted to suit the specific features of a melody: its placement of emphasis, of short and long notes, and so on, and thus a melody became a rather rigorous armature for a stanza form as numerous alternate lyrics were written for it. A *ci* tune-type is referred to by a tag drawn from the circumstances of the tune's circulation or the wording of its best-known poetic setting: these titles and the prosodic features they specify have long survived the disappearance of the original music. (See Appendix A.) As noted above, *ci* compositions were at first performed in extraliterary settings—principally banquets involving female entertainers. Thus, song-lyrics are associated with women, indeed specifically with the female voice. Many *ci* compositions were cast as monologues for female speakers. The elaboration of a male or neutral persona for *ci* was the work of several centuries. *Ci* compositions range in form from the brief *xiaoling* ("short song," which is limited to fifty-eight or fewer characters), often misleadingly similar to a regular stanza of *shi* poetry, to the lengthy, complex, and non-stanzaic *manci* ("prolonged song-lyric").

Dramatic writing, especially in the Yuan dynasty, when an occupation government interrupted the usual occasions of literary culture, contributed a further genre, the *qu*, or "aria." Arias without a dramatic setting—in other words, isolated lyric compositions—were known as *sanqu*, or "dispersed arias." Certain *sanqu* became, like *ci*, templates in which later poets composed their own words. (*Sanqu* titles are also included in Appendix A.) All traditional Chinese theater was sung, which presupposes verse composition. A recitation to instrumental accompaniment, the *tanci*, or "strumming lyric," could take narrative or dramatic form.

In translating these forms, we have not been unduly scrupulous to give every structural feature its English equivalent. No attempt has been made at rhyme. By and large, a line in the English corresponds to a line in the original. In regular verse-forms the correspondence is helpful: the reader can follow the parallelisms and antitheses on which the effect of the original often depends. In the case of *ci* and other asymmetrical forms, it may be that only the most extreme contrasts of line length remain recognizable. Some translators prefer to break a long line midway; others have reconstructed poems on new bases. The line numbers in the text, which are keyed to the lines of the Chinese originals (or approximately so), reflect *shi* stanza structure in marking the eighth verse and every fourth verse thereafter. The commentary that follows the poems is also keyed to these line numbers. (See Editorial Conventions.)

The thematic groupings of Chinese poetry are too numerous to list, but a few types may help the reader look for similarities in the corpus we have provided. There are first of all functional categories: hymns (*song*), elegies (*lei*, *diao*), letter-poems, poems of farewell, jokes. Social occasions often led to *lianju* ("linked-rhyme") compositions, in which one person would start a chain of verses for others to finish. Poems in the *zengda* ("bestowals and responses") mode demonstrated friendship or at the least sociability. Friends would often reply to each other's poems with new poems answering the previous poems' rhyme-words: this is known as "following the rhymes" or "harmonizing with the rhymes" of another. (As a sign of homage, one might follow the rhymes of a famous poem by a long-dead master.)

Palace-style verse (*gongti shi*) emerged from the special circumstances of court sociability, where little of substance could be discussed but where every utterance had to show polish. Among the popular genres for palace poetry was the *yongwu shi* or "poem in praise of an object," which might read as obscurely as a riddle. Another palace genre later adopted by the public (including the female public) was the *gui yuan*, the "boudoir lament": expressions of distress by neglected, offended, or simply unhappy women. The *yongshi shi* ("poem in praise of history") reworked episodes from the chronicles, sharpening them to a few intense images. Poems "on rising from an illness" and "expressing my feelings" fixed moments in the poet's life.

Before the modern period, Chinese poetry did not always reach its reader in single-author collections. If we had not had previous anthologies to go on, this work would have been far shorter. Anthologies of women's writing are discussed in the Editorial Conventions ("A Note on Sources"). Here it is to the point to cite the major general collections in which so much of the work of preservation and judgment takes place. After the *Book of Odes*, the great anthologies are *Wen xuan* (Selections of refined literature, ca. 530), *Yutai xinyong* (YTXY: New songs from a jade terrace, ca. 545), *Huajian ji* (Among the flowers, ca. 940), *Yuefu shiji* (The Music Bureau collection, twelfth century), *Liechao shiji* (LCSJ: Collection from the former [Ming] dynasty, ca. 1650), and the retrospective omnibus anthologies *Quan Tang shi* (QTS: Collected poetry of the Tang), *Song shi chao* (Shi poetry of the Song, transcribed), *Quan Song ci* (QSC: Collected song-lyric poetry of the Song), and so forth.

Other technical matters are covered in the section on Editorial Conventions, Appendix A on tune-titles, or the notes to specific authors.

Part One POETRY

From Ancient Times to the Six Dynasties (222–589)

班捷妤

P.1. Ban *jieyu* (ca. 48–ca. 6 B.C.E.)

Favorite Beauty Ban (Ban *jieyu*) came from a family of prominent officials and scholars; she was the great-aunt of the famous historian Ban Gu. At the beginning of the reign of Emperor Cheng of the Han (r. 37–33 B.C.E.), Lady Ban entered the imperial harem as a junior maid, which conferred rank eleven in the fourteen-rank system of palace personnel. She rapidly rose to rank two, the position of *jieyu* or Favorite Beauty, which theoretically had a status above that of the Nine Chamberlains, or heads of the chief divisions of the imperial government. She bore the emperor two sons; both died in infancy. She was known for her learning and strong sense of propriety. On one occasion the emperor invited her to ride with him in the imperial chaise. Lady Ban refused on the grounds that the ancient paintings always depicted the degenerate last rulers of the three pre-imperial dynasties (Xia, Shang, and Zhou) with their female favorites at their sides, and she feared that if she shared the emperor's cart, he might be deemed a negligent wastrel like them.

Lady Ban enjoyed Emperor Cheng's favor until the Hongjia period (20–17 B.C.E.), when he began to bestow his affection on a dancer, Zhao Feiyan (Flying Swallow Zhao, d. 1 B.C.E.), and her younger sister, later known as the Brilliant Companion Zhao (Zhao *zhaoyi*). In 18 B.C.E., Emperor Cheng's principal wife, Empress Xu, was accused of using black magic against pregnant palace ladies, and she was deposed. Zhao Feiyan accused Lady Ban of conspiring with Empress Xu and even trying to put a curse on the emperor himself. When interrogated by the judicial officers, Lady Ban eloquently replied with a quotation from the *Analects* of Confucius (12.5): "Life and death are determined by fate, but wealth and honor reside with Heaven." She then went on to say: "If I have cultivated uprightness, but have yet to receive good fortune, what could I expect to gain by doing evil? If the spirits and gods have sentience, they will not accept the plaint of a disloyal subject. If they do not have sentience, what good would it do to complain to them? Thus, I would never do such a thing." Her reply so impressed the emperor that he took pity on her and rewarded her with a gift of one hundred catties (well over a hundred pounds) of gold.

However, fearful of further accusations from the ruthless Zhao sisters, Lady Ban requested permission to leave the imperial palace, giving as an excuse her desire to care for the aged Empress Dowager Wang. The emperor granted her request, and she took up residence in the Palace of Eternal Trust, one of the halls of the Palace of Eternal Joy, which was the principal residence of empresses in the Han. After Emperor Cheng died in 7 B.C.E., she was assigned to the staff of his funeral park, yet a further remove from palace rivalries. She died there and was buried, ca. 6 B.C.E.

Lady Ban is traditionally credited with three poetic works: two *fu* and one pentasyllabic poem. The pentasyllabic poem, most commonly known under the title "Yuan ge xing" (P.1.1, "Song of Resentment"), is often cited as one of the earliest examples of this verse form. The attribution of this poem has, however, been questioned since the late Six Dynasties period.[1]

The two rhapsodies, or *fu*, ascribed to Favorite Beauty Ban are "Rhapsody on Pounding Silk" ("Dao su fu") and "Rhapsody of Self-Commiseration" (P.1.2, "Zi dao fu"). As for the first, the style and the theme of the woman pining for her lover as she fulls cloth on a cold autumn night seem more appropriate for the Six Dynasties than the end of the Former Han dynasty. Thus, it is probably not authentic, and it is not included here.[2]

The "Rhapsody of Self-Commiseration" is contained in Lady Ban's biography in the *Han shu* (History of the Former Han), and there is no question about its authorship. According to the *Han shu*, Lady Ban wrote this rhapsody after she had left the court and taken up residence in the Palace of Eternal Trust. It is a poem highly charged with emotion, one of the few truly personal rhapsodies of the Former Han period. For commentary on Lady Ban, see C.23.1–2.

P.1.1. Song of Resentment

Newly cut white silk from Qi,
Glistening and pure as frost and snow:
Fashioned into a fan of "conjoined bliss,"

Round, round as the bright moon.
It goes in and out of my lord's breast and sleeve;
Waved, it stirs a gentle breeze.
But I always fear autumn's coming,
When chilling winds dispel blazing heat.
Then it will be thrown into a box,
And his love will be cut off midcourse.

(*Wen xuan*, 27/17a–b)

P.1.2. Rhapsody of Self-Commiseration

Heir to virtue bequeathed by my ancestors,
Endowed in life with a noble genius,
My humble person was presented to the palace towers,
To fill a low rank in the rear court.
Basking in the sage sovereign's generous grace,
I faced the resplendent brilliance of sun and moon.
Surrounded by the fiery glow of majesty,
I received highest favor in the Storied Lodge.
Having been inordinately blessed by an undeserved position,
I thought perhaps this was a propitious time.
Whether awake or asleep, I sighed repeatedly;
I'd loosen my sash and reflect on myself.
I spread out paintings of women to serve as guiding mirrors;
Consulting the lady scribe, I asked about the *Odes*.
Saddened by the monition of the hen that crows,
I lamented the transgressions of Bao and Yan.
I praised Huang and Ying, wives of the Lord of Yu,
Extolled Ren and Si, mothers of Zhou.
Although stupid and uncouth, and unable to emulate them,
Dare I still my thoughts and forget them?
With the passing years I have become sad and fearful,
Sorrowing for the lush blossoms that no longer flourish.
I painfully remember Yanglu and Silkworm Thorn lodges,
Where, still in swaddling clothes, my infant sons met disaster.
How could this be the fault of this lowly concubine?
For one cannot seek to undo Heaven's decree.
Suddenly, the bright sun shifted its light,

And as dusky evening fell, all was dim and dark.
Yet I still received generous grace of shelter and support,
And was not cast aside for my faults and transgressions.
Now to care for the Empress Dowager in the eastern chamber,
I am assigned a lowly rank in the Palace of Eternal Trust.
I dutifully sprinkle and sweep amidst the curtains;
Ever shall I do so, until my death.
May they return my bones to the foot of a hill,
To rest in the lingering shade of pine and cypress.

The Coda says:

I am hidden in the dark palace, secluded and still:
The main entrance is shut, the forbidden gates barred,
Dust lies in ornate halls, moss covers jade stairs,
In its courtyards, green grass thickly grows.
Broad chambers are somber, curtains darkly drawn,
Through empty window gratings the wind blows biting cold.
It stirs curtains and gown, blows red chiffons;
Swish, swish, the sound of rustling silks.
My soul flies away to some secret, quiet place;
My lord no longer favors me with his presence—who could feel honor in this?
I look down over the vermilion walkway
And recall where my lord used to tread.
I look up at his cloud-enshrouded chamber
And twin streams of tears pour down my face.
With pleasant expression, I look at those around me;
Pour a winged goblet to dispel my sorrow.
I think how one is born to life,
Only suddenly to pass as if drifting in a stream.
Already I've enjoyed eminence and honor,
And lived a life of unmatched blessings.
I shall cheer my spirit, enjoy myself to the full,
For good fortune and felicity are hard to predict.
"Green Jacket" and "White Flower"—
From ancient times, such has been the state of affairs.

(*Han shu*, 97b/3985–87)

line 4: The rear court is the location of the women's apartments of the palace (the harem).

line 8: The Storied Lodge was one of eight lodges in the women's quarters of the palace.

line 12: The reference is to the instruction Lady Ban received from her mother at the time of her sash-binding ceremony. Performed just before a young woman left for her new home, the binding of the sash was intended to signify the devotion of the new bride to her husband and his family.

line 14: The *Book of Odes*.

line 15: Zhòu, the degenerate last king of the Shang dynasty (d. ca. 1040 B.C.E.), was said to be dominated by his wife. The *Shang shu* records that King Wu, the founder of the Zhou dynasty, addressed his troops before the decisive battle with Shang in these terms: "The ancients had a saying: The hen should not call the morning. If the hen calls the morning, the house is at an end" (Karlgren, *The Book of Documents*, p. 29, translation modified; *Shang shu*, "Mu shi," SSJZS 11/16b).

line 16: Bao Si, presumably a member of the princely family of the state of Bao, was offered to the Zhou monarch You after his victory over Bao. She refused to smile despite all You's efforts to amuse her, until one day You had the idea of lighting the beacon fires and announcing a military emergency. The sight of the counselors and generals anxiously assembling for no purpose drew a laugh from Bao Si, and the trick was repeated again and again until one day, when a real emergency presented itself, no one answered the call, and King You was killed (*Shi ji* 4, "Zhou ben ji," 4/62–65). The word *Yan*, paired with Bao in this line, is problematic. It seems to derive from a line in poem 193 of the *Book of Odes*, where the Lu version of the classic has "wife of Yan" and the Mao version has "beautiful wife." According to the Mao commentary, "beautiful wife" refers to Bao Si. However, the Tang dynasty commentator to the *Han shu*, Yan Shigu, says Yan is the name of a favored clan in the time of the Zhou king Li.

line 17: Ying and Huang are Nü Ying and E Huang, daughters of the sage ruler Yao, who married them to Shun, also known as the Lord of Yu (reportedly ca. 2300 B.C.E.). They were known for their humility, frugality, intelligence, and devotion to their husband.

line 18: Ren is Tairen, the mother of King Wen of Zhou. Si is Taisi, the mother of King Wu of Zhou. Both are revered examples of virtuous motherhood in the Confucian tradition.

line 59: "Green Jacket" ("Lü yi") is the title of poem 27 in the *Book of Odes*. According to the Mao commentary, this song was a complaint by the wife of Duke Zhuang of Wei (r. 758–35 B.C.E.), known as Zhuangjiang, against a concubine who had usurped her place. "White Flower" ("Bai hua") is poem 229 in the same collection. According to the Mao commentary, this song criticizes Bao Si for usurping the rightful place of King You's queen. Lady Ban probably uses these references to allude to the improper conduct of the two Zhao sisters at the court of Emperor Cheng.

BIOGRAPHICAL NOTE AND TRANSLATION BY DAVID R. KNECHTGES

P.2. Cai Yan (176?–early 3rd century)

Cai Yan, courtesy name Wenji (Lady of Literary Refinement), was the daughter of the eminent poet and statesman Cai Yong (133–92; see P.85.5), who died in prison after his associate, the frontier general Dong Zhuo (d. 192) rebelled against the Han dynasty. Even as a young woman, she was noted for her poetic talent and scholarly knowledge. Cai Yan was captured in 192 by a raiding party of barbarian mercenaries. Although already a widow and so by Chinese custom no longer eligible for marriage, she became the wife of a chieftain of the Southern Xiongnu. Cai Yan bore two sons to her husband in exile, then was forced to leave them behind when she was ransomed by Cao Cao (155–220) in 206. Cai Yan was the last surviving member of a distinguished and influential clan, which had been destroyed in the struggles that brought Cao Cao to power after the fall of the Han. He therefore needed her to placate the ancestor spirits of her family, lest they exercise a baneful influence on his fledgling Wei dynasty. Upon her return, she was given a new Chinese husband, Dong Si. Although her clan, as represented by her, had been restored to its former status by Cao Cao, Cai Yan found herself ostracized at court because of both her family connections and her degrading multiple marriages.

Upon her return to the capital, Cao Cao is said to have called Cai Yan to an audience and tested her by asking if she could remember any of the books in her father's famous library. She obliged him by writing down several thousand titles. Her new husband later offended Cao Cao and was condemned to death. Cai Yan, taking advantage of her notoriety, challenged Cao Cao's sentence before the court and asked him if he would provide her with yet *another* husband. Dong Si was spared.[1]

Three poetic compositions have been ascribed to Cai Yan. Two appear in her *Hou Han shu* biography, which dates from 424–45, and are narrative poems, one in the regular *shi* meter and the other in the more rhapsodic *sao* form; both describe her life among the nomads. The third, translated here, is a poem sequence in *shi* form, the "Eighteen Songs of a Nomad Flute" (P.2.1). It is probably the most influential of her works, but its authorship is also the most debated, for it is not transmitted by any text earlier than Guo Maoqian's anthology *Yuefu shiji* in the late eleventh century.[2] After the compilation of that anthology, Zhu Xi included the "Eighteen Songs" in his *Chuci houyu* (Sequels to the songs of Chu; late twelfth century), and his assertion of its authenticity was accepted by the majority of critics until the modern period.[3] While it may never be possible to prove Cai Yan's authorship, the sequence is unique in early poetry for the direct, passionately expressed identity of the woman's voice. Many later variations and rewritings of the Cai Yan theme—notably that of the mid-Tang male poet Liu Shang (fl. 770), which immediately follows Cai's sequence in Guo Maoqian's anthology—give it a self-consciously "feminine" voice, endowed with the virtues of compliance and passivity most often emphasized by men writing in female personae. In stark contrast, the poems translated here stress the particularity of the speaker's voice with repeated personal pronouns and raw emotion. They ring with unassuaged grief—a style impossible for the formulaic voice of female narrators after the fifth century.[4]

P.2.1. *Eighteen Songs of a Nomad Flute*

SONG 1

In the early part of my life, equity still governed the empire,
But later in my life the Han throne fell into decay.
Heaven was not humane, sending down rebellion and chaos,
Earth was not humane, causing me to encounter such a time.
War gear was a daily commonplace, and travel by road was dangerous,
The common people fled, all plunged in wretchedness.
Smoke and dust darkened the countryside, overrun by barbarians;
They knocked aside my widow's vows, and my chastity was lost.
Their strange customs were so utterly foreign to me—
Whom can I possibly tell of my calamity, shame, and grief?
One measure for the nomad flute, one stanza for the *qin*,
No one can know my heart's agony and anger!

SONG 2

A barbarian of the northwest tribes took me to wife by force,
He led me on a journey to the lands at the horizon,
Ten thousand strata of cloudy peaks, so stretched the returning road,
A thousand miles of piercing winds, driving dust and sand.
The people extravagantly savage, violent—like reptiles and snakes,
They draw their bows, they wear armor, their bearing arrogant and
fierce.

My second song stretches the strings, stretches them to the breaking point,
My will shattered, my heart broken, I lament and sigh.

SONG 3

I traveled across the land of Han and entered barbarian domains,
My home was lost, my body violated; better never to have been born.
The felts and furs they make into clothes are a shock to my bones and flesh,
I cannot hide my disgust for the taste of their rank-smelling mutton.
War drums pulse through the night until it grows light,
The barbarian wind roars with great noise and obscures the border camps.
Appalled by the present, regretting the past, my third song is done,
My sorrow builds, my anger mounts; when will there be peace?

SONG 4

Not a day, not a night when I do not long for my home,
Of all beings that live and breathe, none can be as bitter as I.
Heaven unleashed calamity upon an empire in crisis, leaving the people without a leader,
But only I have this miserable fate, to be lost among the barbarians.
Their customs different, their minds unlike, how can I survive among them?
What we like and want are not the same, with whom can I even speak?
I brood on what I have been through, how adverse my fate,
My fourth song is finished, and my suffering more intense.

SONG 5

The wild geese fly to the south; I wish I could send my thoughts from the border,
The wild geese return to the north; I might get news from China.
The wild geese fly high, so remote they are hard to see;
I break my heart in vain, my thoughts dark and hidden.
With knitted brows I face the moon and strum my elegant *qin*,
My fifth song is quiet and desolate, emotion deepening.

SONG 6

The ice and frost are shattering, my body bitterly cold,
Though hungry, when faced with meat and milk I cannot take the meal.
At night I listen to the waters of the Long, its sound sadly murmuring,
In the morning I see the Great Wall—this road spreads out forever!
My thoughts go back to the days past, the travel so very hard,
With the sixth song sorrow comes—I wish I could stop playing.

SONG 7

At sunset the wind is melancholy, its frontier strains rise all around,
I do not know if there is someone to share my grieving heart.
The border wastes are desolate, ten thousand miles of beacons,
Their customs despise the old and weak, in favor of the young and strong.
They wander wherever water and grass may be, and there set up camps and defenses,
Cattle and sheep fill the land, swarming like bees or ants.
When the grass is finished and water used up, livestock and horses all move,
(8) My seventh song flows with resentment—I hate living in this place!

SONG 8

Heaven is supposed to have eyes; how can it not see me drifting alone?
Spirits should have some power; how came I south of the sky and north of the sea?
I did not offend Heaven; how could Heaven match me with such a strange mate?
I did not offend the spirits; how could the spirits have cast me into the distant wilderness?
I composed my eighth song to give form to my grief,
How could I know when the piece was done my sorrow would be more intense?

SONG 9

Heaven has no horizon, earth no borders,
My heart's grief is likewise boundless and unceasing,

Human life passes swiftly, like a white horse flashing by a crack,
Here I am in the prime of life with never a happy day!
I am angry, and wish to question Heaven,
But Heaven is so vast, I have no way to reach it.
I raise my head and gaze up into its empty clouds and smoke.
(8) My ninth song conveys my feelings, but to whom may I tell them?

SONG 10

The beacons on the fortress are never allowed to die out,
When will the warfare over this wilderness ever cease?
The urge to kill, day in, day out, assaults the border gates,
The nomad wind, night in, night out, cries to the frontier moon.
I am severed from my home town, cut off from any news,
I cry without a sound, my breath about to choke.
Separation from my home has caused a lifetime of bitterness,
(8) My tenth song deepens in melancholy, tears turn into blood.

SONG 11

I am not one who clings to life on account of a fear of death,
But I could not do away with myself; my heart had its reasons:
If I lived I could still hope to return to the land of mulberries and catalpas,
But if I died my bones would be buried here, in the empty plains.
Days and months I dwelt among the nomads,
My nomad husband was fond of me, and we had two sons.
I nurtured them, brought them up, I can feel no shame for this.
(8) I felt for them, pitied them, born in the far frontier.
My eleventh song has risen from this emotion,
Its sad harmonies entwine to penetrate heart and marrow.

SONG 12

The east wind responds to natural recurrences, with plenty of warm air,
I know that the Han Son of Heaven is spreading energy and peace.
Now the Qiang and the Hu dance the measures and sing in harmony,
The two nations make a truce and put an end to conflict.
Suddenly we meet an envoy from China, bearing a direct order;

He offers a thousand pieces of gold as a ransom for me.
I rejoice that I lived for a chance to return to greet our enlightened ruler,
But I grieve at parting from my two young sons, with no chance of meeting again.
My twelfth song balances sorrow and joy,
My twin emotions—go, stay—to whom can I reveal them?

SONG 13

I had never dreamed I would ever go home again;
I caress, I embrace my nomad sons, the flowing tears soak our clothes.
To escort me the envoy from China has a team of horses,
My nomad children wail till they lose their voices—alas! who could have known
That while we still lived there would come a time that would separate us like death?
My longing for my children makes the sun lose its light,
Where can I find wings to carry me back to you?
Step by step I am farther away, though my feet can hardly go on,
Our souls devastated, our shadows cut apart, just our love is left to us.
In my thirteenth song the strings are passionate, the tones melancholy,
My bowels feel cut to pieces, and no one knows what I have known.

SONG 14

My body returns to my country, but my sons cannot know how to follow;
My heart lingers with them, the distance will forever keep me starved for news.
The four seasons and the myriad creatures have their natural flourishing and waning,
Only my grief and bitterness cannot change.
The mountains are high, the earth is broad—we can have no hope of meeting—
Deep in the night I dream that you have come here,
In my dream we clutch each other's hands—one part joy, one part sorrow,
After I wake the pain in my heart leaves me without a moment's rest,

In my fourteenth song, alas, tears stream down my face,
As the waters of the Yellow River flow east, so my heart flows with
these thoughts.

SONG 15

In my fifteenth song the tempo of the melody quickens,
The spirit which rises in my breast, who understands its song?
I lived in a yurt with the nomads, their customs so different and
strange,
I longed to return to my home, and Heaven granted my wish,
My return to China should be enough to gladden my heart.
But my heart is full of memories that feed my ever-deepening sorrow,
The sun and moon are impartial, yet they fail to shine on me.
(8) The thoughts of children and mother separated are hard to bear;
Though the same sky is our canopy, we are like distant constellations,
Not knowing if one or another lives or dies, or where we might find
each other.

SONG 16

In the sixteenth song my thoughts range over vast distances,
I and my children in different places,
Like the sun in the east, the moon in the west, we may only gaze
toward each other,
But never come together again, in vain our vitals are crushed.
I contemplate the forget-all-care lily, but my sadness is not forgotten,
I play the sounding *qin*—how wounded are my feelings!
Now I have parted from my children and returned to my old home,
(8) My former anguish has been set to rest, but my new anguish grows
with time.
Weeping blood, I lift up my head and rage at the high heavens,
Why was I born to suffer such unheard-of disaster?

SONG 17

In my seventeenth song, my heart and nose are sore as if they inhaled
vinegar,
Passes and mountains, dangerous and long—the road brutal to travel,

When I left, I longed for my home soil, I had no idea what would happen;
When I came back, separated from my sons, my thoughts of them flowed on and on.
Wormwood on the frontier lands—brittle twigs, dry leaves,
White bones on the desert battlefields—blade wounds, arrow scars.
Wind-borne frost chills, chills; spring and summer are cold,
(8) Men and horses hungry, weary; bones and flesh too meager.
How could I know I would come again to Chang'an?—
I give a great sigh, as if to break; tears fill my eyes.

SONG 18

The nomad flute originally came from the nomads themselves,
Matched with the *qin*, their music follows the same patterns.
With these eighteen stanzas, my song is finished,
But the tones continue, and my longing is without end.
From this we know how subtle strings and pipes may be; they reflect the work of creation,
In sorrow and joy they follow men's hearts, and transform to match them.
The nomads and Han, different lands, different customs,
(8) Heaven and earth separate us, alas!—children west, mother east.
Bitter am I, angry my spirit, flooding to the great void,
The length and breadth of the universe cannot contain this feeling!

(Su Zhecong, 34–37)

Song 1, line 1: This line comes in its entirety from the *Book of Odes*, poem 70, as does the first half of the second line.

Song 1, line 4: Compare the words of Laozi, "Heaven and earth are not humane; they regard the ten thousand things as straw dogs" (*Dao de jing*, chap. 5; trans. Henricks, *Lao-tzu*, p. 57).

Song 1, line 7: The Hu and Qiang were two of the principal "barbarian" or nomad tribes living on China's northwest frontier throughout early Chinese history (see Song 12).

Song 1, line 11: The nomad flute was a reed pipe, known for its plaintive sound. Technically a zither rather than a lute, the *qin* is a 7-stringed instrument that is placed on the floor or on a table before the player; the strings are fingered with the left hand and plucked with the right.

Song 5, line 2: Cai Yan here recalls the heroic endurance of the Han emissary

Su Wu (140–60 B.C.E.), who was held captive for nineteen years by the nomadic Xiongnu (known to European history as the Huns). When he refused to betray his sovereign, the Xiongnu threw him into a dungeon to die; he survived by eating snow. Concluding that he must have supernatural powers, the Xiongnu sent him into the northern steppe to tend sheep. He refused many entreaties to switch his allegiance to the Xiongnu court, and for some time the Xiongnu Khan answered all Han inquiries with the report that he was dead. Finally, a Han envoy told the Khan that the Emperor had shot a wild goose with a message from Su Wu attached to its leg, thus he knew that Su Wu was still alive and living in Xiongnu territory. The Khan was so impressed with this news that he released the now white-haired old man. Su Wu is thus an example of steadfast loyalty and integrity despite the bitterest hardship, and on account of his story wild geese are a conventional symbol for letters from far away.

Song 6, line 3: The Long is a river in present-day Gansu province.

Song 9, line 3: An expression derived from the Warring States philosopher Zhuang Zhou (ca. 350–300 B.C.E.). See *Zhuangzi*, chap. 29; also *Li ji*, chap. 37.

Song 11, line 3: That is, to her own home in China. Mulberries and catalpas are trees of a milder climate and are cultivated for silk production and for beauty; hence they evoke the difference in lifestyle between the Chinese and the nomads.

Song 12, line 7: This would be Cao Cao, who sent the ransom for Cai Yan.

Song 16, line 5: *Xuancao* (forget-all-care lily) or *Hemerocallis flava* (*H. lilioasphodelus*) is an early-blooming species of daylily native to China. Its delectable, fresh scent was thought to dispel melancholy. Cf. poem 62 of the *Book of Odes*: "Where does one find the *xuan*-plant? It is planted north of the house [i.e., near the women's quarters]." The Mao commentary adds: "The *xuan* causes people to forget their sorrows" (*Mao shi*, in SSJZS 3.3/14a.)

BIOGRAPHICAL NOTE AND TRANSLATION BY DORE J. LEVY

P.3. Zuo Fen (255?–300)

Zuo Fen was the younger sister of the renowned Western Jin poet Zuo Si (ca. 250–ca. 305). She was a native of Linzi prefecture (modern Zibo City in Shandong). Although she came from an undistinguished clan, she acquired a good literary education. In 272, she was selected as a lady-in-waiting for the Western Jin emperor Sima Yan (Emperor Wu, r. 265–90). Zuo Fen was a rather homely woman, and her literary talents, rather than her beauty, seem to have been the reason for her entering the palace and winning the title *xiuyi* (Lady of Cultivated Deportment). During her first year in the palace, she composed "Rhapsody of Thoughts on Separation" (P.3.3) upon imperial command. Despite its being written under imperial auspices, Zuo Fen actually uses the piece to express the frustration of a concubine who is sequestered in the recesses of the palace, unable even to see members of her own family. In 274, she was promoted to her highest rank, *guipin* (Honorable Companion). Zuo Fen was often ill, and except for her writings to imperial command, she did not play an active role in palace life.

Throughout her stay in the imperial palace, Sima Yan frequently summoned her to compose poems and prose pieces for special occasions. In 274, she wrote a long dirge upon the death of Empress Yang. In 276, Sima Yan commanded her to write a dirge for his deceased daughter, Princess Wannian. Zuo Fen's extant corpus includes *fu* rhapsodies, eulogies (*song*), dirges (*lei*), and two lyric *shi*. Her most admired pieces are "Heartfelt Feelings on Separation" (P.3.2) and the "Rhapsody of Thoughts on Separation," both of which trenchantly express her personal feelings of loneliness and longing for her family.[1]

P.3.1. Woodpecker Song

There is a bird in the southern hills;
It calls itself "woodpecker."
When hungry it pecks a tree;
At dusk it sleeps in a nest.
It seeks nothing from man,
And does as it pleases.
Such is the nature of the birds and beasts.
(8) Honor shall come to one of pure character,
But he who sullies himself shall fall into disgrace.

(Lu Qinli, ed., *Xian Qin Han Wei Jin Nanbeichao shi*, 1: 730; Su Zhecong, 56)

This poem is preserved in Li Fang, comp., *Taiping yulan*, 923/7a, and Ouyang Xin, comp., *Yiwen leiju*, 92/1604, which identify it as a poem by a Lady née Zuo contained in the *Paixie ji* (Collection of humorous writings) by Yuan Shu (408–53). We are thus not certain that it is actually by Zuo Fen. The poem probably is a fragment.

P.3.2. Heartfelt Feelings on Separation

From the time I left our parents,
Suddenly two years have passed.
The distance separating us has become gradually greater;
When shall I pay my respects to them again?

I have perused what you kindly told me in your letter,
And I savor the words of your sorrowful song of separation.
I can almost imagine your face before me,
And I sigh and sob out of control.
When will we meet again
To amuse ourselves with prose and verse?
How can I recount my misery?
I'll express my feelings in writing.

(Lu Qinli, ed., *Xian Qin Han Wei Jin Nanbeichao shi*, 1; 730; Su Zhecong, 56)

Zuo Fen's brother had sent her a set of poems titled "Sorrow at Separation, Sent to My Younger Sister." This poem is her response. She probably wrote this piece in 274.

P.3.3. Rhapsody of Thoughts on Separation

I

Born in the humble seclusion of a thatched hut,
I knew nothing of state documents.
I never saw the splendid portraits painted on palace walls,
Or heard the canons and counsels of the ancient sages.
Despite my foolish vulgarity and meager learning,
I was mistakenly given a place in the purple chamber.
This is not a place for a rustic,
And I constantly tremble with worry and fear.
My breast is filled with the sadness of longing,
Redoubled by ten thousand unremitting cares.
Alas, heavy sorrows accumulate deep within me!
Alone in my torment, I have no way to vent them.
My mind is vexed and troubled, joyless;
My thoughts are tied in a tangle, and my longing increases.
At night I lie awake unable to sleep;
My soul is restless, fretful till dawn.
Wind, soughing and sighing, rises all around;
Frost, pure white, covers the courtyard.
The sun, dim and dark, casts no light;
The air is sad and gloomy, bitterly cold.
I hear many sorrowful feelings
And am afflicted by tears that fall of themselves.

II

Of old, Boyu, handsome and fair,
Always dressed in colored clothes to cheer his parents.
I grieve at the separation of today;
Like Antares and Orion, long have family and I been parted.
It is not that the distance is far—
It does not even exceed several rods.
How cold and confining the forbidden palace!
I wish to gaze into the distance but lack the means.
I look up at the moving clouds and sob;
Flowing tears soak my gown.
Qu Yuan was beset with sorrow;
Oh, how he grieved at separation!
He who wrote a song at the wall tower
Compared one day to three months.
How much more painful for parents and children who love each other,
Cut off so long and so far.
Long have I been laden with sorrow, afflicted with grief;
I look up at the blue sky and weep tears of blood.

The Coda says:

Parents and children, the dearest of kin,
Have been transformed into strangers.
We bid a final farewell,
And I was sorrowful and sad.
I dream that my soul returns home,
And I see my loved ones.
I wake with a start and cry out:
My heart cannot comfort itself.
Copious tears pour down my face;
I pick up a brush and express my feelings.
Tear upon tear falls
As I make my plaint in this poem.

(*Jin shu*, 31/957–58; Su Zhecong, 57–58)

ii, lines 1–2: Han Boyu was a legend of filial piety. Even at the age of seventy his absence of self-regard allowed him to dress in motley to amuse his parents. See Cao Zhi, "Song of the Magic Polypore," cited in *Song shu*, 22/627.

ii, line 4: Antares (*shang*) and Orion (*shen*) are used proverbially to mean "poles apart."

ii, lines 11–12: Qu Yuan's grief at being cast off by his king is recorded in Qu's "Li sao" (Encountering sorrow; the title may also be translated as "Bemoaning separation"); see P.37.

ii, line 14: Zuo alludes to poem 91 from the *Book of Odes*, a lover's lament: "I pace to and fro / By the wall tower. / One day that I do not see you / Is like three months."

P.3.4. *Rhapsody on Pine and Cypress*

How grand and luxuriant these wondrous trees,
That rest on the towering heights of lofty peaks!
Girded by a dark stream that twists and twines,
They look down upon a green river's white swells.
Their tall trunks rise up in stately majesty,
Their emerald foliage grows in rank profusion.
Spreading forth lush exuberance of tender stalks,
Displaying the verdure of lovely needles,
They are arrayed with green cones thickly clustered,
And their fragrance is ever heavy and strong.
Splendidly growing, they are broadly spread;
Their aura is solemn and grave, pure and cold.
Responding to the wind, their branches sing,
Just like the echoing sounds of strings and reeds.
Endowed from nature with firmness and strength,
They endure harsh winter and never shed their foliage.
Even in freezing frost their trunks stand tall,
And as verdant spring approaches they remain lush and luxuriant.
They are like the gentleman who accords with the season,
And resemble the unyielding steadfastness of the True Man.
Chi Songzi wanders below them and attains the Way;
Wen Bin, eating their cones, achieves long life.
Poets sing of their lush luxuriance;
Like the southern mountains they are forever tranquil.

(Yan Kejun, *Quan shanggu sandai Qin Han Sanguo Liuchao wen*, 13/2a; Su Zhecong, 58)

This rhapsody is a fragment. Extracts of it are found in *Yiwen leiju*, 88/1516, and Xu Jian, comp., *Chuxue ji*, 28/688.

lines 21–22: Chi Songzi (Red Pine) and Wen Bin are both legendary Daoist immortals.

BIOGRAPHICAL NOTE AND TRANSLATION BY DAVID R. KNECHTGES

P.4. Bao Linghui (fl. ca. 464)

Bao Linghui was a native of Donghai in Jiangsu province and the younger sister of the renowned poet Bao Zhao (ca. 414–66). Little is known about her. Her seven extant poems, all examples of the "boudoir lament" genre—poems in which a woman narrates her longing for an absent lover—are largely imitations and reworkings of earlier models, especially the "Nineteen Ancient Poems" and *yuefu* ballads.[1] For an early commentary on Bao Linghui, see C.23.4.

P.4.1. After "Green, Green, the Riverside Grass"

Slim, slim, the bamboo swaying by my window;
Lush, lush, the phoenix tree overhanging the gate.
Bright, bright, the lady by the green window,
Cold, cold, in her high terrace.
Her pure sentiments outshine autumn frost;
Her jade face eclipses spring blossoms.
Who, in life, can avoid parting?
(8) But I grieve that you're enlisted so soon.
Quavering strings shame me by the night moon;
Indigo kohl abashes me in the spring wind.

(YTXY, 152; Su Zhecong, 69)

The poem imitated is number two in the anonymous series of folk lyrics known as the "Nineteen Ancient Poems," *Wen xuan* 29/2a–b.

P.4.2. After "A Visitor Came from Far Away"

A visitor came from far away,
He brought me a lacquered singing lute.
Its wood displays a "mutual longing" design;
Its strings diffuse a tone of separateness.

All my life I'll keep to this key;
No season's cold will change my heart.
I'd like to compose a "Sunny Spring" tune
(8) With *gong* and *shang* notes ever in tandem.

(YTXY, 153; Su Zhecong, 70)

The poem imitated is number eighteen of the "Nineteen Ancient Poems," *Wen xuan*, 29/7b–8a.

line 3: A pattern exhibiting symmetry in its two halves—like the grain of a piece of wood split in two to form the body of a lute—might be described as a "mutual longing" design.

line 7: An ancient tune. Its repute in poetry stems from the following passage in Song Yu (290–223 B.C.E.), "Answering the King of Chu" (*Wen xuan*, 45/1b–2b): "When your servant composed the 'Sunny Spring' and 'White Snow' music, in the whole country there were no more than a few dozen people who could perform it. . . . The loftier the music, the fewer those who can appreciate it."

line 8: *Gong* and *shang* were the lowest and second-lowest notes in the ancient musical scale. They were believed to stand for the ruler and his minister and were expected to "respond" to each other in a composition.

P.4.3. Postscript Sent to a Traveler

Ever since you went away,
The face by the window has not lit up.
The clothes-pounder and block are mute at night;
The tall gates are closed during the day.
Into my bed curtains fireflies glide;
In front of the courtyard purple orchids bloom.
As nature withers, I know the season's changing;
(8) When wild geese arrive, I know the traveler is cold.
Your journey will end at winter's close;
I'll await your return at the start of spring.

(YTXY, 153)

line 3: The sound of women pounding laundry on distant wash-blocks frequently indicates the speaker's melancholy and sleeplessness: for early instances of the motif, see Cao Pi, "On Hearing the Clothes-Pounder at Night" (Lu Qinli, *Xian Qin Liang Han Jin Nanbeichao shi*, 1: 889); Xie Huilian, "Clothes-Pounding Song" (*Wen xuan*, 30/5a–b).

P.4.4. An Old Theme for Someone in the Present

A cold land allows no other clothing—
Wool takes the place of patterned silk.
Month after month I pine for your return;
Year after year I find no relief.
In Jing and Yang spring has long turned balmy,
But You and Ji still suffer frost and hail.
Your cold in the north I already know;
My heart in the south you do not see.
Who will convey my bitter pain?
I'll send my love through a pair of flying swallows.
My figure looks gaunt as I trim silk at the shuttle;
My face has aged, battered by lightning and wind.
One day my lovely looks will be gone;
Only my heart will stay unchanged.

(YTXY, 154; Su Zhecong, 70–71)

lines 5–6: The reference is to the two southern cities of Jingzhou and Yangzhou, and to the northern cities of Youzhou and Jizhou.

P.4.5. Two Poems Written on Behalf of Guo Xiaoyu, Wife of Monk Ge

I

The bright moon is white, so white;
Through hanging drapes it shines on my silken mattress.
It seems to share my night of longing,
To join me in my dawn of grief.
How would fragrant flowers pity my face?
Frost and dew do not spare anyone.
You may not be a blue cloud flown away,
But your drifting tracks have brought you to serve in Qin.
I will hold to a lifetime of tears,
As I pass autumn and weather spring.

II

My love is going on a distant campaign,
He gave me a pair of inscribed brocades.

Toward the moment of his leaving,
He also left a pillow of mutual longing.
His inscription I'll always etch in my heart;
His pillow reminds me of our sleep together.
On and on, each day further away,
(8) As I feel my pining deepen.

(YTXY, 154–55)

i, line 8: Qin is an area of northwestern China, remote from the capital and other cities.

P.4.6. Sent to a Traveler

The cassia has put forth several twigs;
The orchid has sprouted a few leaves.
If you do not return this moment,
The spring wind will just mock me.

(Qian Zhonglian, *Bao Canjun ji zhu*, 425; Su Zhecong, 71)

BIOGRAPHICAL NOTE AND TRANSLATION BY CHARLES KWONG

P.5. Found Voices in *Yuefu* Poetry (3rd–4th century)

These three sets of poems are examples of "western tunes" (*xiqu*) associated with the early medieval genre of *yuefu shi* (Music Bureau poetry). These anonymous poems originate in the lower reaches of the Yangzi River. While the authors are not identified, such poems were often associated with upper-class women of the time and these seem to adopt such a voice.

P.5.1. Here's a Willow Bough: Songs of the Thirteen Months

I. FIRST MONTH OF SPRING

And still the spring wind is gloomy and cold
Out with the old and in with the new
Our troubles are more than a morning's worry
  Here's a willow bough
Sad thoughts tangle my heart in knots
There's no knowing their number or profusion

II. MIDDLE MONTH OF SPRING

Into the village the crows swing on tireless wings
On the road I meet swallows flying two by two
Look, we are now in the height of spring
   Here's a willow bough
To send a message to the one I love
Come back soon, stay away no longer

III. LAST MONTH OF SPRING

As the boat floats through the curved pool
We lift our eyes to the spring flowers
The cry of the nightjar threads the woods
   Here's a willow bough
They come two by two, fluttering here and there
My love and I shall have each other

IV. FIRST MONTH OF SUMMER

When the lotus is just coming to bud
Where would I find a kindred soul to love
To share our lives in the Buddha's presence
   Here's a willow bough
Offering incense and these fine flowers
We shall have each other, each other forever

V. MIDDLE MONTH OF SUMMER

Wild rice standing three or four feet high
For whom will this pure body be a jewel?
Lovely it is in full growth
   Here's a willow bough
With it I'll make sweet buns
Intending them for my love's own hand

VI. LAST MONTH OF SUMMER

Midsummer burns like fire
The lattice is open on the north window
I sit on a couch across from my man
   Here's a willow bough

Cool hydromel stored in a bronze jar
We drink it straight and undiluted

VII. FIRST MONTH OF AUTUMN

The Weaving Girl wanders beside her river
On the other side the Herd Boy watches and sighs
Meeting only once with each turn of the year
  Here's a willow bough
Knotting together the flowers of long life
Kindred souls will not fail each other

VIII. MIDDLE MONTH OF AUTUMN

I make clothes to welcome my love
Days and nights flow on like water
Sparkling dew freezes into courtyard frost
  Here's a willow bough
At night hearing the washing blocks pound
Whose wife is this lovely lady?

IX. LAST MONTH OF AUTUMN

Sweet mums burst into yellow flower
It's not that we have no cups for wine
Ah, but what about the cold
  Here's a willow bough
I give my love these silken clothes
He says no, but with a smile

X. FIRST MONTH OF WINTER

The great trees turn lonely and stark
The sky is dark but the rain does not come
A heavy frost builds in the middle of the night
  Here's a willow bough
In the woods with pine and cypress
The year grows cold; we shall not fail each other

XI. MIDDLE MONTH OF WINTER

Again the snow is in wind-blown drifts
The branches of the tree turn barren

But pine and cypress have no need to worry
Here's a willow bough
Bundled in winter clothes, I tread on thin ice
Will my love recognize me like this?

XII. LAST MONTH OF WINTER

The sky is cold, the year about to close
Spring and fall, winter and summer too
Let's put these troubles to rest
Here's a willow bough
Sunk between pillow and mat
Sweetly entangled, time passes us by

XIII. INTERCALARY MONTH

The intercalary comes in the heat and the cold
Spring and fall rounded out by a lesser month
But there's no time that I don't think of you
Here's a willow bough
The flux of *yin* and *yang* presses me to leave
How will I ever get a steady one to care for me?

(Guo Maoqian, *Yuefu shiji*, 49/722–24)

The title literally reads "To Break Off a Willow Branch": willow branches were a token gift for someone leaving on a trip. This custom was based on the homophony in classical Chinese between the word for "willow" and the word "to stay"—by giving a willow branch one was symbolically saying "please stay." The songs are merely subtitled "first month," "middle month," and so forth. These are designations for the lunar year, which began somewhere between January 15 and February 15, depending on the year; the first month was considered the advent of spring. On the thirteenth month, see note to *xiii*.

ii, line 2: Paired swallows were harbingers of spring and a cliché for human lovers.

iii, line 3: According to legend, Du Yu, the ruler of Shu during the late Zhou dynasty, was infatuated with the wife of a court official. He died of lovesickness and was transformed into the nightjar—or cuckoo, as *dujuan* is usually translated. In some versions of the story, the cuckoo spits blood while emitting his cry. *Dujuan hua* are red azaleas—flowers said to be spotted with the cuckoo's blood.

iv, line 1: The lotus was an erotic symbol for a beautiful woman, but it also had Buddhist associations, which are developed in the following lines.

v, line 5: The cakes referred to here, *jiuzi zong*, are associated with a goddess of fertility, Jiuzi Mu. *Jiuzi* can mean "nine seeds" or "nine sons"; the number nine suggests completeness.

vi, line 5: Hydromel is a drink made of fermented honey.

vii, lines 1–2: According to legend, the Weaving Girl and Herd Boy, ill-fated lovers, were transformed into stars separated by the Milky Way, which in Chinese is called the Silver River. Once a year, on the seventh day of the seventh lunar month, magpies made a bridge for them to meet. Their reunion was celebrated on earth by various rituals, all with a focus on the lives and arts of women. The Weaving Girl was worshiped as the consummate exponent of her craft, and it was traditional on Double Seventh eve to "beg her for skill" in the coming year. On the meanings of Double Seventh in later Chinese history, see Mann, "The Education of Daughters," pp. 28–30.

viii, line 1: For a woman to make clothes for a man was a traditional sign of devotion and would indicate betrothal, perhaps marriage.

ix, line 1: *Gan ju* ("sweet mums") is the *chrysanthemum indicum, L. var. procumbens*. Its late blooming season made it a symbol of a vigorous old age; on the ninth day of the ninth month (Double Ninth, *Chongyang*), children invited their parents to drink a "longevity brew" of chrysanthemums soaked in wine.

x, line 6: This imagery is related to a passage in the *Analects* (9.28), "It is only after the year turns cold that one knows the pine and cypress are the last to lose their leaves."

xiii: The Chinese method of aligning the lunar and solar calendars is to insert intercalary lunar months every few years (seven times in nineteen years), such that there are occasionally repeated months—two "third" months, etc. The intercalations moved through the year, but never occurred in the eleventh, twelfth, or first month.

P.5.2. Peaceful Dongping

I

The north wind chilly and cold
Blows in the biting snow
Boats trapped in ice
The roads are lost in drifts

II

Fine fabrics of southern Wu
In wide bolts and long rolls
From the length of cloth I own
I will make a jacket for my man

III

Only a trifle, but
Made with my own slow hand

There are several yards more
Something for my man at parting

IV

I fashion a summer kerchief
For my old friend
Perhaps not finely made
Just to dust off my man's clothes

V

The fellow called Liu of Dongping
Always fills me with desire
To know him as my man
Would free me a thousand years

(Guo Maoqian, *Yuefu shiji*, 49/712)

Dongping is a common place name and cannot be specified.

ii, line 1: Wu is an area in the lower Yangzi River valley (near the location of present-day Shanghai). The beauty of women from Wu, like their skill in weaving, was celebrated in antiquity. "Songs of Wu" was a general name for songs like those in this selection, short compositions with a female speaker.

iii, line 4: The lines contain southern dialect words of uncertain meaning; the translation is partly conjectural.

P.5.3. *The Music of Shouyang*

I

The Range of Eight Lords is lovely
   Here in Shouyang
Once we part, please don't forget me

II

The Eastern Terrace rises a hundred feet or more
   Like wind-blown clouds
Once we part, I will never forget you

III

The bridge spans the meandering stream
   Bright as a mirror
With the steadfast tree does my man compare

IV

Leaving home, you travel afar
　It's only for you
I sense how the days and months pass me by

V

The latticed window catches the cool breeze
　Strumming a simple lute
A sigh, and then a song

VI

At night, thoughts of you
　Waiting, but you do not come
Everyone else is happy, only I am sad

VII

How splendid is the mighty Huai
　The road goes on and on
With such joy, loneliness is forgotten

VIII

Climbing up the Lai River bridge
　I watch the way home
The autumn wind dies and then rises again

IX

Going out Shang Gate, traces of my tears
　Shouyang left behind
Surely you will return, but in how many years

(Guo Maoqian, *Yuefu shiji*, 49/719–20)

Shouyang was a district in present-day Anhui province. These poems have an unusual form: five syllables, three syllables, then five syllables.

i, line 1: Bagong Shan (literally "Eight-Duke Mountains") is located in present-day Anhui province.

iii, line 3: *Shuanglin* (paired woods) is an abbreviated form of *shuangshu lin* (woods of paired trees). A "paired tree" is two trees that grow from a single base, thus representing steadfast devotion.

vi, line 1: Two characters are apparently missing from this line, which has only three syllables instead of the standard five.

ix, line 1: There is perhaps a scribal error in the name of the gate; *shang* (to wound, injury) is an unlikely name for a city gate. The similarly shaped character *yang* (bright, sunny) is probably meant.

PREFATORY NOTE AND TRANSLATION BY JOSEPH R. ALLEN

Tang (618–907) and Five Dynasties (907–60)

武則天

P.6. Wu Zetian (624/627–705)

Wu Zhao, often referred to as Empress Wu or Wu Zetian (her posthumous name), was without question the most formidable and flamboyant female figure to appear in Chinese history. For almost half a century she enjoyed supreme power, first in partnership with her husband Emperor Gaozong (r. 649–83), later as de facto regent for her sons, and finally as China's sole ruler in both fact and name. Later traditional scholars looked on her with tremendous bias, making the task of writing a reliable, objective biography today an impossible one. As Denis Twitchett notes, "Everything concerning this remarkable woman is surrounded by doubts, for she stood for everything to which the ideas of the Confucian scholar-official class were opposed—feminine interference in public affairs, government by arbitrary whim, the deliberate exploitation of factionalism, ruthless personal vendettas, political manipulation in complete disregard of ethics and principles. From the very first the historical record of her reign has been hostile, biased, and curiously fragmentary and incomplete."[1]

Wu Zhao was the daughter of the wealthy official Wu Shihuo and Madame Yang (579–670), a descendant of the Sui imperial family. Wu Zhao was most likely born in 627 and entered Emperor Taizong's harem as a fifth-rank consort, *cairen* (Lady of Talents), in 640 at the age of thirteen. After Taizong's death in 649, Wu Zhao managed to escape the typical fate of being consigned to a Buddhist convent for the rest of her life by attracting the favor of the new emperor, Gaozong, and the support of the childless Empress Wang. As a result of the new emperor's constant favor, her ability to bear a number of male children, and, most important, her own natural genius for politics, she rose to the position of empress in 655. Empress Wu's unprecedented skills are demonstrated by the fact that she became the first woman ever to perform the imperial Shan sacrifice on Mount Tai in 665. When Empress Wu's son Ruizong (r. 684–89) abdicated, she proclaimed herself the Holy and Divine Emperor of the new Zhou dynasty, reigning from 690 to 705. In 705 a sudden attack organized by the Tang loyalist Zhang Jianzhi in the name of Wu Zetian's seventh son, later Emperor Zhongzong, forced to her to retire, and she died shortly thereafter.[2]

Wu Zetian was a lavish patron of Confucian and Buddhist scholarship, and countless compilation projects are listed under her name.[3] Forty-six of her own poems are recorded in the *Quan Tang shi*, including the three poems selected here to represent three different stages of her life. There are also sixty-one essays recorded under her name in *Quan Tang wen* (see C.1.1). Although it has been suggested that many of her poems and essays are from the hands of ghostwriters, these at least reveal her concerns, and some, no doubt, are hers alone.

P.6.1. Set to the tune Ruyi niang

Watching red turn to green, my thoughts entangled and scattered,
I am disheveled and torn from my longing for you, my lord.
If you fail to believe that of late I have constantly shed tears,
Open the chest and look for the skirt of pomegranate-red.

(QTS, 5/58–59; Su Zhecong, 98)

Empress Wu may have composed this poem while temporarily cloistered in a Buddhist temple after Emperor Taizong's death, in hopes of attracting the attention (and the attentions) of Emperor Gaozong.

P.6.2. Accompanying the Emperor on a Visit to the Shaolin Temple

Upon seeing the place that my deceased mother once patronized, lonely feelings deepen in my heart, and I am saddened recalling my longing for her. I thus composed this poem to express my sorrow.

Accompanying my Emperor, I tour the restricted garden,
Granted this favor to leave the fragrant chambers.
Clouds recline, enshrouding mountain peaks,
Rosy mists descend, speared by waves of banners.
Sun Palace leads to a scene of stream-side dwellings,
Moon Hall opens to a view of cliff-perched homes.

Golden wheels revolve above the golden land,
In incensed chambers move long, fragrant robes.
Bells ring; the humming of Buddhist chants lightly rises;
Banners flap; the mists faintly disperse.
Once upon a time it met with the disaster of fire,
A mountain of flame flew over the serried fields.
Of Flower Terrace no trace is left,
But Lotus Tower maintains its glory.
Truly it depends upon those with benevolent means
To aid the Almighty One's power of perfecting the world.
Compassion gives rise to good fortune,
At this place I linger with thoughts of devotion.
But a branch in the wind cannot find peace,
Even tears of blood will not bring her back.

(QTS, 5/58)

Though undated, this poem must have been written between the death of her mother in 670 and Wu Zetian's becoming emperor in 690. Wu Zetian's mother, a devout Buddhist, undoubtedly influenced her daughter, who became a great patron of the Buddhist church. This is the only extant poem by Wu Zetian that reflects her more private side.

lines 19–20: These last two lines are derived from a passage in *Han shi waizhuan* describing Gao Yu's lament for having missed his opportunity to serve his parents as a filial son: "The tree would be still, but the wind will not stop; the son wishes to look after them, but his parents will not tarry" (Han Ying, *Han shi waizhuan* 9/3, trans. Hightower, *Han Shih Wai Chuan*, p. 292).

P.6.3. Proclaiming an Imperial Visit to the Shanglin Park on the Eighth Day of the Twelfth Month

On the eighth day of the twelfth lunar month, the second year of the Tianshou reign [691], some officials intended to deceive me into visiting the Shanglin Park by announcing that flowers were already in bloom there. In fact, they were planning a conspiracy. I agreed to their invitation but soon after suspected their scheme. Thus, I dispatched a messenger to release this proclamation. The next morning the Shanglin Park was suddenly filled with the blossoming of well-known flowers. The officials all sighed over this unusual phenomenon.

Tomorrow morning I will make an outing to Shanglin Park,
With urgent haste I inform the spring:
Flowers must open their petals overnight,
Don't wait for the morning wind to blow!

(QTS, 5/46; Su Zhecong, 97–98)

headnote: Traditional commentators have treated this poem and the incident for which it was composed as evidence of Wu Zetian's strategy for manipulating power through the creation of personal legends. By the time this poem was written, Empress Wu had already established herself as sole ruler in her newly formed Zhou dynasty. Her status is revealed by her use of imperatives in the poem; see Ji Yougong, *Tang shi jishi*, 3/24.

BIOGRAPHICAL NOTE AND TRANSLATION BY HUI-SHU LEE

上官婉兒

P.7. Shangguan Wan'er (664–710)

Despite the small size of her extant corpus of poems, Shangguan Wan'er probably played a larger role in male literary culture, both as writer and arbiter, than any other woman in Chinese history. The granddaughter of the courtier and poet Shangguan Yi, she was taken into the palace as a baby when her grandfather and the other male members of her household were executed for Shangguan Yi's part in a plot against Empress Wu. Despite the facial tattoo that marked her family's crime, she rose quickly in the empress's service, drafting edicts and eventually becoming the empress's personal secretary. After the death of Empress Wu, Zhongzong was restored to the throne, but effective power was still in the hands of the women of the court, the Empress Wei and several imperial princesses. Shangguan Wan'er became a nominal consort of Zhongzong and continued to exercise immense influence over the literary world. She served as ghostwriter for the emperor and great ladies of the court, and her few surviving poems could probably be augmented by some of the surviving poems attributed to Zhongzong.

Shangguan Wan'er presided over the great poetry competitions of the court and was said even to have served as an examiner. The last decade of her life, when she was at the height of her power, was also one of the most notoriously corrupt periods in the Tang, and Shangguan Wan'er played no small part in the sexual and political intrigues of the court. She was executed in the coup of

710, in which the Empress Wei and her party were overthrown. Although the future emperor Xuanzong was the Tang prince behind the coup, he nonetheless later ordered her collected works to be compiled and entrusted the preface to one of the outstanding literary and political figures of the day, Zhang Yue (see C.25.1). Like many other writers of her times, Shangguan Wan'er was more revered than read in the changing tastes of Xuanzong's reign. Her collected works were lost, probably in the destruction of the imperial library during the great rebellion of the mid-eighth century.

P.7.1. Reproach in a Letter on Colored Paper

When first leaves fall on Lake Dongting,
I long for you, thousands of miles away.
In heavy dew my scented quilt feels cold,
At moonset, brocade screen deserted.
I would play a Southland melody
And crave to seal a letter to Jibei.
The letter has no other message but
(8) This misery in living long apart.

(QTS, 5/61; Su Zhecong, 100)

line 6: Jibei, in the far northeastern corner of China, represents a region of frontier warfare, thus suggesting a woman writing to her husband away in the army.

P.7.2. Three Poems Presented to His Majesty on Visiting Xinfeng and Warmsprings Palace

1

The very last of winter's three months,
in the years of the Jinglong Reign,
The Prince of Hosts left the River Ba
to view the ways of his land.
I see in the distance lightning leap,
dragons are his steeds;
I turn and spy the frosty plain
whose fields are all of jade.

II

Wind-rattled phoenix pennons
 turn brushing through the sky,
Shaggy-hoofed steeds of the horse guard
 come stamping beams of light.
Mount Li lies sunk in shadow,
 jutting beyond the clouds,
While far in the distance the royal tent
 opens beside the sun.

(QTS, 5/61; Su Zhecong, 101)

The third poem has not been included. An occasional note, appended later, dates the imperial excursion to January 16, 709, which was the third year of the Jinglong Reign. Warmsprings Palace was built around the thermal springs on Mount Li, mentioned in the second poem, and was, for obvious reasons, a favorite spot for imperial excursions in the dead of winter.

ii, line 2: This image plays on the name of one of the First Emperor Qin Shihuang's famous horses, "Light-Stamper."

ii, line 4: This describes the imperial guard surrounding the emperor, the embodiment of the sun.

P.7.3. Visiting Princess Changning's Pool-for-Setting-Winecups-Afloat

Propped on my staff, I looked over wispy peaks,
Then with hazardous pace descended frosty trails.
My goals grew serene the deeper I went in the hills,
I strayed on the path that bent with the mountain stream.
Slowly I sensed detachment in my soul,
And noticed at once how fogs were sinking low.
Be not dismayed I wrote upon that tree—
(8) It was because I cherished this hidden rest.

(QTS, 5/63)

Princess Changning was a daughter of Emperor Zhongzong by a concubine. This poem was composed at imperial command during one of the emperor's visits to his daughter's residence and is one of twenty-five by Shangguan Wan'er on the same subject in QTS.

BIOGRAPHICAL NOTE AND TRANSLATION BY STEPHEN OWEN

P.8. Other Court Women of the Tang: Xu Hui and Bao Junhui

P.8a. Xu Hui (627–50)

Xu Hui came from Changcheng in Huzhou (modern Zhejiang province). Traditional Chinese biographies mark her as a born poet; we are told that she was a child prodigy, uttering her first words five months after birth, reading the *Analects* and the *Book of Odes* at age three, and writing poems and prose essays before she turned eight. As with other female poets, her father is said to have had some misgivings about his young daughter's display of talent—or the notoriety it was likely to bring. In recognition of Xu's literary gifts, Emperor Taizong summoned her to court and gave her a position as a "Lady of Talents" (*cairen*), later promoting her to "Lady of Complete Countenance" (*chongrong*), placing her at a rank just below his principal wives and his secondary consorts. When Xu wrote him criticizing his military policy and urging peace, the emperor reportedly thought highly of her words. The closeness of their relationship is implied by the tradition that, upon his death, she became ill from grief and refused medication. Still in her early twenties, she died the following year.

Taizong's successor posthumously awarded Xu the title of "Worthy Consort" (*xianfei*) in 650. Her father, Xu Xiaode, himself a writer of some note, was promoted to prefect of Guozhou on his daughter's account. She is believed to have written approximately a thousand poems, of which five survive and four are included here.

P.8a.1. Regret in Changmen Palace

You used to love my Cypress Rafter Terrace,
But now you dote upon her Bright Yang Palace.
I know my place, take leave of your palanquin,
Hold in my feelings, weep for a cast-off fan.
There was a time my dances, songs, brought honor.
These letters and poems of long ago? Despised!
It's true, I think—your favor collapsed like waves.
(8) Hard to offer water that's been spilled.

(QTS, 5/59)

These lines recall the plight and poetry of Ban *jieyu* (P.1). The residences of rival Han consorts named in lines 1 and 2 imply a parallel situation between Xu and a newly favored woman. However, there is a twist in the poem's title, which evokes the Han dynasty empress Chen, who retired to Changmen (Far Gate) Palace after Emperor Wu (r. 141–87 B.C.E.) lost interest in her. Empress Chen commissioned the poet Sima Xiangru (179–118 B.C.E.) to write a poem, the "Changmen Rhapsody," whereby she might regain Emperor Wu's favor; according to the poem's preface (*Wen xuan* 16.8b) she succeeded.

P.8a.2. Poem Modeled on "There's a Beauty in the North"

It's been said for all these years, she stands alone:
She calls herself "a beauty who topples walls."
Willow leaves—her green-black brows—spring forth,
And peach tree flowers blossom on her face.
She shakes her wrists, makes golden bracelets chime;
She shifts her feet and rings of jade sing out.
Her costly bodice suits her slender torso;
(8) Gold threads, fine weaving make her red gown glow.
I know what's coming: a single look weighs heavy—
Don't take it lightly, that swinging, swaying waist.

(QTS, 5/60)

The poem "modeled after" another poem was one of the genres represented in the Tang examinations. The original "There's a Beauty in the North" was written by the Han court musician Li Yannian to arouse Emperor Wu's interest in Li's younger sister, a talented and attractive dancer. For that poem, see YTXY, 1/8a, and Birrell, trans., *New Songs from a Jade Terrace*, p. 41.

P.8a.3. Offered to Emperor Taizong

Morning comes: I face the mirror stand.
Make-up done, I walk back and forth a while.
"A thousand in gold!"—to prompt a single laugh.
A single summons? You think I'd come for that?

(QTS, 5/60)

This poem is supposed to have been composed by Xu after a tiff with the emperor. "A thousand in gold for a single smile" is proverbial for a beautiful woman's haughtiness.

P.8a.4. *Autumn Wind at Hangu Pass: Written on Command*

Autumn winds lift up
  this Scabbard Valley.
Keen vapors shift and stir
  these streams and hills.
Flattened pines along a thousand ridgelines;
Scattered rains between two tongues of land.
Lowering clouds: grief for swamps spread wide.
The setting sun: gone gloomy, the double pass.
There floats up in this season a purplish mist
(8) Attesting to the mystic sage's return.

(QTS, 5/59)

Hangu (Scabbard Valley) Pass, in what is now Henan province, was an essential strategic point in many battles for control of central China throughout history. Through it passed the main routes between the Wei River heartlands and the coastal plains. By sealing up the Hangu Pass, for example, Liu Bang, the first Han emperor, was able to render the capital city of Xianyang inaccessible to his rival Xiang Yu.

line 8: Similar auspicious signs in the sky were said to follow Liu Bang; the poem is thus an indirect compliment to its imperial inspirer, Taizong.

鮑君徽

P.8b. *Bao Junhui (fl. 798)*

Bao Junhui (courtesy name Wenji) was widowed at an early age and, having no brothers, was forced to depend on her mother for her living. Because of her reputation as a poet of quiet elegance she was summoned to the imperial palace in 798, during the reign of Dezong (Li Gua). Soon thereafter, however, she had to leave to care for her aging mother. The poems she exchanged with officials at court met with high regard, but only four of her works remain; three are included here.

P.8b.1. *Tea Ceremony in the East Pavilion*

At ease this morning, turn toward dawn,
  go out past windows and blinds.
Meet for tea in the East Pavilion—
  clear views, in four directions.

Staring far: the moat round the walls,
  see it in mountains' colors.
Looking down: strings and pipes,
  hear them in watery sounds.
Deep bamboo thickets pull at the pond,
  and sprout a lush new green.
Sweet hibiscus draw down the eaves;
  soon they'll burst out red.
Linger, sitting amid all this—
  high spirits, boundless, rise.
(8) And more love now, for this round fan
  that gives off cooling winds.

(QTS, 7/69; Su Zhecong, 113)

This poem, written in the elevated heptasyllabic regulated-verse form, celebrates aesthetic experience despite reminders of evanescence (such as the short-lived blossoms of hibiscus) and of gender-based restrictions (the window blinds often associated with the women's quarters).

P.8b.2. Sung Out in Sympathy for Flowers

Flowers on a branch;
  someone beneath the flowers.
A blush on both that catches hearts:
  both are in their spring.
Flower-gazing yesterday—
  flowers bright with bloom.
Flower-gazing at dawn today—
  flowers soon to fall.
Best drain it dry, this joy, this pleasure,
  underneath the flowers;
Don't wait for those springtime winds
  to gust them all away.
Warblers sing, butterflies dance,
  bright scenes linger long.
(8) Brewing tea on a dark-red stove:
  pine-flowers loose their scent.
Makeup finished, singing ended,
  done with wandering free,

Alone, hold on to a fragrant branch
  and go back to the cave of your room.

(QTS, 7/69)

The poem has been read as Bao's lament for the loneliness of her widowhood, likened to a hermit's retreat. The phrase "fragrant branch" in the last line, borrowed from the "Nine Songs" attributed to Qu Yuan (see P.3.3), suggests that poet's purity and resolve.

P.8b.3. Moon at the Frontier Pass

High, sky-high: fall's moon glitters bright
And off in the north illumines Liaoyang's fort.
The border so far, yet that light covers all—
The wind so great, a glory-ring grows round.
Soldiers stare toward their villages, and brood.
Cavalry mounts hear battle drums, and shy.
Northern winds blow sorrow through frontier grass,
And barbarous sands obscure the enemy camps.
Frost crystallizes swords within their scabbards.
Winds wear out feathered banners above the steppes.
Some day, some day—reporting near palace towers,
No more to hear the clangorous camp-gongs' clash.

(QTS, 7/69; Su Zhecong, 113)

Like many of the *yuefu* poems on which it is patterned, this poem details the miseries of the garrisons sent to guard the empire's northern fringe. Unlike other "Moon at the Frontier Pass" poems, however, this one cites a specific and much fought-over place—Liaoyang in present-day Liaoning province.

BIOGRAPHICAL NOTES AND TRANSLATION BY JEANNE LARSEN

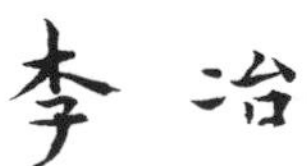

P.9. Li Ye (8th century)

Relatively little is known of Li Ye (courtesy name Jilan). True to her biographical type, she is supposed to have displayed precocious talents, composing a couplet on roses at the age of seven, at which her father commented on her literary promise and prophesied that she would therefore not be a respectable woman. As one of those "Daoist nuns" who doubled as courtesan and entertainer, she was much admired, but indeed never entirely respectable. The terms that contemporaries used to describe her suggest an aggressive vigor that is usually exclusively masculine. She seems to have been well known among the poetic groups of the lower Yangzi region in the 760s and 770s (a poem by the poet-monk Jiaoran suggests that she made romantic as well as literary advances). At some point, probably because of her poetic reputation, she was summoned to the palace, but was soon released because her age redeemed her from the imperial fancy. She was in the capital again when the brief usurpation of Zhu Ci caused the young emperor Dezong to flee. Perhaps under coercion, she wrote a congratulatory verse to Zhu Ci; and when Dezong retook Chang'an, she was executed for treason in 784. Of her eighteen extant poems, two are clearly spurious; however, twelve of the remaining sixteen were preserved in Tang anthologies, which is a good indication of her popularity.

P.9.1. Sending Han Kui on a Journey to the Western Reaches of the Yangzi

We look at each other and point to willows,
Parting's pain brings increase of fondness.
On thousands of miles to the western Yangzi
Whither will your lone boat go?
The high waters do not reach to Pencheng,
Surely letters from Xiakou will be few.
All I will have are the Hengyang geese,
(8) Flying back and forth, year after year.

(QTS, 805/9058)

line 1: On the snapping of willow branches, see P.5.1.

line 2: The term for "fondness" here, *yiyi*, also alludes to a scene of departure narrated in poem 197 in the *Book of Odes*.

lines 5–6: Pencheng is in Jiangxi. Xiakou is present-day Hankou, farther up the river from Pencheng.

line 8: One spur of Mount Heng was reputedly so high that geese could not fly over it; "Returning-Goose Peak" (*Hui yan feng*), as it was dubbed, was considered the southernmost point in the annual migration of the geese. On wild geese as a symbol for letters, see P.2.1. Li Ye's anxiety about receiving letters has caused her to treat the north-south axis of the conventional poetic symbolism as equivalent to the east-west axis of her separation from Han.

P.9.2. A Song Written on the Topic "Streams Flowing Down in the Three Gorges"

My home used to be up there
  in Wu Mountain's clouds,
Where streams flowing from the mountain
  always can be heard.
As the jade zither plays these sounds,
  they grow more sharp and clear,
Just as they were in days of yore
  when heard within a dream.
The Three Gorges are far away,
  many thousands of miles,
But all at once they come flowing
  into my secluded chambers.
Huge boulders crash down cliffs,
  audible under his fingers,
Waterfalls and rushing waves
  rise from in the strings.
It seems at first some bursting rage,
  thundering gales within,
Then as if choked with sobbing sounds—
  some current can't get through.
When force of winding rapids
  and whirlpools runs its course,
The liquid notes fall drop by drop
  upon the level sand.
I recall how long ago
  Ruan Xian composed this tune—
This could make even him
  ever hear his fill.
You've played it once and finished,
  now play it once again,
I want those flowing streams
  to continue forever.

(QTS, 805/9058)

This topic was a traditional piece of the *qin* repertoire, supposedly composed by Ruan Xian in the third century. There are numerous variations on Li Ye's title, some of which suggest that she composed her song after one by Xiao Shuzi. The opening lines recall the story of the King of Chu's sexual encounter in a dream with a mysterious woman who, on parting, told him: "At dawn I am the morning cloud, at evening I am the moving rain." Recognizing her as the goddess of Wu Mountain, the king dedicated a temple to her. (See Song Yu, "Gaotang fu," in *Wen xuan* 19/2a.) Li Ye is clearly identifying herself with the goddess in the opening, but some scholars have taken this to suggest that she was a native of the region.

P.9.3. Reproach in Love

People say the sea is deep—
  it's not as deep by half as love.
The sea at least still has its coasts,
  love's farthest reaches have no shore.
Take your harp and climb the tower,
  where moonlight fills the empty rooms.
Then play the song of longing love—
  heart and strings will break together.

(QTS, 805/9058)

P.9.4. Eight Extremes

What is closest and farthest apart?—
  east and west,
What is deepest and most shallow?—
  the clear brook.
What is highest and brightest?—
  the sun and moon,
Most intimate and most estranged?—
  a man and wife.

(QTS, 805/9059)

BIOGRAPHICAL NOTE AND TRANSLATION BY STEPHEN OWEN

薛濤

P.10. Xue Tao (768–ca. 832)

Probably one of the most famous courtesan poets in Chinese literary history, Xue Tao was a native of Chang'an (now Xi'an). In her youth she migrated with her father to the state of Shu (the modern Sichuan province) and became a "song-courtesan" (*geji*) at sixteen, after his death. Since Xue was reputed to be able to write poems and parallel couplets when she was merely eight or nine years old, her literary talents were greatly prized. A wide circle of literati became her friends, correspondents, patrons, and suitors, including such well-known poets as Yuan Zhen, Bo Juyi, Niu Sengru, Du Mu, and Liu Yuxi, with all of whom Xue often exchanged poems.

As gifted in calligraphy as she was in poetry, Xue was said to have been fond of writing on small stationery dyed crimson. In later times this kind of paper, bearing her name, became a popular artifact. Legend has it that when Xue was thirty-eight, Wu Yuanheng, the Governor of Shu, who was deeply appreciative of her literary accomplishments, recommended to the throne that she be appointed as "Lady Collator of Books" (*nü jiaoshu lang*). Although it seems hardly probable that the Tang emperor would grant her such a post in the Palace Library, since it had to do with work on the imperial diary and was thus reserved for men of great literary promise, Xue was nonetheless addressed by the title after Wu's efforts became known. Henceforth, *jiaoshu* became a literary reference for courtesan.

When Xue was forty years old, she apparently was attracted to Yuan Zhen, who was then serving in Shu as the Investigating Censor. Yuan, however, did not reciprocate the affection enough to marry her. After his demotion and departure from Shu, Xue remained single till her death, living by herself at Huanhuaxi. The collected edition of her poetry is named *Jinjiang ji* (The River Jin collection). Eighty-nine of her poems are preserved in the *Quan Tang shi*, a total unequaled by any other woman writer of the period.[1]

P.10.1. A Poetic Gift for Someone Viewing Bamboos After Rain

In southern clime and spring rain times,
Who could see faces tried by snow?
One species, thriving amidst many,
Finds strength in true pudicity.
A shelter to drunken Jin worthies,
It shares the grief of Shun's consorts.
In old age you appreciate
(8) Its joints both hoary and sturdy.

(QTS, 803/9035)

line 5: During the Jin period (266–316) there was a famous group of talkers and tipplers known as the "Seven Worthies of the Bamboo Grove," who included the poets Ruan Ji and Ji Kang, the philosopher Xiang Xiu, and the legendary drinker Liu Ling. Many stories recount their unconventional behavior, their quips and revelries. See Liu Yiqing, *Shishuo xinyu*, 23.1; Mather, *Shih-shuo Hsin-yü*, pp. 371–72.

line 6: When the sagely legendary emperor Shun died, his two consorts (see P.1.2) wept profusely before drowning themselves in the river Xiang. Their tears, according to this legend, became permanent stains on the mottled bamboo by the river.

P.10.2. *The Moon*

Her soul curls like a slender hook
Or rounds off like a Han-loom fan.
This small form growing to fullness
Is seen at how many spots on earth.

(QTS, 803/9036)

P.10.3. *Cicadas*

Dew drops bathe their clear, distant tones
When wind blows together a few leaves.
Sound after sound seems closely joined,
Though each lives on a different branch.

(QTS, 803/9036)

P.10.4. *Listening to a Monk Playing the Reed Flute*

Dawn's sobbing cicadas or sad orioles at night—
Such earnest speech is of ten digits born.
Just play when you have read the Sanskrit tome:
It will join gold bells to mix with autumn.

(QTS, 803/9037)

line 4: "Gold bells" refers to the handheld recitation bells used by Buddhist or Daoist priests.

P.10.5. *A Pilgrimage to Wu Mountain Shrine*

I visit Gaotang where anarchic apes cry,
Where all roads end in mist and fragrant plants.
The mountain hues can never forget Song Yu,

And water sounds still mourn the Prince of Xiang.
Day and night below the Sun-Cloud Terrace
In acts of love the State of Chu would die.
How many wistful willows before the Shrine
Vie vainly in spring for length like painted brows!

(QTS, 803/9037)

line 3: On the female spirit of Wu Mountain and her amorous encounter with King Xiang of Chu, see P.9.2.

P.10.6. Sending Off Mr. Yao, a Supernumerary

Of countless willows one early autumn branch:
Wind-swept, earth-draping, its colors remain.
I'd break it off to make a farewell gift,
So mist and moon at two spots will not feel sad.

(QTS, 803/9038)

P.10.7. A Farewell for Mr. Li, Bureau Director

A phoenix leaves his mate as *wutong*-blossoms fall,
Sadder still when he climbs the peaks of Qin.
Though Anren has poems he's about to write,
Half his lyrics are mixed with elegies.

(QTS, 803/9038)

line 1: The legendary phoenix would nest only in a *wutong* tree (*Sterculia platanifolia*, the "scholar's tree" or "parasol tree"). The wood of the *wutong* makes the finest musical instruments.

lines 3–4: Anren was the style name of Pan Yue (247–300), a famous poet of the Jin period. The prevailing mood in many of his compositions was one of grief: his elegies (*lei*) were among the best known of the genre, and some twenty of his surviving tetrasyllabic or pentasyllabic poems are on sorrow or bereavement. His "Three Poems on My Deceased Wife" were especially acclaimed.

P.10.8. A Poetic Gift for Courtesan Li

Your talents past compare though far away,
Your world-filling learning is readily known.
I who now languish by the River Zhang
Admire your winged dance atop the clouds.

(QTS, 803/9039)

P.10.9. Two Poems for Someone Faraway

I

Hibiscus newly fallen on the hills of Shu,
And grief arrives when the envelope's unsealed.
A girl who does not know the affairs of war
Still climbs at full moon the mate-watching tower.

II

New rushes, though weak, show a steady green
When late-spring blossoms drop in frontier creeks.
Your steed, I know, has yet to round Qin forts:
My sleeve's tear-soaked, the moon lights a thousand gates.

(QTS, 803/9042–43)

P.10.10. Ten Versions of Separation

I. A DOG SEPARATED FROM ITS MASTER

Behind crimson gates for four or five years
  a docile, obedient beast,
Its sweet-smelling pelt and cleanly feet
  won the master's affection.
Then for no reason it took a bite
  of a dearly loved friend,
And no more is it allowed to sleep
  upon the red silk rug.

II. A BRUSH SEPARATED FROM THE HAND

Reed of Yue and Xuancheng bristles
  suit the owner's pleasure,
On sheets of pink writing paper
  it scattered flowers and gems.
Only due to such long use
  the hairs have lost their point,
And now it won't be taken up
  in the hand of Wang Xizhi.

III. A HORSE SEPARATED FROM THE STABLE

Ears like snow, a russet coat,
pale sapphire hooves,
This wind-chaser tracked the sun
horizon to horizon.
It reared and threw the gentleman
whose face was white as jade,
And never will it neigh again,
drawing the splendid coach.

IV. A PARROT SEPARATED FROM ITS CAGE

It goes alone through Longxi,
a solitary bird,
To and fro it flies, then lights
upon the brocade cushion.
Just because it spoke some words
discomforting its owner,
Never again can it summon folk,
calling from its cage.

V. A SWALLOW SEPARATED FROM THE NEST

In and out through crimson gates,
it cannot bear to leave them,
The owner always doted on
its captivating trills.
Some mud fell from its beak and soiled
his pillow of coral,
And no more can it pile its nest
up among the rafters.

VI. A PEARL SEPARATED FROM THE PALM

Glistening thing, bright and round,
radiant throughout,
Its clear light seemingly reflects
palaces of crystal.
But due to just a single speck,
it's ruined by a flaw,

And no more can it pass the night
  in the owner's palm.

VII. A FISH SEPARATED FROM ITS POOL

In the lotus pond for four or five years
  it has leapt playfully,
Always waving its crimson tail,
  it sports with fishing lines.
By accident it bumped and broke
  a blossom of the lotus,
Now no more can it swim about
  through the clear waves.

VIII. A HAWK SEPARATED FROM THE GAUNTLET

Talons sharp as blade-point,
  eyes like bells,
To pounce on hares in the meadow
  suits its noble mood.
By accident it disappeared
  up beyond blue clouds,
No longer will it be lifted
  upon the ruler's arm.

IX. BAMBOO SEPARATED FROM A PAVILION

Exuberant growth, newly planted,
  four or five rows,
Always bearing strong resolve
  they brave the autumn frost.
It was because their springtime shoots
  pierced holes through the wall,
They can no longer cast their shade
  over the jadelike hall.

X. A MIRROR SEPARATED FROM ITS STAND

The molten gold was poured,
  a mirror then appeared,
A full moon first rising
  and hanging in the sky.

Because it suffered endless
layers of dust and grime,
It cannot be set on the stand of jade
within the splendid hall.

(QTS, 803/9043–45, with reference to
Chen Wenhua, *Tang nüshiren ji san zhong*, 74–78)

Scholars long doubted the authenticity of the attribution of this poem to Xue Tao, in particular because the style, which sometimes approaches doggerel, was felt to be unworthy of her known mastery. Doubts were laid to rest when a Tang anthology, preserved in Japan and published in China in the mid-twentieth century, was found to include the first poem of the set under Xue Tao's name. A circumstantial anecdote attached to the poems interprets them as Xue Tao's attempt to regain the good graces of the poet Yuan Zhen, who during his brief tenure in Chengdu in 809 was supposed to have become angry with her over some matter. The application of the poems to a woman rejected by a man is appropriate, but we can never be certain whether the poems were merely an exercise or were written to some specific occasion. Making extensive use of clichés, filler phrases, and repeated patterns, these poems are characteristic of Tang popular verse and the verse that more literary poets might compose extempore.

i, line 1: Crimson gates were a standard synecdoche for a great household.

ii, line 1: Reeds from the southeastern region of Yue and wolf or rabbit hairs from Xuancheng in modern Anhui were said to make the finest writing brushes.

ii, line 4: The great fourth-century calligrapher Wang Xizhi is here used as a figure for the brush's owner.

iv, line 1: Parrots (particularly white ones) were brought to the capital from Longxi, a mountainous region incorporating parts of present-day Gansu, Sichuan, and Shaanxi provinces.

ix, line 2: This line employs a commonplace pun on *jie*, which means both "resolve" and the "joints" between bamboo segments.

BIOGRAPHICAL NOTE AND TRANSLATION OF P.10.1–9 BY ANTHONY C. YU;
TRANSLATION OF P.10.10 BY STEPHEN OWEN

P.11. Yu Xuanji (844–68)

Yu Xuanji was, with her fellow courtesan Xue Tao, one of the most famous woman poets of the Tang dynasty. An inhabitant of the Tang capital of Chang'an, she was taken on as a concubine early in her life by an official named Li Yi (whom she addresses in her poetry by his personal name, Zi'an). Later, he abandoned her, purportedly at the instigation of a jealous wife. Yu then took Daoist vows and entered a nunnery, although, as was common at the time, she seems not to have renounced her courtesan's life. Like Xue Tao, Yu appears to have formed friendships with various members of the male literary world; in particular, her collection contains two poems addressed to the Late Tang poet Wen Tingyun (personal name Feiqing). Legend links the two poets romantically; however, Yu's poems to Wen do not appear to be love poems, and there is no other evidence of an affair. She is supposed to have been executed at the age of twenty-four after beating her maid-servant to death in a jealous rage; however, this semilegendary account of her death may be influenced by traditional society's distrust of a woman who was evidently strong-willed and sexually independent.

Yu seems to have been well aware of the constraints imposed upon female talent, complaining of "these gauze robes of mine which hide my lines of verse." Her dissatisfaction with these constraints appears in various guises —among them her attribution of value to wilted peonies (the reference to the shelf life of female beauty is clear) and her occasional discussion of the courtesan-client relationship in the same terms a male literatus might use in addressing a potential patron. About fifty of her poems exist today, making her one of the earliest woman poets whose works have survived in any number. The existing poems vary widely in metrical form, topic, and, indeed, quality.

Yu's poetry and life have understandably fascinated a number of modern writers, and Yu appears as a character in works as diverse as a short story by Mori Ōgai and a detective novel by Robert van Gulik.

P.II.I. Selling Wilted Peonies

I sigh into the wind at how often the flowers fall;
Their tender feelings melt away unseen: another spring gone by.
It must be because their price is so high that no one wants them,
And because their scent is so strong that butterflies won't love them.
These red blooms are fit to grow only within the palace:
How can their jade-green leaves bear to be sullied by the dust of the road?
When, at last, their roots are transplanted to the Imperial Park,
(8) Then, my dear prince, you will regret that they are no longer for sale.

(QTS, 804/9048)

P.II.2. *Sent to Feiqing*

On the stone steps crickets chirp, unsettled;
Misty dew is pure on the boughs in the courtyard.
In the moonlight, echoes of nearby music—
From an upper story, glow of distant mountains.
The fine mat is touched by a cold wind,
My pains lodged in notes from a jade zither.
Master Ji is too lazy to write letters,
(8) So what can console my autumn feelings?

(QTS, 804/9053)

line 7: Master Ji is Ji Kang, the third-century poet, member of the "Seven Worthies of the Bamboo Grove" coterie.

P.II.3. *Traveling on the Yangzi (Two Poems)*

I

The great Yangzi curves and embraces Wuchang,
Ten thousand households stand before Parrot Island.
Spring sleep on a painted barge is interrupted by the dawn:
I dream that I am a butterfly still seeking flowers.

II

Misty flowers have already entered Cormorant Bay,
But on the painted barge I still write of Parrot Island.
Drunk, I sleep; sober, I chant—unaware of everything,
This morning startled to find myself at the Han River's mouth.

(QTS, 804/9051)

P.II.4. *On the Double Ninth, Kept in by Rain*

Filling the courtyard, chrysanthemums bloom beside the hedge,
While, in the mirror, two lotus blossoms open.
Before Fallen-Cap Terrace, kept in by wind and rain,
I don't know where I can get drunk from a cup of gold.

(QTS, 804/9051)

line 1: The Double Ninth festival falls on the ninth day of the ninth lunar month. Nine is the culmination of the *yang* (odd) series of numbers, and the identity of the day's number with the month's suggests a harmonious alignment of celestial cycles.

The day is therefore associated with the preservation of the *yang* energies and with long life. The custom on Double Ninth is to climb to high ground (heights being geomantically *yang*), drink wine in which chrysanthemum petals have been dropped, and compose poetry. Since the chrysanthemum blooms in autumn, it suggests a hale and hearty old age.

line 2: Lotus blossoms here represent a woman's cheeks.

line 3: The warlord Huan Wen (late fourth century) was holding a banquet one Double Ninth when one of his ministers, Meng Jia, failed to notice that the wind had blown off his cap. Huan thought to tease him by keeping the fact concealed from him, and when Meng went to visit the privy, Huan composed a satiric essay extempore on the subject. Upon his return, Meng immediately countered with an essay of his own. The site of the banquet was thereafter called "Fallen-Cap Terrace."

P.11.5. Deeply Moved, I Send This to Someone

I entrust my bitterness to a lute's crimson strings,
Hold back passion—my thoughts unbearable.
Long ago I knew that a cloud-rain meeting
Would not give rise to an orchid heart.
Fresh and shining, the peach and the plum—
Nothing prevents eminent scholars from seeking them out.
Grey-green, the pine and the cassia—
Still they long for honor from the people of the age.
The moon's hue is pure on mossy steps,
Song comes from deep within the bamboo garden.
Before my gate—ground covered with red leaves,
I don't sweep them away, waiting for one who understands me.

(QTS, 804/9052)

lines 3–4: On "clouds and rain," see P.9.2. The orchid, by allusion to the "Li sao" of Qu Yuan (see P.37), signifies an upright and virtuous mind.

line 5: Peach and plum trees occur in the *Book of Odes* as images for marriageable women: see poems 6 and 20.

line 7: Pine and cassia are proverbially enduring plants. The meaning of this pair of couplets is not exclusively sexual: similar wording might be used by a man bemoaning his lack of a patron.

P.11.6. Spring Feelings, Sent to Zi'an

The mountain road slants, the rocky steps are steep;
But I don't lament the hardships of travel, it is my longing that is
bitter.

Ice melts in far torrents—I am touched by your clear rhymes,
Snow lies distant on cold peaks—I think of your jade-like beauty.
Don't listen to common songs and grow sick on wine in spring,
Don't invite guests to while away the time, eager for games of chess at night.
I am like pine—I am no stone—my oath will always endure,
(8) Like paired-wing birds or two robes joined, how could I want to delay our meeting?
Though I regret traveling alone through a whole winter's day,
In the end, I'll wait to see you when the moon is full.
Parted, what is a worthy present to give to you?
(12) Tears that fall in the bright light—and this single poem.

(QTS, 804/9049)

line 7: Poem 26 of the *Book of Odes* was reputedly composed by a young widow who refused to obey her family's demand that she remarry: "My heart is not a stone; you cannot roll it about," she protests.

line 8: The *biyi*, a legendary bird, had only one wing and could not fly without a mate. Like "two robes joined," it became a symbol of conjugal felicity.

P.II.7. *Sent to Zi'an*

Drunk at parting: a thousand goblets of wine won't wash away my sorrow;
My heart in separation tied into a hundred knots—no way to undo them.
Orchids fade away and die in the spring garden,
While willows, east and west, detain the traveler's boat.
Meeting, parting—already I grieve at the drifting cloud,
My love must imitate the ever-flowing river.
When flowers are in season, I know that we can't meet,
(8) But I'm not yet willing to stay languidly drunk in my jade tower.

(QTS, 804/9054)

P.II.8. *Inscribed on Mist-Hidden Pavilion*

Spring flowers and autumn moon enter my poems,
Bright daylight, clear night—these belong to an immortal at ease.
I do nothing but roll up my beaded blinds—and never lower them,

I've moved my couch for good so that I can sleep facing the mountains.

(QTS, 804/9051)

P.11.9. *An Allegory*

Red peaches everywhere don their spring colors,
Green willows by each house are bright with moonlight.
In the tower, freshly made-up, I await the night,
In my chamber I sit alone, burdened with emotions.
Fish sport beneath the lotus flowers,
Sparrows call out beside the distant rainbow.
In the mortal world sorrow and happiness are equally a dream,
So how can I become an immortal like Shuangcheng?

(QTS, 804/9054)

line 8: Shuangcheng was a maidservant of the immortal Queen Mother of the West.

P.11.10. *On a Winter's Night, Sent to Feiqing*

With bitter longing I sought a poem, sang it beneath the lamplight,
Sleepless through the long night, fearing cold coverlets.
Tree leaves fill the courtyard—I grieve at the rising wind,
Through sheer gauze window curtains, I pity the sinking moon.
Estranged, but not for long—in the end I shall follow my will,
In flourishing and fading I emptily perceive the nature of my original mind.
I haven't settled upon a spot on the *wutong* for my hidden resting place;
The evening sparrows twitter, vainly circling the forest.

(QTS, 804/9049)

line 8: Cf. the "Duan ge xing" of the warlord Cao Cao: "The moon is bright, the stars few, / Crows and magpies fly south. / Thrice circling the forest, / On what branch can they roost?" (*Wen xuan*, 27/117b–18a.)

P.11.11. *Telling My Feelings*

Idle, at ease—with nothing that I must attend to,
I travel alone through the sweep of the scenery.

Through broken clouds, moonlight shines on the river;
Its moorings unfastened, a boat on the sea.
I play my zither by Xiao-Liang Temple
And sing a poem at Yuliang Tower.
Thickets of bamboo are worthy to be friends,
And pieces of rock serve well as companions.
Swallows and sparrows alone I consider noble,
For gold and silver are not my aim.
I fill a goblet with green spring wine,
Face the moon—night windows hidden.
Winding steps clear in the transparent water,
I pull out my hairpin—it shines in the rippling current.
I lie on the bed, my books spread everywhere,
And then, half-drunk, I rise and comb my hair.

(QTS, 804/9052)

lines 5–6: Because Emperor Wu of the Liang Dynasty, whose family name was Xiao, was the greatest early patron of Buddhism in China, Xiao-Liang Temple was a generic name for Buddhist places of worship. Yuliang Tower is the South Tower in Wuchang, Hubei.

line 11: Rustic unfiltered wine was greenish in color.

P.11.12. Rhyming with a Friend

What can melt away the melancholy of lodging at an inn?
When I open the red notepaper, I see the fine lines of your writing.
Rain sprinkles Penglai—all other peaks grow small,
The wind blows in Xie Valley—myriad leaves touched by autumn.
In the morning I read word after word, more precious than green jade,
And at night beneath my coverlets I recite page after page.
I'll pack your poem away in a fragrant casket,
But for now I'll take it in hand and chant it.

(QTS, 804/9050)

lines 3–4: Penglai Mountain, beyond the eastern sea, was the abode of the immortals; the Xie Valley to the remote west was held to be the place of origin of musical pipes.

P.II.13. *Moved by the End of Spring: Sent to a Friend*

The oriole's song startles me from the remnants of a dream,
Light make-up alters my tear-streaked face.
Through shady bamboos the new moon is dim;
Over the quiet river the evening mist is thick.
Damp-mouthed swallows carry mud,
And bees, their feelers scented, gather pollen.
Alone I pity my endless longings
(8) And finish my song beside the low-limbed pine trees.

(QTS, 804/9049)

P.II.14. *Following the Rhymes of a New Graduate's Poem Mourning the Death of His Wife (Two Poems)*

I

Those enrolled among the immortals don't linger in the human world,
For them, a moment goes by, while we have passed a million autumns.
Beneath mandarin-duck curtains, fragrance is still warm,
And the parrot's words have not yet ceased in its cage.
Morning dew beads the flowers—the sorrow on her cheeks;
Evening wind bends the willows—the melancholy of her eyebrows.
Once the many-hued cloud has gone, there comes no word,
(8) Pan Yue is so filled with grief that his hair is turning white.

II

Blending with the mist, a single branch of moon cassia is graceful,
Bearing the rain, myriad river-peach trees are red.
Get drunk a while in front of your goblet—stop your sad gazing,
For, since olden times, sorrow and joy have been the same as today.

(QTS, 804/9050)

i, line 8: On Pan Yue and his elegy for his dead wife, see P.10.7. Pan's hair was said to have turned gray overnight with grief.

ii, line 1: "Cassia" is homophonous with "honor"; successful examination candidates were therefore said to have "plucked cassia" (achieved honor).

P.II.15. *Elegy on Another's Behalf*

The young peach I glimpsed calls to mind her jade beauty,
Willows trailing in the wind—I recognize her moth eyebrows.
The pearl has returned to the dragon's cave, who shall see it again?
The mirror remains on the phoenix stand, but to whom shall I speak?
From now on, in dreams I will grieve through nights of mist and rain,
Unable to bear bitter chanting when I am lonely.
As the sun sets on the western mountains, the moon rises in the east,
But there is no way to end my regretful thoughts.

(QTS, 804/9053)

line 3: Cf. *Zhuangzi*, chap. 32: "A pearl worth a thousand gold pieces certainly belongs in the nine-layered abyss, beneath the chin of a black dragon."

line 4: According to legend, the king of Jibin (Kashmir) once bought a female phoenix. Despite being fed the most expensive delicacies, she refused to sing. After three years the king's wife said to him, "I've heard that if a phoenix sees its like, it will sing. Why not hang a mirror in front of her?" The king followed her advice. The phoenix saw her reflection and cried out broken-heartedly. Spreading her wings, she rose into the air once and died. (See Liu Jingshu, *Yi yuan*, chap. 3, in SKQS, 1042: 506.)

P.II.16. *Following the Rhyme Words of a Poem Written by My New Neighbor to the West, in Order to Beg Some Wine from Him*

Your single poem came, and I chanted it a hundred times.
New feelings with every word—along with its sounds of gold.
Looking west, I've already a mind to climb the fence;
Gazing afar, how can I help having a heart like hers who changed to stone?
But the tryst at the Silver River is distant: in vain I gaze to the horizon;
The dream of Xiao and Xiang is broken off: I cease tuning my lute.
Even worse, this season of chill adds to my longing for home—
So don't pour out Shuye's excellent wine alone!

(QTS, 804/9050)

line 3: From Song Yu's poem "Master Dengtu the Lecher." The fourth-century B.C.E. poet Song Yu, accused of being a libertine, countered with the argument that his beautiful eastern neighbor had been making eyes at him over the fence for three years, but he had refused to respond to her (*Wen xuan*, 19/9b–11a).

line 4: Many local stories tell of a woman who waited faithfully for her husband's return from the army—until she was changed to stone (see, for example, Liu Yiqing, *Youming lu*, p. 183). For another poem on the subject, see P.24.3.

line 5: On the Silver River (Milky Way) and the Double Seventh festival, see P.5.1.

line 6: The Xiao and Xiang Rivers were associated with the river goddesses of the *Chuci* (see "Xiang jun," "Xiang furen," *Chuci buzhu*, 2/8b–13b; Hawkes, *Songs of the South*, 104–9; and see P.74.3), as well as with the mourning wives of Shun (see P.10.1).

line 8: Shuye was the personal name of the famous poet Ji Kang.

P.11.17. *Presented to the Girl Next Door*

Shying from the sun, I shade myself with gauze sleeves,
Made melancholy by spring, too listless to rise and put on my
  make-up.
It's easy to seek a priceless treasure—
But hard to find a man with a heart.
I let my tears fall unseen on my pillow,
I am secretly downcast among the flowers.
But if I can steal glances at Song Yu,
(8) Why should I regret Wang Chang?

(QTS, 804/9047)

lines 7–8: On Song Yu, see P.11.16. Wang Chang is a name often used for a handsome and elegant lover. The line may also allude to an anonymous *yuefu* poem that describes a young bride as having every possible good fortune, except for one: "A life of wealth and honor—what more could she desire? / She only wishes she had married her eastern neighbor Wang." See Morohashi, *Dai kanwa jiten*, entry 20823.522.

P.11.18. *Visiting the Southern Pavilion of Chongzhen Temple, I Saw the Place Where the Names of Successful Examination Candidates Are Written*

Cloudy peaks fill my eyes, the clearness of spring is released,
The silver hooks spring to life one by one beneath their fingers.
I resent these gauze robes of mine which conceal poems' lines,
I raise my head, envying the names on the roster of successful
  candidates.

(QTS, 804/9050)

line 2: "Silver hooks" here represents the writing of the successful candidates.

BIOGRAPHICAL NOTE AND TRANSLATION BY JENNIFER CARPENTER

P.12. Other Courtesan-Poets of the Tang: Sheng Xiaocong, Zhao Luanluan, and Xu Yueying

P.12a. Sheng Xiaocong (9th century)

The courtesan Sheng Xiaocong, who came from southeast China, was noted for the earnest sound of her singing. This quality caught the attention of the Investigation Commissioner, or civil governor, of Zhedong, Li Na. He had Sheng perform at a farewell dinner for another official who was departing for the capital. When the guests made the usual exchange of poems composed on this occasion, she presented a poem of her own.

P.12a.1. A Turkic Santai Song

In the Wild-goose Range,
  above the pass, wild geese
    begin to fly.
Warhorses in Horse-town's stables
  grow sleek and strong.
Day fades in the West-Ridge borderlands:
  you meet army couriers,
Come up from the south,
  taking pains with winter
    uniforms
      sent to the north.

(QTS, 802/9032)

The words of this song have also been attributed to the well-known male poet Wei Yingwu.

P.12b. Zhao Luanluan

Zhao Luanluan was a courtesan of considerable repute who lived in the Pingkang quarter, the entertainment district of the Tang capital. Her five extant poems have been given the collective title "Five Lyric Outcries from the Boudoir."

P.12b.1. Cloud Curls

Tossed and tumbled, those perfumed curls,
  their dampness not yet dried:
A raven's feathers! cicadas' wings!
  slick shine that's winter-cold.
Off to one side, slip in aslant
  a phoenix made of gold—
Hair done up, and then that man
  looks, looks with that smile.

P.12b.2. Willow-Leaf Eyebrows

Arching, arching, willow leaves
  that play on sorrow's brink:
Bright caltrop flowers, deep with dew,
  shine beneath a frown.
Coy, cajoling, they don't bother
  with dark conch-shell dye—
These spring hillcrests paint themselves
  with their own vital force.

P.12b.3. Sandalwood Mouth

A sip from a cup subtly moves
  that cherry, that rosy peach.
It coughs a cough, and lightly wafts
  the fragrance of jessamine.
You've seen the poet Bo Juyi's
  beloved's singing mouth:
Teeth white and even, like melon seeds,
  catch a pomegranate's scent.

P.12b.4. Silk-Slim Fingers

Slight and slender, soft white jade,
  scallions peeled in spring—

They bide their time in scented sleeves
  of gauze kingfisher-blue.
But yesterday upon the strings
  of a lover's lute:
Every nail distinct and clear,
  dyed scarlet, blood-dark red.

P.12b.5. Succulent Breasts

A whiff of powder, damp with sweat,
  rare jade tuning-pegs:
Aroused by spring, they glisten, gleam,
  sleek as silkfloss-rains.
When, fresh from the bath, her sweet-scent man
  teases with a touch,
Those magical buds feel shivery-wet—
  those dusky-purple grapes!

(QTS, 802/9032–33)

徐月英

P.12c. Xu Yueying (9th–10th century)

Xu Yueying lived just at the end of the Tang dynasty in the region between the Yangzi and Huai Rivers (now included in Jiangsu and Anhui provinces) in east-central China. A collection of her poems was once in circulation, but only two pieces remain today.

P.12c.1. Getting It Off My Chest

I've broken the rules—
  obedience to father, husband, son.
    That's why I cry so much.
This body? What way, what
  use, to stick
    to what proper people do?
Though day after day
  I chase the glee
    of mouth-pipes' elegant songs,

Here's what I can't
  stop wanting: thorns
    for my hairpins, one
      cheap cotton skirt.

(QTS, 802/9033)

P.12C.2. Saying Good-Bye at a Parting Pavilion

Grief and regret:
  in the human world, everything
    goes wrong.
Two set out
  together. One
    comes back.
I hate with all my life
  the look of peace
    on this river where we part,
That can bear to mirror
  love-duck and love-drake,
    flying, each
      headed its own way.

(QTS, 802/9033)

BIOGRAPHICAL NOTES AND TRANSLATION BY JEANNE LARSEN

張窈窕

P.13. Zhang Yaotiao (9th century)

Zhang Yaotiao came as a refugee to live in Chengdu (in modern Sichuan province) and there became a courtesan. Her official hometown, where her family would have been enrolled in the government registry, is unknown. Her works were highly regarded by poets of her day, at least in part because, like Xue Tao, she went beyond the tones and attitudes generally expected of courtesan-poets.

P.13.1. Poem Sent to Someone from My Past

When a thin spring wind
  brings petals down,

It's just too much—
  sad faraway stares,
    more thoughts of you.
No gold to buy
  a poem
    to win a lost
      love's heart.
I have: regret
  and an empty chant,
    the song of a cast-off fan.

(QTS, 802/9029)

P.13.2. What I Did When I Got to Chengdu

Yesterday, I sold
  a blouse, a skirt.
Today, another blouse,
  another skirt.
All my blouses, all
  my skirts, are sold.
Ashamed, I steal
  a glance at my dowry chest.
With things to sell,
  I still held off
    these griefs.
Now, in nothing
  flat, my heart's
    come round to pain.
My old garden?
  Past checkpoints
    and blockades!
(8) Where shall I tend
  a good wife's silkworm-trees?

(QTS, 802/9029)

P.13.3. Spring Thoughts (Two Poems)

I

Out in the dooryard: plum trees,
willows, bright,
too bright, with spring.
Closed up in the depths
of the women's rooms,
I stitch
a dancer's dress.
This pair of swallows—unaware
how my heart, my belly,
twist—
On purpose, on
purpose, fly right up close—
beaks filled with clay
for their nest.

II

This phoenix tree beside the well:
I moved it here myself.
During the night, flowers
opened, up
on the farthest
branch.
If I hadn't planted it
deep in the compound,
near the women's rooms,
Spring would pass
the household gate,
and I—
how would I know?

(QTS, 802/9030)

P.13.4. Song: West of the Yangzi River

Sun going down
back of the Westbourn Hills,

Come up from the south,
this traveler
from Cave-Garden Lake.
Cloudless skies: a white
bird crosses over.
Miles and
miles of autumn
light—sapphire,
turquoise,
jade.

(QTS, 802/9030)

BIOGRAPHICAL NOTE AND TRANSLATION BY JEANNE LARSEN

程長文

P.14. Cheng Changwen (9th century)

What little is known of the Tang dynasty maiden Cheng Changwen comes to us from her long narrative poem, "Writing My Feelings to the Regional Inspector While in Prison," one of only three compositions that survive from her hand. Of humble origins from near Boyang, in Jiangxi province, she was a beautiful young woman of sixteen when she became the victim of an act of violence by a local ruffian. Cheng fought for her chastity and apparently killed her attacker in the course of defending herself. Put into jail without a trial, she composed this narrative poem in order to vindicate herself. Her later fate is unknown.

P.14.1. Writing My Feelings to the Regional Inspector While in Prison

I was raised in a secluded place near Boyang,
With chaste heart, as pure as solitary bamboo.
That year I was sixteen and full of youthful grace.
On ruled paper calligraphy emerged from my flying brush.
All day I would sit at ease, embroidering by the window,
Occasionally by the water I would pluck lotus and return.
Who was this person living humbly in her hometown,
Alone in her hidden chamber, unknown to others?

Sea swallows returned each morning, chilling coverlet and pillow;
Mountain blossoms fell at night, dampening the outside stairs.
That evil man, what were his intentions?
Knife shining in hand, he moved towards the curtain.
This single life would yield to the steel blade,
But could the value of my honor be darkly compromised?
My resolve was rock-firm, my feelings unwavering,
My will like autumn frost, my mind unshakable.
Blood splattered my silk garment, but to the end no regrets,
Stained my embroidered sleeves, but how could I turn back?
The district official had not learned the details of what passed
When he ordered me locked in the prison.
My red lips now taste falling tears, alone I bear this wrong,
My jade tears flowing criss-cross, I sigh over this injustice.
The cold watches of the tenth month make one long for a friend;
Each beat of the night watchman's clapper renews my grief.
My hair, uncombed, now falls like scattering clouds,
Moth-eyebrows, unswept, are still like the new moon.
The severe sentence I have been dealt is hard to escape,
This eternal matter of my heart, to whom can I express it?
I only hope to be cleared and released from this jail,
So others will trust this white jade is without flaw.

(QTS, 799/1961; Su Zhecong, 129–30)

line 2: *Guzhu*, "solitary bamboo," may possibly refer to Bo Yi and Shu Qi, who lived at the end of the Shang dynasty (ca. 1040 B.C.E.) and who renounced their succession to the throne of Guzhu to chose a reclusive life. In that case the sense of the phrase would be "as pure as the hermits of Guzhu."

P.14.2. *Sorrow in the Spring Chamber*

Field paths interweave in the floating fragrance, willow floss like
threads,
Time passes so swiftly, like the glide of lightning.
Where has my beloved gone in pursuit of fame and glory?
Ten years of longing, but no chance to see him.

(QTS, 799/1961; Su Zhecong, 130)

BIOGRAPHICAL NOTE AND TRANSLATION BY HUI-SHU LEE

花蕊夫人

P.15. Huarui *furen* (fl. ca. 935)

The identity of this person (whose name literally means "Lady Flower Stamen") is subject to considerable dispute. One theory gives her family name as Fei, and another as Xu. The traditional view identifies her as a native of Qingcheng (now Guanxian of Sichuan province) and the consort of Meng Chang (919–65), the Prince of Shu during the Later Tang. She received her title because of her extraordinary beauty. When the prince surrendered to Song troops at Kaifeng, Huarui *furen* was supposed to have written the poem "Narrating the Fall of the State" (P.15.2). After Meng Chang was put to death as a prisoner, she supposedly gained favor with the first Song emperor. Displeased, the Song heir apparent (Prince Jin, later Emperor Taizong) shot her to death with an arrow, claiming it was a hunting accident.

A long and complex essay by the modern scholar Pu Jiangqing argues that there actually were two poets called Huarui *furen*. One was active in the kingdom of the Former Shu (907–25, in Sichuan) and another under the Later Shu (934–65).[1] In Pu's view, the Huarui *furen* of the Former Shu was the daughter of Xu Geng, the consort of Wang Jian, and the mother of Wang Yan. Both Wang Yan and his mother were put to death by troops of the Later Tang (923–34).

P.15.1. Palace Poems (4 from a series of 157)

I

The dragon moat of nine bends all connects,
While willows detain the wind along both banks.
It's like the comely scene of River South Land
Where painted skiffs ply the jade-green waves.

II

Spring's daily tributes—those royal garden blooms
Of crimson stamens wreathed in pinkish hues—
Are tendered bedewed by those on jade steps kneeling
And then by edict on palace girls bestowed.

III

Taiyi Pool is clear, the water-palace cool.
The painted boats stir up the resting ducks.
Darkened brows can't match the poolside willows
Who send at will their blossoms into Jianzhang.

IV

Who teaches the parrot to wag her tongue?
By palace folks nurtured she is ever sly.
More words seem to bring greater favor still:
She tells the king oft how she misses Mount Long.

(QTS, 798/8971, 8974, 8980)

The numbers assigned here do not reflect the order of the poems in the sources.

i, line 3: "River South Land" refers to the rich and fertile area south of the Yangzi.

iii, line 4: Jianzhang was a palace of the Han, west of the Weiyang Palace and outside the city of Chang'an. In this Tang poem, the Han name imparts a flavor of antiquity and distance.

iv, line 4: According to the eccentric Mi Heng (173–98) of the Latter Han, who wrote a "Rhapsody on the Parrot," the bird's breeding ground is located on Long Mountain, in the present Henan province (see *Wen xuan* 13/20a–23b). Mi's composition details the bird's frustration over its captivity; the allegory of protest is in turn blatantly evoked by Huarui *furen*.

P.15.2. Narrating the Fall of the State

The king on the rampart flies the white flag.
Deep within the palace how could I know?
One hundred forty thousand all disarmed!
Among these was there not one single man?

(Su Zhecong, 155–56)

BIOGRAPHICAL NOTE AND TRANSLATION BY ANTHONY C. YU

Song Dynasty (960–1279)

魏夫人

P.16. Lady Wei (fl. 1050)

Wei Wan (style name Yuru), customarily known as Lady Wei, was the wife of the Northern Song statesman Zeng Bu (1036–1107). She received the title Lady of the Kingdom of Lu while her husband was a Grand Councilor. The great Neo-Confucian philosopher Zhu Xi is reported to have said: "In our time there are only two women who can write, Li Yi'an [Li Qingzhao] and Lady Wei. Lady Wei's *ci* style has some surpassing qualities. Although she is no match for Yi'an, such talent is nonetheless no easy thing."[1] Lady Wei's son was proud to claim her as his first teacher of poetry. The poems of Lady Wei were issued in a collection of her own writings, *Wei furen ji*, now lost.[2]

P.16.1. Pusa man

As the sun sets, the play of light and dark
　Throws mountain and creek into relief.
Mandarin ducks and drakes take flight,
　Startled by the shadows on the tower stairs.
Red almond flowers have burst over the garden walls
　Of two or three houses on the other bank.

Beneath the dike, on a road lined by green poplars,
(8) 　Travelers leave the creek at all hours.
Three times I've watched the willow catkins fly,
　Yet the one who left still has not returned.

(Su Zhecong, 162)

P.16.2. Pusa man

The east wind has turned the grass of Yingzhou green,
The curtains of the painted tower are drawn in the morning frost.
Pure are the plum trees against the lake,
Their blossoms opening, not yet filling the branches.

Beneath the vast sky there is no word of him.
I watch the geese flying south again.
Where lies our sorrow in parting?
(8) At the bright moon tower of Chang'an.

(Su Zhecong, 162)

line 1: The mythical mountain Yingzhou is one of the realms of the immortals.
line 8: Presumably the lovers parted at the tower of Chang'an.

P.16.3. Pusa man

The red tower leans at an angle to the bend of the creek,
The waters near the tower grow still as cool jade.
A magnolia boat bobs on the waves,
Its passengers young indeed.
To the sound of laughter, the boat enters the bay of mandarin ducks and drakes.
Surrounded by lotus flowers so charming they seem about to speak.
On the waves, dark mists lower,
(8) In time with the caltrop-picking song, they go home in the moonlight.

(Su Zhecong, 162)

line 3: A magnolia boat is shaped like a magnolia petal.

P.16.4. Jian zi mulanhua

By the West Tower the light of the moon
Dances over a thousand trees of snowy apricot blossoms.
The one in the tower has gone,
In sorrow I listen to a single goose flying above the lonely city.

Where has the jade one gone?
I watch the colors of spring in Jiangnan come to a close again.

It has been hard to find news of you
(8) Since you departed, leaving only peach blossoms in deep-flowing
water.

(Su Zhecong, 163)

line 8: A reference to Tao Yuanming's "Peach Blossom Spring," a tale of an agrarian paradise discovered by a fisherman who followed peach blossoms swirling on the water. Once he left the paradise he was never able to find his way back again. See "Tao hua yuan ji" in Lu Qinli, ed., *Tao Yuanming ji*, pp. 165–68.

P.16.5. Ding fengbo

It's not that I have no pity for the falling flowers,
But just that the falling petals care nothing for the glory of spring.
Yesterday they smiled on the branches in all their beauty.
Who would have thought
That this morning they would float down upon someone else's home?

Winecup in hand, I face the wind with a thousand regrets—
Hard to put into words!
(8) As I wake, the clouds scatter and my gaze knows no bounds.
Wondrous dancing, clear song—who is the host at this feast?
Turning round,
I cannot see the evening sun set beyond high walls.

(Su Zhecong, 163)

P.16.6. Xi qunyao

Sparks from the lamp flicker, the water clock slowly drips.
My beloved has left
And the night grows cold.
The west wind blows wildly, waking me from a dream.
Who thinks of me
As I go to my lone pillow
With furrowed brows?

(8) Brocade screen and embroidered curtains await the coming of autumn.
My heart is about to break
And my tears fall in secret
As moonlight retreats to the west of the window.

(12) I hate you,
I cherish you,
But how would you know?

(Su Zhecong, 163–64)

BIOGRAPHICAL NOTE AND TRANSLATION BY SOPHIE VOLPP

P.17. Li Qingzhao (1084–ca. 1151)

Li Qingzhao (studio name Yi'an jushi), native of Licheng (modern Jinan), Shandong, bridged the Northern and Southern Song periods. Historians consider her a major link in the poetic tradition—the successor to Su Shi (Su Dongpo; 1037–1101) and a precursor of Xin Qiji (1140–1207). She ranks among the finest *ci* poets. The daughter of a distinguished man of letters, she became the daughter-in-law of a minister of state in marrying Zhao Mingcheng, a minor official who was an antiquarian, a book collector, and an epigrapher. Her reputation as a poet was established early. Unfortunately, only a small portion of her total poetic output—some fifty lyrics out of some six volumes—is now extant. Yet these fifty poems give ample evidence of a remarkable poet. Her happy marriage figures in most of her poems, either actively celebrated or nostalgically recollected. At one time husband and wife collaborated on the *Jin shi lu* (Record of stone and metal), a monumental catalogue of stone and bronze objets d'art constituting a resource of considerable archaeological interest, to which she added a postscript after Zhao's death. Her "On the Song-Lyric" is included as C.3.1. Commentary on Li Qingzhao is included at C.27.1.

When in 1127 the Song court, threatened by the incursion of Jürchen armies in the north, retreated to southern China, Li and her husband followed. This was the beginning of Li's lifelong exile from her home region. Zhao died on the way to his new official post. Of Li's last years, little is known except that they were certainly difficult. A legend (inspired perhaps by envy) has her marrying a low-ranking military man and divorcing him soon thereafter.

P.17.1. Yuan wangsun

On the lake the wind comes, the waves spread far and wide,
End of autumn: the reds are sparse, the fragrance fades.

The glimmer off the water, the foliage of the hills, make us kin:
No way to describe it:
This ineffable beauty!

Lotus pods have ripened, lotus leaves grow old;
Dewdrops sprinkle the duckweed, speckle the island grass.
(8) The herons on the banks, dozing, won't turn their heads.
They seem sad, too, that
We should leave so soon.

(QSC, 929)

P.17.2. Zhegu tian

Wintry day whistles through the window shut tight.
The *wutong* should dread the onset of evening frost.
The wine's finished, pleasant the bitter taste of tea.
A broken dream favors the smell of incense.

Autumn is over
But the day still seems long.
Zhongxuan pined for home; I too am lonely.
(8) Why not accept our portion, and be drunk before the cup?
We mustn't fail the yellow chrysanthemums at the eastern hedge.

(QSC, 929)

line 7: Zhongxuan is the style name of Wang Can (177–217), one of the Seven Masters of the Jian'an period, who spent a portion of his life as a neglected exile. Li's reference is doubtless to the homesick utterances of Wang's "Rhyme-Prose on Ascending the Tower" (*Wen xuan*, 11/1b–3b).

line 9: A reminiscence of Tao Yuanming's (Tao Qian) famous lines, "Picking chrysanthemums by the eastern hedge / I catch sight of the distant southern hills" ("Drinking Wine," number 5; Lu Qinli, ed., *Xian Qin Han Wei Jin Nanbeichao shi*, 2: 998).

P.17.3. Cai sang zi

In the evening gusts of wind and rain
  Washed away embers of daylight.
  I stop playing on the reed-pipe
And touch up my face in front of the mirror.

Through the thin red silk my cool flesh glistens
  Lustrous as snow, fresh with fragrance.
  With a smile I say to my beloved:
"Tonight, inside the mesh curtains, the pillow and mat are cool."

(*Li Qingzhao ji*, 43)

P.17.4. Huan xi sha

I

In the little courtyard, by the vacant window,
  Spring's colors deepen,
With the double blinds unfurled
  The gloom thickens.
Upstairs, wordless,
  The strumming of a jasper lute.

Far-off hills, jutting peaks
  Hasten the thinning of the dusk,
Gentle wind, blowing rain
  Play with light shade.
Pear blossoms are about to fall
  But there's no helping that.

II

Mild and peaceful spring glow, Cold Food Day.
From a jade censer, incense curls out in wisps of smoke.
My dream returns me to the hills of my pillow, hiding my hairpins.
The sea swallows have not yet arrived,
  Idly we duel with blades of grass.
By the river the plum trees have bloomed,
  Catkins sprout from the willow,
And at dusk scattered showers
  Sprinkle the garden swing.

(QSC, 928)

ii, line 1: Cold Food Day (*Hanshi jie*) is an important festival from ancient times, which fell at or around the spring equinox, when all fires were allowed to go out and only cold food was eaten (in commemoration of the ancient statesman Jie Zitui, burned to death by an overzealous sovereign who started a fire in an attempt to bring Jie back from a mountain retreat). New fires were then kindled in a ritual of purification. See Bodde, *Festivals in Classic China*, pp. 292–98.

P.17.5. Yi jianmei

The scent of red lotus fades: the jade mat feels autumnal.
Gently loosening the silk gown,
I board the orchid boat alone.
Who's sending a gilded message in the clouds?
When the migrating geese bring word
The moon will be full in the western chamber.
Flower petals drift down, the river flows.
One kind of longing
In two places: idle melancholy.
No way to dispel these feelings.
For just when they brim in the eyes,
They go straight to the heart.

(QSC, 928)

P.17.6. Ru meng ling

I

How many evenings in the arbor by the river
When flushed with wine we'd lose our way back.
Our revels ended, returning late by boat
We'd stray off into a spot thick with lotus
   And rowing, rowing through
Startle a shoreful of herons by the lake.

II

Last night, a bit of rain, gusty wind,
A deep sleep did not dispel the last of the wine.
I ask the maid rolling up the blinds—
But she replies: "The crab apple is just as it was."
   Doesn't she know? Doesn't she know?
The leaves should be lush and the petals frail.

(QSC, 927)

P.17.7. Niannu jiao

Lonely courtyard,
There's also slanting wind, misty rain,
The double-hinged door must be shut.
Graceful willow, delicate blossoms,
Cold Food Day approaches,
And with it every kind of unsettling weather.
I work out a few tricky rhymes,
Raise my head, clear my mind of wine,
Exceptional, the taste of idleness.
Migrating wild geese wing out of sight
But they cannot convey my teeming thoughts.

In my pavilion, cold for days with spring chill,
The curtains are drawn on all sides.
I am too weary to lean over the balustrade.
The incense sputters, the quilt feels cold,
I am just awake from a dream.
No dallying in bed for one who grieves,
When clear dew descends with the dawn
And the *wutong* tree is about to bud.
There are so many diversions in spring.
The sun is rising: the fog withdraws;
Let's see, will this be a good day?

(QSC, 931)

P.17.8. Jian zi mulanhua

From the pole of the flower vendor
I bought a sprig of spring about to bloom,
Tear-speckled, slightly sprinkled,
Still touched by rose mist and dawn's early dew.

Should my beloved chance to ask
If my face is as fair as a flower's,
I'll put one aslant in my hair,
Then ask him to look and compare.

(QSC, 932)

P.17.9. Xiao chong shan

Spring has come to the gate—spring's grasses green;
Some red blossoms on the plum tree burst open,
Others have yet to bloom.
From the "azure cloud" jar we grind "jade" tea cakes into dust.
Let's keep this morning's dream:
Break open a jug of spring!

Flowers' shadows press at the gate;
(8) Translucent curtains spread over pale moonlight.
It's a lovely evening!
Over two years—three times—you've missed the spring.
Come back!
(12) Let's enjoy this one to the full!

(QSC, 929)

line 4: Tea cakes are bricks of dried tea leaf, to be ground for making tea.

P.17.10. Zui hua yin

Thin mists—thick clouds—sad all day long.
The gold animal spurts incense from its head.
Once more it's the Festival of Double Nine;
On the jade pillow—through mesh bed curtain—
The chill of midnight starts seeping through.

At the eastern hedge I drink a cup after dusk;
Furtive fragrances fill my sleeve.
(8) Don't say one can't be overwhelmed:
When the west wind furls up the curtain,
I'm more fragile than the yellow chrysanthemum.

(QSC, 929)

line 3: On the Double Ninth festival, see P.11.4 and P.5.1. The festival was especially important to Li Qingzhao because it was associated with Tao Yuanming (Tao Qian), the poet she and her husband preferred above all others, who was known for his poems on chrysanthemums. Note the use in line 6 of the "eastern hedge," as in P.17.2.

P.17.11. Die lian hua

Long night's malaise, welcome thoughts few;
In vain, I dream of Chang'an,
Recalling the road to Chang'an.
But I must say, the spring is lovely this year,
Radiance of flower and glow of moon set each other off.

The food and drink are just right, though prepared in haste.
The wine is good, the plums sour,
(8) Just the kind of fare I take to heart:
Don't stick flowers in my hair when I'm drunk, and blossoms, don't you laugh!
Such a pity that spring—like me—must grow old.

(QSC, 932)

P.17.12. Pusa man

The wind is soft, the sun mild, it's still early spring.
Wearing a light shift suddenly brings out a happy heart.
When I woke up, there was a touch of chill,
Withering the plum blossom in my hair.

Where is my home?
I forget except when I'm drunk.
The incense was lit when I slept:
(8) It's faded now, but the wine has not lost its spell.

(QSC, 927)

P.17.13. Dian jiang chun

Lonely in my inner chamber.
My tender heart, a wisp; my sorrow tangled in a thousand skeins.
I'm fond of spring, but spring is gone,
And rain urges the petals to fall.

I lean on the balustrade:
Only loose ends left, and no feeling.
Where is he?

(8) Withering grasses stretch to the heavens:
I can't make out the path that leads him home to me.

(QSC, 932)

P.17.14. Tanpo huan xi sha

Crushed gold, thousands of feather-light dots;
Layer-cut into jade-green, leaves on leaves.
Carried off with panache like Yanfu's,
Brilliant!

Plum petals piled layer upon layer are very vulgar;
Lilacs in a thousand clusters are depressingly coarse.
Their scent pervades the faraway dream of one who's sad—
(8) Heartless!

(QSC, 933)

line 3: Yue Guang, style name Yanfu, Director of the Imperial Secretariat during the Western Jin (265–317), was known for his brilliant conversation, dazzling appearance, and impressive bearing (*Jin shu* 43/1243–48).

P.17.15. Qingping yue

Year after year in the snow
I'd put plum blossoms in my hair, drunk,
Fingering the petals till they fell, and the good mood gone,
Getting my clothes drenched with pure white tears.

This year I'm at the end of the world,
Strand by strand—alas!—my thin hair grays.
Judging by the force of the evening wind
(8) Plum blossoms will be hard to come by.

(QSC, 926)

P.17.16. Nan gezi

In the sky the Milky Way turns;
Here on earth a curtain drops.
A chill collects on the pillow-mat, wet with tears.
I get up to untie my silk gown, wondering what hour of the night it is.

The blue-tinted lotus pod is small,
The gold-spotted lotus leaves are sparse.
Old-time weather, old-time clothes
Only bring back memories
But nothing like the good old times.

(QSC, 926)

P.17.17. Xing xiang zi

Sky and autumn are both radiant!
My feelings churn inside.
I see the profusion of golden yellows: the Double Nine approaches.
I try on a thin shift,
Taste the new vintage.
In time, it turns windy,
Then turns rainy,
Then turns cold.

Dusk falls on the courtyard
Desolate and disheartened.
The wine has worn off, and now the memories hurt.
How do I survive the long night,
The bright moon on the empty bed?
I hear the sounds of washing clothes, pounding;
The sounds of the crickets, chirping;
The sounds of the water clock, dripping . . .

(*Li Qingzhao ji*, 25)

P.17.18. Hao shi jin

The wind dies down; flower petals are piled deep;
Outside the curtains, mounds of red, drifts of snowy-white.
I remember that when the cherry blossoms bloom,
That's the time when spring starts to fade.
No more wine, no more song, the jade goblets are empty.
The blue-green lamp dims and flickers out.
My haunted dreams can't bear any more secret sorrow:
Listen! the cuckoo's call!

(QSC, 929)

line 8: On the associations of the cuckoo or nightjar with sorrow, see P.5.1.

P.17.19. Wuling chun

The wind subsides—the dust carries a fragrance of fallen petals;
It's late in the day—I'm too tired to comb my hair.
Things remain but he is gone, and with him everything.
On the verge of words, tears flow.

I hear at Twin Creek spring's still lovely;
How I long to float there on a small boat—
But I fear that at Twin Creek my frail grasshopper boat
Could not carry this load of grief.

(QSC, 931)

P.17.20. Sheng sheng man

Search . . . seek
Dreary . . . desolate
Dismal . . . downcast . . . disconsolate
A warm spell—then it's back to winter
Hard to find rest.
A few swallows of weak wine
Can hardly fend off the urgent wind towards evening.
The wild geese have gone—
Breaks one's heart!—
They are acquaintances from the old days.

The yellow petals are piled all over the ground,
Forlorn and damaged: now, what's worth the plucking?
At the window,
Alone, how do I brace myself against the encroaching dark?
The *wutong* tree soaks in the drizzling rain,
Drip-drops, drip-drops into the dusk. . . .
These things, this moment,
How can one word—"grief"—say it all?

(QSC, 932)

P.17.21. Gu yan'er

Mornings, I get up from my rattan bed with its paper-thin curtains,
Unhappier than I can say.
Incense smoke nearly extinct, the jade burner cold,
Accompany my feelings that flow like water.
The sound of a flute, a melodic air,
"Burst open, plum blossoms":
How much nostalgia there is in the spring.

Light breeze, sparse rain, whisper on the ground,
Urging forth, once more, streams of tears.
The flutist leaves, the jade pavilion's empty.
Against whom can one lean with a broken heart?
I break off a branch of blossoms:
But on earth and in heaven
There's not a soul to send it to.

(QSC, 925)

P.17.22. Su zhongqing

Night found me so flushed with wine,
  I was slow to undo my hair.
The plum petals still stuck to a dying branch.
As I awoke, the scent of wine stirred me from spring sleep;
  My dream once broken, there was no going back.

  Now it's quiet:
  The moon hovers above,
  The kingfisher blinds are drawn.
Still: I feel the fallen petals;
Still: I touch their lingering scent;
Still: I hold onto a moment of time.

(QSC, 930)

BIOGRAPHICAL NOTE AND TRANSLATION BY EUGENE EOYANG

朱淑真

P.18. Zhu Shuzhen (1063?–1106)

Zhu Shuzhen's story is dramatic and detailed, involving an unhappy marriage to a merchant who could not appreciate her literary talents, an adulterous liaison with a man who shared her interest in literature, and her parents' burning of her literary corpus (supposedly only one in a hundred poems survived). But certainty about her dates, her place of origin, and the major events of her life is elusive, and the particulars of the tradition must be treated with some suspicion.

In fact, there is no firm evidence of Zhu's existence. Zhu's poems were first collected by a twelfth-century official named Wei Duanli, who stated that he happened to hear them in inns in the area of Hangzhou. He titled her collection *Heartbreak*. His preface (see C.28.1) created the legend of Zhu Shuzhen, a frustrated talent misunderstood by her parents and husband. Although Wei cites a biography by one Wang Tanzuo of Hangzhou, which is not extant, the research of Huang Yanli has established that most of the detailed traditions regarding Zhu first surfaced in the writing of Ming anthologists.[1]

For example, Tian Rucheng and Tian Yiheng, father and son, established competing claims regarding Zhu's place of origin. Tian Rucheng, who believed Zhu to have been a Yuan poet, called her a native of Hangzhou, following Wei Duanli; Tian Yiheng asserted that she was a Southern Song poet, the niece of the philosopher Zhu Xi, and that she came from Haining. Others have claimed that Zhu Shuzhen was a Northern Song poet, based on the speculation that the poem cycle in her collection subtitled "Meeting Lady Wei at a Banquet" refers to the famous Northern Song poet of that name. However, several women with the title "Lady" (*furen*) were social acquaintances of Zhu's. Her collection also mentions a "Lady Xie," and one cannot assume that the Lady Wei referred to here is the famous poet.

The first annotated edition of Zhu's work was by Zheng Yuanzuo of Hangzhou. While Zheng is commonly supposed to be a Song editor, there is no evidence to support this, and his dates are uncertain. The work of Qing and modern editors has brought the total number of her poems to three hundred *shi* poems and thirty-three song lyrics.

P.18.1. Qingping yue*: Going to the Lake on a Summer's Day*

Mist and dew, painfully enticing,
For a moment detain me here.
On the road beside the lake, we hold hands among the lotus plants:
A moment of "yellow plum rain."

I act foolishly, not caring if anyone guesses.
Like an ordinary mortal, for a moment I forget my sorrows.
The moment our hands part, I am overwhelmed,
Returning home, I lean wearily against my dressing table.

(Huang Yanli, *Zhu Shuzhen ji qi zuopin*, 278)

line 4: "Yellow plum rain" refers to the drizzly season of early fall that coincides with the ripening of yellow plums.

P 18.2. Jiang cheng zi*: Admiring Spring*

Driving wind and fine rain make for a chill spring.
A wine cup before me,
I remember our past love.
Once, clutching pear flowers in hand,
I shed streams of tears in the gloomy stillness.
Fragrant grasses and patches of mist on the road to South Bank;
With tears of parting in my eyes,
I gaze at the azure hills.

Last night I dreamt that I followed him
Through waters and mists,
Silent, without a word.
When I woke I could not control
My sorrow, deep as before.
Tossing and turning in my quilt I am vexed to no end.
It's simple enough to watch the sky,
Hard to catch a glimpse of him.

(*Zhu Shuzhen ji*, 275)

P.18.3. Die lian hua

Before the tower, thousands of strands of hanging willow.
I'd like to tie down the green of spring.

I could detain it a short while, but in the end it would vanish.
Willow catkins float in the wind
As though following spring just to see where it calls home.

All through the mountains and rivers filled with green I hear the cuckoo,
A bird without feelings of its own.
(8) It must be grieving for another's sorrow.
I take wine and make an offering to spring, but there is no response.
At dusk, though, comes a driving rain.

(*Zhu Shuzhen ji*, 281)

P.18.4. A Vehicle for My Feelings [first of two poems]

Pale moon, sparse clouds, the sky in the ninth month.
Reckless leaves drunk with frost fall into the chill river.
Alone by the window, I pass a day of boredom and lethargy,
Editing my poems and songs, experimenting with words erased and changed.

(*Zhu Shuzhen ji*, 102)

P.18.5. Jian zi mulanhua*: Spring Plaint*

I walk alone, sit alone
Chant poems and raise my glass alone
Even go to bed alone.
I stand still, my spirit grieving,
No way to defend myself against the troubling spring chill.

Who notices these feelings of mine?
Tears have washed away the powder and rouge till not even half is left.
(8) Sorrow and sickness have each had their turn.
I've trimmed the lamp's cold wick to the quick, but dreams won't come.

(*Zhu Shuzhen ji*, 275–76)

P.18.6. Abashed Before the Swallows

As my needle pauses, tears wordlessly fill my eyes,
Not only in spring do I grieve; summer has its sadnesses as well.

A pair of swallows fly over the flowers;
Each time they pass, I feel shame.

(*Zhu Shuzhen ji*, 82)

P.18.7. The Double Ninth

Last year on the Double Ninth I thought my sorrow knew no bounds.
This year it breaks my heart still more.
Autumn tints and setting sun—both pale and weak;
Trace of tears, thoughts of parting—both chill and bleak.

Though the migrating geese have come from afar, they bring no message,
Yellow chrysanthemums hold scent but no feeling.
Lately I sense that I have grown gaunt,
(8) But lack the strength to raise my phoenix mirror and check my reflection.

(*Zhu Shuzhen ji*, 101)

line 1: On Double Ninth, see P.5.1, P.11.4.
line 5: On geese as bearers of messages, see P.2.1 (Song 5).
line 6: Yellow chrysanthemums are a common metaphor for autumn; on the association with longevity, see P.5.1.
line 8: On the legend of the phoenix and the mirror, see P.11.15.

P.18.8. Peonies

With thousands of fetching poses they display their exquisite scents,
Royalty among flowers.
Don't compare them to those beauties for whom cities are lost,
For whole kingdoms have fallen for them.

(*Zhu Shuzhen ji*, 213)

P.18.9. Rhyming After Two Poems I Received in a Packet

Suddenly I receive a letter from the South,
Your earnestness comforts my heart.
Reading your new poem, I cherish your carefree talent;
Your clear tunes remind me of your face and voice.
The road to our hometown is long, farther than eyes can see.
The tower is high and the traveler's grief deep.

In three years we will meet again,
(8) And watch the shadow of the thornbush once more.

(*Zhu Shuzhen ji*, 248)

line 8: Zhu alludes to a story concerning three brothers who were persuaded to keep the family fortune intact by a magical thornbush, which withered and died when it overheard the brother's plan to divide it along with all the other goods (Wu Jun, *Xu Qi xieji*, in SKQS, 1042: 554–55). Her allusion suggests that she hopes to be united permanently with the poems' addressee.

P.18.10. Asking After Spring: An Old-Style Poem [one of a series]

Spring is here, so let's stop talking about the love we had in days past.
The atmosphere is washed with newness again.
The orioles and flowers address their sorrows to me alone;
The silent peaches and pears merely vex me.
Tears charged with powder have washed my gaunt face clean;
My sash falls loosely around my slender waist.
The Lord of the East owes me three months of spring—
(8) Or is it I who owe him a full spring, three months of it?

(*Zhu Shuzhen ji*, 11)

P.18.11. Feelings Evoked by an Autumn Night [three poems from a series of six]

I

A sliver of new moon hangs in the dusk,
In the secluded chamber, a heart is about to break.
I open the envelope, unfold the pale paper, and amend my letter once more.
Too weary to lift the wine cup, I nonetheless have it warmed again.
Sparks from the lamp consume the cares of the heart.
My gauze sleeves have always served to wipe the tracks of my tears.
And I regret even more that romance only leads to dissatisfaction,
(8) It is time to realize that love is the root of all sorrow.

II

Beyond the eaves the autumn chill penetrates the lattice window.
Mist shrouds the chrysanthemums speckled with their moonlit dew, their scents floating in the chill.

In the cold, the fifth watch sounds,
And in response, my sorrow stretches as long as the night.

III

A hundred illnesses arise from idle frustration and sorrow,
It's better, in the end, to lack feelings than to have them.
Let the shell of romance be engraved and polished to perfection;
Then the heartbreak of separation may be cast and stamped forever.

(*Zhu Shuzhen ji*, 11)

P.18.12. Five Extemporaneous Quatrains

When I met Lady Wei at a banquet, she ordered the dancer Xiao Huan to perform her marvelous dance. When the tune ended, she asked me for a poem. I used the line "Flying snow fills the many peaks" to set my rhymes, and composed five quatrains.

I. RHYMING ON "FLYING"

When the pipes and strings urge her to dance on the brocade mat
Her body is so light it seems about to fly.
If Emperor Ming of the Tang had seen this
Aman would not have seemed a second Yang Guifei.

II. RHYMING ON "SNOW"

Her fragrant dress and neat petticoat are like a slender crescent moon,
Her steps ripple to and fro and vanish as easily as a cloud's shadow.
The strings quicken and the clappers reach a crescendo, rushing the
 melody to an end,
Her two sleeves whirl like floating snow.

III. RHYMING ON "FILLS"

Her willow waist is not bound by spring,
The phoenix twirls and the *luan*-bird swirls on her sunset-colored
 sleeves.
When she has finished dancing to the Yizhou tune, her strength is
 almost gone.
Nearing the banquet tables she brushes past the flowers, and the air is
 filled with flying petals.

IV. RHYMING ON "MANY"

She dominated the spring season in the capital,
Her pure song and wondrous dance surpass the rest.
I am afraid that, come dawn,
She will melt into a streak of Wu Mountain cloud.

V. RHYMING ON "PEAKS"

Her powdered beauty stands idly in the shadows cast by the candles,
A spot of sadness steals between her brows.
Unafraid of the jealousy of Zhao Feiyan,
Wordlessly she goes along to watch the "Curved-Bow" dance.

(*Zhu Shuzhen ji*, 103)

i, line 4: The dancer Xie Aman was much favored by Yang Guifei, the chief concubine of Emperor Ming (Xuanzong, r. 713–56). When rebels led by the mercenary general An Lushan forced Xuanzong and his court to flee the capital, Xuanzong's guard, blaming the emperor's infatuation with Yang Guifei for his neglect of state affairs, demanded that she be put to death. After Xuanzong's return to the capital, Xie danced once more for the emperor and presented him with gold armbands that had been a gift from Yang Guifei.

ii, lines 2 and 4: "Rippling steps" and "whirling snow" allude to Cao Zhi's "Rhyme-Prose on the Goddess of the Lo" (*Wen xuan*, 19/11b–16a).

iii, line 2: The *luan* is a mythical phoenixlike bird usually regarded as female in opposition to the male *feng* bird. (See also P.29.9.)

iv, line 4: On the goddess of Wu Mountain, see P.9.2.

v, line 3: Zhao Feiyan (Flying Swallow) was the victorious rival of Ban *jieyu* (see P.1).

BIOGRAPHICAL NOTE AND TRANSLATION BY SOPHIE VOLPP

P.19. Yan Rui (fl. ca. 1160)

The primary source of information regarding Yan Rui (style name Youfang) is a short entry in *Qidong yeyu* (Rustic talk from east of Qi), a miscellany compiled by the Southern Song author Zhou Mi (1232–1308). According to this narrative, Yan Rui was a popular courtesan who excelled at playing the *qin*, singing, dancing, calligraphy, and painting. This entry also contains the three poems attributed to Yan Rui. Unfortunately, we cannot be sure that Yan Rui ever existed.

Zhou Mi embeds Yan's three poems in a narrative involving the leading neo-Confucian thinker Zhu Xi. According to this tale, Yan was entertaining the official Tang Zhongyou when he asked her to compose a lyric on the peach flower. She responded with the "Ru meng ling" (P.19.3). Zhu Xi, who had been appointed to the area, bore a grudge against Tang Zhongyou, and Tang's liaison with an unofficial entertainer gave him his chance. Hoping to cut short Tang's official career, he threw Yan Rui into jail and tried to make her give evidence. Despite beatings, she refused to confess to anything, saying that her involvement with Tang was not a capital crime and that she would not slander him, even under the threat of death. Thereupon she was jailed, bound, and beaten once more. After Zhu Xi was posted elsewhere, an official named Yue Linshang took pity on Yan Rui and asked her to tell her story. She replied with the song-lyric to the tune "Bu suanzi" (P.19.1). Yet another official named Xie Yuan, having heard of her fame, asked her for a composition regarding the festival of the seventh month. The result was her third recorded lyric, "Que qiao xian" (P.19.2). Xie is said to have become so enamored of her that he kept her at his home for half a year.[1]

Zhou Mi stated that his information came from old families of Tiantai (in present-day Zhejiang province), where Yan Rui lived. This suggests that the poems may have circulated orally as a part of Yan's legend before Zhou wrote his account.

P.19.1. Bu suanzi

It is not that I love the courtesan's life;
It's the karma of a past life that has wronged me.
Blossoms fall and blossoms open; each has its season.
All depends on the god of spring.

In the end I must leave,
For how can I stay?
If I could fill my hair with flowers of the mountain—
(8) Don't ask where I would go to dwell.

(Su Zhecong, 220)

P.19.2. Que qiao xian

When the deep blue of the *wutong* leaves first appears
The cassia has just begun to bud,
And the flowers of the pond have begun to wither.
The women threading needles are in the Tower of Conjoined Bliss
As lunar dew
Drips from the jade basin on high.

Spiders are busy, magpies lazy.
The plow slackens, the weaver is weary.
This is just a fine tale of past and present.
In the human world, we think that one year has passed.
But in heaven—look—
It was just a night.

(Su Zhecong, 221)

line 4: A reference to the practice of "begging for skill" on Double Seventh night (see P.5.1). In one custom, a group of women would each put a spider in a small box. The woman whose spider had woven the most intricate web on the next morning would become most skilled in weaving. Another ritual was to thread needles by the light of the moon in hopes of improved skill in needlework.

line 8: On the story of Weaving Girl and Herd Boy, see P.5.1.

P.19.3. Ru meng ling: *Peach Flowers Red and White*

People call them pear flowers, but they're not,
People call them almond flowers, but they're not.
Their whites and reds
Have a special quality in the east wind.
Do you remember
Do you remember
That someone grew a bit tipsy in Wuling?

(Su Zhecong, 221)

line 7: Wuling was the home of the fisherman who discovered the agrarian paradise described in Tao Yuanming's "Peach Blossom Spring"; see P.16.4.

BIOGRAPHICAL NOTE AND TRANSLATION BY SOPHIE VOLPP

楊太后

P.20. Empress Yang (1162–1233)

Empress Yang was the talented and powerful second consort of Emperor Ningzong (r. 1194–1224). A force behind the throne through Ningzong's reign and into that of his successor, Lizong (r. 1225–64), Empress Yang was also an active patron of the arts. It has been established that Empress Yang is the same as Yang Meizi, author of numerous poetic inscriptions that accompany paintings by Southern Song court artists. Her family origins are unclear. She arose from the humble background of court entertainer, adopting the surname Yang in order to establish alliance with a powerful clan and secure legitimacy for her bid to the throne. She played a key role in the choice of Lizong as emperor and helped to arrange his marriage as well. Once established, Lizong rewarded her patronage by establishing her as Supreme Empress Dowager.[1]

Empress Yang's official biography in *Song shi* describes her as bright and witty in nature, "one familiar with calligraphy, history, and matters of past and present."[2] This character portrait is substantiated by Empress Yang's extant inscriptions to paintings, which testify, in remarkably subtle cooperation with the pictures they accompany, to the intersection of art, gender, and politics in the imperial court. Empress Yang's poetic compositions are also found in a collection of verses entitled *Yang taihou gongci* (Palace lyrics of Empress Dowager Yang).[3] This book of poems has become corrupted over time, with a few verses of Tang and Yuan dynasty date creeping in, but it remains an invaluable document. Its poems are generally consistent in style and many relate to specific Southern Song state occasions and personages.

P.20.1. [Untitled]

Gentle and soothing the light breeze of the second month;
Willow catkins, windblown, are ever more winsome and pitiable.
Quietly I rest against the decorated balustrade, with nothing to do but
Count, one by one, swallows darting through the flowers until their
 shadows slant.

(Yang Meizi, *Yang taihou gongci*, 1b)

P.20.2. [Untitled]

Spring breeze is light, water flowing,
Hand in hand we seek fragrant blossoms across the small bridge.
But how annoying the scene of the wild pond where my eye chances upon
Innumerable mandarin ducks resting pair by pair!

(*Yang taihou gongci*, 1b)

line 4: Paired mandarin ducks are a symbol of lifelong fidelity. The implication is that this woman has been disappointed in love or her mate is away.

P.20.3. [Untitled]

Provisions for my Kunning Palace: just a single goat.
Since assuming the proper seat, I manage literary affairs.
Cherishing life and frugality, I pursue models of the ancient past;
As exemplar for the palace ladies, I apply only light rouge.

(*Yang taihou gongci*, 4b)

This is a poem from the standpoint of an empress: her frugality, learning, and modesty set an example for her subordinates in the time-honored Confucian way.

P.20.4. [Untitled]

Deep layers of curtains and drapes deeply hung on all four sides:
Clear and harmonious weather, the clock announces the late hour.
In the inner chamber of the palace, an urgent call for the spinning of thread:
I hurry forward to take part personally in the making of colored silks.

(*Yang taihou gongci*, 6a)

P.20.5. [Untitled]

It is our family tradition in brushwork to study Guangyao;
The great man's writing in all of the scripts has prevailed for two reigns.
With heaven-bestowed talent he naturally formed his own style,
Likened by many to the stalking tiger and leaping dragon.

(*Yang taihou gongci*, 4b)

line 1: Guangyao was the literary name of Emperor Gaozong of the Southern Song, whose calligraphy was widely renowned.

P.20.6. Crab Apple Blossoms

Her thinly fading rouge is lightly fragrant,
When before one's eyes spring's scene can still be enjoyed.
It is said that in a year's time to flourish and wither is easy;
Can it be you tire of luxuriant blooming and cherish instead the
 drunken realm?

This poem is inscribed on a round fan, now in the possession of the Metropolitan Museum of Art, bearing Empress Yang's signature "Yang Meizi" and her single-dragon seal. The poem seems to allude to Yang Guifei, the "drunken beauty" (see P.18.12) and perhaps to compare her to Empress Yang. For an art-historical discussion, see H. Lee, "The Domain of Empress Yang," pp. 199–202.

P.20.7. [Untitled]

Golden millet-like blossoms cluster on the emerald tree;
Under the bright moon, dew wets the jade step terrace.
Still some traces of lingering fragrance remain
From the last time he came visiting the Kunning Palace.

(Yuan Hua, *Gengxuezhai shiji*, 10/9b–10a)

This poem was originally inscribed on a fan painting by Empress Yang's favorite court painter, Ma Yuan. Since the poem celebrates cassia, the other side of the fan probably bore an image of that tree. Its allegory is to be decoded as follows: the cassia tree is Empress Yang, and the moon that visits her with favor is the emperor.

P.20.8. [Untitled]

Those who are able to be without attachments worry no more;
The ten thousand scenes merge together and end with a single laugh.
How could it be only the mid-autumn moon that is worthy of
 appreciation and feasting?
When the day is cool and the moon is fine, that is mid-autumn.

This poem is inscribed on a fan now in the possession of the Tianjin Art Museum.

P.20.9. [Untitled]

Occasions and events of the four seasons urge us on in haste;
By seeing through our mundane lives one dwells in the realm of happiness.
Ninth month, by the side of the fence: although the mood is desolate,
After the chrysanthemums bloom comes the Double Ninth Day of autumn.

This poem is inscribed on a fan now in the Elliot Family Collection, Princeton University Art Museum, Princeton, N.J.

line 4: On Double Ninth, see P.5.1, P.11.4.

P.20.10. [Untitled]

He carries a staff to push aside the grass and gaze into the wind,
Unable to avoid climbing mountains and crossing waters.
Not realizing that the Way streams throughout the world,
No sooner does he look, head bowed, than a smile rises from within.

Encomium inscribed on a painting, "Dongshan Wading Through Water," by Ma Yuan, hanging scroll now in the Tokyo National Museum. This scroll is believed to have been one of a set of five paintings of Chan patriarchs (two others from the set are in the collection of the Tenryu-ji, Kyoto, Japan). "Pushing aside the grass and gazing into the wind" alludes to Chan discipleship. "Wading through waters" is symbolic of the hardships of the search for wisdom; in addition, Dongshan was said to have gained enlightenment after gazing at his reflection in a river. See Daoyuan, *Jingde chuandeng lu*, 15/12a–13a, 17a–b; and Powell, *The Record of Tungshan*, pp. 3–5, 27–28.

BIOGRAPHICAL NOTE AND TRANSLATION BY HUI-SHU LEE

P.21. Wang Qinghui (fl. 1270)

Wang Qinghui, one of the Nine Concubines during the reign of Emperor Duzong (1265–74), last emperor of the Southern Song, is also known by her official title Wang *zhaoyi*—"Brilliant Companion." She, along with the other members of the imperial entourage, was taken north to the Mongol capital Dadu (Beijing) after the fall of the dynasty. Once there she requested permission to become a Daoist priestess and changed her name to Chonghua.[1]

The beautiful Wang Qinghui is said to have been talented in composing both *shi* and *ci* poetry, though very few examples are extant today. Her only surviving *ci* song-lyric, set to the tune "Man jiang hong," is very well known, however. According to Zhou Mi (1232–1308) and Tao Zongyi (1316–?), Wang composed the poem and wrote it on the wall of the Yishan Inn near Kaifeng (Henan province) during her forced journey to the north.[2] The Song loyalist Wen Tianxiang (1236–83), touched by it, wrote a poem in response. He also wrote a second one, "representing Wang Qinghui," that rejected the air of resignation in her ending lines, in order to assert his own unwavering loyalty to the Song.[3] In addition, Wang Qinghui is known as one of the seventeen Song imperial ladies who wrote farewell poems for the scholar and musician Wang Yuanliang upon his release from the Mongol captivity to return south as a Daoist.[4]

P.21.1. Man jiang hong: *Inscribed on the Wall of an Inn*

The lotus of Taiyi Pond
Has nothing of the color she displayed in the past.
Still she remembers
The imperial favor that fell like rain and dew
In jade towers and golden pavilions.
Her fame spread, an orchid hairpin among the imperial consorts,
A radiant blush suffused her lotus face as she accompanied the
emperor.
Suddenly one day
War drums approached across the heavens,
Splendor came to an end.

Dragons and tigers are dispersed,
Winds and clouds have vanished.
A thousand years of sorrow—
To whom can she tell them?
As she faces this vast land of mountains and rivers,
Tears stain her sleeves with blood.
At an inn she is startled one night: a dream of the dusty world,
Palace carriages roll at dawn, moon over the mountain pass.
She prays to Chang E, Goddess of the Moon,

(20) To be her guardian and allow her
To follow, be she full or waning.

(Zhou Mi, *Haoranzhai yatan*, 2/8b; QSC, 3344; Chen Xin, 138–39)

lines 1–2: Taiyi was a pond in the palaces of the Han and Tang dynasties. Here it alludes to a line from the Tang poet Bo Juyi's poem on the concubine Yang Guifei, "Song of Everlasting Sorrow": "When [the emperor and his suite] returned to the palace [after Yang Guifei's execution], the ponds and gardens were as before— / The lotus of Taiyi Pond and the willow of the Weiyang Palace" (Bo Juyi, *Baixiangshan shiji*, 12/117–20; see P.18.12). Wang Qinghui thus suggests her own desolation as an imperial consort of the defeated dynasty.

lines 9–10: These lines also borrow from Bo Juyi's "Song of Everlasting Sorrow": "The war drums of Yuyang approach, shaking the earth."

lines 11–12: Dragons and tigers refer to the emperor of the past dynasty; wind and clouds, to virtuous officials. The allusion comes from the commentary on the *qian* hexagram of the *Yi jing*: "Clouds follow the dragon, wind follows the tiger. Thus the sage arises, and all creatures follow him with their eyes" (Wilhelm and Baynes, *I Ching*, p. 9).

line 19: Chang E, the goddess of the moon, escaped to the moon after stealing the herb of immortality from her husband Yi (see *Huainan zi*, "Lan ming xun" 6/10b). Now she spends eternity wishing she could be reunited with him.

BIOGRAPHICAL NOTE AND TRANSLATION BY HUI-SHU LEE

Yuan Dynasty (1264–1368)

元代藝人

P.22. Yuan Entertainers: Pearl Screen Beauty, Little Bit, Swallow Song Liu, Zhenzhen, Mother's Compassion Liu

The women represented in this section are named, yet nameless. They are known primarily through one small text, *Qinglou ji* (The record of the green lofts), a collection of biographical notices of some 117 entertainers (predominantly female) from the middle and late Yuan. The focus of the collection is on performers, particularly of drama but also of other stage acts, including martial arts and various forms of speech and song performances. Our knowledge of them is further fashioned out of the writings of their literate clients and paramours. All of the women represented here were subjects of prefaces, poems, and essays written by influential scholars. But one will look in vain for any hint of personalized character. They are treated as literary playthings, their physical shape, their skills, turned solely into surface features of created "things" (*wu*), objects to be fetishized as poets fetishized other exotic, beautiful creations.

Even the surname of the most famous of them, "Pearl Screen Beauty," subject of prefaces and poems by the most famous literati and dramatists of the day, is uncertain. Her family name has been transmitted both as Song and as Zhu, two words that are easy to confuse orthographically. In any case, entertainers were known principally by "talent names," as they are called in Chinese, stage names that captured some essence of their physical beauty or skill in performance: "Swallow Song Liu," "Mother's Compassion Liu," "Pearl Screen Beauty," "Little Bit," and "Zhenzhen" (meaning "true and pure") are the women represented here.

Such women were most valued as the performing voice of scholars' own poems: first and foremost they were singers whose clear voices could "shake the dust from the rafters." Yet they were often extremely talented in their own right. Many were extolled for their prodigious memories: one could rehearse the complete songbooks for more than three hundred dramas; another could recite on command from the massive *Zizhi tongjian* (Comprehensive mirror for the aid of government), an extraordinarily long and detailed chronological history. They were also calligraphers, painters, and most notably, quick creators of verse, able to pick up a proffered line or sentiment and extemporize a lyric as they sang it. It was the performance of the lyric, not the substance, that counted in the eyes of their male audience—the verbal dexterity and wit to create, on the spot, lyrics and poems that danced in the fetters of the strict tonal and rhyme patterns of Chinese verse.

In keeping with this pattern of reception, the poems we have left are all written as responses, created on demand, on the spot at a banquet, or prompted as a reply, both thematically and metrically, to a poem written by one of their clients. These are playful verses, provoked and provocative, stripped of the intentionality and ethical weight normally given to personal expressions of sentiment. They are performance pieces—and yet the language and imagery of such poems are often identical to those found in poems thought to be complex expressions of deep feeling. Their value to us is to show how poetry operates in the extraliterary world: they show us the usefulness of poetry as a tool, a method of operation, a way to win favor or fame, and through those actions as a means of attaining some security and wealth in a highly literate and powerful segment of Chinese society. Of course, this function mirrored the structure of the male literary world, where the curious dynamic between intentionality—personal expression—and personal fame as a writer took place in a vastly more influential world of real social and political power.

But an entertainer's poetry never has the last word: rather, it is the accompanying stories and biographical notes that carry historical and ethical weight. So we read that many attained favor on the basis of their skill and beauty and were taken into prominent families as a kind of special concubine: "placed in a side room" was the term used to describe this process. After favor waned or their paramour died, these women were often thrown out by the family. Like others of their profession, some wound up married to merchants or Daoist priests; some simply disappeared. The most dramatically appealing ending, from the point of view of male audiences at least, was that chosen by a significant number who disfigured themselves to repel sexual predation or committed suicide rather than return to a life of prostitution and entertainment.

These women are remembered because of their playful exchanges with prominent men. The aesthetic and ethical judgments proffered by the documents of context often make their poetic exchanges seem natural and uncalculating. Most of the interchanges took place in the *sanqu*, "free aria" (see Appendix A), a form that was stamped as a performance art. But, as noted, the posed sentiments of these exchanges were couched in a vocabulary of words and images that matched more serious forms of response verse. Since the poems of entertainers were so clearly designed to win favor and acclaim, the stories of famous entertainers problematized both favor and the receiving of favor, and comment subtly, yet subversively, on *any* fame won through the discourse of poetry. This may account in part for the fact that the poems themselves are never commented on; only the creative moment of their composition and the beauty of their performance ever drew the attention of writers.

P.22a. Pearl Screen Beauty (Zhulian xiu; b. ca. 1270)

Among the intimate paramours of this renowned actress and slightly hunchbacked beauty were the great dramatist Guan Hanqing (fl. ca. 1240) and a plethora of famous Yuan scholars, including Hu Zhiyu (1227–93), Wang Yun (1228–1304), Feng Zizhen (1257–1314), and Lu Zhi (d. after 1314). All these men wrote suites of songs about Pearl, sent love songs to her, or wrote prefaces extolling her beauty or her skill. The *Qinglou ji* has a small note on her:

> Her surname was Song, and she was born fourth in sequence. She strides alone in the contemporary world of *zaju* drama. "Emperor role," "flowery female lead," and "soft male lead"[1]—in every case she creates the wonder of the role. Hu Zhiyu once sent her a poem to the tune *Chen zui dongfeng* that read:
>
> Jade green bamboos by the edge of a damask-embroidered river;
> Strings thread ocean's bright pearls.
> At the time the moon is pale,
> And where the wind is fresh,
> Everything is cut off from the world of falling red dust.
> A swatch of idle passion is furled and unfurled at will,
> Hanging up all of the morning clouds and evening rains.
>
> Feng Zizhen also sent her a poem to the tune *Zhegu tian* that read:
>
> Leaning into the eastern wind, a distant reflected loft,
> Flowing orioles peek at her face, swallows bow down their heads.
> The slender shadows of shrimps' whiskers finely, finely woven,

> The perfumed patterns of tortoises' backs lightly, lightly float.
> The red mists gather away,
> The colored clouds retreat.
> Sunset over the sea for a strap, the moon for a hook—
> Night comes and it rolls away all the rains of western hills,
> And lets not a speck of sorrow into the world of men.
>
> Now Pearl's back was slightly hunched, so Feng intentionally made a metaphor using the hook of a curtain. Even to this day, all the younger generations designate her as "Momma Pearl."[2]

Her designation as Momma Pearl (*Zhu niangniang*) speaks to her status among entertainers. *Niangniang* is a term of respect, often used for local female deities. Indeed, Pearl trained many students who went on to become famous in their own right. She began her career in the Yuan capital at Dadu (present-day Beijing) and later moved to Yangzhou, where she held sway over the acting world. In the end, she married a Daoist priest in Hangzhou and stayed with him until death.

Pearl was a talented poet. The number of writings addressed to her from literati demonstrate that it was this gift, above all, that gave her access to the world of the powerful. The two poems of jest in the above passage, playing on her name, the pearl screen that closed off her boudoir, and even the soft curve of her slightly hunched back, provide a measure of contextualization for her poems. Only two of her own compositions are left, one a short "small lyric" written in response to a poem sent her by Lu Zhi and the other a longer suite that laments the loss of a love. While we may be tempted to read these poems as sincere expressions of "love longing," we should remember that, in the first case, she was intimate with many influential men and that this intimacy called for a kind of posed exchange of verse. The longer poem is highly reminiscent of songs of self-pity often sung by entertainer-prostitutes in drama, who themselves are likely to be rejected by a scholar of some merit and comeliness.

P.22a.1. Shouyang qu: *In Response to Lu Zhi*

Mountains beyond number,
The mist a myriad intertwining threads—
Turn the Scholar of the Jade Hall pallid with sorrow.
I lean against the bramble window, my whole body alive with pain,
Hating that I cannot follow that Great River to the east.

(Xia Tingzhi, *Qinglou ji*, 87)

Lu Zhi's poem reads as follows: "Just enjoying pleasure, / We part too soon. / So painful—hard to tear ourselves apart, / The painted boat carries spring away, / Leaving vainly behind a half river of bright moon" (*Qinglou ji*, 87).

P.22a.2. Untitled Suite to Qu *Tunes*

I. *ZUI XI SHI*

Recalling with care the romantic elegance of former times,
These last few days I've gradually become aware that Xiao Man's waist is thin.
Thought, then, of the myriad sorts of care and passion at the start,
Turned now, the whole lot, to nothing but dream of enervating vexation.
It strikes me so hard my willow brows crinkle,
Raceways for the water of autumn billows,
Teardrops that dribble on the sleeves of my spring gown.
Like peachblow in the rain, my rouge peeks through.
"Lush leaves, petals frail"—
This *is* the time to sorrow!

II. *BINGTOU LIAN*

The wind is weak,
Curtains hang on jade hooks.
I fear pairs of swallows,
Oriole mates, two by two,
Abiding by each other in matched sets.
What house of pleasure does that ingrate haunt now?
I'm left with naught but new sickness piling on the old,
New sorrow pushing out old sorrow.
Cloud mountains fill the eyes,
Listless, I climb the loft for evening toilet.

III. *SAI GUANYIN*

The flowers bud with smiles,
Willows carry embarrassment,
But everywhere in this arena of dance are the sorrows of separation.
I want to send a length of silken letter, but whom shall I trust to write it?

One brush stroke to wipe clean all of this love longing.
Seeing the cold, sere, fragrant grasses increases infinite sorrow.
Enough, enough—
(8) Broken heart, the Xiang River, about to reach their end.

IV. *YU FURONG*

When will loneliness end?
I hope for news from heaven's edge.
Adding to human illness—a branch-tip oriole,
Augmenting human sorrow—fading willows at Wei City.
Even if the "spring river that fills the eyes were all made of tears,"
It could never "float away this much sorrow."
If, on his return we can
(8) Walk as one, sit together,
Even if I should die beneath the peony itself,
I'd still be a romantic ghost.

V. CODA

The whole night the eastern wind probed with light chill,
Reporting that peachblow was carried away on river's current—
Don't imitate that Lord of the East,
Who never even turns his head.

(Xia Tingzhi, *Qinglou ji*, 86)

i, line 2: Xiao Man was a performer in the house of Bo Juyi. A slim beauty, she was famous for her dancing.

i, line 9: A reminiscence of Li Qingzhao; see P.17.6.

iv, line 3: An allusion to a poem by the obscure Tang writer Jin Changxu: "Scare away those yellow orioles, / Don't let them chatter on branches' ends! / When they chatter, they startle my dreams / And I cannot reach Liaoxi" (QTS, 8724).

iv, line 4: A light twist on Wang Wei's famous lines: "Morning rain in Wei City sprinkles light dust, / By hostel side, green, green, the color of willow is new. / I urge you, sir, to finish one more cup of wine. / Forth to the west from Yang Pass, there are no old friends!" (QTS 1307).

iv, lines 5–6: A reference to a lyric by Qin Guan (QSC, 458):

West city willows sport spring's suppleness,
Incite the anxiety of separation.
Tears are hard to stop.
I still recall, full of passion, tying up the homing boat,

The blue wilds, red bridge, events of that day—
The person is gone,
The water flows vainly by.
(8) The wonders of youth do not linger for the young,
Vexation goes on and on.
When will it cease?
When willow floss flies, flowers fall, I climb the loft once more.
(12) Even if we make the spring river all of tears,
It cannot float away
So much sorrow.

v, line 3: The god of spring.

P.22b. Little Bit (Yifen'er; mid–14th century)

Little is known of the life of "Little Bit," except for her biographical notice in the *Qinglou ji*. One of the people mentioned in that record was still living during the early part of the Ming (that is, very late in the fourteenth century), therefore we can estimate her dates to have been sometime between 1320 and 1400. Yifen'er was "surnamed Wang, and a top geisha in the capital [Dadu, present-day Beijing]. Her singing and dancing were without peer, and she was incomparably quick and intelligent. One day, Commander Ding gathered with playwrights Liu Shichang and Cheng Jishan at Riverhome Park for a little banquet. Madame Wang was in attendance. At this time there was a young beauty singing a song in southern mode from 'A Gathering of Chrysanthemums,' which said, 'Red leaves let fall their fire—the dragon sheds its scales, / Green pines withered and weird—the python grows teeth.' Ding said, 'These are the first lines of "Deep Drunk in the East Wind," and Madame Wang can fill them out.' Wang immediately replied. . . . Everyone at the feast mat sighed appreciatively, and from this time on her fame grew even greater."[3]

Yifen'er's—Madame Wang's—response has been recorded as follows:

P.22b.1. Chen zui dongfeng

Red leaves let fall their fire—the dragon sheds its scales,
Green pines withered and weird—the python grows teeth.
A theme worth singing about,
A painting worth sketching—
But flagons and wine tallies lie scattered on the feast mat,

And *darasu* keeps getting poured into the *lisima*.
If I'm not drunk, don't put me up on my horse!

(Xia Tingzhi, *Qinglou ji*, 211)

line 6: *Darasu* is the Mongolian word for wine cup; *lisima* is unknown.

P.22C. Swallow Song Liu (Liu Yan'ge; ca. 1240)

Nothing is known of Liu apart from the brief biography that contains one of her two extant lyrics. Qi Rongxian, the person addressed in her poems, was a prominent official during the late Jin and early Yuan eras. He retired from service in roughly 1260, and the last post he held before retirement was as Special Consultant to the Route Commander of Dongping, in Shandong. Some scholars suggest these poems were written in commemoration of his retirement from that post. This would place Swallow Song Liu in the early or middle part of the thirteenth century. She was noted for her *ci* poems. The first poem quoted here is given this commentary: "[Swallow Song Liu] was skilled at dancing. When Special Consultant Qi Rongxian returned to Shandong, Liu wrote a song to the tune 'Taichang yin' to send him off. . . . These lines are on everyone's lips to this very day."[4]

P.22C.1. Taichang yin: *To Special Consultant Qi on his Return to Dongping*

My old friend parts from me, "goes out of Yang Pass,"
I have no plans to chain up the carved saddle.
Past to present, nothing is as hard as parting,
Now who sketches these black brows, distant mountains?
One stirrup cup for parting,
One sound of the cuckoo—
Forlorn and lonely, and at spring's tattered end.
(8) In the bright moonlight in the little loft,
The first night's lovelorn tears are flicked away.

(Xia Tingzhi, *Qinglou ji*, 99)

line 1: See the note on Wang Wei's poem to P.22A.2.

line 4: Meaning a husband or intimate; a reference to the story of Zhang Chang. Zhang was not one who bothered much about decorum, and he enjoyed painting his wife's eyebrows when she did her makeup. When authorities reported this behavior and the emperor asked Zhang about it, he replied that in the privacy of the bedroom, more shocking behavior than this was known to go on. See *Han shu*, 76/3222.

P.22c.2. *Moved by Emotion*

Remembering old happiness and pleasure, I stay in bed,
Our vow was the equal of mountain and sea: "We shan't forget each
other."
How can you bear to let it suddenly turn to rejection,
Master Li the tenth, and produce a grudge that lasts forever?

(Xia Tingzhi, *Qinglou ji*, 99)

P.22d. *Zhenzhen (ca. 1300)*

Madame Zhen was a descendant of the house of the famous Southern Song scholar, Zhen Dexiu (1178–1235). She was sold into prostitution by her father, who found himself unable to repay moneys he had pilfered from government coffers. Her story, as related in Tao Zongyi's *Chuogeng lu* (fifteenth century), was the basis for several poems by sympathetic literati.

> When Yao Sui [1238–1313], the Duke of Letters, was Recipient of Rescripts in the Hanlin Academy, he held a feast in the academy hall. The singing girls were all lined up, and there was among them one who was a particularly gorgeous and refined beauty, and who had a trace of accent of the Min dialect. The Duke had her brought forward and asked her about her life history. At first she did not reply truthfully, but on being asked again, she broke into sobs and said, "I am from Jian'ning and am a descendant of Zhen Dexiu. When my own father was in service in the north, the salary he received was too meager to survive on. He dipped into the government treasury and could not pay it back, so he sold me into a prostitute's household [to be trained as a geisha]. And I gradually drifted here."
>
> The Duke had her sit down, then sent a messenger to the Prime Minister Salbuliu, requesting that she be dropped from the [tax] status [as entertainer]. The Prime Minister had long respected the Duke and thought that he probably wanted her to personally "serve [him] with cloth and comb." Therefore, he ordered the Inspector of the Music Bureau to cleanse her from the rolls.
>
> When the Duke got this report, he told one of his clerks, "I am making

> this girl your wife, and having her take me as her father." The clerk happily heeded his command. People of the Capital all thought this a splendid affair.[5]

P.22d.1. Jie san cheng

I was first a bright pearl held in someone's palm,
But somehow fell into this Pingkang Ward.
In front of others I feign all kinds of coquettish manners,
But out of sight my tears flow by the thousands.
At the end of spring in southern kingdoms, I pity being tossed adrift,
Always at the beck of the eastern wind, planless, powerless.
Increase, painful sorrow!
(8) Where are ten bushels of precious pearls
To ransom *this* cloud girl?

(*Quan Yuan sanqu*, 2: 1144)

line 2: The district in Tang dynasty Chang'an where the Music Bureau was located; later a common term for the brothel and entertainment districts.

line 9: A reference to the story of Cloud Blossom and Pei Hang. Pei Hang spied a beautiful immortal named Cloud Blossom at Indigo Bridge Hostel and sought her hand in marriage. Cloud's mother gave him one hundred days to find a jade mortar and pestle before she would assent. He was successful and was allowed to marry Cloud and ascend into the heavens as an immortal.

P.22e. Mother's Compassion Liu (Liu Poxi; fl. ca. 1350)

Virtually all that is known of Mother's Compassion Liu is found in the short biography in the *Qinglou ji*:

> Mother's Compassion Liu was the wife of entertainer Li the Fourth. She was from "Right of the River," and was a contemporary of Spring's Blossom Yang. She was very capable in arts of the brush and ink and was a fine, quick-witted singer and dancer. She far surpassed her peers, and many of the nobles of that time valued her greatly. At first, she had an affair with the son of Penal Superintendant Chang of Fuzhou—Chang Sanshe. Fearful that his wife would come between them, they ran away together one night. The affair came to light, and she was sentenced to be beaten. She bore her shame and was about to go on to Guanghai to live. When she passed through Ganzhou, she encountered Quan Buyan Sari,

known as Ziren, who had been selected to be the Darhaci of Ganzhou from the post of Secretary of Board of Rites, after encountering a plethora of political problems.

He was a man who had long held government office with purity and integrity, and his administrative documents and skill in administration were praised to the Central Secretariat—but he could never get over his addiction to women and wine. Every day, after his official duties, he would drink and compose poetry with local scholars. He loved to stick flowers into his hat, or else fruits or leaves; sometimes he stuck in whole sprigs.

One day, when Liu was passing by Gan on the way to Guanghai, she visited Lord Quan. Quan said, "A woman, remnant of punishment? Hardly worth meeting with." Liu spoke to the gatekeeper, "I am about to go to Guanghai, and I have vowed not to return. I have long heard of the pure reputation of the Secretary. Should I obtain one visit as I pass by, then I would die without regret."

Quan was moved to grief by her wish, and allowed her to be advanced. At that time his guests and friends filled the feast seats, and Quan, a sprig of green chrysanthemum stuck into his hat, was passing out the wine. Quan extemporized a line to the tune *Qingjiang yin* ("Green, green, fruits form along the branch"), and asked his guests to complete the poem. None of the assembly could come up with a proper match, when Liu gathered together her lapels [as a sign of respect] and came forward, saying, "May I be allowed a word?" Quan said, "All right." Liu then shot back [the poem given here]. Quan greatly praised her poem, and from this time on she was favored without cease and taken into his side room. After the rebellion, in which Quan died with integrity, Liu came to a good end in his household.[6]

P.22e.1. Qingjiang yin

Green, green, fruits form along the branch,
Enticing someone to pull them down and pluck them.
But they are "all seed in the middle,"
And inside have a special taste—
Hard to reject, just because they are so sour to the taste.

(Xia Tingzhi, *Qinglou ji*, 213)

lines 3–5: A clever play on Quan's family name and courtesy name, which sound like the phrase "all seeds." On that understanding, these lines would read: "Among them all is Quan Ziren, / Who has a special 'taste' all his own— / Just because you are so sour, you are the hardest to put out of mind."

BIOGRAPHICAL NOTES AND TRANSLATION BY STEPHEN H. WEST

P.23. Guan Daosheng (1262–1319)

The earliest woman painter of China so esteemed by male critics that they collected and preserved her works, Guan Daosheng (style name Zhongji) became the paradigm of the cultivated Chinese gentry woman. The writings of her husband, the well-known painter and official Zhao Mengfu (1254–1322), indicate that Guan was born to a local scholar-gentry family in Wucheng, Wuxing, Zhejiang province.[1] Her styles in painting and in poetry are closely related to those of the male literati coteries in which she participated. The painters Qian Xuan (ca. 1235–after 1301), Li Kan (1245–1320), and Wu Zhen (1280–1354) and the monk Zhongfeng mingben (1263–1323) were among the scholarly friends of her husband who had a profound influence on her life and work. Unlike most gentry women of her time, Guan Daosheng experienced much of the world beyond the women's quarters of her home. She is recorded as having painted temple murals, and she traveled throughout southern China with her husband on official business.[2]

Zhao Mengfu, a scion of the Song imperial family, made a difficult and controversial decision to serve the Mongol conquerors of China in their newly established capital of Dadu (modern Beijing). In 1289, Zhao returned home from his post to wed Guan: she was twenty-eight, he thirty-six.[3] They resided in Dadu for three years and departed for Wuxing in 1292. It was after her return to southern China that Guan Daosheng began to paint and write poetry: her extant paintings show her active as an artist from 1296 until the time of her death in the second decade of the fourteenth century.[4]

Guan's fame as an artist was such that Emperor Renzong requested that she copy the *Qianzi wen*, to be mounted with examples of the calligraphy of her husband and son so that "future generations [will] know that in my reign there was a woman good at calligraphy and that, moreover, her whole family was equally talented. How rare indeed!"[5] Impressed with her talents, Renzong conferred on her the title Lady of the Kingdom of Wei (Weiguo *furen*) in 1317.

Guan Daosheng integrated her skills in poetry, calligraphy, and painting by embellishing her paintings with poetic inscriptions, and many of her poems are extant today because they were recorded in catalogues of painting collections. Her secular works often include the image of bamboo, a favorite theme of her male contemporaries, including her husband, and one well suited to her unusual position as a woman of extraordinary creativity working among the leading male scholars of her era. The feminine tradition of painting bamboo began with Lady Li of Shu [Sichuan] (fl. 923–34), who used a brush to trace shadows of bamboo cast by the moon on her paper window;[6] the masculine tradition of bamboo painting and poetry emerged with the rise of the literati arts during the Northern Song dynasty and is most closely associated with the painter Wen Tong (1019–79). For Northern Song scholars, particularly those with a hermit streak, bamboo evoked the gentleman's purity of character in the midst of adversity.

In her poetry Guan manipulates the image of bamboo, fashioning it into an autobiographical emblem. The bamboo often reflects her presence in poems that describe her thoughts and feelings about her children, about her husband and his career, and about growing old. Stylistically, Guan's poems are similar to those of her husband, Zhao, though crafted of more elegant images and language. In 1299, Guan Daosheng inscribed a rhyme-prose, "Xiuzhu fu," on a painting of bamboo made for her sister Guan Daogao, herself a poet and frequent recipient of Daosheng's poetry and painting.[7] This rhyme-prose is the most formal and polished of her bamboo poems; it exhibits a virtuoso command of the history of the bamboo image in Chinese poetry, a technical proficiency equal to that of her male contemporaries, and an expressive mode different from, though no less personal than, her shorter, more intimate poems on the theme of bamboo.

P.23.1. On an Ink Bamboo Sent to Zi'ang [Zhao Mengfu]

On the day milord left, the bamboo was first planted;
The bamboo has already formed a grove and milord has yet to return.
Once my jade visage has faded it can hardly be restored—
Unlike a flower which dies to bloom again.

(Chen Yan, *Yuan shi ji shi*, 36/815)

P.23.2. Inscribed on a Painting

As Spring is fair, today is also fair,
Casually I stroll with my children under the bamboo.
The sense of spring is recently much stronger;
Leafy, leafy my children grow by the side of the stone.

(*Yuan shi ji shi*, 36/815)

P.23.3. Inscribed on My Own Painting of Bamboo

I returned home after the banquet before the sun had set,
Wrapped in garments still bearing the fragrance of an Imperial censer.
My maid needn't incessantly flap her fan,
For tall, slender bamboo soughs, soughs, producing tender coolness.

(*Yuan shi ji shi*, 36/814)

P.23.4. A Four-Stanza Cycle to the Tune Yufu *("The Fisherman's Song")*

I

From a distance I think of the Mountain Studio, its many plum trees
In freezing cold—jade blossoms emerge on southern branches.
The mountain moonlight shines,
The dawn wind whistles,
Just for their pure fragrance, I long to return home.

II

Looking South four thousand miles along the Wuxing road—
When will I return to the banks of Zha Stream?
Fame and wealth—
Leave them to Heaven;
Laughing, put your angling rod in the fishing boat.

III

My body at Yanshan, close to the Imperial Residence;
My returning heart daily, nightly recalls eastern Wu.
Pour good wine,
Mince fresh fish—
Remove pure leisure, and nothing remains quite the same.

IV

The great positions in human life belong to princes and marquises,
But fleeting wealth, fleeting fame are not freedom.
How can they compare
With a single boat,
Appreciating the moon, chanting with the wind, and returning home
to rest?

(*Yuan shi ji shi*, 36/814–15)

i: "Mountain Studio" refers to Zhao Mengfu's studio name "Songxue zhai" ("Pine-Snow Studio"). During the Yuan dynasty the flowering plum was a popular symbol of the retired scholar. This verse of "Fisherman's Song" is recorded under Guan's name in the collected writings of Zhao Mengfu, *Songxuezhai ji*, 3/18b, and is the only poetic work attributed to Guan Daosheng in an extant anthology of the Yuan dynasty.

ii, lines 1–2: Wuxing was the home of Guan and her husband, Zhao Mengfu, and the Zha was a stream near that home.

iii, line 1: In the Yuan dynasty the Imperial Residence was built at Yanshan near the capital, Dadu.

iii, line 2: Eastern Wu is the district in which Wuxing was located.

P.23.5. *Rhyme-Prose on Tall, Slender Bamboo*

Leafy, leafy, tall, slender bamboo,
Neither tangled nor creeping,
Neither grass nor tree.
Its virtue, exalted, rises above the world;
Its bearing, dignified, stands above vulgarity.
Leaves deep like kingfisher plumes,
A trunk dark like teal jade:
It alone grows on Mount Tai's side
And in the thousand acres of the Wei River's bends.
It brings a cool whirlwind from the distant peak,
And gladdens the beautiful woman in the empty valley.

One sees how it faces the bending balustrade,
Overlooks pure ripples.
Its beauty overtakes that of the Milky Way;
Its shadows flow in pliant waves.
Azure clouds gather over it in summer;

Verdant dew drops down from it at dawn.
Pattering, pattering rain washes it clean,
Swirling, curling breeze spreads it out.
A morning crane's long call,
The autumn cicada's solitary cry;
The intermittent sounding of *zhong* and *qing*
And the mingled shrillness of *sheng* and *yu*.

Then, on fine moonlit nights
Or at winter's end when snow is piled high,
Shadows sweep the rocks' surface,
And snapping is heard from the midst of the grove.
Its meaning reaches that of Greatest Antiquity,
While sound sinks into an empty cave.
Ears and eyes are opened, washed clean by it;
Spirit and emotion are pleased by it.
For its match is the exquisite teal *wutong*,
And it finds a friend in the green pine.
Before it, rushes and willows are ashamed of their weakness;
Peach and pear trees, abased by their emptiness.

It makes the song of the fishing pole for the Maiden of Wei,
And intones the "River Bend Tune" in the "Airs of the States."
Thus Ziyou chanted beneath it,
And Zhongxuan rested in its midst.
The Seven Worthies acted in harmony [under it];
The Six Idle Ones left their lofty imprint [upon it]—
All with good cause.
What's more—the voice of the phoenix at Xie valley,
The transformation into a dragon at Gepo!

Its heart is empty,
Its joints substantial,
And its trunk and leaves unchanging throughout the four seasons:
From these I perceive a gentleman's virtue.

(Zhao Mengfu, *Songxuezhai ji*, 1/5a–b)

line 11: This line paraphrases the first couplet of Du Fu's "Jia Ren."
lines 22–23: The *zhong* and *qing* are bronze bells and stone chimes used for the

most ancient music; the *sheng* is a reed instrument with thirteen bamboo pipes, sounded through a gourdlike wind box; the *yu* is also an ancient wind instrument.

lines 36–37: In the "Airs of the States" section of the *Book of Odes*, see the opening of poem 59—"Tapering are the bamboo rods, with them they angle in the Qi river; do I not think of you?" (spoken by a woman of Wei to her absent lover)—and poem 55—"Look at that cove of the Qi, the green bamboo is luxuriant" (Karlgren, *Book of Odes*, pp. 41, 37; second translation modified).

lines 38–39: Zhongxuan is the style name of Wang Can (see P.17.2). Ziyou is the style name of Wang Huizhi (d. 388), the eccentric fifth son of the great calligrapher Wang Xizhi (see P.10.10). Huizhi had bamboo planted everywhere he lived, even in temporary lodgings, asking: "How could I live a single day without this gentleman?" (Liu Yiqing, *Shishuo xinyu* 23/46; Mather, *Shih-shuo Hsin-yü*, p. 388). "Gentleman" subsequently became one of the standard epithets for bamboo.

line 40: The Seven Worthies of the Bamboo Grove; see P.10.1.

line 41: The Six Idle Ones of the Tang, who met alongside Bamboo Creek and thus are associated with bamboo.

line 43: Xie Valley lies in the Kunlun Mountains, far to the west of China. The Yellow Emperor obtained bamboo from this place to establish the Chinese musical scale. According to a parallel story, the Yellow Emperor based the scale on the phoenix's call, hence the equivalence of phoenix and bamboo as sources of harmonious sound.

line 44: At Gepo in Henan during the Eastern Han dynasty, Fei Changfang transformed his bamboo staff into a dragon. See *Han shu*, "Fang shu lie zhuan," 82/2743–44.

BIOGRAPHICAL NOTE AND TRANSLATION BY JENNIFER PURTLE

鄭允端

P.24. Zheng Yunduan (ca. 1327–56)

Zheng Yunduan, style name Zhengshu, was a native of Pingjiang (Suzhou), Jiangsu province, and a fifth-generation descendant of the Southern Song grand councilor Zheng Qingzhi (1176–1251). Zheng Yunduan writes in a preface to her collected poetry, *Suyong ji* (Solemn harmonies) that she was born into a gentry family of scholars and teachers, showed an early interest in letters, and enjoyed writing poetry in her spare time. This interest was encouraged by her marriage to Shi Boren, a local scholar from a family with an equally long tradition of involvement with the literary arts. In 1356, following the designation of Pingjiang as the new capital of the pretender Zhang Shicheng, the area around the city was subject to heavy fighting and looting. Zheng Yunduan's home is said to have been ransacked by troops, a disaster that led to her family's poverty and to her debilitating illness and death at the young age of thirty.

In her preface to *Suyong ji* (see C.5), Zheng Yunduan claims that her poetry speaks with the sober voice of Confucian morality, without the flowery sentimentality typical of women's verses. In fact, the admonitory tone that her preface promises proves to be less didactic than personally meditative, as the poet muses on the limitations of a life constrained by both her social position as a gentry woman and her illness. The subjects of her poems range from everyday objects around her to flights of fancy spurred by legends of female immortals. The willingness to dwell on mundane concerns that characterizes the content of much of her poetry and the direct simplicity that characterizes her diction are perhaps what led the editors of the *Siku quanshu zongmu* to criticize some of her poems as shallow and weak. In direct contrast, however, others have described her poetry as "lofty and chaste, profound and long-lasting." Her ancient-style poems are singled out as her most skillful.

The extant collection of Zheng Yunduan's poems is said to have been formed after her death by her husband and originally included a preface (now missing) by the renowned scholar Qian Weishan. A fifth-generation descendant first had the collection printed during the Jiajing reign of the Ming dynasty (1522–66). Because of the inclusion of a couple of poems suspected not to have been written by Zheng Yunduan, the editors of *Siku quanshu zongmu* raise the possibility that the manuscript text did not survive intact following the Yuan dynasty and was subject to the meddling of later hands.[1]

P.24.1. Song for a Landscape Screen

I own a piece of fine eastern silk
Upon which are painted the countless hills of the south.
Could the brushwork be less than Li Yingqiu's?
I wager it surpasses Yang Qidan.
The work of skilled hands is not easily found,
But this painting is rich and capably composed.
Layered hills and stacked peaks converge and open,
(8) Strange rocks and tall pines solemnly face one another.
Plank bridge and grass hut are by the forest's edge,
A quick stream splashes the rocks, sounding like thunder.

Revealed, I feel as if seated under Mount Lu,
(12) And sense that all worldly dust has been cleansed from my breast.
But this body is destined to age in the inner chambers,
I hate that there is no chance to go seeking hidden places.
This life has been consigned to cloth socks and grass slippers,
(16) Long I face this painting with these useless, deep regrets.

(Zheng Guangyi, 1149–50)

lines 1–2: The first lines of this poem are lifted from Du Fu's "Song Playfully Composed for Wei Yan's Painting of Twin Pines," Qiu Zhao'ao, ed., *Du shi xiangzhu*, 9/757–59. The original reference is to silk produced in Yanting prefecture, Zizhou (Santai), Sichuan province.

lines 3–4: Li Yingqiu is the Five Dynasties landscape painter Li Cheng (919–67), a native of the Yingqiu region of Shandong. Yang Qidan was a Sui dynasty (589–618) artist known for his paintings of figures and religious subjects.

P.24.2. A Verse on the Wu People's Marrying Off Their Daughters

I have seen how common families often aspire to marry their daughters to highly placed officials and noblemen. Though they may have their moment of glory, in the end husband and wife rarely grow old together harmoniously. For this reason, in the *bingshen* year of the Zhizheng reign [1356], I write this poem of warning.

When planting flowers, don't plant them by the official highway,
And when marrying daughters, don't marry them to noble princes.
Flowers planted by the official road get plucked by passers-by,
Daughters married to noble princes do not enjoy long unions.
Flowers fall, colors fade, feelings change.
Departing phoenix and broken mirror—a separation in the end.
Much better to marry her to a lad who works the fields,
(8) So that with graying heads they can regard one another, and she won't fear losing her place.

(Zheng Guangyi, 1144–45; Su Zhecong, 257–58)

line 6: The phrase "departing phoenix" (*liluan*), from the zither tune composed by the young Han dynasty poet Qing Anshi, "Double Phoenixes and Departing *Luan*," is a metaphor for a lost lover (Liu Xin, *Xijing zaji*, 2/6). "Broken mirror" refers to the parting of husband and wife. During the chaos that accompanied the decline of the Chen dynasty (557–89), Xu Deyan and his wife were forced to endure a long separation. They broke a mirror and vowed that they would one day unite the two pieces (Li Fang, *Taiping guangji*, 166/1212–13).

line 8: The final line's expression *xia tang* (literally, "to descend from the hall") referring to a wife who is cast off by her husband, is derived from the biography of Song Hong of the Eastern Han. Song Hong is said to have remarked, "Your official has heard that the knowledge of those who are impoverished is never forgotten, and the wife who has accompanied a man through his days of youthful poverty [lit. 'the wife of dregs and husks,' these being the food of the poorest] is never made to descend from the hall" (*Hou Han shu*, 26/905).

P.24.3. *On Husband-Longing Rock*

Her husband left for conscript labor,
Summoned to a distant corner of the realm.
He planned to return after three years' time,
But since his departure so many winters have passed.
She climbs a mountain that soars with precipitous peaks
And stretches her neck, watching for returning boats.
But no returning boat meets her gaze;
(8) She paces back and forth, lingers in vain.
She turns into a mountaintop rock,
Standing alone against the sky.
Never has her resolve shifted,
(12) Day and night, distantly gazing.
Rock is solid, but with time it crumbles,
And oceans dry to become fields and orchards.
When the rock crumbles and the oceans dry,
(16) Only then will the traveler return home.

(Zheng Guangyi, 1147–48; Su Zhecong, 258–59)

On this legend, see P.11.16.

P.24.4. *Arising from Illness, I Try a Staff*

Fifty canes in the house,
My years barely add up to thirty.
I have been ill now for a year,
Sitting and reclining, rarely walking and standing.
This morning I try ambling about,

But as I move my feet an uneasiness persists.
When I lean on a cane and slowly walk,
My four limbs find peace of mind.
Truly, beauty follows to where one reaches,
I begin to know the strength of this staff.
Thin in circumference—barely a palm's width,
It rises past my head—about six feet.
No river-heart bamboo, this
Truly is mountain-born chestnut.
Its knots are full of rocky bumps,
Its surface pattern is dense and fine.
Sufficient to support an infirm body,
It can also assist one who is sickly and thin.
No need to mention the danger of high places;
How useful it is to have something to lean on.

(*Suyong ji*, 3b)

P.24.5. Song for a Mirror

Sparkling, this mirror in its case,
Accompanying me year after year.
To what can I liken its pure shine?
The bright moon hanging in the sky.
In the past, when barely fifteen,
With a complexion as fresh as a flower,
I would face it, arranging my morning makeup,
Daubing and rubbing, vying for beauty.
Since then my years have gone on quite a bit,
Poverty and illness fuel constant worry.
My appearance has gradually aged and worsened,
No longer do I apply rouge and powder.
This morning the mirror too is dim,
Dust and grime destroy its circled decor.
My reflection appears so dark,
How can I tell uncomeliness from grace?
Human life has its rise and decline,
Feelings for things accordingly change.

Such being the way of the world,
Of what use to add my lament?

(*Suyong ji*, 4a)

P.24.6. Recording a Dream

Magu, that immortal of old,
Suddenly took form in my dream.
At first I did not recognize her,
She seemed so real, a chaste young maiden.
In age, maybe seventeen or eighteen;
Her fingernails were long.
Her locks were set high, and her clothes blue and rose,
The rest of her hair spread down like thread.
She said: since she began serving Wang Yuan,
Three times oceans have changed to fields;
That recently when she passed the mountain Penglai,
Even weak streams flowed crystal clear.
She invites me on a journey to her western home.
By the pond I see an old woman.
I laugh but don't say a word,
And lightly drift high above.
I gaze up at the sky's clouds and mist,
Returning from my dream I emit a long sigh.

(*Suyong ji*, 4b)

During the reign of Huandi of the Eastern Han (146–67), an immortal named Wang Yuan is said to have descended to the home of Cai Jing and summoned Magu. Magu was eighteen or nineteen and beautiful in appearance, with extremely long fingernails. She said to Wang Yuan, "Since the time I began serving you, three times the deep blue ocean has turned to mulberry fields. I have journeyed to the immortal isle of Penglai, and there, too, the water has become shallower; now, at this time that we finally meet, it is about half of what it used to be. Will it one day all become dry land?" See Ge Hong, *Shen xian zhuan*, in *Siku quanshu*, 3/8b–9a. On Penglai, see P.11.12.

P.24.7. Listening to the Zither

Deep in the night all sounds hush,
A half moon shines brightly in the sky.

The secluded one leans into the dry wood:
From untrammeled sounds clear tones rise.
Strummed once, then three times more:
Feelings of antiquity are harbored within.
Seated in rapture, I listen long,
The landscape echoes with feeling.
Long ago Ziqi passed from this earth—
What kindred soul is left to accompany Bo Ya?
Melancholy, long I dwell on such thoughts,
The lofty wonders of heaven and earth are for naught.

(Su Zhecong, 259)

lines 3–4: *Gao wu*, "dry [firmiana-]wood," is derived from *Zhuangzi*, chapter 5, where the sophist Hui Shi is described as leaning over his *gao wu* and dozing. Some commentators take the *gao wu* to be a zither: such is Zheng Yunduan's sense here. See *Zhuangzi jishi*, p. 222.

lines 9–10: Zhong Ziqi, of the Warring States Period, is the famed appreciator of the zither playing of Bo Ya. When Bo Ya played a piece describing mountains, Zhong could see the peaks, and when he played a piece with a river theme, Zhong could see the rushing waters. After Zhong Ziqi died, Bo Ya never played the zither again, for the only one who "understood the sounds" was gone. See Liu Xiang, *Shuo yuan*, 8/7b–8a.

P.24.8. Writing My Feelings

Originally an immortal from beyond the seas,
By accident I clung to this vulgar world.
Mistakenly I fell into this dusty net,
And now twenty years have passed.
Recently a letter from Magu arrived,
Asking the date of my return.
Facing the wind, hollow, I tarry,
Raise my head to the three fairy isles.

(*Suyong ji*, 6b)

lines 3–4: These lines recall Tao Yuanming, "On Returning to Live in Garden and Field," number one: "By mistake I fell into the dusty net / And once I was in, I was lost for thirty years" (Lu Qinli, ed., *Tao Yuanming ji*, p. 40).

P.24.9. Reclining in Illness on the Day of the Flower Festival

Lonely feelings under a vacant window;
Disjointed, this body wracked with illness.
Like an empty sack it relies on medicine,
Though a raised pillow joins it to a fragrant hour.
Garden plants are filled with life;
Thicket flowers, knowingly, smile.
Daily I dwell on my feelings of decline and fatigue;
By this scene the spirit is wounded even more.

(*Suyong ji*, 7a–b)

P.24.10. As I Face the Moon in the Central Courtyard, Feelings Arise

In the central courtyard the night air is cooler than water,
Seated, I gaze at the moon's turning jade disk in the cerulean sky.
Over ten thousand miles its pure rays illumine all within the four seas,
For ten years the chill of death has darkened Chang'an.
Secluded women only remember the suffering of loyal hearts,
Wartime ghosts cling piteously to the cold of bleaching bones.
I wish to peel back the clouds and shout at heaven's gate,
But it is an endless road that leads to the jade towers of the moon.

(*Suyong ji*, 9a; Su Zhecong, 262)

P.24.11. Riverside Railing

Those houses near the water—little more than simple huts,
Their windows and railings more neglected than a hermit's dwelling.
Against the railing I suddenly hear a paddle beating the prow,
And know a small boat has come to peddle fish.

(Zheng Guangyi, 1141–42)

P.24.12. Courtyard Locust Tree

Wind encircles the courtyard locust, coaxing the fence gate open,
Green shade like a spreading dye, clean, unsullied by dust.
The gentlewoman does not partake in dreams of merit and fame,
Casually she watches the ants of the southern branch come and go.

(*Suyong ji*, 15a)

This poem refers to the story of Chunyu Fen of the Tang dynasty, who one day fell asleep under an old locust tree in his courtyard. He dreamed that two envoys approached him to extend an invitation from the king of the great country of Huai'an (Locust Peace). Chunyu followed them into a cavity in the tree and met with the king. Chunyu was assigned the duties of Prefect of the Southern Branch, to which he devoted his energies for twenty years before being escorted home to his drunken sleep. Awakening, he found a swarm of ants inside the tree, and one particularly large ant which he understood to be the king of Huai'an. See Li Gongzuo, *Nanke ji*, in Wu Zengqi, ed., *Jiu xiaoshuo*, 2: 45–50.

P.24.13. Wutong

To the *wutong*'s leaves autumn first arrives,
Whistling and rustling, facing the tree they sing.
As payment to this west wind that never ceases blowing,
I sit long in the night, listening to autumn's sounds.

(*Suyong ji*, 15a–b; Su Zhecong, 264)

P.24.14. Thoughts of the Inner Chamber

Thin, the hibiscus curtain cannot resist autumn's march;
Pillowed, I listen to the water clock mark the passing time.
It is not that my husband has forsaken me and left;
Coming of age, the young man must seek an official career.

(*Suyong ji*, 16a)

P.24.15. Gauze Net

Deep in the mountains, the Jade Maiden in her cave of roseate mists;
In the heavens above, an immortal at her window of clouds.
My bamboo pillow dream is broken by the clean dripping of the water clock;
A sudden coolness, like water, permeates the autumn river.

(*Suyong ji*, 16a–b)

line 1: A beautiful immortal maiden is sometimes said to live on Mount Huashan, where she attends to the jade nectar; she is also known as the Star Jade Maiden. See Li Fang, *Taiping guangji*, 59/362.

BIOGRAPHICAL NOTE AND TRANSLATION BY PETER C. STURMAN

吴氏女

P.25. Wu *shi* nü (14th century)

Wu, whose exact dates are unknown, was a Yuan-dynasty writer of love lyrics that seem to have been inspired by the circumstances of her own life. She is said to have fallen in love with her neighbor, a young scholar named Zheng Xi, who enjoyed composing poems, and she sent her old woman servant next door to request verses from him.[1] He responded with several for her to the tune of *Mulanhua man*. The first poems presented here are her lyrics composed to the same tune, sent in reply to him. These are followed by several regulated-verse poems that offer more details of their star-crossed relationship. Zheng apparently sought permission from Wu's mother to marry her, but because his request was denied, she was forced to send her answering poems surreptitiously. Realizing that she could not look forward to a future with him, she is said to have died of a broken heart. In the last of her poems translated here, she tells Zheng she is ill and wasting away with grief.[2]

P.25.1. Mulanhua man: *Replying to Zheng Xi and Echoing His Rhyme*

How I admire talent and elegance—
See how his brushstrokes sweep away mist.
I was just leaning wearily against my study window,
Idly holding my needlework,
Lazily intoning a piece of poetry.
Red leaves of love—to whom can I send them?
Slowly pacing
Without words by my little window.
Swallows understand human intentions
As pair by pair they fly over the flower hedge.
With an earnest smile I consult the wise—
Truly they say, "Man is a woman's Heaven."
But I fear lest a sketch of Xue Yuan
Which could cause Chucai to sigh
Would just stir the past to life.
Plum blossoms fill the branches, layer upon layer.

Taking stock of my life, I know
I have no destiny to share with Su Dongpo.
Nothing for me but a handkerchief of mermaid silk
Stained with teardrops beyond counting.

(Su Zhecong, 266)

line 12: A quotation from Ban Zhao's (d. 116) *Nü jie* (Admonitions for women; see P.60.9): "A man is obligated to take a second wife, but nothing is written about a woman marrying twice. Hence the saying, 'A husband is one's Heaven; one cannot flee Heaven; one cannot leave a husband' " (cited in Su Zhecong, p. 480; trans. from Ebrey, *Chinese Civilization*, p. 75).

lines 13–15: An allusion to a Tang dynasty story. Nan Chucai and Xue Yuan were husband and wife. Nan was posted to an area that is now central Henan, where the magistrate of Yingzhou took a liking to him and offered him his daughter in marriage. Xue learned of this and, looking into a mirror, drew a sketch of herself and wrote a poem to accompany it. Upon receiving her sketch and poem, Nan was filled with remorse, and returned to her to live happily ever after (QTS, 799/8991).

line 18: This reference indicates the already legendary standing of Su Shi (Su Dongpo; 1037–1101), the prolific poet, outspoken official, and frequent target of imperial rancor. While governor of Hangzhou, Su often kept company with singing girls, and composed for them many of his best-known song-lyrics.

lines 19–20: Mermaids were said to weave silk of supernatural delicacy. The conclusion of the poem suggests otherworldliness and disappointment, probably alluding to a poem by Li Shangyin: "I had a glimpse of the Water God, who looked wistful; / Sell the mermaid-silk no more, for the sea has turned into fields!" (J. J. Y. Liu, *Poetry of Li Shang-yin*, p. 114).

P.25.2. [Tune title lost]: Begging Jixian to Send Down Divine Writings

Though destiny is cruel to this phoenix pair,
My soul is still lost in love.
The secret words of a pure heart are by my side—
Like seeing into the poet's face.

Tender feelings yet remain—
Why can't Heaven grant a mortal's will?
My jasper and jade flesh waste away.
An empty dreaming soul is left
With how much bitter pain?

(Su Zhecong, 267–78)

Jixian was a popular divinity; when called down by sorcerers, the spirit would leave brush-written prophecies through the human intermediary.

P.25.3. Given to Master Zheng

My mother didn't know my heart,
So never will you paint moth eyebrows for me.
Though now the apricot blooms more brightly,
The earlier plum holds more old memories.

(Zhao Shijie, ed., *Lidai nüzi shiji*, 6/4b)

line 2: On a husband painting his wife's eyebrows, see P.22C.1.

P.25.4. A Reply to Master Zheng, Written While Sick

Pearl tears drip drip, wetting silk gauze,
Illness has taken its toll of fragrant flesh.
Don't blame me if nights bring few spring dreams—
I no longer even know the day or season.

(*Lidai nüzi shiji*, 6/4b)

BIOGRAPHICAL NOTE AND TRANSLATION BY FRANCES LA FLEUR

張玉娘

P.26. Zhang Yuniang (13th century)

Little is known of Zhang Yuniang other than the name of her small collection of poems, *Lanxue ji* (Orchid snow collection), her style name, Ruoqiong, and her native county, Songyang (in present-day Zhejiang). Brief references from Yuan and early Ming texts place her in the late Southern Song or beginning of the Yuan dynasty, but her exact dates are unknown. The earliest extant record of her life and work appears in a Yuan text that states Zhang's poems were addressed to her male cousin. The hint of an ill-fated love affair was repeated in later texts and was most fully elaborated on by a sixteenth-century Ming literatus from Songyang, Wang Zhao, in a biography of Zhang. According to this and later accounts, Zhang's early betrothal to her cousin Shen Quan was inexplicably broken by her parents. Zhang remained faithful to Shen, refusing to marry, and upon Shen's death she, too, sickened and died. Thus Zhang became known as "The Ever-Chaste Recluse." Although the story is charming, it is difficult to determine how much of it is true. Fortunately, we do not need the story to appreciate the many striking images, the clever plays on clichéd images of women, and the spectrum of emotions found in Zhang Yuniang's poems.

P.26.1. Xian xian yin: *Summer Night*

The heavens roll up wisps of clouds;
The water clock sounds from the high chamber.
A few bits of firefly light flow along flowered paths.
Wordlessly, I stand before the mountain-painted screen;
New bamboo and tall locust trees
Wildly scatter transparent shadows.
I look at my painted fan, at my gauze gown,
As moonbeams freeze into cold moon-flowers.

As the night wears on,
I wonder if my recent languor comes from thinking on things past,
From facing scenery turning into remembrance.
The Dipper sinks in the sky;
In pale metallic waves, the Milky Way still glitters.
My mat spotted and wrinkled, I turn into my coral pillow,
Not feeling chilly or tired.
I let my hairpin dangle wildly from my chignon
Then listlessly rise to push it straight.

(Su Zhecong, 269)

P.26.2. Yu hudie: *Feelings on Parting*

Gazing out to the sky's emptiness, the distance of the trees,
She crinkles her "spring-mountain" brows
And leans on the carved balustrade.
Kingfisher-green bamboo rustles and clatters,
Her round jade pendants clink and tinkle.
Snowy skin fragrant, gleaming like the jade of Mount Jing,
Temple-knots tousled, cold as the clouds of Wu Gorge.
She wipes away the tear marks
As the mirror's light shines on her shyly—
An abandoned blue mandarin duck.

When will they once again turn the cold into warmth
(12) Under the moon and stars?
Autumn in the far north is fierce,
But her fine gentleman must not yet have saddled up to return.
A few new swans: she'd like to send a loving letter with them,
(16) But she lays down her rabbit-hair brush—too hard to write her grief and bitterness.
In the twilight, amid the faded lotus and light rain,
How often has she felt her soul melting!

(Su Zhecong, 270)

P.26.3. Yulou chun: *Spring Evening*

Leaning out from the tower, I seek signs of spring;
The curtains roll up to reveal mists and rain.
Bamboo paints screen and netting with kingfisher-green silhouettes;
Breezes invite a riot of red to rest in my boudoir.

Baby orioles play in the willows, fluttering golden strands;
Purple swallows make their nests, beaks full of dancing floss.
I'd like to rely on these new rhymes to break up this new sorrow;
(8) Laughing, I ask the fallen flowers, but the flowers do not speak.

(Su Zhecong, 270–71)

P.26.4. Yunü yao xian pei: *Autumn Feelings*

Frigid skies split the night:
A blast of cold wind
Wildly whooshes through curtains, pierces my windows.
I fall asleep drunk on the coral pillow
And dream of returning to the shores of the Xiang:
The sound of dawn bells comes across dividing waters.
But this is no "Gaotang Rhapsody"!
(8) I laugh at the Divine Woman of Wu Mountain
And the passing clouds of morning and evening.
When I reckon closely that past affair,
I'd say in the end he was heartless to abandon her so suddenly.
(12) Just at this moment, when my illness is grave, my grief deep,
I still hear the mournful plaint of barbarian flutes from the frontier.

Making myself get up, pushing aside the tattered embroidered quilt,
I face the caltrop-lily mirror alone:
I've grown thin and weak, my spirit off in the South.
Why was it that our wine debts and poetic reveries
In moonlit tower, song pavilion, flowered courtyard,
Were so carelessly cut off?
I wait for him to hurry back on the old road.
If only we could ride out together,
Coming home in my fine carriage.
We would let spring fill our emerald chamber and painted hall,
Incense curling in front of the mat,
And he would turn out new verses for me.
So we could be happy as before:
The man of the capital painting his lady's brows.

(Su Zhecong, 271–72)

line 5: The Xiang River, in south China, was the home of the deified wives of Shun; see P.1.2 and *Chuci buzhu*, "Xiang jun" (*Wen xuan* 32/20a; Hawkes, *Songs of the South*, pp. 106–7).

lines 8–11: On Song Yu's "Gaotang fu" and the goddess of Wu Mountain, see P.9.2.

line 27: See P.22C.1.

P.26.5. Niannu jiao: *On the Mid-Autumn Moon, Following Yao Xiaozhu's Rhymes*

The icy wheel rides on the sea,
Breaking up cold mists—
   ten thousand bits of dark mountain green.
The chill presses on the stillness of Chang E's autumn palace;
The cassia tree swirls fragrance in golden grains.
A plain of berylline,
A sky of white silk—
Radiance penetrates the soaring crystalline chambers.
But no trace remains of Chu clouds—
My dream is cut off by the splashing of silvery streaks of rain.

The night of the fifteenth is better than any other night—
The lofty river now pouring down

(12) Snowy waves in frosted cascades.
My arms are cold, fragrance gone—I find myself sitting alone,
Looking out on the shadows [ ] a thousand gallons of sorrow.
Swallow Tower is empty,
(16) The piper far away—
I secretly lament and grieve for "Yellow Crane."
The night wears on, the water clock runs down—
The sound of "Plum Blossoms" moves the Jade Lady of the Xiang.

(Su Zhecong, 272)

lines 3–4: On Chang E, see P.21.1. Other denizens of the moon are a hare and a toad; the moon's spots are said to be the dark areas between the flowers of a cassia tree that grows there, or the Palace of Vast Coldness of Chang E. "Icy wheel" and "plain of berylline" are also metaphors for the moon.

line 11: "The lofty river": the Silver River, or Milky Way.

line 14: One character is missing from the text of this line.

lines 15–16: A Tang official was reputed to have placed his lover in Swallow Tower and deserted her; after his death, she died of grief (see Bo Juyi, "Yanzi lou san shou bing xu," QTS 438/4869–70). The piper refers to the tale in which Duke Mu of Qin married his musically talented daughter Nongyu to his chief flute player. The music played by Nongyu and the Piper attracted phoenixes, on which the couple took flight to an unknown place (Liu Xiang, *Lie xian zhuan*, 1/29–30).

line 17: "Yellow Crane" was a song composed by a woman named Tao Ying who lost her husband while still young yet refused to remarry. See Liu Xiang, "Lu gua Tao Ying," *Gu lienü zhuan*, 4/21b–22a.

line 19: The "Plum Blossom" tune dates from the Tang.

P.26.6. Shuidiao ge tou: *Following [Su] Dongpo's Rhymes*

The Pure-White Maiden refines her cloud draught;
Ten thousand pipes are stilled in the autumn sky.
From the crystalline towers, endless fine vistas—
Everyone says it's better than in years past.
Breeze-borne fragrances from the cassia palace are gently diffused;
In gauze stockings, she stands long by the silver bed
Steeped in the chill of that single cold hook.
(8) Snowy waves toss over her silver chamber—
She is inside a vase of jade.

With this Jade Pass sorrow,
This Golden Chamber plaint,

She can't get to sleep.
Since her handsome man left,
How many times has she seen the bright moon wane and wax?
Why can't she of the cloud-chignon and fragrant sleeves
Fly into the moon's jeweled pavilions and silver palaces,
To be safe with the hare and the crane?
Secretly Chang E stole the herb of longevity,
So that woman and moon would grow full of beauty.

(Su Zhecong, 273–74)

line 1: The "Pure-White Maiden": Chang E.

line 7: "That single cold hook": the new moon.

lines 10–11: The Jade Gate Pass on the northwestern frontier was one of the traditional boundaries between China and its "barbarian" northern neighbors and a heavily guarded stronghold. The Golden Chamber was built by the Han emperor Wudi for one of his concubines.

P.26.7. Huilanfang yin: *Autumn Thoughts*

The stars give way to a dawn sky;
From frontier towers, the khan's war-horns sound piercingly.
I clutch at the kingfisher-green blanket's lingering fragrance,
As frosty clothes-beaters clatter beneath the setting moon.
My dream of Chu rivers is cut off—
Only tears, like blood, flowing privately beneath the bed-curtains.
I see my thinning arms in their golden bracelets,
And my brow tied in a thousand knots.

Rains block the silver screen,
Winds carry away my love-letters—
How can I stop this longing?
We shouldn't have parted so lightly!
I'll sharpen my precious hairpin and use it on myself.
The jade capital is distant and hazy,
And the messages from geese and fish are cut off.
My sorrow will not cease—
Outside the windows, brown leaves tapping again.

(Su Zhecong, 274)

line 4: On the motif of clothes-beaters, see P.4.3.

line 15: On geese as a metaphor for the sending of letters, see P.2.1 (Song 5). Carp, too, are associated with letter writing on account of a *yuefu* poem attributed to Cai Yong in *Yutai xinyong* (1/12b–13a): "A traveler came from far away, / He brought me a brace of carp. / I call my children and cook the carp. / Inside I find a white silk letter" (Birrell, *New Songs*, p. 48; translation modified).

P.26.8. Yi Qin e: *Singing of Snow*

The heavens are shrouded,
Red clouds dark and murky, cold wind rising fiercely.
Cold wind rising fiercely,
Shards of shattered gems
Ride the wind, swirl on gusts.

Those beauties ought to despise their own lightness,
Snow-white shapes recklessly tossed against the bed-curtains.
Tossed against the bed-curtains,
They cannot but feel chilled—
But to whom can they speak?

(Su Zhecong, 275)

P.26.9. Han gong chun: *On the Fifteenth of the First Month, Using Jing Zhongyuan's Rhymes*

Beneath the radiance of the jade hare,
I see the crystalline flow from the Milky Way,
And chill seeps into my tall pavilion.
Just now a song carries over the flowered city;
The clouds are poised in the starry paths.
Orchid and sandalwood incenses
Penetrate the golden lotus-lanterns,
Shadows dizzying in the fragrant dust.
Beyond anything [ ] three thousand beauties:
Coming home together in the moonlight.

It seems that the spring breeze means
To set out a year's worth
Of beautiful scenes all at once.
Who is that man carelessly galloping his jeweled horse,
All flushed with drink from his golden cups?

(16) Elegantly clad,
He embraces his "divine one" as they linger beyond the flowers.
Only pity me, locked in embroidered gauze curtains,
Year by year growing haggard in my gowns and hairpins.

(Su Zhecong, 275)

Jing Tang (Zhongyuan, d. 1200), Southern Song literatus and poet.
line 9: One character is missing from the text of this line.

BIOGRAPHICAL NOTE AND TRANSLATION BY ANNA MARSHALL SHIELDS

Ming Dynasty (1368–1644)

THE FIFTEENTH CENTURY

張紅橋

P.27. Zhang Hongqiao (fl. ca. 1400)

Zhang Hongqiao came from Min county in Fujian province. She was betrothed to a certain Lin Hong. The couple's poetic dialogue forms the basis of Zhang's surviving poetry, recorded as *Hongqiao yi gao* (Surviving drafts of Hongqiao) in the *Fujian tongzhi* (Gazetteer of Fujian province).[1] Liu Shi's (P.67) biographical commentary on Zhang Hongqiao is included at C.14.1.

The following poems rely on punning for much of their effect. Zhang took her pen name Hongqiao ("Red Bridge") from a landmark located near her residence; Lin's given name, Hong, means "wild goose." Red bridges and wild geese are evoked in a variety of ways to suggest the poets' feelings of longing and intimacy. (On wild geese as bearers of messages from far away, see P.2.1, Song 5.)

P.27.1. In Reply to Lin Hong

I

Pear blossoms contend in silence with the beauty of the moon;
The Milky Way curves to reach the embroidered chamber.
I love to burn incense, passing the eternal night,
And have never implored heaven for anything.

II

Water lilies, layer on layer, form a silken drape;
As the jade clock counts time, wings are matched in flight and tender
    cries exchanged.
Spring is vast as the sea in the Jasper Pond of Paradise;
Beneath the brilliant moon fly a pair of wild geese.

III

The osmanthus moon drips to shine upon my empty dressing-room;
Ding-ding sounds the water clock and flickering shadows surround the red candle.
The night dew is moist with hidden fragrance, pearls and jade turn cold;
By the red railing of the bridge, I wait for the return of the wild goose.

IV

Thousands of flowers beside the bridge mirror the azure sky;
Far away a beautiful maiden is separated by water and clouds from the east.
A fine steed neighs to the bright moon;
Wild geese fly up in alarm from a sandbar.

V

The scent of fragrant grasses and warm flowers intoxicates the spring breeze;
My love comes toward the west and I go east.
I lean on the stone railing and watch with a pining glance;
The bright moon and a lonely shadow laugh at the flying geese.

(LR, 24b)

iii, line 1: "Osmanthus" is a name for jasmine.

P.27.2. Farewell to Lin Hong

I

At the head of my bed crickets weep in the autumn wind;
The flicker of a dying lamp illuminates a jumble of medicines.
Neither nightmares nor good dreams matter;
Day and night, I look for a wild goose flying back from the north.

II

The golden vase has dropped into the well and communication is broken off.
The misty mountain, remote and indistinct, darkens the red maples.

My light silk dress is moistened by the night dew; mandarin ducks feel cold;
Through the tedious hours of the night I hear the cry of wild geese.

III

Jade tears stream from eyes and my cheeks turn red;
Through what place in the mountains and passes can my letter be sent?
The green screened windows are lonely and no one comes.
The sea is vast, the sky is high, and I resent the descending wild geese.

IV

Cold bedclothes and jade ornaments are intimidated by the autumn wind;
My love is in the south, I am in the east.
We see each other thousands of times, but only in dreams;
During the long day I envy the pair of wild geese glimpsed from my terrace.

V

Through the screen, the shadow of the bright moon is blurred;
It illuminates mandarin ducks against the shining silken drapes.
In my dream the man of jade has just dismounted from his horse.
I hate the cries of the wild geese that awaken me.

VI

One is in the south, one in the north; we are like whirling motes in the air.
I regret that my intentions and your heart are not the same.
Even if you return some day, it will be useless;
In the grave, message-carrying wild geese should be few.

(LR, 25a–b)

BIOGRAPHICAL NOTE AND TRANSLATION BY PEI-KAI CHENG

朱靜庵

P.28. Zhu Jing'an (fl. 1450)

Zhu Zhongxian, chiefly known by her style name Zhu Jing'an (and also by the courtesy names Miaoduan and Lingwen) came from an old office-holding literati family in Haining, Zhejiang province. Intelligent and well educated, she won a reputation for her poetry and lived to the age of eighty. Married to a man of similar background, a schoolmaster named Zhou Ji, she found little joy in her conjugal life, and her feelings often found expression in her poems. Her contemporaries remarked on her refusal to write in predictably "feminine" ways, praising her for having captured "the tone and manner of the ancients, without any of that rouge-and-powder tone of delicate prettiness." After having been preserved for generations as a family treasure, her poetry was collected into a ten-*juan* book with the title *Jing'an ji*; later her poetry and prose were brought together in the fifteen-*juan Zhu Miaoduan ji*. Her poems are also featured in seventeenth- and eighteenth-century anthologies of women's poetry. Xu Xian wrote of her: "For womanly virtues and purity of character, not even Zhu Shuzhen and Li Yi'an [Li Qingzhao] can compare with her."[1]

P.28.1. The Consort Yu

Strength exhausted, Xiang Yu lost the hegemonic light in his
  double-pupiled eyes.
Surrounded by the singing of Southern songs, he felt endless regret.
A faithful soul, she turned into grass on the battleground,
Refusing to follow the east wind into Han territory.

(Su Zhecong, 289)

Yu was the favorite consort of Xiang Yu (232–202 B.C.E.), hegemon of Chu and the arch rival of Liu Bang in the struggle for control of the empire that preceded Liu's founding of the Han dynasty. When Xiang (who was said to have double pupils) was cornered in Gaixia, Liu had his soldiers sing Southern songs at night, leading Xiang to believe that his home territory, Chu, had joined Liu's forces. Consort Yu committed suicide before Xiang's defeat in the final battle the next day.

P.28.2. *Reflecting on Antiquity on Wu Hill*

Blood of war washed the ten-thousand-mile Central Plains.
Thereupon the Song court moved to the south:
Loyal ministers were determined to clear the desert,
But incompetent lords had no intention of recovering the lost capital.
In northern passes, cuckoos of Shu cry in spring breeze;
On West Lake the night moon shines on the jade zither.
Past glory and disgrace are but empty traces—
(8) I turn to gaze at the setting sun still glowing on Wu Hill.

(Su Zhecong, 289–90)

line 1: The Chinese heartland; the reference is to the fall of northern China to the Jürchen armies in 1127.

lines 5–6: On the "cuckoo of Shu," see P.5.1. The allusion here is also to a poem composed by the loyal general Wen Tianxiang between his capture and execution by the Mongol invaders; see Qian Zhongshu, ed., *Song shi xuan zhu*, p. 353. "West Lake" refers to Hangzhou, the Southern Song capital-in-exile.

P.28.3. *Impromptu on a Trip*

I have traveled long in foreign lands,
Prevented from going home by wind and rain.
Emerald mountain peaks along the shore,
The lone boat light as a feather.
By the broad window, a dying candle,
Hazy trees, morning crows cry.
Waiting for the sun to rise,
(8) I seem to see a city at sea.

(Zheng Guangyi, 1220)

P.28.4. *Spring Rain*

Dark rain clouds, drizzle like silk yarns,
Flowers fill the west garden, unknown to butterflies.
In the morning chill of the golden mansion, orioles' bitter songs,
Late spring in the adorned boudoir, swallows have not returned.
Resentful peach blossoms in the palace shed crimson tears;
Passionate willows in the haze knit their emerald brows.

Sandalwood clappers and gold goblets have long stood still—
(8) Grieving in a lonely city, I listen to the sad sound of horns.

(MYSG, 26/2a)

P.28.5. Songs on the Lake [two from a series of four]

I

Shimmering lake and mountain glow refracted on the bramble door,
Behind the makeshift fence, in the thatched hut, visitors are few.
In leisure I pluck juniper berries to brew spring wine
And tailor water lily leaves into an autumn gown.
Red flames in the night illuminate my studio;
Green waves on a clear day immerse the fishing rock.
Only a pair of white birds at the head of the stream—
(8) Standing side by side they have forgotten the world.

II

Autumn in Hengtang is deeper while lotus flowers fade.
Two by two, southern beauties return rowing their boats.
Startled, the mandarin ducks stop swimming
And fly swiftly over White Duckweed Beach.

(MYSG, 26/2a–b)

P.28.6. Late Spring

Fallen petals on green moss like snowflakes,
The double door tightly shut even during the day.
Not knowing spring has gone,
Butterflies flit over the wall with willow catkins.

(MYSG, 26/3b)

P.28.7. Early Summer

Fading reds have all fallen and the sun has set,
Roses withering in the warm breeze of the night.
By the pond after the rain, no one is there—
Elm seeds like gold coins cover the ground while orioles sing.

(MYSG, 26/3b)

P.28.8. *Spring Silkworms: A Song*

Peach blossoms have all fallen and the day is longer.
On the path after the rain, mulberry leaves have turned yellow.
After praying to the patron goddess, she makes an offering to the silkworm nursery
And lights a low fire in bamboo baskets to warm up the room.

(MYSG, 26/3b–4a)

P.28.9. *Coloring My Fingernails*

In a golden plate dew is mixed with dawn sunlight,
Applying red to fingers slender and white like young bamboo shoots.
Green sleeves with an exquisite scent play the zither—
In green shade crab apple flowers newly in bloom.

(MYSG, 26/4a)

P.28.10. *Written in Illness*

Wide awake, I trim the remaining wick of the cold lamp.
With a quilt over me, I sit up till midnight.
Where is the flute coming from?—
Plum blossoms fall in a moonlight-washed town.

(MYSG, 26/4a–b)

P.28.11. *Impromptu on a Trip*

The splendid mansion is quiet, young swallows fly.
In the deep shade of green poplars, orioles sing.
The breeze is gone, the light curtain still,
I sit and watch flower shadows shift in the garden.

(MYSG, 26/3b)

P.28.12. *Grievance from the Boudoir*

Awakened from daydreaming by twittering birds,
She leans languidly on a silver screen.
Her slender brows have not been painted by Scholar Zhang—
She's too shy to see green willow eyes in the east wind.

(MYSG, 26/3b)

line 3: See P.22C.1.

P.28.13. Seeing a Butterfly on an Autumn Day

Vast river, falling leaves, eagles' sorrowful cries,
Frost dyes crimson maples, all plants wither.
Not knowing itself a dream, a butterfly
Flits toward a cold twig in this autumn scene.

(MYSG, 26/3b)

P.28.14. Selling My Vacant Home

Moss on the wall, dust on earthen cooking pots:
Now that my house belongs to the west neighbor,
I can't bear to see the willows in front of the door
For fear they'll treat me like a stranger tomorrow.

(MYSG, 26/4a)

BIOGRAPHICAL NOTE AND TRANSLATION BY MICHELLE YEH

陳德懿

P.29. Chen Deyi (fl. 1476)

Chen came from a literati family in Changxing in present-day eastern Zhejiang and later moved to Hangzhou. She was married to a provincial graduate who became a high-ranking official. Best known for her regulated verse, she early achieved a reputation as a landscape poet; her later work expresses grief over an unhappy life and the wish to renounce the mundane world. Chen corresponded with Zhu Jing'an (P.28) in verse, and her poetry is collected in a four-*juan* volume, *Chen Deyi ji*.[1]

P.29.1. Spring Grass

No one planted the spring grass
Sprouting in clumps as it pleases—
Greenness reaching beyond the countryside,
A blue haze returning from far to near.
An enveloping mist dampens fallen willow catkins;

Mixed with rain, spring grass a foil for fading flowers.
Not knowing why the prince has left,
(8) Sadly it faces the evening breeze.

(MYSG, 25/5a)

P.29.2. *Impromptu on a Summer Day*

Bamboo in the garden, layers of green,
Sheer windows covered with emerald gauze screen.
In a bowl, gold-thread grass is planted;
On the terrace jade-hairpin flowers grow.
After the rain, the setting sun lingers,
But returning clouds take the sunset away.
In the remaining summer heat,
(8) I stroll at ease listening to frogs in the pond.

(MYSG, 25/5b)

P.29.3. *Written for Zhu Jing'an, Who Promised to Pay Me a Visit*

The Fair One promised to pay me a visit.
Why hasn't her carriage of clouds arrived?
In the deep yard, snow has melted and sweet grass is green.
When a breeze brushes by, plum blossoms fall like rain.
To go on immortals' white-stone diet, we must take herbs first.
We'll enjoy copying the *Yellow Court Scripture* so much, we won't trade
it for a goose.
I'd like to cultivate the great Way with you.
(8) In days to come, we'll rub the bronze man together.

(MYSG, 25/6a–b)

line 5: The *Biographies of Immortals* alludes to a man who subsisted on white stones and lived on Mount White Stone; thus, he was known as "Master White Stone." See Ge Hong, *Shen xian zhuan, juan* 1 (*Siku quanshu* edition, 1059: 261).

line 6: The fourth-century calligrapher Wang Xizhi copied the Daoist *Huangting-jing* (Yellow court scripture) in exchange for a white goose he admired for its grace and elegance of movement.

line 8: The *Hou Han shu* (History of the Later Han) records a magician named Ji Zixun (fl. 196–220), said to be able to raise the dead. After disappearing in a white cloud, he was later seen in Chang'an together with an old man, rubbing a bronze statue of a warrior that had been set up by the First Emperor of Qin (r. 221–210

B.C.E.). He was overheard to say: "Do you remember? A moment ago we saw this being cast, and almost five hundred years have already gone by." See *Hou Han shu*, 72b/2745–46. The allusion suggests that Chen Deyi sees herself and Zhu Jing'an as immortals whose meetings transcend ordinary time and space.

P.29.4. Arriving in Huaiyin

By the western Huai River, I moor my boat and stroll.
The sight of smartweed and wild flowers on the sandy shore
saddens me.
The shadow of the sail retreats with rippling water,
Clattering oars follow the sound of waves.
Clouds drift over distant peaks, nightfall in the grove.
Rain has stopped on the long dikes, autumn on the riverbank.
The most enchanting sight of mist and smoke—
(8) Swift gulls bathe in the depths of white duckweed.

(MYSG, 25/6b)

P.29.5. A Walk on Mount Min

I walk a long way to the end of the mountain stream,
A few thatched huts facing the setting sun.
A spring is guided through a bamboo pipe into the kitchen;
Scented pines laden with cones surround the compound.
No one on the woodsman's path except an occasional dozing calf;
In the stony field, rainwater splashes between rice sprouts.
All my life I've yearned for mountains and woods—
(8) I'd like to build a straw hut by the stream.

(MYSG, 25/7a)

P.29.6. Bidding Farewell to Mrs. Chang, Wife of a Fellow Official of Tongyin

Flapping banners move our hearts as we say goodbye.
I hesitate to leave, unable to walk away.
After the rain, farming in Bianliang thrives.
In receding waves, the traveler's westbound boat is swift.
It's hard to say good-bye, cross the passes and hills.
Trudging on tortuous paths, I'll find it hard to reckon the distance.

Not knowing when we shall meet again, let's write letters.
Looking at each other, we only pick up cup after cup of wine.

(MYSG, 25/9a)

P.29.7. Autumn Evening

The water clock has stopped dripping.
Newly awake, I see the moon at the zenith of the sky.
Feeding the fire under the herb-brewing cinnabar burner,
I light incense in the chamber before bowing to the stars above.
The whistling wind knocks on leaves on the trees,
The glowing lamp shining on my bed curtain.
With a quilt over me, I suddenly have a strange dream
Of riding on a long whale, crossing Lake Dongting.

(MYSG, 25/9b)

P.29.8. Writing About My Thoughts

It's been years since my husband became an itinerant official.
Now home again, I conceal my trails for the love of groves and springs.
I know I'll lose track of human affairs when I study the Way;
Often I stay awake at night in search of poetry.
The door closed behind me, I go looking for a sweet grass field.
Rolling up the curtain, I am sad to see the apricot-blossom sky.
How can I become a reclusive immortal in the mountain
When I still allow mundane things to enter my mind?

(MYSG, 25/8a)

P.29.9. Weeping for My Husband

For four decades you were an accomplished minister.
Never did I expect to be separated from you by the Yellow Springs.
Your writings naturally stand as a paradigm for contemporaries;
Your political achievements will be remembered by posterity.
Before the mirror, I'm sad to see the reflection of a solitary *luan*;
To continue the lineage, I'd need the sagacity of a *feng*.
Forlorn wind, bitter rain, under a cold lamp,
Many times I grieve and bitter tears fall.

(MYSG, 25/8a–b)

line 2: The Yellow Springs are the abode of the dead, the underworld.

lines 5–6: *Luan* and *feng* are both phoenixlike mythical birds; the *luan* is usually spoken of as female and the *feng* as male.

P.29.10. *Autumn Night*

Dyed by the frost, how many trees in the maple grove have turned red?
Blue sky, shifting clouds, the crescent moon like a bow.
For ten years I have roamed beyond rivers and lakes,
Wandering freely in a dream on my pillow.
Everywhere in nature I see traces of Yu the sage-king,
All over town, people dress in Tang caps and gowns.
My melancholy heart and pure thoughts find no relief—
(8) Night insects chirp loudly in the four walls.

(MYSG, 25/8a)

BIOGRAPHICAL NOTE AND TRANSLATION BY MICHELLE YEH

孟淑卿

P.30. Meng Shuqing (fl. 1476)

Meng Shuqing was the daughter of a minor scholar-official, a district-level assistant instructor of studies named Meng Cheng. She was a native of Suzhou, in modern-day Jiangsu province, and although styled "The Recluse of Mount Jing" for failing to find fulfillment in marriage, she was actually quite sociable, and even faulted in her day for being too ready to meet guests and display her cleverness.[1] Her disputational skills were much respected in scholarly circles, as were her literary talent and discrimination. She particularly enjoyed discussing poetry, saying that it should be free of conventional shackles—with "Buddhist verses not reeking of incense and paper money, feminine themes not overwhelmed with cosmetics and rouge, humble scholar poems not imbued with shabbiness and misery, Daoist poems not steeped in life-prolonging quackery, or mountain hermits' poems mired in seclusion and misery." These critical sentiments were applauded by her poetry-writing contemporaries.[2] Comments attributed to her on other women poets are included as C.7.

Meng Shuqing's poems reveal a mind deeply tinged with melancholy and discontent. Although her themes are not necessarily novel, she weaves poetic precursors' lines seamlessly into her work and manages to express herself with a subtlety that moves without seeking to overwhelm.

P.30.1. *The Palace of Everlasting Trust*

Stairs thick with red leaves, geese urgently calling—
Autumn deep in palace alleys tortures one's very being.
Once my lord's will like the season changes,
Fragrant grass no more enjoys an endless spring.

(MYSG, 25/3a)

The Palace of Everlasting Trust was the residence of the cast-off Ban *jieyu* (see P.1.2).

P.30.2. *Presented to a Singing Girl at a Banquet*

A pomegranate skirt becomes her wasp waist,
New songs sung, she takes up jade flute strains.
But turning from the spring breeze she dabs secret tears.
For whom does she pine, and for whom ply her charms?

(MYSG, 25/4a)

P.30.3. *Occasional Couplets on a Spring Day*

The light turns into dancing rays as the days begin to lengthen,
Shrimp-feeler curtains are rolled up, and swallows dart about.
Beside the painted tower, dark willows undulate,
And on the dancing stage a red profusion of sleepy crab apple blooms.

(MYSG, 25/4a)

P.30.4. *Spring's Return*

Water brimming with pear petals pats the riverbank,
While my gaze is lost in flourishing grasses.
Most heartless of all is the bird on the branch
Heedless of human sorrow in his cries.

(MYSG, 25/3b)

P.30.5. *Climbing the Tower*

Deploring the passing of spring
  I wouldn't climb the tower.

Now ascending its southern story
stirs yearning for someone afar.
Fallen petals are scattering everywhere
in red-rained confusion
And fragrant grasses stretch endlessly skyward
as dense green clouds.

(MYSG, 25/4b)

P.30.6. *Inscription for a Painting*

Trees on the ridge coil up to the clouds,
The stream winds and the road turns steeply.
Evening comes, blending mist with murky sky—
Where can I seek out a mountain lodge?

(MYSG, 25/3a)

P.30.7. *Writing of Feelings on an Autumn Day*

The cicada's chirp from the courtyard acacia branch
turns to a sob in the autumn drear.
A few more columns of wild geese
pass over my southern tower.
I can't look toward that hook-shaped moon
just clearing the horizon!
Or it will stab me with fresh sadness
and stir old sorrows anew.

(MYSG, 25/4b)

P.30.8. *Lament*

Teardrops on my gauze sleeve retrace wet paths,
Why must I lack the magic scent to lure a dead soul back?
A cardamom flower I remain, but the man is no more,
Only the bright moon through a curtain comforts me at twilight.

(MYSG, 25/4b)

line 3: The cardamom flower was a symbol of chastity.

P.30.9. *Fragrant Boudoir Poem*

Deep in her chamber she silently sits,
with far too many thoughts.
Gradually she feels the fearsome frost
invading her robes.
The green damask coverlet is chilly
without any dreams of love,
And bitter cold days at the Great Wall
have stopped the arrival of letters.

The sound of wind playing through bamboos
invades the entrance door,
Plum blossoms and a mellow moon
ascend the window in vain.
How can her moth eyebrows
match the courtyard willows,
(8) Which will suddenly open and smile
when spring arrives?

(MYSG, 25/2b–3a)

P.30.10. *Facing the Mirror*

At break of day she turns to the phoenix case,
Feelings in check, she wills herself to finish her face and hair.
Since her destiny is already dust
What need has she for a face like jade?

(MYSG, 25/3a)

P.30.11. *Viewing the Picture of the Lotus Beauty*

Sounds of cicadas in the *wutong* tree,
the day needlessly long;
Too lazy to light the blended incense
in the golden brazier.
Don't go wading in the pool
looking for lotus seeds,
You'll find the greater part of them
have only empty pods.

(MYSG, 25/3b–4a)

P.30.12. The Yang Guifei Chrysanthemum

The dance of the rainbow robes is over
  for the small waist and stem.
Head lowered to brace the wind,
  I wonder how many thoughts?
Don't blame her for a beauty
  too radiant—
Half her red blush was morning wine,
  the other half was rouge.

(MYSG, 25/3b)

line 1: The Dance of the Rainbow Robes was Yang Guifei's most celebrated performance. (On Yang, see P.18.12 and P.21.1.) Like Wang Qinghui, Meng Shuqing borrows heavily from Bo Juyi's "Song of Everlasting Sorrow" in composing her reminiscence of Yang Guifei.

P.30.13. Autumn Night

Ample bean-flower rains
  have turned the evening cool;
In the forest lodge I lie alone,
  afraid the night will be long.
It's the weight of sadness alone
  that keeps me from falling asleep
And not the little cricket crying
  within the golden well.

(MYSG, 25/5a.)

BIOGRAPHICAL NOTE AND TRANSLATION BY FRANCES LAFLEUR

沈瓊蓮

P.31. Shen Qionglian (fl. 1488–1505)

Born to a scholarly family, Shen Qionglian was a precocious child. At the age of thirteen, she was chosen to become a female scribe (*nü shi*) at the imperial court. When the Ming emperor Xiaozong (Zhu Youcheng, 1470–1505) set an examination on the theme "gecko," Shen Qionglian's answer, punning on the word *shou gong* (gecko), which sounds exactly like "defending the palace," pleased the emperor greatly and won first place. She was later made Female Chancellor (*nü xueshi*) and held this position until her death. Shen Qionglian's work includes "Ten Palace Poems" ("Gongci shi shou") and the well-known regulated-verse poem addressed to her brothers. Some commentators and readers have compared her to Huarui *furen* (P.15) and Shangguan Wan'er (P.7), but others have considered her superior to both.[1]

P.31.1. To My Older Brother

Bright stars are thinning out—the night is ending,
Their faces fair and flowering, the palace women stand arrayed.
Breezes carry the heavenly music of the palatial bells,
Melting snow chills the Zhique Tower at daybreak.
Lady Zhaoyi leads the imperial carriage toward the crimson screens,
The Matron of Shangqin lights incense burners with sandalwood.
Solemnly hung on all six palace gates are the sacred creeds and images;
(8) In the balmy air the front hall awaits the belled chariot.

(Xie Wuliang, 3/2/12)

line 4: The Zhique (Jaybird) Tower, located in Sweet Springs Park, was built by Emperor Wu of the Han dynasty; here the name is applied to the Ming palace buildings.

line 5: On the title *zhaoyi*, see P.21.

line 6: *Shangqin* refers to the housekeeping service, one of six agencies among which palace women were distributed. The Matron of Shangqin is the lady in charge of this service agency.

P.31.2. To My Younger Brother Pu on His Spring Examination

In my adolescence I left home to attend at the inner palace,
Heaven and earth have remained remote from each other since.
In the morning I follow the phoenix carriage to the Gate of Blue
  Chained-Pattern,
In the evening I carry imperial letters to the Hall of Purple Tenuity.
No matter how many candles are burnt, my dreams are of no avail,
Many a jade hairpin broken, I have yet to return home.
Year after year I expect your name to appear on the golden list,
(8) Together we can mend the robe of the mountain dragon.

(Su Zhecong, 292)

line 3: "Phoenix carriage" usually refers to the carriage used by the empress. Blue Chained-Pattern (*Qingsuo*) refers to the pattern of blue overlapping circles decorating the palace gate.

line 4: Purple Tenuity (*Ziwei*) was originally the name given to a star north of the Dipper that was supposed to be the site of the Heavenly King's palace; it later became the unofficial designation of the Central Drafting Office (*Zhongshu ge*), which was attached to the Grand Secretariat.

line 7: The list of top-ranked examination candidates.

line 8: The dragon is a symbol of the emperor; "to mend the robe of the mountain dragon" is to serve the emperor at the court (cf. poem 260 of the *Book of Odes*).

BIOGRAPHICAL NOTE AND TRANSLATION BY WAN LIU

夏雲英

P.32. Xia Yunying (15th century)

Xia Yunying was a lady at the court of Prince Zhu Youdun (1379–1439), one of the grandsons of the first Ming emperor, Zhu Yuanzhang. Xia was known for her tenacious memory and erudition, and for the refinement of her writing. Ninety-one of her poems are recorded as having been collected in a volume, the *Duanqing ge shi* (Poems from the Tower of Utter Purity); she also left Buddhist writings in prose. She later became a nun and died at the age of twenty-four.

P.32.1. First Day of Fall

The autumn winds bring rain across the southern pavilion,
After the refreshing coolness overnight, the first day of fall arrives.
In the jeweled and duck-shaped burner the incense dies out, the fire grows cold,
At her leisure, the maid plays the *konghou* by herself.

(Xie Wuliang, 3/2/14)

line 4: The *konghou* was a small zitherlike instrument with seven strings, of Central Asian origin (although the *Old History of the Tang* claims that Emperor Wu of the Han commanded his chief musician Hou Diao to create it for use in sacrifices to the Great Unity; see *Jiu Tang shu*, 29/1076–77). A tune called the "Konghou Prelude" was celebrated as a moving expression of conjugal fidelity.

P.32.2. Clear Skies After the Rain

Crab apple trees are newly planted and bamboo moved;
A flowing stream gurgles into a small pool.
The spring rain suddenly stops, yielding a pleasant breeze,
A chirping bird flies past the blossoming branches.

(Xie Wuliang, 3/2/14)

P.32.3. Observation on an Autumn Night

The west wind, soughing, stirs up the gauze curtain,
In the twilight the incense's fragrance descends the jade stairs.
The sacrificial ritual ends, the courtyard quiets,
The silvery moon shining high, we watch the chess game.

(Xie Wuliang, 3/2/14)

BIOGRAPHICAL NOTE AND TRANSLATION BY WAN LIU

鄒賽貞

P.33. Zou Saizhen (fl. 1496)

Zou Saizhen was from Dangtu in Anhui province. She was the daughter of the censor Zou Qian and the wife of Pu Weixuan, an aide in the Directorate of Education. She was awarded the honorary title *Ruren* (Child nurturess), which was bestowed upon mothers and wives of high officials. Her son Pu Shao was a *jinshi* (presented scholar) degree recipient of 1496 and was made a junior compiler in the Hanlin Academy. Her daughter Pu Xiulan married the Grand Secretary Pei Ehu.[1]

Zou Saizhen showed signs of great intelligence and refinement while still young. She was superb at chanting poetry. Whenever she encountered a new sentence, she could read it without hesitation. Because of her talent she was given the courtesy name Shizhai, "The Scholar's Studio." Her collected works (in three *juan*) are entitled *Shizhai ji*.[2]

P.33.1. A Letter from My Younger Sister Arrives at the Official Residence

I seal my letter and ask the geese to deliver it.
Despite many sicknesses we have remained inseparable.

Wintry chestnut trees have encroached on your flesh of jade,
Autumn raspberries have mussed your cicada curls.
Your letter from the village had still not arrived,
When flesh and bones had started to tug at each other.
When will we return to our secret place,
(8) Light a lamp and talk of when we were young?

(MYSG, 26/5b)

P.33.2. Encouraging My Son Shao to Study and Abstain from Wine

Your benevolent forebears passed on purity and honor
To you, my son, who are now no longer a child.
Heed your father's teachings and strive to emulate him;
Trace things to their roots and know the value of study.
Do not set out on the easy path of drinking wine,
Instead punt your boat upstream.
And though your wife may have no goods to pass on,
(8) The Classics and Histories will be your family's legacy.

(MYSG, 26/5b)

P.33.3. Grieving over the Spring

Who cherishes longing and dwells on pain?
My brushwood door stays shut all day long.
Purple swallows settle on the beams and speak,
Faded flowers, adorned with rain, scatter.
Lazily I sleep behind kingfisher curtains,
Mournfully I weave with my "mandarin duck" loom.
The spring colors are here again,
(8) But the one who is gone has not yet returned.

(MYSG, 26/5b)

P.33.4. In the Capital on the Double Ninth Festival, Thinking of My Absent Husband, Weixuan

Ten years of pure bitterness, my bedfellow a cheap green blanket:
You sought high office, but your luck was poor, and we were forced to live miserably apart.
Maple leaves whistle with the wind and add to my morning dizziness;

I find those chrysanthemum flowers beautiful, blooming in defiance of
 the cold.
The autumn Yangzi has not seen Zhang Han's return,
In a lonely house who pities old Zheng Qian?
I long to encounter a white-robed wine steward
(8) Who will come from afar bearing ease and joy to my rude bamboo
 fence.

(MYSG, 26/6a)

line 5: Zhang Han, a Latter Jin dynasty (936–47) resident of Wu, near present-day Suzhou, was a careful scholar who served at the court of Qi Wang as administrator of the Eastern Section. When the autumn breezes arose, he thought of the local cuisine of the Suzhou area and left his post; see *Jin shu* 92/2384.

line 6: Zheng Qian was a Tang-dynasty resident of Yingyang, in Henan province. From a poor family, he would practice his writing on leaves because he could not afford paper. Emperor Tang Xuanzong recognized his abilities and made him an Erudite; see *Xin Tang shu*, 202/5766.

lines 7–8: After the pastoral poet Tao Yuanming (Tao Qian; 365–427) had retired from office to lead a recluse's existence on the outskirts of a village, he once went for nine days without wine. In desperation he left his small house and went beyond his bamboo fence in search of it and saw someone in white clothing approach him, a steward from the official Wang Hong bearing a gift of wine; see *Zhongwen da cidian*, no. 23191.166.

P.33.5. A Tiny Scene of an Egret

A slim, bending egret
Flies to alight on a high riverbank.
Like a patch of snow that does not melt,
It dots the emerald of the river sky.

(Su Zhecong, 291)

BIOGRAPHICAL NOTE AND TRANSLATION BY NORMAN KUTCHER

王素娥

P.34. Wang Su'e (16th century)

Wang Su'e was from Shanyin in Zhejiang province; her courtesy name is variously given as Nie Zhai, "Tree Stump Studio," and Nie Ping, "Tree Stump Screen." She was the wife of the clerk Hu Jie, who died in service at the capital. Wang pledged to remain faithful to him until death. Her moral character won the respect of many. She was skilled in both poetry and writing, and was adept at needlework. She died at age forty-one.[1]

P.34.1. Feeling Melancholy

My tears are not easily released,
Even so, my home village is a thousand miles from here.
Cares of the heart and grief of the entrails,
To whom can I speak of these?

(MYSG, 26/9b)

P.34.2. Ferrying the Qiantang River

The wind is gentle, the moon low, the water calm.
In river country the weather has just turned clear and my joy is
boundless.
I try to make out a small boat, light as a leaf,
Carrying the mountain colors across Xiling river.

(MYSG, 26/9b)

The Qiantang and Xiling Rivers are both in the Hangzhou area.

P.34.3. *Dusk*

At the foot of the stairs the crickets chirp and it is late autumn again;
As I lean alone against the railing, long is my plaint.
How many cares, in these three years of tears,
Have I endured flowing onto this coral pillow?

(MYSG, 26/10a)

P.34.4. *Solitary Grief*

At dusk I listen sadly to the sawing of the rain;
I lengthen the dying lamp wick to its end.
I do not pick up needle and thread—my heart is about to break.
The fragrance from the brazier has gone cold—the fire is out.

(MYSG, 26/10a)

BIOGRAPHICAL NOTE AND TRANSLATION BY NORMAN KUTCHER

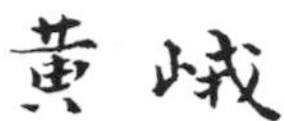

P.35. Huang E (1498–1569)

Huang E, better known by her courtesy name Huang Xiumei, is known for her role in one of the most famous husband-wife poetic dialogues in Chinese literary history The daughter of a high official in the Ming government, she received the equivalent of a man's education, both because she was extremely bright and because she was pampered by a family of the established elite who could indulge a precocious daughter in that way. She probably was born in the family home at Suining in central Sichuan, but as a young woman she also lived in her father's home in the capital and elsewhere. When she was twenty-one and (unusually for a young woman of her status and time) not yet betrothed, her father reached retirement age and took his family back to Sichuan. Later in that same year, 1519, she was married to the newly widowed Yang Shen (1488–1559), the scion of another prominent Sichuan family. Yang's father, Yang Tinghe, appointed a grand secretary in 1509, became Chief Grand Secretary in 1513. Yang Shen himself had been awarded the *zhuangyuan* or "optimus" title in the Palace Examination in 1511.[1] The marriage undoubtedly seemed very appropriate to both their families, and on more than one account. Yang Shen was well known as a young star of learning; Huang Xiumei, equal to him in education, shared his zeal for poetry. They symbolized the ideal pairing of genius and beauty.

But their lives were transformed shortly after the Jiajing emperor (posthumously known as Shizong) came to the throne in 1521. Yang Tinghe, as chief civil official of the realm, had arranged for the childless Zhengde emperor to be succeeded by a cousin, then only fourteen years old, not suspecting that this successor would refuse to perform the ritual tasks placed upon him as a successor from a collateral branch. So began a long and tortured struggle at the court, in which Yang Tinghe and his son Yang Shen opposed the strong-willed new ruler. Early in 1524, Yang Tinghe retired from government, unable to contest longer with the inimical emperor, and later that year Yang Shen, along with more than a hundred like-minded officials, took part in a demonstration within the palace grounds against the emperor's policies. The demonstration so enraged the ruler that he had them all beaten severely; a number died.[2] Yang Shen survived, only to be banished to the malarial far southwest borders of Yunnan. He and Huang Xiumei left the capital together to travel by inland boat to central China, whence he went on alone to Yunnan as she traveled with her servants and retainers back to the Yang family home at Xindu, just north of Chengdu. Yang Shen was never granted amnesty; he lived out his life and died thirty-five years later in Yunnan.

The young couple whose prospects had seemed so brilliant now faced a dismal life of separation. Huang Xiumei became the central figure in the Yang family household, responsible for running the estate, rearing the children and grandchildren (none of them her own), and providing for their education and general well-being. While Yang, lionized as a literary giant in Yunnan, lived a relatively free if frustrated life embellished by a number of romantic encounters, she lived the proper and constrained life of an upper-class lady, seeing to her husband's financial needs and those of the entire Yang clan with hard work and devotion. They had been married three years when Yang was banished; in the late 1520s she spent about three years with him in Sichuan, but after that they were together rarely, and only for a few days or months at a time.

As long as Yang Shen lived (she survived him by ten years) they communicated through letters and poems. None of the letters are extant,[3] but their exchange of poetry has become famous. Some have suggested that Huang Xiumei should be considered the first woman of letters of the entire Ming period. The couple's poems began to be circulated in manuscript and recited at literary gatherings within their lifetimes, obviously because Yang Shen shared them with his literary colleagues; Huang is said never to have sought to preserve, much less to publish, her writings. By late Ming times anthologies had begun to include some of her poems alongside Yang's.

Huang Xiumei's poems mostly are written in the *sanqu* genre, but some are in *ci* or even in regulated-verse form.[4] Many of the *sanqu* attributed to her are startlingly frank. Some bitterly reproach Yang for living his unrepressed and irresponsible life in Yunnan while she was cloistered in the Yang family home, doing her duty to his family and having no pleasures. Some recall their days of youthful bliss and express her physical longing. Some are playful, some are tormented, some reveal the deep sadness of resignation. They are often linguistically brilliant, prosodically innovative, provocative. Their vivid emotional content gives them all the appearance of genuineness.

The *appearance* of genuineness—for the one problem that the reader of Huang Xiumei's poetry faces is the certainty that she did not write all, or even probably most, of the poems attributed to her.[5] For several centuries scholars have argued about which poems are genuine. Did her brilliant husband (known and admired as a parodist), seeking literary amusement for himself and his companions, actually write them in her voice and let them be circulated, claiming that they were hers? Was he in that way expressing his continuing love and admiration, or was he adding to a public image of his wife and himself for his personal gratification? Did others plagiarize and fabricate poems, for personal, even commercial reasons? It has been argued in recent years that a woman of Huang Xiumei's background and status simply could not have expressed herself so directly on matters that in Ming times were not to be spoken of openly. Those poems that seem more likely to be hers reveal remarkable qualities as poetry. Other, "out of character" poems may in fact be from her husband's hand, or even from the hands of other literary figures of the age, or have been cribbed from other writings and attributed to her by booksellers, in the characteristic late Ming printers' fashion of falsely attributing writings to well-known persons. Perhaps future research will resolve these issues.

In order to facilitate the understanding of her more interesting *sanqu* lyrics, we offer here translations of two of the poems sent to her by Yang Shen:

> The flowering branch suggests a face; her face is like a flower.
> Her lovely face has no flaw though even jade has flaws.
> Yellow gold has its price, but spring is beyond all price.
> For sensual elegance, who can compare?

One to be pitied: ill-fated, of many talents.
She plucked a lotus blossom and sadly poured the parting wine;
Facing the chrysanthemums, silently she suffers the melancholy of
separation.
Seeing the plum blossoms, may she then quickly write to me.

In the first poem the allusion is to a line by the Song poet Su Shi (Su Dongpo) that "a quarter-hour of a spring night is worth a thousand pieces of gold" ("Chun ye," in Su Shi, *Su Shi shiji*, p. 2592). The phrase "spring night" also recalls Bo Juyi's "Chang hen ge," describing the Tang emperor Xuanzong's passion for his favorite, Yang Guifei (see P.18.12): "Within the warm gauze bed-hangings they pass the spring nights; but spring nights were bitterly brief, and the sun rose early." In the second poem the progression of flowers reflects to the passage of time from summer to autumn and winter and suggests the hope that seeing the winter plum, the first flower of spring, will restore Huang's spirits so that she will write to him.

P.35.1. Sent to My Husband

"Wild geese have never flown as far as Hengyang";
How then will my embroidered words be carried all the way to
Yongchang?
Like the willow's flowers by the end of spring, I am ill-fated indeed;
In the mists of that alien land, you feel the pangs of despair.
"Oh, to go home, to go home," you mourn to the year's bitter end.
"Oh, if it would rain, if it would rain," I complain to the bright dawn.
One hears of vain promises that you could be set free;
(8) When will the Golden Cock reach all the way to Yelang?

(Wang Wencai, *Yang Shen ciqu ji*, p. 430; Su Zhecong, 296)

line 1: "Wild geese," the bearers of messages (see P.2.1, Song 5), were said to fly no farther south than Hengyang (in Hunan; see P.9.1).

line 2: "Embroidered words" is traditional, since Su Hui's "Palindrome Poem," for a wife's messages to her husband (see C.1.1, C.4.1).

lines 5–6: "Oh, to go home" is quoted from poem 167 of the *Book of Odes* and "Oh, if it would rain," from poem 62. Both poems lament the separation of husband and wife because of military duties. On the use of these allusions, see Liang Rongruo, *Zhongguo zuojia yu zuopin*, p. 32.

line 8: A figure of a golden cock was raised at the palace gates whenever a general amnesty was announced. Huang's allusion recalls lines from a poem by Li Bo (701–

62), who was banished to Yelang (roughly modern southwest China) and benefited from an imperial amnesty while en route (see Waley, *Poetry and Career of Li Po*, pp. 87–88).

P.35.2. Sent to Sheng'an

The time for watching the harvest moon is scarcely gone
When again we pass through the season of chrysanthemums.
Through the months and years the waters ever flow on to the east
While our human lives are still, oh, so far apart.

(Wang Wencai, *Yang Shen ciqu ji*, 432)

"Sheng'an" is Yang Shen's courtesy name. This poem is one of the handful of *shi* poems early attributed to Huang Xiumei.

lines 1–2: "Watching the harvest moon" is something done particularly at the midautumn festival, normally an occasion for family reunions. Chrysanthemums are regularly used in poetry to allude to the melancholy of the passing year's end.

P.35.3. Sanqu *Lyric, to the Tune* Zhe gui ling *[second in a set of four]*

I remember when we were together: shared pillow, same coverlet;
Together we drove out all sadness, together expelled all ills.
Jade-green sleeves, richly carved saddles,
Through cold and ice, to far streams and distant peaks.
But that good time of joy was not to endure;
This blighted marriage has now worn my spirit thin.
I sigh long sighs, sunk deep in gloomy thought,—
(8) No need to pursue those old promises.
The mood for billing and cooing has long since been swept away,
So don't bring up again that old line about "one quarter-hour being
worth a thousand pieces of gold."

(Wang Wencai, *Yang Shen ciqu ji*, 409–10)

lines 1–4: Probably a reference to the journey on which Huang Xiumei accompanied her husband back to their homes in Sichuan in the early years of their marriage, nominally on a mission for the emperor.

line 10: A direct response to her husband's own indirect reference to Su Shi's poem "Chun ye." Yang Shen's reference can be taken to mean "A spring night spent with you would be priceless to me." Knowing all too well that his spring nights, unlike hers, were not spent alone, she throws his slightly improper endearment back at him.

P.35.4. Huang ying'er *[number one of four]*

Incessant rain brings on light chill.
I see luxuriant bloom on all the trees now battered;
My eyes are filled with muddy roads ascending to the immortals,
How many layers of peaks in the clouds?
How many bends in the rivers?
To the edge of the heavens as far as eye can see, and my heart breaks in vain.
It is so hard to send a letter,
(8) The heartless migrating geese will not fly all the way to Yunnan.

(Wang Wencai, *Yang Shen ciqu ji*, pp. 169–70)

The problems of authenticity are well summed up in the evaluations of this poem—one often considered to be among Huang E's best, but also often credited to Yang Shen. It is the first of a set of four *sanqu* bearing the tune name "*Huang ying'er*" and the subtitle: "In rain, giving vent to my feelings." Editors of Yang's and Huang's poems have variously assigned all four to him, the first to her and the last three to him, or all to her. Many literary editors through the centuries have acclaimed the first in particular as among the finest, many indeed saying that she sent the first one to him, and that he responded with matching poems three times, each time failing to match the quality of hers. See Wang Wencai, *Yang Shen ciqu ji*, pp. 169–71, 391, 436–38, 441; Wang believes the first as well as the following three all were probably written by Yang.

P.35.5. Two Sanqu *Lyrics, Again to the Tune* Zhe gui ling

1

I'll write to that thoughtless ingrate, that callous fellow:
"You don't care that I've been sick abed for days;
You don't care that a sea of pestilence brings grief to the spring;
You don't care that my bed has an extra pillow, empty blankets;
You don't care that I'm in a lonely house amongst desolate hills;
You don't care that I sleep alone, to face a solitary dawn."
My tea isn't like tea, food doesn't seem like food;
(8) Drained of all feelings.
Dying, I don't die; living but not alive.
What spirit could I have?
Cut off from all traces of him, and for what reason?

The good things of life are all beset by trials; even heaven has turned peevish.

II

Heaven must have produced you just to torment me.
"So fair a flower," into whose house have I fallen?
"Sensual within the bed-covers"; "faithful love clasped to the breast"—
Such phrases grow stale in the mouth.
In all the romances, justice eventually is achieved;
How was the fledgling phoenix matched to a crow?
At some corner of the seas, some edge of the heavens, beyond endless waters, distant clouds,
Eventually even mountains are supposed to meet.
Until we meet, my itching heart cannot be scratched.

(Wang Wencai, *Yang Shen ciqu ji*, pp. 416–17)

The first line of the first lyric in this set seems to have been written in direct response to Yang Shen's entreaty "May she then quickly write to me." Other lines—the "You don't care" sequence—also are responses to words and phrases of his. (To avoid lengthy explanations of allusions, the line "In all the romances . . ." has simply been paraphrased here.) In their wit and high spirit and frank expression of sexuality these lyrics anticipate the tone of the late Ming.

BIOGRAPHICAL NOTE AND TRANSLATION BY CH'EN HSIAO-LAN AND F. W. MOTE

P.36. Li Yuying (1506–after 1522)

Li Yuying is thought to have written during the early decades of the sixteenth century. Her father was Li Xiong, a member of the prestigious imperial bodyguard. After her mother's death, her father married a woman surnamed Jiao. When he in turn was killed in a military conflict in the west of China, Li Yuying's stepmother moved against the children of the first wife to ensure that her own son would inherit the father's property. She poisoned Li Xiong's ten-year-old son, sold a daughter as a servant, and sent another into mendicancy. Armed with Li Yuying's poetry manuscripts, the stepmother charged her with unfilial behavior and lechery, asking that she be given the "lingering death" (slow dismemberment, a punishment reserved for truly egregious offenders). Li Yuying sent a memorial to Emperor Jiajing (r. 1522–67) detailing these events, and her life was spared.[1]

P.36.1. A Farewell to Spring

Lonely behind my brushwood door I sit locked away from the late spring,
While the elm seeds covering the ground do not relieve my poverty.
My cloud-like hair and clothes are half muddied;
Why do you, wildflowers, choose to arouse me?

(Su Zhecong, 299; MYSG, 28/2a)

P.36.2. Taking Leave of the Swallows

New nests dribble mud while the old nests lie aslant,
Dust half covers my door curtain, almost concealing the stitching.
Mournfully I face the twittering of the swallows, who finally must leave.
The painted hall is as before, but the master is gone.

(MYSG, 28/2a–b)

BIOGRAPHICAL NOTE AND TRANSLATION BY NORMAN KUTCHER

P.37. Wen *shi* (16th century)

Little is known about this author, who is referred to only by her maiden surname. Miss Wen was born into an office-holding family of Binzhou in Shaanxi, northwest of present-day Xi'an—a far cry from the southerly river landscapes of her poems. She married a man named Ge Dashou but early became a widow. Her surviving poems, a series of nine rhapsodies in the *sao* style, are directly modeled on the "Li sao" (Encountering sorrow) of the ancient poet and statesman Qu Yuan. Evidently, Wen saw similarities between Qu's misfortunes and her own.

Qu Yuan's "Li sao" is said to have been composed in response to rejection by King Huai of Chu. Its first-person narrator protests his virtues and devotion to the "Fair One," that is, King Huai, who has been led astray by a bevy of jealous concubines (i.e., rival advisors). After unsuccessfully attempting to recapture the king's affections, the narrator seemingly resumes a masculine guise to embark on a visionary tour of the cosmos in search of the perfect mate. Repeatedly frustrated in this aim, he is about to depart entirely from the known human world when he catches sight of his homeland and is unable to make another step. This plot provided Wen a framework for expressing the sorrows and slights of her young widowhood.

Xie Wuliang found that Wen's "Ni sao" series "perfectly captured the ancient tone" of the difficult and rarely imitated original, calling her "a singular talent among women." At the very least, they demonstrate a thorough familiarity with the *Chuci* and *Wen xuan* anthologies. Her poems, collected in a volume as *Junzi tang ji* (Poems from the Hall of the Noble Soul), were deemed of sufficient interest to be entered in the gazetteer of her home district.[1]

P.37.1. *In Imitation of the "Li sao" [preface and three poems from a series of nine]*

PREFACE

In my youth my paternal aunt and I used to study works setting out the principles of life in the women's quarters. With my revered grandfather I studied the *Analects* and the *Book of Odes*. But then, taking up the duties of married life, I found myself separated from my own relatives. And then, alas, I experienced the griefs of the ode "Bo zhou" [the early death of her husband]. A similar misfortune befell my aunt. My loneliness was more desolate and terrifying than the steep climb up a twisting peak! Night and day I had always to be on guard against the slightest fault, trusting only in my inward virtue. Above me I saw the towers of the heavenly capital; below me, a realm of deathly darkness. Human life is indeed fleeting like the dust raised by a galloping white horse. The days of Guirui are past, those of Xiayang are long gone, and the Way of womanliness has sunk low. Forgetful of sleep and food, I read through the night with a single lamp in my hand, studying the principles of the ancients and striving to follow their virtuous examples. My sorrow and indignation being without end, I have cast my feelings in an antique form and written these nine elegies in the form of the *Sao*. I transcribe them here in obedience to the head of my household.

1. *SIC TRANSIT*

In a winter of hardship my life draws to completion:
I cling to the pure heart within me as my only handhold!
Exhibiting the sincere and fragrant breath of virtue,
I have knocked on loneliness and come to know my true nature.
Having washed away the filthy currents of vulgarity,
I dress in threads of fragrant grasses that soothe my mind.
The Wind God slipping into my secluded room
Strikes and scatters my melancholy thoughts.
As I dwell on the fine rhymes of the "Pine Boat,"
My soul dissolves and sorrow sets in.
Clinging to the notes of honor, unwilling to alter them,
I remember with regret my true and short-lived mate.
Once, as I pored over the mournful "Rhyme-Prose on Widowhood,"
Tears coursed down in parallel streams and wet my dress.
Thrice I heard the bedewed rooster cry;
Then night came on slowly and took possession of my thoughts.
But my will was wandering past the high cliffs of heaven:
There I adorned myself with autumn orchids and gathered green moly.
My heart had not chimed as one with its desire:
Encountering pitfalls and high walls I sighed aloud.
I opened my untutored thoughts to the white clouds;
I gathered *qiongmao* among the Nine Doubts.
Above me, the bright sharpness of the city of purity!
I drank mist and vapor, feasted on dewy heliotrope.
—When Yao said, "Go down, and serve Shun in the nook of the Gui,"
They obeyed the kingly command, and their fame is still bright.
But Heaven no longer moves its favors for the lady of Xiayang;
The Way is corrupt and daily grows worse.
No matter: my inner beauty is straight, like hair never shorn,
I cling to it as to a hook, I preserve my steadfast will.
When the gentle night departs, I lie dreaming, though still dressed,
And receive the goddess Nü Wa as my teacher.
Aligning purest perfumes on the tip of my brush,

She refines away every grain of dross and leaves the essence.
Now I emulate the canons and patterns of the past:
(36) My thoughts bend to the deeps and my gaze reaches far,
To praise the pure thoughts of the girl of Tushan
And execrate the laughter of the beautiful Bao Si.
With devotion I read over the writings of women past,
(40) After nine detours I grasp and extend their lessons.
Others may envy, in their blindness, a woman's delicate beauty,
But I adopt purity, heaven's own virtue.
When I recall my departed husband's fine manner
(44) My heart sways to and fro as if I were drunk.
My hair is uncombed and tangled like a mourner's;
Though I have planted forget-all-care, I cannot sleep.
Whoso holds pure chastity in the square inch of her heart
(48) Flies on wings of fame to be honored in Heaven's court.
Though trapped in the stifling air of this dusty realm,
How could I lapse in my will and reject the Way?
With glorious thoughts I make the inner quarters my hermitage,
(52) Or in a drumming of hoofbeats charge up to the sky.
My purpose is brilliantly numinous, not hazy or obscure:
It is to follow heaven's decree and leave an enduring name.
I have fulfilled the wifely tasks prescribed by ancient custom,
(56) Tempered womanly teachings as one would season a soup.
As I think of the loving and pliant ways of the "gentle and retiring girl,"
I feast on jasper and drink decoctions of jade.
Treading with virtue's perfumed step, I am ever mindful;
(60) Touching my inlaid pillow, I am lost in thought.

II. A MEMORY OF THE XIANG RIVER

Look across to the flowing waves of Lake Dongting!
The emperor's child is sporting on the Xiao and Xiang.
The fleeting shapes of gods indistinctly glitter
As clouds swollen with rain rise and go.
Wave-hammered stones groan until the cliffs tremble;
The lake's vast surface shudders in long bars.
Climb precipitous crags and noble hills,

Grasping hollow branches as birds take flight about one;
When a blast of wind comes to shake the tree
The tender twigs drone mournfully like flutes.
Here are autumn orchids that have not yet burst forth;
Hibiscus buds, green and fresh, still store up their fragrance.
As I recall the pure example set by the two consorts,
Fragrant grasses dazzle the sight with bending waves;
Causes of Chonghua's magnificence,
Their gentle voices still linger in pepperwood halls.
Ren and Si, mothers of Zhou!
Your very nature was deep, pure, and good.
An exquisite maiden is a rare thing ever sought for,
But you are a double-headed tulip bursting with scent.
Dare I match you with Wenji and Su Hui?
Mao Qiang and Xi Shi?—their lives devoid of deeds.
How I admire the "gentle and retiring girl," that pattern of virtue,
And point to the "Inner Regulations" as my model!
Holding fast to the odorous pepper, I cast my clear eyes about,
And break a branch of cassia to make a flag.
I tread the path of the ancients, quiet yet firm,
Minutely attentive to my steadfast models.
What is it that summons me to tireless, sleepless labor?
I will delve into the Classics and deftly arrange jasper and agate.
Under a rack of bright lanterns, I read the annals of the past,
Trusting only in virtuous effort to yield me renown.
Indeed the stimuli to correctness are found in ancient works.
My mind is ever vigilant, as from fear.
I lack the will to arrange my hair or my appearance,
But my mind is sincere and will not change.
Desiring the mystic wind of the Great Purity,
I shall set my hand on my woman's armory and swear to keep my old vow.
Recoiling from all lust for filth and muck,
I praise "The Green Robe" and preserve my good name.
I knock at heaven's gate, and it opens for me;
Welcomed, I pay homage to the Female Spirits.
I look up to the blaze of the southern Heavenly Throne,

(44) Then turn towards the spot where my slight frame had its birth.
Renewing the past so as to leave a name for the future,
I trim my compositions and reveal my thoughts.
Should my coming into this world not have been entirely in vain,
(48) I may look at my shadow and not feel shame for its shape.

IX. BRUSHING THE JADE MIRROR

From my jade mirror I brush away the fine dust:
How pure and brilliant its empty light!
I gaze upon this holy and mysterious object:
Revealer of impurities and terror of false hearts!
Bronze prized in the time of the Yellow Emperor
For pure luster as of emerald depths!
Alas, that my own fresh coloring should so rapidly fade!
(8) But my inch of heart will never change.
Riches and fame I have thrown to the vulgar without;
To shape my acts in accordance with ritual is my only vow.
At the cock's first crow I have already dressed,
(12) And I watch the break of dawn in the east.
Far from me, the side-paths of the robber Zhi!
I follow the sages of old and take as my teacher the maiden Yijiang.
I have read the "Palindromic Verses" both backwards and forwards, and chanted the mournful airs of the "Nomad Flute";
(16) But all my "plangent thought" is to know how I may strengthen the "Three Bonds."
Wenji and Su Hui lived in vain times: mere floating pleasures were esteemed by all;
Women went adorned like kingfishers, but in them virtue was dead.
I look to the "gentle and retiring girl" for my model of purity,
(20) Submitting to womanly virtue, I remember the Xiayang bride.
Her benevolent influence spreads through a hundred generations,
Her virtuous deeds endure in the pepperwood halls.
I sweep my orchid side-chambers
(24) And in beast-figured burners light precious scents.
Wreaths of flying cloud enfold my window;
A gentle west wind steals in through my book-lined corner.
Or when stark winter hangs icicles from the eaves,

Bright chrysanthemums burst out in yellow flower.
Dense stands of cypress never lose their needles,
Although blue-green pines are capped with frost.
If grasses and trees can show such determination,
Can I, a woman, display less splendid garb?
Because of the mercy shown by old Duke Jing of Song,
Even the Fire Star retired to the third house;
And the elder daughter of Tushan,
Devoting herself to one man, fostered the rise of Xia.
Desiring nothing that ritual excludes, I live in quiet,
Pursuing my feminine tasks and revering what the sages have made.
I worship benevolence and loyalty, I make them my bulwark,
Transcending vulgar mores to serve the Way.

(Xie Wuliang, 6/22–30)

preface: Wen's phrase "works setting out the principles of life in the women's quarters" may refer to such works in general, or it may cite by title the *Kun fan* of Lü Zuqian (1137–81), an eminent neo-Confucian and associate of Zhu Xi. On the place-names Guirui and Xiayang: the legendary sage-emperor Yao, wishing to test his potential successor Shun, sent his two daughters to serve as Shun's wives in his home place of Guirui, the nook of the Gui River (see *Shang shu*, "Yao dian"; Karlgren, *Book of Documents*, p. 4; and see P.1.2). Similarly, when King Wen, the founder of the Zhou dynasty, had begun to show signs of preeminent virtue, "Heaven made for him a mate, to the north of the Xia [River], on the banks of the Wei" (poem 236 in the *Book of Odes*; see Karlgren, *Book of Odes*, p. 188).

i, lines 3–4: Here and elsewhere Wen uses fragrant things as emblems of virtue, and foul and sordid things to signify the opposite—a set of analogies directly inherited from the "Li sao." "Knocking on loneliness" (*kou jimo*) derives from Lu Ji (261–303), "Wen fu" (Rhyme-prose on literature). In keeping with Wen's use of it, the passage might be translated as follows: "[The writer] investigates absence in search of presence; knocks on loneliness to demand an answering voice" (*Wen xuan*, 17/4a).

i, line 5: Citing Liu Xiang (77–6 B.C.E.), "Jiu tan," "Xi xian" (Lament for the worthy man): see *Chuci buzhu*, 16/15a; Hawkes, *The Songs of the South*, p. 292.

i, line 7: Cf. Zhang Heng (78–139), "Si xuan fu" (Rhyme-prose on longing for the mysterious), *Wen xuan* 15/1–19b: "I will call Ji Bo, master of the winds, to cast off the filth and make everything pure."

i, line 9: "The Cypress Boat," poem 26 of the *Book of Odes*, was in Han times attributed to the young widow of a marquis of Wei and interpreted as her protest against her late husband's family's wish that she remarry. See Liu Xiang, *Gu lienü zhuan*, 4/5a–b.

i, line 13: The poem mentioned here is most likely Pan Yue's "Gua fu fu" (Rhymeprose on the widow), *Wen xuan* 16/19a–24b.

i, line 18: Cf. "Li sao," verse 12: "I gathered autumn orchids to make my belt" (*Chuci buzhu*, 1/4b; Hawkes, *Songs of the South*, p. 68); "moly" here represents the fungus of immortality (*zhi*).

i, line 20: Literally "pits and granaries," low and high places representing obstacles on the worthy's path. Liu Xiang, "Jiu tan," "Yuan si," line 2 (*Chuci buzhu*, 16/8b).

i, line 22: Just before setting out on his last journey, Qu Yuan, too, had searched for *qiongmao*, described by commentators as "a divine herb" (*Chuci buzhu*, 1/27a–b; Hawkes, p. 75). Nine-Doubt Mountain (Jiuyi Shan), so called because of the confusing similarity of its nine peaks, is said to be the site of Shun's grave. See "Li sao," *Chuci buzhu*, 1/29a; Hawkes, *Songs of the South*, pp. 76, 86.

i, line 23: The "city of purity" is the dwelling place of the Heavenly King (Tian Di), according to *Liezi* 3, "Zhou Mu wang" (3/32ab).

i, line 29: Closely paraphrasing "Li sao," line 9 (*Chuci buzhu*, 1/4a; Hawkes, p. 68).

i, line 37: After taming the flood waters, the legendary sovereign Yu of the Xia dynasty received a woman from the barbarian tribe of Tushan (or, by some accounts, the female spirit of that mountain) in marriage: see "Tian wen," *Chuci buzhu*, 3/10a–b; Hawkes, p. 129.

i, line 38: On Bao Si, see P.1.2.

i, line 46: On the *xuan*, or forget-all-care lily, see P.2.1 (Song 16) and *Book of Odes*, poem 62. Wen further alludes to Ruan Ji's "Singing of My Feelings, No. 2": "Such intense feelings give rise to sad thoughts, / And one plants the herb of forgetfulness [*xuan*] near the orchid chamber" (*Wen xuan* 23/2b; trans. Holzman, *Poetry and Politics*, p. 120).

i, line 54: Cf. "Li sao" (*Chuci buzhu*, 1/9b; Hawkes, *Songs of the South*, p. 70).

i, line 57: Cf. poem 1 of the *Book of Odes*: "A gentle and retiring girl, / A good match for our lord." The poem is traditionally supposed to praise Tai Si, bride of King Wen of the Zhou (see note to preface).

ii, line 2: "The emperor's child" refers to the Lady of the Xiang; in her mortal life this Lady was one of the daughters of Yao who was married to Shun. Much of the language in this poem derives from the poems "Xiang furen" (*Chuci buzhu*, 2/8a–12a; Hawkes, *Songs of the South*, pp. 108–9) and "Bei hui feng" (*Chuci buzhu*, 4/29a–36b; Hawkes, *Songs of the South*, pp. 179–83).

ii, lines 13–16: Shun, husband of the Two Consorts, is also known as Chonghua. "Pepperwood halls" describes the living quarters of wealthy families.

ii, line 17: Cf. Ban *jieyu*'s "Rhapsody of Self-Commiseration," P.1.2.

ii, line 21: Wenji is Cai Yan, P.2. Su Hui of the Eastern Jin dynasty was famous for her "Silk-Woven Palindromic Verse"; see C.1.1, C.4.1. Despite their literary glory, these two are not to be ranked with Ren and Si, the two great ladies of the early Zhou.

ii, line 22: Mao Qiang and Xi Shi are stereotypes of female beauty, often alluded to in early anecdotal literature. Both caused the ruin of royal houses.

ii, line 24: "Inner Regulations" is a chapter of the classic *Li ji* (Records of ritual) dealing with the domestic realm, particularly with the role of wives and mothers.

ii, line 38: This line's wit is for the eye as well as the ear: like a hero of old swearing on the hilt of his sword (*fu jian*), Wen *shi* lays her hand on her cosmetic case (*fu lian*).

ii, line 40: "The Green Robe," poem 27 of the *Book of Odes*, voices the complaint of a cast-off official who nonetheless takes heart in thinking of the men of old. This reference, too, echoes Ban *jieyu*'s "Rhapsody of Self-Commiseration," P.1.2.

ii, lines 43–44: Compare the ending of the "Li sao": "But when I had ascended the splendour of the heavens, / I suddenly caught a glimpse below of my old home" (Hawkes, *Songs of the South*, p. 78; *Chuci buzhu*, 1/36b).

ix, lines 11–13: These lines take their point from *Mencius*, "Jin xin," part A: "He who gets up with the crowing of the cock and never tires of doing good is the same kind of man as [the saintly] Shun; he who gets up with the crowing of the cock and never tires of working for profit is the same kind of man as [the robber] Zhi" (trans. Lau, *Mencius*, p. 187; SSJZS, 13b/3a).

ix, line 14: Yijiang was the consort of King Wu of the Zhou.

ix, line 16: "Plangent thought," a phrase from the traditional "Preface" to the first poem of the *Book of Odes*, represents the virtues of Tai Si, who showed "thoughtful concern for promoting worth and talent" (in the event, by recruiting the best young women to serve King Wen as concubines). The "Three Bonds" (*san gang*, a term current from the Han dynasty) are those between ruler and subject, father and son, husband and wife.

ix, lines 29–30: Alluding to Confucius, *Analects* 9.28, a standard parable for endurance and loyalty: "When the year grows cold, then one knows that the pine and cypress are the last to lose their leaves." See P.5.1.

ix, lines 33–34: A story from the Warring States period, used here to expand the theme of unselfish service. In the thirty-sixth year of Duke Jing's reign, the Fire Star (prevalent influence over hostile armies) crossed into Xin, an area of the heavens corresponding to Song. This presaged disaster for the ruler, and the duke called in his astrologer to discuss it. The astrologer said: "I can transfer the baleful influence to your ministers." The Duke answered: "But my ministers are virtually my own arms and legs!" "Then I can transfer it to the common people." "But any prince is dependent on his people!" "Then I can transfer it to the crops." "But if the crops are lost, the people will suffer! For whose benefit do you think I rule?" The astrologer answered: "You have answered three times as a true ruler would. The Fire Star is sure to move; wait for it." Presently the Fire Star moved to a spot three celestial houses away from Xin, and the Duke ruled for nearly thirty years more ("Song Weizi shijia," *Shi ji*, 38/39–40).

ix, line 36: I.e., the Xia dynasty (traditional dates 2205–1766 B.C.E.), founded by Yu the Great.

BIOGRAPHICAL NOTE AND TRANSLATION BY HAUN SAUSSY

王娇鸾

P.38. Wang Jiaoluan (16th century)

The editors of the *Mingyuan shi gui* (Compendium of poetry by renowned ladies) give the following account of Wang's poetic career:

> Wang Jiaoluan was the daughter of a petty military officer from Lin'an. Her father was demoted to the post of military commandant in Nanyang. There was a certain Zhou Tingzhang of Wujiang, whose father was serving as Instructor in the Confucian school at Nanyang at the time. It so happened that the school was located quite close to the guards' headquarters; and Zhou and Jiaoluan formed a secret liaison, swearing that they would never betray each other as long as they might live. Afterwards, Zhou returned to his home district and married someone else. When Jiaoluan heard of this and knew that there was no way to remedy the situation, she assembled all the poems they had previously exchanged into a volume and secretly tied it to a dispatch her father was preparing to send to the Provincial Court in Suzhou. That evening she hanged herself. When the document reached Suzhou, Xiu Yeshi and Fan Gongshe read it and, outraged by her story; they punished Zhou in accordance with the law. This occurred at the beginning of the Tianshun period.[1]

Wang's "Chang hen ge" (Song of everlasting resentment) shares a title with Bo Juyi's famous ballad on Xuanzong and Yang Guifei (see P.18.12), but the two have nothing more in common. Rather, Wang's is a long lament over the heartless behavior of her lover and an explanation of her own suicide.

P.38.1 Song of Everlasting Resentment

This song of lasting resentment—for whom is it written?
Once I begin writing, I become sick in my heart.
Brooding at dawn, longing at dusk—no end to it at all;
So again I take paper in hand to tell of my fickle lover.

My family originally were folk from Lin'an;
My grandfather won merit, was honored by emperors.
Once he was granted the rank of a general;
(8) He guarded state and people, bowed to his lord's pleasure.

Later, because my father erred in his military duty,
He was demoted to Nanyang, an outpost of a thousand families.
Father cried, the children wept to have come to such a pass;
(12) Earth frozen, the sky cold—who then would look after us?

He had raised me deep within the women's chambers;
Never had I ventured even to play in our house's court.
My parents cherished me—I was their pearl, their jade;
(16) And I loved my parents—for me, they were treasured jewels.

How could I know the ruin I'd meet at twenty?
I went out with a girl friend, left dressing table behind.
We went off to visit West Garden and played on a swing;
(20) And there amid the flowers I met a talented lad.

The swing ride over, I soon faced him across a banquet mat;
Amid sounds of fine stringed instruments our gold cups passed about.
Grateful I was that you should present the wine to me;
(24) Romantic feelings without end were written on your brow.

Our eyes sent out words of love—we couldn't help ourselves;
Raising your head, your single smile was a fortune in gold.
When I left, I happened to lose my scented silk kerchief
(28) And had to send my maid back to find it and bring it back.

I didn't think its scented silk would fall into your hands.
In vain I sent my Meixiang back and forth to look.
Then I kindly received the scented silk poem you wrote,
(32) Stirring in me fits of longing till I lay in illness.

Love notes came, letters went—though our love was great,
Never could we chant our verses hand in hand together.
Your father's office was next door, as far as Heaven!
(36) A torrent of idle grief poured forth from me in a cascade.

Once I could trim rush-mats, present them on Duanwu day—
Happy before, I could not know the bitter sadness to come.
Longing for you oft and again, two years then went by;
(40) Then my father adopted you as a child of my mother's.

Adopted then by my mother, you became my brother—
My family now accepted you, and we could stroll together.

Yet I feared our passions would soon turn improper;
So we then bound up our hair, swore an oath upon the hills.

Swore upon the hills and seas, yet on this I did not rely—
And I asked Aunt Cao as well to act as our go-between.
Then we wrote our marriage vows, sent them off to Heaven—
Now united in married bliss, for it was Heaven's decree.

Then I took my husband's lead—our hearts were then as one;
Side by side, holding hands, we strolled among the flowers.
I can't recall the hundreds of times we played at clouds and rain,
But only remember the three thousand "moon and wind" verses we wrote.

Though my name was Wang, and yours was Zhou,
A heaven full of lovely weather marked our wedded bliss.
We'd gaily plan our secret trysts off in the western hall,
Chant together hand in hand as we strolled in South Garden.

For two years, then, our union was as sweet as honey;
We swore we'd stay together in life, to stick like lacquer.
Then suddenly all at once you thought of home—
All day you longed for your kin, your regret without end.

Missing your kin, yet loving your wife—the two were hard to bear.
You gave up sleep, forgot to eat; bit by bit you grew ill.
My heart couldn't stand to see the grief of your heart—
So I urged my love to return once more to his former home.

Over and over I told you, as you left Gusu City—
"Don't listen to the song of spring in the brothel lanes.
As soon as you have seen your mother, turn back—
For you must recall the lonely one in her scented room."

So I earnestly entreated him, at the time of parting—
"Forsake the old or cherish the new—it is up to you while away."
Once he left, I never thought that he'd forget to return.
To long for you till end of day was worse for me than death.

Many came to tell me that you had married again;
Many times I was almost persuaded, but found it hard to believe.

Then I heard from Sun the Ninth, just returned from a trip:
(76) A newly married couple held Zhuo Wenjun in jest.

How I despised my love for such a fickle man!
Even over a thousand miles, our bonds should not be severed.
You obtained your wish, and then you betrayed all my love;
(80) Once you got what you had wanted, amorous feelings vanished.

Don't wonder at how great my grief then became—
Everywhere were trunks and sacks filled with my poems.
Letter-paper, brocade notes—five thousand sheets;
(84) I wore three hundred ink-brushes down to the nub.

In my jade chamber I grew thin—delicate and weak.
Our happy years now became a time for eternal longing.
In vain I cast the eight characters of my natal fate;
(88) Idly sought my destiny in a Changes hexagram.

The coins were thrown out of shape, my heart in flame within;
The mirror shattered to pieces, my grief was hard to bear.
I leant on tower balustrades, where my soul melted away;
(92) Tried to devise some plan to flee far off to where you were.

I recalled every event from the beginning, one by one:
How we joined in days past and I loved you in my folly.
How you, drunk or sober, were always at my side;
(96) Desire moved our loving hearts, you close beside my body.

At times you laughed and drew me within the silken curtains;
Gold hairpins and jade pendants then would shake and jingle.
Under the silken coverlet, after clouds and rain had ceased,
(100) Many whispered endearments would bring love's passion again.

And so time and again I would surrender my love to you—
Who'd have known that in a moment you'd leave me behind?
Since we are now poles apart, east and west,
(104) How much better if, from the start, we had never met?

On the Qingming Festival the rain fell everywhere;
I sighed by painted railings, for the flowers had no master;
The east wind vainly possessed a springtime of emerald peach;
(108) I trod on the last red petals—there was no one to talk to.

The cuckoo's cry will break the heart of an abandoned one;
I'm ashamed I've lost my virtue, all because of Master Zhou.
Then I'd hoped that we together might worship the moon,
But I was left—who'd have known?—to grieve alone at dusk.

Orioles and swallows, each formed their pairs;
Why did Heaven give no mate to me alone?
My little sister, Jiaofeng, two years younger than me,
Had a fine boy at home then, already two years old.

Amid chestnut and lotus scent a southern fragrance came;
In cold gardens alone I look—who here can speak of poetry?
In the end I forgot to put the blossoms in my hair;
The pendants have long since ceased to swing from the waist of my red skirt.

With the west wind falling leaves rustled and whispered;
So chill, I could not bear to climb the high tower.
Idly I took my painted zither and strummed it once or twice;
Who would fill my hair now with the chrysanthemum blooms?

Flying snow blew about, the cold made me tremble;
Lost in gloom, then I brooded, ailing by my pillow.
Under the curtain there was no one who would share my sleep;
There was wine in my cup, but no one to drink it with.

Those times I sometimes thought that I would tell Aunt Cao;
For after Master Zhou left, whom could I deceive?
Yet always still I forced myself to enjoy the seasons;
And she watched me solitary, my heart lonely and sad.

While I toyed with rouge and powder, my heart took no joy in it.
At the time of tea or meals I couldn't taste a thing.
Savory things I had no mood to bring to my mother's room;
How longer could I do my needlework at the window?

I'd surrendered my body to you, precious as gold;
But where now were the oaths and intentions of times past?
For this grievous fault you have made no recompense;
But right above you there are gods who will avenge.

You've gone south of the river, I remain to the north;
A thousand miles of mountains and passes keep us far apart.

If I could all at once sprout a pair of wings,
I'd fly off then to Wujiang, to be by your side.

But now even the sight of your face is impossible for me;
My soul, silent before, is now moved to laments and sighs.
In the underworld I will express my injustice;
To complain against the severing of our conjugal love.

When we first were joined, Heaven and Earth knew it well;
Now people without number tell of their disapproval . . .
[two lines are missing]

I resent it—that your crime will send me to my death!
It's just as if Heaven above had not given birth to me.
And now I send this letter for a former friend to read;
Don't bother to send any reply to the place where I dwell.

How sad that the family of a noble, armored general
Should raise in jade rooms such a girl, lovely as a flower!
Just because I well knew the love of books and music,
My amorous feelings will in a trice return me to the dust.

A long white silken sash will hang me from high rafters;
And drifting, lost in a sleep, my soul will then disperse.
As soon as it's reported that Jiaoluan has died,
The whole town will laugh to scorn the Lin'an Wangs.

Oh, how ashamed am I that I was not a good girl!
I dared to take too lightly the conduct of the women's chambers.
My debt of love is now paid—I return to the springs below;
Down below in those springs I still will not forgive you.

The way you loved me at first is not the way you now behave;
And the fury that I have for you is as deep as the sea.
I know that my intentions were kind, upright as well—
Not knowing that your heart was no different than a beast's.

So again I take a length of the finest silk
And send it sincerely far off to where you are.
Alas! That my rise and fall should be due to this!
Murder may be forgiven, but never the death of feeling.

Over and over I lament, but it still turns out the same;
This idle grieving of the past ends with today.
If you are still willing to remember our old love,
Read to the end this letter that your Jiaoluan sends you.

(MYSG, 27/ 9a–11b)

line 30: Meixiang is a standard name for a maid.

line 31: Zhou has written a love poem on her handkerchief and has sent it back to her.

line 37: One of the customs on Duanwu (the Double Fifth festival, a holiday of purification on the fifth day of the fifth month; see P.54a.16) was to weave mats out of rush and present them to friends.

line 44: Married persons bound up their hair.

line 47: The lovers burned the marriage oath so that the ashes could drift to Heaven, where the gods could testify to it.

lines 51–52: "Clouds and rain" are a euphemism for lovemaking; see P.9.2. "Moon and wind" verses are romantic poems.

line 58: "Like glue and lacquer" is a Chinese cliché for the closeness of lovers.

line 65: Gusu City is a poetic name for Suzhou, famous for beautiful women; it is only a few miles from Zhou's home in Wujiang.

line 76: Zhuo Wenjun was the wife of the Han dynasty writer Sima Xiangru. Xiangru was preparing to take in a girl from Maoling as a concubine, but his wife won him back with her poem "Bai tou yin" (Song of white hair.) See Liu Xin, *Xijing zaji*, 3/5b.

line 87: The specific time of one's birth may be defined by four sets of two characters each; in Chinese astrology, these eight characters are thought to determine a person's fate.

lines 88–89: Those consulting the *Book of Changes* often cast hexagrams through the throwing of coins; here the poet has cast so many hexagrams her coins were worn out.

line 105: The Qingming (Clear-Bright) festival occurs in late spring; it is an occasion for excursions to the countryside and for the sweeping of ancestral tombs. See Bodde, *Festivals in Classical China*, pp. 391–95.

line 111: A deity who lives on the moon is said to influence the fates of married couples.

line 113: In this and the following three stanzas the poet refers to the four seasons to describe her loneliness throughout the year.

lines 135–36: These two lines refer in passing to a daughter's duties: to serve her mother fine food and to keep up with her needlework.

line 168: "Those springs" are the Yellow Springs, the Chinese abode of the dead.

BIOGRAPHICAL NOTE AND TRANSLATION BY PAUL F. ROUZER

楊文儷

P.39. Yang Wenli (16th century)

Yang Wenli lived during the sixteenth century in Renhe (present-day Hangzhou). She was the daughter of Yang Yingxie, a vice director in the Ministry of Works, and the second wife of Duke Wenke, Sun Sheng, whose father was a vice censor-in-chief. Having been given the official title of Lady, she is also known as Lady Sun (and is listed under that name in the *Mingyuan shigui*). In addition to being considered a fine poet, she was renowned for the fact that her sons and grandsons all attained high office.

P.39.1. Playing the Zither by Moonlight

A small inner chamber, bright moon in the night,
I furl the curtains, tune the silk and wood.
Moon's white spirit glistens on a thousand doors,
Pure tones penetrate the courtyard.
Sinking clouds fly beneath my fingers,
Flowing streams cascade amidst the strings.
The tune stops, for a while I stand still, waiting;
(8) In the lofty sky, distant geese are crossing.

(MYSG, 27/3b)

P.39.2. Lotus-Picking Girl

On Ruoye Creek a girl picking lotus
At sunrise lightly plies her pole.
Jade fingers grip magnolia oars,
Gold hairpin clasps kingfisher feathers.
Her gossamer skirt could pass for leaves,
Her powdered face daintier than flowers.
Well she knows her way through the Creek,
(8) Her song carries under the painted bridge.

(MYSG, 27/4b)

line 2: This poem may be intended as an indirect description of Xi Shi (also known as Yiguang), the famous beauty of antiquity who was discovered washing silk on the banks of the Ruoye. See also C.36.1, note to par. 2, and Appendix A, "Zui Xi Shi."

P.39.3. Sent to My Son Ting

I think of you, away in the capital,
And spring blossoms twice have reddened.
You read your texts inside the vermilion palace,
And test your brush within the halls of jade.
Your talents are fine, your name should resound,
Though lowly your post, your way is unbounded.
For a hundred years you must drive yourself on,
For pure and clean are our family's ancient ways.

(MYSG, 27/4a–b)

P.39.4. Moon over Mountains and Passes

Over the Han capital, tonight's moon
For ten thousand miles shines upon mountains and passes.
Autumn leaves, one still sees them falling,
The man on the march has yet to return.
Cold light congeals on his thick armor,
A solitary shadow faces her sorrowful self.
Those in high halls feasting in merriment
Have not yet stilled their pipes and songs.

(MYSG, 27/4a)

P.39.5. On an Autumn Day, the Weather Having Just Cleared

Swish, swish, a cool gust comes,
Last night's rain's just passed.
Clouds break up, brightening a sky of jade,
The sun comes out, rippling a river with gold.
In the trees, calling cicadas scatter,
Across the sky, passing geese are many.
Heaven and Earth soothe my distant gaze,
Autumn colors merit intoning and chanting.

(MYSG, 27/4a)

P.39.6. To Be Shown to My Son Jun

Again it's the season of clear, mild weather
When plums turn yellow, days of drizzling rain.
People strive to make the most of the flowing time,
You must be bent on study, nothing else.
Fine talents are specially hard to rely on,
Empty fame is also gained in vain.
When able to fulfill his vow inscribed upon the bridge-post—
(8) Only then was Master Sima deemed a worthy man.

(MYSG, 27/4b)

lines 7–8: A few miles north of Chengdu on the road to Chang'an, there was a bridge nicknamed "The Immortals' Ascent" (*Sheng xian qiao*). As a poor youth setting out for the capital, the Han-dynasty poet Sima Xiangru is said to have inscribed on one of its pillars: "Unless in a red carriage drawn by a team of four horses, I shall not cross this bridge again." Use of such a carriage was, of course, the exclusive privilege of high officials.

P.39.7. On a Winter's Day, My Son Jun Travels North to Take the Examinations

Young and unused to going to other places,
From here in a skiff you'll sail a thousand miles.
On your long journey, at times you must comfort the pages and
servants,
In bitter cold, always wear thick clothes and furs.
Leaning at the gate in days to come, I'll gaze into the distance;
Loosening the mooring ties this morning, you must not linger.
For now in Radiant Palace you can present your rhapsodies,
(8) As the Son of Heaven in this age of peace
Nods the jade pendants on his cap.

(MYSG, 27/5a)

P.39.8. Thinking of My Three Sons, Long, Ting, and Jun, in the Capital, Matching Your Rhymes

Ill, in temporary lodgings, I hesitate, wavering;
Bit by bit the flow of time presses another year's end.
From the edge of sky, a double-fish letter is nowhere seen;

Beside the sun, just how are those three phoenixes of mine?
In literary gardens, Sima Xiangru polished his rhapsodies;
At the Han palace gate, Gongsun Hong waited to present his memorials.
But now at court there is many a "capped bandit"—
(8) As I lean against the door, how to find relief for my worried heart?

(MYSG, 27/5b)

line 6: Gongsun Hong, the marquis of Pingjin and chancellor for the Han emperor Jing, was proverbial for his frugality. More relevant to the present context is the fact that both Sima and Gongsun rose rapidly to high office through the personal patronage of the sovereign.

P.39.9. *Random Jottings Facing the Rain*

Overnight rain pounds and patters, summer heat abates,
Garden flowers thoroughly drenched, doubly plush and fragrant.
Peaches and plums in my garden of old—what are they like now?
My gaze fixed on clouds over the river, alone I lean against the door.

(MYSG, 27/5b–6a)

P.39.10. *Upon Hearing of the Arrival of the Recruited Wa Family Troops*

The Wa family is famed for extraordinary bravery—
Recruited from ten thousand miles away to purge the bandits.
How many able officers are stationed on the sea coast!
Yet for merits to record they rely on a woman general.

(MYSG, 27/6a; Su Zhecong, 305–6)

The Wa family troops were recruited from the Zhuang minority in Guangxi to help guard against the Japanese pirates that plagued the southeastern coast of China during the poet's time.

P.39.11. *New Year's Eve*

Spring has just come, the year's about to end,
Lanterns and fireworks smoke up the sky; this night's not so cold.
Aware that tomorrow my age will turn,
With joy all night I'll requite the change of seasons.
Seats arranged in the painted hall, gold and jade plates set,

Scent of burning musk and orchid wafts from precious tripods.
A chance is won to appreciate spring in advance:
(8) Plum blossoms fill my sight as I gaze at them, all smiles.

(MYSG, 27/4b)

P.39.12. Hearing Wild Geese

Carrying the moonlight, cutting through clouds, passing too at night—
Loud and clear, several sounds, nearing the Milky Way.
The river's source ten thousand miles afar—how far a way to come!
Passes and barriers a thousand-fold and more you have crossed.
A single letter carried once, returning to the imperial garden;
Then, still, trailing autumn shadows into the chilly ripples.
Travelers at the sky's edge feel sad indeed to hear you,
(8) Calling up their homeward hearts—what ever can they do?

(MYSG, 27/5a)

line 5: On wild geese carrying a letter, see P.2.1 (Song 5).

P.39.13. Remembering the Past at the City of Yue

Desolate state beside the sea, regrets of a thousand years
Surging on and on, all given over to waters flowing east.
Where is he now, the Hegemon of Yue, meant to rule a thousand years?
In one battle Wu was swallowed—the event is now just emptiness.
Delicate willows begin to sway, as yellow orioles twitter,
Deserted terraces still remain, shrouded in green mist.
Now there is only the moon above Mount Ji,
(8) Once scattering golden rays all over ancient palaces.

(MYSG, 27/5a–b)

P.39.14. Thinking of My Family on an Autumn Day

Wet is the jade dew that borders the flowers,
Cool the metallic breeze that penetrates the curtain.
Emerald green the autumn waters stretching to the sky,
Hazy blue the evening mist that winds around the mountains.
I ponder the scene, sigh at the season's changes,

Think of my family, recall my native place.
Leaning on the balustrade, I stand for a long while fixed,
(8) My heart chasing wild geese that soar towards the south.

(MYSG, 27/3a–b)

line 2: Metal is associated with autumn.

P.39.15. Skies Clearing After Snow

Through the night snow fell heavily,
Grayish clouds blurring distant skies.
Dawn comes and I watch the clearing scene,
Splendor sparkles against the curtains and lattice.
Over pure white isles fly wild geese in the cold,
A jasper picture from a skillful painter's hand.
When the bright moon rises over eastern mountains
(8) I stand, it seems, within a vessel of jade.

(MYSG, 27/4a)

BIOGRAPHICAL NOTE AND TRANSLATION BY NANCY J. HODES AND TUNG YUAN-FANG

P.40. Kuaiji nüzi (16th century)

Nothing is known about this "Woman from Kuaiji" aside from what can be gleaned from the short preface she left to her three extant poems, found inscribed on a wall of a government hostel. She had been acquired as a concubine by a northerner and, by the time she wrote her poems, had been taken from her native Kuaiji to the northeast. Her words, though brief, convey vividly enough the essential circumstances of her life.

P.40.1. Poems Written on the Wall of New Blessings Station

PREFACE

I was born and raised in Kuaiji, and in my youth I studied the Classics and Histories. When I came of age, I was married to a northerner. I grieve that my "Bamboo Grove manner" now serves "a general whose belly has betrayed him." To make matters worse, the lioness of Hedong roars several times each day. Today, when I went to tell him of my plight, she confronted me in anger. The blows of her whip rained down on me, abusing me as if I were a servant. Feelings of anger and bitterness filled my breast, and I found it nearly impossible to stand up again. How awful! I am a person caught in a cage. What would there be to regret about my dying? Yet I fear that if I gave my body to the grasses and weeds, I would vanish and be forgotten. That is why I have chosen to forgo death a little while.

Tonight, having waited until the other concubines were sound asleep, I stole out to the rear courtyard. Using tears to moisten the inkstone, I have inscribed three quatrains on the wall and given this account of their origin. If persons of understanding read them as they pass by, they will grieve for my untimely life. Then, although I die, I shall not be forgotten.

I

My pink gown is half covered with dirt,
A single lamp is my only companion.
I resemble pear blossoms after a rainstorm,
Pitifully fallen, spring of the past.

II

My days are spent in the company of tigers and wildcats,
I sit silently, not showing my bitterness that knows no end.
Heaven had its reasons for giving me this life—
To make me an entertaining topic of conversation!

III

Ten thousand sorrows, but whom can I tell?
Facing others I force a smile, behind them I grieve.
Don't think these poems are just the ordinary kind,
Each line is a thousand tears shed.

(MYSG, 28/12b–13b)

preface: The text of this preface is taken from LR, p. 741. An abbreviated and textually inferior version of the preface is contained in MYSG, 28/12b–13b, which, however, supplies the text of the poems.

par. 1: For the meaning of "Bamboo Grove manner," see C.24.1. The Song dynasty general Dang Jin, after boasting to his attendants that he had never betrayed his stomach (i.e., his appetite), was told that his stomach (i.e., the seat of intelligence) had betrayed him by not producing any worthwhile plans or stratagems. See Morohashi, *Dai kanwa jiten*, 9: 350 (no. 29722:74), who cites Li Tao, *Xu zizhi tongjian changbian*, as the source. "Lioness of Hedong" is a set phrase for a wife who is jealous of her husband's concubines; it derives from a poem by Su Shi, "Ji Wu Deren jian jian Chen Jichang," *Su Shi shiji* 25/1341.

par. 2: The original text reads "two quatrains," presumably a misprint.

BIOGRAPHICAL NOTE AND TRANSLATION BY RONALD EGAN

端淑卿

P.41. Duan Shuqing (CA. 1510–CA. 1600?)

Duan Shuqing was from an important office-holding family of Dangtu in Anhui. She flourished throughout the Jiajing reign period (1522–67). She learned to read from her father, Duan Tingbi, a Confucian schoolmaster who apparently served some branch of the imperial family. Accompanying him on his official duties, she was exposed to such texts as the *Book of Odes*, *Nü fan* (Instructions for women), and *Lienü zhuan* (Biographies of virtuous women), from which she went on to read more broadly. Her husband, Rui Ru, a native of Danhu in Jiangsu, was also a Confucian scholar. Duan Shuqing was a writer of *shi* and *ci*, some of which survive in a collection entitled *Lü chuang shi gao* (Drafts of poetry from the green gauze window). Her poems are said to have followed Tang models. At her death she was past ninety years of age.[1]

P.41.1. Random Composition

Leaves fall, the face of autumn tranquil;
Orioles call, who can stand to hear?
Letters so late in arriving!
Feelings I cannot bear to speak.
Open lattice—the sun angles past;
Broken mountains—clouds whirl by.
Bright flowers fear the wind and rain;
(8) Paulownia leaves chaotically fall.

(MYSG, 30/6b)

P.41.2. Sui Willow

Emperor Yang's willow on the embankment—
Withered by how many autumns?
Cicadas call in despair for the lost nation;
Orioles cry laments by the tomb mounds.
Where are the foundations of the Traveling Lodge?
Water in the deserted river flows on its own.
Traveler, do not break all the willow twigs:
(8) Breaking them all arouses more sadness.

(MYSG, 30/6b–7a)

lines 1–2: "Emperor Yang's willow" refers to the well-known "Parting Poem" sometimes attributed to Yang Guang, Emperor Yang of the Sui dynasty (r. 605–17): "Green, green the willows, brushing the ground / Wild, wild the catkins, roiling in the air / Willow twigs have all been broken, catkins have all flown / I ask the traveler, will he return?" The text is listed among anonymous Sui "Miscellaneous tunes and song-lyrics" in Lu Qinli, ed., *Xian Qin Han Wei Jin Nanbeichao shi*, p. 2753. The "embankment" mentioned is probably a reference to the Grand Canal, completed during Emperor Yang's reign.

line 5: The "Traveling Lodge" refers to one of the elaborate palaces built for Emperor Yang's travels around the country.

P.41.3. Taibai Tower

Amid the clouds, the tower of an earthbound immortal,
In loneliness looking down at the river islands.
Spirit that presses low two mountain peaks;
Clarity that pervades a running stream.
A brocade robe still shines and glitters;
The bright moon continues to dip and float.
Never-ending is the gentleman's plaint—
(8) Year after year it moves travelers to sadness.

(MYSG, 30/7a–b)

Taibai Tower, dedicated to the memory of the Tang poet Li Bai (701–62), was at Caishi ji below Ma'an Mountain in Dangtu, Anhui, at the place where, according to legend, the poet died. The third couplet of this poem is an allusion to the supposed circumstances of Li Bo's death: drowned while attempting to catch the moon's reflection in the water.

P.41.4. Chrysanthemum

Hoarded for holiday wine,
Yellow chrysanthemum grows next to the low wall.
Sadly lacking in competitive bright color,
But now and then giving off extraordinary fragrance.
When soil is deep the flowers bloom in profusion;
When fences are sparse butterflies are not obstructed.
Move it here next to the railing:
(8) Together we will conquer the fifth-watch frost.

(MYSG, 30/7b)

line 2: This poem combines a number of motifs associated with the Double Ninth festival; see P.11.4.

P.41.5. Autumn Night

The single cry of a goose after frost:
Troubles on my mind—so many still remain.
A cool moon now and then peeks in the window;
A hard wind incessantly bangs on the door.
My dream travels to my distant homeland;
My heart pursues the running clouds and water.
Alas, the washing-blocks are pounding fast—
(8) Layered clothes collect the tracks of tears.

(MYSG, 30/7b)

lines 7–8: On the motif of the clothes-beaters, see P.4.3.

P.41.6. Hearing the Rain

Autumn rain spatters the withered leaves,
Chilling vain butterfly dreams.
Sorrow over the old garden has not abated;
The grief of the wayfarer is hard to overcome.
Sleepless, I am alarmed by wind bells on the eaves;
Concerned at heart, I think of the border geese.
When sorrow is great, the water clock is never-ending:
(8) Matters of the heart, amid the sound of rain.

(MYSG, 30/8a)

line 2: An allusion to the story of Zhuang Zhou's dream that he was a butterfly; on awakening he could not be sure if he was Zhuang Zhou who had dreamt he was a butterfly or a butterfly who was dreaming he was Zhuang Zhou (*Zhuangzi*, chap. 2).

P.41.7. Spring

Second month: orioles call beyond the courtyard.
Sunlight on the mirror stand shines on the blinds and window.
Moisture returns to wild grass—downy growth of green;
Warmth enters jade branches—clustered blooms in red.
First trying on of light silk, wet by festival rain;
From time to time sampling the new vintage, drunk in the east wind.
At leisure I come to examine matters of the blooming season:
(8) On dark strands beneath the flowers, little spiders descend.

(MYSG, 30/8a)

P.41.8. Spring Night

In the remains of night a sliver moon rises above the tranquil garden.
Silently taking in the clear light, I'm not sound in my sleep.
The cuckoo's cry despairing—breaking a butterfly dream;
Mandarin ducks' water warm—protecting the sandy islet.
Groundless spring regrets lengthen with the season;
Limitless indolent sadness waits for wine to awaken.
Morning comes: I casually stroke an old pine and watch—
(8) Enduring the sight of garden forms all green.

(MYSG, 30/8b)

line 3: On the cuckoo or nightjar, see P.5.1.

P.41.9. Hearing Geese on an Autumn Day

Northern geese fly to the south—for what do they hurry?
The sound carries to red mansions, tears wet my robe.
In sadness I take up the green wine by the autumn chrysanthemums,
And bear to face the red maple covered in evening frost.
Layered mist and layered clouds obscure the road I traveled;
Driving wind and driving rain pursued me to unfamiliar lands.
Where is home to one a thousand miles away?
(8) My heart is set on returning home—hopelessly I grieve.

(MYSG, 30/9a)

P.41.10. *Writing My Feelings*

Dew cold on the high terrace, geese come late.
Flowers yellow in late autumn, waiting for whom?
In my sadness I write letters, but something catches my eye;
In my sickness I see chrysanthemums, which in turn engender sadness.
When boiling water bubbles, pound tea in the mortar;
When grapes ferment, send round the wine cups.
I wish to release what's in my breast, but the wind is so lonely:
(8) Trim the lamp and sit alone—not a time for speech.

(MYSG, 30/9b)

P.41.11. *Thinking of My Niece*

A river reaching the sky in the distance;
Sadness great, both temples mottled in gray.
In dreams my soul knows no danger:
In wind and rain it crosses streams and mountains.

(MYSG, 30/10a)

P.41.12. *Mooring on an Autumn Night at Dan Lake*

Autumn waters vast and vague, belted by white duckgrass;
Fishing boats and crab nets crowd the lakeshore.
The great sky comes to twilight, mist and clouds rise;
I hear the sound of song, but see no one.

(MYSG, 30/10a)

Dan Lake is Danyang hu, also known as Nanhu, located on the border between Dangtu in Anhui and Gaochun in Jiangsu.

P.41.13. *Plum Tree*

A tree of plum flowers, its adornment light and even;
The sparse branches carry the moon and befriend a sad woman.
Don't play the nomad flute facing the clear night,
For I fear the cold blossoms cannot bear the spring!

(MYSG, 30/10b)

lines 3–4: This couplet is an allusion to the Han and Six Dynasties *yuefu* title "Meihua luo" (The falling plum blossoms). According to its classification in the *Yuefu shi ji*, it must have been a tune for the flute.

P.41.14. Cassia Tea

In dreams on my couch I cross the clear night—
Meandering on the Starry River, walking the Magpie Bridge.
Entering the cold Palace of the Moon, flowers everywhere!
Tea steeps on the bamboo brazier, cassia fragrance drifts.

(MYSG, 30/11a)

line 2: A reference to the Double Seventh festival; see P.5.1.

P.41.15. Chamber Lyrics

I

Late makeup just complete, jade hairpin askew;
Five-colored flames dim on low candle stands.
In dreams entering the imperial capital—my heart almost broken!
I cannot bear it when wind and rain join the washing-block sounds.

II

Layered gates locked tight, growing green moss;
Petal upon petal of drifting flowers drop on the mirror stand.
In sadness not knowing that spring has already gone:
Swallows that flew away before mid-spring have now all returned.

(MYSG, 30/11b–12a)

BIOGRAPHICAL NOTE BY ELLEN WIDMER AND CHARLES H. EGAN;
TRANSLATION BY CHARLES H. EGAN

P.42. Dong Shaoyu (fl. 1545)

Dong Shaoyu was a Ming-dynasty gentry woman from Xiling in Hubei province. She married Zhou Hongyue (style name Yuanfu), of Macheng county in Hubei, after his first wife died. Zhou Hongyue was so outspoken and direct that he twice offended the emperor with his frank criticisms, and was demoted and transferred or exiled as a result. Dong Shaoyu was known for loyally following her husband in exile, no matter how great the hardships they suffered. However, she had a weak constitution, and while in a fairly remote area of Zhejiang province she took ill and died at the young age of twenty-eight. Her husband published one volume of her poetry, which was widely praised for its distinctive style and its combination of strong feeling and moral sentiments.[1]

P.42.1. On the Border in Late Spring, Thinking of Home

New grass fills the long embankment;
With thoughts of home, I linger to watch the moon.
Dew-drenched peach blossoms are as if deeply drunk with wine;
Haze-filled willows are like lightly painted eyebrows.
Autumn in the borderlands: you cannot shut it out;
Springtime on the river: the oars are easily moved.
I am just like the bird of the south,
(8) Night by night recalling its southern perch.

(Su Zhecong, 307)

P.42.2. Cutting Out a Shirt

North of Hibiscus River the swallows fly and fly;
Here beside Swallow Cliff, my beloved has not returned.
I only fear Master Shen out there is already thin;
So I hesitate to send him last year's size.

(Su Zhecong, 308)

lines 3–4: Shen Yue (441–513) served in a variety of official posts, but so often complained of his weariness, his ill health, and his preference for Daoist-style retirement that he was canonized as the "hermit marquis." A painstaking stylist, Shen reportedly worked so hard on his poetry that "his waist grew thin."

P.42.3. Two Verses on Seeing You Off [first verse only]

Amidst the last flurry of poplar blossoms we said goodbye,
We share a mutual gaze but are not free.
A traveler gazes at the distant border;
A young wife leans on the rail of her bare balcony.
Colors of spring are easy to change;
Sad sounds of the horn are difficult to bear.
On the river that has no feelings
(8) Parting boats are borne day by day.

(Su Zhecong, 308)

P.42.4. Recalling Our Parting

I

I recall our parting at the willows by the bridge;
Amidst the green I watched your horse trot away.
I longingly play the flute the Qiang tribes use,
Not a day passes that I don't think of Liaoxi.

II

Flowers will soon bloom on the courier road;
At our parting pavilion, willows are now bent with growth.
I lean on the balcony rail with nothing to do,
Day after day counting when you'll return.

(Su Zhecong, 308)

i, line 4: Liaoxi is in Hebei province, the dwelling place of the person addressed here.

P.42.5. Writing My Husband in Kelan [Shanxi]

Still stuck out there on the frontier,
Scabbard hung by your horse's head.
Don't think too much of the willow's beauty,
Just go for high rank!

(Zhou Shouchang, *Gonggui wenxuan*, 22/5a)

BIOGRAPHICAL NOTE AND TRANSLATION BY PAUL S. ROPP

許景樊

P.43. Hŏ Kyŏngbŏn (Xu Jingfan, 1563–89)

Hŏ Kyŏngbŏn (Mandarin: Xu Jingfan) is now considered Korea's leading female poet. Commonly known in Korean as Hŏ Nansŏrhŏn (from her studio name; in Mandarin, Xu Lanxue xuan or "Xu of Orchid Snow Studio"), she had the given name Ch'ohŭi (Mandarin: Chuji) and the style name Kyŏngbŏndang (Jingfan tang). She was from a well-known and highly educated family. She was particularly close to her younger brother Hŏ Kyun (Xu Yun, 1569–1618), the author of Korea's earliest vernacular work of fiction, *The Tale of Hong Kiltong*. It is commonly assumed that she learned to read and write Chinese and Korean from her brothers, all three of whom had outstanding talent. She was married to a man surnamed Kim, but it was not a happy marriage. Her mother-in-law was uncomfortable at the thought that her son was less talented than his wife. In addition, Hŏ lost more than one child. These troubles, along with the political turmoil that brought adversity to her brothers, led her to pour her energies into poetry. Hŏ's husband died during the Hideyoshi invasion of Korea in 1592.

Though she had burned most of her work before she died, in 1607 her younger brother edited what remained of her Chinese poems and presented them to the Chinese ambassador to Korea, Zhu Zhifan. Zhu subsequently published them in China, where they created a sensation, attracting the attention of the great dramatist Tang Xianzu, among others. However, Liu Rushi (P.67) later questioned Hŏ's originality in the *Liechao shiji* (see C.14.4).[1] Subsequently, Hŏ's poems were published in Japan (an edition of 1711 survives) to favorable notice. Her younger brother was executed for treason in 1618, and her poetry was not circulated in Korea until late in the seventeenth century, when an edition was published in Pusan.[2] Hŏ is also celebrated for her poems in Korean, among them the *kasa* entitled "A Woman's Sorrow."[3]

P.43.1. Song of Longing for an Immortal

The immortal Wang Qiao summons me to travel:
He waits for me at Mount Kunlun.
In the morning we climb Xuanpu peak
And look at Purple Cloud Dwelling in the distance.

How brilliant Purple Cloud Dwelling is!
Its jade beaches are truly boundless.
He suddenly rides the Milky Way—
Turns, and flies toward the mulberry tree at the end of the world.

This mulberry is a thousand miles to the east,
The wind and waves are immense.
I want to take off from this world and go away,
Yet how can I forget my wedding date back on earth?

And you, my beloved, what are you thinking?
As for me, I feel nothing but pain.

(MYSG, 29/1a)

lines 1–8: The dwelling of the immortals is on Mount Kunlun. Wang Qiao (or Wangzi Qiao), the son of King Ling of the Zhou, loved to play the *sheng* (bamboo mouth-organ) in imitation of the phoenix's call. He encountered a Daoist, Fuqiu Gong, and spent more than thirty years with him on top of Mount Song. He then summoned his family to the mountain for the seventh day of the seventh month. They saw him riding over the mountain on a white crane; then he raised his hand and flew away (Liu Xiang, *Lie xian zhuan*, 1/23–24).

P.43.2. *Separating Long Ago*

Rumble, rumble go the two cart wheels,
In one day they turn ten thousand times.
Our hearts are together, but we're not in the same cart.
After we separated, the seasons of our hearts kept on changing.
Your cart left tracks that can still be traced,
But no matter how much I think of you, I just cannot see you.

(MYSG, 29/1b)

P.43.3. *Song of Youth*

The young man commits himself to his pledges,
Befriending many a knight errant.
At his waist was a white windlass;
On his silver robe a pair of unicorns.

He departed in the morning from the Mingguang palace,
He hurried his horse to Changle hill.
He bought some Weicheng wine;
Amidst flowers, he passed a full day.

The young gentleman spent the night at a brothel,
Enjoying pleasures, debating where to linger.
Does anyone pity Yang Ziyun
Who closed his door to write the *Taixuan jing*?

(MYSG, 29/2a)

lines 5–6: These sites are parts of the Han imperial Northern Palace complex.
line 12: A philosophical book modeled on the *Book of Changes*, the *Taixuan jing*, composed by the Han-dynasty poet and essayist Yang Xiong (style name Ziyun), was often said to be impenetrably obscure. (For a complete translation, see Nylan, *The Canon of Supreme Mystery*.) Owing to its difficulty, the text also connotes reclusiveness.

P.43.4. *Mountain Mist*

The evening rain invades the river, the dawn begins to break,
The morning sun dyes the mist, turning it green.
The warp of clouds and the woof of fog create a rich brocade.
One recognizes the fall scenery of the Xiao and Xiang Rivers.

The mountain mist changes with the wind, as a beautiful woman
 might change her moods.
The mountains are slender eyebrows arching like moth antennae.
Suddenly the mist scatters and the rain falls hard:
Behold the green mountain, emerging as if newly bathed.

(MYSG, 29/2b)

P.43.5. *Song of the Fisherwomen*

I married a seaman who rides the tide.
In fantasy, I follow him along the banks of the river.
The north wind, the south wind blow the wind sock.
Boats up the river, down the river rowing in unison.

Splashing like peach blossoms, tall waves reach the sky,
The obscure sails of returning boats disappear in the evening sun.
I shall not wait on the beach to observe the weather.
If the joyful moment of his return doesn't arrive, grief will
 overcome me.

(MYSG, 29/2a–b)

P.43.6. *To a Female Friend*

I built a house near Bai ford.
By day I see the great river flow.
The *luan* bird on my mirror case is almost old.
The butterflies in my garden find it's already fall.

In the cold mountain, the wild geese have just arrived.
In the evening rain, I go home alone by boat.
I keep my silk curtains closed all evening:
How can I bear to remember my travels with my old friend?

(MYSG, 29/4b)

P.43.7. After the Rhymes of My Brother Kyun [Yun]

At Kasan to the east you look out on lush and rugged mountain scenery.
A banished official chanting sadly, what's on your mind?
A lone goose bears the pain of separation from her beloved across the Milky Way.
Yet the north wind swirls around the great river waves.
As the dawn bugle sounds over the elms at the pass, your military clothes are too thin.
The roads at the frontier startle your heart; there, falling leaves abound.
A silver candle stands in your military tent by night,
(8) As your dream of homecoming wanders by.

(MYSG, 29/6b–7a)

P.43.8. Song of Meeting You

We met below the pleasure house.
You tied your horse by the willow at the front door.
Laughingly I took off my brocade and mink fur.
We reached for the Xinfeng wine.

(MYSG, 29/7a)

P.43.9. [Untitled]

A *wutong* tree grew at Yiyang;
Then they chopped it down and made it into a *qin*.
This *qin* is played to repeated sighs,
But there's no friend with whom I can feel in tune.

P.43.10. [Untitled]

I have a bolt of silk,
I give it today to my beloved.
I don't mind if it becomes a pair of trousers for you,
But please don't make it into clothes for someone else.

P.43.11. [Untitled]

Fine gold shines like moonlight,
I give it to you to make belt ornaments.
Don't worry about losing them by the roadside,
But don't let them be tied to a new lover's belt.

(P.43.9–11: MYSG, 29/7a–b)

P.43.12. A Pledge to Ch'oe Kukpo

I have a golden hairpin,
A head ornament that's been mine since I married.
Now I give it to you as you leave:
Think of me when you are a thousand miles away.

(MYSG, 29/7b)

P.43.13. Boudoir Feelings

Swallows brush against the setting sun, flying in pairs.
Flowers fall sparsely on my silken clothes.
In my nuptial boudoir I am beset by spring laments:
The grass is green in Jiangnan, but my beloved has not yet returned.

(MYSG, 29/9b)

P.43.14. Autumn Regrets

The crimson gauze reflects the color of the evening lamplight in the distance.
Awakened from a dream I find my silk coverlet is half empty.
In the cold frost the parrot talks to himself in his jade cage,
The whole staircase is covered by *wutong* leaves, blown by the west wind.

(MYSG, 29/10a)

P.43.15. Crying for My Children

Last year I buried my beloved daughter.
This year I buried my beloved son.
Mournful is the earth at Guangling
Where their paired graves face one another.

The white poplars sough in the wind,
Will-o-the-wisps illuminate the evergreens.
With paper money I summon your souls,
With "dark wine" I venerate your grave mounds.

Your sibling spirits
Must play together every evening.
Even if I were to conceive other children,
How could I count on their living to adulthood?

As I chant "The Song of the Yellow Terrace"
I shed tears of blood, but stifle my mournful sounds.

(*Lanxue xuan shi* [*Nansŏrhŏn si*], 2a)

The source for this poem is the Harvard-Yenching library's copy of *Nansŏrhŏn si*, colophon dated 1608.

line 8: In ancient times, water was used as an offering to the dead and in such cases was called "dark wine."

line 13: A reference to the "Song of the Yellow Terrace Melons," composed by the Tang prince Xian (sixth son of Emperor Gaozong). After Prince Hong was assassinated by Empress Wu, Prince Xian was made crown prince. Concerned that he might suffer the same fate, he composed the song, which reads in part: "I planted melons beneath the Yellow Terrace; / When they ripened, they were luxuriant. / Pick one and there are still many left, / Pick two and they start to thin out" (*QTS*, 6/65). Prince Xian was eventually banished by Empress Wu and died on his way to Qian (modern Guizhou province).

BIOGRAPHICAL NOTE AND TRANSLATION BY ELLEN WIDMER

P.44. Yi Sugwŏn (Li Shuyuan; late 16th century)

Yi Sugwŏn (Mandarin: Li Shuyuan) is commonly known in Korea by her studio name Yi Okpong (Li Yufeng). She was the child by a concubine of the celebrated poet Yi Tal (Li Da) and became the concubine of Cho Wŏn (Zhao Yuan), a scholar and an official who passed the *jinshi* examination in 1564 and who may have died during the Hideyoshi invasion of 1592. Yi's poems have been passed down to us as an appendix to her husband's published collected writings; if a collection of her poetry was published as a separate volume, it does not survive. Thirty-two of Yi's works were salvaged and republished by her husband's grandson in 1684. After Hŏ Kyŏngbŏn, Yi is the best-known Korean woman of the early and middle Chosŏn dynasty. She became known to Chinese readers through the inclusion of a selection of her poems in *Mingyuan shigui*.[1]

P.44.1. Regrets of the Mottled Bamboo

As the two concubines long ago mourned Emperor Shun's death,
They rushed south to the Xiang River region.
Their tears splashed the Xiang bamboo:
From that moment on Xiang bamboo has been mottled.
Clouds cover his shrine at Nine Doubts Mountain.
The sun sets at Cangwu.
What remains of their grief is entrusted to the river water
(8) Which moves endlessly and will never return.

(MYSG, 30/1a)

line 1: On Shun and his two wives, see P.1.2 and P.37.1.
line 6: Cangwu, where Shun died, is a deserted area near Nine Doubts Mountain (see P.37.1).

P.44.2. Song of Lotus Picking

At South Lake the girl picks lotuses.
Every day she returns to South Lake.
The shallow sandbars are full of water caltrop
But in the deeper pools, lotus leaves are few.

She rows her boat in a frail and charming way.
Drops of water splash her silk clothes.
She churns the oars, her thoughts are distant,
(8) Eager to see the mandarin ducks fly.

(MYSG, 30/1a)

P.44.3. Separating Long Ago

When the girl in the western house was fifteen years old,
She laughed at her eastern neighbor for grieving over separation.
Little did she know she would now be suffering so much pain,
Her black hair tossed and twisted all night long.

Her beloved has no intention of tying his horse;
Expectations of high position fill his mind.
A young man has plenty of time to establish his name,
(8) A young woman's potential passes more quickly.
Stifling her sobs, she dares not express the pain of farewell,
Covering her face to cry, she regrets they met so late.
Hearing that he has already reached Kangcheng county,
(12) She holds her *qin* and, alone, faces the shores of Jiangnan, singing:

"I'm sorry I can't be like the river goose
Who can follow you to remote places, wings fluttering.
I have abandoned the makeup table and the mirror,
(16) I no longer sway in my light spring clothes.
My soul dreams of being far away but it can't find the road.
In life what good does it do to dwell on grieving thoughts?"

(MYSG, 30/1b)

P.44.4. *In Praise of Swallows*

Deep in the painted house, the blue screen drooping,
Pairs of swallows fly back and forth, then perch at their nests.
Great poplars line the doors and lanes, the east wind arrives late in the day.
Green grass and ponds are indistinct in the fine rain.
Chasing butterflies, how many times do the swallows enter the garden?
Building their nests they peck at sticks and mud all day long.
Thus do they build a safe and convenient home
(8) In which to bring up their fledglings year after year.

(MYSG, 30/3b)

P.44.5. *Double Seventh Evening*

The stars meet yearly, what is there to be sad about?
Not like in the human world where parting looms so large.
In heaven it's no more than a morning and a night;
For humans the separation lasts a year.

(MYSG, 30/3a)

BIOGRAPHICAL NOTE AND TRANSLATION BY ELLEN WIDMER

薄少君

P.45. Bo Shaojun (d. 1625)

Bo Shaojun was the wife of Shen Cheng, a talented and unconventional scholar of the late Ming from Loudong (modern Taicang county in Jiangsu province).[1] Shen Cheng was known to people close to him as a man who loved to laugh and to read unusual books, an accomplished writer of poetry and prose, and a man who was endowed with such a stubborn and upright character that he could not mix well with ordinary people. Dedicated to his study for the civil service examinations, he was unable to make a decent living for his family. Unfortunately, he was not destined to succeed in the examinations and died late in the year 1624 at the age of about thirty. Exactly one year after Shen Cheng's death, Bo Shaojun was so overcome by grief that she starved herself to death. They had been married for twelve years and had a daughter and a son—the latter was born after Shen Cheng's death and was raised after Bo Shaojun's own death by Zhang Pu, a scholar of some prominence from the region who knew them well.

A cultivated person herself, Bo Shaojun was said always to have supported her husband's scholarly pursuits and to have shared his enjoyment in discussing the art of poetry and Buddhist texts as well as in writing poems together. After Shen Cheng died, Bo Shaojun reportedly wrote one hundred poems in the seven-character-line quatrain (*qiyan jueju*) form under the general title of *Daowang shi* (Mourning for the dead). When several close friends of Shen Cheng obtained Bo Shaojun's manuscript, three quatrains had already been lost.[2] They then selected eighty-one poems out of the remaining ninety-seven and published them, together with Shen Cheng's collected works. The sequence was later included in the anthology *Mingyuan shigui*.[3]

In the first quatrain of "Mourning for the Dead," Bo Shaojun says that she would not weep plaintively for her husband but, instead, would sing with metal clappers (i.e., like a marketplace performer) of the brevity of life. "Mourning for the Dead" is thus the work of a tough woman, determined to show no self-pity about her fate in losing a husband so early in her life. According to Zhang Sanguang, who helped compile the poems, they evoke, for the most part, Shen Cheng's subtlety of mind, unyielding character, indifference to fame and wealth, and extraordinary literary talent. They also seem to show some resentment at Shen Cheng's somewhat impractical devotion to the system of civil service examinations, which had brought him poverty and untimely death rather than glory and wealth. Considered stylistically, the poems are characterized by a forceful rhythm, a sense of spontaneous execution, and a plain and straightforward diction. They can be regarded as examples of good poetry that comes directly from a poet's *xingling* or "native sensibility" rather than from the imitation of the works of previous masters.

P.45.1. Quatrains from "Mourning for the Dead"

5

Common pulse for food, clothes of abaca: the breath of your life was always thin;
Old Heaven needn't have laid murderous hands on you.
Although he's robbed you of years as a man of letters,
Can he steal even half of one of your written lines?

18

At the end of a man's days, cheap and hollow fame—
Looking back at your whole life, what else did you achieve?
Left behind—an eighty-year-old father, his white hair wild,
Tears dried up in his old eyes, unable to utter a cry.

27

Through seven battles in Jinling, your morale never flagged—
Alas! this brave hero gave his life at the scholar's cold window.
Glory at the civil service exams lured you to this end;
I want to kick over the Gold Mountain, let the Great River flow dry!

31

The yellow crane has gone afar, never to return—
Our son wailed, our daughter cried out, pressing around you.
You turned your head away, uncaring! abandoning them!
You let go and fell down the Ten Thousand Foot Cliff.

34

In this dusty world, why should people strive for longer life?
True longevity resides in one's literary works.

Your writings will endure for ever;
You may look back to scoff at Pengzu for having died young!

40

Azure sky and Yellow Springs—I don't know where you are;
Will I have a chance to talk with you face to face in another life?
My love for you is so strong, I'll turn into a husband-gazing rock—
At the end of this *kalpa*, I'll still wonder when this rock will dissolve.

45

An ice-cold heart to chill the white sun—
Let the demons display thousands of their ferocious forms.
It's said that etiquette in the Underworld is stern,
Don't write any new poems to mock the nether officials!

58

When others cry for us, we're not aware;
When we cry for others, we're the ones who grieve.
I grieve here today, but you don't cry—
You've been severed from suffering—how convenient!

64

As a man of letters, you were strong-spined:
You felt it beneath you to seek fame, and failed the exams.
The wall by the bed was broken, no need to make a hole—
You read on your pillow by the moonlight.

67

I was shocked to meet you in a dream this clear night;
In my dream I worried only about being in a dream:
I quickly clutched at your robe
And woke with empty hands.

69

Deep, deep in the ditch of night, the dim torch burns away;
My grave was dug into the roots of pines, threatening my place of rest.

Who knows my wretchedness in the wind and the moonlight?
On nights like this, I speak to the stone statues before the mound.

(MYSG, 34/3a–13b)

27, line 1: Jinling is an old name for Nanjing. This line seems to refer to the civil service examinations Shen Cheng took.

27, line 4: The Gold Mountain, or Jinshan, refers to the mountain in the section of the Yangzi River in the northwestern part of Zhenjiang county in Jiangsu province.

31, line 1: Shen Cheng is here compared to the Daoist immortal Zi'an, who rides on the back of a yellow crane. See the entry on "Huanghelou," in Chen Zhi, *Zhongguo gudai shici diangu cidian*, p. 164.

34, line 4: This line alludes to a famous paradox in *Zhuangzi*, chap. 2: "No one has lived longer than a dead child, and Pengzu died young." Pengzu is a legendary character said to have lived to an incredible old age.

40, line 1: On "Yellow Springs," see P.29.9.

40, line 3: On the "husband-gazing rock," see P.11.16.

40, line 4: *Kalpa* is a Buddhist term for the duration of the world, the equivalent of 430 million years.

64, line 4: The allusion here is to Kuang Heng, a poverty-stricken worthy of the Han dynasty who pierced a hole in his wall in order to benefit by the neighbor's light and continue studying.

BIOGRAPHICAL NOTE AND TRANSLATION BY SHUEN-FU LIN

謝五娘

P.46. Xie Wuniang (late 16th century)

Xie Wuniang was from Chaozhou, in Guangdong province. Her *Liechao shiji* entry reports that she was once arrested for some unknown charge. Her single volume of writings, entitled *Duyueju ji* (Poems from the Moon-Reading Residence) included poems addressed to her husband, away to attend the civil service examinations, and many poems sent as letters or recalling absent friends. Qian Qianyi and Liu Shi cite the first poem translated here, written "in taking leave of my father after accepting a second offer of engagement," as evidence of her "reckless and independent character." (In traditional China, marriages were typically arranged by the parents, and an engagement was legally binding; it is not known what the maker of the first offer thought of Xie's independence.) Hu Wenkai has assembled a total of twenty-three poems by Xie Wuniang from Guangdong local chronicles and women's anthologies.[1]

P.46.1. *On Taking Leave of My Father After Accepting a Second Offer of Engagement*

First betrothed to the excellent student Li,
I later fell in love with the dashing son of the Zhong house.
Once the peach blossom has fallen into the hand of Liu [Ziji],
The fisherman may not seek the ford again.

(LCSJ, 2:771; see also Hu Wenkai, 204–5)

LCSJ quotes this quatrain in Xie's biographical notice rather than including it among her poems.

lines 3–4: These lines, announcing that the earlier engagement has been superseded, allude to the epilogue of Tao Qian's (Yuanming) "A Record of Peach Blossom Spring" (see P.16.4): the fisherman who first wanders into the mountain paradise of Peach Blossom Spring and back again is unable to lead others to his discovery. "Liu Ziji of Nanyang desired to go there too, but before he could carry out his plan, he grew sick and died. Since then there have been no seekers after the ford" ("Taohua yuan ji," in Lu Qinli, ed., *Xian Qin Han Wei Jin Nanbeichao shi*, 2:985–86).

P.46.2. Liuzhi

Close to the water, a thousand withes brush the painted oar.
At the six bridges, the storm soughs and moans.
Every branch, every leaf holds the sorrow of parting.
Add the oriole's cry: it is still more forlorn.

(LR, 4/77a)

line 2: As governor of Hangzhou, Su Shi constructed a causeway that included a series of six bridges across part of the West Lake. Some three hundred years earlier, his predecessor Bo Juyi had built a causeway or dike that contained a single steep bridge known as the "Broken Bridge." Willows are planted along both these causeways. The two poets are thus indelibly associated with the Hangzhou landscape.

P.46.3. *Spring Dusk*

The cuckoo cries "Blood!," reporting spring's return.
It stirs withered flowers into flight over the earth.

Only a pair of swallows outside the blinds
Pity the flowers, picking up the sweet-smelling mud.

(LR, 4/77a)

line 1: On the cuckoo, see P.5.1.

P.46.4. Early Summer

A mild breeze in the courtyard, the headrest is cool.
The persimmon tree starting to bud, the rain just cleared.
The incense goes out, my dream ends, I am at a loss—
I can hear the first sounds of the new cicadas.

(LR, 4/77b)

P.46.5. Impromptu on a Spring Day

Nesting swallows gather mud in the long spring day.
I lean silently on the railing, standing in the slanting sun.
Peach blossoms—a red rain—and pear blossoms—snow—
Chase each other in the east wind over the white wall.

(LR, 4/77b)

P.46.6. Early Summer

Amidst birds' cries, I return from my midday dream.
I probe the incense block again: already turned to ash.
The east wind, as if regretting spring has gone,
Blows poplar flowers into the house.

(LR, 4/77b)

line 2: *Zhuan xiang*, incense shaped to resemble the meandering lines of sigillary characters, could be used to mark time.

P.46.7. Recollection

The blinds surrounding me hang from green jade hooks.
The depths of the secluded yard lock spring sorrow in.
The distant traveler has sent no word home.
Flowers fall in the east wind—too listless to go downstairs.

(LR, 4/77b)

P.46.8. Spring Night

The silver candlestick burns low to the clock's late night chime.
On the painted screen and table, my shadow is all alone.
A yard full of spring splendor, no one concerned with it.
Have the pear blossoms accompany the moonlight!

(LR, 4/77b)

P.46.9. Spring Evening

In the fresh green park when the rain has passed,
An oriole silently mourns the return of spring.
Poplar blossoms afraid to go with the east wind
Cling to the railing, refusing to fly.

(Yang Ruicong, *Mingren jueju xuan*, 2/27a)

P.46.10. Encountering Rain on the Seventh Night

Seeking skill they pass the wine cups without pause.
In the realm of mortals and heaven above, there is one love.
The west wind stems the cowherd's tears.
Falling outside the blinds they make the sound of rain.

(*Mingren jueju xuan*, 2/27a)

On the Weaving Girl and the Herd Boy, see P.5.1. On the custom of *qi qiao* ("begging for skill") on Double Seventh night, see P.5.1 and P.19.2.

BIOGRAPHICAL NOTE AND TRANSLATION BY KATHRYN LOWRY

景翩翩

P.47. Jing Pianpian (late 16th century)

Jing Pianpian (given name Yao; courtesy name Sanmei) was a famous courtesan from Xujiang in eastern Jiangxi. Because she frequently traveled to Jian'an in Fujian, many works classify her as a Fujian courtesan. She was known for her erudition, was on good terms with many well-known Fujian literati, and was widely praised as one of the best courtesan poets of the Ming period. She was once engaged to Mei Ziyu, but the marriage never took place. Su Zhecong reports that she died in extreme poverty. According to Zhang Gongchang, she eventually married a man named Ding Changfa. When he was arrested and taken away in chains, she committed suicide.[1]

P.47.1. Don't Wash Off the Rouge

Don't wash off the rouge.
The more you wash, the less the beauty;
Once gone it can't be recovered.
Too weak and fragile to put it back on—
Just let my red tears join the eastward flow.
When the color has faded, there will be no face to weave fallen flowers.

(Zhou Shouchang, *Gonggui wenxuan*, 16/14a)

P.47.2. Poem of Resentment

How can you complain that the distance is great
When it is your hesitation that keeps you away?
My heart, like the wheel of a cart,
Travels ten thousand miles and more each day.
I am like water in a mountain stream,
Never flowing far from the streambed stones.
Your heart is like a blossom of the poplar tree,
(8) Drifting in the breeze with no set track.

(Zhou Shouchang, *Gonggui wenxuan*, 16/14a)

P.47.3. Copper-Shod Hoofbeats of Xiangyang

I

You are a Xiangyang man
Used to drinking Xiangyang wine.
When you were not yet drunk I gave you some advice,
Once sober again, you should recall.

II

Your fine horse treads on copper shoes,
Its gold bridle shines in Longxi.
You should intensify your determination,
How then could I cry to others?

(Zhou Shouchang, *Gonggui wenxuan*, 16/14b)

Xiangyang is a county in Hubei province. Jing Pianpian is apparently urging her friend to become more serious about his official duties, perhaps so that with a higher rank and higher pay, he would be in a better position to take her as a concubine. The reference to Longxi, on the frontier in Gansu province, suggests that he is stationed at a military outpost. These songs allude to Li Bo's famous "Song of Xiangyang," which contains the line, "I offer my thousand-gold steed for a singing girl."

P.47.4. Song of Qingxi

Every day you ride in fancy carriages,
On intimate terms with upper-class friends.
But no one here is from Suzhou
And I miss those Suzhou soft sounds.
I return late at night with my love;
After I've softly played the *zheng*,
We sit and tie a lover's knot,
(8) Inviting the moon into the room.

(Zhou Shouchang, *Gonggui wenxuan*, 16/14b)

line 7: A *tongxin jie* is a knot uniting two hearts, suspended from one's belt as a pendant.

P.47.5. Peach Leaf Song

I call myself "Peach Leaf"—
My face is like a peach blossom.
Peach blossoms easily fall
While you're in who knows whose bed.

(Zhou Shouchang, *Gonggui wenxuan*, 16/15a)

Peach Leaf (Taoye) is the name of the courtesan who became the concubine of the famous calligrapher Wang Xianzhi (344–88). One of the landmarks on the Qinhuai River in Nanjing was the Peach Leaf Ford, after Wang's poem commemorating the spot where his love parted from him and crossed the river.

BIOGRAPHICAL NOTE AND TRANSLATION BY PAUL S. ROPP

薛素素

P.48. Xue Susu (ca. 1564–ca. 1637)

A gifted courtesan in an age of talented women, Xue Susu (that is, Xue Wu; her sobriquets include Xuesu, Sujun, Runqing, Qiaoqiao, Wulang, and Runniang) was classed as one of the Eight Famous Courtesans of the Ming. She was known for her paintings of orchids and bamboo, for her poetry, and for her skill at shooting with bow and arrow from horseback; she called herself a "female knight-errant." Sources disagree on the place of Xue's birth, and record it as Suzhou in Jiangsu province or Jiaxing in Zhejiang province.[1] Active in the pleasure quarters along the Qinhuai River in Nanjing, Xue Susu met and befriended many distinguished men of letters.

Dong Qichang (1555–1636), the foremost painter and theorist of painting of the day, held her work in high esteem, writing: "As for [painting] landscapes, orchids, and bamboo, she lowers her brush swiftly, sweepingly. None [of her paintings] lacks an intention and spirit that approaches the divine."[2] Hu Yinglin (1543–81) added: "What famous painter with skilled hands can surpass her?"[3] The judgment of Dong and Hu is echoed by their contemporary Fan Yunlin (1558–1641) in a colophon attached to her "Flowers," a painting of 1615: "Later generations have not seen many women who paint as well as Madame Guan [Daosheng; P.23]. . . . I obtained from a friend an ink-orchid fan by her [Xue Susu]. It was like having obtained a precious jade: to this day I store it away as a treasure."[4]

Xue Susu's paintings were enhanced by her poetry, also highly regarded. Hu Yinglin in his *Jiayi shengyan* wrote of her literary accomplishments: "Susu was interested in Buddhism which she studied with Yu Xianzhang. She was fond of poetry which she learned from Wang Xingfu. Her poetry, although lacking in freedom, shows a talent rare among women."[5]

In the economy of social exchange between courtesan and patron, Xue Susu's talents in painting and poetry served her well. She produced paintings and poems for her lovers as tokens of their shared affection. In return she received the poetic attentions of her lovers and admirers, who included some of the most prominent writers of her day—the dramatist Shen Defu (1578–1642) and the painter and author Li Rihua (1565–1635), among others.

Her liaisons with and social connections to leading literati placed Xue Susu at the center of late Ming cultural life. Yet Xue, unlike many courtesans, did not accept the prolonged tutelage of a single man and never formed a lasting bond with any of her lovers. She married several times during her life and was left alone in her last years.[6] Yet even age did not dim Xue's reputation. Xu Jing inscribed on a portrait of her:

> In spite of her long life, ingenious Xue retained her glamorous reputation. After she passed away, legends grew up around her saying that she had possessed witchcraft by means of which she attached younger men to her. But this is fiction only. Studying her portrait, one sees a fastidious but unpretentious woman. It is more likely that, as Daoist tradition has it, her high spiritual power preserved her charm.[7]

P.48.1. *Lines Inspired by an Autumn Day's Invitation to Censor He to Drink*

In the pleasure quarter within the stone city walls,
I'm deeply embarrassed to be the most prominent one.
River brimming, water clear, gulls bathe in pairs;
Sky empty, clouds pure, geese aloft form rows.
An embroidered robe half-borrows the hibiscus's color;
Green wine equals the water lilies' fragrance.
If not sharing deep affection with you,
(8) Dare I offer soup and pastries to Master He?

(MYSG, 31/8a)

P.48.2. *Written as a Gift When Passing Cai's "Shadowy Cloud" Tower*

Leaning idly against a tall tower, lingering a little;
Irises before the window delicately exhale fragrance.
Milky light from a hidden table reflects on the bare wall;
Mountain air rests on books, dampens the couch.
I have heard of nights lit gray by bramble fires,
I like the coolness of jade trees the wind produces:
In its midst one finds competent poets,
(8) But who is as talented as Master Cai?

(MYSG, 31/8b)

line 6: The word *liang* ("coolness") can be read "to be faithful, sincere"; and "jade tree" (*yu shu*) may be used to refer to a handsome or talented young man.
line 8: Master Cai: Cai Yong, on whom see P.2.

P.48.3. Pouring Wine Alone

Fragrant taste of wine beneath the blossoms;
Kingfisher covers the door among bamboo.
Alone, watching gulls by myself:
Quiet and tranquil with no contention.

(MYSG, 31/8b)

P.48.4. Painting Orchids

In the empty valley a lady of surpassing beauty;
Blue silken gauze for a belt, and jade for flesh.
Except, alas, that it gets mingled with the weeds;
Its secluded fragrance rare, but unnoticed.

(MYSG, 31/8b–9a)

BIOGRAPHICAL NOTE AND TRANSLATION BY JENNIFER PURTLE

楊玉香

P.49. Yang Yuxiang (late 16th century)

Yang Yuxiang was a courtesan from Jinling, near present-day Nanjing in Jiangsu province. She possessed outstanding beauty and talent. At age fifteen she became close to the Fujianese Lin Jingqing through poetry exchanges and consented to marry him. They were separated for six years, while Lin Jingqing traveled again in the south. On a moonlit night, while his boat was anchored at Baisha in Jiangxi province, he saw Yang Yuxiang in the boat, and they were as happy as ever. When dawn approached, she disappeared. Later he returned to Jinling to look for her, and learned that she had been dead for over a year.

P.49.1. Replying to Lin Jingqing

After the incense in the burner dies out, I go alone to close the door,
And the lute's sounds are broken in the moonlit dusk.
My sad heart is afraid that the flowers would laugh at me,
And I do not dare wipe my tears away before them.

(Su Zhecong, 330)

BIOGRAPHICAL NOTE AND TRANSLATION BY NORMAN KUTCHER

秦淮四姬

P.50. The "Four Talented Courtesans of Qinhuai": Ma Shouzhen, Zhao Caiji, Zhu Wuxia, Zheng Ruying

Beauty, talent, and learning distinguished Ma Shouzhen, Zhao Caiji, Zhu Wuxia, and Zheng Ruying. The Qing scholar Mao Yuchang gathered their poems and published the collection under the title *Qinhuai siji shi* (Poems by the four talented courtesans of Qinhuai).[1]

馬守貞

P.50a. Ma Shouzhen (1548–1604)

Of the "Four Talented Courtesans," Ma Shouzhen was undoubtedly the most famous. (See commentary on her at C.31.1, a preface to a collection of her poetry, *Xiang lan zi ji* [Collection of Master Orchid-of-the-Xiang-River].) Aside from her talent in writing poetry, Ma was also an accomplished painter and dramatist.[2] She was especially known for her spirit of chivalry in literati circles.

P.50a.1. Since You Went Away: Two Poems

I

Since you went away,
I am afraid to hear the maid's song.
When the song enters the abandoned one's ears,
The green robe is spattered with teardrops.

II

Since you went away,
No more lifting of jade cups together.
Wine is a grief-dispelling thing,
But how much can it dispel?

(LR, 68b)

P.50a.2. Parting in Sadness

Ailing bones drag on during the long days.
Master Wang loved me before.
Often we faced the orchids and bamboo;
Every night we gathered poetic works.
The chill rain brings tidings across the three rivers,
The autumn wind blows through the night's sleep.
In the deep boudoir, with nothing to do,
(8) All day long I wait for the returning boat.

(LR, 68b)

P.50a.3. The Parrot

All day long I watch the parrot
Pass its life in a golden cage.
Emerald-plumed, it is skilled in brushing its feathers;
Its vermilion beak is good at harmonizing sounds.
By the mound trees the heart is wont to break;
Taught Wu music, it manages to learn quickly.
For your snowy plumage, I cherish you,
(8) Always companion to my boudoir feelings.

(LR, 68b–69a)

趙彩姬

P.50b. Zhao Caiji

P.50b.1. Facing a Visitor at Mid-Autumn

The moon is full tonight;
Autumn divides at this hour.
Do not stint the golden goblets;
In the clear light I'm glad to be with you.

(LR, 70a)

P.50b.2. *Seeing Off Wang Zhongfang on His Return to Xin'an*

Dusk's snow falls over the road to Yangzi South;
The lone wall marks the time for a goblet of wine.
Ardently I break the willow
Yet still I turn towards last year's branches.

(LR, 70a)

P.50b.3. *Swallows Coming*

Sitting alone I lower the silk curtain;
Sadly I watch a pair of swallows fly.
I think you are not equal to the swallows
Which return once every year.

(LR, 70a)

P.50b.4. *Farewell by the River in Late Spring*

A wave of tidal sounds descends the rocks;
Seeing off a traveler at the riverside pavilion saddens one.
What a pity that the hanging willows, whose threads stretch a thousand feet,
Do not hold fast the boat on its way to the spring river.

(LR, 70b)

P.50b.5. *Seeing Off Zhang Youyu on His Return to Wumen*

Before the flowers tears soak my robe and skirt;
We hold our wine cups at the riverside pavilion as the setting sun lingers.
This time towards Wujiang the frosty moon is full;
Whomever you meet, entrust him with a letter to Lake Tai!

(LR, 70b)

P.50b.6. *Seeing Off Shen Jiaze on His Travel to Guangling*

The autumn wind whiffs away the wooden orchid boat;
Everywhere the green hills await the recluse.
Do not sing the "Jade Tree" song to the green hills;
The flowers and moon of Yangzhou sadden one.

(LR, 70b)

朱無瑕

P.50c. Zhu Wuxia (fl. 1569)

P.50c.1. Facing the Moon

A curtain of bright moon shines profusely white;
The precious duck incense is burnt out, the heart about to break.
The maid wrongly conveys the matters of my heart,
Wrongly blaming the flowers and willows at dusk.

(LR, 71a)

P.50c.2. Boudoir Dream

The cold frosty dust flies swiftly while the water clock drip is slow;
In the long night and lonely curtain, I recall our parting.
The remote dream is almost fulfilled, but the bright moon leaves;
Where can I find the source to light up my longing?

(LR, 71a)

P.50c.3. Autumn Boudoir Song

The dew on the lotus is cold, the moon is dim;
In the small yard the wind is keen, wild geese fly past above.
I have heard the Jade Gate is thousands of miles away;
In the deep autumn whither can I send winter clothes?

(LR, 71a)

P.50c.4. Rain on the Banana Leaves

It shatters my dream of grief;
I have heard all the sounds on the leaves.
New poems are hard to finish,
Except to vent feelings of separation.

(LR, 71a)

P.50c.5. Composed upon the Moon on a Frosty Night

The night's atmosphere is cool as water;
The frost's radiance is bright as the moon.
Who will invite the Green Maid to come out
And accompany this White Beauty in her walk?

(LR, 71a)

P.50c.6. The Wanderer

The northern wild geese eagerly fly south;
The cold wind is blowing keen.
The traveler's thoughts grow weary of the protracted journey,
My heart grieves over the long separation.
I tire of hearing the last dripping sounds,
Am sad to see a waning moon.
Day after day I reckon the time of your return—
Letting my tears turn into blood for nothing.

(LR, 71a)

鄭如英

P.50d. Zheng Ruying

P.50d.1. Parting at Qinhuai River, a Plaintive Poem Sent to Qilian

By Qinhuai the new willows are yellow in the second month;
I break a willow branch for a gift, but the recipient is heartbroken.
What a pity to see the slender Qinhuai willow
Once again grasped in a parting lover's hand.
The parting one looks at the yielding twig in his hand,
Mournfully brushing the saddle on his fine steed.
The steed is about to neigh and the lover drops tears;
Who at this moment can still feel light-headed?
Tenderly I hold your hand, asking about the future—
"When the lotus flowers bloom, I will return."
I fear I'll see the lotus but not you,
And vainly recall the peach-blossom face.

Green, green the grass on Changgan Road;
It makes the lonesome lover's face waste away.
Ascending the Qinhuai, you reach Fengxi,
(16) But my heart, like the water, flows east, not west.
Look at the Qinhuai, its waters that flow on and on—
Doesn't it make a loving heart die of longing?

(LR, 71b)

line 2: On the symbolism of willow trees, see P.5.1.

P.50d.2. *In Reply to Pan Jingsheng's Poem Expressing His Feelings*

You sent me a bright mirror
That reflects my tangled hair.
I requite you with curdled cassia grease
And fragrant oils to smooth your hand.
You gave me gold-dusted ink,
I requite you with hibiscus paper.
If anything prompts me to chew the brush, lost in thought,
(8) It's probably you, a thousand miles away.

(LR, 72a)

BIOGRAPHICAL NOTE AND TRANSLATION OF P.50A–C BY KANG-I SUN CHANG;
TRANSLATION OF P.50D BY KANG-I SUN CHANG AND CHARLES KWONG

胡文如

P.51. Hu Wenru (fl. ca. 1590)

Hu Wenru (courtesy name Zu) was a well-known official courtesan (*yingji*) during the Wanli period (1573–1620).[1] From Jiangxia in Hubei, she was accomplished in poetry, painting, and playing the *qin*. Her sister, Hu Wenju, was also a famous courtesan. Hu Wenru fell in love with a *jinshi* named Qiu Qianzhi, but his father would not permit their marriage. When he wrote to her confessing his failure to get his father's consent to their wedding, she wrote back vowing never to renounce her love for him. Unfortunately, her father cared only for money, so he sold her to a merchant to be his concubine. She detested this man, so she ran away and fled to find Qiu Qianzhi. Qiu wrote to his father and married Wenru immediately, in the winter of 1582. Later Qiu was dismissed from his official post and spent his time with Wenru traveling to famous scenic and historic sites, playing the *qin*, and writing poetry. He eventually had her poems, with many matching rhymes between them, published under the title *Yaojibian* (Collected pieces from distant places).

P.51.1. *A Poem in Blood Sent to Qiu Qianzhi*

In the Changmen Palace of days gone by, she sighed over life's
vicissitudes;
But a single *fu* won back the emperor's heart.
How could yellow gold alone secure a retainer?
Xiangru was in fact only moved by a lover's lament.

(Su Zhecong, 316)

This poem alludes to two events in the life of the Han court poet Sima Xiangru: his writing the "Lament of the Changmen Palace" for Empress Chen, and his wife's composition of the "Song of White Hair"; see P.8a.1 and P.38.1.

P.51.2. *A Letter to Qiu Qianzhi, Heading East Toward Guangdong*

Your horse without a guide is like a giant spider,
Leaving on the road a drifting gossamer strand.
My heart is like the spring silkworm's cocoon;
I "pull the thread" all day, but never leave my hut.

(Su Zhecong, 317)

This poem is a play on the word *si*, thread, which is a homophone for *si*, "thinking (of you)." The "thread" also symbolizes strong ties of affection that, however far they may be stretched, cannot be broken.

P.51.3. *Tearful Improvisation After Getting Drunk with Qiu Qianzhi*

A sad song substitutes for tears, but sadness overflows;
Tonight getting drunk with you, this I finally understood.
Then leaning on a chair, I lost all control;
A pair of tears dropped at once into the golden goblet.

(Su Zhecong, 317)

P.51.4. Sending Off Qiu Qianzhi with a Meal on the Road to Lin'gao

Heading east from Wuchang, the waters are boundless;
In one day a tiny craft goes far by itself.
Don't blame people for doubting the story of Peach Leaf Ford;
It has always been hard to find a man of deep feeling.

(Su Zhecong, 317)

lines 3–4: These lines allude to Yu Xuanji's saying: "It is easy to seek a priceless treasure— / But hard to find a man with a heart" (see P.11.17). On Peach Leaf Ford, see P.47.5.

P.51.5. After Parting, Another Letter Sent from My Boat Amidst Wind and Rain

I cannot bear the night of wind and rain;
All haggard and forlorn in this lonesome boat.
Tears and waves both make a splashing sound,
My lamp winds through the autumn twilight round and round.
In my dreams I wonder if I am still at the Red Cliffs,
Though the line of sight is already blocked by Huangzhou.
Here at this moment, can you understand my state?
(8) From the crying consorts of Shun you can know.

(Su Zhecong, 318)

line 6: Though she can no longer see them because her boat has passed on to Huangzhou, Hu Wenru still dreams of the famous Red Cliffs on the Yangzi River, near where she parted from Qiu.

line 8: On the consorts of Shun and the mottled bamboo native to Hunan, see P.10.1 and P.44.1.

P.51.6. Unable to Follow Qiu Qianzhi Going to the Capital, I Send a Letter

The letter you sent to me, who else could understand it?
My tears gush out, intensifying my sense of longing.
Music of "Tall Mountains" and "Flowing Waters" for a thousand
years!
In life or death, our tie will last to the end.

(Su Zhecong, 318)

line 3: A reference to the great lute player Bo Ya and his friend Zhong Ziqi; see P.24.7.

P.51.7. After Our Parting

After we part, at the river's mouth, the night rain feels cold;
My pathetic face is all forlorn now that I've given up rouge.
If my belly does not contain the road on which you are traveling,
Why do I feel your coach's wheels daily grinding my entrails?

(Su Zhecong, 319)

P.51.8. A Letter to Master Qiu upon Hearing of His Dismissal from Office

What's so joyous about holding office?
What's so sad about dismissal?
Once you retire from office,
That's when I can marry you.

(Su Zhecong, 319)

P.51.9. Confirming My Earlier Engagement with Master Qiu

I

Like the flowing water is your carriage;
Like the hanging willow are the silky locks that grow from my temples.
The spring river turns beautiful by itself;
One by one the scenes enter into my longing.

II

Any time you can visit the flowers,
Anywhere you can purchase wine.
Of calamities here, you've no idea;
Deathly sad, the woman in the mansion.

(Su Zhecong, 316; Zhou Shouchang, *Gonggui wenxuan*, 22/10b)

BIOGRAPHICAL NOTE AND TRANSLATION BY PAUL S. ROPP

陸卿子

P.52. Lu Qingzi (fl. 1590)

During her lifetime, Lu Qingzi was widely recognized as an outstanding poet. She was among the few Ming women whose work was selected for anthologies devoted predominantly to literati poetry, and since the inclusion of her poetry in Qian Qianyi's anthology *Liechao shiji* in the mid-seventeenth century, her poetry and prose have been represented in numerous late imperial and modern anthologies of women's writings.[1] In addition to poetry, Lu wrote prose of distinction, excelling in rhyme-prose (*fu*) and elegy (*lei*), in which she has been considered the equal of literati writers of the Six Dynasties period (third to seventh centuries). Her preface to Xiang Langzhen's (P.57) collection *Yongxue zhai yigao* is included as C.9.1. Lu and her contemporary and literary friend Xu Yuan (P.53) were known as "the two learned ladies of Suzhou." Critics have generally followed the *Liechao shiji* editor in regarding Lu as the better poet of the two.

Lu was from Gusu (Suzhou) in present-day Jiangsu province. Her father, Lu Shidao, served under the Ming emperor Shenzong (r. 1572–1615) as Chief Minister of the Office of Seals. At the age of fifteen, Lu married Zhao Huan'guang, courtesy name Fanfu, who took her to live a "rustic" private life on Cold Mountain, where it was said they cleared the land and dredged the streams with their own hands. Echoing the *Analects* of Confucius, Zhao said of Lu that at fifteen her heart was set on study, and that among subjects of study her heart was set especially on poetry. In her middle twenties, Lu's first collection of poetry, *Yunwoge ji* (Poems from Resting-in-Clouds Lodge), was printed, but this work was laid aside and lost before being circulated. Her two later collections, *Kaopan ji* (A recluse's perfect joy), published in 1600, and *Xuanzhi ji* (The fungus of immortality) contain all her extant poetry.

Lu and Zhao were regarded as a model companionate couple, sharing a passion for literature and a leisurely private life without separations or the pressures of a large household. Though they chose to live remote from political and social entanglements, their Cold Mountain home received many prominent literary figures of the day as guests. Zhao Huan'guang's learning and literary ability were said to fall considerably short of Lu's, yet his preface to *Kaopan ji* (C.33.1) is full of enthusiasm for her achievements and betrays no sense of dismay at his own more modest stature in the eyes of contemporaries.[2]

Lu is said to have disregarded the boundaries of social status and to have written her poems to whomever and about whatever interested her. The addressees of her many poems to other women include gentry women, entertainers, and servants. Her latitude in this regard seems to have provoked the criticism that some of her social poetry is of lesser quality—"forced and bland" is Qian Qianyi's characterization; see also Liu Shi's (P.67) comments at C.14.2.

Lu wrote in a wide range of conventional literati topics and themes, among them friendship, descriptions of life in the mountains and landscape, parting, imitations of great literati poets of the past, poems in the heroic mode, and lyrics to ballad captions. Her style has been praised as *youqing gudan*, "reclusive and unsullied, with the deep composure of the ancient poets."[3] To a modern reader, Lu's poetry is interesting for her meticulous care in structuring couplet dynamics and in word choice, as well as for her willingness to experiment with masculine topics and textual voices. A mature subjectivity, a fresh lyricism, and ease of control over language characterize her best poems. Of special interest is her representation of the details of women's lives in poems that speak of trying on clothes, small household tasks, and gestures of friendship with other women.

P.52.1. In the Manner of Tao Qian

Living quietly, little to do
  with the busy world,
It is my nature to forget
  elaborate hairpins.
Green water brims
  in flower-scented pools,
Cool winds are stored
  in leafy woods.
Minnows play in
  wavelets and ripples,
Wild birds sing out
  their pleasing notes.
At evening comes
  a timely rain,
(8) White clouds deepen
  on the highest peaks.

Plants in the yard are bathed
  in nourishing moisture,
Clouds over mountain meadows
  send showers flying down.
Completely relaxed,
  I set thoughts free
    to range far, far—
(12) And when I like,
  pour for myself
    some unstrained wine.

(MYSG, 32/1a)

Lu borrows here from the characteristic themes and diction of the poet Tao Yuanming. The translations of Lu's poems here employ some freedom in representing the individual lines of the originals.

line 12: "Unstrained wine" is homemade or local country wine. This poem captures the mood of personal satisfaction expressed in some of Tao's poetry; see especially "Twenty Poems After Drinking Wine," number 7, and "On Reading the Classic of Seas and Mountains" (Hightower, *Poetry of T'ao Ch'ien*, pp. 133, 229).

P.52.2. In the Manner of Li Bo's "Poems in Ancient Style"

Heavy gloom blocks the daytime sun,
Mild and bright has cycled to cold and harsh.
What a chaos of mingled snow and sleet!
Leaves fall, scatter from all the plants and trees.
Ceaseless winds sweep cruelly through the night,
Where can the roosting bird find shelter?
The traveler's fur-lined coat wears thin,
(8) The jobless scholar hoards his grains and beans.
So it was, when the old men of Shang Mountain
Took to the road, bound for a hidden valley.

(MYSG, 32/1a–b)

line 10: *Shangshan sihao*, the four old men of Shang Mountain, fled civil and military disorders at the end of the Qin dynasty, went to live as recluses deep in the Shang Mountains, and refused to return even after the establishment of the Han dynasty. Both Tao Yuanming and Li Bo refer to these men in their poems; Lu is demonstrating her familiarity with both poets and hinting at the hermit ideal she shares with the *sihao* and their admirers.

P.52.3. Living in the Mountains

I

Everywhere under the earth
jade lies buried deep;
Never a mountain slope
not grown with pines.
If rains are heavy
we gather mushrooms early;
When the sun turns warm,
spend the afternoon tending bees.
Musk deer, as we climb the cliffs,
are coming down;
Foxes, where we gather herbs,
may show up.
When peach blossoms open
in full bloom everywhere,
(8) The passing woodsman, dazzled,
almost forgets his way.

II

The spreading hazelnut
overshadows a vine-grown lodge;
Shouldering the void,
a hidden path through flowers.
In the stillness of moonlight
demonic foxes weep;
From deep recesses of pine forest
strange birds cry out.
On the mountain in autumn
cloudlight shines on my door;
In springtime valleys
stream water bursts its banks
And, flying down, becomes
a thousand-foot sheer waterfall
(8) That households everywhere may draw from
to irrigate their fields.

III

Double door-panels at mid-day still barred,
Green water flows
around a sandy point.
On the other bank
a beautiful woman is speaking,
Her voice carried along the stream
to the servant girl who listens.
Cliffside flowers
compete with embroideries,
Willows at water's edge
imitate graceful girls.
Day after day, songs
shake dust from rafters;
(8) In the inner courtyard
grass is turning green.

IV

In the warmth of flowers
a white ox sleeps;
With my own hands I cook
milk for butterfat.
Teaching my sons,
sometimes we recite sutras;
I let the servant girl go
to practice sitting meditation.
In deciding to leave
the world of human affairs,
I've committed my life
to "freedom from delusion."
Fruits like red jades
fill an immaculate mat;
(8) A guest sits in conversation
touching on deep mysteries.

V

The deep reach of blue sky
one unbroken color,
Receding, merging, vectors
of force impossible to define.
Red millet is stored
in a stone house;
White clouds rise
from vine-covered rooms.
Birds fly away
beyond the bright skyscape;
A spring echoes
from just behind the trees.
Tossing and trembling
in the sparkle of waves,
(8) Mists and sunset clouds
entice twilight.

VI

Color of trees
a thousand layers of green,
Sound of streams
spilling down ten thousand gorges.
Birds call
in flowers warm on the slope;
Maple leaves fall
by the stone gate in autumn.
Children are listening
to the pure sound of sutras;
In the house, a lady ascends
to a well-kept upper floor.
Her sole desire
is to fathom Buddha's teaching,
(8) Not to search out
the way to Cinnabar Hill.

(MYSG, 32/7b–8b)

iv, line 1: Whether or not Lu's household did, in fact, include a white ox, this creature was important in religious iconography as a symbol for Gautama Buddha and the highest spiritual wisdom. "Ride an ox to seek an ox" means to use Buddha's teachings to find Buddha, or realize Buddhist enlightenment. In the following lines, butterfat is another reference to Buddhist wisdom: the rich essence of milk, obtained through a process requiring several stages of heating and skimming, is symbolic of spiritual cultivation. Butterfat is used in Buddhist votive lamps.

iv, line 6: *Zizai tian*, in Sanskrit *Ishvaradeva*, refers to Siva, King of the Devas; it is also a title for the Bodhisattva Guanyin. In Buddhism, this expression often refers to the mind free from delusion (Soothill and Hodous, *Dictionary of Chinese Buddhist Terms*, p. 218).

v, line 8: Lu's Buddhist values appear to shape the conclusion of this poem, where the actual sky, first described as a vast energy field, has become merely a reflection that seeks its own obliteration; *han*—"lure, beckon, entice"—suggests the Buddhist view that it is the beautiful but illusionary passions that bring about spiritual loss. The poem is properly read as a description of physical circumstances experienced in the mountains, but a Buddhist subtext seems implied.

vi, lines 7–8: "Buddha's teaching" (*fazang*): the treasure-house of Buddhist teachings, the canon. This phrase may also, more abstractly, refer to the absolute reality of the Buddha-mind. "Cinnabar Hill" (*Danqiu*) in Daoist lore is a place where immortals dwell, described in the *Songs of Chu* as the land of the "feathered ones," *yuren*, who do not die. Lu denies here any interest in Daoist immortality-seeking.

P.52.4. *To Lady Gu, née Yan*

I

In those days, just married,
little more than thirteen,
You were a marsh-orchid
in your sweet plenitude
An elegant epidendrum
so soft and delicate—
Even jade could not compare.
You lived sequestered, alone
In a fine mansion, behind
screens strung with pearls,
And no one ever got to see
your beautifully embroidered dress.

II

Moonlight illumines an empty court
  half the double door is shut;
A sweet aroma emanates
  from silk bed curtains—
    you've just awakened from dreams.
Petals from trees
  have finished falling,
    restless crows have settled;
Not raising the pearl blinds,
  you chant sutras in the night.

III

Sunlight draws a clear spring
  to flow over fine sand;
In the sand is white jade
  pure, without flaw.
Intending to keep butterflies
  from flitting among red maples,
You didn't plant peonies
  in your spring garden.

(MYSG, 32/13a)

P.52.5. To Lady Xu of Taiyuan

I remember how we met by chance
  that day in empty autumn hills;
    hills empty, air so chilled
      it wilted thickets of sweet herbs.
But your silken garments swept away
  the lonely-cloud-of-autumn mood;
Autumn brilliance shone like fire
  bathing the green hibiscus.
Your rosy face, with a flower's grace
Glowed and seemed to hold spring breeze.
You did not want to tell your name
And only said of land and home
  they were the same as mine.

(8) Met but not yet friends, alas,
parted, we kept thinking of each other;
It was thinking of each other
that finally brought us close.
Thus I met the charming one
When pink buds made the dawn moon lovely
(12) And lush green gave a splendor to the sunny spring.
In sunny springtime's second month the fair one came.
This fair one was so hesitant
to make her feelings known to me,
So hesitant yet wished to tell
the story of her life.
(16) She spoke at last of everything
of all the troubles in her heart.
The fair one's home is west of the misty sea;
She was twenty when her phoenix husband died,
leaving the phoenix mate to roost alone.
Weeping dew in the spring courtyard,
the purple orchid suffered;
(20) Her fragrance spent itself
by autumn draperies as the sun went down.
Year after year, time and again,
she saddened when the sweet green came;
Filled with grief, filled with heartbreak,
so soon did autumn once again arrive.
By lamplight she was moved to sing
the song called "Cypress Boat";
(24) Under flowering trees, could she stand
to listen to the calling birds?
Birds calling, flowers falling
springtime and autumn again;
As time passed, the flower of youth
was carried away on the current.
When mother was thirty and son sixteen,
(28) Screens opened, a peacock soared
magnificent in many-colored plumage.
Newly whitewashed were the walls,
the bright mirror gleamed;

At the gauze window, beautifully adorned,
  an orchid swayed, sweet upon the breeze.
Wild weeds were promptly cut away
  before the darkening of autumn;
Peach and plum were planted everywhere
  to make a blaze of beauty in the spring.
In the night, when no one knew,
  she held her beloved grandson;
By day she watched the careless maid
  for errors in her weaving.
She traveled with her elder brother,
  a pleasure-trip to the capital;
He took her with him everywhere,
  her happiness knew no end.
But for every three thousand held prisoner
  ten thousand is paid in ransom,
And when she returned she found someone
  had stolen in, a present made to Xiangru;
A beautiful Maoling girl, her face like jade,
Now sang at banquets in the tender evening light.
Wenjun in grief composed her complaint:
  "Together till our heads are white."
Anguish over the young lord
  has caused no end of pain.
But why the need for so much pain?
Why the need for sorrow?
This family of so proud a name—
  whom can we call its equal?
Elder brother is a great minister,
  nephew an important scholar;
What's more it has an immortal,
  the Immortal of Red Palisades, who's come
    to make a pleasant sojourn there.
Oh, Red Palisades Immortal!
  Visitor from Penglai!
The dark blue sea
  is vast and dim,
    fog and mist divide us.

Why do you not inhale
essences of moon and stars,
Con your spirit texts of gold?
Then when white clouds disappear,
leaving the tiers of heaven clear,
Seize the motion of yin and yang,
ride it boldly where you will
anywhere in the universe!

(MYSG, 32/5b–6a)

This poem contains unusual variations in the pattern of characters per line. In general, its lines are composed of seven characters, but at moments of emphasis (lines 4–5, 9–12) Lu varies this pattern with 5-character lines. See also note to lines 43–53 below.

line 18: On "phoenix" and "phoenix mate" (*feng* and *luan*), see P.29.9. These fabulous male and female birds whose calls were musically harmonious symbolize marital harmony and devotion.

line 23: The title of poem 26 of the *Book of Odes*; see P.37.1.

line 28: The soaring peacock refers to Lady Xu's son, who has reached the age of marriage. The following lines describe the preparations for and arrival of the bride.

lines 38–40: A reference to the story of Sima Xiangru and his wife; see P.38.1. Lu suggests in the next lines that Xu's son will, like Sima Xiangru, eventually return his affections to his wife.

lines 43–53: According to the editor of MYSG, "The ending [of this poem] is extremely forceful and sublime." The structure itself is unusual in that lines 43 and 44 have five characters, lines 45 and 46 have seven, line 47 has nine, lines 48 and 49 have seven, line 50 has five, line 51 has three, and lines 52 and 53 have seven.

line 47: Red Palisades is the name of a mountain in Tiantai district, Zhejiang province, on the route to Tiantai, one of the five most sacred mountains of China. People wishing to climb Tiantai had to traverse Red Palisades, so named because of the color of its soil. The sixth-ranked of the Daoist cave-heavens (*dongtian*) was believed to be located on its western flank. Lu praises Xu by saying she was originally an immortal from the Red Palisades paradise.

line 48: On Penglai, see P.11.12.

lines 50–51: "Essences of moon and stars," literally, "fluid beams of light," *liu guang*. In Daoist religious practice, one technique for cultivating immortality was to imbibe, absorb, or breathe in the "pure" essences of the heavenly bodies by drinking dew, exposing the body to the stars and moonlight, or inducing a meditative trance in which the spirit was believed to travel to a constellation. "Spirit texts," literally "golden tablets," *jin ce*, refers to tablets said to contain instructions from Daoist spirits and immortals about ritual procedures for gaining power to transcend mortality and other human limitations.

P.52.6. *Living the Quiet Life*

Closing the gate,
  I am free to do as I please;
My humble lane
  is overgrown with vines.
The color of willows
  excites birds' noisy chatter;
The glitter of waves
  makes shades of evening calm.
Quietly, falling petals
  blanket the ground;
Clouds in the void, serene,
  lean upon forest.
You ask why I roost here,
  hidden away—
(8) Beside my bed there is
  a stringless zither.

(MYSG, 32/9a)

line 16: The poet Tao Qian (Yuanming) "was no musician, but he kept a plain zither with no strings. When stimulated by wine he would strum it as a way of expressing his feelings" (*Song shu*, p. 2288).

P.52.7. *A Young Wife's Lament*

Above a tall house
  clouds drift across the sky,
The bright moon shines down
  with a light pure and clear.
A young wife wakes and sadly sighs,
The pitch of her grief resonates
  with the clear *shang* note of autumn.
"White clouds cover the pass to Qin,
Green water blocks the bridge to Jing;
My absent one defends a distant border,
(8) Vast, the strange country between us.
The Wolf of Heaven burns with steady fire,
The Horsetail Whisk is flashing fitfully.

In the courtyard, orchids on dry stalks;
Their leaves are injured by the freezing air.
Flowerlike youth, with passing days
  has lost its sweetness,
Cloudlike hair
  is blown in tangles by the wind.
My mirror of former time I break
  in two,
Sending half to you
  long miles past dikes and terraced fields.
When my chaste heart
  is buried in yellow earth,
Bright sun shall say
  farewell to rouged cheek.
Don't dwell upon the joy
  we had here, hand in hand,
Just swear to meet your death
  there on the field of battle.
When a young man's body
  is promised to his country,
Should his wife have any cause
  to feel the wound of grief?"

(MYSG, 32/10b–11a)

line 4: The musical note *shang* was associated, in the traditional system of correspondences, with the season of autumn.

lines 5–6: Qin and Jing were two rival feudal kingdoms of the Warring States period (475–221 B.C.E.) during the Zhou dynasty. Jing is another name for the ancient state of Chu.

lines 9–10: The Wolf of Heaven corresponds to the star Sirius in the constellation Canis Major. Changes in the Wolf's luminosity were understood to portend rebellion or war. The Horsetail Whisk was one of the twenty-eight constellations of the Chinese zodiac, the seven stars known in the West as the Pleiades. Astrologers interpreted distinct flashing or twinkling in this constellation as a sign of imminent catastrophe, such as flood or military uprisings. The constellation was also called the Barbarian Stars, *huxing*; when the stars appeared to fade out completely, a serious nomad invasion was expected.

line 15: On the broken mirror as emblem for the separation of husband and wife, see P.24.2.

P.52.8. Brief Song

I

Haven't you noticed—
Flowers of radiant beauty
on a bough in the breezes of spring,
And how, in a matter of days,
spring breezes blow the flowers down?
Let us not glamorize
the joys and sorrows of life;
Rosy faces will melt away
in the heat of joys and sorrows.
There's no end to joys and sorrows
but our lives will have an end,
Leaving only the moon at night
to shed its pure and fluid light,
(8) And among the flowers
beneath the leaves
mist in the vacant air.

II

Haven't you noticed—
How the boy whose hair
hangs down in tufts
Is all at once somebody's father?

Haven't you noticed
How the girl with brows
so lovely and dark
Ends up as the matron next door?

And haven't you noticed—
(8) How fancy banquets are spread
in the grandest of halls
With crystal-clear songs and
all kinds of music and dance,
Then before you know it
the candles burn out
music falls still

It's quiet and empty
with nothing at all
left to see?
Our human lives
are just like this;
Once we pass on,
no present or past.

The sun is unwilling to stay,
Pink cheeks in time turn to earth.
Brief songs are the saddest of songs.

(MYSG, 32/4a–b)

In this poem Li Qingzi imitates Li Bo, who uses a free style signaled by changes in syllable count and frequent apostrophes.

P.52.9. To a Courtesan

In skirt of kingfisher blue
robes of peony crimson
You halt your cloud-carriage
at a hidden spot deep
in a mass of flowers.
Reaching for a red leaf
you casually inscribe some words,
Feeling no less a poet
than Collator Xue of long ago.

(MYSG, 32/13b)

line 2: Immortals are described in literary texts as riding through the skies in carriages made of clouds, drawn by rain dragons or other fabulous beasts.

line 4: Collator Xue is Xue Tao, P.10.

P.52.10. A Beautiful Woman Asleep in Springtime

Behind the "mother-of-clouds" screen
in a "seven treasures" inlaid bed
Where tasseled curtains are warm,
scented with aromatic "bunched gold,"
This beautiful woman who last night
sang and danced her heart out

Now twists and turns mothlike brows
  trying to evade the morning light.

(MYSG, 32/12b)

lines 1–2: "Mother-of-clouds," *yunmu*, was the Chinese name for mica, which was used decoratively in the accessories of the wealthy. The details of the bedroom's decor suggest that this woman is a very successful entertainer. The list of the "seven treasures," or seven precious substances used ornamentally varied with time and taste. A representative list appearing in the Song dynasty history includes gold, silver, agate, cowry, amber, and coral. "Bunched gold," *yujin*, was a popular name for the turmeric plant, the tuber of which was used in cooking, as a medicament, and as an aromatic. The best turmeric was imported from Malaya and was thus a luxury item.

P.52.11. *The Sick Songstress*

She leans for support upon a silver screen;
  lately she doesn't allow herself to sing.
Her Chu waist is thin and weak,
  hardly able to bear a silk dress.
In her small courtyard the moon sets,
  flowers have nothing to say;
Sadly, anxiously, she listens
  to rain in the night, falling faster.

(MYSG, 32/12b)

line 2: Literary convention used women of the south, from the region of the ancient state of Chu, to represent an ideally delicate and graceful figure.

P.52.12. *Song of Sorrow*

On the path of a great endeavor
  I set my foot, and traveled far;
In a young and gallant heart
  fierce passion was running high.
My aim: sweep clean the Tartar dust!
Smite the Wolf of Heaven with a flying sword!
Then the Silver River vanished from the blue,
In the Fusang tree the sun remained concealed.
The world grew overcast, obscured and dim,
(8) Dark winds came blasting wild, chaotic.
On the trip back, in misery at my failure,

I felt knots of sorrow twisting in my gut.
Deeds of worth and a good name—
  not achieving these has brought me pain.
(12) A lifetime is a bright vision
  that quickly passes away—
When it's gone, it's gone,
  what more is there to say?
When they bury this body
  let it be on Beimang Mountain.

(MYSG, 32/2a)

lines 4–6: On the Wolf of Heaven, see P.52.7. The Silver River is the Milky Way. The Fusang tree is the cosmic tree at the end of the world; the sun was said to set on it each night.

line 14: Beimang, north of the medieval captital city of Luoyang, was the final resting place of many princes and chancellors and thus a favored site for melancholy musings. See Guo Maoqian, *Yuefu shiji*, 94/1322–23, for some examples.

P.52.13. In Response to Lady Fan

Thousands of valleys
  wind in the pines,
    thousands of valleys
    autumn.
Each separate note
  of the crying birds
    is a separate note
      of sorrow.
I want to send you
  my sorrowing heart—
    with whom then shall I send it?
I'll send it with the flowing stream
  that bears my flowing tears away.

(MYSG, 32/13a–b)

The addressee of this poem was probably Xu Yuan, whose husband's family name was Fan.

P.52.14. *Hardships of the Road*

With orchid and musk
   tapestried quilts perfumed;
Behind silk screens
   breezes of spring still cold.
When I bound up my hair
   and became your bride
We were always together
   like a bundle tied:
      you were my heart's beloved.
We were lacquer and glue—
   who could come between?
We were metal and stone—
   enduring to the end.
Then a mere word, by chance
   caused the ruin of all my hopes;
(8) Your angry glance
   was the first sign of ill will.
The lady's beauty
   gradually faded away;
The shining mirror
   took leave of the soaring phoenix.
I mounted the carriage,
   went out the gate and left,
(12) The knot of our bond
   for a thousand miles unraveled.

When I was young
   I enjoyed your loving favor;
Who could know then
   my road would be hard to travel?
Though it hasn't been long
   they speak of someone new;
(16) Your generous love for me
   is truly already spent!

(MYSG, 32/1b)

P.52.15. Song of the Border

Frontier geese fly high
  autumn is in the blossoming reeds
Towering clouds, motionless
  he feels now the melancholy of borderlands.
Miles and miles of yellow sand
  strand the traveler
At evening, his spirit overwhelmed
  he cries as he waters his horse.

(MYSG, 32/12a)

BIOGRAPHICAL NOTE AND TRANSLATION BY MAUREEN ROBERTSON

P.53. Xu Yuan (fl. 1590)

Xu Yuan, who lived and wrote during the Wanli reign of the Shenzong Emperor (1573–1620), was, in her time, the foremost woman poet of Suzhou. Born in Suzhou, she was the eldest daughter of the imperial retainer Xu Shitai. According to her biographers, Xu Yuan displayed her talents at a tender age, mastering literary writings and earning the nickname "Xie reincarnate" in reference to Xie Daoyun (on whom see C.24.1).

As an adult, Xu Yuan assumed the name Xiaoshu, "Petite Lady." She married Fan Yunlin, a lover of books like herself, but found that her wifely duties took her away from her own literary work. Because of her in-laws' financial difficulties, Xu Yuan spent her evenings weaving cloth; she even sold jewelry and other items of her dowry to help the family and make it possible for her husband to apply himself to his studies. Despite their relative poverty, however, Xu Yuan and Fan Yunlin seemed to have been a model "talented couple." They cultivated a relationship based on mutual honor and respect, not only for each other's person, but for each other's work as well, as each read and polished the style of literary pieces the other had written.

Eventually, Fan Yunlin's diligence paid off, and he succeeded in securing an official position, which took him to Nanjing, Yunnan, and Guizhou. Xu Yuan, with what must have been a driving curiosity to see the many places she had previously only read about, did not remain at home, as did so many gentry women of her time, but rather traveled with her husband around the country. Thus, her lifetime experiences were both broad and deep.

Like many poets of her day, Xu Yuan held the Tang dynasty masters in high esteem, but she chose as her favorite the eccentric Li He. Still, as her husband put it, "In most cases, she took her own heart and mind as her teacher and created [her poems] herself, without models to imitate." The Qing critic Qian Xiyan commented that her poetry was "splendid, like rose-colored clouds at daybreak, brilliant as moonlight, with a fragrance like delicate orchids in ancient fields . . . and without too much ornament, like scattered stars in the Milky Way."

Also characteristic of Xu Yuan was her love of personal and even intimate expression through verse. The Qing critic Qian Qianyi notes that she exchanged verses with a number of literati, many of whom were leading scholars in the Jiangsu area. But she also dedicated verses to or exchanged poetry with a number of women, including Lu Qingzi (P.52), often employing the vocabulary of a lover.[1]

In order to commemorate many difficult years of nighttime weaving and studying, Xu Yuan's twelve-*juan* collection of poetry is entitled *Luowei yin* (Silk-reeling chants).[2]

P.53.1. Written Impromptu While Passing By Dragon Lake, at the Courier Station

I look out into the expanse of green with white clouds floating,
With winding, winding pointed spring hills, straddled by a tiny
  bridge.
Ten thousand trees of misty smoke coil round woodland peaks;
Halfway to heaven, wind's adumbration sweeps the river tides.
Mountain dwellers' wine is fully matured, overflowing with grapes,
And the ferry launch's fish is so fresh that the fine-weave net's still
  stirring.
The sun sets at the courier lodge, we settle in for the night;
(8) Tremulous, the slender moon is overlaced with a forest of branch-tips.

(MYSG, 33/9b)

P.53.2. *A Toast, Following the Rhyme-Pattern of Another's Poem (Composed some time ago, seeing my husband off to the northwest)*

Unabating winds sweep through outlying fields, the high mountain
clouds are yellow;
At the distant border, migrating swans, and night upon night of frost.
On the "vast ocean" of Gobi sand, as on a floating raft: just a man and
his shadow;
Near the frontier, your spur on your horse, and this raft serves as your
bridge.
Willow catkins are startled to flight by the scene atop my tower;
Plum blossoms, all of them fallen to the sounds of the flute.
The road has not yet been opened for your passage to Yanran—
(8) Whom shall I enlist to take up his arrow and shoot down the Wolf of
Heaven?

(MYSG, 33/9b)

line 7: "Yanran" is Hang'ai Mountain in Outer Mongolia.
line 8: On the Wolf of Heaven, see P.52.7.

P.53.3. *Presented to My Younger Brother's Wife, Ye Niang*

Her marvelous beauty possesses the fragrant spring,
Her manner effortlessly steals the hearts of others.
Pacing back and forth, leaning against the curtain screen,
Coming and going, her shadow spills across a carpet of flowers.
The dressing table mirror reveals the lovely curves of her face;
Lowering her head, coiled hair forward, she folds an embroidered
kerchief.
To her pair of moth eyebrows she lightly applies black kohl,
(8) With delicate hands she smoothes on flesh-colored powder.
Her *qin* plays, and flowing water echoes its tune;
Pipes perform, and colored clouds unfurl.
She composes songs on the River Xiang,
(12) Leaves pearls on the Luo River's banks.
Patterned curtains obscure the moonlight;
Sheer silk awnings ward off fragrant dust.
Dreams are broken by dawn at her window;
(16) Flowers are bright, fledgling swallows tame.

May we meet someday at the riverbank's bend
To gather greenery and enjoy a fine day together.

(MYSG, 33/10a)

P.53.4. *Observing Change*

Autumn cicadas die in the withered mulberry trees;
Wispy clouds screen out the sun's bright rays.
Objects' conditions alter, following changing circumstances,
And because of this, my pensive heart holds sobs choked with grief.

(MYSG, 33/10b)

P.53.5. *Walking at Daybreak [two poems from a set of three]*

I

The crescent moon's jade pendant begins to recede,
The last rosy clouds sink behind the ancient hills.
Fading stars linger in daybreak's trees,
River shadows intertwine with currents of mist.

II

The sheet of Canglang River is white;
Morning's brilliance lights upon the purple screen.
Dawn's Raven caws unceasingly,
Calling attention to winter's light touch of cold.

(MYSG, 33/10b–11a)

i: The moon resembles a semicircular pendant (*huang*) of which the discreet tinkling would be heard during a lover's early-morning departure.

ii: Canglang is a river in Suzhou. The raven is the three-footed bird that inhabits the sun.

P.53.6. *A Spring Day, Tending the Family Garden*

Precious flowers push forth around stone steps;
Wild bamboo, in every shade of green.
A slight breeze rolls open the curtain,
A secret fragrance wafts down the footpath.

(MYSG, 33/11a)

P.53.7. For a Beautiful Woman

Pretty eyebrows, envy of the aromatic spring;
Eyes with wave-like glances: autumn moons.
Gracefully, she walks among the blossom-covered shrubs.
A breeze arrives; her light sleeves slightly flare.

Her fragile frame cannot withstand the autumn,
Listless, she can't bear the endless day.
What is it that most touches her emotions?
(8) Bamboo shadows swaying over clear waters.

(MYSG, 33/11a)

P.53.8. The Herd Boy and the Weaving Girl

The Magpie Bridge breaks apart over the Silver Han,
Parting sorrows darken the clear flow.
A belt of mist, then morning comes, making it more transparent,
Yet wind-swept hair bespeaks midnight worries.
She removes her ornaments, washes off old makeup,
And tidies the case which holds her new clothes.
They stare across at each other; she leans against her loom;
(8) Their paired hearts are just as in autumns past.

(MYSG, 33/7b)

On the Herd Boy and the Weaving Girl and the Double Seventh, see P.5.1. Xu refers to Li He's poem "Seventh Night" ("Qi xi," QTS, 390/4394), which focuses on the contrasting perceptions of the festival as seen from heaven and from earth.

P.53.9. Autumn Night (After Li He)

The purple incense-stand's lonely column of smoke sweeps across
white walls;
Pervasive coolness moves the precious zither's strings.
A leaf of maple floats by—suddenly it's autumn;
Silk-reeling sounds are sad amid the soughing of wind.
Congealed dew on red orchids, creamy rouge weeping;
Frost flies from ancient locust trees, reflecting the moonlight.
Longing deep in my chambers, I hear evening's pounding of laundry
rocks,

And the cutting of set lengths of silk: sounds of knives and rules.
Vivid stars across the sky build the Magpie Bridge;
Chang E, in her cassia palace, sits throughout the night.
The needle-threading moon is bright, the flowers are resplendent;
Clothes-Sunning Tower is obscured, auspicious smoke disappears.
The vault of heaven is hushed, the Bright River shines,
A turning well-rope sounds *yi-ya*.
At the wood's edge, hibiscus grows by the pond,
On the pool's fresh water floats a pair of ducks.

(MYSG, 33/2b)

line 4: On the "silk-reeler," whose sound is characteristic of autumn, see note 2 to the biographical note.

line 8: The silk is being cut to make winter clothing.

lines 11–12: These lines build on one couplet of Li He's poem: "Magpies take leave of the needle-threading moon, / Flowers [or, in another reading, "fireflies"] enter the Clothes-Sunning Tower." "Clothes-Sunning Tower" was built during the time of Emperor Wu of the Han dynasty (r. 141–87 B.C.E.); court ladies aired clothes out in the sun there on Double Seventh day. On needle-threading by moonlight and other rituals of "begging for skill" on Double Seventh, see P.5.1.

line 13: The Bright River is the Silver River, or Milky Way.

P.53.10. Palace Lament

I

From magnificent chambers fragrance blows forth; fragrance of powder and kohl;
In the night, so cold, high in the blue, I see the river's bridge.
The Star Couple fails to turn and shine down upon mortals;
Cold fills the pear flower on the white jade bed.

II

Gazing, gazing, deep in the palace, the cassia halls are cold;
The magnificent rooms of the beauty A-jiao are filled with night-flying frost.
Don't spend a thousand in gold to buy Xiangru's *fu*;
White-haired Wenjun's lament is long enough.

(MYSG, 33/13a)

i, line 2: The Magpie Bridge across the Silver River (Milky Way).

ii, line 3: The Star Couple are Weaving Girl and Herd Boy.

ii, line 2: II. A-jiao, the beautiful daughter of Chen Yinghui, became a favorite of Emperor Wu of the Han (r. 141–87 B.C.E.). For her the emperor built magnificent rooms.

ii, line 4: On the two episodes in Sima Xiangru's life alluded to here, see P.8a.1 and P.38.1.

P.53.11. Chanting of Aromatic Grasses

The year's commencement, the sun's first light;
The trees' green shade, luxuriant.
Flying brightness scatters the clouds;
Multicolored dew appears at morning.
South of the river, sapphire splendor;
Far off at the border, a coil of silk threads.
Returning to my chamber, bound up in my thoughts
That on the expedition, his horse is slow.
Climbing the mountain, gathering handfuls of herbs,
I look as far as I can, to heaven's edge.
Following one after the other, folks enjoy the country,
Plucking aromatic grasses from the beautiful bank.
My thoughts are of resting here
Where coolness rises on a pure fresh breeze.
Footstalks are fragrant between my fingers,
Leaves and stems pliant and moist.
Yet I'd rather be like the spring pine—
Not shrinking from frost's imposition.

(MYSG, 33/1a)

line 7: This line plays on the homophony of "silk" and "longing," both pronounced *si*.

P.53.12. On Sending a Gift of a Lamp

Clouds set ablaze by trees of fire;
The moon is warmed by stars.
The Lantern Festival, a gala affair;
Spring forests of feasting and toasts.

Pepper plates' fragrance spills over;
Cypress wine shines as it floats.

(MYSG, 33/1a–b)

lines 5–6: At the New Year it was a custom to offer one's parents wine flavored with pepper and cypress as a wish for their longevity.

P.53.13. *Parting Words to Uncle's Wife as She Returns to Chu*

Our hearts lingering at the Northern Bridge;
Our steps disconsolate as we hold hands.
The cold pond's wild flowers wither;
The hidden path's fragrant orchids fade.
Forever cut off from Wuchang fish scales,
Afraid that we'll never see Hengyang feathers.
How can I ease my troubled thoughts—
(8) Ever clinging with the firmness of metal and stone?

(MYSG, 33/2b)

lines 5–6: Fish and birds are elements of the scenery by Dongting Lake in the former kingdom of Chu. Both are also messengers that carry correspondence between friends; see P.2.1 (Song 5) and P.26.7.

P.53.14. *Traveling to the Xu Family's Mountain Villa*

Autumn's emptiness: I gaze far, clouds merge with the sea;
Setting sun in a village market, the tower I see seems to hang in
mid-air.
A thousand piles of hibiscus reach up to the sky;
An arc of water and moon is imprinted upon the heart's quietude.
Autumn wind, half faded colors of the *wutong* tree;
Fragrant haze, half tangerine and half pomelo mist.
Crying birds, sun's slanting rays, the traveler is weary;
(8) But that does not keep her from leaving her couch to sleep amid forest
and stream.

(MYSG, 33/9a)

P.53.15. *Crossing the River*

Setting aslant its lightweight sails, I ride a tiny boat;
The clear river is like white silk, its water peacefully flowing.

In the misty mountain scenery, heaven and earth are merged;
In the distance, hazy smoke and light seem to float high and low.
In brush thickets, a profusion of flowers suited for breeding butterflies;
Wild duckweeds and shoreline reeds are good for sheltering gulls.
Xiao xiao the wind whips up, the waves chill my heart;
(8) Dusk falls to the sound of a clear reed whistle throughout the garrison watchtowers.

(MYSG, 33/9a–b)

P.53.16. Written in Fun for My Cousin in Celebration of Her Wedding

I

In cassia rooms the orchid censer burns brightly;
Though cloud-like windows, drums beat anew.
A person like the one who sits in the moonlight:
A scene rivaling spring in the Han Palace.
Perfecting your beauty, you steal glances in the phoenix mirror;
Refreshing your makeup, you adjust a green hand scarf.
Full of tenderness, yet shy to come from behind the curtain;
(8) Wavering light shines upon your back, your waist, your body.

II

Painted sheer silk, floating scarf upon your forehead;
Soft thick canopy, richly ornamented bed.
Standing screen panels carved from mother-of-cloud;
At the heart of the chamber hangs a crescent moon of jade.
Hiding from the wind, a lacquer stand reflects green shadows;
As you take lotus footsteps, silk stockings emit perfume.
You have a husband who will forever serve as your companion;
(8) Bring him round to share a cup with us amidst the flowers!

(MYSG, 33/7a)

ii, line 6: "Lotus steps" are steps made with bound feet (often described as resembling lotus buds). Another explanation of the phrase refers it to the lotus-patterned walkway made by Emperor Fei (r. 559–60) of the Northern Qi for his consort Pan. The rest of the line alludes to Cao Zhi, "Rhyme-prose on the Goddess of the Lo": "Her gauze stockings give off a fragrant dust" (*Wen xuan*, 19/14b).

BIOGRAPHICAL NOTE AND TRANSLATION BY MARY ELLEN FRIENDS

P.54. Shen Yixiu and Her Daughters, Ye Wanwan, Ye Xiaowan, and Ye Xiaoluan

Shen Yixiu (style name Wanjun) and her three daughters, Ye Wanwan (style name Zhaoqi), Ye Xiaowan, and Ye Xiaoluan (style name Qiongzhang), form a literary constellation unparalleled in Chinese history. Born into a distinguished family of scholars in the Wujiang region (in modern Jiangsu province), Shen was married to the talented official Ye Shaoyuan (1589–1649) and gave birth to three daughters and five sons. Shen was particularly proud of her three outstanding daughters and educated them alongside their brothers.

Shen's early poems were marked by a melancholy born of her long separations from her husband and her sensitivity to others' suffering. This melancholy later gave way to mourning for the early death of her daughters. Xiaoluan, the youngest daughter, died at the age of seventeen, five days before she was to be married. According to Cao Xuequan (1574–1646), who wrote a preface to Ye Shaoyuan's anthology *Wumengtang quanji*, this unexpected loss led to the death soon after of the grief-stricken Wanwan, the eldest daughter. (Dorothy Ko suggests that they were both more likely victims of one of the epidemics that swept through China in the seventeenth century.) [1] Shen's later poems are saturated with the memory of these two daughters. Their language obsessively echoes the wording of the poems she had exchanged with them in earlier years.

Although Shen herself lived only to the age of forty-five, she wrote or edited several collections of poetry, including *Lichui ji* (Oriole melodies) and *Meihua shi baishou* (One hundred quatrains on plum flowers). Her poems, along with those of her daughters, all appear in Ye Shaoyuan's *Wumengtang quanji*

(Collected works from the Daydreamer's Studio; see C.38). She also edited an anthology of women poets, *Yiren si* (Thoughts of one far away; see C.8). The *Yujing yangqiu* describes Shen's compositions as "overly ornate and resplendent, falling short of succinctness and serenity."[2] One may counter, however, that as they walked the tightrope between sensibility and sentimentality, Shen Yixiu and her daughters managed to convey their observations of the world with thoughtfulness and insight. Shen Yixiu's later poems, occasioned by the loss of her daughters, tackle questions about women and writing, suffering and transcendence, with deep pathos.

Among the three daughters, Xiaoluan was renowned as a child prodigy, excelling in the style of seven-character ancient-style poetry and quatrains. She was also a talented artist.[3] Many of her poems collected in *Fansheng xiang* (The fragrance of reincarnation) follow the tradition of "poems on objects" (*yongwu shi*), with one sequence celebrating the female body part by part. This poem series invited her parents' poetic responses and is revealing evidence of the mutual literary inspiration among the family members. The poems produced by this exchange, centering on the unusual topic of bound feet, have been translated and discussed elsewhere.[4]

Wanwan's works in *Chouyan* (Melancholy words) reveal her desire to retire from the world and transcend worldly concerns; she is remembered particularly for her seven-character quatrains and song-lyrics.[5] The surviving daughter, Xiaowan, did not specialize in poetic composition, and her literary reputation was founded on her four-act play entitled *Yuanyang meng* (Dream of the mandarin ducks), in which three brothers suffer early death and achieve immortality on the occasion of their reunion. The three brothers are usually identified with Xiaowan and her two sisters. The play therefore exemplifies the female fantasy of cross-dressing and emulating male literary counterparts, even though Xiaowan lived in an intellectually liberal family and enjoyed an education that did not distinguish between the sexes.

Ye Xiaowan was one of the first Chinese women to explore this genre, dominated by male playwrights.[6] Her achievements may seem natural in light of the tradition of her family: Shen Yixiu was the cousin of the famous dramatist Shen Jing (1553–1610) and the sister of the late Ming *zaju* writer Shen Zizheng (1591–1641).

沈宜修

P.54a. Shen Yixiu (1590–1635)

P.54a.1. Recording My Thoughts

In ancient times the poet Yu Xuanji
Without sufficient reason discussed feelings thus:
"It is easy to seek a priceless treasure,
  but hard to find a man with heart"—
How greatly mistaken was her statement!
When is the world ever short of passions?
But all in all these are not genuine feelings;
One party may harbor intense passion
While the other's feeling is thinner than paper;
The impassioned one cannot forget the remote other,
And pursues daily her obsession in vain.
Compare Plum Blossom with Yang Yuhuan:
Which woman is more beautiful?
One passionate and the other heartless—
But how can we tell them apart?
Like illusions when seen through an enlightened eye,
Everything disappears like flowing water.

(*Lichui ji*, in *Wumengtang quanji*, 4)

lines 1–4: On Yu Xuanji, see P.11.17. Compare Hu Wenru's treatment of the same sentiment, P.51.4.

line 12: Jiang Caipin, a literate and talented concubine of the Tang emperor Xuanzong, had plum trees planted all around her residence; Xuanzong called her his Plum-Blossom Consort (Mei Fei). Subsequently, however, Mei Fei was supplanted in the emperor's affections by the plump dancer Yang Guifei (Yuhuan). In her retirement, Mei Fei composed a "Rhapsody from East of the Tower" that recalls Ban *jieyu*'s "Rhapsody of Self-Commiseration" (P.1.2) and Sima Xiangru's "Changmen Palace Rhapsody" (see P.8a.1). See the *chuanqi* tale "Meifei zhuan," Lu Xun, ed., *Tang Song chuanqi ji*, pp. 282–86.

P.54a.2. An Autumn Night in Jinling

Crickets chirp with deep sorrow,
Crumbling walls are deserted in a ghost-haunted evening.
Antique casements capture the moonlight,
Cold cypress trees luxuriate in the bleak swamp.
The place differs, my sorrow differs not,
The river flows, my remorse flows with it;
Carefree clouds drift in uncertainty,
Fleeting shadows grow idle by the day.

The frail leaves of the leaning willow
Still remain as the relics of the Six Dynasties.
But where is the Jingyang Palace to be found?
Devastated, the Brocade Terrace exists no more.
I suddenly realize how time has passed!
Wilting flowers hasten the silvering of my hair;
Writhing with worries, I lament to no purpose.
My garden plants bring no relief from sorrow;
I advise you: never be born a woman—
Wealthy or humble, you will end sorrowful all the same;
Why bother to consult Junping's soothsaying?
One exerts no control over destiny.

The bugle announces the setting of the moon,
A broken dream descends into the Xiao-Xiang basin.
The bell in a distant temple ceases its tolling,
I raise the curtain, stirring the reflected dim light of daybreak;
The thin garment dreads the morning's freezing cold,
The autumn fan laments the coming of cold seasons.
Holding my dress, I try to raise myself,
Pressing against my pillows, I feel the endurance of my resentment.
Uncertain and lonely, with only my melancholy,
Tears wet my clothes.

Leaning against the threshold, I first look into the mirror,
Still hearing the chirping of the yellow birds;
Their trills intertwine with the wind,
Like those of birds singing in my hometown.

Fragrant grasses, haunted by sorrowful thoughts,
Stretch their footprints to the ends of the earth.
Baffling, baffling, the autumn landscape,
Forlorn, forlorn, feelings past and present.

(*Lichui ji*, in *Wumengtang quanji*, 4–5)

lines 11–12: Both the Jingyang Palance and the Brocade Terrace were lodgings for the consorts of the last emperor of the Chen dynasty.

line 16: Literally, "my garden plants are not daylilies." On the daylily, see P.2.1 (Song 16).

line 19: During the Han dynasty, the famous soothsayer Junping ran a business in Chengdu. Once he had earned a certain amount of money, he would close his shop and lecture on the *Dao de jing*.

line 35: *Fangcao* (fragrant grass), used since Qu Yuan's "Li sao" (see P.37) as an image for the uprightness of the rejected official, is here associated with departure and separation.

P.54a.3. *On Double Seventh Festival, Missing My Two Dead Daughters*

"Begging for skill" is an annual event,
But this time my sorrow exceeds all times past.
The magpies constructed the bridge to fulfill an old promise,
And melons and fruits introduce the coming autumn.
But colored silk cannot thread tears,
The golden needle only rends the heart.
I want to tell the weaving girls:
Don't sport your artful threads.

(*Lichui ji*, in *Wumengtang quanji*, 26)

On the Double Seventh festival, see P.5.1, P.19.2.

P.54a.4. *On an Autumn Day, I Wait for Zhongshao's [Ye Shaoyuan's] Letter from the Capital, Which Never Arrives*

The chill of the west wind sets in, dyeing my fragrant skirt green,
Your white-haired mother waits for your return every evening at the door.
Isn't there a single goose left in the capital?
Must you deprive the paired carp of their silken voice?

Wang Can climbs the tower, pondering—
When will Qin Jia at the frontier write to his wife?
All the white duckweed is swept away, and the waves turn green,
Pine trees swish in the wind, dew congeals on the paulownia, yet behind the evening curtains: emptiness.

(*Lichui ji*, in *Wumengtang quanji*, 33)

lines 3–4: On geese as carriers of letters, see P.2.1 (Song 5), and on carp, see P.26.7.
line 5: On Wang Can, see P.17.2.
line 6: The correspondence between Qin Jia (fl. ca. 147) and his wife, Xu Shu, is one of the earliest masterpieces of the literary exchange between husband and wife. With his third poem, Qin sent gifts, among them a mirror (in later literature a frequent reference for separated couples). For the poems exchanged between the two, see Xu Ling, *Yutai xinyong*, 1/11a–12 (Birrell, *New Songs*, pp. 45–47).

P.54a.5. *Late Spring: Parting from Junhui, I Compose This Poem to Rhyme with His Farewell Poem*

Drizzle woven with threads of mist: a doleful flute plays melodies of Yizhou and Liangzhou,
Green plums sprout daily like beans.
Young orioles and soft willows enchant the spring colors,
Painted barques and seagoing craft send off the setting sun.
Don't lament that the pond constantly enters your dream,
I alone indulge in wine as I pity the fragrant plant.
Drifting clouds wreathe around a thousand green mountains,
Yet I rue that Antares and Orion never meet.

(*Lichui ji*, in *Wumengtang quanji*, 35)

line 5: At the age of ten, Xie Huilian (397–433) was greatly admired by the famous poet Xie Lingyun (385–433), who came from the same clan and was Huilian's senior. Lingyun acknowledged Huilian as his poetic inspiration by recording an anecdote. When Xie Lingyun was in West Pond of Yongjia region, he could not bring his own poem to conclusion for months. Once he dreamed of Huilian, he came up with his famous line: "Spring grass grows from the pond." See "Xie Huilian zhuan," *Nan shi* 19/21a.
line 8: On Antares and Orion, see P.3.3.

P.54a.6. *Autumn Night: Lamenting My Feelings*

In this endless chilly evening, dew refreshes the air,
In the lush meadow hidden insects quaver in bitterness and sorrow;

He left me, just as the first leaf fell from the high trees;
Awakened by the third watch, I feel the brevity of dream, the
transience of life.
Alone, I lament the haunting thousand Melodies of Whirling Waves,
In vain the waning moonlight shines through half the casement.
Wenyuan, ill and frustrated, travels far in autumnal melancholy,
(8) The west wind incites sentiments of ten thousand years.

(*Lichui ji*, in *Wumengtang quanji*, 38)

line 3: "One leaf" is short for "one [fallen] leaf reveals the coming of the autumn" (*yiye zhiqiu*); see *Huainan zi*, "Shuoshan xun," 16/7a.

line 5: "Melodies of Whirling Waves" (*Huibo qu*) is a musical composition created during the reign of Emperor Zhong of the Tang dynasty. This music was often performed in the banquets held by Emperor Zhong, in which officials composed poetry according to the tune and danced to the music. When the poet Shen Quanqi (ca. 650–713) returned from exile, he delivered poems set to these melodies to request the restoration of his official position. The song is therefore associated with self-promotion.

line 7: Shen Yixiu compares her husband to the great Han poet Sima Xiangru (style name Wenyuan; see P.8a.1), who was frustrated in his official career and fell victim to illness despite his unsurpassed talents.

P.54a.7. Mourning for My Eldest Daughter Zhaoqi [Wanwan]

I stored your clothes in the chest, but who would wear them?
Then I sold them to finance the sacrifices to Buddha.
Heroic and carefree, you departed from this world!
Now in utmost pain, I am even more perplexed and lost.
I do know that illusive transformation is not reality,
But without the enlightenment of true emptiness I only come to
deeper sorrow.
I only hope that in our next three reincarnations our souls will not
bypass each other,
(8) By the Ge River we will exchange smiles, fortuitously met.

(*Lichui ji*, in *Wumengtang quanji*, 41)

lines 7–8: In Buddhist teaching, the three incarnations are the previous one, the present one, and the next. The phrase evokes the idea of fated meeting in a future life through the tale of the Tang-dynasty monk Yuanguan. Yuanguan and the former playboy Li Yuan were great friends, and Yuanguan, shortly before his death, promised to meet Li again twelve years later at the Tianzhu Monastery outside Hangzhou. At the appointed time, Li, arriving at the monastery, heard a shepherd boy on the far bank of the Gehong River singing: "At the Rock of Three Incarnations waits a former soul; / Admiring the moon, chanting the wind [i.e., literary pursuits] are no longer its affair. / I'm touched to see a dear friend come from so far away; / The body may be different but the spirit is the same." It was, of course, Yuanguan's reincarnation (Li Fang, comp., *Taiping guangji*, 387/3089–90).

P.54a.8. Expressing My Feelings, Rhyming with Zhongshao's Poem

Thick incense, misty grass, and a symphony of warblers,
Spring's charm is disturbed, but what can I do?
In my utmost destitution, I can no longer resist the demon of illness,
Upon finishing each poem, I come to lament the hallucinating power of writing.
The storm has subsided, vermilion blossoms climb up the branches in the small courtyard.
A curtain of drooping willow refreshed by the rain: its green shadow dances.
The slender setting sun remains silent in melancholy,
(8) The distant mountains frown in the twilight, shaped like glossy hair-knots.

(*Lichui ji*, in *Wumengtang quanji*, 46)

P.54a.9. Poverty and Illness

Poverty and illness come upon me in succession, leaving me defenseless,
Poor me!—poverty and illness reinforce each other.
In desolation, I am ill and fearful of the piercing west wind
Which aggravates my poverty and lengthens the somber autumn days.
Ill, I lie in my freezing house, enduring months and years.
Since few guests visit a poor person, I have no need for hurry.
The demon of illness asks the ghost of poetry to compose an apology,
(8) Yet when will the devil of poverty retreat to a remote place?

(*Lichui ji*, in *Wumengtang quanji*, 47)

P.54a.10. A Reminiscence

Endless ancient routes share the same twilight,
Chirping orioles disturb the shiny willow leaves,

In vain I compose a new poem to mourn an old event,
When evening clouds herd home the harvest boats.

(*Lichui ji*, in *Wumengtang quanji*, 58)

P.54a.11. *The Double Seventh*

The mother-of-cloud screen reflects the glare of crystal,
Green jeweled trees are drenched in the evening chill.
When we reunite, don't dwell on the last year's events,
Let us only lament the deep sorrow of impending parting.

(*Lichui ji*, in *Wumengtang quanji*, 62)

P.54a.12. *The Pine Tree*

In my leisure I take shelter under you to capture the chilly breeze,
In your green shade I become oblivious of the bawling world of dust.
Where else can I find a resting-place of flowing waters
And listen to the cranes wing through the lucid evening sky?

(*Lichui ji*, in *Wumengtang quanji*, 74)

P.54a.13. Huan xi sha: *An Occasional Composition*

High noon, a leaf flies about the palace gate,
In the human world, don't ask what is right or wrong,
Now watch the migrating geese skirt the overhanging clouds,
The footprints on the moss thin out,
In front of the balustrades, the languid shadows of flowers move,
We don't need to debate about the past and the present.

(*Lichui ji*, in *Wumengtang quanji*, 88)

P.54a.14. Ta suo xing

[My brother] Junyong had often promised to return home, but no time had been set for his coming. Then I saw him in a dream. Upon awakening, I was stricken with sorrow and composed poems to express my feelings.

I

Dream broken, hope abandoned,
Poems finished with dripping tears.

I want to return to the dream, but it has already vanished,
As I look on the ranks of cloudy mountain-peaks, my gaze is lost;
Boundless regions of misty forest fade into heaven's blue.

II

The traveler's lodging—clouds are thick,
The village far, roads are cut off.
To meet night after night—this is an impossibility;
The whole world becomes an insubstantial dream.
Orion slides, the moon falls, the darkness goes on forever.

(*Lichui ji*, in *Wumengtang quanji*, 106)

P.54a.15. Sheng sheng man: *In Ancient Style, Rhyming Eight Times on the Word "Sheng"*

Spring charms are no more,
Mist and grass seem to have no feelings;
As I set up the motley instruments and new music,
The pale makeup has just vanished from my forehead.
Purple swallows warble among the sculpted pillars,
The half-rolled bamboo curtain casts a green shadow,
Painted balustrades, several trees with twittering cuckoos;
(8) Under the apricot trees, I try to play my jade flute,
Attempting to learn the melodies of Qin.

On resplendent routes, perfumed carriages compete in splendor,
Loitering, I listen to the pure songs.
(12) The place is immersed in spring chimes.
I feel free in the small courtyard,
Flying petals remain reticent,
Pine-scented winds descend on the embroiled casements.
(16) The resonance of these sounds begets the music of Liang, blowing the whirling waves.
Still more,
several orioles trill around the willow trees.

(*Lichui ji*, in *Wumengtang quanji*, 112)

line 9: To "learn the melodies of Qin" suggests both true love and departure from this world; see the story of Nongyu and the Piper, P.26.5.

P.54a.16. Baizi ling: *Mourning on the Double Fifth Festival and Recording My Feelings*

Time of melancholy:
Again the ambiance of the Double Fifth Festival
Fills my view.
From dark willows emerges the orioles' music, thousands of trills,
Flowing through the painted curtains and wind-shaken bamboos.
With old regrets I meditate on flowers,
With new sorrow I weep over my dreams.
Drizzling rain beads on the green rush,
Tears spoil the fragrant grass,
Where shall this pining soul find the will to go on?

Don't tell me about the yearly flutes and drums,
Racing dragon boats,
Jade cups brimming with Linglu wine—
Present and past, rise and fall, how many alterations!
Endless, the ten thousand songs of Yuan and Xiang.
The bright moon shines on empty mountains,
The green pine stands alone in the dew,
Ducks fly as always through mist and water.
In the shadow cast by the descending evening glow,
Nothing is sadder than my shabby lodge.

(*Lichui ji*, in *Wumengtang quanji*, 114)

line 2: The fifth day of the fifth lunar month is called Duanwu, an ancient holiday of purification with which many festival observances have become associated. In particular, people commemorate the death of the poet Qu Yuan by holding dragon-boat races and tossing steamed rice dumplings into rivers. Shen Yixiu feels the tragedy more than the festivity.

line 13: "Linglu" is the legendary wine, famous for its green color, produced from the water of Lake Ling and Rivulet Lu.

line 15: The area watered by the Yuan and Xiang Rivers was Qu Yuan's birthplace. These songs are Qu Yuan's poetry—and, by extension, any poetic lament.

lines 18–19: The images in these two lines allude to the famous lines of Wang Bo (649–76): "The evening glow takes flight with the solitary duck, / Autumn water merges in one color with the long sky" (*Quan Tang wen*, 181/1: 814).

P.54a.17. Shuilong yin

On an autumn day of the year *gengwu* [1630], I composed two *ci* poems set to the tune "Water Dragon Chant," which became the rhyming model for my children. They followed my example and wrote down their poems on a fan. Now, three years later, I open a storage basket and chance upon the fan. And yet my two daughters have already passed away. The object still remains, while my beloved ones exist no more. I restrain my heart from breaking, but am unable to hold back my tears. I now follow the earlier poems' rhyme and compose these verses.

Glittering moonlight splinters the swift flux of time,
This instant, my tangled mind cannot recapture the past.
Fresh flowers have died out,
But what does the chilly toad intend?
Willows here and there seem half bent to the ground
With fluttering leaves that awaken melancholy.
Frozen clouds are intertwined with grief,
Again and again, ceaselessly.
I bemoan the autumn evening, forlorn and empty,
Night insects call lonesomely in their sorrow,
I bow my head in misery.

My hope of seeing your faces and hearing your voices is forever cut off.
For my broken heart only your embroidery-like writings are left.
Transverse mist dusts the Milky Way,
Migrating geese are about to cross.
The moon cold, flowers shriveled,
The setting sun swallows the stream.
Mountains hem in the unvisited path.
I think of the happy past—
Now my tears of pain flow like the river,
An accompaniment to the west wind's sighs.

(*Lichui ji*, in *Wumengtang quanji*, 116)

line 4: The "chilly toad" is the moon; see P.26.5.
lines 14–15: The migrating geese, usually associated with letters and the theme of the lonely traveler, here perform the crossing of the Milky Way usually done by the Herd Boy's magpies on Double Seventh Eve.

P.54a.18. Shuang ye fei: *Inscription on Junshan's Portrait of a Tonsured Cleric*

It is hard to express my pent-up feelings.
The west wind brings sorrow, causing people to lose their paths,
With a laugh I comb my white hair, resigned to my heartrending
  sorrow.
The dew mourns for the aging hibiscus;
Its dream broken under the misty willow, the butterfly awakens.
I mutter: why not cast aside the mirror and remove these chilly clouds?
Worldly matters always come to an end:
(8) All I ask is that the moonlight filtered through the dark window
Retain its midnight luster.

Haggard and agitated, yes—but I am not crazed;
Though melancholy, I am not drunk.
(12) The person in the painting must know.
Yellow leaves tumble over the cliffs in drifts,
As if to shriek with mournful apes.
Don't be vexed by the flowers fallen into the Chu
(16) Or the aromatic sandbars covered with melancholy grass.
Idle clouds float and accompany me,
Pines and moon in this empty mountain,
Cassia in groves, with boundless mist.

(*Lichui ji*, in *Wumengtang quanji*, 117)

line 6: "Chilly clouds" is a familiar kenning for women's luxuriant hair. The speaker is here considering cutting off her hair to take up the monastic life, in imitation of the person in Junshan's picture.

葉紈紈

P.54b. Ye Wanwan (1610–32)

P.54b.1. Autumn Day, Village Life: Rhyming After My Father's Poem

Floating life is nothing but a dream,
Ambitious people are pitiable creatures.
Predisposed to purity and seclusion,
I used to disdain worldly pursuits.
Furling the curtains, I rake off the fallen leaves,
And draw water to clean the silver pulley.
The river waves dissolve in the distant mist,
(8) Autumn leads waters to the Five Lakes.

(*Chou yan*, in *Wumengtang quanji*, 5)

line 8: The Five Lakes may be identified with different locations. In this case, they most likely refer to various lakes connected to Lake Tai, where the legendary hermit Fan Li (ca. 5th century B.C.E.) allegedly retreated with his lover Xi Shi, on whom see P.39.2.

P.54b.2. Double Seventh: Two Quatrains on the Weaving Girl

I

Jade terrace, agate courtyard, are aglow with the twilight,
Magpies build a bridge along the remote Milky Way.
Lest the Moon Goddess should get away so easily,
I resume working on my interrupted weaving, with barely stifled resentment.

II

Dusting the mirror, taking out the cosmetics, I trace my green eyebrows,
Decked out in my finest dress and makeup, I step from behind the purple cloud curtains;

One night's intimacy after a year-long separation,
At my happiest moment I feel the deepest sorrow.

(*Chou yan*, in *Wumengtang quanji*, 10)

i, line 1: "Jade terrace" and "agate courtyard" are metaphors for the moon.

P54b.3. Elegy for My Sister Qiongzhang [Xiaoluan]

Having just composed a poem to urge on Qiongzhang's wedding
makeup, I already have to mourn for her death,
O heaven, this agony—how you perpetuate this agony!
The ladies of Jade Terrace should have envied her new crimson-tube
brush,
In the human world remains eternal sorrow.

(*Chou yan*, in *Wumengtang quanji*, 12)

line 1: "Urging makeup" (*cui zhuang*) was a ritual performed before the wedding night, in which the bride's sisters and friends joyously helped her with her toilette. It became a theme for occasional poems.

line 3: On the "crimson [or vermilion] tube" as proverbial for a woman's writing instrument, see C.36.

P.54b.4. Pusa man: *Expressing My Feelings*

Who understands my drifting spring-day dream?
All of a sudden the green willow ages with the east wind;
I lament my own futile excess of feelings,
Floating in this dusty world, I always feel bitter and resentful.

The humble cottage surrounded by green mountains,
The winding shore where a creek faintly gurgles—
When can we fulfill our eternal wish
(8) And hand in hand head for the Jade Capital?

(*Chou yan*, in *Wumengtang quanji*, 21)

line 8: In Daoist usage, paradise or the abode of the gods.

P.54b.5. Shuilong yin: *Early Autumn Provokes Nostalgic Feelings; Composed by My Two Sisters and Myself, Following Our Mother's Rhyme*

This autumn I recall our parting at the river shore,
Objects remain as they were, but the past will not return:
My silk handkerchief is soaked with tears,
The soul spellbound at the ancient ford.
Willow branches are bent and broken by wisps of fog.
Crickets mourn the mounting chill,
The wind howls through the moonlit pass.
(8) How often have I been startled by autumn's return!
Lamenting that life in this world should be so inconstant,
So lacking in order and reason.
In vain I rehearse the past, scratching my head in perplexity.

(12) I still remember: we promised to meet
In Stone City, by the Huai, where mountains are like embroidery.
I pursue you still, but my wish will not be granted.
My brows are still knitted
(16) In remorse for our separation.
Pillow and bamboo mat, a touch of autumn chill,
The dream vanished from the ends of the earth,
A heartbreaking moment!
(20) Now I want only to enjoy the beautiful flowers,
Never ask why fleeting time proceeds in such a march.

(*Chou yan*, in *Wumengtang quanji*, 26–27)

葉小紈

P.54c. Ye Xiaowan (b. 1613)

P.54c.1. Elegy for My Sister Zhaoqi [Wanwan]

Your nature loved cloudy seclusion, you never betrayed your will.
Facing the bamboo casements, together we composed poems about the twilight.

Your expressions, your words, your jests still play on my mind as before,
But your supernatural clothing—where is it now?
When you go to the Turquoise Pond, you must have company,
But in the six corners of the world I have few understanding friends.
Alas, my recital of the Six Songs is choked by sobs,
(8) Blood and tears flow from every inch of my breaking heart.

(Appendix to *Chou yan*, in *Wumengtang quanji*, 32)

line 4: The phrasing suggests that Xiaoluan was an immortal in human form. In legends, such beings leave no corpse behind, only their clothes, after their return to heaven.

line 5: The "Turquoise Pond" is a name for the heavenly realm.

葉小鸞

P.54d. Ye Xiaoluan (1616–32)

P.54d.1. Langtao sha: *Spring Boudoir*

Translucent twilight, piercing chill,
Silky blanket, bamboo mat, burnt incense.
The painted wall detains the shadow, sports with the sunset,
A wisp coils from the dream-brewed tea,
Once again, dusk comes upon me.

The twisting smoke draws the embroidered pattern of Xiang,
Quietly covers the clouds on Mount Wu.
(8) Flowers blossom and fall, in spite of the East Wind's will,
All that flowers and withers
Belongs to the God of Spring.

(*Fansheng xiang*, in *Wumengtang quanji*, 28)

P.54d.2. Zhegu tian: *Recording a Dream on a Spring Night in the Year* Renshen *[1632]*

One volume of the *Surangama Sutra*, one stick of incense,
A prayer mat accompanies me, the world and I have forgotten each other.

Traveling through the three mountains and through green waters, my soul is no longer far away,
With half a pillow of pure wind I slowly fall into a dream.

Aside by the winding paths,
Next to the arcade,
Bamboo hedges and thatched huts complete a charming landscape.
In vain I pity the swallows that return and depart:
Why do they busy themselves daily with their nests?

(*Fansheng xiang*, in *Wumengtang quanji*, 29)

P.54d.3. Shuilong yin: *Autumn Thoughts, Rhymed After Mother's Poem on Things Past, When Father Was in the Capital*

The drizzle saturates the banana trees,
The patter of rain resonates with the pounding of mallets against washing boards,
Leaning over the balustrade, I extend my view to the distance,
The flat forest is like a painting.
Overhanging clouds press against the evening mountains,
The metallic wind has just arisen,
Jade dew settles,
A slight chill creeps gently in.
When the river reaches its end, all leaves will have fallen,
Only the slender green mountains will remain.

Let me ask the elusive autumn air
If in the past Song Yu knew such sorrow.
Half a curtain of fragrant mist,
A courtyard of misty moonlight,
Several broken chimes of the water clock,
Four walls of chirping crickets,
Lines of traveling geese.
I casually sip a goblet of wine,
Waiting for the yellow chrysanthemums to flower on the east hedge.
Then I will pick them, and a subtle fragrance will fill my sleeves.

(*Fansheng xiang*, in *Wumengtang quanji*, 37)

line 12: Song Yu is the poet most closely associated with Qu Yuan. Here the allusion is to his "Jiu bian" (Nine arguments) and particularly to the opening of the first piece in that series: "Alas for the breath of autumn! / Wan and drear: flower and leaf fluttering fall and turn to decay" (*Wen xuan* 33/8a; trans. Hawkes, *Songs of the South*, p. 209).

BIOGRAPHICAL NOTE AND TRANSLATION BY CH'IU-TI LIU

P.55. Fang Weiyi (1585–1668)

No biographer, however sympathetic, can depict the hardships of Fang Weiyi's life better than she did herself in her poems. This native of Tongcheng, Anhui province, lived most of her life in a state of perpetual loss. At the age of seventeen, Fang Zhongxian (Weiyi is her style name) was married to Yao Sunqi, a man who had been suffering from an unidentified illness during the six previous years. Although she toiled tirelessly to nurse her ailing husband, he died later the same year, leaving her pregnant with their daughter who, in turn, died before her tenth month. Fang did not remarry but observed a studious and chaste life, helping her sister-in-law Wu Lingyi raise her nephew, the renowned political activist and philosopher Fang Yizhi (1611–71).[1]

As a member of a well-respected and prosperous family, Weiyi had access to a superior education at home. At an early age, she became proficient in both poetry and painting. Her elder sister, Fang Mengshi, was also a noted poet, and according to Mengshi, the arts—their appreciation as well as creation—became Weiyi's sole spiritual haven after the loss of her husband and child. She left behind a great deal of work: her own *Qingfen ge ji* (Collection from the Tower of Clear Fragrance, variously described as containing either seven or eight *juan*) and the one-*juan* anthology *Chujiang yin* (Songs from the River Chu). Weiyi also edited a volume called *Guifan* (Models for the women's quarters) and produced a series of studies on women's literary history.[2] Most of her writing is no longer extant. What texts have survived were recorded by contemporary critics and anthologists; her preface to her sister's collection appears as C.10.1.[3]

Weiyi's style is spare and unadorned. The author of the *Shenshitang cuoyu* points out that Weiyi was one of the rare woman poets who mastered both new- and old-style poetry. She applied herself with customary elegance to the subject of social problems and unrest (as in the poems "Setting Out from the Passes" and "While Traveling in Autumn, I Hear of the Invading Bandits," P.55.8 and P.55.10 below). She also continued to develop her talents as painter and calligrapher well into her old age. A master of the *baimiao* or "ink drawing" style of painting, she is listed as one of the Painters of the Boudoir alongside Ni Renji, Zhou Xi, and Li Yin.[4]

P.55.1. To My Older Sister on Her Departure to Yue

You came last year from Changxi,
And this year depart for Yue.
Separated as we shall be for years to come,
What remains to be said of our parting pain?
At dawn you'll set out from Wanjiang town,
The mountain river veiled by smoky mist.
A bright white moon shall survey blue-green waves,
(8) And spring's wind shall fill the river's trees.

(GGZSJ, 10/18)

Yue refers to the southeastern region of China, especially the provinces of Guangdong and Guangxi. Changxi is in northeastern Fujian province. Wanjiang town is probably Wancheng, on the Wan River in northern Anhui province.

P.55.2. On Ancient Themes

I

Since dawn I've watched the airy skies,
As flying birds return from the mountaintop.
A crust of stone is all that's left,
We face each other as white clouds drift by.

II

Break off a branch from a wayside willow,
The spring wind blows to shatter your heart.
Sounds of spring escape the eye,
But the river waters flow on without end.

(CLEJ, 106)

P.55.3. *In Response to My Niece, Ziying*

The night is calm, my roaming boat at rest,
Reed-flowers stir the ripples to whisper.
Wicker window bright beneath a shining moon,
—How it brims with parting's sorrow.

(CLEJ, 106–7)

P.55.4. *One Night, Missing My Younger Sister*

Through the fallen leaves of empty forests cries the evening crow,
The Milky Way lies in the distance, beyond the river Wan.
Our late-night departure from Cangwu—a wintry dream now far;
A gleaming moon of southern skies shines west of the pavilion.

(CLEJ, 107)

line 3: Cangwu, located in modern-day Hunan province, is best known as the place where the legendary sage-king Shun died.

P.55.5. *Spring Rain*

Along the springtime river, new rain reaches my western window,
Clouds darken the mountain light, the distant trees are lost.
Scattered showers of pear blossoms in never-ending flight,
In the old garden that must be a partridge calling.

(CLEJ, 107)

P.55.6. *Sitting Alone*

I sit alone on an empty step, the crystal dew is chill;
As night grows deep a certain shadow falls upon my robe.
From whence that sound of pestles pounding, hurrying the moon,
Gazing down on a forlorn figure—heart about to break?

(CLEJ, 107)

line 3: On the motif of the clothes-beater, see P.4.3.

P.55.7. *Parted by Death*

Since times of old we hear of separation;
Who has spoken of partings by death?
Yet whether it be by life or by death—

I face it all alone.
The north wind buffets the barren mulberry,
It mourns for me night and day.
I lift my eyes to the broad azure sky—
Below, no wide-mouthed babe.

To live thus is worse than death,
Still, mother and father cling and weep.
Two orioles fly—one east, one west,
The autumn grasses, too, are in disarray.
I live—and what do I serve?
I die—why should I refuse?
That under the white sun there can be such torment,
My heart knows well, in vain.

(Yi Boyin, 5/131)

lines 7–8: She raises her eyes to heaven in supplication, like the speaker of poem 65 in the *Book of Odes*. The expression *huang kou er* describes a fledgling chick or a baby. This couplet alludes grimly to the *yuefu* poem "Leaving from the Eastern Gate" ("Chu dongmen xing"), in which a wife pleads with her husband not to depart: "Other families only care for wealth and fortune, / Your humble wife would simply share the plainest gruel / For the sake of the bounty of blue heaven above / And our wide-mouthed babes below" (Guo Maoqian, *Yuefu shiji*, 37/550).

P.55.8. Setting Out from the Passes

Left home for an outpost ten thousand miles away
Where the mountain roads are severed by wind and smoke.
Too many taxes, no extra victuals,
The frontier is barren—no planting of fields.
Foot soldiers ever mindful of death,
A grasping official still demanding his sum—
Relying on the bounty of our lord and king,
When will we sing out: Victory!—and home!

(Yi Boyin, 5/131)

P.55.9. Returning Alone to My Childhood Home

No need to ask about my old hometown,
Arms of war torment it without rest.
Our family is poor, but no use in planning,

Taxes multiply—then add to our grief.
The distant trees and blue mountains are ancient,
Barren fields and white waters autumnal.
In sorrow had I left behind the haven of my parents' care,
I peer out to see them but first my tears flow.

(Zheng Guangyi, 1362)

Fang Weiyi wrote this poem as a newly widowed young woman returning to live with her parents.

line 2: The poet is referring here to the peasant uprisings that were common in the early part of the seventeenth century and that led to the fall of the Ming dynasty. In 1635, a group of rebels led by Gao Yingxiang, Li Zicheng, Zhang Xianzhong, and others, entered Anhui province, first desecrating the ancestral tombs of the Ming emperor in Fengyang and then moving on to the towns of Luzhou (modern-day Hefei) and Anqing. Fang's hometown, Tongcheng, was located between these two towns.

P.55.10. While Traveling in Autumn, I Hear of the Invading Bandits

At autumn portals crickets hum,
A cool wind rises amid dusky peaks.
In my declining years, I run into troubled times,
When will I return to my native land?
Bandits invade the southern townships,
Military orders are dispatched to the northern passes.
Human horror is at its height:
Layers of blood coat our swords to the hilt.

(Yi Boyin, 5/131)

BIOGRAPHICAL NOTE AND TRANSLATION BY PAULA VARSANO

P.56. Yin Renrong (early 17th century)

Yin Renrong was born in the early seventeenth century in Sichuan's Yibin prefecture. Daughter of Administration Vice Commissioner Yin Shen, she married Liu Jinzhong, the top candidate of his province's civil service exam. It was only after her marriage, it seems, that she began her poetic career. She saw the works of her husband's younger sister, Wenyu, and was so taken with them that she resolved to master the art of poetry herself. Her years as a poet were few, for she died young—apparently at the age of eighteen (nineteen *sui*). Her husband compiled both the finished works and the unfinished drafts of poetry she had saved and published them in a volume appropriately entitled *Duanxiang ji* (Broken fragrance collection).

In his preface to her works, her husband wrote: "A sorrowful timbre cuts short the resonance of a voice—as when a flute breaks or a string snaps in two. Perhaps not all of her poems tell of heartbreak, but the sorrowful tone is common to them all." The "Inscription" (attributed to Zhong Xing) to the *Mingyuan shigui* selection from *Duanxiang ji* comments: "As for Renrong's poetry, it is the rise and fall of her spirit that sets her apart from other people. The disjointed structure and desolate tone of her poetry, matched with the purity and abruptness of its articulation, reminds one of dying leaves drawn down by the wind which sometimes land on a branch and, rustle as they may, cannot reach the ground on their own. Her poetry is like a hidden spring that is obstructed by rocks and thus is unable to bring forth the fullness of its sound." The *Yujing yangqiu* further comments: "Renrong's verse does not show completeness in structure and organization [lit. 'tendon and bone']. To bring together what in it is separate and unrelated is like appreciating 'the music that lies beyond the strings.' Accordingly Zhong Xing gave it such high praise." It is useful to keep this seemingly double-edged compliment in mind when reading Yin Renrong's poetry, for, upon first reading, one may indeed too hastily criticize its relatively weak structure rather than appreciate its delicate subtlety.[1]

P.56.1. Staring Out at the River, After the Rain

After the rain, the water is brighter than ever;
Autumn wind whispers *xi xi*.
Wintry sky, filled with white dew;
River surface cloaked in morning mist.

(Zhou Shouchang, ed., *Gonggui wenxuan*, 32/4a)

P.56.2. Gazing Over the Countryside

Gazing over the countryside, there is no mountain scenery;
The vast sky is a single limpid stroke.

Pathside trees aligned as in a painting;
Beneath them there are people strolling by.

(*Gonggui wenxuan*, 32/4b)

BIOGRAPHICAL NOTE AND TRANSLATION BY MARY ELLEN FRIENDS

項蘭貞

P.57. Xiang Lanzhen (fl. early 17th century)

Xiang Lanzhen (alternate name Shu, style name Mengwan), of Jiaxing in Zhejiang, was the wife of Huang Maoxi of Xiushui or Zuili, also in Jiaxing.[1] After her marriage into the Huang family, Xiang Lanzhen is said to have spent more than ten years learning from her husband to write verse. Her husband's aunt, Huang Shude, also cultivated the art of poetry.[2]

Although Lanzhen's parentage is unknown, it is likely that she was a member of the large and prominent Xiang family of Xiushui, which had settled in the region during the twelfth century, thereafter producing generations of scholars, officials, and artists.[3] In the Ming dynasty, men such as the military commander Xiang Zhong (1421–1502), the art collector and connoisseur Xiang Yuanbian (1525–90), and the painter, calligrapher, and poet Xiang Shengmo (1597–1658) sustained the family tradition. Xiang Lanzhen was approximately of the same generation as Shengmo, and may have been his sister or cousin. She may also have been related to Xiang Pei (fl. mid–17th century) of Xiushui, a competent woman poet and skilled painter.

Xiang Lanzhen was a talented and prolific poet who produced at least three collections of her own poetry, including the *Caiyun cao* (Cloud-tailoring drafts), *Yuelu yin* (Moon-dew chants), and *Yongxue zhai yigao* (Manuscripts from the Snow-Praising Studio). Unfortunately, these collections have all been lost, known to us only as titles recorded in catalogues of literary works. Her extant poems, preserved in various anthologies, show the elegance of diction and high technical skill that won her renown. Xiang Lanzhen's talents were evaluated in the preface to her *Yongxue zhai yigao* by her contemporary, the reclusive woman poet Lu Qingzi (P.52) of Cold Mountain (see C.9).[4]

The active cultural life of the Jiaxing area in the late Ming would have provided a stimulating background and a discriminating audience for Xiang Lanzhen. It is not surprising that she took up the brush and established contacts with other men and women through the medium of poetry. Representing two familial traditions allied by marriage, her poetic voice is evidence of the richness of literary friendship and exchange that might be experienced by a gentry woman of the late Ming dynasty.

P.57.1. Willow Branch Lyric

Green trees, shady and cool, make the tavern flag flash,
About to draw spring colors forth onto their pliant branches.
Year after year I grieve over the traveler's farewell,
All the willow branches broken by the springtime wind—and still he
does not know.

(Su Zhecong, 337)

line 4: On the custom of offering a willow branch to a departing traveler, see P.5.1.

P.57.2. At Luo City, Listening to Geese

Bright moonlight shining on darkest moss;
Crossing the sky, a lone goose comes.
As its shadows turn, flying leaves fall,
Its sound brings an eddying evening wind.
North of the ramparts, the traveler reflects,
While in her boudoir, the young woman laments.
South of the river, where my country place lies,
(8) When will the cassia thicket bloom?

(Su Zhecong, 337)

The walled city of Luo was located in Sichuan province, just north of Guanghan county.

BIOGRAPHICAL NOTE AND TRANSLATION BY JENNIFER PURTLE

P.58. Wang Fengxian and Her Daughter Zhang Yinyuan

Wang Fengxian (style name Ruiqing, sobriquet Wenruzi) was born in Huating in Shanghai municipality. Her literary talent became known from a very early age. She married Metropolitan Graduate Zhang Benjia (style name Mengduan), the magistrate of Yichun, and lived to the age of sixty-nine. The most representative of her surviving works is the poetry collection *Guanzhu ji* (A string of pearls). She used to exchange poems with her daughters, Zhang Yinyuan and Zhang Yinqing. Zhang Yinyuan, the elder, was a precocious talent who died at the age of twenty-six.

王鳳嫺

P.58a. *Wang Fengxian (fl. early 17th century)*

P.58a.1. *"A Mountain Exhales the Moon"*

I

At the first watch a mountain exhales the moon,
Reflections of pine branches bob in the waves.
Putting aside my embroidery, I offer up incense in worship;
Putting down my wine cup, I gaze up in tears.
The mountains brighten as at dawn;
Shrouded in mist, the waves turn chilly.
Pity this secluded boudoir's sojourner,
(8) Her cloudlike coiffure looks disheveled.

II

At the second watch a mountain exhales the moon;
Wishing to sleep, I dread the long night.
Night birds, roosting, again wake with a start;
The drifting *wutong* leaves flutter and fall.
My husband won't be returning again,
On whom shall our children rely?
Facing my shadow I seek solace in vain,
(8) My innermost feelings hard to declare.

III

At the third watch a mountain exhales the moon;
Nipped by cold dews, cawing crows take flight.
Through the vacant window the chill begins to seep in;
How can I bear it with only a thin quilt?

The red cassia wafts a nocturnal fragrance,
The silver vase grows frigid with autumn water.
Whence come those thuds of a laundry mallet,
Drumming into anxious ears with every beat?

IV

At the fourth watch a mountain exhales the moon,
Illuminating my emerald pond.
In tranquil waters fish sleep soundly;
Beside an anxious person, a pillow stretches unused.
Tears follow the dying night watches, drip on for long.
My shadow chases after my thin figure, pacing up and down.
As I toss and turn, sleep seems ever elusive.
From a stone fortress a Tartar pipe mournfully blows.

V

At the fifth watch a mountain exhales the moon,
Incense embers darken in the jade burner.
Languidly, I abandon myself to Consort Ban's grievances;
Indolently, I ascend the tower of the stymied Wang Can.
Congealed dews herald the coming dawn,
An icy quilt signals mid-autumn's arrival.
With a broken heart I complete this tune,
Pray do not dismiss it as but a ditty.

(MYSG, 31/1a–2a)

The title and first lines of this poem series repeat a famous line by the Tang poet Du Fu. For the translation of *tu* as "exhale," see J. J. Y. Liu, *Art of Chinese Poetry*, p. 109.

iii, lines 7–8: On the melancholy tones of clothes-beaters, see P.4.3.

v, lines 3–4: On Ban *jieyu*, see P.1. On Wang Can, see P.17.2.

P.58a.2. Bidding Adieu to a Singsong Girl Now Bound for a Nunnery

Washing off rouge and powder, you bid farewell to Chu Terrace,
Awakened through transcending the worldly realm.
As you reach the Three Celestial Terraces,
Colorful clouds, broken dreams, songs scatter like dust.

On hearing Buddhist prayers your wisdom shall unfold;
In meditation you will transcend the present *kalpa*.
Surely the prefect couldn't have broken your heart?
No need to look beyond the ripples and mists.
The firs and cypresses by the imperial tombs will sooner or later turn
to ash.

(MYSG, 31/3a)

line 6: On the Buddhist term *kalpa*, see P.45.1.

P.58a.3. Reply to My Daughters, Yinyuan and Yinqing, on an Autumn Evening, Using Their Rhymes

In the frosty cold crows and magpies huddle together on the southern
branches.
How can a lonely traveler bear to hear the late-night sounds of the
water clock?
Our grief, divided among three places, rests on the same dream.
A heart full of sorrow causes my eyebrows to droop down.
Song Yu composed a rhapsody when saddened by autumn.
Xiangru neglected his lute when afflicted with rain.
The yellow leaves rapping on the window compound my sleeplessness.
The sinking moon by the beam keeps my distant thoughts company.

(MYSG, 31/3a–b)

lines 5–6: On Song Yu and autumn, see P.54d.3. Xiangru is Sima Xiangru, the great Han poet.

P.58a.4. The Empty Boudoir

The wall collects cobwebs, the mirror collects dust.
Head ornaments lie on the floor, I know nothing of spring.
Grieving, I dread to see the twittering swallows
Still seeking their master among the carved beams.

(MYSG, 31/4a)

P.58a.5. Remembering My Late Husband

The icy orb has just set, the night watch is almost over.
A hush descends upon all creatures, as the frost grows cold.

The phoenix has left its emerald *wutong* tree, and autumn winds mourn.
As incense goes cold in the ornamental chamber, the night stretches long.
When will your soul return from Penglai of the Three Fairy Isles?
In my empty room's desolation, tears silently fall.
I recall former times when we shared joy and laughter,
(8) Who would have thought that meeting you would become so difficult?

(MYSG, 31/4a)

line 5: On Penglai, see P.11.12.

P.58a.6. Passing by Yan Guang's Fishing Terrace and Hearing That One of His Descendants Studies in the Hall

The Fishing Terrace, still and tranquil, rises from cold ripples.
Mists and waters are the same as before, yet another traveler passes.
For ages the mountain spirits have conferred hereditary honors on this marsh,
While again and again the Han palaces suffered pillage and ruin.

(MYSG, 31/4b)

Yan Guang went into reclusion after his good friend had ascended the throne to become Emperor Guangwu of the Eastern Han.

P.58a.7. Weeping Over My Husband Mengduan on Returning Home

The year was drawing to an end when I returned from a far-off land.
Living in retirement, I can do nothing about the cold north wind.
Startled by the mournful cries of the wild geese in the sky,
I dream of our parting at the grave; fabulous pheasants weep in their dance.
The "three paths" remain the same, only I have grown old.
Who sits with me to gaze at this desolate lamp?
Were there a way to find you in the dark grave,
(8) I'd look upon death as homecoming and not fear its pain.

(MYSG, 31/2b)

line 5: "Although the three paths [of my garden] have grown desolate, the pines and chrysanthemums survive" (Tao Qian [365–427], "Guiqulai xi ci," in Lu Qinli, *Tao Yuanming ji*, pp. 159–62). "Three paths" thus refers to the dwelling of a recluse.

P.58a.8. Chang xiang si: *To My Husband Mengduan*

Peach blossoms flutter,
Apricot blossoms flutter,
But you are so far away,
Who will paint my eyebrows?
Orioles chirp prettily,
Swallows twitter prettily,
The long day locks my loneliness in the idle yard.
(8) At this moment I'm secretly overwhelmed by thoughts of love.

(GXCC, 2/13a)

line 4: See the story of Zhang Chang, P.22C.1.

P.58a.9. Yi Qin e: *Remembering My Deceased Daughter Yinqing on a Moonlit Night*

I

I tugged at her robe at parting,
About to leave, she stopped again, my heart was broken,
Quite broken.
Our silk sleeves soaked with tears,
Our hearts pounding with blood.
I leaned against the door till she disappeared in the distance,
Then our correspondence came to an abrupt end.
(8) I was shocked to hear that she had chased the waves and floated with the moon,
With the moon.
In vain I mourn for my aging self,
Snow hanging from my locks.

II

The long song chokes,
The fragrant soul no longer returns, I mourn and grieve in vain,
Quite in vain.
Cold mists, somber trees,
Serve to congeal my sorrow.
Perching crows caw, gone is the human voice.

An expanse of sadness fills up, the moon in the middle of the sky,
In the middle of the sky,
Sadly, still shines
On her old dressing case in the empty chamber.

(GXCC, 2/13a–b)

P.58a.10. Lin jiang xian: *Autumn Feelings*

Through closed pearl blinds the moonbeam penetrates,
Alone in the cool night I lean against the balustrade.
Wishing to tune the jasper lute, my fingers begin to freeze.
The crane has gone to roost, pine-dews grown cold.
No more human voices can be heard,
The *wutong* tree by the well withers.

A sudden cry resounds in the sky—
A young goose making its first migration.
It soars as if seeking an eddy pool.
Oft in my floating life have I witnessed times both sad and joyful.
The three autumn months are half over.
Maple leaves lie as if drunken in the crimson forest.

(GXCC, 2/13b)

P.58a.11. Chun guang hao: *On the First Day of Spring*

Scented paths are soft to the tread,
Myriad mountains are bright;
I try on my light silk robe.
Green grass buds and spreads onto a distant islet in the stream;
Our joy from the excursion lingers.

Warbling, skillful birds compose songs;
Cooing pigeons call up rain and sunshine.
On the twelve pearl-decorated chambers the blinds have all been raised,
New tunes come to be made.

(GXCC, 2/14a)

P.58a.12. Huan xi sha: *On Another Outing with Madame Qiao*

New bamboo groves surround the winding path,
Amidst wild flowers' perfumes.
Butterflies' busy wings flash in the wind,
Fluttering willow floss dots gauze dresses.
In these surroundings we grieve over our thin shadows.
Swallows whirl on the ripples, dancing the whole spring long.
Over a rustic bridge by an ancient ferry, the sun has set halfway.

(GXCC, 2/14a–b)

張引元

P.58b. Zhang Yinyuan (mid–17th century)

P.58b.1. Casually Composed at the Beginning of Autumn

Emerald *wutong* trees sway in the wind, water chestnuts and lotuses wither.
Jadelike dew drops chill amid crickets' chirps.
I spent the long day reading the *Surangama* sutra,
Now and then gazing at the white clouds through the latticed window.

(MYSG, 31/7a)

P.58b.2. Living in the Mountains

In the dense forest, birds' chirping sounds clear.
In the high sun, flowers' vapors feel thin.
Beside a secluded cliff, a hut stands.
At its window, a flying waterfall hangs.

(MYSG, 31/6b)

P.58b.3. White upon White—A Poem Written in Jest

A crane struts on the clean jasper terrace,
Fireflies fly into the slanting Milky Way.
A jade beauty lifts a white silk curtain,
A gentle moon plucks a pear blossom.

(MYSG, 31/6b)

P.58b.4. Boudoir Thoughts

As the one I yearn for travels on a distant road,
My youthful complexion withers in the mirror.
I strain my eyes on the great dike,
Too shy to tread on its grass.

(MYSG, 31/6b)

P.58b.5. Inscribed on a Painted Fan Presented to My Husband

The thousand pieces of jade surround a lonely pavilion,
As a fountain gurgles in the night.
In it stands a man who has deserted the world,
Discoursing with the bright moon about poetry.

(MYSG, 31/6b)

P.58b.6. Inscribed on the Painting "Tall Bamboos and the Beauty"

She awakens beside the latticed window; the white silk feels cold.
Like distant hills, her knitted eyebrows envelop spring sorrows.
Don't shed your tears in the wind,
Lest they stain the tall bamboos.

(MYSG, 31/6b–7a)

lines 3–4: A reminiscence of the tears shed by the consorts of the ancient sage-king Shun on his death; see P.10.1.

P.58b.7. Lament for the Plum Consort

Lean not against the Changmen Palace, sigh not over the bright moon.
From days of old the fair have had sorry fates.
Your talents composed the "Rhapsody from the East of the Pavilion,"
But it will never be adopted in the orchestral music of the Temporary
Palace.

(MYSG, 31/7a)

line 1: On Sima Xiangru's "Changmen Palace Rhapsody," see P.8a.1.

lines 3–4: On the rivalry of the Plum-Blossom Consort (Mei Fei) and Yang Guifei, see P.54a.1. The Temporary Palace is a euphemism for the emperor's court in its southern exile, where the Emperor Xuanzong withdrew after his infatuation with Consort Yang and neglect of state duties led to a garrison revolt; see P.18.12.

P.58b.8. Written in Snow to Be Shown to My Younger Brother and Sister

Masses of clouds darken the wind and the fog.
Lustrous snowflakes scatter in four directions.
A flute has finished playing the village boy's tune.
An old fisherman sleeps, bundled in a straw raincoat.
The horse before the mountain seems to seek its companion in plum
 blossoms.
A sailboat on the river seems to return without seeing Dai Kui.
Together we lean against the thatch window; the dusk is falling.
Wild geese align their wings, migrating south.

(MYSG, 31/5a)

line 6: Wang Huizhi of the Jin dynasty once set out by boat to pay his friend Dai Kui a visit on a snowy evening, but turned back without so much as knocking on Dai's door, saying that he had already exhausted his original impulse (Liu Yiqing, *Shishuo xinyu*, p. 23; Mather, *Shih-shuo Hsin-yü*, p. 389).

P.58b.9. Song of the Brilliant Consort

Knitting eyebrows, she took leave of the royal gate.
Covering her face with her sleeves, she departed from the palace.
Who would take pity on that pretty face
Soon to become a tiger's or jackal's bride?
Among wailing gibbons she retained Han tunes,
A jade pendant covered by Tartar dust.
Send these words to the Glorious One:
"A picture caused this unjust dismissal!"

(MYSG, 31/4b)

Wang Zhaojun, later given the title Brilliant Consort (Mingfei), was a palace woman in the time of Emperor Yuan of the Han. Legend has it that she refused to bribe the court painter Mao Yanshou, whereupon Mao made her portrait so ugly that the emperor, studying his albums for a disposable concubine, married her off to the chief of the nomadic Xiongnu. She was thus forced to live out her days among the steppe barbarians.

P.58b.10. "At the Fifth Watch a Mountain Exhales the Moon"

At the second watch a mountain exhales the moon,
My collar opened, I sit through the long night.

Fallen leaves fill the empty courtyard,
Descending profusely from up high.
With bygone days the world presses me forward,
What means do I have to lodge my tracks?
As I ponder the setting, hundreds of emotions emerge—
I'd have to confide them to the immensity of the sea.

(MYSG, 31/4b)

Note that although the title refers to the fifth watch, the poem begins with the second watch.

P.58b.11. Seeing Off the Summer

Cicadas cease chirping, summer clouds pass.
I'm startled by sadness—how days and months advance!
Amidst cursive drifts of incense magpie tails float.
Sharply outlined, bamboo shadows shelter whiskered shrimp.
To pick lotuses, temporarily release the oars;
To buy wine, first procure the river perch.
Best of all, the moon by the small window tonight
Shall dispatch poetic thoughts to the *wutong* tree in my yard.

(MYSG, 31/5b–6a)

P.58b.12. Dian jiang chun: *In Reply to My Mother*

The season is summer.
Warm wind begins to blow into the plantain court.
Daily I yearn for your return,
My golden bracelets hang loosely about my wrists.
In the southern chamber I arise after illness.
Sadly I observe the fledgling swallows.
But where will I see you?
How illusory are the white clouds.
I crane over each of the twelve balustrades.

(GXCC, 2/16b)

BIOGRAPHICAL NOTE AND TRANSLATION BY YENNA WU

P.59. Cao Jingzhao (fl. 1620)

Cao Jingzhao lived during the early seventeenth century in Wanping (present-day Beijing). She entered service in the imperial palace in 1620 and later became a Buddhist nun.

P.59.1. Palace Poems [two from a series of six]

II

A tree full of chilly flowers blooms right in the snow,
Faintly fragrant, utterly silent, dazzling tower and terrace.
Palace maids cluster around, their calls draw near,
Making known the Phoenix Palace chosen attendants are here.

III

Bejeweled makeup, cloud-coiffure, trailing golden garments,
Small and dainty the pose she strikes beside the door of jade.
A newcomer still unfamiliar with palace matters,
Head lowered, first she bows to the number one concubine.

(Su Zhecong, 335–36)

iii, lines 3–4: "Still unfamiliar" (*wei an*) and the situation of the poem suggest a discreetly humorous allusion to the third of Wang Jian's "Xin jia niang ci" poems (The new bride, QTS, 301/3423): "Not yet familiar with her mother-in-law's tastes, / First she begged her sister-in-law to taste the soup."

BIOGRAPHICAL NOTE AND TRANSLATION BY NANCY HODES AND TUNG YUAN-FANG

P.60. Gu Ruopu (1592–ca. 1681)

Gu Ruopu (courtesy name Hezhi) was born in Qiantang (present-day Hangzhou). Her husband, Huang Maowu, was a scholar from the nearby area of Renhe. He died in 1619, and thereafter Gu Ruopu gained a name for chastity and filiality. Her writings were published as *Woyuexuan ji* (Poems from the "Sleeping Beneath the Moon" Studio, 1651). In prose and poetry she displayed the straightforward vividness of the Jian'an period at the end of the Han, tempered with a bent for Du Fu's later verse of the Dali period. Her contemporaries remarked on her zeal for studying the dynastic histories and noted the influence of such reading on her poetry. She was compared, often favorably, to her learned near-contemporary Fang Weiyi (P.55).[1]

P.60.1. Harmonizing with the Rhymes of My Husband's Poem, "Plum Blossoms Falling at West Creek"

We follow a winding way
   and emerge into West Creek.
Its current carries us
   deeper and deeper, round many bends.
Above sheer banks
   fishermen's net frames are suspended;
Thatched eaves hang out
   over the tall bamboo.
Iridescent green feathers—
   such chatter and birdsong!
Overflowing the plum groves
   waves of sweet air assail us.
Sparkling snow, the tattered blossoms fly;
(8) We sit enchanted by the green
   of frothy spring wine poured out.
If the trail to Deer Gate
   has not yet disappeared,
I would return here with you
   and we could stay, together.

(GGSC, 1: 3/2a)

West Creek in Hangzhou district, Zhejiang province, winds through the hills of Lingyin Mountain; its high banks were, by report even into the present century, luxuriant with bamboo and plum trees. The translations of Gu's poems here employ some freedom in representing the individual lines of the originals.

line 9: Deer Gate Mountain, in Xiangyang district, Hubei province, was named for two stone deer that flanked a "spirit way" to a temple built there. Tang dynasty poets Meng Haoran (689–740) and Pi Rixiu (fl. mid–9th century), both known for having retired from the political arena into private life on Deer Gate, are called up by this reference, as is the Song dynasty poet, painter, and official Mi Fu (1051–1107), who was known as "The Retired Gentleman of Deer Gate."

P.60.2. *Palace Songs, no. 7*

In early spring she steals out
   for a romp in the imperial garden,
Chasing the yellow orioles,
   kicking a bright red cloth ball.
When she goes, misbehaving,
   into a thicket of flowers,
      no one knows—
Her peals of laughter
   carry to the high, red-walled residence.

(Gu Ruopu, *Woyuexuan ji*, 1/3a)

P.60.3. *Palace Songs, no. 6*

She has learned to comb her own hair
   and to put in the phoenix hairpin;
From blue-green dress to pearl slippers,
   everything is newly made.
Now her makeup is done, but still
   it doesn't have that Eastern Palace look!
Again she takes cosmetics from the case
   and meticulously redoes her face.

(*Woyuexuan ji*, 1/2b–3a)

P.60.4. *Refurbishing a Boat for My Son, Can, to Use as a Study*

I was always conscience-stricken
   before the zeal of those ancient mothers
Until I found it, at a scenic spot
   beside a bridge where in other days
It used to skirt the trees,
   following the chaste moon (not like
Those craft that cruise the mist
   in search of frivolous ladies).
You have long hoped to study
   in Yang Zhu's school, but now

Passers-by will see the scholar Mi Fu's barge.
Don't mistake it for a pleasure boat;
(8) I've fixed it up with old coverlets
woven of blue silk.

(GGSC, I: 3/4a)

line 1: Gu alludes to the stories of virtuous mothers included in educational material for girls, such as the Han dynasty *Lienü zhuan*. Such women went to extraordinary lengths to provide moral and academic training for their sons.

line 5: Mentioned in the *Zhuangzi* and the *Mengzi*, Yang Zhu was regarded as a "hedonist" thinker by orthodox Confucians. He placed the nurture of life before any other imperative. Gu seems to be teasing her son for his laziness or self-indulgence.

line 6: Mi Fu is said to have put his extensive library of books and paintings onto a barge so that he could take them with him wherever he went.

line 8: Blue coverlets symbolize a family heritage of learning handed down from generation to generation.

P.60.5. Going Out to See Plum Blossoms in the Moonlight, I Imagine My Husband Might Come Riding Back on a Cloud

I

The blossoms, just to enchant the moon,
give even more scent, are more beautifully fresh.
Deep in shadow, loved one gone,
I am awake in the night.
Alone, I lift the winged goblet, sing
"Whiter than snow."
My silk lutestrings invite the moon:
we'll keep vigil here
for the immortal spirit of the plum blossom.

II

How easy for beauty in the world to deepen sorrow,
But hard for this new poem to figure forth the pain.
I confront the flowers, and the flowers say nothing;
I invoke the moon, and the moon radiates coldness.

(*Woyuexuan ji*, 2/3a)

i, line 3: A reference to Ban *jieyu*'s "Song of Resentment" (P.1.1).

P.60.6. Moved to Deep Distress

It is the year *jiazi* [1624]. Five years ago, in the second month of spring, on the sixteenth of the month, my husband left this life. On the first day of the third month of spring, my mother also died. In the years since, I have been easily moved by things, and this has increased my feelings of grief until I do not know where to turn. Thus, I take up the brush to compose this poem, wishing to report my grievance to the Ninefold Deep Springs.

Now is the season of splendor,
  the "green and sunlit" time,
Third month's "Great Burgeoning."
A thousand branches burst with beauty,
Ten thousand trees send sweetness flying.
As the flow of change transforms all things,
Sad reflections suddenly arise.

Oh, misery! That my birth was so untimely!
(8) I did not turn my back on heaven,
  oh, why did heaven send disaster?
I was not heartless to my parent,
  oh, how could my parent be the one
    to leave me with none to trust to?
I want to "climb that bare hill,"
  but, oh, my pace is slow, too late.
I want to turn myself to stone,
  oh, I would not "fly up and away."
(12) My vitals are torn in shreds,
  oh, anguish enwraps me completely.
My heart beats faster, faster,
  oh, pain cuts sharper, deeper.
North Hall is silent now,
  oh, the daylilies all are picked.
The jade tower was completed,
  oh, orchid fragrance was extinguished.
(16) Now melodious orioles' choral songs
  are poison to sensitive feelings;

The waterfowls' incessant calls
wound my heart still more.
Wounded at heart, I scratch my head,
alone before the vast blue sky.
Cloud paths there are endless
and thoughts too run beyond control.
When shall I ever dance again
in a brightly colored dress?
A full moon shines upon the lofty hall;
For a time, there in the moonlight,
we once cared for one another.
Playing the zither, enjoying the lute,
we found our pleasure in orchid rooms.
Sighing, whispering, wind in the trees
now spreads a desolate chill.
The phoenix is stranded in a different region,
there is no way to reach him.
Spotted stains of bloody tears
dye my empty bed.
Hoping in dreams to be with him,
I counted on his spirit presence.
But since such dreams have failed to come,
oh, my loving thoughts are lost
in a vague and endless emptiness.
These loving thoughts
with nowhere to go
destroy my heart.

(*Woyuexuan ji*, 2/5a–6a)

headnote: The Ninefold Deep Springs (also known as the Yellow Springs; see P.29.9) are the abode of the dead.

line 1: "Green and sunlit" (*qingyang*) is an ancient designation for the three months of the spring season.

line 2: "Great Burgeoning" was a designation for the third month of spring and also for the third pitch on the bamboo pipes, believed to have been attuned in ancient times with the resonances of the cosmos and its changes.

line 7: A quotation from poem 257 of the *Book of Odes*.

line 10: Gu again quotes the *Book of Odes*, poem 110: "I climb that bare hill / and look far off toward my mother." In the ode, the speaker, who is away from home, is concerned for the worry he is causing his parents and brother.

line 11: On the story of Husband-Gazing Rock, see P.11.16. "Fly up and away" is a quote from poem 26 of the *Book of Odes*, which has been interpreted as the complaint of a wife, presumably widowed, who is being pressed to remarry and who wishes to escape the criticisms of her family. Gu associates herself with the chastity theme of Husband-Gazing Rock but rejects the thematic of escape.

line 14: "North Hall" is a conventional euphemism for the mother of the household or for the mother's quarters in the household. From ancient times, flowers of the daylily were used for medicinal and nutritional purposes. They were believed to ease the suffering of bereavement and were called "the herb of forgetting." On the belief they could dispel melancholy, see P.2.1 (Song 16).

line 15: A tower of jade is an emblem for the death of a talented scholar. The image is derived from Li Shangyin's biography of the Tang poet Li He (791–818), who died in his twenties. A spirit messenger is said to have appeared as Li lay dying to explain that the ruler of heaven had just completed a new jade tower and needed someone of his talent to come and write a commemorative essay on the occasion. Gu is saying her husband had so much talent that he was summoned prematurely to heaven. "Orchid fragrance" symbolizes the attributes of integrity and cultivation.

lines 16–17: Orioles are emblems for happy lovers, while the calls of mated waterfowl symbolize harmonious marriage.

line 18: "Scratch my head": A gesture used in poetry as a sign of helplessness, being at the end of one's rope.

line 21: "Lofty hall" is a courteous phrase used to refer to parents or the family residence. Gu is referring to her husband's household.

line 23: A reference to their apartment in the inner courtyard.

line 25: "The phoenix" represents Gu's husband.

P.60.7. Endless Longing: Did Spring Come First?

I

Did spring come first?
Or did sorrow come first?
Young orioles deliberately
  call out in new-leaved groves.
Spiritless, she cradles her zither.

II

Did sorrow come first?
Or did spring come first?

Gay flowers, rioting butterflies
  and a sinuous east wind.
She picks one, but
  the flowers understand.

(*Woyuexuan ji*, 2/7a)

P.60.8. Spring in the Jade Tower: Moon-Viewing on Midway Bridge in Late Spring

Petals fly down into brocaded ribbons
  where spring ripples rise;
A waning moon's fluid shimmer
  gleams in the water's depths.
Thousands of pearls brilliantly ignite,
  reflecting light on her new dress;
She is holding the goddess of the moon
  in her small hands.

(*Woyuexuan ji*, 1/5a)

Midway Bridge is located on West Lake in the city of Hangzhou.

P.60.9. When I Hired a Teacher to Instruct the Girls, Someone Ridiculed Me, So as a Joke I Have Written This Retort to Explain Matters

Since first the Primal Forces were discrete
  and human relations, engendered thus, complete,
Men must be the arbiters of Right
  and in the home all virtuous women Chaste.
But if we fail to practice poetry and prose,
  how shall we display our natural gifts?
An elder woman scolded me for this:
  "You don't pursue the true and wifely way,
Engaging teachers to instruct the girls
  as if they sought to win the world's regard.
They put aside our normal women's work
  and waste their efforts to recite and learn."
I listened well to what she said
  but it left me unimpressed.

(8) In human society sexes segregate
and yet preserving chastity is hard;
How can we in women's quarters
fail to take the ancients as our teachers?
Yi Jiang and Da Si, royal women of Zhou,
both were praised for their solid virtue.
Ban Zhao wrote *Instructions for Women*
that we might know the code of proper conduct.
(12) I am ashamed of my own stupidity,
unable to correct my faults,
Yet I pity those today who cultivate
appearances—they are only pretty dresses.
Not treating moral training seriously
will visit shame upon the family name.
Bring girls together, let them study,
debate the issues, inquire into fine points.
(16) The Four Virtues, the Three Obediences—
make the ancient ways their standard.
Prune their character, refine and beautify;
make their persons fine and good.
Who expects them to be famous?
Seek only that the bad will be restrained.
Do this, then test them, and if something is amiss,
take your complaint to the worthy men of old.

(*Woyuexuan ji*, 2/1b–2a)

line 1: The two elemental cosmic forces whose unending interaction generates the material world and its processes of change in time, *yin* and *yang*. Yin is identified with the feminine and yang with the masculine.

line 10: Yi Jiang, also called Tai Jiang, was the queen of King Wu, first ruler of the Zhou dynasty. Tai (Da) Si was the consort of King Wu's father, who under the Shang dynasty first settled the Zhou people in the area from which they conquered the Shang. Tai Si was praised throughout history as a model for all women and an important source of the civilizing power of early Zhou rule.

line 11: Ban Zhao's work, *Nü jie* (Admonitions for women), describes the proper deportment and duties of the governing class wife. Ban was also known as a great scholar; see P.69.5.

line 16: The four women's virtues were respectful speech, chaste conduct, proper women's work, and modest demeanor. In theory, a traditional Chinese woman was subject all her life to the authority of men. She was expected to obey her father as a child, her husband as a wife, and her (eldest) son in her old age. For the Three Bonds expected of a man, see P.37.1 (note to xi, line 16).

P.60.10. Elegy for My Deceased Husband

I

Shadows of the *wutong* tree
attenuate, the moon still low.
Whose jade flute plays on,
its song making free with
currents of autumn cold?
It calls me from my bed in this dark wing
and takes me to your study
where books and lute are cold.
Blowing long into the night
it breaks the crystals of autumn frost.

II

Day after day, toward the mountains
straining eyes to see—
Where beyond the clouds
can I discover the immortal ones?
For all I know, my love
lives there at the fountainhead
in their hidden world,
Forgetting how he came
on his fragile, leaf-like boat.

III

For twenty years your books and sword—
spider silks and dust,
But the fine trees you planted before the hall
have new leaves.
I sketch your likeness and then,
Foolish as ever,
softly whisper to the person in the picture.

IV

Flowerlike lamps with orchid-scented oil
attend the pursuit of learning and letters.
In early autumn pistils of cassia bloom
are utterly, brilliantly beautiful.
What remains are the pleasures
of lute, books, and the "three paths."
What need to search for bright clouds
of pink blossom reflected in a stream?

V

Like piles of snow, layers of ice
they were impenetrable,
Then as we returned, the undercurrents
began to flow and ripple.
The clear tones of emerald lutestrings
are no different from those of long ago;
Beautiful as ever, the landscape
still waits for the old friend's return.

VI

I remember when with your own hands
you planted and nurtured these banana trees,
And I write a new poem, trying to outdo
the "Summons to the Soul" of Chu.
As I chant the poem till the moon falls
and the water clock runs out,
Tears mix with cold dew
soaking my thin silk dress.

VII

Lithe and slender branches of the willow—
An autumn wind sends their green
through the window curtain.
When I was young, my brushtip
had the finest point; now it's worn.

Today what use are fine words
Except to let this idled heart cling
  tight, as willow floss clings to mud.

(*Woyuexuan ji*, 3/1b–2a)

i, line 4: "Frost" (*shuang*) is a homophone for "widow" (*shuang*), and autumn is analogous to middle age in the human life cycle.

ii, line 2: On "Peach Blossom Spring" see P.16.4. In later treatments of the theme, residents described in the story of the utopian community deep in the mountains came to be represented as immortal beings.

iv, line 3: The phrase "three paths" implies a secluded life; see P.58a.7.

v, line 1: The images of layers of snow and ice refer to lotus flowers thickly covering a pond where the speaker and her husband used to go boating. The language of this passage may also hint at physical intimacy.

v, line 3: In this context, lutestrings signify "wife." Gu says her feelings for her husband remain the same.

vi, line 2: The third century B.C.E. *Chuci* includes two literary treatments of the ancient shamanistic ritual of summoning the soul of a sick or recently deceased person back to the body.

vii, line 4: The willow tree, in Chinese poetry, often connotes femininity. At maturity, the seeds of the willow, airborne with a silky floss, eventually come to rest on low ground, a metaphor for the loss of youth and beauty and a "descent" into the harder realities of life. The speaker claims that her writing, which was skilled and versatile in her youth, has become in widowhood merely a means by which she has sustained herself in her loss while fulfilling the duties that faithfulness to her husband requires of her.

P.60.11. Early Chrysanthemums

Having a special love
  for the gold blooms that come early,
I have transplanted their fragrance
  to the innermost courtyard.
When all the other flowers
  have been blown away,
They rise brilliant and proud
  under the frosts of autumn.

(*Woyuexuan ji*, 1/4a)

BIOGRAPHICAL NOTE BY REN ZIPANG; TRANSLATION BY MAUREEN ROBERTSON

商景蘭

P.61 Shang Jinglan (1604–ca. 1680)

Born in 1604, Shang Jinglan (style name Meisheng) is known to have been still living in 1676; the exact date of her death is not known.[1] Both her father, Shang Zhouzuo, and her husband, Qi Biaojia, were from Kuaiji (Shaoxing), where she resided throughout her life.[2] Shang and her husband were widely celebrated as a talented and handsome couple. The tradition of educating women was strong in both her natal and her marital families. Her sister, Shang Jinghui, was also known for her poetry, and Jinglan's two sons, four daughters, and two daughters-in-law all received literary training under Jinglan's supervision.

Shang Jinglan's father had been minister of personnel during the last decades of the Ming. Her husband also held a minor office under the Ming. Jinglan was forty years old (forty-two *sui*) when her husband drowned himself in despair at the fall of Nanjing in 1645.[3] Literature and painting were central to her life in the thirty or more years that remained to her. During those years she organized numerous excursions of family women to scenic spots in the vicinity of her home. Reports of Shang directing her academy of female relatives in bouts of composition made her the wonder of the area. She was pleased to welcome Huang Yuanjie, a celebrated woman poet and painter of Jiaxing, whose trip to Shaoxing was arranged by the poet, loyalist, and playboy Wang Ruqian (Ranming) of Hangzhou during the mid-1650s. A collection of poems written during Huang's visit was published in 1661.[4] Shang Jinglan's collected *shi* and *ci* were published under the title *Jin nang ji* (The brocade bag collection; also known as *Xiang lian ji*, or The fragrant dressing-case collection).[5] Other pieces appear in anthologies of her day.

P.61.1. Sending Huang [Yuanjie] Off to the Provincial Capital

The wind drives the lone sail away,
The empty curtain makes me sad.
Petals scatter on the barren, zigzag path,
Fallen leaves gather on the wild, deserted hill.
The river moon chills the fisherman's boat,
Mountain clouds escort the traveler's skiff.

Though we take leave of one another today,
(8) I shall long remember our nighttime excursions.

(MYSW, 11/1b)

P.61.2. *Rejoicing That My Second Son Studies in the Purple Fungus Studio*

Lotus flowers once laughed at the sun.
Wutong leaves startle me by degrees with their signs of fall.
The water is white; in its light, trees seem broken.
Flowers are red; in their reflection the tower moves.
My son's literary talent stands out from the pack.
My white hair—in the mirror it reveals my grief.
I rely on the books my husband left behind,
(8) And on the empty staircase the light of his moon never recedes.

(MYSW, 11/1b)

Purple Fungus Lodge was the studio of Qi Biaojia; its name alludes to the Four White-Haired Ones, wise men who escaped to the mountains to avoid the exactions of the First Emperor of Qin. Shang's son is following in his father's footsteps. The first lines, with their contrast of spring and fall, suggest both personal mourning and a loyalist subtext.

P.61.3. *Night Rain*

Rain crosses the jade stairs, the fragrant grass is green.
The beautiful woman dreams of crossing the Jiao river to the north.
The Jiao river is ten thousand miles long, where can she seek him?
At midnight the returning swan spends the night on the river bank alone.

(MYSW, 11/2a)

P.61.4. *In Celebration of the Visit of [Huang Yuanjie] of Jiaxing*

A pair of candles helps to detain our guest.
As our wine vessels float, the night scenery takes on new luster.
We enter deeper into conversation, incense swirling around our chairs.
Once the curtain is raised, the moon follows us everywhere.
A fan covers your face, as if your grief has no outlet.
Riding the waves, your thought is free of contamination.

The bright pearl of your worth is encased in its sack,
(8) But your spirit cannot help shining through.

(MYSW, 11/2a)

P.61.5. Traveling with Huang Yuanjie to Yu Mountain

The *sheng* plays as a song evokes the long-gone storied tower.
A path stretches far through the bamboos, lined with green moss.
The lake and the sky are of one color; the cold air makes us feel old.
Over endless layers of mountains and ravines the evening clouds open.
Plum blossoms surround the path as our spirits aimlessly roam.
Though there's a bright moon over the balcony, dreams do not come.
Now the affairs of the world have faded away.
(8) How can I bear to know that my lovely guest is not yet at peace?

(MYSW, 11/2a–b)

line 1: For the *sheng*, see P.23.5.

P.61.6. Sitting in the Book Room at the Garden of What Remains

The peaceful lake is vast, the white clouds are light.
The frost illuminates the yellow flowers, the bottoms of the stones are bright.
As I sit behind my curtain at the decorated railing, it's really quiet.
Bird songs accompany me as I read alone.

(MYSW, 11/2b)

P.61.7. Climbing Up the Book Storage Tower and Printing Rhymes

A light sun and yellow clouds overhang northern mist.
Ten years of remorse are preserved in the sweet springs.
The official doesn't worry if a storm damages his jade hall.
When will the bronze hand give off round drops of dew?
The books bestowed by my husband are worth sharing with guests.
Newly grieving over my silk fan, I intend to seek the immortal realm.
Though I "climb high," I am no match for you in writing *fu*.
(8) A dry trunk of wood, I sadly lack that freshness after rain.

(MYSW, 11/2b)

line 1: This sentence may present an allegorical protest against Qing rule (the fog obscuring the "sun," i.e., the legitimate Ming heir).

line 4: As part of his cult of the Supreme Unity (*Taiyi*), Emperor Wu of the Han set up a bronze statue of an immortal with a dew-collecting bowl in its hand (the dew doubtless being intended for alchemical purposes). After the disintegration of the Han dynasty, Emperor Ming of the Wei (r. 226–39) had the statue moved to his own palace. On its removal the statue wept. The bronze immortal thus symbolizes dynastic integrity and legitimacy. For a predecessor poem, see Li He, "The bronze immortal's farewell to the Han capital: a song with preface," QTS, 391/ 4403.

line 6: On the silk fan and its associations with Ban *jieyu*, see P.1.1.

line 7: The ability to "climb high and compose" (later taken to mean specifically "compose a *fu* rhyme-prose") is recorded as early as the Mao *Commentary* to the *Book of Odes* (in SSJZS, 3: 2/16b) as one of the nine accomplishments of the gentleman.

P.61.8. *Traveling to the Secret Garden*

Quietly the peaceful woods are enveloped by green mist.
Coldly the mountain streams emerge from flowing springs.
The light off the lake is pale where it meets the storied tower on the far side.
The frost on oranges and pomelos accentuates their round, yellow forms.
Like the chickens and dogs at the cave opening, we seek to escape the world.
Clouds and sunset under my pen give expression to poems of wandering immortals.
Visitors to a fragrant landscape, we never tire of climbing high and looking into the distance.
(8) Still more do we appreciate the special purity of pear flowers.

(MYSW, 11/3a)

line 5: When Liu An (180–122 B.C.E.), prince of Huainan and practitioner of Daoist immortality magic, ascended to heaven, the chickens and dogs in his courtyard licked the elixir from his bowl and attained immortality, too (Ge Hong, *Shen xian zhuan*, 4/5a). The *Dao de jing*, chapter 80, advises that countries be kept small and their inhabitants few, so that "neighboring states might overlook one another, and the sounds of chickens and dogs might be overheard, yet the people will arrive at old age and death with no comings and goings between them" (trans. Henricks, *Lao-tzu*, p. 156). These two allusions are frequently employed together in order to suggest the Daoist hermit's life: see, for example, Tao Yuanming's "Peach-Blossom Spring," the probable source of the "cave" mentioned here (see P.16.4).

P.61.9. *Thinking of Huang [Yuanjie]*

A yellow cloud completely hides the green of the mountain top.
A bird on its way home flies to its old tree.
In the garden a hidden fragrance rises from the base of the flowers.
As the sun sets on a peak far away, I hear the ringing of chimes.
Wind and rain howl with the mountain ghost's cry.
Silent behind a brushwood door I copy the *Tai xuan jing*.
From a hundred miles away, I think of you in my high tower.
Your lonely wall seems dimly visible in the white clouds.

(MYSW, 11/3a)

line 6: On Yang Xiong's formidably difficult *Tai xuan jing*, see P.43.3.

P.61.10. *Celebrating Huang's [Yuanjie] Arrival*

For ten years I've lived behind locked doors among brambles.
How could I have dreamed of catching sight of you from a thousand
  miles away?
In talent you are a descendant of Lady Ban [Zhao],
In elegance you are more than a match for Miss Zuo [Fen],
In calligraphic style, you outdo Cai Yong,
In writing one-thousand-character *fu*, you resemble Sima Xiangru.
Only now as we sit here finding delight in the same poems
Do I realize I am in the presence of a modern-day Xue Tao!

(MYSW, 11/3a–b)

lines 3–5: See Ban *jieyu* (P.1) and Zuo Fen (P.3). Cai Yong, the father of Cai Yan (P.2), was also a poet; he is credited with creating the eight calligraphic styles.

P.61.11. *In Honor of My Second Daughter, on the Birth of a Grandson*

You're propped up in bed, and I'm kneeling next to you, what
  happiness for both of us!
I rejoice all the more because it will take time for you to recover your
  strength.
I used to be afraid that beautiful women would have bad fates.
But today, white hair and all, I look upon your beautiful boy.

May your son's reputation reach the Luo region, following your example,
And his virtue be manifest in Jingnan, never to be outshone.
Fortunately all the brothers of the Xi family are present.
Greater and lesser officials will find it hard to bully him.

(MYSW, 11/3b)

P.61.12. A Lament for My Father

The southern clouds, like the signal fires, are dark,
The tall tree of our hereditary house is ruined.
Though we face national shame there are still loyal hearts.
Your children cannot honor you enough for your pains.
Your image, in official hat and attire, still fills our imaginations.
Your table and walking stick inspire tears.
Preparing to leave, I stand in the empty courtyard
And grievingly watch the stars descend.

(MYSW, 11/4a)

P.61.13. Seeing [Huang Yuanjie] Off Again

After our farewell you disappeared among mountains and clouds.
I thought of you on the road.
Your lone sail reached the river
As your elegant beauty returned home under the moon.

(MYSW, 11/4a)

P.61.14. Chun guang hao

The mountain's cape is elegant,
The ripples on the water are clear,
The falling flowers dainty.
Along the sand, mandarin ducks play in clear water
And one hears the sound of oars returning.
Little birds chirp as if in conversation;
In the spring vista, spells of rain are followed by clearing.
A burst of purple sends the sun below the horizon,
Then the moon rises in the east.

(Zheng Guangyi, 1346)

P.61.15. Mourning the Dead: In Memory of My Husband

Your name will be known forever:
I chose to cling to life.
Loyal officials are called great,
Parents who cherish their children are merely human.
You lived as a righteous official;
Your epitaph carries your name past death.
Though the living and the dead walk on different roads,
(8) My chastity complements your integrity.

(Zheng Guangyi, 1347)

BIOGRAPHICAL NOTE AND TRANSLATION BY ELLEN WIDMER

王 微

P.62. Wang Wei (ca. 1600–ca. 1647)

Wang Wei was a distinguished courtesan and poet of Guanglin (Yangzhou). Orphaned early, she took up the courtesan's profession. She called herself the "Daoist Master in the Straw Garment," but her habits were more those of a Buddhist. One of the few women poets to make nature her poetic concern, Wang Wei explored in her verse the natural quietude of mountains and rivers and is reported to have written a work in several hundred chapters called *Ming shan ji* (Records of the famous mountains). Her prefaces to her collection *Wanzai pian* (As if I were there) and *Yueguan shi* (Poems from shaded halls; see C.11) underscore the effect scenery had on her mind and feelings.[1] She loved to travel with her library on a boat, visiting freely with male literati and constantly exchanging verses with them. Zhong Xing and Tan Yuanchun, founders of the Jingling School of poetry, were among her intimate acquaintances. Wang Wei was later married to Xu Yuqing, a Ming loyalist who participated in various resistance activities against the Manchu invaders. A commentary on Wang Wei by Liu Shi (P.67) appears at C.14.3.

P.62.1. Getting Up for a Stroll

I

So many leaves give color to the hills,
At sunset they look deep green.

Since the hills and waters have found each other,
They would rather have their wonders hidden.
Floating clouds emerge from the front ranges
And veil the fading sunlight.
My ears and eyes delight in this new spectacular scenery;
(8) All my past travels sink into oblivion.

II

River and lake give aspect to each other;
The evening hues cannot be distinguished.
As I walk along the reddish-yellow path,
Birds descend to the ox and sheep herds.
Away from the crowd, I have attained loftiness;
My hands reach the layered clouds.
Each assimilates what it sees,
(8) Hearing the rest contentedly from afar.

(MYSG, 36/1a)

P.62.2. *Inscribing a Poem on "The Dream" for Wang Ranming*

Emotion is the root of dreams;
The emotion may be real, but the dreams are mostly unreal.
Not that dreams can become indistinct,
For indistinctness generates even more shapes.
You, Master, are one who has forgotten emotion,
Alone awakened from where others are stuck.
Would you, for no reason in the spring,
(8) Let a dream wander and flutter?
In the dream and in the heart—
Is it one or is it two?
Reading your "Dream" poems in my boat on the lake
(12) Makes me understand the reach of emotion.
At this moment the setting moon is here;
All around is a stretch of emerald drizzle.
The arousal and dispersal of dreams
(16) Both depend on the pear blossoms.

(MYSG, 36/1b)

P.62.3. Parting in the Boat on an Autumn Night

Mist rises from the desolate grass;
The moon descends into the cold stream.
The soul goes home as autumn ends,
Sadness comes in the dim night.
When will this disquiet end?
Will my inner heart grow cold?
You point your oars to the edge of the sky;
Seeing you off, I feel hesitant and uncertain.

(MYSG, 36/1b)

P.62.4. Farewell on an Autumn Night

Holding hands, we are without words.
As you leave the pavilion, time gradually elapses.
In the cold frost the sky does not dawn;
The moon is lovely, but dreams will be few.
Say not that you're about to go,
For I think of following the waves.

(MYSG, 36/2a)

P.62.5. Seeing Off Mr. Meigong on His Return to Yunjian

Last time you saw me off
The moon shone all over the flowering grove.
Fantastic clouds emerged from truncated peaks;
Wild ostriches rested near the water surface.
The servants all received poems;
You freely obliged them.
A hundred poems, then a hundred cups;
Roaring in laughter, we both forgot fatigue.
Now as I see you off,
The flowers and the moon are both in bloom.
The dew is wet, the autumn light cold;
The wind whirls; the shadow of the sail trembles.
Who knows when we will meet again?
Let not the boat go like an arrow!

(MYSG, 36/2b)

P.62.6. Song at Late Spring

Spring days are long, the spring grass is lush;
The empty stairs are wet, disturbed birds chirp.
Flowers wither, trees bloom by themselves;
Only longing cannot be forgotten.
My love is not yet cut off, my plaint not ended:
Who is playing the flute to add to my grief?

(MYSG, 36/4a)

P.62.7. Sunset Song

The sun longs to set, the birds to return;
The deep chamber is quiet, I think of lowering the silk curtain.
My dream not realized, I am heartbroken, feeling empty,
Many times I look back, but my thoughts are dim and remote.
The birds, unconscious, return home at dusk;
My heart is sad, but you do not know.

(MYSG, 36/4a)

P.62.8. Boating with Zhong Xing and Other Gentlemen at Night on the Two Streams of the Jiashan Grassy Marsh

Whither does the light boat float?
The grassy marsh between the Jia hills.
When leaves fall, cool waves move;
Mist rises in the quiet of the night.
Tea by the stove deepens the travelers' talk;
Water and rocks relax one's countenance.
Shall we do as the courtiers' sons do—
(8) Enjoy ourselves freely for a thousand years before we return?

(MYSG, 36/5a)

P.62.9. Writing to Mr. Meigong on a Cold Night

The moon rises over a quiet grove of light;
A quiet heart fears the cold winter.
By the terrace is a fire lit for studying;
In the mist pounding is heard across the creek.
Wild birds eat in the evening;

The stony brook's coldness reaches the pines.
When again can I ask you about a word
(8) As we face each other at the highest peak?

(MYSG, 36/6b)

P.62.10. *Written in Regret at Being Prevented by Other Matters from Joining My Friends Yongqi and Youxia Sojourning at Faxiang Monastery*

I heard that Zonglei was a companion to the monk,
Living secluded in an ancient monastery.
Now the fragrance of your robe exudes with the mist;
The shadow of your cane falls into the mountain void.
As you finish writing on a grove of leaves,
Your talk animates the wind from the valleys.
Too bad that I have no wings to fly away
(8) And listen to the bells in the dawn mist with you!

(MYSG, 36/7a)

line 1: Zonglei was a recluse who lived in a temple on Mount Lu. He often played chess with the monk in the monastery.

P.62.11. *Quatrain with Preface*

On an autumn night in the year *gengshen* [1620], I was lying sick at Solitary Mountain. As I slowly read the "Autumn Dream" poems by Lady Ma of Huguan, my spirit was carried away by melancholy. Unable to sleep, I casually wrote a quatrain to register my deep feelings. Even though I have already become one of wood and stone, I could not be free of emotions; what about readers after me?

Cold rises from the lonely pillow, sweet dreams come often;
Several times I thought I saw you, suddenly wondering if it were real.
I know sweet dreams are of no use,
But I still wish to be the one in your dream.

(MYSG, 36/13a)

preface: Lady Ma was the wife of a general stationed at Huguan (Tiger Pass). She wrote a series of a hundred poems, entitled "Autumn Dream," to express her longing for her husband during the war. These poems became lost but a copy was later discovered in an old country house in Shaoxing, Zhejiang (LCXZ, 2: 747).

P.62.12. Bidding Farewell on Another's Behalf

I recall the time when the lotus blossomed,
And the lotus seeds were bitter.
Now the frost and dew are cold,
Where have the paulownia seeds fallen?
The moon draws near, I feel the courtyard is empty;
The wind comes, and I love to see the leaves dancing.
The autumn mist embraces the truncated hills;
(8) A lone cloud darkens the southern riverbank.
With no way to tie your boat tight,
I would fain break its pole and oars.

(Xie Wuliang, 61)

P.62.13. Meeting Someone in Early Autumn, Missing My Female Companions for the First Time

I recall that in the past, every year before the Autumn Equinox,
During the dawn coiffure the yard was filled with dense mist.
Before the stairs we stamped our vermilion silk slippers softly;
Inside the window we sewed white silk skirts together.
When midnight singing was done we yet entertained the moon;
When the day's meditation was over we felt enlightened by the passing clouds.
Now, as I pick emerald and gaze by the brook,
(8) The cool dewdrops fall like beads, rousing ripples.

(Xie Wuliang, 62)

P.62.14. For Lin Tiansu at Parting

With fishing gear and tea-things in my light boat,
Glad I am to be nearing your house under the willows.
Here and now at parting my thoughts are endless;
The lake and hills cannot express the autumn of this moment.

(MYSG, 36/15a)

P.62.15. Passing Rain Blossom Terrace Again

The forms of spring are quiet in the eastern hills,
The shadows of the clouds fashion a distant radiance.
Sitting, I feel the high terrace is empty,
Not realizing the greenish mist has shrouded half of it.
Falling flowers make their own past and present;
Crying birds change from dawn to dusk.
Reflecting on transformation, one easily goes along with change;
Things at hand serve as enjoyment for a while.
How much more so when the river opens out,
And the clear waves are lapping against the banks!

(Xie Wuliang, 34)

P.62.16. Parting from Chen Zhongchun by the Ripples of the Jia Hills

From the Jia hills the chill water flows down,
Leaves are falling in profusion.
Parting is hard enough in the setting sun,
How more so, to see you off in a boat!
Once the jade flowers are plucked,
The falling dew cannot be heard.
Inscribe on the silk fan for me
A new poem entrusted to the white clouds.

(Xie Wuliang, 341)

P.62.17. Boat Mooring by the Riverside

A boat floats on in the void without end;
Chill clouds, the wind keen, the water flows west.
Reeds in the moon, pounding in every village;
Crickets amidst the frost, autumn all over the place.
At night the traveler's thoughts reach a dream a thousand miles away;
The sounds of bells cannot drive off sadness at the fifth watch.
My lone track—where may it be remembered?
Vast, vast the desolate mist, an angling boat all alone.

(Xie Wuliang, 342)

P.62.18. Dao lianzi

A heart of scattered threads,
Sorrow in utter solitude.
The bright face may follow spring and leave.
In my dream, he still has a heart that cherishes flowers;
Awakened, again I hear the rain that hastens the blossoms away.

(Yi Boyin, 154)

P.62.19. Yi Qin e

The sentimental moon
Steals out from behind the clouds and shines on the cruel parting.
Cruel parting—
The moon's clear light can do nothing;
Full for a while, but often waning.

My sad heart would fain speak to the West Lake.
But the lake's shimmer is dreamlike, its flow blocked.
Its flow blocked—
The sorrow of separation lingers by the lamp,
As it suddenly flickers, and goes out.

(Yi Boyin, 154)

P.62.20. Asking the Maid How Far the Moon Has Climbed Atop the Flowering Trees

Quietly the evening fragrance exudes from the flowering branches;
In the cool night, I sit up late before the window gauze.
I'm most fond of the moon's brightness, though sad to see the moon;
But I do love the moon's shadow, and the maid knows it.

(LR, 4/61)

P.62.21. Ru meng ling

One can only call him dreamlike;
Altogether I've played the new tunes in vain.
When the wind rises I'll hoist the sail;
Quickly the parting robe grows cold.
Don't see me off,

Don't see me off:
Tonight the moon is chilly, take care.

(Xu Shumin and Qian Yue, eds., *Zhongxiang ci*, "Shu ji," 11b)

P.62.22. Sheng zhazi: *Thinking of Lady Han on a Winter Day*

The wild geese pass, the paper window is cold;
The moon comes, the empty stairs turn chill.
Already sick, I cannot bear more grief;
Now the dream is gone, I have just woken up.

I still remember the times of our youth
When our wandering track was like a duckweed stalk.
Wearing scarves with patterns of fallen plums,
Hand in hand we explored the flowers' shadows . . .

(*Zhongxiang ci*, "Shu ji," 11b)

P.62.23. Zui chun feng

Who urges my love to be drunk so fast?
The window is cold behind the lamp.
Putting down the lute, embracing me, you lean against the fragrant curtain,
And sleep, sleep, sleep.
Silently I ponder, how is our love?
But you are indulging in a drunken dream.

I am ashamed of using slipper riddles,
For detaining you in this mandarin duck quilt.
I ask, have you taken off your silk robe?
"No, no, no."
Perhaps even when the divine maiden meets her love,
She too frets over the ease of parting.

(*Zhongxiang ci*, "Shu ji," 11b)

P.62.24. Tianxianzi: *Parting Feelings*

Misty water, reed catkins, all blend into a stretch of sadness;
Tidings of you are hard to obtain.
Raising my cup to invite the moon does not make three:

You can meet me,
I can meet you,
But now you are facing the cold lamp alone.

I would like to send a letter, but my feelings will be restrained,
Lest I write a whole story of longing.
Several times holding my brush, I ponder over and over again:
You miss me,
I miss you—
A frosty saddle wends the dawn road as the cock crows in the inn.

(*Zhongxiang ci*, "Shuji," 12a)

BIOGRAPHICAL NOTE AND TRANSLATION BY KANG-I SUN CHANG

馬如玉

P.63. Ma Ruyu (early 17th century)

Ma Ruyu lived in Jinling (present-day Nanjing). Originally surnamed Zhang, she took the name Ma after the "house mother" in charge of her training as a courtesan. Known to be clever and talented in various forms of amusement, well schooled in the *Wen xuan* and in Tang verse, and a fine calligrapher and painter, as a courtesan she created a sensation among the gentry of her time. It is recorded in the *Liechao shiji* that "women as well were drawn to her in intimacy, and there were those who cut off their hair and burned their arms [in oath], unwilling to part with her even unto death." Later she studied under a Buddhist monk, took the Buddhist name Miaohui, and visited several of the sacred Buddhist mountains. She died in her thirties.[1]

P.63.1. Kicking the Leather Ball

Her dainty waist sways with gentle force,
Swirling red dust brushes her plumed garment.
By moon-covering cloud coiffure a single star pin dangles,
Under pomegranate skirts a pair of phoenixes fly.

(LR, 33b)

P.63.2. *Dueling with Grass Blades*

Gathering emerald greenery, roaming fragrant paths,
Plucking flower blossoms, crossing an azure pool.
In the game people fight for win or lose,
Startled, butterflies scatter, male and female.
Break not the Forget-Worry-Grass,
And cherish the Trample-Anger-Branch.
A riot of color, really rather enviable,
(8) At the end succumbs to roadside mud.

(LR, 33b)

This was a children's game, the point being to see whose grass blade was strongest. Ma Ruyu may have in mind a poem by Li Qingzhao (see P.17.4, ii).

P.63.3. *Candle Flowers*

Silver candlelight suffuses window curtains,
In her orchid chamber, auspicious color melts.
Red flowers go to make a jealous moon,
Yet purple candle-snuff frets because of breezes.
The cup reflects like pearls returning to Hepu,
The light flickers like stars that cross the sky.
Lacking fragrance, it lets down doting butterflies,
(8) Possessing flame, it draws darting insects.

(LR, 33b)

line 5: A reference to the revival of the production of fine pearls in Hepu (present-day Guangdong province) through the elimination of pilfering in the second century, under the celebrated governor Meng Chang.

P.63.4. *Passing the Grave of Ma Shiniang*

I

In the southern state, a splendid flower withers,
On the western mound, pine and cypress flourish.
Beautiful or ugly, finally both are spent,
Long or short, what can be said about life?
Your dance was like homebound cranes in flight,

Your song made gibbons sob in the night.
My feelings are wounded for you, my dear companion,
(8) From time to time I mourn you on these highlands.

II

Flower moon lady, gone forever,
Between heaven and earth a mound of dirt.
I thought the frost was face-powder left behind,
The moss I took for an emerald hairpin that remained.
A solitary grave buries your hidden regret,
A chilly mist saddens my evening grief.
To see me you'd pity my ailing bones,
(8) Clear tears sprinkle the pines and catalpa.

(LR, 33a)

Ma Shiniang was probably a fellow courtesan in the same household as the poet herself.

BIOGRAPHICAL NOTE AND TRANSLATION BY NANCY HODES AND TUNG YUAN-FANG

P.64. Bian Sai (early 17th century)

Bian Sai (Bian Yujing) was a courtesan and painter in the Qinhuai area during the late Ming, famous enough to have sparked the couplet: "Near the tavern, we sought after Bian Sai, / But from beneath a mass of flowers emerged Chen Yuanyuan."[1] She was immensely popular with the scholar-officials of her day. Bian befriended Qian Qianyi and exchanged poems with him. She had an intimate relationship with the major poet Wu Weiye (1609–71), and for more than thirty years—from around 1630 to some time in the 1660s after her death—Wu continued to write poems about her. One of Wu's poems for her contains the following frank statement of love:

> The student in the blue gown so distraught—you took pity on me then,
> Now that your beauty is fading, I think of you fondly.
> I remember that wonderful autumn night we had in Hengtang:
> Our vow of love with the jade hairpin began in a previous existence.[2]

After the fall of the Ming, she became a Daoist nun and remained secluded for many years. Her work was published in *Yujing daoren ji* (Writings of the Daoist of the Jade Capital), now lost.[3]

P.64.1. Jiu quan zi*: On the Mirror*

Wiping away the light dust
Sets off the mirror-stand's brilliance.
Here are the round moon and its shadow;
Both most pleasing.

Preparing for the spring *kṣamā*, I quietly match ornament and rouge;
Outside the window the flowers shade draws near.
I coil my hair, make up my face,
So as to convey my spirit.

(Xu Shumin and Qian Yue, eds., *Zhongxiang ci*, "Shu ji," 10a)

line 5: *Kṣamā* (*chanhui*) is a periodic Buddhist ritual of repentance and confession.

P.64.2. Zui hua yin*: Spring Plaint*

How long can spring stay for mankind?
Sadly I pass the Pure and Bright Festival.
On the path is a time of bloom;
Soft, soft, float the gossamer threads,
The cuckoo cries blood.

Dim and remote now the landscape through long years of separation;
As I reflect, my homing heart aches.
There is no way to detain the spring:
Puffs of willow catkins
Stir up a sky of snow.

(*Zhongxiang ci*, "Shu ji," 10a)

line 2: On the Qingming festival, see P.38.1 (note to line 105).
line 5: On the cuckoo, see P.5.1.

P.64.3. Ta suo xing

Fragrance has faded from the night burner;
I admire the lonely flowers in the day.

The painted wall is ten feet high, my grief is ten thousand.
Tender spring dreams have long abandoned me;
Every night I leave the silk bed in search of you.

Your beautiful words are imprinted in my heart;
Past meetings tie down my thoughts.
(8) Just when I am saddest, spring comes and brings more grief.
Soul-searing slim willows droop low throughout the day,
Heartbreaking lush grasses spread to the edge of the sky.

(*Zhongxiang ci*, "Shu ji," 10a)

BIOGRAPHICAL NOTE AND TRANSLATION BY KANG-I SUN CHANG AND CHARLES KWONG

P.65. Yang Wan (ca. 1600–ca. 1647)

The Nanjing courtesan Yang Wan was known for her poetry and calligraphy. At sixteen, she married a scholar-official named Mao Yuanyi (style name Zhisheng). "Zhisheng valued her literary talent and was extremely courteous toward her. But, disloyal to her husband, Wan had a great number of extramarital affairs. Zhisheng adopted the attitude of a man of the world: although he knew about it, he did nothing to stop her." After Mao's death, she deserted his family and traveled with a succession of men. At one point, dressed as a beggar-woman, she was on her way back to Nanjing when she was captured and killed by a rebel band. "Yang Wan and the Straw-Coat Daoist [Wang Wei; P.62] called each other sister. The Daoist often urged her to change her way of life, but Yang Wan would not listen. The Daoist was as bright and clean as the blue lotus blossom, gracefully rising above the mud. But Yang Wan ended up being defiled by mud and became a laughingstock to all. Sad indeed!"[1] As these quotations show, Yang Wan was often judged unfavorably according to historians' moral biases. Her poetry builds on the seductive *topoi* of the "poem on an object" subgenre, but now and again reveals ambitions that reach beyond the conventions of courtesan verse.

P.65.1. Five Poems on Watching a Beautiful Woman Fly a Kite

I

Together we watch a jade wrist hold a light thread;
If the wind is slow to come do not complain it is late.
For instantly, where one looks afar toward the sky's edge,
The penetration of the clouds and swaying of the trees mark the
appointed hour.

II

I would fain relax my sad heart but find no reason for it;
A held thread may be cut off, but grief cannot.
If the kite were as heavy as my grief,
It would not be able to reach the loftiest heights.

III

I envy your crossing the bright welkin for thousands of miles,
Sigh that my body is not as light.
Were you to reach the sky's edge and meet the wanderer,
Could you take him a few lines from me?

IV

Paper-thin its love, its heart is of bamboo;
Never will it reward your deep affection.
Once in flight, it cannot be detained;
At sky's edge vanishing, it sends no word.

V

When the time comes, it departs in the wake of floating clouds.
Set on fluttering, it renders a myriad of intentions void.
Passionate, but in the end frivolous:
Like a beautiful lady, it vainly blames the east wind.

(LR, 81a)

P.65.2. In a Dream I Returned to the Immortal City. The Dim Traces Seemed Real, the Empty Room Was Silent. Only a Jade Inkstone Was Kept in It. I Recognized Long-Remembered Names.

The absence of a plaintive dream allowed for a sweet one;
Last night I unexpectedly had the joy of my life.
A few low houses stood beyond the floating clouds;
Several curves of clear brooks welcomed the bright moon.
Startled I was to see the Daoist books newly worm-eaten,
But touched to see half an inkstone inscribed with old names.
A single strand of literary thought is the work of three incarnations:
(8) I only resent the cold grief that disturbs my inkbrush.

(LR, 81b)

line 7: On the "three incarnations," see P.54a.7.

P.65.3. Recovering from Sickness

This happening goes against the heart—
For weeks I have not opened my door.
The carefree flowers are gone with the receding water;
The slender willows sway in the bright light.
Swallows pass by the curtain,
Fish grow by the angling rock.
Every year at this moment
(8) I recover from sickness, afraid to don spring clothes.

(LR, 82a)

P.65.4. Amid Sickness

I lie within a closed and empty house;
A fragrant breeze circles the brush-rack.
Composing on flowers produces amorous words;
Writing on willows leads to frivolities.
Matters are few, yet the body is weary;
Feelings are deep, but dreams do not run long.
Year after year I grieve through days of sickness,
(8) Yet laugh at myself for making so much of poetry.

(LR, 82a)

P.65.5. Two Extempore Poems Sent to Xiuwei

I

The east wind is lovable but also hateful,
Bringing all flowers to bloom then sending them away.
Alas that a courtyard of colors dark and light
Has gone with the wind—to fall on whose house?

II

The east wind equally shields all within the curved fence:
Every branch in flower, yet blossoming variously.
Though spring is incapable of binding the petals fast,
Don't let them be strewn wildly east of the Songs' house!

(LR, 82a)

BIOGRAPHICAL NOTE AND TRANSLATION BY KANG-I SUN CHANG

Qing Dynasty (1644–1911)

THE SEVENTEENTH CENTURY

P.66. Xu Can (ca. 1610–after 1677)

Xu Can (style names Xiangpin and Mingshen) was a native of Changzhou (modern Suzhou) in Jiangsu province. She married Chen Zhilin (style name Su'an), who obtained his *jinshi* (presented scholar) degree in 1637 and served both the Ming regime and the Qing, which came to power in 1644. Chen eventually became a Grand Secretary with the added titles of Junior Guardian and Grand Guardian of the Heir Apparent. Xu was named a lady of the first rank, but had to follow her husband into exile when he was accused of graft. He was sent to live in Manchuria but was allowed to retain his official titles. Soon summoned back to the capital, Chen was subsequently charged with bribing a palace eunuch, whereupon he was stripped of his property and banished again to Manchuria, where he died in 1666. Eventually, in 1671, after more than ten years of life in exile beyond the frontiers, Xu successfully petitioned Emperor Kangxi to have her husband's remains reburied in his native Haining (Zhejiang province), where she spent the last years of her life.[1]

Skilled in poetry (especially *ci*), painting, and calligraphy, Xu was a prominent member of the Banana Garden (*Jiaoyuan*) Poetry Club, which also included Chai Jingyi (P.75a), Zhu Rouze (P.75b), Lin Yining (P.77), and Qian Fenglun (P.78). Mainly written in the style known as "delicate restraint" (*wanyue*), her poems are nonetheless more than boudoir laments; personal vicissitudes and grief over dynastic change often led her to project her feelings onto nature, lending added depth and poignancy to her artistically dexterous lyrics, which have been compared with those of Li Qingzhao (P.17). Xu left over three hundred *shi* and *ci* poems, collected respectively in *Zhuozhengyuan shiji* and *Zhuozhengyuan shiyu* (Poetry collection and Lyric collection from the Garden of the Unsuccessful Statesman).

P.66.1. Dao lianzi: *Spring Plaint*

Verdant as before;
Blooming brightly for whom?
Grasses and flowers fill a tearful grove.
I would hold to the incense smoke and linger in my sweet dream,
But a cuckoo cries on a branch, scattering spring away.

(*Zhuozhengyuan shiyu*, in XTLS, 1/1a)

P.66.2. Bu suanzi: *Spring Sorrow*

Light rain breeds spring sorrow,
Sorrow that reaches the brows and stays.
We say sad moods are brought by spring,
But from where does spring come?

I count the flowers' days on my fingers;
In a blink the flowers will be gone.
Before the flowers I, too, would learn to cherish spring—
(8) When spring is gone, the flowers will lose their ground.

(*Zhuozhengyuan shiyu*, in XTLS, 1/3a)

P.66.3. Ru meng ling: *Spring Evening*

Like a face in parting, the flowers show little color;
As with a heart of sorrow, the plums turn sour early.
I fear the cuckoo's voice,
Lest it prematurely scorch the grass before the courtyard.
Spring fades,
Spring fades;
A few weeping willows still sway slender and soft.

(*Zhuozhengyuan shiyu*, in XTLS, 1/3b)

lines 3–4: On the cuckoo's voice, see P.5.1 (iii).

P.66.4. Pusa man: *Spring Boudoir*

The flossy rain vexes the flowers and weighs down the buds;
Unable to bear it, they speak to the sad one.
The funnel-like bed curtains wrap a spring chill in;
Where lie the hills in my dream?

Furling the curtains, the wind blows with an ill will;
Tears fall with dying blossoms.
I envy the willow catkins so—
They'll reach home before I do.

(*Zhuozhengyuan shiyu*, in XTLS, 1/5b)

P.66.5. Mulanhua: *Autumn Night*

The night is cold, I cannot bear the keen west wind;
The passionate one has become a victim of insentience.
The moon's tracks move faintly to the south tower,
Where the drums and bugles have stopped at midnight.

The cicadas are dying, their tunes muffled—my soul cannot be stilled
Amid a hundred torments and a thousand regrets.
I rise to examine the deepening dew-florets,
While along the four walls autumn crickets compete in shrieking.

(*Zhuozhengyuan shiyu*, in XTLS, 1/6a)

P.66.6. Shaonian you: *Moved*

Wilting willows, frost all over Baling Bridge—
What thing resembles that in the last dynasty?
At night the bright moon
Shines as before,
Still recognizing the slim waists of the Chu palace.

The golden goblet half drowns the lute's grief;
For whom shall I play the old tune?
In front of the emerald tower,
By the rouge well,
My soul drifts with the falling petals.

(*Zhuozhengyuan shiyu*, in XTLS, 1/7a)

line 1: Baling Bridge stands near present-day Xi'an in Shaanxi province.
line 5: King Ling of Chu (r. 540–529 B.C.E.) was fond of slender waists in women.

P.66.7. Xi fen chai: *Spring Boudoir*

The east wind is vexing,
The oriole's voice low;

Willows sporting in spring sway their flossy wisps.
The dream lingers;
When shall we meet?
I implore a homing swan
This bit of perfumed paper
To deliver! deliver!

The flower season is gone early,
Joyous feelings are few;
The split hairpin, regrettably, ages on the dressing-table.
Lying on the paired-ducks pillow,
When did I ever sleep?
Let me just go near the golden cage;
The parrot can talk . . .
Proceed! Proceed!

(*Zhuozhengyuan shiyu*, in XTLS, 1/8b)

P.66.8. Yi Qin e: *Spring Sentiments, Following Su'an's [Chen Zhilin] Rhymes*

In the season of spring:
Yesterday it looked like rain, but today it snowed.
Today it snowed;
Half a spring of fragrant warmth
Has been cast away.

The wasting of my heart needs no word from you;
Miserable it is, like a pang, and a whimper.
Like a whimper:
Old love, new favor,
Are but dawn clouds and flowing moon.

(*Zhuozhengyuan shiyu*, in XTLS, 1/9a–b)

P.66.9. Yi Qin e: *Spring's Leave-Taking*

The east wind is waning;
I rise to survey the few remnant blossoms.
The remnant blossoms are few:
A drape of sparse rain;
Half a courtyard of misty grass.

The swallows and orioles purposely vex one,
Their thousand cries and myriad strains singing "Spring is gone!"
(8) Spring is gone:
Who will unknit the eyebrows,
Their image in the mirror tinged with grief?

(*Zhuozhengyuan shiyu*, in XTLS, 1/9b)

P.66.10. Ta suo xing: *Early Spring*

Fragrant grasses are just sprouting,
Pear blossoms not yet battered down by rain,
But spring's soul is already a catkin at the edge of the sky.
The crystal curtain is softly hanging—but for whom?
Orioles fly up to the cherry tree.

Vast and dim is the bygone kingdom,
Where may the small boat be?
(8) A stretch of setting sunlight flows away with the stream.
Slate clouds still shroud the old rivers and hills;
May the moon's tracks not reach that deep, deep spot!

(*Zhuozhengyuan shiyu*, in XTLS, 1/11a)

P.66.11. Huan xi sha: *Spring Boudoir*

Incense from the iron circles the painted curtain;
Now and then a breeze brushes my brow-tips.
When did the needlework on the embroidery frame progress?

A few fallen blossoms dot the lonely spring;
The courtyard's lush grass bathes in the drizzle:
One needs no spring illness to be weary.

(*Zhuozhengyuan shiyu*, in XTLS, 1/11b–12a)

P.66.12. Nantang huan xi sha: *The Night of the Fourteenth*

They've used decorated lanterns to light up damask seats;
Now wondrous touches are added, new hangings rival one another.
The bright moon seems averse to the lovely sights' haste,
And doesn't readily round.

I love best the day before a festival,
Often reckoning how long past happiness did last.
Too bad the capital guards still enforce curfew,
Urging back the roving whips.

(*Zhuozhengyuan shiyu*, in XTLS, 1/12a)

The fourteenth day of the first month of the year is the eve of the Lantern Festival, held on the first full moon after the New Year.

P.66.13. Nantang huan xi sha: *The Night of the Fifteenth*

The warmth is faint, the chill light, the night air mild;
Picking a red dress for my spring jaunt, I try on sheer gauze.
The moon is like a languid beauty about to sleep,
Its halo diffusing waves.

Too idle to follow the fragrant dust or watch the splendid lights,
I write new verses in place of pipes and songs.
Half-leaning toward the flowing clouds, two or three cups—
No need for more.

(*Zhuozhengyuan shiyu*, in XTLS, 1/12a)

P.66.14. Nantang huan xi sha: *The Night of the Sixteenth*

Jade awry and fragrance swirling in the midnight light:
On red soft carpets the feast has just begun.
The fair moon's favor on man waned not a bit;
Last night it was full.

Crimson candles have burnt out in the wind, but the merry mood is
 not yet sated;
A stroll amid lanterns will have to wait for next year.
Better to have the phoenix flutes play until dawn,
Lest the flowers close their lids.

(*Zhuozhengyuan shiyu*, in XTLS, 1/12b)

P.66.15. Lin jiang xian: *Boudoir Feelings*

I did not know autumn had entered the mirror;
How often it shows my tearful rouge!
Green ripples and clear dew have vexed the red fragrance;

The lotus hearts are shy to bear fruit—
Over half are empty pods.
Bending low by the room, the hanging willows have stopped swaying;
Through the curtain, I see homing wild geese formed in line.
In dream my soul has traveled to the misty land.
Here, light breeze and rain
Chill the silvery pond through the night.

(*Zhuozhengyuan shiyu*, in XTLS, 2/1b)

P.66.16. Tangduo ling: *Reflections*

The jade flute sends off cool autumn;
On the red plantain, dew has not dried.
The night fragrance is fading—don't lean from the high tower!
The cold moon and the traveler are both sojourners;
She keeps me company in a somber land.

Into the small courtyard comes frontier grief;
Iron weapons litter old haunts.
Where can one find a small boat in the five lakes?
In my dream the river's cries blend with sobbing tears;
Why don't they flow toward my old home?

(*Zhuozhengyuan shiyu*, in XTLS, 2/3a)

P.66.17. Die lian hua: *Stirred by the Frequent Loss of My Letters to Su'an*

Often I send brocade letters, but the wild goose fails to go;
I fear the creeping of dusk
Into the depths of my curtains.
How much sadness is there in a single look?
Specks of tear stains form a shower of rouge.

I've leaned long over the railing, but remain listless;
Casually I trim the leftover incense—
All by myself, with whom can I speak?
Through the day I feel weary as in a dream;
A flash of the setting sun and I'm a thousand miles away.

(*Zhuozhengyuan shiyu*, in XTLS, 2/3a)

line 1: On geese as messengers, see P.2.1 (Song 5).

P.66.18. Die lian hua

The butterfly does not love the flowers, though the flowers love the butterfly;
It leaves the green for the red,
But not because its heart is cruel.
There is a deep feeling that runs uniquely keen;
It loves nothing but for kindred hearts to be tied.

A few lines of spring ice gradually crack in the breeze;
I must thank the east wind,
For consenting to dispatch the homing boat.
Day and night I have followed you, never once parted;
Did you have to leave for the Suzhou moon?

(*Zhuozhengyuan shiyu*, in XTLS, 2/3b)

P.66.19. Qingyu'an: *Mourning Antiquity*

Heartbroken, by mistake I took the road to Desolate City;
I've brought my blood and tears,
But there's nowhere to shed them.
The half-moon looks blurred, frost covers a few trees:
Once purple flutes sounded low and far,
Kingfisher ornaments shone bright and dim,
And goat-carriages passed indistinctly by.

Towering blue waves have buried the chains across the river;
Old ramparts lie forlorn by the reed shore.
Mist and water know not the flaws of human affairs:
A thousand miles of warships,
A stretch of sails pulled low in surrender—
Don't blame them on women's lotus steps!

(*Zhuozhengyuan shiyu*, in XTLS, 2/4a)

line 1: Guangling (Yangzhou) in Jiangsu province.

lines 5–7: These lines recall leisurely scenes of court life in days long past.

line 8: In 280, the Jin general Wang Jun captured Jinling (Nanjing, capital of the Wu kingdom), which had been defended by iron chains laid across the Yangzi River. The second stanza alludes to an earlier poem on the historical site by the Tang poet Liu Yuxi (772–842), "Xisaishan huaigu" (QTS, 359/4058).

P.66.20. Yijian mei: *Seeing Off Spring*

Three months of spring radiance have all abandoned one:
Seeing it off consumes the soul;
Keeping it consumes the soul.
The Eastern Lord sends word to bid the enchanting adieu—
Leaving makes one listless;
Staying makes one listless.

On the jade bed the perfumed quilt displays its light silk;
Tonight is long,
Tonight is short.
Sad flowers, fear not the green shadows twining with you—
Tomorrow will be early,
Tomorrow will be late.

(*Zhuozhengyuan shiyu*, in XTLS, 2/5a)

P.66.21. Yujie xing: *The Lantern Festival in Beijing*

Having watched the decorated lanterns, I move away on fragrant clogs.
Now on the imperial avenue
All roving dust is gone.
With white skirt, powdered sleeves and jade for a face,
There is no difference between lady and moon.
The clouds over the cinnabar tower look pale;
The frost on the golden gates turns cold—
My delicate hands are afraid to touch them.

Along the Third Bridge I wind in light wave-traversing steps.
My kohl brows knit,
I say in a subdued voice:
"Year after year, may I always roam the Phoenix City,
Knowing that I've gazed upon those flower-beaded palaces.
But it's vague and dim even at close hand,
A thousand miles just before the eyes—
Let alone next year's moon."

(*Zhuozhengyuan shiyu*, in XTLS, 2/5a–b)

line 9: A reference to a phrase from Cao Zhi, "Lo shen fu" (Rhyme-prose on the goddess of the River Luo; *Wen xuan* 19/14a): "Traversing the waves with light steps."

line 12: The "Phoenix City" is the capital, Beijing.

P.66.22. Man jiang hong: *Shown to Fourth Sister*

By the blue sea and reedy creek,
Gone is another year, parted in the snap of a finger.
Before my eyes I see weary willows turn yellow,
Plaintive peach blossoms lose their rouge.
We often hoped to greet each other on a lamplit night,
But always meet under the moon by the palms and pomegranates.
The dying lamp calls forth half a lifetime's sadness,
All expressed on this night.

In the lotus-picking pond
The fragrant waves are sobbing;
On the grass-treading path
All traces of aroma are gone.
I'm pained by the misty desolation—where are
The splendid rafters of our old home?
Delicate are our ancestors' phoenix plumes, early the foundations they laid;
Now disheveled is the cicada coiffure, forlorn the lintel of the door.
As I stroke the silver stand and play the jade flute,
Every note drips blood.

(*Zhuozhengyuan shiyu*, in XTLS, 3/3a)

P.66.23. Man jiang hong: *Moved*

A homeland after upheaval—
The gloomy mood within is hard to describe.
Spring is almost gone, the mugwort has just sprouted;
The window adornments overlap one another.
The eaglewood in the burner has turned to ashes, but still I am loath to get up;
The small window faintly shows the clouds and moon.
Sad it is, that life isn't like a lotus in the water,
With hearts entwined.

Tears of parting
Brim with blood,
Flowing without end,
Their waves swelling with sobs.

Seeing wild geese return in groups
Often compounds my biting grief.
More and more my kohl brows pale in the mirror;
Now and then the waning moon appears at bedside.
This spring, did I dream of visiting my hometown
And startling the cuckoos?

(*Zhuozhengyuan shiyu*, in XTLS, 3/3a–b)

P.66.24. Man jiang hong: *Sent to Su'an upon Approaching the Capital*

The willow bank leans aslant;
From beyond the sail's shadow the east wind is blowing hard.
The traveler's sorrow comes before the body rises;
Now and then the dawn chill stirs.
Before my eyes the rivers and hills draw an old grief;
Vast and dim—where in the ravine can I hide my boat?
I recall how jade flutes and golden pipes resonated in midstream—
But the present is not the past.

Spring is still here;
My clothes are woefully thin.
The wild geese are gone;
There is no messenger for my letter.
Alas, the journey has made me wan and sallow,
My sickly waist as though pared.
It is a stone's throw from the capital, but he hasn't appeared,
Again missing our morning appointment.
Perhaps in the dying watch I'll read a book in silence
And drink a sad cup alone.

(*Zhuozhengyuan shiyu*, in XTLS, 3/4a)

line 6: A hidden boat is supposed to be safe, but someone may come in the middle of the night and carry it off—an allusion to the sixth chapter of the Daoist philosophical classic *Zhuangzi* (*Zhuangzi jishi*, 243–44; Mair, trans., *Wandering on the Way*, pp. 53–55). The sentiment here is that the poet cannot stand above the uncertainties of human life.

P.66.25. Yong yu le: *In a Boat, Moved by the Past*

Intact are the peach blossoms,
As always are the swallows,
But the spring sights are greatly changed.
The Master Liu of former days,
The Director Jiang who returned—
Who can bear recounting past events?
Receding waters in the dying sun;
Dragons gone and swords vanished:
How much of heroes' tears and blood!
Ah, eternal plaint
For rivers and hills like these,
Their grandeur cast away in a blink.

Before the White Jade Tower,
By the Yellow Gold Terrace,
Night after night only the bright moon remains.
Do not mock the weeping willows
Whose golden hue has now faded,
Or the lush plums that likewise have withered.
Flowing clouds of world affairs,
Flying catkins of human life,
All are consigned to the lost gibbon's mournful sobs.
The western hills survive,
Their sad visage a gloomy kohl,
As though sharing one's desolate grief.

(*Zhuozhengyuan shiyu*, in XTLS, 3/6b)

line 4: Liu Yuxi was repeatedly banished to distant posts. In a poem reflecting on human vicissitudes, written upon returning to the capital (Chang'an) after fourteen years of absence, he refers to himself as "the Master Liu of former days."

line 5: Jiang Zong (519–94) who was forced by military riots and dynastic transition to live far away from the southern capital at Nanjing for more than ten years.

line 8: A reference to two magical swords, which vanished and changed into two dragons after the heroes who discovered them had died (*Jin shu*, "Zhang Hua zhuan," 36/1074–75).

lines 13–14: On the Jade Tower and the Tang poet Li He, see P.60.6. King Zhao of Yan built a terrace for literary gatherings and kept a great deal of gold there to reward visiting worthies. Both allusions evoke past glories.

P.66.26. Fengliuzi: *Reminiscing with Su'an*

It's just like looking back on yesterday's events,
Though they must already be ten years past.
By the ink-washing pool
We built a study,
Where Sichuan paper and ivory brushes
Brought a special romantic freedom.
Several times spring almost left our yard of dying blossoms,
But stayed behind for our sake.
The night rain weighed down the flowers,
The light breeze tilted the butterflies;
And when the crystal blinds were rolled up
It was time to comb my hair.

The western hills are still here:
Do they know why I'm leaning against the balustrade,
Afraid to raise my eyes?
That even if I brew wine with the daylily,
It will only stir my grief?
I bid the peach blossoms of former days
Not to bloom in the green pond,
The swallows of old times
Not to pass the vermilion tower.
Ah, how regrettable that those newly joined wings
Should have mistakenly flown to Fairy Isle!

(*Zhuozhengyuan shiyu*, in XTLS, 3/7b)

line 17: On the daylily as a cure for melancholy, see P.2.1 (Song 16).

P.66.27. Shuilong yin: *Matching Su'an's Rhymes, Moved by the Past*

Under the silk tree's flowers we lingered;
Then, I once tried to explain to you:
Joy and sorrow turn in the blink of an eye,
Flowers, too, are like a dream—
How can they bloom forever?
Now indeed
The terrace is empty, the blossoms are gone,
Leaving weeds enwrapped in sprawling mist.

I recall the time of splendid sights,
The time of bustling glamour,
Each seizing on the spring breeze to show its charm.

Sigh not that the flower-spirit has gone afar,
There are fragrant flower poems inscribed on floral paper.
Here, pink blossoms open and close,
Green shade hangs dense and sparse,
Greeting us as though with a smile.
Holding a cup, we may chant softly,
As if our old companions
Have returned in our dream.
From now on,
Candle in hand, let us admire the flowers;
Never wait till the flower sprigs have grown old.

(*Zhuozhengyuan shiyu*, in XTLS, 3/8a)

line 1: The Chinese name for the silk tree is literally "joy in union" (*hehuan*).

BIOGRAPHICAL NOTE AND TRANSLATION BY CHARLES KWONG

柳是

P.67. Liu Shi (1618–64)

Liu Shi (also known as Liu Rushi) was a distinguished courtesan and poet-painter. She published her first collection of poems at the age of twenty; many literati in the Jiangnan area came to admire her learning and beauty. Her intense love relationship with the young poet and Ming-loyalist martyr Chen Zilong (1608–47) and later her marriage to the literary giant Qian Qianyi (1582–1664) made her a legendary figure in the field of literature. Furthermore, her numerous love poems to Chen (and for that matter, Chen's to her) engendered a whole new interest in song-lyric (*ci*), a genre characterized by intensity of emotion.[1] (Chen's preface to her *Wuyin cao* [Manuscript from the year 1638] appears at C.39.1.) Since traditionally a proficiency in song-lyrics was closely associated with the courtesan culture, we can surmise that Liu Shi, with her deep historical awareness of that culture, greatly influenced the late-Ming revival of *ci* as a serious genre. In "Dream of the South" (P.67.1, subtitled "Thinking of Someone," twenty poems), perhaps her most brilliant song series, she tells a moving story of her passionate and agonized relationship with Chen. Not limited to the *ci* genre, however, in her *shi* poems Liu Shi attempted to create a mingling of self and nature, as may be seen in her poem series, "Eight Quatrains on the West Lake of Hangzhou" (P.67.4)

On Liu Shi's activities as critic and anthologist, see C.14.[2]

P.67.1. Meng Jiangnan: *Dream of the South: Thinking of Someone*

I

He is gone,
Gone somewhere west of Fengcheng.
A thin rain dampens my red sleeves,
New weeds lie as deep as my jade brows are low,
The butterfly is most bewildered.

II

He is gone,
Gone from the Isle of Egrets.
Lotus blossoms turn to emerald remorse,
Willow catkins rise to join the zither's grief,
Behind the brocade curtain the early autumn startles.

III

He is gone,
Gone from the painted chamber tower.
No longer lustrous and beautiful, I sit idle,
Why bother about rouge powder and jade hairpin?
Only the wind coming at night.

IV

He is gone,
Gone from the small water pavilion.
Would you say we "have not loved enough"?
Or that we "have little to regret"?
All I see is trodden moss.

V

He is gone,
Gone from the green window gauze.
All gain is frail sickness. Lighter than a swallow,
Pitiful is my lone self, now that we are far apart.
Secretly we hide sweet memories in our hearts.

VI

He is gone,
Gone, leaving the jade pipe cold.
Phoenix pecked at the scattered tiny red beans,
Pheasants, joyfully embracing the censer, gazed at us,
Apricot was the color of my spring dress.

VII

He is gone,
Gone from the shadow of the green *wutong* tree.
I can't believe this has earned us a heartbreaking tune,
Still I wonder why our love has failed.
Whence this brooding grief? No need to look.

VIII

He is gone,
Gone from the small Crab Apple Hall.
I force myself to rise; the fallen petals are quivering,
A few red parting tears still remain,
Outside the door, willows leaning against one another.

IX

He is gone,
Gone, yet dreams of him come even more often.
Recalling the past: our shared moments were mostly wordless,
But now I secretly regret the growing distance.
Only in dreams can I find self-indulgence.

X

He is gone,
Gone, and the nights are longer.
How can this jeweled belt warm my thoughts about the black steed?
Gently putting on the silk robe in chill jade moonlight,
Behind the rosy curtain, a single wisp of incense.

XI

Where was he?
On the Isle of Smartweed.
The duck-censer burning low, the fragrant smoke warm,
Spring mountains winding deeply in the painted screen,
The golden sparrow ceased to weep.

XII

Where was he?
At the middle pavilion.
Recall once after washing his face,
His carefree laughter seemed so unconcerned—
Who knows for whom he smiled?

XIII

Where was he?
In the moonlight.
In the middle of the night, I clutched his priceless arm,
Lethargic, I looked at the lotus flowers again and again,
My inner sentiments, how hazy!

XIV

Where was he?
In the magnolia boat.
Often talking to herself when receiving guests,
Feeling more lost while combing her hair,
This beauty still broods over his charms.

XV

Where was he?
At the magnificent banquet.
My perfumed arms fluttered up and down,
Words issued in song, like profound thoughts,
Chiefly from my faintly glossed lips.

XVI

Where was he?
At the Autumn Crab Apple Hall.
Fun was playing hide-and-seek,
Round after round, no need to linger for long.
Again, how many sunsets have gone by!

XVII

Where was he?
On the Lake of Misty Rain.
Water rippled by the bamboo oar, the moon shining bright in the
 lustrous and gentle spring,
Our storied boat filled with wind and daphne fragrance,
Willows caressing the delicate waves.

XVIII

Where was he?
At the jade steps.
No fool for love, yet I wanted to stay,
Overly sensitive to any sign of indifference,
It must be that I feared love would run too deep.

XIX

Where was he?
Behind the curtain patterned with thrushes.
A parrot dream ends in a black otter's tail,
Incense smoke lingers on the tip of the green spiral censer,
Delicate were the pink jade fingers.

xx

Where was he?
By my pillow side.
Nothing but endless tears at the quilt edge—
Wiping them off secretly, only inducing more,
How I yearn for his love.

(Chen Yinke, *Liu Rushi biezhuan*, 1: 255–65)

i, line 2: Fengcheng most likely refers to Chen Zilong's hometown, Songjiang (Chen Yinke, *LiuRushi biezhuan*, 1: 256).

i, line 5: On Zhuang Zhou's dream of the butterfly, see P.41.6.

iii: This song alludes to a love poem in the *shi* form by the densely allusive Tang poet Li Shangyin: "Last night's stars, last night's winds / By the wall of the painted chamber tower, east of the hall of cassia" ("Wu ti," QTS, 539/6163).

vi, line 2: An allusion to Li Jing's (916–61) line, "In the small chamber [*xiao lou*] the song of the jade flute has become cold" (Lin Dachun, ed., *Tang Wudai ci*, 1: 220), with which Liu Shi refers subtly to the chamber in the Southern Villa she shared with Chen Zilong in 1635. See Chang, *The Late-Ming Poet Ch'en Tzu-lung*, pp. 34–35, and Chen Yinke, *Liu Rushi biezhuan*, 1: 280.

vi, lines 3–4: The phoenix and pheasant designs are part of the incense burner.

x, line 3: The "jeweled belt" might have been a gift from Chen Zilong. The black steed, a symbol of the male lover, is metaphorically connected with Chen here. See also the ancient *yuefu* song entitled "Black and White Steeds," in Guo Maoqian, ed., *Yuefu shiji*, 49/711.

P.67.2. At Cold Food Festival, After the Rain

Red silk, butterfly mist, all things seem so distant;
Hard to believe tonight the wind is blowing at length.
Even if one could delay the spring wind's going, it would surely
  withher;
A heartbroken one rises, struck by the hanging willows.

(Huang Shang, *Qianchen mengying xinlu*, 164)

On Cold Food Festival, see P.17.4.

P.67.3. Following the Rhymes of "Written While Viewing the Green-Calyxed Plum Flowers at Yongxing Monastery"

Homesickness, spring thoughts—both lie aslant;
Can one watch plum blossoms without thinking of home?

Breaking them for a gift, I love their fine sparse shadows;
Lingering on, I should cherish the light chill.
The small flowers come through the curtains, beautiful as snow;
The flowing light ripples the moon by the fine sand.
I wish to build a plank road here,
(8) To sit and lie down with you to admire the fragrant blossoms.

(Huang Shang, *Qianchen mengying xinlu*, 164)

P.67.4. Eight Quatrains on the West Lake of Hangzhou

I

A small yard with hanging willows lies east of the embroidered curtains;
Bare branches stretch by the oriole pavilion, no thoughts of longing yet.
Truly at the West Chill Bridge on the Cold Food Road
The peach blossoms have the essence of beautiful women.

II

Year after year, red tears dye the green brook;
By the spring waters the east wind bends the willows evenly.
The bright moon has just shifted, the new leaves are cold;
Traces of teardrops lie but west of the cuckoos.

III

Emerald strings of Xiang are tied to the double hoop;
Here the fragrance fades in the violent wind and rain.
Countless red orchids rush towards the body,
But most break off, unable to bound back.

IV

Beyond the south screen, in the misty moon, dawn lies dark and silent;
In the drizzle, delicate orioles shed tears that seem to come from the depths.
Again there is a gentle pair of butterflies
Whose winged rouge touches a loving heart.

V

The low branches have started to put forth lovely flowers;
Green birds fly primly over the wet, sloping path.
The sorrowful heart moves up the willow trees;
Over West Chill Bridge cuckoos are few.

VI

The mist brushes the green grassland in the night cool;
Fallen cherries darken the emerald pond.
Already I resent how the willow catkins resemble tears;
But now the spring wind and spring dream whiff me along.

VII

The fresh water of the bright lake looks like jade emitting smoke;
The grass grows lush, like a coiffure adorned with wild geese.
I think long and hard of the Greenhill Terrace birds of times past:
Crying amid the peach blossoms, they did not return.

VIII

Sadly I watch the water-birds sporting among the flowered rocks;
The purple swallows, flying up and down, soak their glistening coats.
In the lonely spring breeze the fragrance does not stir;
The dying blossoms should turn into rain gossamer and fly.

(Liu Shi, *Hu shang cao*, 6a–7b)

iii, line 1: Xiang is the lush region of lakes and hills associated with Qu Yuan; see P.37.

BIOGRAPHICAL NOTE AND TRANSLATION BY KANG-I SUN CHANG

P.68. Huang Yuanjie (mid–17th century)

Huang Yuanjie was from Jiaxing. Her exact dates of birth and death are not known, but she lived at the end of the Ming and the beginning of the Qing. Throughout her life she was intensely loyal to the Ming. Though she came from an educated family, she married a poor man who was separated from her in the turmoil following the collapse of the Ming. Because her family would not help her, she had to find other means of support. These included living with wealthy friends, such as Liu Rushi, and selling her poems and paintings, as she did in Hangzhou and other cities while living with the woman poet Wu Shan (P.74). Huang's and Wu's work attracted the attention of leading male poets, such as Wu Weiye, and playboys, such as Wang Ruqian. They, along with various officials and members of Ming loyalist circles, also contributed to her livelihood. It was thanks to Wang that she was conveyed by boat to the home of Shang Jinglan (P.61), where she lived for a while. Huang was later invited to be a tutor in Beijing, but her boat capsized in Tianjin as she made her way there, drowning one of her children. Her other child then died young in Beijing.[1] Huang herself became ill after these catastrophes and died in middle age sometime before 1669.[2] Though she published several collections of poems and other writings, none of these volumes are known to survive. However, some of her paintings have been preserved.[3]

P.68.1. Recording My Poverty on a Summer Day

At the bank of the lake the water rises, the *xing* plant looks like mist.
Swallows peck at duckweed threads, casting shadows in the water.
A high wall creates shadows, it shelters me from the sun.
The new lotuses have only small leaves, they are not yet in bloom.
Writing books does not cost anything in my mountain life,
But buying wine uses up the money I make selling my paintings.
My straitened circumstances must not be seen by the outside world.
(8) Fortunately locust trees and willows provide a green cover over my head.

(Hanazaki Saien, *Chūgoku no joshijin*, 320)

line 1: The *xing* plant (*Nymphoides peltatum*) is an edible water plant.

P.68.2. Chang xiang si

Wind fills the tower,
Rain fills the tower,
Wind and rain never cease, year after year.
The leftover fragrance is cold like autumn.

The sound of selling flowers:
Boats are selling flowers.
Purple and red flowers all evoke sorrow.
(8) Spring flows on like a river, never to return.

(Zheng Guangyi, 1458)

P.68.3. *Qingming Festival, 1646*

Leaning against a pillar, I am overwhelmed with worries about the state.
Others, as always, go to pleasure houses.
My thoughts persist like unending drizzle.
Tears fall like dispersing petals, without end.
Since the time of parting, it's already a new year.
Abstaining from burning fires is still an ancient custom we observe.
Thinking of my family I stare off into the white clouds.
(8) My small heart is overwhelmed by grief.

(Zheng Guangyi, 1459)

On the Qingming festival, see P.38.1 (note to line 105).

line 6: A reference to Cold Food Day; see P.17.4. The allusion is to the story of Jie Zitui and the implication is that although the Ming dynasty has fallen (1644), China's culture will persist.

P.68.4. *Written to Accompany a Small Painting*

I'm disinclined to climb a tall tower and observe distant green mountains.
For years I have preferred to close my door and paint from the heart.
Pale ink transmits a dimly visible landscape.
This lone peak lies somewhere between seen and unseen.

(Zheng Guangyi, 1461)

P.68.5. *A Rural Scene at Evening, Viewed from Afar*

Fall grass fills the banks of the pond.
High clouds converge in the evening chill.
A far-off oar divides the water's radiance.
I hear people talking near the setting sun.
The wind penetrates my thin clothes, chilling them.

Flowers give off the scent of rice paddies.
Alone I enjoy looking into the beautiful night.
(8) The stars and moon calmly preside over abundant frost.

(Zheng Guangyi, 1463)

P.68.6. In Praise of Poppy Flowers

She is deeply ashamed that the long sword achieved nothing.
Regretfully, she entrusts herself to the east wind, there lodging her life.
Once a beautiful woman, she is now a flower:
A vanished soul keeps its name from olden times.

(MYSW, 9/3a)

A certain kind of poppy was known as the "Lady Yu" poppy; for her story, see P.28.1.

P.68.7. [Untitled]

In 1656 I visited Shaoxing in the rain; Madame Ding [Wang Duanshu, P.69] came to visit and stayed with me. Madame Qi [Shang Jinglan, P.61] and Xu Ruoyun put on a performance of "The Fresh Cloud Child," prompting me to commemorate the event with a poem.

Spring begins at Nine Bends, the traveler's regret is everlasting.
The east wind moves the drooping poplars, almost imperceptibly.
Looking at the mountain and holding wine, I am not Dai Kui.
Accompanied by rain the returning boat carries a visitor, Wang Huizhi.
Composing poems where we sit, we abandon formal terms of address.
In front of a curtain they measure time with candles and play their music.
Moved by the actors' songs,
(8) I return home sad that you must leave again.

(MYSW, 9/3a–b)

lines 2–3: On the story of Wang Huizhi's non-visit to Dai Kui, see P.58b.8.

P.68.8. *[Untitled]*

On the fifth day of spring, with Madame Qi [Shang Jinglan] and all her daughters, we converge on The Hall of Contemporary Classics to see a performance of "The Fresh Cloud Child."

The east wind blows warmly around the magnificent hall in spring.
The table is set with fine cloths and mats, and foods from everywhere
 are set out.
Your progeny are all virtuous men of integrity.
As always, your female family members get along beautifully.
With red makeup and brocade sleeves the actresses come out before
 the lanterns.
Mimicking sighs and laughter, they are charming and frail.
Twelve rows of matchless beauties—
(8) Enough to enchant three thousand guests arriving in pearl shoes.

We witness the shattering upheavals of the Central Plains,
In an instant we are exiles with broken hearts.
Our jokes and talk exceed the humor of Ju Meng.
(12) Like New Year gods, these actresses amaze us with their brilliant
 reputations.
Filling glasses and cutting meat, people bunch around the candles.
In one time, at one glance, it cannot all be taken in.
Song after song, word after word is new,
(16) As beautiful women congregate to perform a New Year's play.

(SGCJ, 12/23a–b)

line 8: The allusion is to the Lord of Chunshen, who entertained over three thousand guests, all wearing pearl-studded shoes ("Chunshen jun liezhuan," *Shi ji* 68/2395).

line 11: A knight errant of the Han dynasty.

line 12: At the New Year, every family in China would paste up new effigies of the household gods (usually in the form of brightly colored woodblock prints). To be as famous as a New Year god was therefore to be known in every household.

P.68.9. *Bitter Rain*

When traveling, who can bear the wind and rain?
Homesickness pains me, I feel like a broken cloud.

Alone I climb the dilapidated tower and question Heaven's wisdom.
I laugh at my grieving face, afraid to look in the mirror.
Branches shiver, the flowers are cold, as orioles prepare to migrate.
My paint bag is empty, my writing brush has no hair, poems are hard to write.
I most lament the passage of youth, yet I go on living.
In the corner of the house a cricket sings, surprising my eccentric muse.

(MYSW, 9/21b)

P.68.10. [Untitled]

In 1655, on the day of the Lantern Festival, Madame Wu [Zixia] invites me, Wang [Duanshu, P.69] and her sister Wang [Jingshu], along with Zhao Dongwei, Tao Gusheng, and all the members of their poetry society to gather at Fucui Studio. We wait for Qi Xiuyan and Zhang Wanxian [daughter and daughter-in-law of Shang Jinglan, P.61] who do not come, then we draw lots and get the character "yuan."

Holding whisks, we're like immortals.
We gather for a feast on the Lantern Festival.
Talent flourishes, we promote ladies' learning,
Elegantly, we assemble at the Liang garden.

In the green of the bamboo, we can make out a long path.
The fragrance of flowers surrounds us everywhere.
Delicious dishes filled with elegant foods—
It's as if we're sitting at the Peach Blossom Spring.

Ornamental candles add to the light of the torches;
Fine wine repeatedly brims over our cups.
When the moon is round we open the jeweled mirror;
When the lanterns are brilliant we spin a pearl rhyme wheel.

Who first comes up with a wonderful poem?
Obsessed by the character "yuan" we aim to phrase our thoughts.
Looking at each other, we find that much remains unsaid.
Saying goodbye, we sense the strength of our emotional ties.

Returning home we go our separate ways,
We are indeed a group of fearsome traveling souls.

(MYSW, 9/21b–22a)

headnote: "Yuan" means "number one."
line 8: On this utopia, see P.16.4.

BIOGRAPHICAL NOTE AND TRANSLATION BY ELLEN WIDMER

王端淑

P.69. Wang Duanshu (1621–ca. 1706)

Wang Duanshu was the second daughter of Wang Siren (1575–1646) of Shaoxing, who considered her a better student than any of his eight sons.[1] One of the few women to make a genuine career out of her writing, Wang Duanshu has been described as an "honorary man."[2] Her elder sister, Wang Jingshu, was also known as a poet. Wang Duanshu married Ding Shengzhao (1621–1700?) of Yuanping, just west of Beijing. Her husband's family, like her own, had ties to both the Beijing and the Shaoxing areas. Before the fall of the Ming and perhaps again thereafter, Duanshu lived in or near Beijing, but for some years just after 1644 she returned to Shaoxing with her husband and kept company with a group of Ming loyalists that included the historian and essayist Zhang Dai (1597–1684?) and the painter Zeng Yi. Later, she lived in Hangzhou, where she became acquainted with a wide circle of celebrities. She was a sociable and engaging person who did not hesitate to enter into poetical competitions with anyone who came to see her.[3] Her friendships with the novelist and playwright Li Yu (1611–80) and with two well-known female loyalist-poets, Huang Yuanjie (P.68) and Wu Shan (P.74), almost certainly date from her stay in Hangzhou.

Her best-known collection of writings, *Yinhong ji* (Red chantings), was published between 1651 and 1655, probably in Shaoxing.[4] (For Ding Shengzhao's preface to this book, see C.40.) Its thirty *juan* contained writings in an impressive variety of forms and styles—from *fu* rhapsodies to regulated-verse poems, from ballads to palindromic seven-character quatrains. Its publication was financed by her husband, Zeng Yi, Zhang Dai, and other members of their poetry group.[5] This collection made a sensation and established Wang Duanshu's reputation. Uncharacteristically for a woman's poetry collection (or so said contemporary readers), it took as its great subject loyalism rather than love. Wang Duanshu's next datable publication is her preface to Li Yu's drama *Bimu yu* (Soul mates) of 1661.[6] This short preface is interesting in its attempt to link Li's drama with those of the late-Ming playwright Xu Wei, an author with whom her father had studied and in whose house she lived long after Xu's death. A much more substantial piece of work is the collection she edited, *Mingyuan shiwei* (The longitudinal canon of poetry by women of note), published in 1667, one of the most important and durable collections of women's poetry of its time. (For the preface to this anthology, see C.13.) Many of Wang Duanshu's other writings and anthologies cannot be dated on the available evidence, though their titles survive. Wang Duanshu was also widely known and praised for her artistic talent; she was accomplished at both painting and calligraphy.[7]

P.69.1. On Reading a Poem by Huang Yuanjie [P.68] of Jiaxing

Flowered bamboo composed in shades of ink,
Elegant silk preserves your splendid composition.
The bold strokes of your moon make me think of Huang Tingjian.
Your unfurling clouds are like Wang Xizhi's brushwork.
The sound of your hands clapping reaches me amidst the loneliness of fall waters.
The empty echo is picked up far away.
Your inborn nature is highly unusual.
(8) Your subtle fragrance stands out on the page.

(Wang Duanshu, *Yinhong ji*, 8/12b)

lines 3–4: Huang Tingjian (1045–1105) excelled as poet and calligrapher. On Wang Xizhi, see P.10.10.

P.69.2. Reading Yinhong ji

Ink spilled in grief is blurred by tears.
A lady chants, her resentment running deep.
Who understands the poet Ji Kang
Whose work is filled with pain?

(Zou Siyi, *Shiyuan bamingjia xuan*, 1/ 27a)

line 3: The Jin dynasty poet Ji Kang, one of the Seven Worthies of the Bamboo Grove, was put to death for political reasons. On the Seven Worthies, see P.10.1.

P.69.3. *Pawning My Mirror*

When you laugh, I laugh with you.
If I am sad, then you too are sad.
Not that I want to bid farewell to your clear reflection:
I'm only afraid you will reflect my grief-stricken face.

(Zou Siyi, *Shiyuan bamingjia xuan*, 1/28a)

P.69.4. *Following Wu Yanzi's [Wu Shan, P.74] Rhymes*

You draw distant mountains like slender eyebrows and paint a green lake.
Yuan Haowen's poems enter your landscape, which recalls Su Dongpo.
Recently I heard you composed poems after the *Songs of Chu*.
I wonder whether you also wrote to the "Sunny Spring" tune?
Whether or not you wear ornate jewelry, one senses your elegance.
As long as I have your poems and other writings, I will never be lonely.
How could such an immortal have descended to earth?
(8) Like Sima Xiangru, you express your poetic feeling by means of the wine jar.

(*Yinhong ji*, 9/2a–b)

line 2: Yuan Haowen (1190–1257) was the most significant poet of the Jürchen dynasty. After the dynasty succumbed to the Mongol invaders in 1233, he refused to serve the new regime and spent the rest of his life collecting historical and literary records of the Jürchen. The allusion here is probably to the series of poems Yuan wrote while crossing the Yellow River after the fall of the Jürchen. Yuan's rejection of the Mongols would, of course, suggest the sentiments of Ming loyalists. On Su Dongpo (Su Shi), see P.25.1. Wang's reference casts Su as a specifically masculine poet: a friend of Su's commented that while Liu Yong's songs should be sung by young women accompanied by red ivory clappers, Su Shi's songs should be sung by strong men accompanied by iron clappers.

line 4: On the refined "Sunny Spring" tune, see P.4.2.

line 8: On Sima Xiangru, see P.8a.1.

P.69.5. Qian [Qianyi], on behalf of Madame Liu [Shi, P.67], summons me to produce a poem on a painting for his eldest aunt Madame Qian, the wife of the provincial governor Tong Huibai, on the occasion of her birthday.

I am embarrassed by my red writing-brush, a pipe played out of turn.
It describes tranquil streams and mountains, which I set in the painting.
Ban Gu's powerful writing inspired his younger sister,
In Xie's courtyard sisters-in-law lustily chanted poems.
The freshly opened mansion stands near West Lake.
A southern beauty stands peerless in this world.
Green birds flying among the clouds summon us to produce poems and paintings
(8) And enable the Queen Mother of the West to create a cloud thoroughfare.

(MYSW, 42/2b)

line 1: On the "red writing-brush" as a symbol of female authorship, see C.36.1.

lines 3–4: Ban Gu (32–92), assigned to compile the *History of the Han*, died prematurely, and parts of the work were completed by his sister, Ban Zhao (d. 116; see P.60.9). Xie An's courtyard is especially associated with the woman writer Xie Daoyun of the Jin dynasty, on whom see C.24.

lines 7–8: Green birds are the escorts of the goddess known as the Queen Mother of the West. In the ancient mythical geography *Shan hai jing* (Classic of mountains and seas; see C.45.1), she is described as half human and half animal. Later writers represented her as a beautiful woman living in a palace with elegant grounds. The Queen Mother, often depicted in popular literature as receiving homage from many visitors on her birthday, is invoked here as a symbol of Madame Qian's longevity.

BIOGRAPHICAL NOTE AND TRANSLATION BY ELLEN WIDMER

紀映淮

P.70. Ji Yinghuai (fl. ca. 1642)

Ji Yinghuai (courtesy name Maolu, nickname A'nan) is a poet in whose work bright settings both veil and enhance feelings of grief. Writing in the then-popular Yunjian *ci* style, Ji preferred expressive, flowing language to imagistic and composed to *xiaoling* forms of the late Tang and Northern Song dynasties. Ji's collection *Zhenleng tang ci* (Song lyrics from the Hall of True Cold) does not survive.[1]

The younger sister of the minor poet Ji Yingzhong (fl. 1644), Ji Yinghuai was born in Nanjing.[2] She was known as "Buddy" (A'nan)—a nickname recalling the courtesan fashion of dressing in scholar's clothes. Her poems often refer to famous courtesans, the entertainment quarter, and festivals. Widowed in the Manchu invasion, she succeeded in supporting her son and mother-in-law on her own.[3]

For the poet and critic Wang Shizhen (1634–1711) composing his famous series of poems on Nanjing in the early 1660s, Ji was an emblem of the city's vanished artistic life. In a poem on the Qinhuai River, he wrote, "The river whispers in vain to the perching crows, / 'Buddy' Ji, who wrote the poem, is nowhere to be seen," alluding to Ji's famous line, "Autumn light reflects off crows perching and water flowing" (see P.70.6).[4]

P.70.1. Taoyuan yi guren: *Late Spring*

Out front, flowers dance with the east wind.
Only the willow catkins are worth envying,
Stickily filtering through screen and door,
Careless if this sad one stares.

A cuckoo cries so bitterly on the branchtip
  that the setting sun wants to disappear.
Outside the gate, countless petals
Lie strewn across the Hengtang road.

(GXCC, 1/12b–13a)

P.70.2. Nan gezi: *Autumn Thoughts*

Asters enliven fall colors,
Hibiscus gleams golden in the evening light;
Weary and without strength, I lean on thin red silk
And hate to death
  the single speck of a
    wild goose crying at the horizon.

(GXCC, 1/12b)

P.70.3. Zui taoyuan: *Early Spring*

The flimsy bed screen can't be rolled up:
  early spring is cold.
A plum tree with remnants of blossoms
  leans against a stone railing.
The azure sky is boundless, the roads remote,
And only a single cloud comes and goes as it wills.

White silk streaks her temples; her mind is worn out,
Tears keep streaming down.
In the courtyard, the moon would be full and embracing—
(8) The sad one had better not look.

(GXCC, 1/13a)

line 7: A full moon symbolizes the reunion of parted loved ones.

P.70.4. Zhegu tian: *Moved*

Red and fragrant blossoms have dropped off
  and the branches have all gone green.
The season's glories sail by, hard to pursue.
As Spring returns,
  the ancient cuckoo utters cries of blood.
In a small room shades hang down
  and swallow chicks peer in.

With ever-flowing feeling,
  a never-changing mind,
Silent and preoccupied with longing:
The color of grasses stretching to the horizon, hazy-bright.
(8) Why is the east wind so eager to blow?

(GXCC, 1/13a)

P.70.5. Xiao chong shan: *Duanwu Festival*

Alone, sitting idly by the window,
  body weak after illness,
I was surprised to hear the painted drums roll
  at the river ford

And realized it was festival time,
The season for wearing waist amulets
Tied with colored silk, offered to the young.

Every year brings something new,
But its passing harries the hair at my temples
  and quietly hurts my soul.
(8) Feeling time go by, thinking of the past,
  I soak a kerchief with tears:
The Xiang River is vast, indistinct—
Where shall I make grave-offerings for Lingjun?

(GXCC, 1/13b)

On the Duanwu, or Double Fifth, festival and its association with Qu Yuan, see P.54a.16. Lingjun was the courtesy name of Qu Yuan, whose famous poem of lamentation, the "Li Sao" (see P.37), Ji echoes here.

P.70.6. Bamboo Branch Song of the Qinhuai River

Autumn light reflects off
  crows perching and water flowing,
I love these rows of desolate trees.
Don't entangle travelers in long farewells,
But write them into Miss Xie's "snow flying in spring."

(Hongmeige zhuren and Qinghuilou zhuren, eds.,
Qingdai guixiu shichao, 7/3a)

"Bamboo Branch" is a tune (based on a seven-character *jueju* quatrain) first popularized by the Tang poet Liu Yuxi. Poems to this tune were predominantly sorrowful songs of parting, so Ji's last verse goes against expectation. The Qinhuai River flows through the old entertainment quarter of Nanjing.

line 4: "Snow flying in spring" inverts the famous simile of Xie Daoyun, according to which (wintry) snow is like (springtime) willow catkins. On Xie Daoyun and her simile, see C.24.

BIOGRAPHICAL NOTE AND TRANSLATION BY CAROL R. KAUFMANN

P.71. Li Yin (1616–85)

Li Yin came from somewhere in the vicinity of Hangzhou.[1] Her biography by the noted historian of philosophy Huang Zongxi names her and two other courtesans, Wang Wei (P.62) and Liu Shi (P.67), as the three most famous women of their day.[2] She became the concubine of Ge Zhengqi, a Ming loyalist and collector of women's poetry, who committed suicide in 1645 after the fall of the Ming. Surviving her husband by forty years, she lived on at his house in Haichang, where she supported herself with her writing, painting, and calligraphy. Her works were much sought after by tourists to that area. Despite her status as a concubine, her social circle included members of the gentry, and she sustained relationships with talented gentry women.[3] Her collected poetry is preserved under the title *Zhuxiao xuan yin cao* (Draft chantings of Laughing Bamboo Studio). Several of her paintings also survive.[4]

P.71.1. A Fall Day in Chang'an

Amidst tall trees the sounds of fall are late entering my dreams.
When night comes, the wind and rain cool the bamboo mats.
It was at such a time that Zhang Han excused himself from his duties
 and went home.
Even without watershield broth or roast perch to provoke them, my
 thoughts still turn toward home.

(Su Zhecong, 355)

lines 3–4: When the autumn winds began to blow, Zhang Han of the Jin dynasty left office and went home on the pretext of missing these local delicacies (Liu Yiqing, *Shishuo xinyu* 7/10; Mather, *Shih-shuo Hsin-yü*, p. 201).

P.71.2. On a Fall Evening, Writing What's on My Mind

Time presses on, and now it's the season of yellow leaves;
Geese align themselves in the sky.
Grief at being alone adds to my white hair.
Having been so often sick, I'm fearful of fall sounds.
Constantly ashamed at my diminished capacities,

I'm always embarrassed when my work is criticized for its derivativeness.
There's a lot to fear in human interactions.
(8) I scratch my head and sigh over what's left of my life.

(Zheng Guangyi, 1412)

P.71.3. Two Poems for Lady Collator Liu Rushi [P.67]

I

I won't pull off a long branch to mark our separation.
But the sound of breaking willows makes me think of you.
The fall wind raises the fear of becoming haggard.
Better to preserve the willows' youthfulness, and let them stretch long as before.

II

I shut my door against the heat and turn to writing.
When I finish my latest "ten partings" poems, I send them out by letter.
My floating boat passes through the mist and clouds of the Sanmao River
Looking for the watershield to remind me of home in my loneliness.

(Li Yin, *Zhuxiao xuan yin cao* 1/11a)

The term "Lady Collator" signifies a courtesan.

i, line 2: The breaking of willows symbolizes parting; see P.5.1. Li is punning on the word for willow, *liu*, which is also Liu Shi's surname.

ii, line 3: The Sanmao River is in Songjiang.

P.71.4. At Evening, Mooring a Boat on the Autumn River and Rhyming with Madame Li of Yuzhang

Rocks protrude: the wind rises and we moor at a sandbar.
The sun falls: along the cold river gulls and egrets roam.
The autumn waters reflect the sky, lit up by moonlight as far as the eye can see.
Dark mists lock in the many-layered mountains.
The song of a lonely woodcutter spreads through the wilderness.

The broken chimes of a Buddhist temple die away; the door is closed.
A forlorn traveler, I dream by the window of my thatched boat;
(8) Thumbing through Du Fu's poems, I annotate them with my own
hand.

(SGCJ, 12/27b)

Madame Li was related to the Ming imperial family.

line 2: Gulls and egrets are symbolic of hermits.

line 8: The great Tang poet Du Fu (712–77) is here remembered for his wanderings in exile during a time of civil war.

BIOGRAPHICAL NOTE AND TRANSLATION BY ELLEN WIDMER

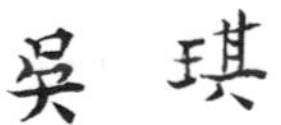

P.72. Wu Qi (mid–17th century)

The daughter of a famous Suzhou family, Wu Qi showed her literary talent at a young age. Her parents, impressed, hired a tutor for her. She was also gifted at painting, and her poems and paintings were much in request by women of the day. Her marriage to Guan Xun was happy, the couple sharing many interests. It appears to have been through Guan that she made the acquaintance of Zou Siyi, who published a number of her poems in his *Shiyuan bamingjia xuan* (Collected poems of eight famous women) and who asked her to write the preface to his *Hongjiao ji* (Red plantain collection).[1] After her husband died, Wu Qi had difficulty supporting herself and a small daughter. She was able to find happiness in friendship with other talented women, however, and she enjoyed writing and painting with them. With her best friend, Zhou Qiong, she traveled around Hangzhou and other scenic sites, and their conversation often turned to history and to women warriors.[2] Later she was much influenced by Buddhism and eventually withdrew to a nunnery, where she took a Buddhist name.

P.72.1. At Morning Sitting in the Study and Writing with My Younger Sister

Paintings and history texts are our friends in the women's quarters.
Our modest skill at poetry composition takes us beyond worldly
affairs.

Trimming the lamp wick, we sigh to see midnight approach.
Holding our books as we sleep, we can't wait for morning to come.
The moon at dawn shuts off our pleasant dreams.
With the morning bell comes the sound of chirping birds.
Our beautiful eyebrows outshine the color of the mirror,
(8) Our sleek hair puts other scholars to shame.

(SGCJ, 12/2b)

P.72.2. Sending Someone Off

A hint of snow fills the fragrant islet.
The departing boat is drawn in by mountains that block its view.
Frost flowers blow into the traveler's dream.
A nomad flute by moonlight recalls the grief of those at the frontier.
You follow military skirmishes for thousands of miles,
Relying on your sword as your only traveling companion.
I remain behind, at home, in the setting sun,
(8) Resisting the urge to climb the highest tower.

(SGCJ, 12/2b)

P.72.3. Following the Rhymes of the Woman Wu Fanghua Who Wrote a Poem on a Wall

Wu Fanghua was the wife of scholar Kang of West Lake. Three months after their marriage, soldiers attacked Qiantang. She followed her husband in taking the road to Tianzhu Temple to escape the trouble but met invading troops on the way who captured her and took her north. The poem that she wrote on a wall as she fled contained these lines: "I only hope to see the moon of Jiangnan as I die, / I do not want to be taken alive to the north of the frontier"—mournful words indeed. Alas, the phoenix is incarcerated and the *luan* bird is imprisoned! I grieve for the masterless beauty, the flower destroyed, the jade smashed, the many troubles of the ill-fated. Thus I have followed her rhyme in sympathy with her sorrow.

With broken zither, divided incense marks immeasurable grief.
Clouds and mountains are boundless, the river flows eastward forever.
In the frontier city the night is still, warning signals glow from afar;

Back in the old country wind rises among the plants of fall.
This black-haired beauty feels the pain of loneliness.
Your tender feelings are stored beside white poplars in a green grave.
Who today can appreciate your jade like beauty?
(8) Wilting grass covers the moat that separates you from this world.

(SGCJ, 12/3b)

headnote: Tianzhu, meaning India, is the name of a temple near Hangzhou. On the phoenix (*feng*) and *luan*, see P.18.12 and P.52.5.

line 1: To "divide the incense," a phrase from the testament of the Wei ruler Cao Cao, means to make preparations for one's death. The originally fifty-stringed zither was "broken" by the legendary ruler Fu Xi, who found its mournful sound unbearable and so reduced it to twenty-five strings.

P.72.4. *Spring Thoughts Sent to Zhou Qiong, Whom I Miss*

In the last days of spring, the scenery has become more forlorn.
The whole mountain is newly green and falling flowers are light.
The river wind naturally bends to the sound of Huan Yi's flute.
The moon above the peaks lends an ear to Wang Qiao's pipe.
Dreams of home are not cut off by the visit of traveling geese.
Travelers' longings inevitably merge with the clouds of evening.
Losing weight year after year, I have become cold in the prime of youth.
(8) Your travel to the ends of the earth with book and sword brings me constant pain of separation.

(SGCJ, 12/5a–b)

line 3: Huan Yi was a famous flute player of the Jin dynasty.

line 4: On the immortal Wang Qiao, see P.43.1. Zhou Qiong is known to have been an excellent musician.

P.72.5. *Selling a Painting*

I pick seeds and vegetables to supply my lunch.
When I have time, I tailor lotus petals to make my fall clothes.
I have never before engaged in commerce.
When I sell a painting, I use some of the proceeds to buy incense for the Buddha.

(Zou Siyi, *Shiyuan bamingjia xuan*, 2/14a)

line 2: This tailoring, factually improbable, repeats the actions of the proud and pure Qu Yuan in his "Li Sao"; see P.37.

P.72.6. Du Liniang

Through your accurate portrait you compared yourself to a divine
 beauty.
You attached your young soul to a far-off site where plum and willow
 grew.
One dies for passion, but such passion defies death.
At Peony Pavilion your reincarnation accomplished fate.

(Zou Siyi, *Shiyuan bamingjia xuan*, 2/17b)

The drama *Mudan ting* (The peony pavilion, also known as *Huan hun ji*, or The return of the soul) by Tang Xianzu (1550–1617) tells the story of a couple, Du Liniang and Liu Mengmei, who have never met but have fallen in love through dreaming of each other and seeing each other's portraits. Worldly obstacles forbid their meeting, and Du Liniang dies of love-sickness. Liu Mengmei's devotion to Du's portrait eventually moves the gods, who bring her back to life and stage a happy ending, with Du's father accepting his new son-in-law, who has just come in first in the examinations. The play's influence on Ming-Qing romantic culture is incalculable. For an English translation, see Tang Xianzu, *Peony Pavilion*, translated by Cyril Birch.

line 2: An allusion to and pun on the name of Du's future husband, Liu (willow) Mengmei (dreams of plum).

line 3: This line paraphrases Tang Xianzu's preface to *Mudan ting*. On the preface's cult status, see Ko, *Teachers of the Inner Chambers*, pp. 78–82.

BIOGRAHICAL NOTE AND TRANSLATION BY ELLEN WIDMER

吴綃

P.73. Wu Xiao (mid–17th century)

According to some sources, Wu Xiao was Wu Qi's (P.72) "younger sister," apparently a reference not to blood ties but to common membership in a circle of women poets loosely connected to Wu Weiye.[1] Wu Xiao was from Changzhou. Her exceptional talent surfaced at an early age. She excelled at both painting and poetry, and she was also an expert musician, skilled at the *qin* and many other instruments. Her writings are likewise unusually broad in their generic range. They include *sanqu* as well as *shi* and *ci*. She was known for exceptional filial piety but also harbored dreams of becoming a Daoist immortal. Her literary acquaintances, in addition to Wu Weiye and Zou Siyi, included the poet Feng Ban of Changshu, who shared her interest in *sanqu*, and she formed literary societies with a number of other notables, such as Yu Huai.[2] Some of her works reached publication through these social contacts. Her poems were published under the title *Xiaoxue an gao* (Manuscripts from Howling-Snow Studio) in 1659; her preface to this collection is included as C.12.1.[3]

P.73.1. *Whistling Pavilion*

Already the dynasties Wei and Jin are as a dream,
This desolate pavilion is all that remains.
While dragon and snake were here locked in struggle,
The regal phoenix just took to the skies.
To avoid vulgarity, just give one long whistle;
On meeting others, never utter a word.
Only now I begin to understand the sense of true reclusion,
(8) Why go as far as Peach Blossom Spring?

(Yi Boyin, 6/175)

lines 4–5: This poem is based on the story of Ruan Ji's visit to the Six Dynasties hermit Sun Deng. According to the "Biography of Ruan Ji," Ruan spoke to the hermit of history past and present, and of the techniques of reposing the spirit and guiding the breath; Sun Deng never replied. Ruan Ji emitted one long whistle and took his leave. When he had descended to the midpoint of the mountain, he heard a sound like the cry of a phoenix, echoing in the mountain valley; it was Sun Deng's answering whistle (*Jin shu*, 49/1362).

line 8: On the "Peach Blossom Spring," see P.16.4. The first line of Wu's poem also seems to echo Tao Yuanming's telling of the story: when the wanderer explained to the denizens of Peach Blossom Spring who he was and where he came from, "they asked him the name of the present dynasty, for they had never heard of the Han, let alone the Wei or the Jin" (Lu Qinli, ed., *Tao Yuanming ji*, 165).

P.73.2. *Words on Willow Branches*

By the house willows burgeon like the painted eyebrows of a beautiful woman
When first we met below the city wall of Wuchang.
Now that spring is here tree after tree is misty green;
But I cannot tell which was the branch you gave me when we said goodbye.

At Cold Food Festival the east wind fills the city.
The delicate branch bends as the singing oriole sings.
The god of spring has no sympathy for our bitterness at parting:
(8) He just produces a new branch where the old one broke off before.

(Zheng Guangyi, 1506)

line 4: On the association of willows with parting, see P.5.1.
line 5: On the Cold Food Festival, see P.17.4.

P.73.3. Qing yu'an: *Remembrance of Old Times in Suzhou*

Suzhou used to be a bustling place
But now I feel lonely. I have no friends.
Time flies by and it's the end of spring.
Many a morning is clear and warm,
But it's often windy and rainy.
How easily spring comes and goes.
My curtains block the full view of the road to my house.
(8) It hurts to think that the swallows have flown away from the engraved roof beams.
When feelings are strong I have only myself to talk to.
I remember poetry and wine amidst the flowers,
Flutes and drums at the banks of the pond.
(12) A misty scene of catkins all over the sky.

(Zheng Guangyi, 1508)

P.73.4. The Eve of the Double Seventh

Sparkling bright the light of stars, the Milky Way flows far and wide,
Sadly gazing at one pair of stars, I lean against the tower, alone.
Do not say parting's pain is sharpest among men—
We sense that same sorrow is felt in the sky.
Liang Qing was banished far, and who stayed by his side?
But when Jin returned, who would not share his journey!
Surely it's Chang E whose jealousy is most bitter—
(8) A wheel of wind and dew, unable to bear autumn.

(Zhou Daorong, Xu Zhixu, and Huang Qizhen, eds.,
Zhongguo lidai nüzi shici xuan, 166–67)

On the Double Seventh festival, see P.5.1 and P.19.2.

line 6: Jin is the formal name of Wang Qiao, on whom see P.43.1.
line 7: On Chang E, see P.21.1.

P.73.5. *Singing of Ancient Times*

Sublime was a certain prince of old, far beyond compare,
As he planned a heroic act to undo the mad emperor of Qin.
No one knows what happened then to our wanderer brave—
He aimed at the wrong lookout and murdered the beautiful maids.

(*Zhongguo lidai nüzi shici xuan*, 167)

Of the three attempts made on the First Emperor's life, as recorded in the *Shi ji*, only one resembles the account given here. Zhang Liang, a member of the ruling clan of Han, seeking revenge against the Qin emperor for the destruction of his kingdom, struck the imperial cortège at Bolangsha while the First Emperor was touring the eastern part of his kingdom (218 B.C.E). Zhang Liang and his followers accidentally hit the wrong carriage. Sima Qian does not say who was in that carriage, although it is reasonable to assume, along with Wu Xiao, that it may have contained women from his entourage. The carriages of the imperial cortège would often be furnished with lookout posts. Zhang Liang subsequently changed his identity and escaped punishment, living on to play a major role in the founding of the Han dynasty (*Shi ji*, 55/2033–34).

P.73.6. *At Yong, Unable to Sleep, I Was Surprised by Rain*

Black clouds blow up on all sides in the strong wind.
Tens of thousands of warring soldiers gallop toward the green sky.
Cracking gorges, collapsing mountains, wolves and tigers grapple;
Stirring up whirlpools, thrashing against the waves, dragons attack
each other.
My spirit is startled, I lie in bed without sleeping.
Dying embers twinkle, on the verge of extinction.
Outside my curtain the noise of waves is ceaseless;
(8) Exhausting my brain with thoughts of poetry, I sit and wait for night
to end.

(SGCJ, 12/46b)

P.73.7. Huang ying'er: *A* Sanqu *in Ten Songs*

I. PAINTING APPLE FLOWERS

No other flower is more delicate.
Soft as silk,
Decorating the green branches,
Only the crab apple can stand comparison.
Her tender red luster threatens to dissolve.
The light rouge surges like a red tide.
The fragrance emerging from her jade dimples contains a smile.
(8) Her immeasurable charm
Is the hardest to draw.
I pause for a moment, not knowing where to begin.

II. CHERRY BLOSSOMS

Its small buds open in spring.
The Qin valley is to blame
For not including it in its gardens.
Men beat a path to its luxuriant flowers, though it does nothing to advertise itself.
Its cheeks are powdered faintly red,
The vivid makeup is accompanied by smiles.
When its flowers disperse, they're like Fan Su's red lips.
(8) Its roots seem useless, but precious birds adore them,
Carrying cherries in their mouths without reserve.

III. LADY YU POPPIES

As their delicate figures play in the light wind,
I recall the sound of singing around the Chu tents.
Easy and graceful, eager to dance, the light body moved.
The hero's options had run out,
The beauty wept tears of blood;
Lotus flowers coughed blood bitterly, looking as though heavily made-up.
Bidding Xiang Yu farewell,
(8) This beautiful soul of all time:
How could she bear to cross the river?

IV. PLUM FLOWERS

All year I have longed to see you.
Coming to my window
At the end of the year
I ask you why you seem so frail?
I'm afraid the god of spring may not recognize you.
I see your southern branches breaking out late
Far, far, goes the courier, but to whom can I send a sprig?
(8) Night brings in pleasant air—
No wind but a moon.
I toast your icy beauty with wine.

V. FLOWERS OF LUOYANG

At how many points do you guard the palace grounds?
Your luxuriant red erupts,
Slanting like trimmed colored silk.
A grove of soft green on your slender twigs hangs low,
Lightly dotted by the colors of the sunset
Your fine buds flourish
Your rouge trembles as it washes over Xu Xi's bird and flower painting.
(8) Please do not drop
The name Luoyang flower.
No need for you to vie with the peony.

VI. APRICOT FLOWERS

In the second month on a really fragrant morning
One hears the sound of flower sellers.
Spring fills the streets.
Red lustrous blossoms each like vermilion prints.
The cherry apple is your reincarnation.
The golden peach is your neighbor.
A beauty's makeup, slightly damp,
(8) One whole branch is new.
At the imperial banquet,
Who will be dubbed the flower-seeking envoy?

VII. QUIET BAMBOO LEAVES

A soft green in front of the long staircase
Like a grove of new bamboo.
Leaf after leaf in mist,
Blackened eyebrows delicately fold into natural luxuriance.
Copper flowers lack your freshness,
Stone flowers lack your charm.
Green spirals on little branch tips start to quiver
Their emerald color forming a green filigree.
At the Jade Terrace when the palace lady finishes making up,
Your green leaves could well substitute for her fine eyebrows.

VIII. IRIS

The sun is warm and the flowers in the grass are fragrant.
Clumps of them open.
Their powdered wings flap against the white light
And vividly come to life like paired butterflies.
They seem to follow the wind in search of scent.
Afraid of taking off and flying over the wall,
They lower their feelers and unroll their wings on green branches
Beside the stone fence.
How many times have I wanted to paint them!
Dipping my brush I celebrate the Prince of Teng.

IX. OLEANDER

Their sparse shadows slant under green clouds.
If one enhances their charm
With a bright red color,
Their cinnabar flowers and soft nodes would be priceless in the spring.
Qin Dynasty people painted them,
And Wang Huizhi loved them.
Slender blossoms under the railing,
They never fail to be themselves.
Your fragrant skin is like delicate bamboo
Finely specked with the colors of the morning.

X. THE "LONG-LIFE" PLUM

Every leaf in its place:
I love to see this perfume-filled tree sway in the light.
Its calyxes rejoice in their ease,
With solicitude preserving their younger brothers:
Sprung from the same root, they admit of no division.
In you take root metaphors and descriptions
Of every kind.
(8) But on careful consideration
I hate to see those who are bound like the branches of the Tian
brothers' bush
Stand apart like the parallel lines of migrating geese.

(Ling Jingyan and Xie Boyang, eds., *Quan Qing sanqu*, 295–98)

ii, line 4: An analogy to virtuous people who silently attract others is implied here.

ii, line 7: Fan Su was the Tang poet Bo Juyi's concubine.

iii: On "Lady Yu" poppies, see P.68.6 and P.28.1.

iii, line 2: On Liu Bang surrounding Xiang Yu's army and having his soldiers sing songs from Xiang's native region of Chu, see P.28.1.

v: The term "Flower of Luoyang" refers both to the peony and to baby's breath. This poem is about the latter.

vi, line 10: "Flower-Seeking Envoy" (*tan hua shi, tan hua lang*) was, in Qing times, the title of the third-ranking graduate in the palace examination. At the banquet held to celebrate the first-ever *jinshi* examination, under the Tang, the name was attributed to the two youngest graduates.

viii, line 4: An allusion to a Warring States period figure who died for love and upon whose grave butterflies and mandarin ducks assembled in pairs.

viii, line 10: A Tang-era prince famous for painting bees and butterflies.

ix, line 6: Wang Huizhi's fondness for bamboo is better documented than that for oleander; see P.23.5.

x, lines 3–5: The Tang emperor Xuanzong had a Tower of Calyxes and Petals built for his enfeoffed brothers. By allusion to poem 164 of the *Book of Odes*, the calyx that supports the petal is an image for the older brother's quasi-fatherly care for the younger brother.

x, lines 9–10: An allusion to the story of the three brothers and the flowering thornbush; see P.18.9.

BIOGRAPHICAL NOTE AND TRANSLATION OF P.73.2–3, P.73.6–7 BY ELLEN WIDMER; TRANSLATION OF P.73.1, P.73.4–5 BY PAULA VARSANO

吴山

P.74. Wu Shan (fl. mid–17th century)

Although little of her work has survived to the present, Wu Shan was praised by her contemporaries as the most talented woman poet of her generation.[1] A widow who struggled to support herself and her daughters with her painting and poetry, she maintained close ties with both women artists and influential male literati of the Jiangnan area.

Wu Shan (courtesy name Yanzi) was originally from Dangtu county in eastern Anhui province. She was married to Bian Lin, an assistant to the magistrate of Taipingfu, Anhui.[2] Bian Lin died in the battles that devastated southern China during the Qing conquest, and Wu Shan began a life of exile, moving first to Hangzhou in 1647 and finally settling in Yangzhou. Many of her poems express deep sorrow at the loss of her husband and at separation from her native place. The preface to her collected works, *Qingshan ji* (Green mountains collection), states: "Sometimes when Wu Shan remembered her native place, she felt an unbearable ambivalence, for she associated her home with thoughts of death."[3]

Bian Lin had not been a wealthy scholar, and his widow had to rely on her talents to gain a livelihood. In her studio beside Hangzhou's West Lake she sold her calligraphy and paintings to support herself and her two daughters, Mengyu and Deji. The three women enjoyed painting and composing poems together, inspired by the local scenery.[4] Both Mengyu and Deji were eventually married to the same man, Liu Jindu of Yangzhou, who proved to be an extremely faithful and devoted son-in-law.[5]

Wu Shan was part of the flourishing network of women artists in seventeenth-century Jiangnan. Her circle included Huang Yuanjie (P.68) and Wang Duanshu (P.69).[6] These women exchanged letters and poems, visited one another's studios, and also met in salonlike settings in the homes of wealthy Hangzhou families.

Male literati with whom Wu Shan was on familiar terms included Wu Weiye, Gong Dingzi, and Huang Zhouxing. Another noted scholar and Ming loyalist, Wei Xi, wrote the preface to her *Qingshan ji*. Several of her poems reveal Ming loyalist sympathies, and Wu sometimes signed her poems "Nü yimin" or "The Loyal Woman Survivor."[7]

The struggles and sorrows of her condition must have weighed heavily on Wu Shan, for late in life she lost her memory, a condition that lasted for two years. As a result of this crisis, Wu gave up writing poetry, shunned feminine ornaments, and became intensely drawn to Daoism. She died in Yangzhou around the age of sixty.[8]

P.74.1. Pusa man: *A Palindromic Ode Written in Leisure*

Cranes and gulls, carefree, join our happy travels.
Happy travelers accompany carefree gulls and cranes.
Pines shed their leaves, revealing tall peaks;
On tall peaks bare pines jut here and there.
In yonder stream, misty water flows white;
White waters are parted by the misty stream.
We do not travel afar to forget our worldly cares,
But forget our worldly mind to leave true and false behind.

(GXCC, 5/4b)

Every second line of this poem repeats the previous line, but in reverse order. A translator cannot hope to reproduce this palindromic device in English, but the reader may imagine the artfulness of the original.

P.74.2. Yulou chun: *Gazing into the Distance at Evening and Remembering the Talented Woman Wang Chenrou*

By the azure edge of the evening clouds—do you know where it is?
Beyond the four mountains—perhaps you dwell in the mountains there.
One sheet of crimson clouds comes, cutting across the bamboo,
Two lines of white birds go, parting the smoke.
I stretch my eyes; my heart is tangled in ten thousand threads.
Leaning against the wall, I softly chant "Jian jia."
My longing makes me dream of the far horizon,
Though I still don't know the way on the far horizon road.

(GXCC, 5/6a)

line 6: The ode "Jian jia," poem 129 from the *Book of Odes*, describes the pursuit of an elusive lover or divinity.

P.74.3. Huatang chun: *Inscribed on a Painted Screen Depicting the Singing Girl Xue'er*

Last night she untied her pendants in a dream of river's edge.
When dawn came, green shadow cloaked the feast-hall screen;
A few orioles chattered beneath the flowers
While breezes blew through successive doors.
Her cicada-wing coiffure is glossy-fresh,
The gorgeous damask she wears still gives off sweet incense.
Singing "Jin lü" with abandon, she presents fine wine to the guests,
(8) Remembering green peaks far away.

(GXCC, 5a–b)

Xue'er was the cherished concubine of Li Mi (Sui dynasty). Whenever Li happened on a memorable phrase, he set it to music for Xue'er to sing.

line 1: A dream with sexual overtones. The legendary Zheng Jiaofu was walking alongside the Xiang River one day and spied two beautiful women. They loosened the jade pendants from their sashes to give to him as love-pledges. Only after the women and their pendants disappeared did he realize they were goddesses (Liu Xiang, *Lie xian zhuan* 1/19–21). See also P.11.16.

line 7: "Jin lü" (Golden threads) is a song associated with happy meetings.

line 8: The "green peaks" allude to Qian Qi's poem "Sheng shi Xiang ling gu se" (The spirits of the River Xiang strum the zither; QTS, 238/2651): "When their song comes to an end, no one is in sight; / Above the river, the many peaks are green." See also Ji Yougong, *Tang shi jishi* 30/484.

P.74.4. Jian zi mulanhua: *Inscribed on a Painted Screen Depicting the Plum-Blossom Consort*

Fallen leaves in the palace courtyard;
Imperial fans in the metallic wind sadly mourn their fate.
As the jade water clock slowly drips through the night,
Distant sounds of a kingfisher carriage come from the Taiye Pond.
The monarch's benevolence is vast and impulsive,
While his concubine is but a wan shadow, her incense is cold.
On the red palace stairs, in the light of the moon,
(8) Who is now singing "A Peck of Pearls"?

(GXCC, 5/5a)

On the Plum-Blossom Consort, displaced by Yang Guifei, see P.54a.1.

line 2: For the fans' dread of cool weather, see P.1.1. Metal correlates with autumn.

line 4: Taiye Pond is associated with the residence of Yang Guifei.

line 8: The Plum-Blossom Consort once refused a gift of pearls from a foreign envoy on the grounds that since Emperor Xuanzong had begun to neglect her, she no longer needed to adorn herself (QTS, 5/64). The music known as "A Peck of Pearls" was composed to commemorate her refusal.

P.74.5. Qingyu'an: *Written at West Lake on the Night of the Double Seventh, Using He Zhu's Rhymes*

The rose-colored mists break before they reach the starry sky:
Like a vast river, the Milky Way flows into the distance.
Beautiful its pure light, but how can they cross?
A year of parting sorrow,
A thousand autumns' sadness
Are all hidden in the depths of the clouds.
Their dragon carriage swiftly arrives at the Indigo Bridge: dusk.
(8) Reluctant to part, they exchange verses on the autumn moon.
They try to express the depths of their pain:
Two lines of loving tears
Fill the sky with autumn dew
(12) Like the rain of love on Mount Wu.

(GXCC, 5/6b)

On the Double Seventh, see P.5.1 and P.19.2.

line 7: The Indigo Bridge was a well-known meeting place for lovers.

line 12: On the clouds and rain of Mount Wu, see P.9.2.

BIOGRAPHICAL NOTE AND TRANSLATION BY RUTH ROGASKI

P.75. Chai Jingyi and Her Daughter-in-Law Zhu Rouze

Chai Jingyi (courtesy name Jixian) and her daughter-in-law Zhu Rouze (courtesy name Daozhu) were talented literatae possessed of markedly different styles and visions,[1] but their relationship went beyond the formal obligations born of Zhu's marriage to Chai's son, the poet Shen Yongji.

柴靜儀

P.75a. Chai Jingyi (fl. mid–17th century)

Chai Jingyi was known primarily for her poetry, publishing her own collection called *Ningxiangshi shichao* (Poems from the Congealed Incense Chamber) and contributing to a joint anthology by the Banana Garden Poetry Club,[2] but poetry was hardly her sole means of expression. She had also been trained by her father, Chai Yunqian, to play the lute and write musical notation, and she apparently enjoyed singing. An accomplished painter as well, Chai Jingyi specialized in the use of color. A telling inscription on one of her paintings has been passed down to us in the *Guochao huashi*:

> Lazing about Incense-Burner Pavilion,
> I paint in color to amuse myself.
> Then I switch and take up my eyebrow lacquer
> To outline distant mountains.[3]

In the *Qingshi biecai*, Shen Deqian declares that her poetry "stems from the purity of her nature and sentiment, and issues from the orthodoxy of her studies. At times, her verses carry [the solidity of] admonitions carved on stone; they cannot be sought among wind, clouds, moonlight, and dew."[4]

The elegant simplicity of her deportment has been captured and passed down to us in this popular story: "In those days, Hangzhou customarily celebrated the spring with great extravagance. The springtime scene of brightly painted boats and embroidered curtains would reflect off the lake, and those on the shore would vie to outdo one another in finery, using brilliant earrings, kingfisher feathers, and silk prints to set off each other's gorgeousness. Jixian floated alone on a small craft, alongside [the boat of] Feng Youling, Qian Yunyi [Fengling; P.78], Lin Yaqing [Yining; P.77], and Gu Qiji. In her simple white skirt and unadorned coiffure, she was counting her writing brushes and putting in order her writing paper. The women drifting on the neighboring boats, upon seeing her, lowered their eyes and faltered, for their beauty could not compare."[5] Chai's poem "To My Daughter-in-Law Zhu Rouze" (P.75a.1) bears eloquent testimony to the closeness and respect she felt for Zhu. Remarkably, Chai is as easily stirred to poetry by her empathetic observation of others' feelings as she is by her own. Her son's long and frequent absences probably inspired, for example, the allegorical *yuefu* "The Palace of Eternal Trust"

(P.75a.3) and the old-style poem "Sustaining My Son, Yongji" (P.75a.2)—in which she both expresses his frustrations and comforts him.

P.75a.1. *To My Daughter-in-Law Zhu Rouze*

Tranquil, the sunlight in your inner chambers,
Musky incense hangs in drapes of gauze.
You rise from your sickbed, too tired to wash,
Mild and gentle as a Milky Way autumn.
Since you've entered my family gate,
Hard have you labored, and without rest.
Supple and pure are the freshwater grasses,
Your windows and doors remain tightly sealed.
Your husband's resolve leads to the world's four corners,
But wealth is not what he seeks.
Alas, the times befit him not;
For now, he wanders about the wood.
He faces you and fingers his lute,
Its serene tune flows along with the wind.
The hidden dragon takes care not to act,
The hen that crows only invites shame.
I send these words to you, in your chambers,
So, gentle and kind, you will not grieve.

(Yi Boyin, 6/168)

line 7: An allusion to poem 15 of the *Book of Odes*, "Cai pin" ("Picking the duckweed"). According to Zheng Xuan's commentary, these aquatic grasses were used in marital rituals to demonstrate that the bride was obedient and had been well instructed in the behavior and obligations of marriage (*Maoshi zhengyi*, in SSJZS, 1.4/3a).

line 8: This refers to poem 155 of the *Book of Odes*, the second verse of which reads, "At the time when heaven was not yet clouded and raining, / I took those mulberry roots, / I twined them and sealed window and door" (Karlgren, *The Book of Odes*, p. 100, translation modified). According to Zheng Xuan's commentary, one seals one's doors and windows in order to avoid impending disaster (*Maoshi zhengyi*, in SSJZS, 8.2/1b). The poet here is praising her daughter-in-law's ability to "plan for a rainy day."

line 15: A reference to the commentary of the *qian* hexagram in the *Book of Changes*, "The dragon is hidden. Do not act." The appended commentary says, "A sage is placed in a lowly rank and there remains hidden" (*Zhouyi zhengyi*, in SSJZS, 1/6a). Here, as in the next line, Chai is exhorting Zhu not to be too aggressive.

line 16: On the "hen that crows the morning," see P.1.2.

P.75a.2. Sustaining My Son, Yongji

Have you not seen—
  Night after night in ducal halls, sumptuous banquets are laid,
But before half-emptied goblets and cold meat dishes, who cares about talent?
After three trips to Chang'an, you have not attained your goal,
Wild-haired, grimy-cheeked, you have come back home.
Alas! This world's humors change a thousand times a day,
To ride in a carriage and dine on meat does man covet and strive.
(8) So, read your books, play your lute, and therein find your pleasure,
Since times of old, thinkers wise endured in poverty.

(Yi Boyin, 6/168)

P.75a.3. The Palace of Eternal Trust

In the jade pavilion, her toilet is finished
  —but no one sees.
Her breast aches: alone, in vain, grieving over a moon-round fan.
Autumn grasses favor the grounds of Changxin Palace,
While spring breezes keep to Zhaoyang Hall.
Within, the prince is half besotted with wine,
Coquettish singers, elegant dancers, contend in a silky whirl.
Three thousand brocade bed curtains float with fragrant musk,
(8) Twelve sinuous robes scatter in colored clouds.

Out among the crowds is another figure of jade,
Her freshly finished powder bright, inviting as the candle's glow.
The winter crow must not caw while bringing out the moon,
(12) For fear he'll wake springtime's swallow, asleep, her beak bearing flowers.
Who pities when, on endless nights, dreams still don't reach their fullness?
Suddenly an oriole passes, he seems to have some feeling.

That disk of moon high above, suspended from the River of Stars—
For one thousand autumns shall mirror the fire of my heart.

(Yi Boyin, 6/169)

On the Palace of Eternal Trust (*Changxin gong*) and its associations with Ban *jieyu*, see P.1.

line 4: Zhaoyang Hall was the opulent court residence of Zhao Feiyan, who displaced Ban *jieyu*.

line 12: The swallow here stands for Zhao Feiyan (Flying Swallow Zhao). This couplet recalls an earlier poem, also called "Changxin Palace," by Wang Changling (698–757): "She [Ban *jieyu*] sweeps at dawn, the Autumn Palace opens, / With her moon-round fan, she wanders awhile, to and fro, / Her jadelike face no match for the winter crow, / As it carries forth the sunrays from Zhaoyang Hall" (*Wenyuan yinghua* 204/1010a).

P.75a.4. *On the Day of the Autumnal Equinox, Missing My Son, Yongji*

A day of festivities—I miss my son,
And chant a poem before the evening sky.
Tomorrow shall the summer swallow take his leave;
At that moment autumn begins.
In traveler's hostels he strokes his sword in vain,
For his living, merely selling compositions.
Better yet to hoist a homeward sail:
Don't wait for snowfall, whirling white.

(Yi Boyin, 6/169)

P.75a.5. *Sending Off Gu Qiji to the North*

A leaf of peach-blossom water
Escorts, in limpid silence, the traveler's boat.
Spring brings out its ten thousand willows—
Blade upon blade of parting's sorrow.
Look at me: nowhere to turn,
Till, finding you, I could share my hopes and dreams.
Before the misty flowers, now and then we moistened our brushes . . .
Under wind and moon—how often did we climb the tower!
Now I sit, only the smoldering incense as companion,
Who could bear to urge your oars on their voyage?

Look back from Yantai pavilion—
(12) Clouds whiten old Hangzhou.

(Yi Boyin, 6/169)

A friend and fellow woman poet, included by some accounts in the Banana Garden Poetry Club, Gu Si, whose style name was Qiji, was also from Hangzhou. She is the author of two collections of poetry, *Jingyutang ji* and *Cuiyuan ji* (Hu Wenkai, p. 802).

line 1: This image alludes to Li Bo's poem, "To Wang Lun," in which the poet takes leave of his host at Peach Blossom Pond (in modern-day Jing prefecture, Anhui province): "The waters of Peach Blossom Pond are one thousand feet deep, / But not so deep as the parting pain of Wang Lun" (in *Li Bo quanji*, 2: 645).

lines 3–4: On the association of willows with parting, see P.5.1.

line 7: Alternate reading of the beginning of this line: "[Beneath] the misty rainbow . . ." (see Zheng Guangyi, p. 1572).

line 11: On the Yantai Pavilion or Yellow Gold Terrace, see P.66.25.

P.75a.6. Thinking of Liang Hongyu at Huangtiandang

Jade-white face and cloud coiffure brushed with the dust of war,
The little "Lotus Batallion" clustered at river's edge.
Carrying—not well-bucket and rice mortar—but the drums of battle,
Who would believe the hero was a fair maid?

(Zheng Guangyi, 1574)

This poem is a tribute to the heroine Liang Hongyu of the Southern Song dynasty, whose exploits in the battles against the Jürchen gained her everlasting fame. She had learned the arts of war as a young girl beside her father, an officer along the frontier, and later fought alongside her husband, General Han Shizhong. In 1129, when the Jürchen were attacking Hangzhou, General Han led the defense at Huangtiandang. Liang Hongyu "took up the mallets and beat the wardrums herself. In the end the Jürchens were unable to cross the river" and so failed to occupy the Chinese heartland (*Song shi*, "Han Shizhong zhuan," p. 11361; see also Zheng Guangyi, pp. 1574–75; Zhuo Chengyuan, ed., *Zhongguo funü renming cidian*, p. 524).

朱柔則

P.75b. Zhu Rouze (late 17th century)

In contrast to her mother-in-law, there is relatively little information on the poet—and painter—Zhu Rouze. One story is consistently repeated, however, not only in accounts of her life, but in entries on her husband as well. It is told that once, while Shen Yongji was sojourning at the home of his patron—Yue Duan, the "Master of Red Orchid Studio"—Zhu sent him a painting called, simply, "Mountain-and-Water Landscape of Our Native Village." To the painting, Yue had added this inscription:

Beneath the willow, a thatched door, beside the river's bend,
The young peach trees blossom again, each and every one.
They should lament that the husband has not sent a reply,
But this painting brings him the mountains from home, far away.[6]

Legend has it that Shen Yongji immediately bid his host farewell and returned home to join Zhu.

P.75b.1. Tunes to Send Far Away

I

I hate the sparseness of the weeping willows
As I mount up the jade saddle with infinite care.
The evening sun warm on the crows' feathered backs,
And spring snow chill under the horses' hooves.
Clumsy our graces as we enter society,
On whom can we rely, whether we leave or stay?
My simple child turns to me and sobs—
Last night he dreamt of Chang'an.

II

Whipping wild, the wind starts hitting hard,
The rain drips deeper, not yet at an end.
My pity for our child with blanket bare
Recalls the unlined jacket of my man on the road.
The nesting swallow raises her chicks in suffering,
The goose on the wing, without mate, feels the cold.
Whether you stay at home or tread the byways—
The hardship you bear is one.

III

I've heard that, on the road to Yantai,
Life is to be pitied.
Too shameful to strum the protégé's sword,
Unthinkable to beg for an instructor's stipend.
Endless wandering is no long-term plan,
Should you come back to farm, there's still our meager land.
By a lonely coffin, grieve for your gentle mother;
(8) Then hurry—find the spot where the ox has slept.

(Yi Boyin, 6/175)

i, line 8: By referring to Chang'an, the capital of China during the Han and the Tang dynasties, the poet intends the capital of her own epoch, Beijing, where her husband is staying. This line echoes a well-known verse written by Du Fu: "From far away, I miss my young children, / Who do not yet understand that they should miss Chang'an" ("Yue ye" [Moonlit night], QTS 224/2403).

iii, line 1: See P.75a.5. Here, the "road to Yantai" refers to the arduous path of the aspiring scholar.

iii, line 3: This is an allusion to the story of Feng Xuan, a poor man of Qi who lived during the Warring States period (see Sima Qian, *Shi ji*, p. 75). Too poor to support himself, he became a protégé of the aristocrat Mengchang Jun, known for his extraordinary hospitality. Unsatisfied with his treatment, Feng continuously sang songs, strumming upon his sword handle, demanding more and better food, a cart and, eventually, a house. Feng Xuan has come to represent the perpetually dependent and demanding man.

iii, line 4: The full expression is "Guangwen money." *Guangwen* refers to an institution founded in the Tianbao reign (742–56) of the Tang dynasty to prepare students for the civil service examinations. By the time of the Ming and Qing dynasties, the word referred to teachers of the Classics.

iii, line 8: In the Jin dynasty, Tao Kan was mourning his father who had just died. As the time for burial approached, the family suddenly lost one of their cattle. While searching for it, Tao encountered an old man who said that he had just seen an ox sleeping by a water hole on the mountain, and that if they buried someone on that spot, a member of the family would attain high honors (*Jin shu* 58/1586).

P.75b.2. Seeing My Husband Off to Daliang

Unsuccessful in the past, you regret traveling to the north,
Now you leave for the central plains; I pity myself in vain.
Endlessly drifting, you suffer like Su Ji,

But my conduct is put to shame by the virtue of Meng Guang.
Measure the distance between us, already three thousand miles,
Remembering our farewell, how can we bear four or five years?
The grass bends toward the parting pavilion, I sing "Breaking the Willows,"
—Though it quicken the wanderer's tears falling on the banquet mat.

(Yi Boyin, 6/175)

line 3: Su Ji was a governor general of Liaodong during the Han dynasty who wrote one *fu*, apparently no longer extant (*Han shu* 30/1749). The exact sense of this allusion remains unclear.

line 4: Meng Guang was a woman of the Eastern Han, known for her respectful treatment of her husband, Liang Hong, even when he was reduced to menial labor. Theirs is considered a model marriage (*Hou Han shu* 83/2765–68).

line 7: On the custom of "breaking willow branches," see P.5.1.

P.75b.3. *After Making a Rendezvous with Gu Chunshan to View the Plum Blossoms on the River Isle*

We promised to meet on the river isle to frolic amid flowers of spring,
With one stroke of my oar, I greet the wind—the distance is not long.
Outside the pavilion plum trees stand, three hundred strong.
If the fair one does not come, their blossoms shall rest unopened.

(Yi Boyin, 6/175)

Gu Chunshan was the poet's husband's concubine. The compilers of the *Qingdai guige shiren zheng lüe* cite this poem as evidence of Zhu's remarkable lack of jealousy and claim that by writing it, Zhu caused Chunshan's reputation to improve "tenfold."

P.75b.4. *A Song on Watching the Tide at Qiantang*

Outside the "Tide-Waiting Gate," people are like ants,
When, after noon, a wild wind buffets the earth and rises.
The flowing waters of the Thrice-Twisted River come rolling, swelling,
A startled wave crashes into Heaven's Gate.
Heaven's Gate grows pale, clouds and wind transform,
Distant cliffsides, layer upon layer, disappear from sight.
At first you think it is merely some clouds emerging from the sea—
Then you start at seeing a bolt of silk cut across the river.

The silver sea surges and pours into whiteness of snowcapped
    mountains,
And roars like thunder drumming in the vault of bright blue sky.
A great high-masted barge is unceasingly tossed,
Armed with powerful crossbows and mighty bows—who would dare
    to shoot?
Amid the smoky azure of dusk, we descend the tower,
While residual ripples still flow without end.
To where have the white horse and chariot returned?—
A bend of blue river, ten thousand miles of autumn.

(Zheng Guangyi, 1615)

The opening from Hangzhou Bay into the Qiantang River is horn-shaped, and the pressure of the relatively sudden constriction of water into the smaller space of the river makes high tide a spectacular sight. Every year, on the eighteenth day of the eighth lunar month, the famed Qiantang (or Zhejiang) tide is at its highest and most dramatic, and the crowd of spectators at its most dense. This phenomenon has been the subject of many poems and essays, the earliest of which may be by the Eastern Jin poet Gu Kaizhi (346–407).

line 1. "Tide-Waiting Gate" is located near the Star Bridge, southeast of Hangzhou. Its name seems to mean both "Waiting-for-the-Tide Gate" (as an advantageous point from which to observe the tide) and "The Gate Where the Tide Waits." Legend has it that Qian Liu, Prince of Wu and Yue (852–932) feared that the tide would prevent his constructing the Qiantang embankment. He ordered three thousand archers and crossbow-men to shoot into the tide and hold it back long enough to allow completion of the work (Chen Xin, p. 236; Zheng Guangyi, p. 1616).

line 4: At the mouth of the Qiantang River, two mountains stand face to face across the water: Mount Kan and Mount Zhe. Together they form what is alternately known as the "Sea Gate" or "Heaven's Gate."

line 15: The white horse and chariot are associated with Wu Zixu, forced to commit suicide for having admonished the Prince of Wu against making peace with the Prince of Yue. His body was drowned in the river; resentful of his fate, he is said to return every year upon the Qiantang tide, riding a white horse and chariot, to seek his revenge (Chen Xin, p. 236; Zheng Guangyi, p. 1616).

BIOGRAPHICAL NOTE AND TRANSLATION BY PAULA VARSANO

王 慧

P.76. Wang Hui (later 17th century)

"Luminous and pure, to be assigned the highest rank," proclaimed Shen Deqian, introducing the poems of Wang Hui (style name Lanyun), a native of Taicang prefecture in modern-day Jiangsu. And the great critic Wang Shizhen, in his *Yuyang shihua*, also admired her poems in five- and seven-character verse, noting their "many beautiful phrases."[1]

In view of the acclaim that Wang Hui was to garner, the modesty with which she developed her gift is surprising. Her husband, a student named Zhu Fanglai, died young, and Wang led the rest of her life in profound seclusion, devoted to study and the writing of poetry. She never shared her poems with anyone; her younger brother Wang Jiwu, a *jinshi* scholar, discovered them when she was over seventy years old. He had them published and distributed under the title *Ningcuilou shiji* (Poetry collection from the Tower of Shimmering Green). This collection was also included in Cai Dianqi's 1844 anthology *Guochao guige shichao*.[2]

P.76.1. Moving Back to the House in Qian Village

Where the Xintang waters round the road's east side
Was our home—fenced in and just large enough for the planting of
mulberries.
Pines and chrysanthemums still stand, evoking ancestral virtue,
Wild weeds, uncut, reveal our family's spirit.
Wildflowers have thickened, dogs and chickens settle beyond the
thinning woods,
When the tide is low, fish and shrimp are seen in our small town.
But I do love that pair of swallows before the hall—
(8) Still seeking their stony niche of old, they pass through the curtained
windows.

(Yi Boyin, 6/170)

line 2: For the precise dimensions meant here, see *Mencius*, book 1, part a: "If the mulberry is planted in every homestead of five *mu* [a little under 200 square meters] of land, then those who are over fifty can wear silk" (Lau, trans., *Mencius*,

p. 51; SSJZS, 1: 1/7a). Wang Hui indicates the humbleness of her abode and suggests the great length of time that it has been in her family.

line 3: Pines and chrysanthemums suggest lasting life (the pine because it is evergreen, the chrysanthemum because it blooms in autumn; see P.5.1). Both are prominent in the poems of Tao Yuanming, on whom see P.17.2 and P.33.4.

line 4: These "wild weeds" (*penghao*) recall Zhang Zhongwei, a learned recluse of the Eastern Han. Zhang "excelled in composing essays and loved poetry and rhyme-prose. He lived ever in ascetic simplicity, where the wild weeds could engulf a man. Closing his gate and cultivating his inner nature, he did not establish a glorious name, and his contemporaries knew nothing of him" (Huangfu Mi, *Gao shi zhuan*, 2/10b–11a).

P.76.2. Upon Hearing That My Neighbor, Married into a Scholarly Family While Young, Was Sent Away to the Frontier Because Her Husband Is Without an Official Post

With the girl next door
  I shared the "red banner."
We'd tailor the clouds and sing of willows,
  vying in petal-fresh youth.
Fragrance drenched our embroidered book-covers—we'd separate the threads;
When spring warmed our dressing tables, we'd send each other flowers.
All say that Luofu, after all, had her husband,
But pity Cai Yan who found herself alone.
Now you plait your hair in two long braids:
(8) As the sun sets over purple passes, you weep with nomad flutes.

(Yi Boyin, 6/170)

line 1: The red banner refers to the Han dynasty scholar-official Ma Rong (79–166), best known for his erudite exegeses of the ancient-text versions of the Confucian Classics. Whenever he wanted to assemble his students for scholarly discussion, he would hoist aloft a vermilion banner (*Hou Han shu*, 60/1972).

line 5: The story of Qin Luofu appears in the *yuefu* poem "Moshang sang." Glimpsed one day by the Prince of Zhao, Luofu resisted his advances by improvising a song about her absent (and possibly fictional) husband, a military officer on campaign (Guo Maoqian, ed., *Yuefu shiji*, 28/410–11).

line 6: On Cai Yan, see P.2. This couplet criticizes the common conviction to which the poet's neighbor seems to have fallen victim: that a woman's source of happiness is life with her husband, not a life devoted to literature.

P.76.3. The Tomb of Yu the Great

The firmament filled with virtue illustrious,
His divine deeds surpassed those of Da Ting.
"Water swallowed the mountains, submerged the hills"
  Then did he exert his utmost strength,
"Callused and coarse his hands, his feet"—
  The picture of labor most strenuous.
Grass and trees burgeoned in darkening density,
Dragons and snakes wallowed in putrid backwaters.

His tribute from the nine provinces: tripods in smelted metal;
In his Record of the Eight Realms, he noted all the world's wonders.
The immortal Cangshui first presented the divine book;
Fangfeng, though, was punished for arriving late.

Here, it is said, where Yu left bow and sword,
He went down to his Yellow Spring abode.
In this, his shrine handed down since the Three Epochs,
For ten thousand autumns have we presented prayer mat and incense,
The beasts and jade disks of ceremonies of yore,
Inscriptions on stele and plaque throughout the dynasties.
While deep in the palace a host of followers is worshipping,
On the empty mountain wander one hundred souls.

Long have we heard of imperial banners stopping here,
And today we see the kingfisher pendants pause.
His heart's teaching was transmitted through the valleys of the Yellow
  and Luo Rivers,
Sovereigns' praise set sun and stars aflame.
Later generations still bask in his far-reaching benevolence,
Ceremonies unique are proclaimed by imperial courts.
With great solemnity I gaze upon the newly cast image,
Then climb aloft to look down at the moored little boats.

Walls and balustrades are bare of ornate carvings,
Doors and windows gleam in red and green.
Search not for his Cavern of Hidden Books;
Simply look upon the Pavilion of Burial Pillars.

And while trailing vines grow long, night-squirrels hide their traces,
Amidst aging pines, pheasants preen their plumage.
The many rivers belt the fertile lands,
(36) Through throngs of peaks open plunging cliffs.

The man of Qiao Mountain accomplished all this—
Alone, he faces the autumnal plains.

(Zhou Daorong, Xu Zhixu, and Huang Qizhen, eds., *Zhongguo lidai nüzi shici xuan*, 171–72)

The tomb of the legendary sovereign and culture-hero Yu the Great (traditionally dated to the twenty-third century B.C.E.) is located just outside Shaoxing in Zhejiang province. He is credited with taming the great floods, regulating and mapping the lands, establishing a system of measurement and naming all the things of the earth. His success in flood control (a task that defeated his father, Gun) enabled him to succeed Yao and Shun as ruler of China. He then became the first king of the Xia dynasty.

line 2: Da Ting was a legendary sovereign of antiquity, possibly Shennong, the deity of farmers, credited with identifying the uses of plants and developing the cultivation of grain. See Mathieu, *Anthologie des mythes*, pp. 67–68; Gan Bao, *Sou shen ji*, 1/1a.

line 3: These words are drawn from the account of the floods found in the *Book of Documents* (*Shang shu*, "Yao dian," in SSJZS, 2/12a; Karlgren, *Book of Documents*, p. 9).

line 5: These words are drawn from Huangfu Mi's *Diwang shiji*, as cited in Chen Xin, p. 263.

line 9: During Yu's tenure as supreme king, "the distant regions sent pictures of various objects and tribute of metal was submitted from the governors of the nine provinces. This was used to cast cauldrons with various objects depicted on them . . . so that the people could learn about the gods and the malevolent spirits" (*Zuo zhuan*, Xuan gong, third year; trans. B. Watson, *The Tso Chuan*, p. 82).

line 10: "The Record of the Eight Realms" probably refers to the *Shanhai jing* (Classic of mountains and seas), traditionally attributed, at least in part, to Yu.

line 11: Searching for a sacred book at the top of Heng Mountain, Yu encountered a youth clad in crimson-embroidered robes who called himself "the Xuanyi Cangshui messenger." He ordered Yu to fast for three days. Yu followed his instructions, then climbed to the top of Wanwei Mountain, overturned the stones, and found the gold-bound book hidden there. One interpretation has it that this book was the *Shanhai jing* (*Wu Yue Chunqiu*, as cited in Chen Xin, p. 263).

line 12: The *Guoyu* (Conversations of the states) recounts that Fangfeng was prince of Wangmang (alt. Wangwang, in modern-day Zhejiang) and committed the egregious error of arriving late at a meeting called by Yu. His punishment was execution, after which he became renowned for the immensity of his bones—each bone had to be transported in a separate cart (*Guoyu yinde*, "Lu yu," 5: 2/51).

line 13: To "leave bow and sword" is a periphrasis for the death of an emperor. The legendary founder of Chinese civilizaton, the Yellow Emperor, left this world on the back of a dragon and, once in the heavens, dropped his bow to earth (*Shi ji*, 28/1394).

line 14: On Yellow Springs as the abode of the dead, see P.29.9 and P.38.1.

line 15: The Three Epochs are the first three dynasties: Xia, Shang, and Zhou.

line 22: Imperial banners were mounted on staffs decorated with kingfisher feathers.

line 31: The Cavern of the Hidden Books probably refers to the spot where Yu found the gold-bound book noted above.

line 32: In contrast to the Cavern of the Hidden Books, the stone pillars supposedly used to lower Yu's coffin into its grave must still have been preserved in a pavilion on the site.

line 37: Qiao Mountain, located in modern-day Shaanxi province, is the legendary burial site of the Yellow Emperor.

P.76.4. On the Road to Shanyin

When I exit the city
from the watchtower gate
I lose completely
all sense of spatial limits,
Passing ten miles through
the cool shade of the hills.
Water and land rise to view
by turns and sink away;
My course lengthens out
open and endless.
Hills and mountains draw apart,
each contour like no other;
Bamboo and trees interlace
making dense forest.
Who would know
under this impenetrable growth
(8) A stream is gliding through?
On the stone bridge
the road is obvious
Then I round a bend
and confuse east and west.

No one else in sight
  here in the mist
(12) Hushed, alone
  mountain flowers so red.

(QSBC, 31/9a)

P.76.5. Waiting for the Tide to Rise at Iris Banks, I Think of My Daughter Who Died

Aground in shallow water
  sun halfway in decline
I fasten the line,
  free to enjoy the view
    that seems to reach to the horizon.
Mist thickens in bamboo on the shore
  where doves croon for rain,
Low tide exposes roots of rushes
  as small crabs cluster on the sand.
Sad thoughts start to unreel,
  snare me like tangled vines;
When time-bound beauty fades and falls,
  heart grieves for the broken blossom.
Deeply I loved my little daughter—
  often we would moor our boat to sit
(8) Together at the rush-mat cabin window
  counting blackbirds in the evening sky.

(QSBC, 31/11a)

P.76.6. Staying Overnight at a House in the Country, I Happened to See Pasted over a Hole in the Window a Page from Han Wo's Collection, The Scented Dressing Case. *Thinking It a Pity, I Wrote This.*

Sentiments of great beauty in elegant verse—
  and who is there to understand?
I catch a glimpse, here at the window
  of lines running sideways.
Moved to pity that style and grace
  have fallen to such obscurity,

I bring the red lamp over,
  brush away the cobwebs.

(GGSC, I: 7/5b)

The *Fragrant Dressing Case Collection* (*Xianglian ji*) is a well-known collection of erotic poems on women attributed to the late-Tang poet Han Wo.

P.76.7. Cold Spring Pavilion

The voice of the spring
  beyond eaves and railing
Comes from far and deep
  in a wooded ravine.
Why dwell in the heat
  of the human world?
When I come here
  coolness spreads to mind and heart.
In groves of pine the stream
  hides patches of sunlight;
On the floor of its deepest pools
  the mountain's shadows sleep.
Since Letian wrote of it long ago
(8) The special beauty of this mountain
  remains, to this day, cold.

(GGSC, I: 7/3b)

line 7: Letian is the courtesy name of Tang dynasty poet Bo Juyi (772–846), who wrote an essay on his visit to the Cold Spring Pavilion. The Cold Spring stream referred to here is located in the West Lake area of Hangzhou district in Zhejiang province.

P.76.8. Asleep One Night, I Was Awakened by the Cry of an Owl and Felt Distressed

Faint breeze moved
  curtains at window and bed,
Moonlight pierced
  the window's paper.
Such a lonely night
  at the third watch,

Everything in the world
more still than water.
Up on the wall
an owl was perched,
Its drawn-out cry came
like mourning to a human ear.
When I heard it, my heart shuddered,
(8) Turned cold, and a hundred thoughts
came crowding up.
Death! My vitals wrenched
in silent pain;
At the thought of this adversary
my hair stood up in dread.
It made me remember
those beneath the Springs,
(12) As I lay in my sickbed
facing the onset of autumn—
Blood so thinned out
I was sleepless at night,
Spirit so vacant
I could not concentrate.
Suddenly hearing the bird's cry
(16) I missed, from surprise,
what it was saying to me.
But I feared it was
an inauspicious message,
And thus with grief
the children came to mind.
I took their hands, my soul
already overwhelmed,
(20) I gazed at them
in tears like rain.
Turning, I observed
the lantern on the wall—
Its flame was trembling, blue,
small as a pea!
What sadness!

(24) I have dwelt on this scene
already two winters and summers.
All this time, so many times
I relived it, with imaginings too many to record:
How malicious people
would often treat them badly,
(28) How orphaned and alone
they would be in constant danger.
And they, lonely and unhappy,
weak fledgling chicks,
How could they fend off rats and foxes?
Anguish assailed me, aggravation mounted
(32) Until all these feelings
have gradually choked my breast.
I fear to ignore this warning
But to whom can I entrust
the burden of my dear ones?
To manage my medicines
is as much as I can do,
(36) Curative mushrooms—
nothing is more costly.
Preparing healthful foods
requires hard labor.
However will I find the strength?
So let my small life float
or sink, as it will;
(40) To succeed or fail, in truth
depends on heaven.

(Xu Shichang, ed., *Wanqingyi shihui*, 183/8078)

The owl, considered a bird of ill omen, was thought to perch on a house where there would soon be a death. Wan's poem recalls a rhyme-prose by Jia Yi (201–169 B.C.E.), which also opens with the cry of an owl and goes on to address the issue of human mortality (*Wen xuan* 13/16a–20a; translated by Burton Watson, *Chinese Rhyme-Prose*, pp. 25–28). Jia's piece is, however, an allusive and philosophical Daoist reflection on change and fate, while Wang's poem is very personal and practical.

P.76.9. *On a Summer Day, I Write About the Place Where We Are Staying*

When we are away for the summer
  nothing at all happens;
The brushwood gate is closed
  the whole day long.
Weary, I throw down books and scrolls,
  lie back and take a rest;
Bored, I go to pull weeds
  and clear the herb garden.
Greens I borrow from trees
  growing in the neighbor's yard;
Blues I share with mountains
  beyond the city walls.
Living quietly apart
  I've left all ordinary cares behind;
(8) In following my own inclinations
  I am really quite obstinate!

(GGSC, I: 7/4a)

BIOGRAPHICAL NOTE AND P.76.1–3 TRANSLATED BY PAULA VARSANO; P.76.4–9 TRANSLATED BY MAUREEN ROBERTSON

林以寧

P.77. Lin Yining (1655–after 1730)

Lin Yining, courtesy name Yaqing, was a member of the well-known Banana Garden Poetry Club (both the original group of five members and the later reorganized group) in the Qiantang township of Hangzhou district, Zhejiang province during the 1670s.[1] Her father was Lin Lun, a *jinshi*. She was a sister-in-law and an especially close friend of Qian Fenglun (P.78), another member of the Banana Garden group. Lin married Qian's brother, Qian Zhaoxiu, a *jinshi* of 1696 who eventually won promotion to the position of Investigating Censor. Lin's mother-in-law, Gu Zhiqiong (style name Yurui), was a niece of Gu Ruopu (P.60) and the founder of the original Banana Garden Club. Members of the club, women of prominent Hangzhou-area families whose men often held high-ranking positions in the civil bureaucracy, were intellectual, literary, and social models of considerable influence for other educated women of Jiangnan in their day and later.[2]

Lin was known for her accomplished poetry, parallel prose writings, calligraphy, and painting of ink bamboo. Like others in the Banana Garden group, she admired the poetry and painting of Chai Jingyi (P.75a) and regarded her as a mentor (see P.77.6, "Lament for Chai Jixian"). In her own preface to her collected works, Lin says that she received her education as a child from her mother, taking a special interest in the Classics. She wished, she says, to become a "great scholar," *da ru*, and not a Ban Zhao (see P.60.9) or a Zuo Fen (P.3), the usual early exemplars for Ming and Qing gentry women writers. Lin was one of three members of the Banana Garden Club who contributed prefatory inscriptions and colophons for the 1694 edition of Tang Xianzu's influential drama *Mudan ting* (The peony pavilion), an edition provided with commentaries by three women and titled *Wu Wushan sanfu heping Mudanting huanhun ji* (Wu Wushan's three wives' combined commentary on "The peony pavilion" or "The soul's return"; see P.72.6).[3] Lin's own writings were collected and published in 1697 under the title *Mozhuang shichao, ciyu, wenchao* (Ink Cottage poems, song-lyrics, and prose). A separately printed collection of *ci* poetry, *Fengxiaolou ji* (Songs from Phoenix Flute Tower), is listed in bibliographical sources. Lin may also have experimented with playwriting; a now lost southern drama called *Tenghua xia* (Wisteria Pass) has been attributed to her.[4]

Lin and her husband shared literary interests, and though she comments on how often his official duties kept him from home, after his retirement they were noted for their companionable enjoyment of literature and the arts. Lin's 1730 preface to an anthology of Tang, Song, and Yuan dynasty poems on the subject of plum blossoms collected by Gu Ruopu's fifth-generation granddaughter by marriage, Liang Ying, mentions a son, Qing, who held office in a distant place; a daughter, Tao; and grandsons. Neither her daughter, her granddaughter, nor her grandsons' wives, she says, "dared" to write literature, although they were all capable students of literature. Thus, at the age of seventy-six, she herself had almost decided to give up writing ("burn brush and inkstone"), when her interest was revived by Liang Ying's project. In writing the preface for Liang's work, she was led to reminisce about her sixty years' association with the "great lady" Gu Ruopu and the many literary women surrounding her as relatives and friends.[5]

Lin's poetry is distinguished by its direct and fluent diction, and vivid visual imagery. Her topics reflect personal interests, rather than the conventional themes and scenarios derived from literati constructions of feminine voices.

P.77.1. Presented to the Lady Scholar Wanqiong

The immortal moon-dweller,
Lady of Condensed Radiance,
From her ocean of silver clouds
hurls down winds rippling
blue-green foliage in the sky.
In the moon Palace of Vast Coldness
purple buds appear on a dark cassia tree;
Icy toad fashions the words:
"a pair of mandarin ducks."
Light of the moon shining solitary in the night
illumines the three regions of Wu;
Collecting sweet scents along riverbanks
are many well-praised girls.
A ray of sun penetrates the blinds,
golden magpie's long tailfeather;
(8) By the window she wakes, refreshed
from sleep on the red woolen mat.
Newly made of fine paper from Shu
there is her wedding announcement,
And calamus leaves tied in a double loveknot.
Cold white jades are her hands
rubbed with lychee powder;
(12) Under shining red lanterns, wine
sets hibiscus cheeks glowing.
Breezes scissor spring flowers,
shatter to shreds the sunset clouds;
She imagines that he and she are
the paired butterflies in the pattern of her dress.
Dark clouds, her coiled chignons,
yellow gold, the pendants at her ears;
(16) From her wrist, a moment exposed,
an aroma of fragrant oils deliquescing.

At a scene of otherworldly magnificance
  she becomes his honored wife, and then
The nights's festivities are done;
  in a glittering shower, the cold stars set.

(GGSC, 2: 6/2b–3a)

line 1: The reference is to Chang E, goddess of the moon, on whom see P.21.1.

lines 3–4: These lines are replete with moon lore; on the lunar palace, the toad, and the cassia tree, see P.26.5. Mandarin ducks are a symbol of fidelity; see P.20.2.

line 5: Suzhou, Runzhou, and Huzhou were known informally as Eastern Wu, Central Wu, and Western Wu, respectively.

line 11: Known primarily for its fruit, the lychee tree also provided medicinal substances and a white starch that was used cosmetically.

P.77.2. *Spring Rains for the Crops*

I

A shaft of liquid light
  from the mirrorstand pierces windowsilk;
Where breezes blow along the eaves
  willow tips hang at angles.
I tidy the books on bamboo shelves
  and rid them of silverfish;
When I wash inkstones in a spring pond
  they get splattered with duckweed blossom.
Mulberry leaves are lush,
  silkworms still hang on their frames;
Sun warming, the queen bee
  has already sent out her drones.
The boy hangs a pot at his waist
  and goes after streamwater;
(8) We clean cups in the sunshine
  for tasting the new tea.

II

I've spent my youthful years thoughtlessly
  back in the women's quarters;
My whole life, I've never known anything
  about cultivating mulberry and hemp.

Along the brushwood fence, wild pea vines
  are putting forth first tendrils;
Around the steps, the mountain cherry
  is on the verge of blooming.
Fine rains soak into branches
  to become the willow's color;
Warm sun nudges into bloom
  the budding peonies.
Village girls do up their hair
  in the latest elaborate style
And just before dawn call out
  to their friends next door,
    "Let's pick tea!"

(GGSC, 2: 6/4b–5a)

The title used here translates *guyu*, one of the twenty-four solar terms; it indicates a period in the spring when rains fall that are essential to the sprouting of crop seeds, equivalent to late April and early May.

P.77.3. Thinking of My Father, Yudu

At dawn I climb a hundred-foot tower
To look out at the central massif in the distance.
At the edge of the sky are white clouds
That day and night leave and return as they will.
Going or coming, they remain remote and aloof;
I lean out to them, but cannot catch and hold them.
Who said giving birth to daughters is good?
Child and adult, I have rarely seen my parent's face.
Is it right not to care for one's parents?
Yet how can I serve him in his later years?
I want to ask him, "Have you rested well?"
But we've been far apart so long.
I want to see that his food is nourishing,
But truly it is impossible.
Walking back by way of South Rise,
My steps are halting but my tears come rushing.

(GGZSJ, 2: 4/1a)

lines 1–4: The opening of the poem echoes poem 110 of the *Book of Odes*, in which a soldier son is worried about his father: "I climb that tree-covered hill / and look out toward my father." In this context, white clouds connote thoughts of parents who are far away.

line 15: South Rise, *Nan'gai*, a place name, is also the title of a song in the *Book of Odes*, one of the six songs for which the text is lost. According to the Han dynasty commentary, the song was about filial sons who spoke to each other about their responsibility to their parents.

P.77.4. Painting Bamboo

New bamboo has emerged from the low hedge;
Tall and erect, it seems spun from kingfisher feathers.
When a shining moon rises over the east porch,
Traceries of bamboo shadow cover the ground.
I rub pineblack on a bronze inkstone
And wet the brush to capture its inner meaning.
For unspoiled modesty it is by all means admirable,
But I love most its resolve: to be steadfast, faithful.

(GGZSJ, 2: 4/1b)

line 4: On the story of the origin of ink bamboo painting with Lady Li of Shu, see P.23.

P.77.5. Crossing at the Confluence of the Yi and the Lo Rivers

One by one I have experienced
  all the hazards of mountains and rivers;
Now at last I understand
  "the hardships of the road."
Cold winds wailing through wide gorges,
Grotesque rocks roiled round in rushing rapids.
When I started out my heart was ever fearful,
By journey's end my tears are still not dry.
A sparkle on the waves—they must be amused by me!
Managing it by myself, I step up on the river landing.

(GGZSJ, 2: 4/2b–3a)

P.77.6. Lament for Chai Jixian

The painting of Mahakasyapa on the wall
Is a relic of your work, still beautiful and vivid.
In the cool of night, it gives off such a shimmering light,
I glance at it sideways, not daring to look directly.
I recall seeing you lower your brush to begin,
Living energy full, your spirit whole.
The way you painted was not demure and dainty;
You drew spontaneously, your green sleeves flew!
Often I longed to throw off the duties of worldly life
And follow you in service to cinnabar and white lead.
How could I know you would not be here to guide me?
Suddenly, in death, you abandon me forever.
I am moved to the depths, my sorrow is the clouds;
Your beauty and grace I keep like treasure concealed
In moonlight shining on the beams of my room.

(GGZSJ, 2: 4/2a)

lines 1–2: Mahakasyapa is the Sanskrit name of one of the principal disciples of Sakyamuni Buddha. He became leader of the disciples, the first of the twenty-eight patriarchs, and the first compiler of the Buddhist canon. The Chinese form of his name, used by Lin, is Posa.

lines 14–15: Lin alludes in the poem's closure to one of Du Fu's poems written to Li Bo, older and much admired by Du Fu. When Li Bo appeared to Du Fu in a dream, Du became worried about his welfare, and in one of two poems to Li, he speaks of the lingering dream image: "Light of the setting moon fills the rafters; / I still seem to see your face there where it shines" ("Meng Li Bo," no. 1, QTS 218/2289).

BIOGRAPHICAL NOTE AND TRANSLATION BY MAUREEN ROBERTSON

P.78. Qian Fenglun (fl. 1690)

Qian Fenglun (courtesy name Yunyi) was the second daughter of Gu Zhiqiong (literary name Yurui *furen*, Lady Jade Pistil), who was a niece of the literary woman Gu Ruopu and the original convenor of the Banana Garden Poetry Club in the Hangzhou area.[1] Qian's father, Qian Anhou, was said to have been a *jinshi*, but whether he held office is not known. The Banana Garden poet Lin Yining (P.77) was Qian's close friend and became her sister-in-law when she married Qian's younger brother, Qian Zhaoxiu.

Qian was said to have been much loved by her parents, and as a child she was praised for her paintings of birds and flowers. Before her marriage, she was a member of the first Banana Garden Club group of five women. At sixteen she married Huang Shixu, a "tribute student," *gongsheng*, and the great-grandson of Gu Ruopu; she joined the Huang household, where she often submitted her writings to Gu for criticism. When the Banana Garden Club was reorganized after a period of inactivity, Qian remained a member.

Qian had two published collections, *Sanhua tan ji* (Shore of scattered flowers: Collected poems) and *Guxianglou ji* (Collected writings from Fragrance of Antiquity Tower), the latter including *shi*, *ci*, *qu*, and "miscellaneous writings"; a copy of the 1702 edition of *Guxianglou ji* is listed in the rare books catalogue of Beijing University. In her 1680 preface to *Guxianglou ji*, Gu Ruopu says that after her great-grandson failed in an examination attempt, Qian studied with him to help and encourage him, the two of them often staying up with their books until midnight. Gu herself had similarly helped her own husband prepare for his examination. Gu praised Qian for her natural gift for poetry and expressed the hope that she would continue to work at her writing so as to become the inheritor and transmitter of the literary legacy of Gu's natal and marital lineages (including herself and other women writers).

A Qing-dynasty critic admired Qian's writing for possessing "the elevated style of [writers of] antiquity," *gaogu*, and for being "completely free of the air of kerchiefs and dainty eyebrows." As examples of her *gaogu* style, he cited six of Qian's prose pieces. Unfortunately, these have not survived. Qian is said to have once composed a piece in the prose genre *zhen*, "admonition," in imitation of the Han-dynasty scholar Yang Xiong's "Admonitions to the Twelve Provinces and the Twenty-Five Offices." Since none of Yang's "admonitions" were addressed to women scholars, Qian wrote a *Tongguan zhen*, "Admonition to Literary Women," to remedy his omission.[2]

P.78.1. Banquet on a Winter's Day at the Residence of Chai Jixian

Come full cycle, the stars tell
  the year is almost gone;
The sky is cold
  winter bleak and gloomy.

Plants all wither
 under severe frost;
Scattered dews dry
 in early morning sun.
Happily I meet with
 these good and modest people
And we sit down together
 in a house of iris and orchid.
As we laugh and talk
 spring breezes rise;
In friendly accord
 we busy ourselves with writing.
Pictures and books
 are strewn about the rooms;
On the yew-wood table
 we set out zithers and harps.
Since the birds have left
 the courtyard is even quieter;
When clouds hang low
 shadows on blinds grow dim.
Living a secluded life
 keeps noise and dust distant;
Then thoughts transcend
 range wide and far away.
Time's flowing lights go
 swift as a thrown shuttle;
Such good times together
 I fear are too easily lost.
And so, inspired by wine,
 we raise our voices in song,
From beginning to end
 enjoying to the fullest
  the bounty of this good hostess!

(GGSC, 2: 4/2a)

line 6: Qian alludes here to the ancient poem "Lady of the Xiang," one of the "Nine Songs" in the third-century B.C.E. *Chuci* (Songs of Chu); in so doing she praises Chai and her residence by comparing it to the home of the Xiang river goddess, who was promised a dwelling beneath the water made of aromatic woods and decorated with fragrant flowers.

line 15: "Flowing lights" refers to the movement of sun, moon, and stars, indicating time's passage.

P.78.2. *Meditation on the Past: In Jade Effusion Garden*

Running currents of West Lake sing
of ages long in the past;
Wind is folding the snowy wave,
water dragons dance.
We're told a royal carriage once
held a splendid hunt;
A thousand riders with carved saddles
camped along the river.
Flageolets and songs at dawn
pressed on Phoenix City clouds;
At evening their pennons and banners
furled Dragon Mountain rain.
Across the lake now autumn winds
are blowing in the reeds.
(8) Red cherry-apple's suspended fruits
are the cuckoo's grieving soul;
The glory and beauty of early times
today are truly gone;
From the river village in waning light
washing blocks ring clear.
In the Palace of Renewed Splendor
only moonlight is brilliant;
(12) By the Hall of Virtue and Longevity
only spring grass comes to life.
Events of an age, mere floating clouds,
can they be fixed or secured?
Lake currents, crying and murmuring,
swirl round ruined city walls.
The descending sun strikes dread in my heart,
transfixes my distant gaze;

(16) No purple clouds do I see there
  this evening in the southland.

(GGSC, 2: 4/3b–4a)

During the later Zhou dynasty a Jade Effusion Garden was said to have been constructed under imperial auspices. In 1147, during the Southern Song dynasty, another garden with the same name was created north of Dragon Mountain in the West Lake area of Hangzhou county, Zhejiang province. In 1185, Emperor Xiaozong (1163–90) held a great hunting party there. "Jade Effusion," in Daoist lore, is a substance that confers immortality. In Daoist mystical texts, it is the saliva from the mouth of the spiritual lover, Jade Maiden, with the power to confer enlightenment.

line 3: "A royal carriage" is a metonymic reference to the emperor. It was customary to avoid referring with impolite directness to the imperial person.

line 5: Phoenix City was a name normally used for the imperial capital, but here it designates a temporary residence of the emperor.

line 16: Purple clouds connote imperial authority, the aura of an emperor, suggesting his spiritual as well as temporal power. The poem closes on a dark note, implying perhaps the Ming dynasty's loss of the "southland" in its final battle with the Manchu invaders who established the Qing dynasty.

P.78.3. Matching Rhymes with My Mother's Poem, "An Offering to Zhuge Liang, the Martial Marquis"

We pay our respects
  at the shrine hall of noble Zhu,
And place on the altar
  an offering of white duckweed.
Where birds are roosting
  the lofty trees are ancient;
Where insects nibble
  the tablet has recently crumbled.
His maze of stones
  is lost in bracken and mist;
The golden phoenix
  is reduced to a dancing spririt.
When he commanded an army
  in the name of Han succession,
(8) His "feathered battle standard"
  was a single length of silk.

(GGSC, 2: 4/4a–b)

Zhuge Liang was a hero of the Three Kingdoms period (221–65) who gave up a secluded life to serve as chief strategist under Liu Bei, leader of a group of rebels in the last days of the Han dynasty. With Zhuge's help, Liu established the kingdom of Shu (Han), claiming to be the inheritor of the Han dynasty mandate. Warfare between the three kingdoms of Shu, Wei, and Wu continued until the establishment of the Jin dynasty in 265. Zhuge was enfeoffed as marquis under Liu Bei's successor.

line 5: One of Zhuge's stratagems was said to have involved a maze of stones named "The Eightfold Array"; a formation with eight "gates," its configuration was constantly shifting so that an enemy who entered the formation was unable to find a way out. It is likely that such stones would have been used to model the formation of troops and their movements on a battlefield; however, the tradition that Zhuge's stones were set in the Yangzi River led to a belief in later centuries that certain actual rocks in the Yangzi about a mile from the shrine were the remnants of the Eightfold Array.

line 8: A standard topped with a fan-shaped spray of feathers was a symbol of leadership carried into battle. The "length of silk" alludes to the story legitimating the claim of succession to the Han. When the last Han emperor, Xian, had fallen under the control of the powerful Han minister and general Cao Cao (eventual founder of the kingdom of Wei; see P.2), it was said the emperor secretly smuggled out one of his robes; hidden inside was a length of white silk upon which the emperor had written an edict in his own blood that legitimized the fight against Cao Cao and called for his murder. It was this length of silk that symbolized the Han cause and made the defeat of Cao Cao at Red Cliff (temporary though it was) by means of Zhuge's military strategy a triumph for Han loyalists.

P.78.4. Composed to the Song "A Beautiful Woman Combs Her Hair"

From the new-leaved grove
  a green bird's sudden call;
Over palace women's quarters
  spring dawn is about to break.
By her bed a silken cord
  linked to the well-pulley;
Autumn-clear water gushes,
  her mirror coldly gleams.
Watching the red sun, slowly
  she rolls up pearl blinds;
Twin arcs, half-moons,
  are her brows traced so fine.

Jade phoenix flies atilt,
golden cicada dangles;
(8) Sash pendants swing and sway,
trailing Xiang River mist.
Then down the stair alone she goes
to pick for herself sweet buds:
"These cherry blossoms laugh at me
because I bear no fruit!"

(GGSC, 2: 4/3b)

One of the best-known *yuefu* compositions under this title "A Beautiful Woman Combs Her Hair" is by the Tang poet Li He. Though her style is different, Qian has modeled her poem rather closely on Li's (see QTS 193/4434; trans. in Graham, *Poems of the Late T'ang*, p. 115).

lines 4–7: These lines refer to waking, washing, and painting the brows. The woman then finishes combing her hair and places hairpins and ornaments in her coiffure.

line 8: The Xiang River was the dwelling place of one, perhaps two, alluring female river spirits (see P.11.16 and P.74.3). The woman in this poem is thus represented as divinely beautiful.

P.78.5. Note to Yaqing on an Autumn Day

Your letter arrived from the city's outer gate,
or, I should say, from the ends of the earth!
We've both felt sad, missing each other,
neither aware of the other's mood.
When cool evening breezes and chess games
are played out, soft rain late in the night;
It is the season when wild geese return.
By my window, orange and pomelo
are heavy with hanging fruits;
Outside the door, hibiscus
blooming on countless branches.
Together we enter this clear autumn
but cannot enjoy it together,
(8) So instead, I'll depend on the blue bird
to send my love to you.

(GGSC, 2: 4/4b)

line 8: The immortals were said to use a magical blue-green bird to carry their messages to each other.

P.78.6. Composed to the Song: "Cold at the West Window"

A rainstorm passes through
  sweet blossoms are drenched;
When the wind comes
  green leaves yield to it.
With inkstone and red paste
  I study the *Changes* of Zhou,
More aware than ever
  how remote from the world
    is my little window.

(GGSC, 2: 4/5a)

line 3: The *Book of Changes.*

P.78.7. Man jiang hong: *Lament for My Mother, on the Fifth Day of the Fifth Month*

I keep remembering spring
When fresh dreams shattered.
Young orioles had just begun to sing,
How many days was it?—
Then glorious spring vanished completely.
Rushes bent down in the wind
Iridescent green gone cold;
Pomegranate flowers were cloaked in rain
Their red petals dragging.
What hurt most:
All things proper to the season
Were there, as ever,
And my dear mother I could not find.

I have hung artemisia and tiger,
Set ritual incense winding
Beat a painted drum until
It rumbled like thunder and lightning.

Watching the children play round my knee
Makes me even more heartbroken.
(20) "Beware" was the message sent in vain
To Qu Yuan's aggrieved soul;
River waves seem to speak the complaint
Of filial daughter Cao.
(24) Yet I long to be with her.
I would take offerings of meat and grain
And enter the deep abyss
Just to see my mother's face.

(XTLS: *Guxianglou ji*, 5a)

On the Double Fifth holiday, see P.38.1 and P.54a.16.

lines 20–21: An allusion to the *Chuci* poem "Da zhao," reportedly a magical litany used to call back the soul of the drowned Qu Yuan. On the Double Fifth festival and its associations with Qu Yuan, see P.54a.16.

lines 22–23: The daughter of Cao Xu of the Latter Han dynasty. Her father drowned by accident while singing and dancing for the river god, Lord Wu (the spirit of Wu Zixu). She wailed on the river bank for seventeen days, finally throwing herself into the river. A tablet praising her filiality was erected, and a tomb was built by local officials in Shaoxing, Zhejiang province. The Cao daughter was commemorated in Zhejiang province during the Double Fifth festival.

P.78.8. Yu meiren: *On the Original Theme*

Chu songs, painted horns—a riot of sounds erupted
And blew down the border city moon.
Eight thousand sons and brothers had long been the dragon's men;
In a single night their finely worked saddles
  and golden armor were scattered
    on endless empty wastes.

She chose to be jade crushed at the side of the king;
Her blood stained his battle dress red.
Faithful, her spirit refused to enter the land within the passes;
(8) Year after year, when Wu River waves rise
  in spring, they are red
    with her tears.

(XTLS: *Guxianglou ji*, 3b)

On Lady Yu and the death of Xiang Yu, see P.28.1. Compare Qian's version with Huang Yuanjie's poem, P.68.6.

line 3: The expression here, literally "followed the dragon," describes those supporting the attempt of a leader to establish dynastic legitimacy. The phrase is borrowed from the *Book of Changes*: "Clouds follow the dragon; winds follow the tiger."

line 5: From a saying, "Better to be crushed jade than an unbroken tile." Lady Yu chooses a noble death rather than debasement and life.

line 7: The "land within the passes" was the territory of the Zhou feudal state of Qin and the base of Qin dynastic power, conquered by Liu Bang after Xiang Yu's death.

line 8: Facing defeat at Gaixia, Xiang Yu was offered a route of escape back across the Yangzi to Wu by a village headman with a boat. Xiang Yu refused, saying he would not be able to face the families of the husbands and sons he had led to their deaths. The Wu River flows into the Yangzi. Fallen red petals floating on the river in spring are figured as tears of blood shed by the grieving spirit of Lady Yu.

P.78.9. Man ting fang: *While at the Lake Cottage, I Observe Some Girls on an Outing*

Green is dyeing banana leaves
Red inflaming the peony;
At every turn, bright beauty exhausts its wonders.
In this small house, finished with dressing
I sit quietly apart, talking to no one.
I draw water for myself from the flowing stream
And prepare some aromatic tea.
Exquisitely fresh!
It makes my mood calm.
I roll up blinds to see the sunlight;
Up above, where mist motions for something to lean on,
Spring hills look tranquil.

By the river dike, a group of girls on an outing,
So graceful, so vivid,
More innocent than fragile willow wands before a breeze.
Plied by the river's current, their reflections waver
Until they look like immortals in flight.
Fantastic!
The setting sun falls westward through the void;

As far as eye can see
Distant waters, endless skies.
I would like to be,
Resting in the long, lush, sweet grass,
One of a pair of mandarin ducks.

(XTLS: *Guxianglou ji*, 5a)

P.78.10. Meifeng bi: *Playing Chess with Yaqing on a Spring Day*

In the deepest courtyard, on a quiet spring day
The gold animal puffs "small seal" incense.
With each fresh cup of tea, a new chess game begins.
In the season of apricot rains the air is sweet.

My parrot's chatter has just become fluent when,
Suddenly, he jumps down to the ground.
Distracted, I turn to look, and
To my dismay, needlessly forfeit a jade scratcher!
Leaning on the screen, laughing, we twist off a flowering branch
  to breathe its scent.

(XTLS: *Guxianglou ji*, 2b)

line 2: The "gold animal" is a metal incense burner. On "small seal" incense, see P.46.6.

lines 7–8: A head scratcher carved from jadeite, bone, ivory, or wood was a personal accessory in earlier China. The speaker has wagered her scratcher, sure of winning, but when she looks away she loses her concentration, the game, and the scratcher.

BIOGRAPHICAL NOTE AND TRANSLATION BY MAUREEN ROBERTSON

P.79. Chen Susu (late 17th century)

The life of Chen Susu is known chiefly through her surviving poems, collected under the title *Erfen mingyue ji* (Erfen's bright moon writings) and through the playwright Zhu He's retelling of her story in the *chuanqi* drama *Qinlou yue* (Moon over Qin Pavilion). From these sources we know that Chen was a courtesan from Yangzhou and that she eventually became the concubine of

Jiang Xuezai after many travails, which included capture by bandits and cutting off her ring to send as a keepsake to her lover. Her poems refer to Jiang by his sobriquet Tianshui; Zhu He's drama changes his name to Lu Quan. Chen's poems were published in 1700 as an appendix to the drama, though her story appears to have taken place in the late 1660s.[1]

P.79.1. Describing My Thoughts

I'm from a poor family.
I grew up in Yangzhou.
At the age of thirteen I learned embroidery.
At the age of fifteen I learned to play the zither.
During difficult times I found I was unable to protect myself:
Without intending to I lost my chastity.
Though I have only one blemish in a lifetime,
(8) Who will again believe in my sincerity?
This is very hurtful, how can I talk of it?
My life is cast away like the feathers of a swan.

(Zhu He, *Qinlou yue*, appendix, 1b–2a)

P.79.2. Qinlou yue: *Zhenniang's Grave*

The fragrant flower is at rest.
The green mountain is so shut away you can't tell what year and
month it is,
Can't tell what year and month it is.
The pines are wilting, the cypresses old.
It is hard to connect them with [Zhenniang's] sympathetic heart.

The Lord of Heaven does not care that the flowers fall like snow.
The orioles and swallows while away the hours. To whom can I tell my
story?
(8) To whom can I tell my story?
Autumn mists, autumn rains, a few piles of yellow leaves.

(*Qinlou yue*, appendix, 3a)

Qinlou yue, the tune to which this lyric is composed, is also the name of Zhu He's drama about Chen Susu.

P.79.3. Rhyming with a Poem Sent by Scholar Tianshui

I

Zhuo Wenjun once enjoyed running a winehouse.
When she first met Sima Xiangru, he was indeed handsome.
I don't feel pity that music communicates a smile,
It's that I don't know whether Xiangru ever got the girl from Maoling.

II

Suddenly the parrot announces the visit of a guest.
I lift the curtain and in one smile I already have feelings for you.
How audacious! my gentleman!
By the magnolia flowers, you ask my nickname.

(*Qinlou yue*, appendix, 5a)

i, lines 1–4: When Zhuo Wenjun eloped with Sima Xiangru, they soon found themselves short of funds and opened a wineshop in Zhuo Wenjun's hometown. Her aristocratic father suddenly decided to help advance his son-in-law's literary career. On Sima Xiangru's infatuatation with the girl from Maoling and Zhuo's response, see P.38.1.

P.79.4. Sending Tianshui Off to West Lake

As you depart, my heart follows your boat.
How can the sorrow of our parting be compared to former times?
I hear the tomb of Su Xiaoxiao is located at West Lake:
Please don't forget to visit her at the Six Bridges.

(*Qinlou yue*, appendix, 7a)

lines 3–4: Su Xiaoxiao was a courtesan of the Six Dynasties period, whose grave is situated on the causeway built by Su Shi (Su Dongpo) across part of the West Lake in Hangzhou; see P.46.2.

P.79.5. Supplementing Tianshui's Farewell Poem to Me

I sent your boat off outside Suzhou.
Numerous clouds and mountains inspire grief for the traveler.
The worst is at daybreak beside my red candle
When, awakened, I pull together broken dreams and start combing my hair.

(*Qinlou yue*, appendix, 7a)

P.79.6. On an Old Embroidered Mirror Bag

From whose hands did the mirror bag come?
Such varied and numerous colors are not often seen.
A coiled dragon and overturned phoenix are on the perfume box,
Wonderfully clear and bright where jade fingers have held it.

Don't resent that the light of the mirror is covered.
The roundness of its moon can only be seen by a beauty.
Please don't buy five-color thread:
(8) Only the bright moon in the sky knows my heart.

(*Qinlou yue*, appendix, 7b)

line 3: The terms dragon and phoenix as used here describe sexual positions.

lines 7–8: Five-color thread was often used as part of the Double Seventh Night ritual of "begging for skill"; see P.5.1 and P.19.2. Since Chen already has a lover, she will not need to use spells.

P.79.7. Giving a Garden Balsam Flower to Tianshui

I love garden balsam flowers.
You love garden balsam seeds.
The anxious nature of seeds is like your heart.
The red of the flower dyes my finger.

(*Qinlou yue*, appendix, 9a)

P.79.8. Reading Juanhong furen ji

The clear sound of your pen reaches me
As I read in the middle of the night.
It's like gathering flowers with pale shadows,
It's like hearing the sound of cold rain.

I lament that our experiences are so similar.
Your genuine talents have difficulty finding a male admirer.
If only you could see this scented volume of your works,
(8) On which endless tears of blood have fallen!

(*Qinlou yue*, appendix, 10b)

Juanhong furen ji was the poetry of Gong Jingzhao, a woman poet and painter; see Hu Wenkai, p. 811, and Yu Jianhua, *Zhongguo meishujia renming cidian*, p. 1554. Gong is said to have been Chen's lifelong best friend.

P.79.9. *Cutting Off My Ring and Sending It to Tianshui*

I have worn this gold ring for years,
Today I send it to you as a token.
The union of two lovers is no difficult matter
As long as your heart is firm as gold.

(*Qinlou yue*, appendix, 11a)

P.79.10. *Burning My Poems*

My grieving heart is always in turmoil. It is hard to revise my writing—
Beneath the light as my poems are consigned to fire, I weep tears of blood.
Because the words "love-sickness" are hard to understand,
I don't want to leave my bitterness to the world of men.

(*Qinlou yue*, appendix, 13a–b)

P.79.11. *Writing of My Regrets at Age Twenty*

Year after year I have wandered around as a beauty.
I sketchily set down the facts of my life at this time.
I've had bitter regrets all my life—that there has been no way to control my fate.
In vain do I regret a hundred matters, all come to grief.

The young crow had a dream of returning to her parents, but home is too far away.
Not being a literary phoenix, I keep my thoughts to myself.
I loved the wonderful time of sunny spring,
But learned the secrets of the winter plum when it grew cold.

(*Qinlou yue*, appendix, 9b–10a)

BIOGRAPHICAL NOTE AND TRANSLATION BY ELLEN WIDMER

顧貞立

P.80. Gu Zhenli (ca. 1637–ca. 1714)

Gu Zhenli was the older sister of the poet Gu Zhenguan, who held the office of Secretariat Drafter. She lived during the early Qing dynasty in Wuxi. Her given name was Wenwan, her style name was Bifen, and she took the pseudonym Bi Qin ren (one who shuns the Qin, "Qin" standing for "Manchus," founders of the Qing dynasty). Her pronounced interest in affairs of state is expressed in the first song-lyric translated below, written in her youth at the time when the Southern Ming court was established in Nanjing. Her collection, in two *juan*, is titled *Qi xiang ge ci* (Song-lyrics from the Nesting-Fragrance Tower). Li Wenyuan, in a preface for a copy of Gu's works, describes the tone of her song-lyrics: "The pages are filled with sorrow, constantly questioning [the ephemeral] shadows of plum blossoms. A remote and quiet courtyard, like a meditation on early summer flowers."[1] The Qing author Li Jia compares her phrasing to that of the Northern Song lyricist Zhang Xian. Guo Ling (1767–1831) wrote that the language of Gu's song-lyric to the tune *Manjiang hong* is "impressive, recalling the 'Li Sao' and the *Ya* poems (of the *Book of Odes*) in spirit—it scarcely seems to be [the voice of] a sheltered woman. The author is an unusual woman indeed."[2] Gu frequently composed poems matching the rhymes of Wang Lang (styled Zhongying).[3] Her son Hou Linxun served as a bureau secretary.[4]

P.80.1. Yu meiren

Mourning the fall of the state, I wipe away silent tears.
This night how can I sleep?
What is it that the moonlight shows to so break my heart?
The worst is that they revel and feast in Zhaoyang Palace as before.
These years, I've tasted every kind of sorrow.
One cannot find a place sorrow has left alone.
I would write out my cares and send them to Chang E
(8) To ask: Would she let me live with her in her cold palace?

(XTLS: *Qi xiang ge ci*, 1/10b)

line 4: The Zhaoyang Palace was the residence of Flying Swallow Zhao, on whom see P.1.

lines 7–8: On Chang E, see P.21.1; on her "cold palace," see P.26.5.

P.80.2. Yuzhong hua: *Rising at Dawn*

Swallows' twitters and orioles' sweet cries
Don't let the lady behind the woven screen sleep a wink.
Sun streams through the bamboo curtain.
My maids, meddlesome,
Again prepare the dressing table.

The incense cold, on the painted screen arched blue brows—
All are dispersed before the sallowness in the mirror.
In these ten years of sadness amid travel
I've filled a sack with poetry,
Yet can't turn these scrolls into teardrops on the flowers.

(XTLS: *Qi xiang ge ci*, 1/3b)

P.80.3. Lang tao sha: *Remembering My Female Companions in Our Old Garden*

The gauze canopy floats in the evening chill.
Autumn sounds fill every leaf.
The bamboo shadows move, the north window brightening.
I am too lazy to trim the silver lamp; it lets blossoms fall.
White scrolls are scattered everywhere.
What has startled my thoughts?
The mica screen from the old days:
A caged *luan*-bird and garden phoenix, so delightful.
When will the west wind send the dreaming butterfly
Flying above this melancholy realm?

(XTLS: *Qi xiang ge ci*, 1/11b)

P.80.4. Yan'er mei: *Early Evening*

A scar of new moon hangs among sparse *wutong* trees.
She stands east of the painted gazebo,
Lingering on alone,
Sad, without a word,
She watches the homing wild geese disappear.

A few sharp sounds of weeping ring out past the gazebo.
Clear dew drips from the fragrant foliage.
Her skirt is gradually soaked.
The scented comforter suddenly cold,
She can't withstand the autumn wind.

(XTLS: *Qi xiang ge ci*, 1/11b)

P.80.5. Man jiang hong

Cutting colored silk into flowers,
I've arranged an imaginary palace,
Unfolding the shapes of flying dragon and dancing phoenix,
Blue paulownia and tall bamboo.
Behind closed doors I'll add tonight's strands,
Laying down the needle to soak millet for the morning.
By now, I have surrendered to eternal poverty.
It could make me cry.

The silken thread of the spring cocoon
Is difficult to spin.
The sun at the western hill,
A breeze blows out the lamp.
I laugh at the illusions of this floating life,
The scenario of the deer and brushwood.
Through my long illness I've not sought medicine
From the divine rabbit.
Idle, I arrange old letters and books,
My wrist moving without a pause.
The pen feels just as heavy as a beam.
I ask my son to write this out.

(XTLS: *Qi xiang ge ci*, 1/15a–b)

line 9: The play on the homophones *si* "silk" and *si* "thoughts" carries through the second stanza.

line 14: The expression "brushwood and deer" derives from a parable in *Liezi*. A man poached a deer, hiding his game in a dry lake bed under some branches. Unable to find his way back to his hiding place, he suspected he had been dreaming, but when he told the story, an onlooker followed his account and found the deer. The first man pressed charges, but the judge said only that the onlooker might well have hidden the deer himself, and that it was fruitless to differentiate dream from reality (*Liezi* 3/107–8). A Ming drama is also recorded with the title *Jiaolu meng* (Brushwood and deer dream; author Che Renyuan).

lines 15–16: The hare in the moon perpetually pounds Chang E's elixir of immortality.

BIOGRAPHICAL NOTE AND TRANSLATION BY KATHRYN LOWRY

吴巽

P.81. Wu Xun (1693–1735)

"Daoxian's poems are balanced, refined, and solemn, just as she was as a person. . . . They bear no 'traces of face-powder.'" Such was the assessment of Wu Xun's contemporary editors.[1] Wu, whose courtesy name was Daoxian, was a gentry woman of Jiaxing (Zhejiang province). Her poems express a strong sense of personal history and attachment to her own and her husband's families. Some of her contemporaries considered her the best woman poet in Zhejiang.[2] Her collection *Tinghonglou shigao* (Poems from the Tower for Listening to Wild Geese) survives in a posthumous 1736 edition. Wu wrote almost exclusively in the *shi* form. Only 7 of 172 poems in her collection are *ci*.[3] Her poems are learned, with many allusions to past poetry. Her "Elegy for My Mother," with its 1,460 characters (292 pentasyllabic lines), was considered a tour de force by Qing anthologists.

P.81.1. On a Winter Day While Living in a Village, I Read Tao Yuanming's Line, "The right month, the right day have come around again," and Expanded It into a Poem

The right month, the right day have come around again,
I'm staying in the village amid remnants of the year.
When I mend clothes, the dawn light is warm,
As I weave silk, the night lamp is chill.
The lot of the chaste is disregard and difficulty
But together with my children in poverty
    I am at peace.

My purse is empty, but I forget to be ashamed of it—
(8) I don't even keep a single coin for show.

(QSBC, 31/30a)

Tao Yuanming's poem celebrates the Double Ninth festival (on which see P.11.4); see "Jiu ri xianju," in Lu Qinli, ed., *Tao Yuanming ji*, p. 39.

P.81.2. Hearing Wild Geese

A line of them approaches
  like the frets of a *zheng* harp,
Every sound as sad as the twang of Southern strings.
I wish I had wings to fly away with them:
Even meeting the highest peaks,
  I swear I would never turn back.

(QSBC, 31/30b)

line 4: On "Returning-Goose Peak," beyond which geese were not supposed to fly, see P.9.1.

P.81.3. The Pavilion at the Lake's Heart

We've come to this pavilion for surpassing scenery:
A world forms, transcendent and separate.
Morning clouds emerge from among rafters,
Spring waters are level with the steps.
Misty grasses line the islet banks,
On lakeside hills, roads are half ramparts.
Just as I forget that our oars
  have been stopped a long time,
(8) I look down and am overwhelmed.

(Ruan Yuan, comp., *Liangzhe youxuan lu*, 40/43b–44a)

P.81.4. Passing My Old Home at South Village

When will I set out in a skiff for Sanxiang?
My head is white, yet I haven't ceased roaming passes and rivers.
It's lonely, that streamside house amid plum blossoms:
It has stopped loving spring—to it, the same as fall.

(*Liangzhe youxuan lu*, 40/44a)

P.81.5. In Autumn of the Year Guichou *[1733], Concubine Chen Bore a Son. At That Time My Husband Was Already Forty. I Wrote This to Record Our Joy.*

In poverty and ill luck, we have trusted in our ancestors' grace,
Since morning now, bow and arrow mark our happiness on the gate.
Alas, his mother and father have turned to morning dew
And never got to see a fine grandson.

(QSBC, 31/30b)

line 2: "On the birth of a child, if it is a boy, a bow shall be affixed to the left of the gate; if a girl, a handkerchief shall be affixed to the right of the gate" (*Li ji*, "Nei ze," [Records of ritual: Domestic regulations], SSJZS, 28/11b).

BIOGRAPHICAL NOTE AND TRANSLATION BY CAROL R. KAUFMANN

侯承恩

P.82. Hou Cheng'en (fl. ca. 1722)

Hou Cheng'en (courtesy name Xiaoyi, sobriquet Sigu) was a musician and poet from Jiading, Jiangsu (near present-day Shanghai). The *Zhengshi ji* notes: "Sigu was bright when very young. While still in pigtails, she made the couplet, 'Sadness swells in the moonlit night / One wastes away in the blossom-dropping days.'"[1] She learned from her father to be a sharp chess player and was a skilled performer on stringed instruments such as the *qin*.

Her poetry consists of two collections, *Penshan cichao* (Bonsai Mountain song-lyrics) and *Songyun xiao cao* (Pine and bamboo scribblings),[2] totaling eight *juan*. The poetry anthology *Lianyin chuji* observes that Hou's "poems mostly consist of 'sadness for the reds and grieving for the green' [that is, the passing of spring's beauties]. One is left lamenting her [unrealized] ambitions." The poet Shen Shanbao (fl. early nineteenth century) remarked that she was especially good at the short *xiaoling* form.[3]

P.82.1. Yijian mei

In no mood to make up, I linger in my room alone,
Sadness in my heart,
  Sadness on my brow.
Smartweed breezes blow cold and sere.

About to drop the curtain hook,
Too tired to drop the curtain hook.

The mixed scent of flowers drifts quietly:
Too lazy to play the *qin*,
  Too lazy to wield the brush.
Sun sets west, river flows east,
I fear hearing the clock
  But keep nearing the clock.

(GXCC, 8/13b; Su Zhecong, 435–36)

P.82.2. Venting Feelings

I would now consign ten thousand things to Emptiness,
But when would I tell about the things I love and cherish?
This spring's flower-messages will soon be gone,
Half my life over and never rid of ill-health.
I don't like all this blossoming—
  Stay out of my dreams!
In purity and silence only,
  I spread out my books.
My family's very style is in their green cases.
When I am with the relics of their hands,
  Happiness overflows of itself.

(GGZSJ, 8/8a)

line 9: The expression "green case" is used to refer to a family's tradition of scholarship handed down from generation to generation. It stems from the erudite Jin dynasty statesman Wang Biaozhi (d. 377), who is said to have recorded his family's history and recent anecdotes and sealed these records in a green case, to be passed on.

P.82.3. Dao lianzi

Spring dreams far,
Late fall cold,
Drooping lotus flowers still smell good.
He is away at the sky's very edge:
  The sun is closer,
So sadly I stand wordless
  in its setting light.

(GXCC, 8/12b)

P.82.4. Dao lian zi

Love pulsing,
Thoughts roaming,
Petals whirl down as water rushes on.
Spring birds never came,
  And now the spring is gone.
I stay quietly despairing in my room.

(GXCC, 8/12b)

P.82.5. Xi jiang yue

Innumerable stars fill the sky above,
While in the human world, ten thousand pipings are stilled.
Suddenly I hear the clear clapper of the third watch.
Moonlight calms and cools through the gauze screen.

Feelings are as deep as the sea
And I lament my fate, thin as ice.
Alas! When will I fly up to blue clouds?
(8) Grief! I wake from a dream in guttering lamplight.

(GXCC, 8/13a)

P.82.6. Yu meiren

The New Year passed three months ago,
  leaving fragrant grasses.
The gate is shut, passersby few.
Elusive fragrance is fading
  from my berry trellis.
But in this seclusion butterflies
  still grace the breezes.

I've thrown down my poems
  to cherish the passing spring,
One can't buy a stop for time.
Up the tower I go, feeling cold and alone,
(8) And see only pairs of mandarin ducks
  happily splashing in a lotus pool.

(GXCC, 8/13b)

BIOGRAPHICAL NOTE AND TRANSLATION BY CAROL R. KAUFMANN

P.83. The Sisters Zhang Xueya and Zhang Xuedian

Zhang Xueya (style name Gushi) was a native of Taiyuan in Shanxi province and the eldest of the official Zhang Yi's seven famous literary daughters. Her superior talents, it seems, were predestined, for according to her biography in the *Guixiu cichao*, she may have been a banished immortal. While pregnant with Xueya, her mother dreamed that a Daoist priest came to her and told her that an immortal Flower-Scattering Jade Lady had mistakenly broken a vase in the heavenly halls. The Jade Lady had subsequently been banished to the Zhang household and would have to be looked after with great care.

Xueya was born shortly thereafter and indeed exhibited certain traits of an immortal. She ate neither meat nor strong foods and developed her literary talents to a remarkable degree. She wrote both prose and poetry, but excelled in song-lyrics, and was known for her ability, even in the harshest of environments and even when she was ill and dying, to grind fresh ink, take up her brush, and lose herself in her work.

In Xueya's twenty-second year, when she was betrothed but as yet unmarried, her mother again dreamed that the Daoist priest came to her. This time the monk told her that the Jade Lady had fulfilled her period of banishment. At noon of the following day, Xueya died. It is said that she was with her books on the day of her death.[1]

Xueya's younger sister Xueyi collected drafts of her poems and published them in a volume entitled *Xiu yu cao* (Drafts written after the needlework is done).

The career of Zhang Yi's fourth daughter, Zhang Xuedian (style name Guzheng), while somewhat less spectacular, is far less melancholy. Unlike her eldest sister who died young and unmarried, Xuedian became the wife of Yang Yiting from Wu prefecture, had two sons, and lived to the impressive age of seventy-five. Although she is mainly known for her poetry and song-lyrics, she also painted. When hard times beset her family, she tutored her two sons and is credited with their eventual success in official careers.[2]

The seven sisters appear to have been close, as evidenced by Zhang Xuedian's quatrain "Feelings About My Late Sister's Former Abode" (P.83b.1). A further illustration of this closeness is the last poem translated in this section (P.83b.7), a joint composition by the youngest four of the Zhang sisters, including Xuedian's twin sister, Xuexiang.

張學雅

P.83.a. Zhang Xueya (18th century)

P.83a.1. Huan xi sha: *A Spring Day*

Idle in the quiet yard, not even opening door leaves;
Hope chest fragrant, accumulating old silk clothes, in vain.
The greens deepen, the reds fade, regrets linger on.

Arising from sleep, the fragrant crab apple dream completed;
Beyond the curtain, peonies in a faint haze obscured.
Spring arrives, spring departs; eternally elusive.

(GXCC, 1/1b)

P.83a.2. Huan xi sha

Toward evening, make-up completed, too languid to emerge from the curtain;
Listlessly pacing, facing the mirror, knitting worried brows.
Self-pity—joys are few; what's plentiful is sorrow.

When flowers sported with shadows in the courtyard, it was noontime;
Where there were startling cries of birds, the sun sank in the west.
Upon awakening, I found dreams already hard to trace.

(GXCC, 1/1b)

P.83a.3. Man jiang hong: *Spring Scenery*

A high tower room surrounded by mist,
The light of dawn begins to shine on the courtyard of weeping willows.
Powder-white butterflies and yellow bees pass beneath the flowers—
A glorious moment in which to revel.
While fledgling swallows learn to fly, orioles grow old;
Flowers and grasses without end—my heart, vainly, breaks.
On red paper, I write of resentment,
(8) In tiny script, speak of sorrows,
Wielding a sandalwood brush.

At the gauze-covered window I keep silence;
Books are my companions.
Beyond my balustrade
The red dust is in chaos.
There at the pond, the grass is long;
Mist and waves merge at its banks.
Idly I sit in my orchid chamber behind embroidered hangings;
Beyond the wall I only hear the cries of hidden birds.
They say that of ten parts of spring scenery, nine parts have vanished,
Which only adds to my longing.

(GXCC, 1/2b)

lines 7–9: Red note paper was commonly used for writing poetry of love and longing.

line 13: "Red dust" is a Buddhist term for the mundane world.

line 16: "Orchid chamber" is a conventional phrase for the women's quarters.

P.83a.4. Sheng zhazi

Waking from a dream, the candle askew;
Why this incessant renewal of tears?
The clear night just goes on and on;
The green flame burns the candle's heart till it breaks.

Behind embroidered bed curtains, a cold incense burner;
Fragrant and smooth, the mandarin duck quilt.
Too listless to remove my jade hair ornaments,
I curl up and sleep in my clothes.

(GXCC, 1/3a)

P.83a.5. Pusa man: *Willow Floss*

Flying cotton is strewn on the roads, but no news.
Riding the wind, floss covers all the southeast paths.
Here, inside this small pavilion, I've nothing to do;
It fills the sky like snow blown about in the wind.
Sorrow leaves me too listless to roll up the pearl-sewn curtain.
Adrift without direction, their floating tracks remote.
Timidly dancing, they dot the little pond,
Like duckweeds' floating green, as far as the eye can see.

(GXCC, 1/3a–b)

Floating duckweed is traditionally used as an image of wanderers, usually men. Willow catkins, on the other hand, traditionally symbolize fragile women who are prey to the whims of fate (see P.35.2 and C.24.1).

P.83a.6. Die lian hua: *Night Rain*

Gate covered with green moss, a spring full of loneliness;
Nightfall's rain blows desolate,
Curtaining the window with drops.
In the small courtyard at dusk, someone stands alone;
A pair of flying birds hurry back to their nest.

For ten thousand miles the Xiao and Xiang are soaked with clouds and mist;
Beyond the curtain, sounds of the wind—
(8) It must be blowing through reeds.
My heart breaks and the plum blossoms accompany my weeping,
Then I'm startled at midnight by a flute from the high tower.

(GXCC, 1/3b)

line 6: The Xiao and Xiang Rivers in Qu Yuan's southern homeland are associated with goddesses; see P.11.16 and P.74.3.

P.83a.7. Idly Chanting in My Chamber

Bamboo courtyard, the wind's soughing, empty of human words;
Last night's wind and rain came with harsh urgency.
At dawn I lean alone against the balustrade,
Idly counting what red lotus blossoms remain on the pond.

(GGZSJ, 5/8b)

P.83b. Zhang Xuedian (18th century)

P.83b.1. Feelings About My Late Sister's Former Abode

Embroidered web, a spider's thread, mirror filled with dust;
Idle flower in disarray, oblivious of the spring.

Renewed grief; afraid to see the swallows in the eaves;
Yet still there's chirping as they seek the mistress of the house.

(GGZSJ, 5/9b)

This famous seven-character quatrain was most probably written in memory of Zhang Xueya.

P.83b.2. Huanxisha: *Hearing Geese from My Autumn Chambers*

In the courtyard, spread about, bushels of fallen leaves;
Calling repeatedly, winter geese rise up from river sandbars,
Shattering my butterfly dream of wandering back home.

This green willow withered and spare—such a pity;
The yellow flower worn and haggard—it can't endure the autumn.
I stare upward—paired shadows fill my gaze.

(GXCC, 1/5a–b)

line 6: "Paired shadows" are lines of migrating geese.

P.83b.3. Sumu zhe: *On the Autumn Magnolias, in Reply to My Husband*

Tenderness unfolds into red;
Light, the clean-cut green.
Brushing on new make-up;
A kind of natural allure.
Faint mist of rouge gives shape to a night's intoxication.
Strength sapped, leaning upon the railing;
From fragrant dreams, just now startled awake.

(8) Reflecting faint rose-colored clouds
Surrounded by morning mist
Delicate form, harboring love-thoughts
Wanting to speak, yet too shy to voice them—
(12) Indeed, she's a match for the cinnabar cassia-tree in the moon!
A night of autumn wind
Is blowing toward and building up upon the jasper steps.

(GXCC, 1/5b)

line 12: On the mythical flora and denizens of the moon, see P.26.5.

P.83b.4. Die lian hua: *Two Song-Lyrics Written in Fun About Sixth Sister Flying a Butterfly Kite*

I

With sleeves drawn back, slender jade fingers grasp a thread.
A newly made garment of cloud
Oh-so-slowly rises, stretches into space.
I seem to see the return of Consort Zhao's fragrant soul—
Demoted by the Eastern Lord to a Flower-Seeker's post.

Obliquely chasing the wandering bee, it traverses the willow courtyard;
Weary, the embroidered beauty
(8) Mistakenly strikes a light silk fan,
Floats off by herself, fluttering; the spring pays no heed.
Uselessly, the passionate one blames the eastern wind.

II

Lacking in strength, yet deftly grasping the delicate thread,
On powdered wings it flies with swiftness and ease.
I'm afraid it will follow where the eastern wind leads.
A beginner at chasing fragrance, it passes the flowers by;
As if deceiving those jade beauties' gentle trust.

Light and flimsy, dancing like a willow catkin,
It appeared so suddenly, I doubted it was real.
(8) Then struck, into branch-tips falling:
Ah, now indeed Zhuangzi's mystic dream is broken.
The soul melts away, not knowing the road of spring's return.

(GXCC, 1/5b–6a)

"Sixth Sister" is Zhang Xuesheng, also a poet, whose works are listed in Hu Wenkai, p. 529. The song title, which translates as "Butterflies Lingering over Flowers," puns on the occasion. Compare the poem series on the same theme by Yang Wan, P.65.1.

i, lines 4–5: "The Eastern Lord," sometimes embodied as the sun, is the Lord of Spring. On the title "Flower-Seeker" (here, as so often elsewhere, used for its decorative quaintness) see P.73.7. Consort Zhao is Flying Swallow Zhao (on whom see P.1), called upon here for her nickname as well as her slimness and agility in dancing.

i, line 9: Kite strings were often broken and kites allowed to fly free at the end of a day's sporting with them.

ii, line 9: On Zhuang Zhou's dream of being a butterfly, see P.41.6.

P.83b.5. Pusa man

Distant smoke encompassing green, unfurling new willows;
Spring light muted, lingering in the tower.
Don't push the embroidered curtains open;
The east wind lets sorrow in.

Converging with mountains, a sheet of clouds;
But he is beyond those clouds and mountains.
Fragrant grasses like parting emotions
(8) Converging with spring, rising up all around.

(GXCC, 1/5b–6a)

P.83b.6. Sending a Letter

Wanting to send a letter,
I hesitate, staring at my brush's tip.
Afraid to add to the sorrow of parting,
I'm hard put to release what's pent up inside.
The words in Su Hui's loom,
The phoenix in Qin Jia's mirror—
All this to send so far, and yet on a single sheet of paper.
(8) How to bring comfort and say: "eat more"?

(GXCC, 1/9a)

lines 5–6: On Su Hui and her woven palindrome poem, see C.1.1 and C.4.1. On the poems and gifts exchanged by Qin Jia and his wife, Xu Shu, see P.54a.4. On the phoenix in the mirror, see P.11.15.

line 8: The first of the "Nineteen Old Poems," cast in the form of a wife's letter to her husband, closes with a tender injunction to "make an effort to eat more" (*Wen xuan* 29/2a).

P.83b.7. Linked Verse by the Four Youngest Zhang Sisters, Recorded by Zhang Xuedian: Enjoying the Moon and Composing Linked Verses with My Sisters

Fourth Sister Xuedian:
Clouds disperse, the empty emerald sky stretches on endlessly;
Fifth Sister Xuexiang:
Together we savor clear luminosity, walking winding corridors.
Below the steps colors congeal, pearl-like cowries are cold;
Sixth Sister Xuesheng:
Before the curtain brilliant light is reflected, crystal is cool.
Chanting like the Xie girl, we compete at linked verse;
Seventh Sister Xuexian:
Gazing far at Chang E, we do not raise our goblets,
But distantly recall the Guanghan Palace in the Moon,
Fourth Sister Xuedian:
And the lingering strains of the fairy "Feathered Robe" song.

(GXCC, 1/9a–b)

In linked verse, one person leads off with the first line of a couplet and the next participant is expected to complete the first couplet and add the first line of the next couplet. One rhyme is preserved throughout the series. For a description of linked verse in action, see Cao Xueqin, *Hong lou meng*, chap. 50 (Hawkes, trans., *Story of the Stone*, 2: 488–94).

Sixth Sister, line 2: The Xie girl is the talented Xie Daoyun, on whom see C.24.1.

Seventh Sister, line 1: On Chang E, the immortal who lives in the moon, see P.21.1. The Tang poet Li Bo, in his celebrated poem-sequence "Drinking Alone Beneath the Moon," did raise his glass.

Seventh Sister, line 2: Guanghan Gong is the lunar Palace of Great Chill.

Fourth Sister: The "Song of the Feathered Robe" is said to have originated in the Moon Palace and was taught to the consort Yang Guifei (on whom see P.18.12) when she journeyed there in a dream. The implication here is that the Zhang sisters, like Yang Guifei, are also fairies who have for some reason been banished to this world.

BIOGRAPHICAL NOTE AND TRANSLATION BY MARY ELLEN FRIENDS

徐映玉

P.84. Xu Yingyu (ca. 1720–50)

Xu Yingyu (style name Ruobing, sobriquets Nanlou and Xiangxi) was a versatile poet who wrote on a wide variety of themes in both *shi* and *ci* forms. The classical scholar Shen Dacheng (1700–1771) edited her posthumously published collection *Nanlou yin gao* (Poems from South Tower, 1758; second printing 1765) in two *juan*.[1] Xu was acquainted with famous women poets of her time and with the circle of Jiangsu scholars surrounding the linguist and poet Wang Chang (1725–1806). In a preface to Xu Yingyu's work, Wang noted that she exchanged poems with Xu Deyin and Fang Fangpei (1728–1808) and expressed his admiration of women poets such as Xu for forming poetic relationships far outside their clans. Wang also pointed out that Xu wrote many poems "following the rhymes" of other poets; he called the device of using other poets' rhymes a sign of refinement and modesty but praised her poetry as never diffuse or vague.[2] Critics considered Xu's poem "Sending Off My Younger Brother Yunting to Qinzhong" as approaching the High Tang style.[3]

P.84.1. Sending Off My Younger Brother Yunting to Qinzhong

Look, look—how far it is, Qin Pass!
I know you will miss our parents.
A thousand mountains ring the Purple Pass
As with a single horse you enter red dust.
Trees of Gansu keep their leaves in the cold,
Sand of the borders is warm without spring.
Bitter and hard are the chants of the hills,
No comfort to those left behind.

(GGZSJ, 9/11a–b)

Qinzhong is in Shanxi province.

line 3: The Purple Pass is a point in the Great Wall, marking the transition between China and the "outside."

P.84.2. Shaonian you: *Sent to Madame Yunqing*

You would not stay your rippling steps
  to write a poem on my lapels—

The sail of the boat flapped desolately.
By the snow-fishing riverbank,
Beside the path at Hanging Rainbow Bridge:
All lovely scenes had entered your pure chanting.

How will I see again your wavy cloud tresses,
  your dark and curving brows?
Thinking of you sets my heart at ease.
(8) When persimmon leaves brighten
  or plum trees flower,
I'll seek you again in dreams.

(GXCC, 2/12a)

Madame Yunqing was Xu Yuzhen, a secondary wife of Wang Chang.

P.84.3. Cai sang zi: *Inscribed on a Painting*

Oh, to live in the halls and towers of the immortals' hills!
If we can't ride cloud-carts,
Then we'll ascend a spirit raft
Or mount a dark roc to play with colored mists.

Moss on white stone: the grotto door undisturbed.
Waters and mist spring from the brinks,
Moon and wind, the glories of the season,
(8) Beloved companions forming pairs
To sweep up the falling flowers.

(GXCC, 2/12a)

P.84.4. Double Seventh Eve

The Silver River hangs aslant,
  the water clock presses;
Needles are threaded on a single strand,
  fruits offered on the table—
In one night they must recount a whole year apart
What time do they have to send us skill?

(GGZSJ, 9/11b)

On the rituals surrounding Double Seventh Eve, see P.5.1 and P.19.2. The Silver River is the Milky Way.

P.84.5. Dian jiang chun: *The Day After New Year's*

As I huddle near the clothes warmer,
Who among my old friends is thinking of me now?
Clear frost, the moon high in the sky,
Snow-fragrance on a lonely hill road.

Spring came to Wuchang
  but the East Wind delayed it.
The gauze window darkens.
In the courtyards, the lamps are dying out;
(8) I wrap my hair against the driving rain.

(GXCC, 2/11b–12a)

BIOGRAPHICAL NOTE AND TRANSLATION BY CAROL R. KAUFMANN

P.85. Cai Wan (1695–1755)

Cai Wan (courtesy name Jiyu), from Liaoning, was a poet and scholar concerned with political affairs. Her father was General Cai Yurong (1633–99), a hotheaded man who quelled many rebellions in his eventful career. Her mother was reputedly a former concubine of the rebel Wu Sangui, against whom General Cai had fought. Cai was married to Baron Gao Qizhuo (1676–1738), who held various governorships and governor-generalships in southern China. He was noted as a poet and writer, but Cai is said to have helped him compose official letters and memorials.[1] Her poetry collection in two *juan*, titled *Yunzhen xuan xiaocao* (A little draft from the Latent-Truth Studio), was compiled by her grandchildren and great-grandchildren and published in 1799.[2] Her poetry contains many allusions to the Classics as well as to previous poetry. Many of her poems celebrate her father's military exploits in southern China.

P.85.1. Chenlong Pass

A single path climbs precipitously, lonely and lost,
Pass upon pass locks winter mists in stillness.
The loyal men of that time live on, hair gone gray;
Battlefields deserted in autumn, they hunt outside the ramparts.

I've heard there were ten thousand men following his horse,
That birds of prey plummeted from the sky
  all through the sixth month.
Now soldiers' tears have dried on memorial slabs—
(8) Broken, moss-covered, mounded with forty years of dirt.

(GGSC, 2: 1/4a; Su Zhecong, 406)

lines 5–6: According to Su Zhecong, Cai Wan is here recalling her father's exploits.

P.85.2. Jiangxi Hill

Like arrowheads and swordpoints, the peaks for a thousand miles
Once pressed upon a myriad of cavalry
  as they clambered up sheepgut paths.
Ghost lights flash, bits of congealed green blood,
White poplars whistle over desolate wilderness graves.
—My dream interrupted, layers of indifferent clouds rise,
Such matters have disappeared with water flowing;
Now there remain only old foot soldiers
(8) Pointing out former battlegrounds
  on the bare mountains.

(GGSC, 2: 1/4b; Su Zhecong, 407)

P.85.3. White Swallows [second of two poems]

With new looks, you came from the distant Coral Sea
  in time for the blooming of the pear.
Spring is not cold, of course,
  but here is dancing snow!
If your body could be transformed,
  it would be congealed cream:
Amid the close shadows of pearl curtains,
  I could hardly see you fly.
I only heard your call
  in the deep shade of the fairy-stone tree,
Reckoning your return to immortals' halls,
  you must have been surprised how late it is;
Flutter, flutter—you flew slowly onto
  my jade hairpin.

(GGSC, 2: 1/5b–6a)

line 1: The Coral Sea refers to the strait between Guangdong province and Hainan Island, in China's far south; Hainan was once known as Coral Island.

line 5: "Fairy stone" is a white precious stone.

P.85.4. *Relaxing Among the Pines*

Getting old amid fine scenery, I'm lazy and foolish:
New chess games, old music scores, all too hard to know.
I feel to preserve the body, an easy mind is best,
Avoiding vulgar things helps small ailments.
Amid evening breezes, I amble home on narrow paths,
Slowly climbing an embankment under a bright moon.
I've cleansed my heart completely of mundane cares,
Lean alone on a pine tree, and do nothing but chant poems.

(GGSC, 2: 1/6b)

P.85.5. *Moonlit Walk on the Autumn Plains*

The dew is cold and mists vanish into the empty sky,
Distant mountains are like brows,
  the moon like a bow.
Crickets chant slowly on the riverbank road,
Cicadas rhyme softly on the rustling branchtips.
A few snowflakes whiten the horizon;
In the brush, a glowworm trace gleams red.
If you, sir, are unable to rise, with whom will I go?
Don't let good timber be consumed as worthless kitchen fuel!

(GGSZJ, 5/2b–3a)

line 7: "Sir" is used here to translate the title *zhonglang*, "Palace Attendant" or "Adjutant"; without precise official reference here, it may be an honorific term of address for her husband. "Unable to rise": dead.

line 8: Cai Yong, father of Cai Yan (P.2), was a skilled lute player and had a famous lute that went by the name "Scorched-Tail." The story of the lute is this: once, while passing through a kitchen, Cai Yong heard the distinctive crackle of excellent *wutong* timber emanating from the fireplace. He rescued a partly burnt log and had a fine lute made from it ("Cai Yong liezhuan," *Hou Han shu*, 50b/2004). Cai Wan here speaks in the persona of the lute-to-be, asking an understanding listener to rescue it from the fire. Since the landscape details of the poem set it firmly in the genre of the "frontier poem," evoking the fears and homesickness of soldiers guarding China's northern borders, the last two lines are to be read as expressing concern that a soldier (Cai Wan's husband?) not lose his life pointlessly. The wastage of good timber in the kitchen fire may also suggest the unenviable fate of widowhood.

BIOGRAPHICAL NOTE AND TRANSLATION BY CAROL R. KAUFMANN

P.86. Ye Hongxiang (ca. 1636–1725)

Ye Hongxiang (style name Shucheng, "City-of-Books"), from Kunshan (Jiangsu), was one of the many widow-poets during the Ming-Qing who were admired both for their poetic talent and for their role as exemplary women. She was the daughter of Ye Hongshou, a *jinshi*, and married a government student named Kan Zongkuan. Her two younger sisters were also accomplished poets. Widowed before the age of thirty, she lived to the age of eighty-four. She was well known for her profound knowledge of the Chinese Classics and was particularly well versed in *shi* and *ci* poetry. Her *ci* collection *Xiuyu ci cao* (Song-lyrics composed after embroidering, 1721) was published in an elegant edition with a number of congratulatory prefaces by male and female colleagues and family members.[1] Unusually for a respected gentry woman, she chose to model her *ci* writing after the courtesan-poet Liu Shi (P.67), as may be seen from her *ci* sequence on *Wang Jiangnan*, also known as *Meng Jiangnan* ("Dream of the South"; compare Liu Shi's "Dream of the South" sequence, P.67.1).

P.86.1. Wang Jiangnan: *Two Lyrics*

I

Since his departure,
Alone I lean by the window gauze:
Too idle to sketch branch-intertwined trees in the painting book,
Too shy to needle twin flowers at the embroidery frame.
Recently sad thoughts have increased.

II

Since his departure,
Whom can I ask to deliver my brocade letter?
My heart follows the traveler to Rain Blossom Terrace,

My feelings are tied to the boat at Peach Leaf Ford;
All day long I feel depressed and weary.

(XTLS, 4/9b)

ii, line 4: On Peach Leaf and the Peach Leaf Ford on the Qiantang River, see P.47.5.

P.86.2. Huan xi sha: *Early Summer*

Roses in bloom fill the small yard with fragrance;
The plum rain has just cleared, butterflies are flitting busily.
In the brook's fresh emerald the mandarin ducks are bathing.

Tired from practicing calligraphy after old models all afternoon, I lean on my pillow.
Playing the jade lute at dusk, I feel cool in my light summer dress;
Resting on the parapet, I look afar: again the setting sun.

(XTLS, 4/10a)

P.86.3. Huan xi sha: *Inscribed on the Posthumous Works of the Female Scribe Yang Qianyu*

The twin stars are blown down, the wild goose returns alone;
A heartbreaking remnant of dream circles the flowering branches.
The west wind has forsaken the old silk curtains.

The eyebrow pencil cannot depict the shadow of a lonely smile;
Teardrops shed become dishevelled flying blossoms.
Trimming the lamp, I read Qianyu's *ci* through and through.

(XTLS, 4/10b)

P.86.4. Nan gezi: *Sent to Seventh Sister, Lady Zha*

In the pillared hall pure fragrance has drifted far;
The paulownia stairs float in the night.
As the door closes on a lone light, one sad person remains;
A few drops of cruel plantain rain drip onto her heart.

Wild goose shadows ice the misty trees;
Cricket sounds chill the emerald tower.
From afar the west wind sweeps on like a torrent,

(8) First blowing wan the reed catkins, then invading her autumnal temples.

(XTLS, 4/10a–b)

P.86.5. Ta suo xing: *In the Autumn Boudoir*

The cold geese cry slowly,
Hedge flowers match my embroidery,
A stretch of bleak autumn time.
I've leaned all along the curved railing looking towards the sky's edge;
Where the slanting sun drops, the green hills look gaunt.

The screen hides the silver bed,
Incense wisps spout from the golden beast burner;
(8) Banana shadows crowd the thin crepe curtain.
How can I bear the moonrise for one more evening
As sounds of dew drip from the leaking parasol?

(XTLS, 4/10b)

P.86.6. Pusa man: *At the Lantern Festival*

The willow treetop has just seen off the reunion moon;
Still I thought last night it was snow on the gauze window.
Alone I stand by the small railing;
Tonight is very cold.

Sadly I watch the lanterns, so picture-like;
I only hear the relentless water clock drip.
Swiftly passes the evening,
(8) As plum flowers keep the closed door company.

(XTLS, "Xuji," 3/15b)

line 1: The round moon symbolizes completeness by its shape; in addition, the New Year's season was a time when business was suspended and those posted to far places returned home.

P.86.7. Maoshan feng guren: *A Life of Leisure*

Spring chill and summer heat are just past,
And it's autumn wind and winter snow again.
Worldly affairs pass like clouds,

Time is like an arrow,
Sympathy like a leaf.

When I'm tired, sweet dreams come and seem real;
Waking up, I toy with books and sigh.
(8) No engaging in abstruse pursuit,
No meditation on Buddhist truth,
No talk about wind and moon.

(XTLS, "Xuji," 3/15b)

P.86.8. Xi jiang yue: *Just Past Thirty, Written to Amuse Myself*

Half my life has muddled past in grief;
Now all that's left is me.
Let people mock at my shabbiness;
Since youth I haven't desired fame or gain.

Even Heaven and Earth contain defects;
How can human life be perfect?
Do your part and peace will come of itself;
(8) Just bear with the fickleness of humanity.

(XTLS, "Xuji," 3/16a)

P.86.9. Qiu rui xiang: *Admiring Cassias in the North Garden*

Terrace trees, pavilion, pond, deep mansion;
Plums and bamboos, willows, pawlonias—all verdant and fresh.
Autumn wind and sparkling dew work so many changes
That the world is now a Palace of Great Chill.

Need there be heavenly fragrance sent down by the moon?
Leaning on the railing, I observe clumps of trees.
As sounds from the lute float in the silvery sky,
(8) The autumn hills have half yellowed.

(XTLS, "Xuji," 3/16a)

line 4: The palace in the moon; see P.26.5.

P.86.10. Chuanyan yunü: *Seeing Off Younger Sister Canying Leaving for Her Home Village*

Suddenly the west wind rises,
Shaking down a whole courtyard of cold emerald.
A line of wild geese disperses in fright,
Almost breaking one's tender heart.
I hold your hand and grasp your clothes,
My affectionate tears falling like beads of rain.
It is our lot to part,
But not to meet again.

You depart seeking glory,
All the honors of mankind.
Though in the thick of affluence,
I hope you will write to me.
Do not let this sad one
Watch until her gaze is blocked by clouds and trees at sky's edge.
—The same advice for each other,
But two distinct moods.

(XTLS, "Xuji," 3/16b)

P.86.11. Man jiang hong: *At Mid-Autumn of the Year* Bingyin *[1686], Seeing the Moon After Rain*

I thought that at mid-autumn
The clouds would soon roll up and the rain end.
Now indeed I see the sky-aspiring willows
Suddenly heaped with beads of icy jade.
Shadows fall on the green parasol, their emerald feathers swaying;
Light floats on the cassias, wafting over their millet-golden flowers,
Yet on this night so charged with beauty
I am alone.

Within the gauze window
The lanterns shine;
Beyond the jade stairs
The cricket chirps.
I wonder why Chang E

Sleeps by herself.
How can I find the long bridge leading to the moon's palace
(16) Where pure breeze and purple mist dispel worldly dust?
Tonight I would stay in the Palace of Great Chill
And voice the tunes of my heart.

(XTLS, "Xuji," 3/16b)

BIOGRAPHICAL NOTE AND TRANSLATION BY KANG-I SUN CHANG AND CHARLES KWONG

賀雙卿

P.87. He Shuangqing (b. 1715)

Although she is hailed by many critics as the greatest woman author of song-lyrics in the Qing dynasty, He Shuangqing's background is obscure—so much so that her very existence is sometimes called into doubt.[1] The only source for details of her life and poetry is a work called *Xiqing sanji* (Random records from West-Green) by Shi Zhenlin (1693–ca. 1779), an otherwise little-known literatus who came into contact with He Shuangqing in her native district of Xiaoshan, in present-day Jiangsu.

According to Shi Zhenlin, Shuangqing (who appears in his work without a surname) was born into a family of lowly peasants. However, she showed intelligence and literary talent from an early age as she studied writing and poetry by eavesdropping on her uncle, who taught at the village school. She would exchange embroidery for poems, and her calligraphy was so fine that she could copy the *Lankavatara*, or *Heart Sutra*, on a leaf.[2] She grew up to be a beautiful young woman whose talent was entirely unappreciated by the people in her social milieu. When Shuangqing was eighteen, her family married her off to an illiterate farmer ten years her senior. She suffered much physical and emotional abuse from both her husband and her mother-in-law. Shuangqing appears in Shi's account as a paragon of feminine virtue. Though mistreated, she never complained but bore the abuses with equanimity, and while she suffered from recurring bouts of malaria, she was extremely forbearing and hardworking, both in the house and in the fields.

Shuangqing had the habit of writing poetry, especially song-lyrics, on leaves and flower petals; as a consequence her poems were extremely perishable—

at least until they attracted the attention and admiration of Shi Zhenlin and his circle of literati friends, who in various ways sought, copied, circulated, and made a cult of her poetry. A strong element of fetishization pervades Shi Zhenlin's narrative of Shuangqing and her poetry, but it was through his interest and efforts that her writings were preserved at all. Her surviving works consist of a mere fourteen song-lyrics (one, a misattribution, is not included in this count) and twenty or thirty *shi* poems, some of them fairly long old-style poems and others poem sequences. Her song-lyrics were later gathered together in a collection named *Xueya xuan ci* (Song-lyrics of Snow-Laden Studio) and included in Xu Naichang's *Xiao tan luan shi huike guixiu ci* (XTLS) anthology. Most of Shuangqing's song lyrics were circulated primarily in such collections of women's and Qing poetry and have thus been read separately from their original narrative context.

The power of her poetry derives from her consummate realization of personal emotion. Shuangqing writes about her experiences as a woman in a rural setting, reaching out from her physical and emotional isolation by seeking companionship and communication with both animate and inanimate objects of nature in her everyday life. Shi Zhenlindoes not provide an ending to Shuangqing's story, for he left Xiaoshan in 1736 to take the imperial examination in Beijing, and Shuangqing disappeared from his concerns. Yet—both rescued by and rising above his narrative frame—Shuangqing's song-lyrics break the silence culture and society imposed on those of her class, reaching countless readers across boundaries of time and place.

P.87.1. Fenghuangtai shang yi chuixiao: *Fading Lamp*

Already dimming—I forget to blow on it;
Were it to shine brightly, who would trim it?
Flameless in front of me, glowing like a firefly.
I listen to the cold rain on the earthen steps
Dripping through the third night watch,
Alone by myself, sick and sleepless.
Hard to extinguish—
(8) You too are excessive in feeling.
The scented oil is finished,
But your fragrant heart has not cooled,
Do keep company with Shuangqing for a while.

Star after star
Gradually fades into motionlessness.
But I hope you will suffer through,
And then blossom forth again.
You will surpass those fishing lamps swaying
In the chaotic wind on the wild pond.
When autumn's hard-working moths scatter,
I am already ill,
And when has my illness ever diminished?
Long we watch each other,
Vaguely sleep comes upon me . . .
From sleep I am startled awake again.

(XTLS: *Xueyaxuan ci*, 2b–3a)

P.87.2. Chun cong tian shang lai: *Taking Food to Do Spring Plowing*

Purpled paths bright in spring weather.
Slowly I tie a spring gauze on my head,
And eat by myself during spring plowing.
The small plum tree is thin in spring,
Fine blades of grass glisten in spring.
At each step along the fields spring comes to life.
I remember that year in a fine spring
To a spring swallow
I blurted out spring feelings.
And now,
I think spring letters and spring tears
Have all melted with the spring ice.

I cherish spring, dote on spring—for how many more springs?
By an expanse of spring mist
The spring oriole is locked in.
You present gifts to a springtime me,
And I offer presents to a springtime you:
Am I or are you the spirit of spring?
You can count the start and end of spring,
But it will be hard to tell my spring awakenings from spring dreams.

Why does the spring demon
Make a whole spring of spring sickness?
Spring has misled Shuangqing.

(XTLS: *Xueyaxuan ci*, 4b–5a)

P.87.3. Er lang shen: *Chrysanthemums*

Strand on strand of frail willows,
Swaying gently, breaks through the light mist as before.
I turn toward the shadows of autumn hills in the setting sun,
And rejoice that the flowers' stems have not withered.
Incessant rain they have endured past the Double Ninth,
And fortunately survived to the time of Small Spring.
Knowing that tonight will be dipped in light frost,
The butterflies go off, leaving them to droop their heads alone.

Taking in the hardships:
When new chill penetrates the bones
And illness comes once again.
Is it that I, Shuangqing, am heartless,
Casting you aside after the dusk turns quiet?
Moonlight chills the railing and I am sleepless—
For many nights now you have not loosened your golden clasps.
I wrongly neglected you when you blossomed for a poor household;
Now that I want to water the site of sorrow, I have no wine.

(XTLS: *Xueyaxuan ci*, 1b–2a)

P.87.4. Gu luan

Noon shivers are unfairly punctual:
Early the malarial symptoms appear,
So I put on another green-colored jacket.
With no desire to comb out yesterday's braids,
I hastily tie a kerchief to tidy my side locks.
Too busy with work to wash my plain skirt:
Along its wrinkled pleats
The torn threads are frayed on both sides.
My white wrists seen close up are rough and calloused,
But these fragrant cheeks are still soft and young.

I deem my whole life wretched—but I'll bear it to the bitter end
Even if I turn into powder and ash.
I foresaw this when I married:
Beautiful thoughts and romantic feelings,
All would be suffocated in cooking smoke.
In the eastern field they only complain that the meal is brought late.
The chills return,
But no one asks about my fever.
I return to fetch the cotton quilts being sunned,
And it's almost time to cook the evening meal again.

(XTLS: *Xueyaxuan ci*, 2a)

P.87.5. Xi huanghua man: *A Stray Wild Goose*

Emerald spreads to the end of the distant sky,
Only rosy dusk clouds scattering their fine silk—
Snipped into fragments of fresh red.
When I listen, I worry that it's so nearby,
When I gaze, I dread its being far away:
One lone wild goose—
To whom can it turn?
White frost has already chilled the sandbar's reed flowers,
So don't even ask the gulls and egrets for sympathy.
In the dark, sleep alone.
Though the phoenix may be fine,
When is there ever a bond with it?

Mournful, I have no words to encourage you;
Go along a sandy shore or halfway up a stream
Just to pass the fleeting years.
With the rice grains recently exhausted,
The fowler's nets cannot wait;
Your dream-soul is easily frightened
Many times in the cold mist.
Is your grief like a woman's?
In that tiny heart there is so much tender attachment.
The night is not yet quiet,
Yet, tired from flight, you make the mistake of resting in the flat field.

(XTLS: *Xueyaxuan ci*, 2a–b)

P.87.6. Chun cong tianshang lai: *Plum Blossom*

I laugh at my own sickliness.
I took a moment during the busy spring season
To visit the flowers' pointed buds.
The haggardness of my jade-like face
Has increased, but for whom?
Since my illness I have grown estranged from the flowers.
Now winter clothes have to be washed,
Yet spring waves are cold,
And my white wrists are soaked in grief.
A stubborn east wind
Uselessly blows cold fragrance for a moment
Beneath a wisp of a new moon.

With so much feeling it drops powder to fill the sky,
But it only brings trouble to Shuangqing,
In dreams trying to grasp it in vain.
I summon its soul with the butterflies
And wipe off tears for the orioles;
Deep in the night I secretly chant the *Lankavatara.*
I have beautiful lines lamenting spring,
Pain and bitterness,
Life and death are all sweet.
I pray for the flowers' years.
Bowing to Guanyin,
I pull out all the divining slips.

(XTLS: *Xueyaxuan ci,* 4a–b)

line 23: Guanyin is the goddess of mercy and compassion in popular Buddhism.

P.87.7. Huan xi sha

The warm rain falls unfeeling
  like scattered threads of silk.
A herd boy tucks a flower bud askew behind his ear
While taking new grains
  from the small field to the threshing floor.
Draw the water, plant the melons,
  but he gets mad—too early!

Bear the smoke, cook the millet,
he's mad again—too late!
The day is long and my body is
racked with aches and weariness.

(Shi Zhenlin, *Xiqing sanji*, 2/34)

"He" in this poem is probably Shuangqing's husband. See also the translations in Rexroth and Chung, *The Orchid Boat*, p. 67, and Choy, *Leaves of Prayer*, p. 217.

P.87.8. Wang Jiangnan

No sight of spring;
I've searched through west of the deserted bridge.
The pink that tints the dream
cheats the butterfly;
The dark green that locks in my grief
fools the oriole.
Deep regrets, best not to mention them again.

No sight of him;
The meeting that should be
is still denied to me.
(8) I salute the moon,
incense only troubles my sleeves.
You pity the flower,
but there are no tears to wet your shirt.
The mountains are far away and the sun is low.

(*Xiqing sanji*, 2/34)

P.87.9. On a Frog Set Free by Shi Zhenlin

Lotus leaves open as your multi-tiered pavilion
on the water's surface;
Their slight fragrance brings a joy that
soon turns to sorrow.
The gentleman immortal set you free
from the heartless net;
In the nighttime rain you say your thanks
from spring to fall.

Reflected in the water, you sit on your
  green ledge in solitary leisure;
Fed coarse greens, whether hot or bitter,
  dare you complain of hunger?
How then to affect your transformation into
  the Silver Moon Palace Toad?
After all you want to grow thin not plump,
  the easier to fly to the moon.

(*Xiqing sanji*, 2/38)

line 7: The reference is to the immortal toad that lives in the moon palace with (or, in some versions of the story, as) Chang E.

P.87.10. Yujing qiu: *Inscribed on a Portrait of Shuangqing Planting Melons*

Eyebrows half in a frown:
Springtime color is already faded,
And the old sorrow not yet gone.
A thin figure in the painting,
Ashamed to be seen but hard to avoid it.
New illness still hangs on,
The painter applies light rouge but in vain.
In the cool of the night
The moon shines brightly,
Chang E shows no blemish.
Green sleeves still bear the stains of tears;
The spot by the crab apple flower has been
Drenched with myriad drops.
I wonder why recently combing hair and getting dressed every day,
Fixing dishes salty or sour,
All seem too much trouble.
Powder and sweat in congealed fragrance
While she dips the light cloth in blue water
And wipes down the bamboo mat:
Who is there to recognize her
For a flower spirit in temporary exile?

(*Xiqing sanji*, 2/41)

P.87.11. *Nine Poems*

I

I cannot hope to burn incense and meditate in a cloistered temple,
My heart unrippled as a still clear pond.
Don't blame a starving swallow for bringing nest mud too late;
Who pities an ailing silkworm for spinning a flimsy cocoon?

II

This year torrents break forth from the autumn clouds.
To pay the new rent, I have pawned my skirt.
If I can save a quilt to protect you from the cold,
My heart will be like honey—how could I fault you?

III

Coiling and stitching hemp, I make a pair of shoes,
To ascend the western peak for wood tomorrow.
The sudden cold brings a night of gusty winds;
I implore them to blow my way instead of yours.

IV

In the chilly kitchen, smoke hangs heavy and damp over the room.
With the *wutong* trees all burned, the phoenix has no perch.
Alone I pick wild vegetables and wash them in the cold.
The chrysanthemum, though ill, still has to bear the frost.

V

My fate is thin and insubstantial as a cicada's wing.
I used to be as beautiful as the girl next door.
Would mother recognize me now
With my tired and sallow face, all its cheerful color gone?

VI

My heart is soaked through with springtime bitterness.
In my illness, sparse dreams easily fall into oblivion.
Having sold my few cheap hairpins for a dose of medicine,
I cut a poplar twig to fasten my hair, with water as a mirror.

VII

Mount Siping looms like a platform in the distance,
From where you, carrying cold firewood, descend many times.
On your return I urge you to get up a little later,
Though the sun is high, I privately bar outsiders from rousing you.

VIII

The chickens, sleeping in pairs, mock the phoenix who perches alone,
They fly in pairs as well, their purple crowns aligned.
The dim lamp wick now flares with green—perhaps an omen there?
If so, my humble stove is better to lean on than a balcony rail.

IX

I live in a simple house next to a wealthy establishment.
Incense smoke drifts down at night, rousing my sense of loss.
Opening my sleeves, I pour out these sad lines of autumn.
Withering grass, setting sun, I dream of roaming afar.

(*Xiqing sanji*, 3/7–8)

viii, line 3: The flaring of an oil lamp's wick was often seen as an auspicious omen.

P.87.12. Mo yu'r: *Thanking the Neighbor Girl Han Xi for Her Gift of Food*

Cheered by the end of the rains,
The evening clouds in the west appear;
Beyond the haze the chilly mountains look light blue.
Where strips of moss are dry, fragrant shoes can tread.
Sharp prints stay on the purplish mud still soft.
Clamor of people's voices:
I rush to go lean on the brushwood door
   vainly harboring deep deep desire.
My thoughts of you are all one strand
Spun from the new moon to the full,
Threaded with grief, strung with remorse,
   pearls of tears enough for one whole string.

After dusk, still warm and damp,
Who will sustain my struggle to breathe?

Through the small window the wind
shoots in like an arrow;
Springtime red, autumn white, heartless beauty;
Difficult to pick a bud like me.
Our next meeting is so far off.
I hear the heartbroken one
Has already received her lavish feast.
The sunset hurts the eyes;
Don't look to the horizon,
The horizon only shows a few cold clouds drifting apart.

(*Xiqing sanji*, 3/51–52)

P.87.13. Ten Poems on the Autumn Lotus

I

Waiting for a letter that doesn't come, I cry like the autumn locust,
My heart is like the plantain leaf tightly folded up.
My reclusive nature outlasts the frost, but the frost can't bear to come;
The plum has barely blossomed; the mum's in sturdy full bloom.

II

The mum's heart and the plum's soul understand each other;
At the setting sun when people retire, the egret returns.
Does the gentleman immortal want to worship the flower spirit?
You can use me to sacrifice at the shrine of the world's aggrieved
women.

III

The beauty's pure grievance, at dawn the cold wind blows,
Drops of dew hit the water, the resting fish coldly stares.
The heart of the lotus seed in autumn is bitterest of all;
If I cannot love the moonlight, whomever can I love?

IV

The moonlight looks like water, no butterflies in sight;
My remaining color almost gone, standing upright alone.
Night rains come again, breaking my red petals in pieces;
When the mermaid sees me, she cries her tear ducts dry.

V

Her tears exhausted, she will give up no more pearls;
The sins of a former life create this life's uncertainties.
One stalk consigned, ten thousand threads are broken;
In Jiangnan's seventh month the wild goose comes early.

VI

Among the clouds, a new wild goose; next to the moon, a lonely
person;
The caltrop competes to show up the water-lily's weakness.
Does the yellow oriole know how to pity the white egret?
The wild pond's poor flowers cannot compete with spring.

VII

Pale reflection, ashamed to face spring feelings in the mirror;
Like water the heart stirs, hard to find nighttime peace.
My leaves impede the fierce rain and flowers collect the dew;
Sweet protection of the mandarin duck's dream, is it cold or not?

VIII

The love-crazed duck without a dream grasps hold of spring;
One feels sadness before cassia buds and silver toad.
Repair all the five colors of West Lake's flowers;
Is my broken heart like Nü Wa's in her heaven?

IX

The five colors fill the heavens at lonely dusk,
Under the moon apply autumn powder mixed with tears.
Carefully gather flower petals, lightly, lightly roll them
Into fragrant tablets for burning by the bed curtain.

X

Fragrant tablets all burned, azure smoke abounds,
Fate as fickle as floating duckweed, no exaggeration.
From now on loving couples should not be parted;
I'll cut reds and tailor greens to mend the fisherman's net.

(*Xiqing sanji*, 4/41–42)

ii, line 1: The plum and chrysanthemum, cold-weather flowers that bloom at the opposite ends of winter, understand and sympathize with each other, but they do not understand the lonely lotus. Note the linked-verse style throughout these poems. The first line of each poem repeats one or more key terms from the last line of the previous poem.

v, line 1: The mermaid of the southern seas lives and spins under water; her tears are pearls. An alternative reading of this line could be "My tears are all exhausted, I'll give up no more pearls," meaning that it is too cold for the lotus's buds to open.

v, line 3: In reference to the many threads of a lotus root.

viii, line 2: Both the silver toad and the cassia tree are associated with Chang E's moon palace. The best moment for moon-gazing is the Mid-Autumn Festival, a season of sadness for the summer-blooming lotus.

viii, line 4: The goddess Nü Wa repaired the firmament with five-colored stones after it was damaged by fighting gods, and she propped up the sky with four pillars made from the legs of a giant turtle. However, the god Gong Gong later went on a rampage and broke one of the supports Nü Wa had built, so the firmament sags in the southeast corner (thus China's rivers all run toward the southeast). The suggestion here is that however much the five colors of West Lake may be restored, the lotus in autumn has no hope of returning to its former state.

ix, line 4: Flower petals and pollen were sometimes ground into powder and then mixed with water to be applied as a woman's make-up. Flower petals were also made into "fragrant tablets" to be burned in autumn or winter as a kind of incense.

BIOGRAPHICAL NOTE AND TRANSLATION OF POEMS P.87.1–6 BY GRACE S. FONG; TRANSLATION OF POEMS P.87.7–13 BY PAUL S. ROPP

徐元端

P.88. Xu Yuanduan (18th century)

Xu Yuanduan, whose school name was Yanxiang, was the daughter of Xu Shilin of Ganchuan in present-day Jiangsu; she married a scholar by the name of Fan Maocai. Her *Xiu xian ji* (Poems written in the intervals of embroidery) was chosen by Xu Naichang for his anthology *Xiao tan luan shi huike guixiu ci* (XTLS).[1]

P.88.1. Yu meiren: *Winter in the Boudoir*

I get up, lean on the dressing table languidly,
And fix my luxuriant hair up carelessly.
He promised to return when willows turn green—
Listless all day, I resent the late arrival of spring.

Last night the west wind howled in the garden
Bringing snow from the sky.
The maid feigns a smile as she rolls up the window screen,
(8) Telling me the white plums are in bloom.

(XTLS: *Xiu xian ji*, 4b)

P.88.2. Nan gezi: *Spring Mood*

Sitting alone, I count the days till his return.
In the depth of flowering shrubs, sun's shadow is low.
I pace back and forth, searching for a good line,
My chin in my hand—
There is no other topic than spring melancholy.

I lean on the railing in the west of the adorned boudoir.
Sweet green grass covers the old riverbank.
(8) I still remember when he left
We couldn't part—
A wine shop's banner flapped by red apricot flowers.

(Su Zhecong, 427)

P.88.3. Chongdie jin: *Spring Regrets*

Waking up to broad daylight, I sit with the bed curtain down,
Writing new poems—alas, no one matches them.
Lowering my head, I complain to the Lord of Heaven—
Why did he give me such an unhappy fate?
I ask Heaven, but Heaven does not reply.
I frown; there is so much grief in my heart.
With tears in my eyes, I stroke the zither strings—
(8) At the end of a tune, only the sound of a sigh is heard.

(XTLS: *Xiu xian ji*, 1b)

P.88.4. Bu suan zi: *Boudoir Thoughts*

At the beckoning of the flower season,
Blooming peaches and plums compete in beauty.
Hesitant to lean on the carved rail,
I dare not look at springtime.

I pick up an embroidering needle,
But already I've lost heart.
I call the maid to roll up the kingfisher curtain,
(8) Only to reveal a pair of swallows.

(XTLS: *Xiu xian ji*, 2a)

P.88.5. Mai hua sheng: *The End of Spring*

Counting the days, I fear spring is gone
And I frown.
Willow branches can't bind the setting sun—
Night is falling again,
Misty like a dream.

The chamber door closed, the curtains drawn.
I sit by the west window.
(8) The heartless lamp always deludes me—

Night after night it lights up a blossom in vain,
Leading me to think that spring has returned.

(XTLS: *Xiu xian ji*, 4a)

BIOGRAPHICAL NOTE AND TRANSLATION BY MICHELLE YEH

毛秀惠

P.89. Mao Xiuhui (fl. 1735)

Mao Xiuhui (courtesy name Shanhui) was an eighteenth-century gentry wife from Taicang in Jiangsu province. She was a talented painter and the wife of a tribute student named Wang Su, who was also a skilled painter and poet.

P.89.1. Ballad of the Water Wheel

The green willows droop low, the water in the pond is shallow;
The din of water wheels fills the paddy fields.
A stream is forced upwards, splashing onto the path;
The suspended buckets, hanging from their perches, go round and
round.
This summer drought has long worn down the farmers' hearts;

The west wind scrapes the earth, yellow dust is swirled high.
The ground splits and cracks like an oracle shell;
(8) To water here is like trying to soak Mount Wojiao.
The feet of men and women alike are callused to the point of bleeding;
Oxen are whipped day and night until their hooves break.
The yellowed seedlings in the field are hard pressed to live.
(12) In village after village all cry they have no strength left.

(QSBC, 31/181–82)

line 8: Mount Wojiao is a mythical mountain in the southern East China Sea; "to water Mount Wojiao" is proverbial for an impossible task.

P.89.2. On a Painting of a Fisherman

A bamboo pole slowly wavers in the gentle breeze;
Neither sad to lose a fish nor thrilled to catch one.
Line gathered in, boat sets out from the dense-grown reeds;
A white egret bursts up into flight across the sky.
At water's edge sets the sun, the water is pure and clean;
So clear one can no longer see where the fish have gone.
There is a road to Peach Blossom Spring too indistinct to find;
(8) Clouds and water in vast expanse stir boundless feelings.

(QSBC, 31/182)

line 7: On Peach Blossom Spring, see P.16.4.

P.89.3. Autumn of the Yimao *Year [1735], a Poem to Console My Husband on Not Passing the Examination at Nanjing*

Newly made up and carefully arranged, she strives for delicacy and grace;
But another girl, the gaudily painted one, always catches everyone's eye.
Who notices the one leaning by the tall bamboo in the cold,
Elegantly standing in the dusk, most solitary and pure?

The poor girl toils on her brocade year after year
Lonely and neglected behind the gynacaeum's closed doors.
But, alas, the evil *zhen* bird serves as go-between;
(8) Without prospects, she arranges a trousseau facing the autumn wind.

Double Ninth storms keep him in the hermit's studio.
The dejected one cannot let go of his sorrow.
But the mums by the fence are open, let's drink to them.
(12) I'll pawn my gold hairpin to buy the wine.

(QSBC, 31/182)

line 3: This line borrows from Du Fu, "Jia ren" (QTS, 218/2287): "Her kingfisher sleeves are thin against the cold; / In the dusk she leans against the tall bamboo." The poem has long been interpreted as expressing through allegory the sorrows of the worthy, but unwanted, official.

line 6: This line repeats phrases from Meng Haoran, "Liu bie Wang shiyu Wei" (QTS, 160/1639): "Lonely and neglected, what more do I expect? / . . . All that is left to me is to preserve my solitude, / Return home and close the bramble gate."

line 7: The *zhen*-bird (translated by Hawkes as a "magpie") first appears in Qu Yuan, "Li sao": "I sent off the magpie to pay my court to her, / But the magpie told me that my suit had gone amiss" (*Wen xuan*, 32/12b; Hawkes, *Songs of the South*, p. 74). Wang Yi's commentary informs us that the *zhen* "secretes a fatal poison; here it is a metaphor for slander. . . . The poet says he entrusted the *zhen* with the mission of marriage broker, but the *zhen*, being of a slanderous nature, was untrustworthy." Qu Yuan's many failed "courtships" are traditionally interpreted as his pursuit of a deserving ruler and patron.

line 11: Evoking Tao Yuanming, "Yin jiu," number five (Lu Qinli, *Tao Yuanming ji*, p. 89); see P.17.2.

line 12: A reference to Yuan Zhen's poem of mourning for his wife: "When you saw that I lacked clothing you ransacked your straw hampers; / Entreating the boy to buy wine you plucked out your golden hairpin" ("Qian bei huai san shou," number one; QTS, 404/4509).

BIOGRAPHICAL NOTE AND TRANSLATION BY PAUL S. ROPP

許飛雲

P.90. Xu Feiyun (mid–18th century)

Xu Feiyun was known to her contemporaries as a versatile poet specializing in lyric verse and as a diligent scholar and painter.[1] A native of Jiangsu, she married Wang Wenming from Wu prefecture. When her husband became ill, the family fell into financial distress. Xu seemed undaunted by these misfortunes. Day and night she offered her family cheerful words of encouragement and even traded her jewelry for food. She replied with perfect decorum to the inquiries of important visitors, was at ease with the literati, and was, in short, a source of strength to the household.

Unlike many budding female authors who upon marriage stopped writing because of the demands of housekeeping, Xu Feiyun continued to study and write. Her literary reputation became so great that a Manchu Grand Secretary invited her to become a private teacher in his home in the capital. She accepted the offer and remained in his service for an entire year. Numerous scholars and poets highly praised her lyric verse.

The five song-lyrics translated below offer a glimpse of Xu Feiyun's poetic persona, a persona that stands in definite contrast to many of the more elaborately drawn female figures in Chinese poetry. Rather than evoking the intimate feminine world of the boudoir, her descriptive powers are focused on the natural world around her and on the range of feelings evoked by and embodied in the birds, trees, and flowers passing from one season to the next. Given Xu Feiyun's great social visibility and widespread popularity even in her own day, it seems unexpected that the poetic identity she developed is so reclusive. Yet it may have been this very aspect of her works that made them so appealing then and gives them a refreshing charm today.

P.90.1. Ru meng ling: *Early Summer, Thinking of My Younger Cousin Chen Yuhuan*

Willow catkins, the little pond swelling with green;
Swallows, and the fragrant mud fermenting with red.
Rising at dawn, examining the scenery;
Spring's appearance has certainly changed.
Into the distance, gazing, gazing;
Praying that your traveling coach is safe.

(GXCC, 2/15b)

line 2: Red flower petals have fallen to the ground and are decaying there. The swallows, like the other images in this and the preceding line, indicate that spring is almost over.

P.90.2. Gong zhong tiao xiao: *Seeing Off the Spring*

Spring departs,
Spring departs;
The whole garden is falling flowers and flying catkins.

Sentimental swallows snatch them up,
Prompting this estranged lover's heart to break.
Heartbroken,
Heartbroken;
(8) Green trees chaotically merge with heaven's edge.

(GXCC, 2/15b)

P.90.3. Ye jin men: *Flower Festival*

Spring brilliance splendid;
The whole courtyard is filled with apricot flowers, fully in bloom.
Still, I think of the few trees winding along the river;
Leaning against the railing, I lightly paint my brows.

Rueful: emerald mountain clouds are fragrant;
Hopes dashed: the person in the mirror grows old.
A single pair of swallows—how early they've returned!
(8) On the painted eaves it's dusk, and then, again, it's dawn.

(GXCC, 2/16a)

P.90.4. Zui hua yin: *Seeing Off Spring*

Spring retreats to the edge of the sky, but who is its master?
And when it leaves, to where will it return?
Forsaken, this jade tower person
Seeks drunkenness before the flowers.

The ground covered with flying red rain;
Butterflies busy, bees in a frenzy, while mine is talk of intimate grief.
From this, I see that my emotions will find no sympathy in them.
(8) What of you, beautiful oriole,
With your cry "come back, come back"?
When will we meet with the east wind again?

(GXCC, 2/16a–b)

line 1: The speaker notes the absence of a human subject (i.e., her loved one) in the scene.

line 9: In Chinese the oriole's cry is thought to sound like the words "Come back!"

line 10: The east wind is the harbinger of spring.

P.90.5. Zhu Yingtai: *On an Autumn Day Sojourning in Qiantang*

Wild geese fly in a slanting line;
Autumn's complexion muted.
Tears dye the maples red
By the banks of Wuling Stream,
The immortal's boat urges men to depart.
I see the snow billow into silver heaps;
The western wind whips at my upswept hair.
Heartrending emotions of parting;
I chant harbored thoughts, but softly.

Swallow Mountain Road
Years ago I traveled;
And now once more I journey to heaven's edge
Learning to write with duckling yellow,
Often beset with shame and envy.
The hills of Wu and the waters of Yue bring tangled grief;
This cannot be good for the literary mind—
How could I come up with "Sunny Springtime" sentences?

(GXCC, 2/16b)

line 10: Swallow Mountain Road is located in Hebei province.
line 13: Yellow ink was used to blot out errors in writing.
line 17: On the refined "Sunny Spring" song, see P.4.2.

BIOGRAPHICAL NOTE AND TRANSLATION BY MARY ELLEN FRIENDS

許權

P.91. Xu Quan (18th century)

Xu Quan (courtesy name Yiying), from Jiangzhou (Jiujiang City in Jiangxi province), was skilled in embroidery, especially in the *baimiao* or outline drawing technique. She was the daughter of a government student, Xu Zhenhuang, and was married to a *jinshi* degree holder, Cui Mo. Apparently unable to bear abuse by her parents-in-law, she committed suicide by hanging herself.[1]

In her poem "Double Seventh Eve" (P.91.1), Xu Quan opposes the nonliterate peasant wife living happily with her husband and the talented gentry wife who lives in loneliness, and suggests that the Weaving Girl's outstanding skill may indeed be a cause of her lonely existence separated from her lover. Unstated but implied in Xu's poem is the warning that skill can also breed resentment in others less skilled and make the life of a talented woman with an absent husband unbearable.

P.91.1. Double Seventh Eve

On the seventh evening of the seventh month
All look for the Weaving Girl and the Herd Boy.
The two celestials are nowhere to be seen;
The chilling wind—how it whistles by!
I wonder whether the Weaving Girl has lost her skill;
One in the east, one in the west—hard to fly over such a divide.
One time each year, one separation,
The primeval Milky Way echoes with lamentations.
Don't pray for dexterity from the Weaving Girl;
When she grants it, sorrow is sure to follow.
Have you not seen the diligent farm wife to the east,
Often plowing with her husband or bringing lunch to the fields?
They share disappointments and joys day and night,
Never separated from youth to white-haired old age.
And have you not seen the gifted girl to the west,
Whose husband has risen to the Hanlin's jade halls?
The whole year long these two never once meet,
At two ends of the magpie bridge they dejectedly pine.
Jade dew descends in the lonely silence of the night,
Spider's web and hope both sundered across the plate.
To whom will the gift of cleverness go?
I fear clever people are quickly old.
So I say to all the foolish girls alive:
It is better to be dull than clever.

(QSBC, 31/185)

On the Double Seventh festival observance, see P.5.1 and P.19.2.

P.91.2. A Dream of Heaven

I am summoned away
  to a hideaway of immortals,
Remote, among islands.
I am carried off
  in a car pulled by Cinnabar Phoenix,
A carriage drawn by Red Dragon.
We pass over the Five Sacred Mountains below
  and bow to Pure Emptiness;
Above we touch the sun and moon
  coursing the highways of heaven.
I turn, look back at the human world—
  it is utterly lost in distance!
(8) On level terrain, all is effaced,
  shrouded in haze and dim.
Mountains in clouds make several dots
  like islands in a sea.
I want to leave it all behind,
  to freely soar on high;
Suddenly I hear, out of the void,
  music of flutes and drums.
(12) Beautiful women, reserved and modest,
  come riding on cloudy ethers;
It seems as though we've met before
  somewhere in a far blue sky.
I go with them to Jasper Pool
  as one of the immortal pages;
Star sisters, moon maiden,
  rank after rank they come.
(16) While there I see no spirits
  with tiger tails or leopard teeth;
My only care is to eat delicacies,
  drink wine of liquid colored clouds.
With a single cup my heart feels clean,
  my bones are light and tingling.
But soaked in sweat, the covers grow cold
  and soon I awake from my dream;

Lonely lamp, lonely pillow—
what a dull place this is!
The west wind sighs and whistles
through plane trees in the courtyard.

(GGSC, 4:1/3a–b)

lines 1–2: Immortals were said to live either in grotto-worlds deep inside mountains or on a group of three islands far out in the ocean.

lines 3–4: The cloud chariots of immortals were drawn by fabulous animals.

line 14: A pool in the environs of the mythic Queen Mother of the West (see P.69.5), whose home was said to be on the summit of the Kunlun Mountains to the west of China.

lines 17–18: Those seeking Daoist immortality through elixirs or meditative practices and spirit journeys hoped to eat the fruits and other exquisite foods of the immortals, which they believed had a purifying effect on mortal bodies.

BIOGRAPHICAL NOTE AND TRANSLATION OF P.91.1 BY PAUL S. ROPP; TRANSLATION OF P.91.2 BY MAUREEN ROBERTSON

陳端生

P.92. Chen Duansheng (1751–96?)

Chen Duansheng, from Qiantang (Hangzhou), was the granddaughter of a famous literatus, Chen Zhaolun (1701–71). She apparently had a happy childhood in Hangzhou and was able to travel with her father, probably to Beijing, where he served as supervisor of the imperial stables. Her sister, Chen Changsheng, was also a talented poet. At age eighteen, Chen Duansheng began a long *tanci* (a lyrical narrative) entitled *Zai sheng yuan* (The destiny of rebirth). A few years later, she married a man surnamed Fan. The early marital happiness of this couple was cut short when Fan was indicted for corruption and exiled. For some fifteen years, she awaited his return. She died in her forties leaving her masterpiece unfinished.[1]

Zai sheng yuan was later completed by another prominent woman poet, Liang Desheng (P.118) and became the most famous *tanci* in the Chinese tradition. It features a heroine who, disguised as a man, succeeds spectacularly in the examination system and rises to the position of prime minister. In the last part written by Chen Duansheng, the heroine refuses to reveal her identity because she enjoys her position far too much to return to her "proper" role of wife to a man who is clearly her intellectual and moral inferior. When her identity is forcibly revealed at the instigation of her fiancé, she curses him as a selfish man with no concern for her welfare. The following poem, sent by Chen to her exiled husband, is far more orthodox in tone and sentiment than her *tanci*.

P.92.1. Sent to My Husband

I scratch my head, clouds extend in the sky to the vast wasteland.
"The one I miss"?—autumn waters flood on boundlessly.
So pitiable, so far away, for years seen only in dreams;
Over and again he breaks my deeply sequestered and tortured heart.
In housework dare I not maintain the wifely way?
With reed and pill I continue our tradition of learning.
Filial daughter, loving parent, I have no shortcomings there,
As I can still bear to report with these few lines.

As the pen is dipped in ink, I lose my presence of mind;
The first word barely formed, tears fall in long strands.
Tears dry away, but their traces remain forever,
Too many words too hard to send turn into no words at all.
Ten years of parting sorrow, this spring silkworm now old;
Ten thousand *li* of wandering grief, word from the border delayed.
I close the tiny window, all inside are quiet and still.
The lamp smoke fades away, cold and desolate, ah! who comprehends?

(Qian Zhonglian and Fan Boqun, eds., *Gudai aiqing shi jianshang ji*, 342)

lines 1–2: "I scratch my head" is quoted from poem 42 of the *Book of Odes*: "She gave me a rendezvous at the corner of the wall; / I love her but do not see her; / I scratch my head and walk hesitatingly." The expression *yiren*, "the one [I miss]," is quoted from poem 129 in the *Book of Odes* and suggests an elusive beloved. "Autumn waters," from the opening of *Zhuangzi*, chapter 17, evokes the idea of the sublimity of infinite spaces.

line 6: "Reed and pill" refers to two mothers famous in Chinese history for sternly educating sons in difficult circumstances. The famous Song-dynasty scholar-official Ouyang Xiu (1007–72) was reportedly taught to read and write by his mother, using only a reed in the dirt, after his father died when Xiu was four. Liu Zhongying (d. 864), a famous Tang-dynasty official, was in his youth reportedly kept awake to study by his mother who gave him pills made of bear's gall and gentian.

line 13: Cf. Li Shang-yin, "Wu ti" (QTS 539/6168): "The spring silkworm's thread will only end when death comes, / The candle will not dry its tears until it turns to ashes" (trans. J. J. Y. Liu, *Poetry of Li Shang-yin*, p. 66).

line 14: One mile is about 2.75 *li*. "Ten thousand *li*" is a common expression for a great distance.

BIOGRAPHICAL NOTE AND TRANSLATION BY PAUL S. ROPP

P.93. Xi Peilan (1760–1820?)

Prima inter pares best summarizes the poetic achievement of Xi Peilan, the foremost among the some two dozen women poets who became students of the iconoclastic Qing poet-critic Yuan Mei (1716–98). When Yuan Mei published an anthology of the best poems by his women students under the title of *Suiyuan nü dizi shixuan* (Selected poems by the women disciples of Sui Garden), Xi's poems came first in its table of contents.[1] (For a preface to Yuan's anthology, see C.46.1.) This mark of honor bestowed upon her may be compared to an event from a different era and a different genre, when the lyrics of Wen Tingyun (813?–70) were accorded a similar place of honor in the *Huajian ji* anthology of *ci* poetry (ca. 940). Xi herself was conscious of this distinction, which she acknowledges in a dedicatory poem she wrote on the occasion; but, more appropriately perhaps, she spoke of the new anthology as "the *Yutai xinyong* of our day."[2] Like its two more illustrious (male-compiled) predecessors, this smaller anthology is a trailblazing book.

A native of Changshu (then called Zhaowen), Jiangsu province, Xi Peilan (courtesy names Yunfen and Daohua, style name Wanyun) was already admired for her poetic talent when at age sixteen, in 1776, she was married to Sun Yuanxiang (1760–1829). Although Sun did not earn his *jinshi* degree until 1805, he enjoyed a wide circle of literary friends. Nonetheless, Sun wrote in the preface to his own collected poems, the *Tianzhen ge ji* (1803), that he first learned poetry from his wife after their marriage. As if to commemorate their literary partnership, Xi's collection *Changzhen ge ji* (Poems from the Tower of Enduring Steadfastness) was printed together with Sun's in posthumous editions (1829, 1891).[3]

In the same preface, Sun credited his father, Sun Hao (1733–89), with teaching him the importance of *xingling* or "native sensibility"—a concept that later became the cornerstone of Yuan Mei's poetic theory.[4] But, no doubt, his later friendship with Yuan Mei served to encourage him (and his wife) to take their craft in the same direction.

Xi's poetry undoubtedly earned her teacher's praise through its expression of "native sensibility." It also demonstrates another tendency much favored by Yuan Mei, namely the technique of *fan an*: "turning the tables" or "overturning precedent." Laboring under the shadow of the millennia-long tradition of classical Chinese poetry, poets are always challenged to say something new. And a woman poet might have seen in *fan an* a means of circumventing both the weight of literary tradition and the narrowness of feminine experience. Whether the subject be slight and jocular, or as sad and tragic as infant mortality and the loss of her own six-year-old child, or as weighty and serious as fame in literature and her husband's dismissal from office, Xi Peilan responded with poetry that was thoroughly personal. Perhaps the one poem translated here that best exemplifies the *fan an* approach is "Savoring Parting" (P.93.8) a regulated-verse poem of which every couplet holds a deliberate echo of a familiar Tang quatrain. "Traveling at Dawn to Watch the Sunrise" (P.93.7) deliberately evokes both stylistic and imagistic echoes of the "Southern Mountains" poem by Han Yu (768–824).[5] Even something as familiar as the sound of pestles on a washing block, a motif common in ancient *yuefu* poetry, can be exploited by Xi to say something entirely personal, in an original way (see P.93.5). Speaking both as wife and as loyal critic, she admonished her husband: "Most ruinous to scholarship is worldly success; / Honor comes unsought and with death it ends" (P.93.6)—a fitting *ars poetica* for this much-honored poet.

P.93.1. Embroidery Work

With my hand I split open a gossamer strand of scented silk,
And pondered the choicest of flowers for my task.
Gorgeous beauties too often waste away after frost,
So I will not embroider a Darling Hibiscus, but only a Virginia creeper.

(Xi Peilan, *Changzhen ge ji*, 1/1a)

line 4: *Furong* in the Chinese text refers to *mufurong*, or *Hibiscus mutabilis*, and is also a pun on the homophonous *furong*, "husband's face." *Nüchen* is the common name of *Ligustrum japonicum*, which flowers in the summer and stays evergreen through the winter. Its name can also be taken punningly to mean "a woman's chastity": hence here the somewhat free rendition as "Virginia creeper."

P.93.2. Willow Catkins

White as light frost and soft as cotton—
Driven about by east wind, most pitiable!
Better to fall on a peach-blossom stream,
And turn into an orb of drifting duckweed!

(*Changzhen ge ji*, 1/2a)

On Xie Daoyun's famous simile of snow and willow catkins, see C.24.1.

P.93.3. Bidding Spring Goodbye

Around a peach tree draped in jade-green,
  purple clouds fly about;
Paler grows the amorous red
  as the green turns lusher.
I blame the east wind
  for flagging and languishing:
For sending spring away but not
  bringing my dear one home.

(*Changzhen ge ji*, 1/4a)

line 3: Cf. Li Qingzhao, speaking of flowers after rain: "The leaves should be lush and the petals frail" (P.17.6). And cf. Li Shangyin, "Wu ti" (QTS, 539/6168): "The east wind is powerless as all the flowers wither" (trans. J. J. Y. Liu, *The Poetry of Li Shang-yin*, p. 66).

P.93.4. Rejoicing at the News of My Husband's Long-Awaited Return Home

By the dawn window
  I am startled awake from a shadowy dream;
For a change this morning,
  magpies sing to augur a sunny day.
Just as my fingers were counting
  the day he should start his journey home,
My ears already catch
  the sound of someone coming in.
Though it pains me to see his thin face
  begrimed by wind and dust,

I can still look through to his heart
　as pure as moonlight on water.
Mustn't he hurry to his mother's side
　and earnestly inquire after her health?
And could we dare express
　our feelings over our reunion?

(*Changzhen ge ji*, 1/5a)

P.93.5. Hearing the Sound of Pestles on a Washing Block

What night is tonight?
Cool wind brings me the sound of pestles from afar,
Shattering to pieces a dream beyond the sky,
Striking to smithereens the heart of a traveler.
Its resonance carries autumn frost's chill;
Its sound hurries dawn's sinking moon.
Resting securely in a secluded boudoir,
I go on lamenting sleeping alone.

(*Changzhen ge ji*, 1/3a)

On the motif of beating clothes on washing blocks, see P.4.3.

P.93.6. Upon Milord's Dismissal from Office, I Wrote This Poem to Console Him

Have you not seen:
　the Rustic Old Man of Duling, a poets' poet?
Or the Banished Immortal of high renown,
Hailed as the most talented poet of all time?
They won no name through examination in their day.
Milord is schooled in the poetry of both Du and Li:
Bold, soaring, and not the least over-refined.
Your high spirit often breaks through empyrean clouds,
Your deep feelings are vast and clear as spring waters.
At times your pen lets loose sorrow and anger
As if your wrist were guided by Du Fu's ghost.
At times rapture and gusto leap from your brush,
To show Taibo's spirit is yet alive.
It's perhaps natural to favor one poet over the other,

But a talent like yours avoids making such distinctions.
This spring you packed and headed for the capital,
Confident of picking up your sashes of blue and purple;
More than once we rejoiced in reports of your success;
Now you've returned still a blue-clad scholar!
But troves of treasured manuscript fill your bags,
I call for lamps to read them through by the window.
Mountains, rivers of Yan and Jin rush before my eyes;
Stored in your verse are the breeze and moonlight of spring and autumn.
That which worldly exam officials dare not approve
Is handed over to Li and Du to be their heir.
Even when the Tang valued poetry, the two masters were overlooked;
What can be made of today when officials aren't chosen for their poetic skill?
Write your verse, and keep to your learning;
Having such talent confers fame after life.
Our boudoir is not known for lofty opinion:
But I do know it's shameful to ask for pity.
Most ruinous to scholarship is worldly success;
Honor comes unsought and with death it ends.
Have you not seen
how sages and worthies since ancient days
Have always risen from among poor and humble folk?

(*Changzhen ge ji*, 1/10a–b)

For poems on a similar theme, see P.75a.2, P.89.3. Sun Yuanxiang obtained his *juren* (provincial graduate) degree in 1795 but did not become a *jinshi* until ten years later. Aside from being made a bachelor of the Hanlin Academy, he never received any official appointment; his later career included teaching in various academies.

lines 1–5: The reference is to two of China's greatest poets, Du Fu and Li Bo (Tai-bo) of the Tang dynasty. Du was a native of Duling, and Li's contemporaries called him "the banished immortal."

line 6: *Qimi*, translated here as "over-refinement," often implies disapproval in Chinese literary criticism. See Lu Ji, "Wen fu" (*Wen xuan*, 17/4b).

line 21: Yan and Jin are the ancient names for modern Hebei and Shanxi provinces.

P.93.7. Traveling at Dawn to Watch the Sunrise [over Mount Tai]

Traveling at dawn in these crenellated mountains,
So pitch-dark I could not see the road ahead;
Silently sitting behind the curtain in a cart,
All I felt was frost scraping my face.
Road so icy that my horse slipped,
Courage failed me, my heart beat faster.
Ahead, I feared the steep cliff would give way;
Behind, I fretted the overhanging rock might break off.
I shut my eyes and dared not open them,
Opened, I could see nothing anyway.

Soon amid clouds and fog
Blossomed forth a ray of crimson,
First like a piece of Sichuan brocade spread out,
Then like a length of Suzhou silk snipped.
Swift as the Great Giant God sunders,
Or again as the Goddess Nü Wa smelts,
A splendid hall suddenly took shape,
Then mirage-towers loomed up transformed!
Like the Five Flavors, the Five Colors
Were blended into a harmonious whole.

Or like a sword's gleam bursting through its scabbard,
Or like the Precious Essence warily collected,
And where the gleam and the Essence gathered,
A golden mirror appeared;
Its rays piercing through the void as if whistling,
Darting out like flashes of lightning.
A fiery wheel revolved around a purple palace;
A golden pillar rose to meet heaven.
Murkish miasma took to sudden flight;
Myriad phenomena stood revealed and bright.

(*Changzhen ge ji*, 1/8a–b)

lines 15–16: Juling, the Giant God or Spirit, split the mountains to create the Yellow River. On Nü Wa, see P.87.13 (viii).

line 19: The Five Flavors and Five Colors are sets that are used to suggest all possible flavors and colors.

line 22: *Baojing*, translated as "Precious Essence," is probably used here in the Daoist sense to refer to a life force that might be preserved through breath control or yoga practice.

P.93.8. Savoring Parting

You've forgone good times for the far journey's sake:
But where's a marquis's title to be sought in this wide, wide world?
Too quickly willow catkins rush spring into aging;
Quietly, peach blossoms hold travelers' grief.
While dawn dream is at its sweetest moment, orioles' trill overfills the valley;
My evening make-up freshly done, swallows return to tower room.
Dusk finds me again dreading Chang E's mockery:
(8) Moonlight comes to the beaded curtain which shall remain unrolled.

(*Changzhen ge ji*, 1/3b)

lines 1–3: These lines echo a familiar quatrain by Wang Changling (d. 756) entitled "Boudoir Lament": "A young woman in her boudoir is unacquainted with grief, / On a spring day, all dressed up, she climbs to the upper story; / Suddenly, upon noticing the color of willows on the embankment, / She regrets having sent her husband off to seek a marquis's title" (QTS, 143/1446; trans., Irving Yucheng Lo).

line 5: Compare the lines from a quatrain by Jin Changxu: "Let the yellow oriole flutter, / But don't let it cry on the branch: / When it cries, my woman's dream will be broken / And I will never be able to reach Liaoxi" (QTS, 768/8724; trans., Irving Yucheng Lo).

line 7: On Chang E, see P.21.1.

line 8: The last three words of this line are *bu shang gou* ("it need not be mounted on the hook"), that is to say, "I won't have the curtain rolled up to be hung on a pair of hooks (lest the Moon Goddess espy my loneliness)." This line echoes the sentiment of Li Bo's famous "Jade Steps Lament" (QTS, 164/1701).

P.93.9. Late Spring

Of ten trees that have bloomed, nine are now bare:
One siege of rain and another of raging wind.
Spiders too know how to plead with spring to tarry:
Tenderly they spin their silk to snare fallen petals.

(*Changzhen ge ji*, 2/8b–9a)

P.93.10. *Accompanying a Gift of Fingernails Sent to My Husband*

Long and slender, a lady's fingernails,
lustrously brittle as coral,
Clipped and trimmed with a pair of gold scissors,
to better show my snow-white flesh—
I give them to my lover for remembrance,
So that when his back starts to itch,
He need not ask for the elfish Maid Magu.

(*Changzhen ge ji*, 3/12b)

line 4: On the immortal Magu, see P.24.6. When Magu took human shape and was born into an unsuspecting family, she prompted the master of the house into saying that he would surely desire this maid's fingernails when his back itched. For another instance of the presentation of fingernails as a parting gift, see Cao Xueqin, *Hong lou meng*, chap. 77 (trans. Hawkes and Minford, *Story of the Stone*, 3: 545).

P.93.11. *Elegiac Verses Mourning the Death of My Son An (Named Wenkui): Two Selections*

I

Amid the fragrance of plum blossoms,
he comes to his eternal sleep;
The sky so vast and indistinct,
my eyes are worn with gazing.
To have chosen the Goddess of Mercy's birthday
as his last day on earth—
Even if he had not returned to Buddhahood,
he surely was reborn in paradise.

II

Bright pupils that could cleave the water
lie motionless and cold;
His snow-white flesh still shows, wrapped
in a tiny red quilt.
Though a master-painter's hand could
capture the spirit of his appearance,
It would be well-nigh impossible
to depict the spark of his intelligence.

(*Changzhen ge ji*, 2/8b)

The original title is "Duanchang ci" (Songs of heartbreak). Xi Peilan left a total of sixteen quatrains upon the death of her six-year-old son An, who preceded his three-year-old brother, named Lu, in death by only one day. Translated here are quatrains 11 and 12.

i, line 4: Xi Peilan added this note: "According to the Buddhist calendar, the birthday of Guanyin [popularly known as the goddess of mercy] falls on the nineteenth day of the second month each year."

BIOGRAPHICAL NOTE AND TRANSLATION BY IRVING YUCHENG LO

P.94. Jin Yi (1770–94)

A native of Soochow, Jin Yi (courtesy name Xianxian) was the wife of a government student by the name of Chen Ji. What record we have of her life is largely gained from her preserved writings and through a lengthy grave inscription penned by her celebrated teacher, Yuan Mei (see C.45.1). Her collected poetry bears the title of *Shouyinlou shicao* (Poetry drafts from the Tower of the Slender Reciter; Xianxian means "slender"), and 108 of her poems (mostly in regulated verse) were selected by Yuan to be included in the anthology of poems written by his female students, *Suiyuan nü dizi shixuan*.[1]

According to Yuan's inscription, Jin was a precocious child: "At a very early age she could already read books and distinguish the four tones. She loved to compose poetry, and every time she let fall her brush it was like a fleet horse prancing along unable to stop." Her love for, and skill in, poetry surprised and delighted her husband on their wedding night, and, as her poems testify, they seem to have enjoyed enormously their poetic companionship. Many of her titles describe her poems as "linked verses," "using my husband's rhyme scheme," or "a joint composition with my husband." She professed great regard for Yuan Mei's poetry, and her own compositions show the influence of Yuan's style: simplicity of diction and syntax, linguistic sonority, exquisite scenic constructions, and avoidance of pedantry in the deployment of allusions.

P.94.1. Sitting at Night in the Quiet Green Studio

A courtyard of jadelike *wutong*
Stirs new cool in night's tower.
The fallen flowers are all due to the rain;
Dead trees easily turn autumnal.

Much illness removes tea and wine;
Cloudy hills await my boat's call.
The incense seems to have feelings,
For strands and strands would flow near me

(GGZSJ, 14/19a)

P.94.2. Peonies

I see and care greatly for you
Who come twice in fresh fair weather,
Outdoing all other beauties—
The hundred gems of the tower.
Rain-soaked you vie with spring for glamor;
Wind-whipped you make piles of brocade.
Pity how those butterflies tire
From circling you a thousand times.

(GGZSJ, 14/19a–b)

P.94.3. An Inscription for a Painting on "Four Guests Touring a Mountain on New Year's Eve" by Grand Scribe Wu Yusong [two from a series of four]

II

One skiff will move you far from worldly air.
Bell-talk of mid-Heaven is heard below.
Leave we our shoes unused at winter's end?
Mountain gods should know these four gentlemen.
Tea games are played though the hut turns misty cold;
The cliff's leafless woods will not detain the clouds.
Past journeys' traces are vaguely recalled,
But a sense of pure peace is felt by all.

IV

An outing like a visit to the gods,
This treading of cold is best as night clears.
At snow-packed inns you'd find the wines of old;
Twilight bells cleave the mist across the stream.
Besides a lone monk there's no other guest;

When you return, it will be another year.
You must recall in future New Year's Eves
(8) How oars found rest by the clouds at dusk.

(GGZSJ, 14/19b–20a)

P.94.4. *Rising from Illness*

The green trees move their shadows up the screens.
West court is empty, the morning sun is faint.
I can't burn incense, rising from illness,
After a brief stand beneath flowers, my robe's perfumed.

(GGZSJ, 14/20a)

P.94.5. *The Boat's Immediate Scene*

Water windows opened, the silk drapes drawn,
One leaflike sail in a mirror returns.
Heaven seems to pity my loneliness:
Green hills have moved near to the painted boat.

(GGZSJ, 14/20b)

BIOGRAPHICAL NOTE AND TRANSLATION BY ANTHONY C. YU

P.95. Dai Lanying (fl. late 18th century)

Dai Lanying (courtesy name Yaozhen) was not only among Yuan Mei's students; she was also related to the Yuan family by marriage to a nephew of the poet, although she became a widow early. She first met Yuan in the spring of 1783 at the Official Residence of Yangshan.[1] (P.95.1 is a thank-you note Dai wrote in response to this meeting.) Fourteen years later, when Yuan celebrated his eightieth birthday, she had the opportunity of seeing him again and calling herself his "female pupil" (*nü dizi*).

Although Yuan and Dai lived far apart, they seem to have exchanged frequent poems and letters. In a poetic inscription for a painting that belonged to Dai, Yuan teased her with the line: "Your gifts of fans and poems counted for tuition."[2] The title of Dai's poetry collection is *Yaozhen yincao* (Recitation drafts of Yaozhen), and twenty-seven of her poems were included in Yuan Mei's anthology of his women students' poetic works, *Suiyuan nü dizi shixuan.*

P.95.1. To Thank Uncle Zicai [Yuan Mei], Who Sent a Poem as an Inscription for the Painting Entitled "Giving My Son Lessons by an Autumn Lamp"

Though your art's great fame has long filled the world,
You cherish others' talent like priceless gold.
When in late spring I heard you were to set sail,
I told a skilled master to start painting at once.
Since you had noble guests both night and day,
I had no time to seek an apposite verse.
Still your staff my painting with favor received;
(8) I was made free from all my former fears—
Now admiring you, now flaunting my luck:
Three visits from you in the year's fifth month!
Just ten days after you from Baimen returned,
(12) Your brush leapt up from its coral stand.
I opened and read those flowing lines you sent.
The fine script, the advanced years both amazed—
Like Ninth Heaven's clouds plunging suddenly,
(16) Like a thousand mile river's startled surge.
You wrongly compared me with Wuyan of Qi,
But I'm ashamed that I'm not the gifted Xie.
My nine-year-old's lessons are not yet done,
(20) I can't shirk the duties of one autumn lamp.
To have a long poem from your wondrous brush
Is like Lotus Peak presiding over Mount Hua.
To be among your thirteen rows of students
(24) I have more cause than those women of fame.
My husband came from your old learned house,
Our line of teachers not from outside lent.
Though Mount Cang's hues grow greener when it's late,
(28) Far Maple River has kept us apart.
But on reading your writings, ten thousand scrolls,
Even a weak plant is transformed by seasonal rain.
Poetic art is scarce in deep boudoirs:

Just idle chants, I once thought, would suffice.
I'll thread in secret my gold needle henceforth
To ply my thoughts from day into the night.
My ditty's no exchange for the fields of Xu;
Your lofty verse commands the price of jade.
I dare approach that Han Lanying of Qi,
Though still an unworthy pupil in your gates.

(GGZSJ, 13/17a–b)

line 14: Although Yuan Mei occasionally remarked that his resistance to constant practice during his youth had made him a poor calligrapher, he was nonetheless capable of writing a fine, small script even at an advanced age. See the last poem in his series of regulated verses celebrating his own eightieth birthday in his *Xiaocang shanfang shiji*, 36/6b.

line 17: There was an exceptionally ugly woman named Zhong Lichun who was from the Wuyan district of the State of Qi. Confident of her own learning and sagacity despite her looks, she requested an audience with Prince Xuan of Qi and gained his recognition. Eventually she became his chief consort, and the security of the State of Qi was said to be a result of her wise policies (Liu Xiang, *Gu lienü zhuan*, 6/8b–10a).

line 18: On Xie Daoyun, see C.24.1.

line 37: Han Lanying was a woman poet of the Southern Qi and Liu-Song dynasties who held administrative and teaching appointments in the palace. Because of her great learning, she was promoted to the rank of *boshi*, or "doctor," and was addressed as "Master Han"; see C.23.4.

P.95.2. Spring Miscellanies

When mosses I see first display their green,
I teach my maid to water orchid buds.
I jot down verse fragments for fear of loss;
My sole pastime is to copy texts.
Begonias, rain-soaked, shed coral tears;
Young swallows find mud to mend their nests.
A sudden faint noise disturbs the dream of spring:
Outside the windows horses lightly tap.

(GGZSJ, 13/17b–18a)

BIOGRAPHICAL NOTE AND TRANSLATION BY ANTHONY C. YU

屈秉筠

P.96. Qu Bingyun (fl. late 18th century)

Available information about Qu Bingyun, a student of Yuan Mei, is not abundant. Her name appears in the table of contents of Yuan's anthology of poems by his female students, but no poems were recorded in the stated fifth *juan* of the work. According to Hu Wenkai, Qu (courtesy name Wanxian) was a native of Changshu in Jiangsu province and the wife of Zhao Tongquan.[1] Her printed works include a book of poems entitled *Yunyulou shi* (Poems from the House of Secluded Jade) and one book of song-lyrics, presumably the *Yunyulou ci* (as republished in Xu Naichang's *Xiao tan luan shi huike guixiu ci* [XTLS]) used for the following translations.

P.96.1. Pusa man: *A Portrait of a Beauty Enjoying the Cool Air*

Cool clouds pass mutely, floral shades are dark.
The crescent snares a night of longing thoughts.
Roll up that water-bright screen
To rouse a slight butterfly dream.

Standing idly by the jade steps—
Her bowlike shoes yet to feel cold—
She only fears a nice breeze
May pry open her gown of silk.

(XTLS: *Yunyulou ci*, 1a)

P.96.2. Yu meiren ying

The blossoms' message bears a thousand dreams:
I have not a moment's free time.
An early rise before the screen's hooked up:
Already the birds trill their notes.

Open the windows and I feel my brows weighed down;
Even all that brushing is no use.
A few petals seem unable to fall—
They love spring that's dying for good.

(XTLS: *Yunyulou ci*, 1b)

P.96.3. Chongdie jin: *A Folding Fan of Pear Blossoms and Twin Swallows*

The east wind blows to age the cloud-white pears:
A few feet of moss will soon inter their scent.
Vanish the butterflies' dream;
Fading hues can never revive.

Look at those two small swallows
That show such pity as this:
They pick up speck after speck
Of naught but fine blooms of spring.

(XTLS: *Yunyulou ci*, 2a)

P.96.4. Qingyu'an: *The Fifth Watch*

One lamp, its glow down to a dying wick;
Below the drapes severe cold attacks.
On the pillows I hear the hourly sounds:
When the clock's done striking,
And the cock's done crowing,
  The windows are still dark.

A small dream at this time has just wound up,
But what idle woes accumulate
To make one toss and turn in silk coverlets!
Mourning and moping,
Thinking and brooding,
I miss the east turning white.

(XTLS: *Yunyulou ci*, 3b–4a)

P.96.5. Ta suo xing: *Candles*

  They mock the moon's pure cold
  And aid the people's glamor.
It's fit—in painted rooms, in nights of love—
That they be veiled by blue sleeves afraid of wind.
Flame-sparing gold scissors should not lightly trim.

  Carved for the poetry contest
  And lit for the drinking club,

(8) Their flickering red first dies behind the screens.
I hate their two rows of tears facing me:
Who would in pity borrow their lingering gleam?

(XTLS: *Yunyulou ci*, 4a)

BIOGRAPHICAL NOTE AND TRANSLATION BY ANTHONY C. YU

歸懋儀

P.97. Gui Maoyi (fl. late 18th century)

A native of Changshu in Jiangsu province like Qu Bingyun, Gui Maoyi (style name Peishan) was the daughter of Gui Zhaoxu, a regional inspector, and the wife of Li Xuehuang of Shanghai. Although her name was included in the table of contents of Yuan Mei's anthology *Suiyuan nü dizi shixuan*, none of her poems are found there. Nonetheless, she obviously enjoyed the regard and affection of the aged poet when she paid him a three-day visit. After Yuan attended the sixtieth anniversary banquet for his class of successful *jinshi* candidates held in the imperial palace (1798), he wrote a series of ten quatrains celebrating the occasion. These were copied by Gui in small regular script and then embroidered on Wu silk, which she sent to Yuan along with twenty of her own poems matching the rhyme schemes of his banquet poems. In turn, he wrote another five quatrains to express his gratitude, praising her as "a leader among the gentry of mankind" and the first to match his poem-sequence.[1]

P.97.1. Yi hu zhu: *Sending Off Spring*

Oriole cries slowly grow old;
Light, sated tipsiness adds to my woes.
The traveler's grass is green till heaven's edge.
Butterflies flag and bees tire
  By beauteous spring's early leave.

A court filled with dense shades, the people mute;
A few fallen reds weaving in the wind.
(8) Half a window's sparse rain and the dream awakes:
Romance or heroics,
  Each will wound alike the heart.

(XTLS: *Ting xue ci*, 1b)

P.97.2. Yi hu zhu: *A Farewell for Mr. Liu Chunqing, Leaving for the North*

A slip of sail in misty rain:
I send you off and spring, too, to go back.
We speak in haste a few words on the waves.
Fisher fires twinkling,
We turn to face the river's night.

I've heard your talents match those of "Seven Steps" Cao.
Your steed will tread again the lucent way.
(8) A god still should live in heaven above.
Through miles of forts and mountains
Don't grow weary with wind and fog.

(XTLS: *Ting xue ci*, 2a)

line 6: Cao Zhi (192–232) once composed a poem in the time it took to walk seven paces (Liu Yiqing, *Shishuo xinyu* 4/66; Mather, *Shih-shuo Hsin-yü*, p. 126).

P.97.3. Fenghuangtai shang yi chuixiao: *An Inscription for Magistrate Tang Taoshan's Painting "Aged Friends Find Tranquility on a Zen Mat"*

One stroke of inspiration;
The wise karma of three lives.
From bamboo-urn smoke faintly rises.
Beyond the willows a few dying reds
fly to the mat of Zen.
Now noble writings of statecraft
are mostly traded
for tasty tea and fragrant blooms.
Leave your office early
to flee all stifling tedium
and enjoy this pure coolness.

The river home:
vast, misty Lake Tai.
(8) Rejoice that the Buddha-like magistrate
(his hairs have frosted for the people)
Has planted also ten thousand peaches
to direct the hues of spring.

Sleep gladly in light breeze and quiet day
  or sit on the prayer mat
To let mind beget pure coolness;
(12) Or listen to a gurgling stream beneath the pines
  and its finely wrought song.

(XTLS: *Ting xue ci*, 2a–b)

line 2: On the phrase "three lives" or "three incarnations," see P.54a.7.
line 11: "Pure coolness," *qingliang*, a Buddhist metaphor for enlightened serenity.

P.97.4. Qinyuan chun: *Mourning the Death of My Fourth Daughter*

A cut lotus is still thread-joined;
Pick a melon and you injure the stalk—
I ponder without any choice.
I grieve at such unreason,
  bring forth tears to hang on the lids.
Startled, I'm wide awake
  as pain invades my heart;
I keep rubbing my palms
  or searching in my breast
And wonder whether I'll see her now.
(8) In this fierce grief,
  reckon that love harasses me
    while poor fate befriends her.

O Heaven, whose habit is to scourge us!
There's no way, I suspect,
  to flee from the river of love.
I regret that
  my care for her in normal times
    was filled with a few mistakes,
(12) And recipes for her illness
  most probably had been all wrong.
Pinning flowers on hair-tufts,
  holding the bed to seek a sister—
    like shadows and bubbles they're gone at once.
To sing is to weep,

For the heart is wholly broken
  and not many tears remain.

(XTLS: *Ting xue ci*, 3a–b)

P.97.5. Qingping yue: *On the Night of the Sixteenth, While Listening to Rain, I Duplicate the Rhyme of Young Sister Guizhai's "Spring Moon"*

I

As twilight descends the west,
The moon hangs high before the rails.
A haze of fragrant mist and dreaming flowers evoke
This scene fit for painting and verse.

A strand of light chill cuts through the room;
In deep night lign-aloes are added to the fire.
Last evening, bright candles and clear flasks;
(8) This night, a glimmering lamp and cold rain.

II

Below the glass windows
My mind dwells often on the one who left.
I fear most light rain and slicing wind might cause
A measure of parting grief finely painted.

I hate swallows scanning the room.
In spring chill we still burn charcoals.
On the racks a few tattered books
(8) Will while away bright noons and clear nights.

(XTLS: *Ting xue ci*, 5b–6a)

BIOGRAPHICAL NOTE AND TRANSLATION BY ANTHONY C. YU

張玉珍

P.98. Zhang Yuzhen (late 18th century)

Zhang Yuzhen (style names Lansheng and Yunshan), from Huating in Jiangsu, was the third daughter of Zhang Mengjie and the wife of Jin Hu of Taicang.

Her poetry was published as *Wanxiangju shichao* and *Wanxiangju ci* (Poems and song-lyrics from the Dwelling of Evening Fragrance, 1803), totaling six *juan*, with prefaces and congratulatory messages from many women members of Yuan Mei's poetry circle.[1]

P.98.1. Ta suo xing: *Cooling Off*

A game of chess just over,
The zither idly playing.
A fresh coolness rises in the courtyard,
Below the steps jasmines newly in bloom—
I pluck one to pin in my hair with a delicate scent.

The wind teases my gauze gown,
The moon keeping my white fan company.
(8) Does Chang E know the depth of sorrow?
Leaning on the railing, I'm wordless as I gaze at the bright Milky Way.
Above blue clouds, behind a heavy locked door, the goddess is hard
to see.

(XTLS: *Wanxiangju ci*, 2b–3a)

P.98.2. Liu shao qing

Watching spring leave—
These melancholy thoughts of parting,
With whom can I share?
A path lined with young bamboos,
Half a plot of sweet green
Reaching the thatched gate.

Traces of sorrow where I lean on the railing,
(8) The cuckoo's cry breaks my heart.
Letters written on brocade,
Spilled ink like clouds—
It's hard to bear from morning to evening.

(XTLS: *Wanxiangju ci*, 5b)

P.98.3. Cai sang zi: *Sitting in the Night*

Pale moon outside the curtain projects sparse shadows.
I sit till the night is deep,

Dejected till the night is deep.
How many candles by the window have I idly burnt?

Lately, letters from Mount Yan have ceased.
The road is distant, so are dreams.
Telling fortune with gold coins only makes me lonelier.

(XTLS: *Wanxiangju ci,* 10a)

P.98.4. Chengtou yue: *The Uncle of My Friend Yan Passes by My House and Shows Me His Recent Works; Humbly I Present the Following Verse*

It is sad to be kept apart by a slender river.
Holding each other's sleeves, we are happy to meet again.
We sit till the night is old and
The pale crescent moon
Clings to the tips of pine trees.
To your brocade pouch you have added new lyrics
Resembling dazzling dragons on the move.
Tonight let's chant them,
For tomorrow we'll part reluctantly—
I will gaze at the path by the riverbank to no end.

(XTLS: *Wanxiangju ci,* 9a)

P.98.5. Sheng zhazi

I remember when we parted,
We thought meeting again would be easy.
No means to relax my knitted brows—
It's been three springs and autumns.
The setting moon and the fading sound of a laundering block
Are both heartrending.
Even if I had seven resplendent carriages,
They could not carry my sorrow for a thousand miles.

(XTLS: *Wanxiangju ci,* 9a)

BIOGRAPHICAL NOTE AND TRANSLATION BY MICHELLE YEH

沈珂

P.99. Shen Ke (fl. late 18th century)

Shen Ke (school name Yunpu), was from Jiangyin in Jiangsu province. She was the daughter of Shen Jiaojun, a county magistrate, and the wife of Huang Zengwei, magistrate of Wujing. Her work is collected in *Zuiyue xuan shici* (Poems and song-lyrics from the Drunk Moon Studio).[1]

P.99.1. Die lian hua

Late in the flower season, spring draws to an end.
Half my time as a traveler
Is spent in melancholy.
Twilight in the deep yard, I sit quietly.
With nothing to do, I light a heart-shaped incense cake.

Birds cry on and on, urging me to go home.
Gazing sadly at the cloudy mountains,
(8) I can't see the roads in the Southland.
To whom can I tell my grievance?
Countless tears drop on my lapel.

(GXCC, 15/7a)

P.99.2. Bu suan zi: *Late Autumn*

Autumn scenes are sad to begin with.
How much more so at the end of autumn!
Outside my window autumn insects chirp now and then,
As if trying to keep autumn here.

Startled from my dream, I resent the autumn sounds.
Leaning on my pillow, I listen to the autumn rain.
This forlorn heart as cold as autumn,
(8) I sing a sad autumn song.

(GXCC, 15/8a–b)

P.99.3. Ru meng ling: *In Mid-Summer When It Gets Warmer, Someone Asks Me to Paint Plum Blossoms on a Fan; So I Inscribe the Following Verse on It*

Jade flutes play here and there in the river city;
It's the time of ripening plums again.
On the fan ink flowers bloom—
Their subtle fragrance seems to fill the sleeves.
Do you know,
Do you know,
As it sways, a spring breeze like the old days?

(GXCC, 15/8b)

P.99.4. Langtao sha

Rolling up the curtain,
I smell the fragrance of a hundred flowers.
Willow threads flutter,
Orioles and scissor-tailed swallows dart here and there.
Twenty-four flower periods—
How much youth has passed?
I chant a poem and drink from the goblet—
(8) The wine cleanses my heart of poesy.
I caress the flowers and play with grass—see how they compete in sweetness.
Flowing rivers, falling petals, and dancing willow catkins—
All make fine writings.

(GXCC, 15/7a)

P.99.5. Yuzhong hua

Throughout the night, wind and rain howl outside my windows;
They have no pity for the lush leaves and slender flowers.
Willow catkins caught on the curtains and the door,
Fallen petals in the courtyard—
These are times when the heart breaks.

Nibbling on a plum blossom, I make a secret plan:
To keep spring longer, I will use a piece of cool silk—

(8) On it I'll draw the outstanding form of plum blossoms,
Paint them in the boneless style—
The beauty of spring is still here.

(GXCC, 15/8b)

line 9: The "boneless style" of painting depicts the form of objects through areas of color wash rather than in outline.

BIOGRAPHICAL NOTE AND TRANSLATION BY MICHELLE YEH

汪玉軫

P.100. Wang Yuzhen (late 18th century)

Wang Yuzhen (style name Yiqiu, sobriquet *Xiaoyuan zhuren*, or Mistress of the Little Courtyard) was from Wujiang, Jiangsu. She left one volume of works entitled *Yiqiu xiaoyuan shi ci* (Poems and song-lyrics from the Little Courtyard suited to autumn). Recognized for her poetry and painting, she supported herself by the sale of her works.

The *Mingyuan shihua* by Shen Shanbao cites the second stanza of Wang Yuzhen's "Impromptu" ("Ou yin") as testament to her poverty:

> Willow catkins float in the wind, flowers blow in the rain;
> So much recent sorrow is haunting the green windowpane.
> I venture to ask the pair of butterflies crossing the wall:
> In whose home does spring dwell now?[1]

Guo Ling (1767–1831) copied down three of the song-lyrics translated here (P.100.1, P.100.2, and P.100.3), which he found in manuscript after her collection was published.[2]

P.100.1. Chang xiang si

The night grows cool;
My dreams are startled.
Half-spent orchid incense glimmers in the wall lantern.
A hungry rat scurries by the bed.

Counting the late night watches
Gives rise to longing.

Lying on the pillow to write songs, not a verse finished,
(8) I weigh my words until dawn comes.

(GXCC, 10/11a)

P.100.2. Fengguang hao

Tightly closed flower buds, flowers in full bloom.
I've seen all of spring's colors,
But spring once more fades away,
Stirring deep sadness.
In the empty courtyard, rain left traces of green moss.
The sky is empty and vast,
A short corridor, a winding railing;
(8) I'll linger a while.

(GXCC, 10/11b)

P.100.3. Pusa man

In melancholy, I found one verse, but could not write another.
Sleepless at midnight, I lit the lamp.
The wind brought in dew, a fine mist.
It oppresses me, the autumn air so cold.
To the incense brazier I add animal coals.
The molded incense block gently disperses.
What thing might help me to express my feelings?
(8) An insect beneath the stairs sings.

(GXCC, 10/11b)

lines 5–6: "Animal charcoal," made from bones, was supposed to be especially warming. Coal dust might also be molded into cakes of animal shape. On "molded incense" (*xiang zhuan*), incense shaped in coiling patterns like seal script that kept time as it burned, see P.46.6.

P.100.4. Pusa man

The west wind in the courtyard, I am utterly desolate.
The *wutong*'s last few withered autumn leaves
Knock on the paper window's carved screen.
Alone beneath the coverlet, I listen through my dream.

Long night watches are accompanied by sharp clarions,
Urging the lamp petals to fall.
Everything I see consumes my soul.
(8) Lowering my head, I see traces of tears.

(GXCC, 10/11b)

P.100.5. Haitang chun

For no reason one night the east wind suddenly raged,
Storming so the apricot flowers grew wasted and thin.
Wait until the little peaches are red.
That's late spring.

My pity for the flowers: do they know of it?
Look at my knit brows and deep wrinkles in the mirror.
News of the flowers' arrival comes over and over again,
(8) But fragrant years cannot be relived.

(GXCC, 10/12a)

line 7: The poet puns on "hua xin" (news that the flowers are blooming), which can also refer to a girl who has reached the age of twenty-four.

BIOGRAPHICAL NOTE AND TRANSLATION BY KATHRYN LOWRY

浦夢珠

P.101. Pu Mengzhu (late 18th century)

The series of nine poems included here constitute the entire extant work of Pu Mengzhu, whose school name was Heshuang. Taken as a series, they form the lyric autobiography of a literate Chinese woman of relatively modest background.

P.101.1. Jiang shen zi

1

I remember when I first learned how to embroider in my spring
  chamber:
The stand was as tall as I
And handling the golden needle was quite a task.

Unable to tell the four corners of the floral design,
I could not figure out how to get to the center.

Emerald green and bright red I sorted with my own hands,
Bits of yarns stuck on the vermilion windows.
(8) Innocent and naive, I did not recognize mandarin ducks
And wondered why the other girls
Never tired of embroidering them in pairs.

II

I remember when silken bangs first covered my forehead
Like glossy dark clouds lowering to touch my eyebrows.
People praised me for being clever and smart—
I won throwing coins with Sister Wisdom
And beat Aunt Orchid in grass-blade jousts.
When the moon shadow filled the courtyard, I asked the maid
To play hide-and-seek in the west boudoir.
(8) We shuttled among flower shadows—
Afraid that our clogs might be heard,
We climbed up the stairs in our stockings.

III

I remember the cool ripples standing still
And a skyful of clouds reflected between fish fins.
We were about to board a carved boat but hesitated.
Our gauze gowns were light as leaves,
With scents borrowed from the lotus flowers.

All of a sudden a gust arose from white duckweed.
Our orchid boat was blown to the lakeside.
(8) I cared not to pick any purple water caltrops,
For I resented their endless silken fibers—
Their nature is to entangle you.

IV

I remember on Double-Seventh Eve I secretly prayed to the Lover Stars.
Gently I opened the latticed door, incense smoke entwining,

No one around in the silent deep yard.
Who would have expected a gust of wind
To flutter my lotus-colored skirt?

Rattan bed six feet long, red jade pillow,
Cool traces on the bamboo mat.
(8) I awoke from a dream and turned around abruptly—
Who would fix my undone hair
Resembling a fluffy cloud?

V

I remember the path by Soul-Dissolving Bridge—
For no reason a lean horse carried me home.
Weeds climbed all over my old boudoir,
When I opened the gold-trimmed trunk
I saw my dust-covered light gown.
They say traces of red tears were seen on the rhino curtain,
And the handsome one's waist became trimmer.
(8) The red wall cannot stop swallows from flying in pairs,
But I regret that they can't convey my sorrow—
They only know how to peck mud to build their nests.

VI

I remember lamenting spring while recovering from an illness.
The day was long; languidly I came down the boudoir stairs.
I fear I can attain Enlightenment only in my next life.
When it comes to herbs, I plant only Live-Alone,
As to flowers, I don't pluck Forget-Your-Sorrow.

On the piece of silk unfolding by the window
I paint a portrait in the double-contour manner.
(8) But I won't send it to the Herd Boy,
For it cannot
Trace the autumn in my heart.

VII

I remember getting up at dawn to fix my hair with two bamboo pins.
For the first time I painted my eyebrows with snail dye

Like faint spring traces on spring hills.
I was surprised to see the new look—

Reminding me of last night's crescent moon.
As usual, I applied some almond face powder—
How strange that it would not go on smoothly that time.
(8) They said the man had the beauty of fine jade.
After finishing my make-up, I was too shy to rise
As I stole a look at myself in the mirror.

VIII

I remember when the inauspicious matchmaker came for my
horoscope.
With back to the door, I sat quietly in my chamber
And eavesdropped on every word:
"A portent in a dream commended the green phoenix.
Because of his birthday, red rams are to be avoided."

She said the moon must be accompanied by two stars—
How was I to refute such nonsense?
(8) Born an immortal, I cannot follow just any man;
How can they mistake me for Emerald Liu,
Longing to be some Prince Runan's concubine?

IX

I remember the oars on Lonesome River
Which I mistook for peach roots.
Instead of drifting to a grassy lawn, I fell into a muddy puddle.
Not even the hundred-foot walls of the City of Ladies
Could keep vibrant spring out.

I was assigned an empty chamber to inhabit by myself.
Its carpet of green moss reminded me of the Long Gate Palace.
(8) My name was changed; each time I heard it I frowned—
There is no evening rain,
So why the name Morning Clouds?

(GXCC, 14/1a–2b)

iv, line 1: On the Double Seventh, see P.5.1 and P.19.2.

viii, line 1: Comparing the eight-character horoscopes of the potential couple was the first stage in traditional Chinese marriage negotiations.

viii, line 5: A "red ewe" would be a woman born in the Year of the Ram.

viii, line 6: The "moon" is the man's principal wife, and the "stars" a pair of concubines.

viii, lines 9–10: Emerald Liu (Liu Biyu) was a girl from a poor family who became the cherished concubine of the Prince of Runan, according to a set of songs recorded in the *Yuefu shiji* (45/663–64). Her story is probably more legendary than historical. Pu's meaning is that she will not stoop to being a concubine, even to a very rich man.

ix, line 4: The reference is probably to the city walls of Xiangyang, reinforced on the orders of the mother of the general Zhu Xu, a lady née Han.

ix, line 7: On the allusion to Long Gate Palace, a reminiscence of the rejected Consort Chen, see P.8a.1.

ix, lines 9–10: The last couplet of the poem is a wry reference to the king of Chu and his encounter with the goddess of Wu Mountain (see P.9.2).

BIOGRAPHICAL NOTE AND TRANSLATION BY MICHELLE YEH

倪瑞璿

P.102. Ni Ruixuan (late 18th century)

Ni Ruixuan, a native of Suqian county in Jiangsu province, was the second wife of Xu Qitai. The biographical sketch prefixed to her poems in Shen Deqian's *Qingshi biecai ji* says that "she possessed all the feminine virtues of gentleness and humility, but [in managing a large, extended household] she alone could discover secrets and inappropriate behavior, punish licentiousness and deceitfulness: Is such a person easily to be found among the ranks of women? Even in her reading she preserved the strictest decorum." After her death, Cao Jia found her poems and published them as *Qiecun shigao* (Poem-drafts preserved in a trunk; three *juan*, 1830).[1]

P.102.1. Passing by Ling Cheng Temple to Visit the Graves of Gu Dake and Dai Guozhu

Fall wind trill, high and hollow
Jumbled mountains crisscrossed with slanting light
Old branches braid with the sky
Mosses running over the ancient temple

Go through the gate:
touch a piece from a broken stele
Sigh with respect
at the sight of what has been left behind
Remember the luck
that ran out for the former Ming

The rising bands of bandits
howling
Aggression failed
appeasement failed
Hornets and scorpions became tigers and leopards
Everywhere they went
no town could withstand them
Everything alive
subject to random cruelty

These two men: true heroes
their loyalty and virtue heaven-bestowed
Pure gold, strong iron
fused in one nature
Trained by ice and frost
drilled by the cold

When the rebel lances came that morning
these two rushed in with rocks and arrows
Minor officials, yet sworn to self-sacrifice
for who thinks of himself when the forces are thin?
Generous, noble, at ease, laughing
quarreling over who would go first

Cannons fired against the rebels
heaven and earth
shook and grieved
The rebels using sorcery and demons
ants mobbed
hornets blitzed
The balance of power tipped
hands sliced off
arms still falling

Martyrdom met right conduct
sun and moon
contending for greatest light
Rebel horses spooked
by the loyal blood
scattered across the wasteland

Even now in this wilderness in light of day
one still sees the burnt remains

After eighty years too few
offer sacrifices to these dead
Their families almost vanished
though the old still repeat the tale

Archivists and historians
should bring these events to light
Whoever holds a pen
should seek out this obscure bequest

(QSBC, 31/21a–22a)

Gu Dake and Dai Guozhu both died supporting Shi Kefa (d. 1645) in his efforts to defend the Southern Ming and protect the throne from both internal rebels and the invading Manchu armies. At the time of the incident, Shi Kefa was in charge of grain transportation along the Grand Canal and was based in Yangzhou. By the mid-eighteenth century, Shi Kefa was honored as a patriotic martyr, while Gu and Dai were merely noted on a dusty stele. As Ni states in the preface to this poem, "When I passed through the area with my mother, we stopped to pay our respects at the gravesite. I was deeply saddened to think that their actions had not been recorded in the history books, and so I composed this poem for the use of future ballad-collectors." (The line numbering for this poem reflects the English emphasis and not the original Chinese.)

line 35: Ni adds the note: "The rebels forced naked women to lie down in the line of the cannon fire in order to terrify their enemy."

P.102.2. *Written in Fun for Li, the Old Mountain Man*

Li, old mountain man, years adding up
Hair gone white, but face still rosy
Shrubby mallows your palace, black stick for a son
Heart full of mist, asleep in a ditch
Nighttime groaning your bones are sore, morning groaning with
hunger

One foot steps forward, the other holds back
You are graced by heaven, so don't complain
(8) Think of the famed and the fortunate: never satisfied

(QSBC, 31/23a)

This playful poem was written to Ni Ruixuan's maternal uncle, Li Guanyuan, who was suffering from a foot ailment.

P.102.3. My Great-Uncle Fan, Passing Through Jinling, Composed a Poem upon the Grave of Mr. Fang Zhengxue. I Followed His Rhymes.

The Northern Army at the Jinchuan Gate—
Concerning uncles, you cited Zhou Gong: loyalty till death
Jade blood: this one district saw your tenfold clan buried
Only the green mountains watch over their graves
Honoring the dead is our common will, our fate
But moss crawls over these unread inscriptions
What can the shepherds and woodsmen know of history?
(8) Through this way again, in grief in the slanting setting sun

(QSBC, 31/23a–b)

Jinling is the traditional name for present-day Nanjing. Fang Xiaoru (1357–1402, studio name Zhengxue, "Correct Learning") was a court erudite and advisor of the Ming emperor Huidi. When Huidi was overthrown by his uncle, the Yongle Emperor, Fang wore mourning to court and for this show of loyalty was put in prison. Then Yongle demanded that Fang, whose literary ability was well known, draft an imperial edict to set the people's minds at rest concerning his taking the throne from his nephew. Fang replied by contrasting Yongle's usurpation with the faithful administration of the Duke of Zhou (Zhou Gong), who in the early years of the Zhou dynasty had acted as regent for his nephew but never presumed to take the throne for himself. Fang was condemned to be cut in pieces, and his family was exterminated to the tenth degree of kinship.

line 1: Yongle's Northern Pacification Army entered Nanjing through the Jinchuan Gate.

P.102.4. Remembering My Mother

Wide river that won't let me cross
Not even knowing how you're getting on

In the dark, minutes drop, tears drop
Worrying you're thinking of me, weeping more

(QSBC, 31/24a)

P.102.5. My Fourth Brother Kenzi Wanted to Change His Name and Style Name. Selecting Words from "Wen Wang Shi Zi," I Renamed Him Kexin, with the New Style Name Zhengzi, and Then Composed This Poem to Mark the Event.

Respect, virtue, worth: a man's life is not in his name
Anyone can call himself Li Bo or Bo Juyi
And what good is that, repetition by empty rote?
You're a smart, happy kid, good to be around
A decent job in Xiang, born to an old family
Too soon our father left us to wander here
House in ruins, no way to go back, washed out and poor
(8) Writing letters, mother's family helping out a little
But you found a teacher, worked hard, won first place early
Talented and able, your reputation grew
You'd had your name for many years
(12) But suddenly grew sick of it, wouldn't even answer to it
So you asked me to change it and I couldn't refuse
We found the words in the *Record of Ritual*
In the Sung they turned the swamps into schools
(16) Filled with the fragrance of learning
A new name is like a new house
Fix it up well, and the beams won't collapse
Don't be like one of those Jiangnan oranges
(20) Transplanted north of the Huai: all skin and no juice.

(QSBC, 31/22b–23a)

Changing one's name in traditional China was a step taken either to mark a major life change or to change one's luck. Ni's choices derive from a sentence in *Li ji* (The Record of ritual), "Wen Wang shi zi": "When the Son of Heaven inspected a school, at *daybreak* [*kexin*] the drums gave the *alert* [*zhengzi*], prompting the crowd to foregather" (SSJZS, 20/26b).

lines 1–2: The literal words of this couplet are: "The difficult [*nan*] matches itself with the easy [*yi*], / The red [*chi*] compares itself with the white [*bai/bo*]"—a multilayered pun that the author's own note may help clarify for readers of Chinese.

"The Tang *jinshi* Huang Junan likened his poetry to that of Bo Letian [Bo Juyi] and called himself Junan, adopting Ledi as his style name. Li Chi, on the other hand, compared himself with Li Bo."

lines 19–20: For the proverb, see *Yanzi chunqiu*, 6 (*Wenyuan ge Siku quanshu* [SKQS] 446: 144).

BIOGRAPHICAL NOTE AND TRANSLATION BY IONA MAN-CHEONG AND ELIOT WEINBERGER

談印梅

P.103. Tan Yinmei (fl. late 18th century)

A native of Gui'an in present-day Huzhou, Zhejiang, Tan Yinmei (style name Xiangqing) was married to Sun Tingkun, a registrar of Nanhe. She is often mentioned in the same breath with her older sister, Tan Yinlian. Both sisters studied poetry with Sun Xianyi (some sources have Sun Qiushi) and achieved fame as poets. Apparently, whenever they wrote new poems, scholars would rush to collect them.

Their teacher published a joint work by the sisters entitled *Huayun lianyin ji* (The flower rhymes collection of linked verse). Tan Yinmei's collection of *shi* and *ci* poems, the *Jiuyixianguan shici chao* (Manuscript of poems and song-lyrics from the Immortals' Lodge of Nine-Doubts Mountain), was printed in 1890. Yinmei also wrote the preface to her sister's posthumous work *Pingluo yicao* (The posthumous manuscript of Pingluo, also known as *Huazhong junzi yicao* [The posthumous manuscript of the prince among flowers]) printed in the same year. It is clear from the prefaces she wrote to Yinlian's poems that the two sisters were very close in their emotional and poetic development.

P.103.1. Diao qiu huan jiu: *Talking at Night with My Elder Sister*

Autumn hides us behind double gates.
Sitting on linked beds by the west window, we trim the candle.
How many fine nights can there be?
Days hurry by, the passing clouds an illusion.
I've tasted all the flavors of sorrow
And regret there's nowhere to bury my worries within these walls.
Suddenly I think of that awful day when we shall part:
Then I'll be anxious to see you return for a home visit.

Once we separate
It will be hundreds of miles.

What's the point of writing about famous mountains?
(12) I sigh that this year I've scribbled off and on,
Half treating it as a game.
I am associated with not a few women friends,
Before my eyes, their silk gauze robes displayed in multitude.
(16) On whom can I count to be my companion in these chambers?
I have been unable to abandon my poetic nature.
Still more I'm sorry your features have all grown plain.
When the one lamp flickers out,
(20) We lift up our voices in song.

(XTLS: *Jiuyixianguan ci*, 3b–4a)

P.103.2. Jinlü qu: *Composed in Grief as I Sorted Out My Sister's Posthumous Poems*

It happens when I read the pieces she left behind:
I can feel a chill, clear wind rising, filling the paper,
Its sorrowful sound cracking the bamboos.
In looks she compared with Zuo Fen, only more precocious;
What's more, her talent surpassed Xu Shu's.
She was ready to enjoy the full measure of this world of dust.
Let me ask then: where would be a good place to bury her fragrance?
(8) Even the green hills would gain by her perfection.
Down the road to the Yellow Springs
Ghosts, too, must cry.

Every morning, every evening, we pursued each other's company.
(12) Why now have the clouds disappeared and the rain dispersed?
And my form is single, my shadow alone.
Of course we'll meet again in worlds to come:
Who says that future lives have not yet been divined?
(16) You can invite me to join you on the list of immortals.
I was startled when you came into my dream so clearly last night.
I admired your appearance, warm as jade as in old times.
So I held your hand
(20) And told you my heart's worries.

(XTLS: *Jiuyixianguan ci*, 7b)

line 4: See Zuo Fen, P.3.
line 5: On Xu Shu and her husband Qin Jia, see P.54a.4.
line 9: On the Yellow Springs, see P.29.9.

P.103.3. Qinyuan chun: *Inscribed on My Own Portrait*

Where did you come from?
What year will you depart?
Alone without any companion.
For a short while you stand among the flowers
So thin your bones are showing.
We sit intimately by the lamp,
Friends who have cast off formalities.
You by nature sad
And I still spiritless,
Both are unfortunates at the edge of the world.
I unroll the picture:
Only you can know me
And I cherish you too.

Why not vanish through the Gate of Emptiness?
Early on I threw away the red dust for white clouds.
It's just that in wailing and weeping tears
I cannot avoid the common lot.
Trials and tribulations
Cannot compare with release from the cycle of rebirths.
The lilies for curing sorrow have dried up forever,
The light of spring grew old long ago,
Never again will the parents call for their daughter.
How is it that you too
Have a heart like a game board,
Uneven from holding resentment?

(XTLS: *Jiuyixianguan ci*, 9a–b)

line 20: The daylily; see P.2.1 (Song 16).
lines 24–25: Tan alludes to a poem by the Tang poet Li Shangyin in which an ancient game of throwing chess pieces at a board with a raised center is made into a metaphor for the feeling of resentment at unfairness (QTS, 539/6164).

P.103.4. Dian jiang chun: *Thoughts on a Cold Night*

Lonely solitude, deep in the boudoir:
As I face the window, moonlight feels cool as water.
Late at night, sleepless:
Soaking wet from flood upon flood of tears.

Toss and turn on the bed
With only the orchid-oil lamp for company.
In the quiet courtyard
Insects chirp and a crane cries
Shattering my heart to pieces.

(XTLS: *Jiuyixianguan ci*, 9b)

P.103.5. Wu jiaqi

After parting, the carriage wheels roll on forever,
Yet after death, the silkworm's threads are hard to break.
A hundred kinds of teasing, a thousand sorts of coyness:
Loving you never became mere habit.

At its peak, love turns and breeds hate.
So long together, who cares if we part?
Well aware that news of your return is still unsure,
I first count the miles of your journey home.

(XTLS: *Jiuyixianguan ci*, 11b)

BIOGRAPHICAL NOTE AND TRANSLATION BY GRACE FONG

熊璉

P.104. Xiong Lian (late 18th–early 19th centuries)

Xiong Lian (courtesy name Shangzhen, sobriquets Danxian and Ruxue Shanren) was a native of the Rugao region in Jiangsu province. She was active into the nineteenth century, married a crippled man, and lived in poverty most of her life. The four *juan* of song-lyrics she left behind show a remarkable range of style: from delicate restraint (*wanyue*) to a more heroic mode (*haofang*), the latter being more evident in her poems addressed to male friends and teachers.

P.104.1. Die lian hua: *Inscription on the Painting "Lighting a Lamp to Read* The Peony Pavilion*"*

Closing the doors on dusk in the depths of the courtyard—
Inside the windows, a lone lamp;
Beyond the windows, rain-soaked plantains.
Ten thousand thoughts that cannot be spoken,
The chirping of insects within four walls so cold.

Strange indeed was the music of Linchuan's lingering regrets—
This story of life unto death, death unto life—
So strange that as they turn to the heartbreaking points
The ill-fated and the love-crazed join in a common grief.
Since ancient times a sensibility too keen has undone so many.

One scroll of autumn light, boundless sorrow.
Hands working wonders from nothing
Painted the scene of that moment.
Sitting alone, she spreads open the book in the long clear night,
Pearls of tears come down, her cloud-like hair is cold.

The gentle soul on paper feels so tenderly for Yuming—
Illusory and real
Is the forlorn world of the dream.
Is it true that her grace would come alive with a call?
The setting sun has seen the shadows of peach blossoms.

(XTLS: *Danxian ci*, 2/11b)

The painting's title is a line from a poem attributed to Feng Xiaoqing (ca. 1600), a sensitive, talented, beautiful, and ill-fated concubine who became the object of a passionate cult in the late Ming and early Qing. On Xiaoqing's story and its historical development, see Widmer, "Xiaoqing's Literary Legacy." Xiaoqing was obsessed with Tang Xianzu's *The Peony Pavilion* (*Mudan ting*; see P.72.6), even to the point of modeling many of her actions just before her death on those of the play's heroine. Xiaoqing's poem reads: "I cannot bear to listen to the cold rain by the dark window, / Lighting a lamp I read *The Peony Pavilion.* / In the human world there was one more obsessed than I, / Xiaoqing is then not alone in her sorrow and melancholy."

line 1: A possible allusion to two lines from a famous lyric by Ouyang Xiu written to the same tune: "The depths of the courtyard, how deep? . . . Closing the doors on dusk, / With no means to make spring stay" (QSC, 1: 162).

line 6: Tang Xianzu was a native of Linchuan county in Jiangxi province.

line 9: "Ill-fated" (*boming*) refers to Feng Xiaoqing, "love-crazed" (*qingchi*) to Du Liniang, the heroine of *The Peony Pavilion*.

line 16: "Yuming tang" (White Camellia Hall) was Tang Xianzu's studio name.

line 19: In *The Peony Pavilion*, the self-portrait Du Liniang painted before her death so entrances Liu Mengmei that he calls out to it and it "comes alive" when Liniang's soul visits him. With this story in mind, Xiaoqing also had her portrait painted before she died.

P.104.2. Ta suo xing: *Souls of Autumn*

A somber gloom fit for sorrow,
Mysterious, dissolving shapes about to be transformed.
Who but Song Yu can describe it?
The receding distance seems to be there, yet almost not there.
Chill rises from the hair, inspiring fear.

Will-o'-the-wisp floats among ancient graves,
Rain hits deserted steps.
Withered willows of the Six Dynasties hang in the west wind.
So many times have I searched vainly in my dreams—
Startled, I see an abundance of leaves coming down, coming down.

(XTLS: *Danxian ci*, 3/9b)

line 3: On Song Yu's lament for autumn see P.54d.3.

line 10: A possible allusion to the fourth line of "Lady of the Xiang River" (Xiang *furen*), one of the *Nine Songs* from the *Chuci* (*Chuci buzhu*, 2/27a); see P.11.16.

P.104.3. Zhegu tian: *Autumn Dreams*

For a moment's escape from the demon of sorrow there is the land of sleep.
The evening is pure as water, chill rises from the bamboo mat.
The wind in *wutong* trees, blowing far, confounds the soul in pain,
The rain on plantains—dream's startled return—the night is still long.

Meditation on illusions,
Regrets for time flowing past,
Empty curtains in a fitful light reflecting the silver lamp.
How can all these be the world of Handan,
Coldly mocking the human arena of wealth and glory?

(XTLS: *Danxian ci*, 3/10a)

line 8: In the famous eighth-century story "Zhen zhong ji" by Shen Jiji, later the subject of a play by Tang Xianzu, the protagonist, Student Lu, laments his meager lot on the road to Handan, where he meets a Daoist named Old Lü. Old Lü gives Student Lu a pillow; Lu enters the pillow, lives out a long life of fame, fortune, and unpredictability, dies—and wakes up to find himself still sitting next to the old Daoist in the inn by the Handan road, where a pot of millet porridge has yet to come to a boil (Li Fang et al., comp., *Taiping guangji*, 82/526–28). "Handan" thus stands for the dreamworld. For an English translation of the story, see "The World Inside a Pillow," trans. William Nienhauser, in Ma and Lau, eds., *Traditional Chinese Stories*, pp. 435–38.

P.104.4. He xin liang: *Thoughts and Feelings*

Scroll in hand yet unmindful of reading:
My zither is already burnt,
Crane cooked, pine uprooted, chrysanthemum cut.
Not the many adversities suffered by great talents—
I just believe I am destined for little happiness.
Nothing need be said
for tears about to be shed at the road's end.
Last night I dreamed of sprouting wings,
Listening by clouds' edge to someone singing
the song of flying immortals.
But it was only
the wind knocking the bamboo.

Contentment eludes human existence at every point.
Most worthy of longing are
fragrance of incense burners, vessels for tea,
mountains blue, water green.
I have long wished to avoid the human world and return to purity.
How may I find three thatch huts
And escape from the furor of the world of red dust?
Yet I have not repaid the great debt to the one who raised me:
I bow low repeatedly and secretly invoke the blessing of the tender clouds.
As to what will happen after death:
Who has leisure enough to divine?

(XTLS: *Danxian ci*, 1/1b–2a)

lines 2–3: These images of sacrifice and finality derive from stories of reclusive geniuses.

line 6: On crying at the road's end as a locus classicus of despair, see P.121.8.

P.104.5. Nan xiangzi: *Poem on a Painting*

Cranes set free soar through mist and clouds.
Who is playing the purple jade flute on the other shore?
Unhurried, indistinct poetic sentiments
Enter the painting, all worthy of form.
With his tattered hat he faces the wind and crosses the wooden bridge.

He wanders, stepping on fine jade,
Buying wine at the village ahead where the snow is not yet gone.
Smilingly he points: where is my abode?
Tips of plum branches—waves of
Subtle fragrance floating among the bamboo.

(XTLS: *Danxian ci*, 2/2b–3a)

P.104.6. Xi jiang yue: *Consort Yu Poppies*

Slender grace and supple loveliness:
Even after taking root at Gaixia,
Who has any control over drifting, falling, withering?
Do you remember the sorrow of losing your country in another year?
For you then seem to lower the coiled knot of your hair, wordless.
Is it longing for the fading spring—
Let alone the encounter with the crying cuckoo
Whose grief pierces the evening rain?
The splendor of illusion—
Why not blossom next to the encircling walls?
Say no more about the kingdom-toppling and city-toppling beauty.
Green, green graves
Are only for the likes of the Shining Consort.
So many beauties have come and gone like dreams,
Who would mourn the numberless mounds of yellow earth?
The chaste spirit of the era,
Most ill-fated one in a thousand years
Still dances before the wind.

Where is the palace of Han?
(20) This flower, in the end, will always belong to Chu.

(XTLS: *Danxian ci*, 4/2a–2b)

On the story of Consort Yu, see P.28.1. On the poppies named after her, see P.68.6. and P.73.7.iii.

lines 12–13: The tomb of the Shining Consort, Wang Zhaojun (see P.58b.9), was said to be eternally green.

P.104.7. Baizi ling: *Facing the Moon*

I stand still on the empty steps
In the silent, deserted depths of the courtyard.
Wutong leaves flutter by an ornate well.
The precious mirror in the clear sky—autumn is like water—
Cleanses the heart of dust and impurities.
I stroke my sword and intone a long cry—
There is no home to turn to.
(8) My gaze breaks off at the farthest heavenly streets.
Ice-strings and ivory pipes:
Who is enjoying this pure scene?

I love its subtle light that extends over ten thousand *li*.
(12) In the depths of colorful clouds are
Evanescent shadows of jade palaces.
I want to ask those female companions with rainbow skirts
Whether their minds turn to the grief and loneliness of the human world.
(16) Wandering with immortals on pillows,
Waiting for cranes in front of the wind—
Startled in happy dreams and awakening.
Reluctantly I enter the silk curtains
(20) As slowly, slowly the autumn night deepens with the water clock.

(XTLS: *Danxian ci*, 4/3a)

line 6: An allusion to the story of the retainer Feng Xuan, who strummed on his sword and announced his intention to go home; see P.75b.1.

line 11: On "ten thousand *li*," see P.92.1.

line 14: The celestial maidens in the moon. "Rainbow skirts" may allude to "The Tune of Rainbow Skirts and Feathered Jackets," which the Tang imperial consort

Yang Guifei was supposed to have learned from the fairies of the moon palace; see P.83b.7.

P.104.8. Fenghuangtai shang yi chuixiao: *Sleepless in Sickness*

Lamplight dims in the funnel curtains,
Leaves rustle on empty steps.
From hollow walls the wind comes under the pillow,
Just at a moment of pain without cause,
When in dejection I am about to shed tears.
All kinds of old regrets and new sorrows
Are gathered in the bell of the fifth watch.
How can I bear
Dreams that again have difficulty being formed,
As, rising, I am yet not risen?

Such a state, bones consumed, spirit dissipated:
I ask how can this fragile creature bear it?
How many in the floating world are similarly afflicted?
Thinking back on the limitless heaven and earth
And the boundless expanse of history—
How many hearts and minds fine as brocade have been transmitted?
I am grateful that the great talents over the ages are immortal.
With effort I should yet embrace the blanket and intone pure lyrics,
Release my spirit and let it lodge high.

(XTLS: *Danxian ci*, 3/8a–b)

P.104.9. Die lian hua: *Feelings*

Lakes and seas create wind, sky creates snow.
In this vast, limitless expanse,
Where to escape the travails of evil karma?
A loveless life with a hundred tribulations—
A homeless swallow, leaves in the autumn wind.

Before bowing to distant heaven I dissolve in bitter tears of grief.
I want to ask questions of the moon-goddess Chang E,
But clouds block the moon beyond the flowers.

And yet deep feelings cannot be told:
The wronged souls are bursting with the blood of the crying cuckoo.

(XTLS: *Danxian ci*, 1/3a–b)

line 10: On the cuckoo, see P.5.1.

P.104.10. Man jiang hong

A neighbor girl came back for a visit after her marriage. Shortly afterward she parted from her mother and wept in grief. I heard her, and in sadness wrote the following lyric to mark my sympathy.

She covered her face and wept in grief.
Who can bear to witness this scene?
Clearly like the lute music beyond the frontier,
The Shining Consort on horseback.
Gibbons' laments at the Chu Gorges break off and continue in surprise and fear.
Wild geese traversing the length of the sky share her woe and anguish.
Compared to ordinary farewells—
A greater heartache,
More cause for sorrow.

Clouds hide the trees,
Waves grow quiet by the harbor.
At crossroads she sobs,
Turns back, gazes—
Sees the slanting rays glowing ever lower,
Wild flowers blooming in the cold.
A hundred miles of distant sky entangle her parting dreams,
A gust of wind rises and rocks her light boat.
I sigh that in bygone years,
I was she—
Thoughts and feelings relived.

(XTLS: *Danxian ci*, 2/11a–b)

BIOGRAPHICAL NOTE AND TRANSLATION BY WAI-YEE LI

P.105. The Sisters Bao Zhilan, Bao Zhihui, and Bao Zhifen

The Bao sisters grew up in a literary household in Dantu, Jiangsu; both their father, Bao Gao (1708–65), and mother, Chen Ruizhu, wrote poetry. Their elder brother Zhizhong earned his *jinshi* degree in 1769 and held a succession of official posts; little is known of their other brother, Zhiyong. With their distinguished father, dubbed an "Erudite Literatus" in 1736, often away from home, their mother took charge of the education of her children and the editing and compiling of both her husband's and her son's poetry. Forty-nine of her own poems appeared in a one-*juan* mother-daughter collection entitled *Kexuanlou hegao* (Combined manuscripts from Lesson Selection Gallery), first published in 1882, with an afterword by Zhizhong.

The sisters were married to men who are now best known for their wives: eldest sister, Zhilan (style name Wanfang), to a national university student, middle sister, Zhihui (style name Chaixiang), to a subprefectural magistrate, and youngest sister, Zhifen (style name Huanyun), to a department magistrate. Zhilan's works include a long autobiographical poem written on the occasion of her fiftieth birthday, in which she describes her delight in reading and writing as a girl and how wifely duties kept her from these pursuits for decades. Zhihui was a disciple of Yuan Mei, and her poetry was considered better than Zhizhong's. She may well be the "Elder Sister Chaixiang" to whom Wu Zao (P.122) wrote several poems. Zhifen's works include several poems to her husband and her poetic responses to her reading of the *Chuci*.

Aside from Zhifen's *ci* in Xu Naichang's *Xiao tan luan shi huike guixiu ci* (XTLS) compendium, the most complete collection of the sisters' poetry is *Jingjiang Baoshi sannüshi shichao heke* (Joint edition of the poetry of the three erudite Bao women of the Yangzi region). It was also known as *Xuankelou heke* in homage to the earlier mother-daughter selection. This combined edition was published in 1882 by Dai Xieyuan, one of Zhilan's great-grandsons. This collection (cited below as JJBS) contains Zhilan's *Qiyunge shichao* (Poems from Rising Cloud Pavilion, first published 1798), 320 poems in four *juan* (which, according to Zhizhong, amounts to less than a tenth of her lifetime output); Zhihui's *Qingyuge shichao* (Poems from Clear Joy Pavilion, first published 1811), 413 poems in six *juan*; and Zhifen's *Sanxiuzhai shichao* (Poems from Thrice-Blossoming Herb Studio, first known edition 1878), 170 poems in two *juan*. The sisters' collections are augmented by numerous prefaces and postfaces signed by Zhizhong, by various eminent poets, and by the sisters themselves, discussing one another's work.[1]

P.105a. Bao Zhilan (late 18th century)

P.105a.1. Sunset

Distant peaks fixed in the cloud-streaked dusk sky,
Cooling trees catch the slanting sunlight.
The piping of a reed whistle from the garrison tower,
The faint sound of bells from a nearby temple.
The last leaves rustle as they fall,
A racket of crows flashes in flight.
I sigh as dusk draws near.
(8) Few know this state of mind.

(JJBS, 1: 1/10a)

P.105a.2. Pear Blossoms in the Next Yard

Spring is more lovely over the wall,
Cool moonlight covers half the yard at dusk.
In the night stillness I seem to hear someone sigh,
The swing is motionless in the cold dark.

(JJBS, 2: 3/14b)

P.105a.3. Spring Sacrifice [from a series of five poems]

V

I run into the old man next door and we talk nonstop.
He wears a tall cap and common cotton clothes,
Falling-down-drunk on a cup of spring sacrifice wine.
At sunset his children come to take him home.

(JJBS, 1: 1/1b–2a)

P.105b. Bao Zhihui (late 18th century)

P.105b.1. Sleepless

Sick so long I can't sleep,
My shoulders draped as night drags on.
The lamp is frozen, its orchid flame low,
In heavy frost, the cotton quilt is cold.
I hear the watchman's rattle faint from the street
And wait for the morning light to wander in.
I so love this halt to all activity,
I open a book—reading really hits the spot.

(JJBS, 4: 4/9b)

P.105b.2. Sitting Up at Night

A half moon rises through the *wutong* leaves,
A clear night scene in the still and empty yard.
Autumn air steals into a smattering of stars,
The coldness of the dew starts up the crickets.
Through time's slow passage, I am a candle in the wind,
This fleeting life of mine, a watch hastening toward dawn.
In the capital a thousand miles away it's this same moon.
Geese in line—that wayward one—always make me think of you.

(JJBS, 3: 2/9a)

P.105b.3. Thoughts on a Rainy Day

Day by day light dust scatters through the sky.
I keep the curtains closed up tight, even in broad daylight.
The past comes back like waking from a spring dream,
And idle sorrows are just made more pressing by the sound of rain.
When will we echo each other's rhymes again at Selection Gallery?
Your letter still hasn't come.
How time lapses—I totally forgot—it's the end of the third month.
Suddenly, outside the gate: roses for sale!

(JJBS, 3: 1/10a)

line 5: Selection Gallery is probably short for Lesson Selection Gallery, as in the title of the joint poetry collection by the sisters and their mother.

P.105b.4. Going by the Old House

We moved out when we were small
And haven't been back for forty years.
If you're looking for flowers, the paths are still here,
But ask about names, and the old neighbors are gone.
The trees are so old it must be early spring,
The rafters are bare, but the swallows still come back.
In this unbounded desolation,
(8) I face the setting sun in silence.

(JJBS, 4: 6/1b)

P.105c. Bao Zhifen (late 18th century)

P.105c.1. Getting Through the Summer

Deep in the courtyard, the dirt and noise die down,
Sunlight slants itself on the buffeted curtain.
Sounds of a chess match: clicks of jade.
The scent of ink infuses bright gauze.
Gardenias tie a love knot,
Two lotus blossoms share a single stem.
I love those new young swallows,
(8) Two by two, off to some other home.

(JJBS, 5: 1/7a)

P.105c.2. Out on a Boat, Facing the Moon, Thinking of My Brother and Sister-in-Law in the Capital

It was constant spring rain when I left the capital,
Each day of clouds and hills took me farther and farther away.
I remember spring winds on the banks green with willows then,
Now all that's left are desolate reeds making sounds of autumn.

(JJBS, 5: 1/10a)

P.105C.3. On Hearing a Flute

On drafts through the bamboo curtain, dew comes in.
Blue clouds cover the ground: the scattered shadows of *wutong* trees.
A tall tower leans into the moon. Who is playing the flute?
In the inn tonight autumn strikes my heart.
The frontier geese should listen to these clear tones with me,
But I can't bear to follow that old river plum tree tune.
Craning my neck at midnight, I can't sleep.
Pressing close, the thuds and slaps of pounding laundry from ten thousand coves.

(JJBS, 5: 1/4b)

line 8: On the sound of clothes being pounded clean, see P.4.3.

BIOGRAPHICAL NOTE AND TRANSLATION BY CATHY SILBER

吴規臣

P.106. Wu Guichen (late 18th century)

Wu Guichen lived in Jintan (present-day southwestern Jiangsu province). Her husband was a district magistrate named Gu He. Wu Guichen was talented, not only in poetry and painting, but also in Chinese medicine and swordsmanship (like certain dashing courtesans of the late Ming). Along with her father, she traveled to many Daoist sites, looking for medicinal herbs and partaking in various Daoist practices. As a result, she "put aside her feminine condition" in the role of initiate.[1]

P.106.1. Cai sang zi

Last night the stars and moon, tonight the rain,
My head is like springtime-tangled vines,
Heart like autumn insects.
My feelings, after all, are like that.

Shut away deep in a small chamber, sad but what can I do?
Just heard a few scattered bells,
Now I hear geese on the move.
Don't say that nothing gets us Wu folks down.

(Su Zhecong, 439)

line 8: "Wu folks" refers to the people of the southern Jiangsu area around Suzhou and Lake Tai, whose native language is Wu dialect. This poem, particularly the last line, contains several Wu colloquialisms.

P.106.2. Qingyu'an

Traces of mist hasten the dusk, threads of wind are cold;
Only my heart feels it.
Years go by like flowing water,
  in truth the twinkling of an eye.
With spring blossoms, more smiles,
Autumn flowers, more illness;
All are scenes for sorrow.

In the lofty edifice all day, not a soul in sight,
I stand a little, then cast off the light-clear tea.
When thick heavy wine flows down inside, my heart's alerted.
At joyful times I'm soon drunk,
But when sad, sober to the end—
How to make it come out right?

(Su Zhecong, 439)

BIOGRAPHICAL NOTE AND TRANSLATION BY NANCY HODES AND TUNG YUAN-FANG

蔣紉蘭

P.107. Jiang Renlan (late 18th century)

Although several Qing-dynasty anthologies include her poetry, little is known about Jiang Renlan. It is, however, recorded that her style name was Qiupei, "Autumn Pendant," that she was from Zhejiang's Jiaxing prefecture, and that she was the wife of Qian Yikai, the Minister of Rites and Education.[1]

P.107.1. Dian jiang chun: *The Double Seventh, Written to My Husband*

In the heavens, there's a meeting,
But on earth they miss the joyous date.
Standing for long, watching the emerald green trees,
I gradually sense the slanting sun disappear.

Brushing against a vermilion rail,
My silk sleeves have grown moist with jade-like dew.
Distressing, this secret desire—
(8) Someone's lost the way to the ferry;
The road so near, and yet as far away as heaven's edge.

(XTLS: *Xianjie ting shiyu*, 8/1b)

On the Double Seventh story underlying this and the next two poems, see P.5.1 and P.19.2.

P.107.2. Wu jiaqi: *Written in Fun for the Daughter of Heaven on the Seventh Day of the Intercalary Sixth Month*

Boundless are the joys of this night!
Standing for long in anticipation, they gaze and gaze—
Yet the Silver River's the same as always; there is no Magpie Bridge;
Secretly, she throws her golden hairpin.

Softly she asks the Herd Boy:
What is it that keeps us apart?
The happy occasion so near at hand, and yet it's come to naught.
(8) She counts on her fingers and is muddled as before.

(XTLS: *Xianjie ting shiyu*, 8/2a)

Tian sun (Heaven's Child or Daughter) is another name for the Weaving Girl star of the Double Seventh legend. The premise of the poem is as follows: Had the year of which Jiang writes not contained an intercalary month to readjust the lunar calendar (see P.5.1), the date mentioned would have been the seventh day of the seventh lunar month. Jiang imagines that the immortal Herd Boy and Weaving Girl have not accounted for this and assume that the date of their meeting has arrived. Note also that the title of the song-lyric tune used here, *Wu jiaqi*, can be interpreted to mean "Missing the Lucky Day."

P.107.3. Ta suo xing: *Emotions Aroused on the Double Seventh*

A pure white moon begins to shine,
Light clouds move in clever play;
The Star Couple stubbornly shine on separated lovers.
Last year was lonely, the Silver River brought woe;
Tonight the Daughter of Heaven laughs above the waves.

River pavilions, flower-filled yards;
The visage of autumn all around;

Hengyang wild geese cut off; correspondence quiet.
Insular chambers, sleeping alone, my grief is deep;
Under a thin silk quilt I toss and turn as dawn takes forever to break.

(XTLS: *Xianjie ting shiyu*, 8/4a)

line 8: On geese as messengers, see P.2.1; on the "Returning-Goose Peak" near Hengyang, see P.9.1.

P.107.4. Chang xiang si: *Relating Harbored Thoughts While Ill*

Thoughts far-reaching,
Hope far-reaching;
You've gone to heaven's edge; I want to meet you, but it's hard.
Of news there is no trace.

Worries troublesome,
Illness troublesome;
Worries and ills consign a jade-like face to the grave.
I ask you—Do you pity me at all?

(XTLS: *Xianjie ting shiyu*, 8/1a)

P.107.5. Man ting fang: *On a Spring Evening During My Illness*

The curtain rolls back in the eastern wind;
Flowers fly down southern paths.
Behind the green window illness and grief make me weary;
My precious jewelry box is filled with dust.
Listless, I do up cloud-like tresses;
The passion-filled mandarin duck pillow accompanies me.
Year after year, spring scenery brings me ill luck;
My heart is about to break.
Glow of my countenance faded away;
Drawn, disappointed by the distant peaks.

The deep night's rain; it seems to go on for a year;
Where raindrops fall on empty stairs,
Disturbing my lonely sleep.
I let faded blossoms scatter and fall,
And the wind disperse the frail smoke.
In an instant aromas dissipate, and the red fades away;
Spring takes its departure.

It could grieve the crying cuckoo to death,
But who would attend to its corpse?
(20) On the courtyard pavilion's stone stairway
Fragrant grasses, green, merge with the sky.

(XTLS: *Xianjie ting shiyu*, 8/6b–7a)

line 3: "Green window" (a window faced with greenish gauze) designates a woman's quarters, usually with a suggestion of virtuous poverty.

BIOGRAPHICAL NOTE AND TRANSLATION BY MARY ELLEN FRIENDS

沈湘雲

P.108. Shen Xiangyun (fl. late 18th century)

Shen Xiangyun, whose school name was Qiqin, was from Jiangyin in present-day northern Jiangsu. She was maidservant to a certain Madame Wang. Her poetry collection *Sanxia yuyin* (Lingering echoes of the Three Gorges) was reprinted in the *Xiao tan luan shi huike guixiu ci* (XTLS) compendium and mentioned in the Jiangyin gazetteer—perhaps because of the author's unusual social standing.[1]

P.108.1. Ta suo xing: *Seeing Spring Off*

Orioles sing sweetly,
Swallows twitter,
Begging the East Lord of Spring to stay.
Beyond the roseleaf raspberry trellis, grass is tender,
Green shade like a tent covers the ground.

I awake from a dream
To find the sun setting.
(8) I take the narrow path to see it off.
Along the murmuring stream with flower petals—
Who knows if this is the path by which spring returns?

(Su Zhecong, 448)

P.108.2. Dan huang liu: *Hearing Cicadas Droning as I Returned in a Boat*

The cold cicada drone is low.
By the bridge the orchid boat moors.
In the river village a lingering rain stopped,
I listen till it's almost dawn-
The pale moon betokens autumn.

At a time like this,
How can I sleep and dream?
The rowing oar sounds forlorn
As it paddles hurriedly.
I remember the willows in Dark-Robe Lane
When I hoist the lone sail.
Things of the distant past—
An unfeeling tree still stands green.

(Su Zhecong, 449)

BIOGRAPHICAL NOTE AND TRANSLATION BY MICHELLE YEH

王筠

P.109. Wang Yun (late 18th–early 19th centuries)

Wang Yun (style name Songping, sobriquet Lüchuang nüshi, or "Lady Historian of the Green Window") came from Chang'an. She was the daughter of Wang Yuanchang (*jinshi*, 1748) who served in a variety of official positions. Her son, Wang Bailing (style Zhitian), received the *juren* degree in 1792 and the *jinshi* degree in 1802. As her son shares her father's surname, it seems likely that her husband was adopted as a member of her clan, rather than the more common inverse. Nothing is known about her husband.

Wang Yun was very bright as a child, and as her talent developed, she resented the fact that she could not compete with men for official rank and prestige through the civil service examinations. She expressed her frustrations in a drama entitled *Fanhua meng* (Dreams of glory), in which a woman in male disguise excels in the examinations and becomes a prominent official. (Compare the lyrical narrative *Zai sheng yuan* by Chen Duansheng, P.92.) Wang's drama, which circulated in manuscript form, was eventually published in 1778 through the good offices of Zhang Zao, mother of the famous scholar-official Bi Yuan. *Fanhua meng* won Wang Yun a wide reputation as a talented poet and dramatist; unfortunately only parts of the drama have come down to us.

The song-lyric to the tune *Zhegu tian* translated below (P.109.1) opens *Fanhua meng* and states its central theme.[1] Wang Yun wrote two more plays in the romantic *chuanqi* genre: *Quanfu ji* (Record of wealth) and *Youxian meng* (Dream of the wandering immortal). The title of her collected works (now apparently lost) was *Huaiqing tang ji*.[2]

P.109.1. Zhegu tian

Buried deep in the boudoir for more than a decade,
I can earn neither honor nor immortality.
In my studies, I always envied Ban Chao's determination,
And raised my glass, reciting the verses of Li Bo.

I harbor a bold spirit
Ready to soar the skies,
But the achievements of Mulan and Chonggu are not in my lot.
(8) Nor am I destined for the Jade Hall and Golden Steed.
I prefer to unfold my heart's desires in dreams.

(Su Zhecong, 451)

line 3: Frustrated by the slowness of his civil career, Ban Chao made his name as a general in the northern borderlands and was ultimately enfeoffed as a marquis. See his biography in *Hou Han shu*.

line 7: Mulan, the subject of a Northern Dynasties song, "Mulan shi" (in Guo Maoqian, ed., *Yuefu shiji*, 25/373–75), took her aged father's place in battle for twelve years in male disguise. Huang Chonggu, the daughter of a Tang commander, dressed in male clothes from her childhood and was skilled in literary writing. Imprisoned on account of a fire, she wrote a poem seeking the favor of the Shu minister Zhou Xiang. He pardoned her and employed her as Administrator of Revenue, discovering that she was not a man only through her poem "Declining Marriage" when he offered her his daughter's hand.

line 8: Jade Hall and Golden Steed were both halls in what came to be known as the Hanlin Academy.

P.109.2. Man jiang hong

Perplexed, I call on heaven.
I call, but no response; only endless desolation.

I bemoan injustice; capricious fate
Purposely gave rise to imperfection.
That painted beauties should fade and drift
Is a past and present regret.
That great talents grow old
Is cause for a myriad autumns' resentment.
I query heaven and earth:
Whom may I ask to hone my heart's sword and stem this sorrow?

Discourse on affairs:
Seek fair judgment.
Rest content in fate:
Gain public repute.
I mourn that the Heyang commander's hair has grayed,
And that the reclusive marquis suffers from kidney pains.
The millet dream merely gave the illusion of fortune;
A fool's essays strive to overturn the existing order.
I wipe my tears on an unadorned sleeve;
Alas! I write in the air day after day,
And give private voice to my sorrow.

(Su Zhecong, 451–52)

line 15: Pan Yue (on whom see P.10.7) served as commander of Heyang. In his "Qiuxingfu bing xu," Pan, known for his beauty, describes his discovery that his hair is beginning to turn gray (*Wen xuan* 13/4a, 6b).

line 16: The Southern Dynasties writer Shen Yue (441–513) helped the Liang emperor to take the throne but eventually left office to go into reclusion. A letter Shen wrote to his friend Xu Mian complaining of old age, sickness, and inadequate recognition gave rise to the phrase "The reclusive marquis's kidney pains," used to describe such a sense of disappointment.

line 17: On the "millet dream" of illusory glory, see P.104.3.

line 18: This line probably alludes to Wang Yun's own writing and may refer to the content of her play *Fanhua meng*.

line 20: Writing in the air is an allusion to the demoted general Yin Hao (306–56), who spent his retirement writing with his fingers the words "Alas! Alas! What an awful turn of events!" in the air (Liu Yiqing, *Shishuo xinyu*, 28/462; Mather, trans., *Shih-shuo Hsin-yü*, p. 451).

P.109.3. *Lament for the Brilliant Consort Wang Zhaojun*

The wind sweeps harshly across the Purple Terrace, the goose's cry is sad;
She has left her country, departed from her family, and lost her freedom.
But deep in the night, when the moon illumines her yurt,
Its pure light is no different from the Han palace in autumn.

(Xu Shichang, *Wanqingyi shihui*, 185/66a)

On Wang Zhaojun, see P.58b.9.

P.109.4. *Inscribed on a Painting of Su Wu Tending Sheep*

With staff and signs of office, leave the palace behind;
Treat life lightly, take off for the border.
He thinks only of the importance of his mission;
How could he fear trouble at the barbarian's court?
Such heroic ambition rises as pure and high as the clouds;
When you have ice-like fortitude, living on snow is easy.
Pass the years with only a herd of sheep;
Speak of bitterest hardship only with homeless ghosts.
Integrity as strong and pure as the icy wind,
And a heart as bright as the white winter sun.
Orphaned by all—yet who can paint his loyalty?
For a thousand ages all view him with praise.

(Jiang Minfan and Wang Ruifang, eds., *Zhongguo lidai cainü xiao zhuan*, 365)

On Su Wu, see P.2.1 (Song 5).

line 8: The wild ghosts here refer to the lonely and untended spirits of Han soldiers who had lost their lives far from their families while defending their homeland.

P.109.5. *Chanted with Feeling on a Moonlit Night*

With bamboo blinds quietly raised and hooked,
I face a moon as bright as a mirror.
The cool breeze blows through the courtyard bamboo,
Disturbing the nests of sleeping birds.

On the deep green moss I pace to and fro;
All the world's sounds are silent.
A hundred times turning, I recount this life
(8) And deeply lament my era and my fate.

Desperate grief is like tangled silk;
Feelings of woe come on like an old sickness.
Again and again my breast feels torn apart;
(12) Bowels all withered, tears of blood all drained.

How did my happiness and good fortune get broken
By my crane-like ambition and monkey-like inquisitiveness?
I ask the earth, it gives me no answer;
(16) And I call to Heaven but get no reply.

How can I find a branch of the willow
With which to wash these floating clouds clean?
The phoenix could then face the sun and sing
(20) While springtime colors shine forth again.

(Shen Qingyai and Wu Tingxi, comps., *Xu Shaanxi tongzhi*, 222/11a)

lines 17–18: These lines may refer to the willow and water associated with Guanyin, the goddess of mercy. Among other associations, the willow is regarded as embodying the power to repel demons, and willow twigs were thus worn at Qingming festival, the spring sweeping of the ancestors' graves (see P.38.1, note to line 105).

P.109.6. Spring, 1796: My Son [Bailing] Attended Me on a Northern Trip to the Hot Springs

My feathers have not stretched out these forty years;
How could I have expected to see again the old hot springs?
Flowers' brightness surrounds the road, adding to the color of the trip;
Birds call in welcome to our cart and talk about our former ties.
My white hair streams in the wind, I am already old,
But the green mountains, layer upon layer, are scenic as before.
I cannot bear to turn around and view the setting sun,
(8) On observing the evening mist, what a feeling of final separation!

(*Xu Shaanxi tongzhi*, 222/11a)

P.109.7. *Prompted by Thoughts of the Elderly Mrs. Zhuang*

Feather-like leaves drift down in the humming breeze of autumn;
Who in the world laments the poverty of Ruan Ji?
How dare I not play the tune of "flowing waters" before you?
In the women's quarters, to see another Yuanlong of Han!

(*Xu Shaanxi tongzhi*, 222/11a–b)

lines 2–4: On Ruan Ji, see P.10.1, P.73.1. "Play the flowing waters" alludes to the great lute player Bo Ya and his friend Zhong Ziqi (on whom see P.24.7). Yuanlong is the style name of the Eastern Han knight-errant Chen Deng, known for his expansive personality, courage, and contempt for normal rules of decorum. These references all suggest deep and intimate friendships among unconventional women.

P.109.8. *In the Fourth Month of 1802: Written with Joy on Hearing of My Son Ling's Success in the Southern Palace [two of four verses]*

I've known every kind of trouble for thirty wind-tossed springs,
Today we turn around to find our sufferings repealed.
How could I have known the golden register of the heavenly court
Would name one of our family to receive the splendid silks?

Through a hundred kinds of hardship you traveled to Beijing,
For a fifth try in the soul-breaking spring examination hall.
Today you are honored in the Jade and Gold Horse Halls,
(8) Now we see the infallible judgment of Heaven's Way.

(*Xu Shaanxi tongzhi*, 222/11b)

In 1802, Wang Yun's son Bailing attained his *jinshi* degree through an examination at the Southern Palace (headquarters of the Board of Rites). See Shen Qingyai and Wu Tingxi, comps., *Xu Shaanxi tongzhi*, 219/15a.

P.109.9. Man jiang hong: *Feelings on a Spring Day*

With a snap of the fingers comes springtime radiance,
   It arrives early again—Qingming Festival is here.
I stare in vain: Willows stretch out, peach blossoms burst,
   Spring's east wind sets in.
As my grief piles up, how can I appreciate the beauty of the flowers?
   My ashen heart finds even the oriole's voice drab.
Worse yet, I cannot bear to sit in careful deliberation;
(8)   A thousand knots inside.

This troubled state
The karma of an earlier life;
Endless plaint—
(12) To whom can these be told?
Why has the undaunted spirit of yesteryear,
Vanished like clouds and mist?
Jingwei cannot fill the vast deep blue sea,
(16) Nor can Nü Wa repair blue Heaven's imperfection.
In the vast universe, to whom can I unburden my pained heart?
To the bright evening moon.

(*Xu Shaanxi tongzhi*, 222/24a)

line 15: The *jingwei*, a legendary small bird, was in the habit of dropping bits of wood and stone into the ocean in the vain hope of filling it, and thus came to symbolize great labor performed, sometimes heroically, but in vain. On Nü Wa, see P.87.13.

P.109.10. Xiao chong shan: *Sent to My Elder Cousin Guanhai in Early Summer*

In the deep deep inner courtyard
Last night's rains have stopped.
The last flowers are fallen and scattered,
Green shade is dense.
Passionate swallows circle round the window screen hook,
They don't mind poverty,
But stay here for their old friend.

(8) With whom can I share my idle sorrow?
To pity from afar the traveler who suffers just as I do
Compounds my anxieties.
Throughout the vast, vast universe
(12) With whom, at last, can I communicate?
My fate and my talent,
Why so locked in mutual hate?

(*Xu Shaanxi tongzhi*, 222/24a)

P.109.11. Langtao sha: *Sad Feelings on a Spring Day*

Fragrant green grasses fill the stream;
But when I look, all I feel inside is sadness.

So much sorrow, so many illnesses, I dread the spring.
Peach and plum know not the human realm's permutations,
And compete as always in beauty.

Life and death: sin's retribution,
Brokenhearted years on end.
(8) Ceaseless weeping, red tears fill the flowerbed.
In Heaven or in Hades, where are you?
This sorrow goes on and on.

(*Xu Shaanxi tongzhi*, 222/24b)

P.109.12. Dian jiang chun: *Idle Chant on an Autumn Evening*

Autumn colors all faded away;
Yellow petals haggard and worn in the idle garden twilight.
I try to roll up the bamboo screen;
A leaf falling, wind cuts like a knife.

I want to strum the lute
But grieve that the one who knows the tune is so far away.
I ceaselessly contemplate
(8) Half a lifetime's gratitudes and resentments.
But alas, I find my heart caught in a thousand knots.

(*Xu Shaanxi tongzhi*, 222/25a)

BIOGRAPHICAL NOTE BY KATHRYN LOWRY AND PAUL S. ROPP; P.109.1–2 TRANSLATED BY KATHRYN LOWRY; P.109.3–12 TRANSLATED BY PAUL S. ROPP

沈纕

P.110. Shen Xiang (fl. late 18th century)

Shen Xiang (courtesy name Huisun, sobriquet Sanhua nüshi) was a native of Suzhou in Jiangsu. Her father, Shen Qifeng (b. 1741), was the official instructor at the district school; he was also a dramatist of some renown. Her mother, Zhang Yun, was also skilled in poetry and prose. Shen Xian married Lin Yanchao, a first-degree graduate (*xiucai*) of the imperial examination system.

Shen participated in the Qingxi Poetry Recital Club with a group of women poets from Suzhou, under the leadership of Zhang Yunzi (b. 1756; style Zilan, sobriquet Qingxi) and her husband, Ren Zhaolin (fl. 1776–1823). It is evident from the prefaces to many of Shen's poems how much she was involved with this supportive and encouraging group of literary friends. In 1789, Zhang Yunzi and Ren Zhaolin compiled poetry manuscripts by members of the group into a collection entitled *Wuzhong shizi shichao* (Poetry drafts by the Talented Ten of Wuzhong; Wuzhong is the ancient name of Suzhou), for which the women wrote prefaces and inscriptions for one another's work. Shen Xiang's manuscript *Feicuilou ji* (Collection of the Kingfisher Pavilion), containing ninety-one poems in the *shi*, *ci*, and *fu* genres, was included among them. She also published separately two other collections of her poetry—*Xiuyu cao* (Scribbles after embroidering) and *Huansha ci* (Washing-silk song-lyrics). Shen possessed considerable expertise in playing the flute, for which instrument she composed a score book.[1]

P.110.1. Dian jiang chun: *In Late Spring Matching the Rhymes of My Friend Lu Suchuang*

At the end of the day, curtains are let down.
Petals are scattered all over the grounds, the orioles silent.
A sorrow-filled heart such as mine
Will not leave with the spring.

I stare at the sky's edge
A sash of clouds joined to the trees.
Where is she?
(8) Wishing to convey my longing thoughts,
I call on the catkins in the wind.

(Su Zhecong, 447–48)

Lu Suchuang was Lu Ying, one of the members of the Qingxi Poetry Recital Club.

P.110.2. Die lian hua: *Spring's End*

What remains of the hundred and five days of beautiful spring?
A slight warmth and a slight chill.
Slowly I realize the coming dusk of the fragrant season.
The peach blossoms have all fallen, the catkins all flown away
As I lean against the railing in ennui.
Listen to the pair of swallow up in the rafters,
How could they understand my grief for the spring?

(8) Yet their twitter—grief for the spring.
Inside, my sorrow folds up in a thousand, ten thousand strands,
When night comes, how to bear more wind and rain?

(XTLS: *Huansha ci*, 1a)

P.110.3. Yue hua qing: *Thinking of My Friend Jiang Bicen on a Spring Night*

Door screen a warm kingfisher-green
As the candle light wavers slightly.
A hundred and five beautiful spring days.
The returning swallows come in the wake of people:
They fly through milky mists and scented air.
We've passed the lingering chill, the weeping willows are thick with shade,
I wonder which bend of the railings their green will reach.
(8) Leaning there at leisure,
I look at the evening scene, so full of feeling,
Thinking of you has touched off my mood.

In the past, I felt that precious essays were sent in vain.
(12) I am dismayed at distance—you being so close
And yet far away as the clouds in the sky.
You are peerless among those within the boudoir.
Laughing I cover up my mouth, how can I compare you?
(16) Slowly I turn my head, toward the dressing chamber at the sky's edge.
I imagine that you must be sitting near the silver screen.
Beyond the curtain
The moon is pale through the wide latticed window,
(20) And the night so cool.

(XTLS: *Huansha ci*, 1a–b)

Jiang Bicen was Jiang Zhu (P.111), another member of the club.

P.110.4. Ku xiang si: *Composed with Qingxi as Spring Departs*

Alone I go up to my dressing chamber and stand leaning out;
All I see at my eyes' limit
Is the sky to the north and south.
I truly dislike the east wind for being so hurried.

Pear blossoms, ah,
Blown like snow,
Willow catkins, ah,
Blown like snow.

The whole day long, to whom can I speak about my boredom?
I could only secretly
Tap the railing,
Sighing that the gentle light of spring cannot be detained.
The cuckoos' cries, ah,
Red as blood,
People's cries, ah,
Red as blood.

(XTLS: *Huansha ci*, 2a–b)

Qingxi was Zhang Yunzi, the head of the poetry club, the name of which is taken from this sobriquet.

lines 13–14: On the cuckoo spitting blood with its cry, see P.5.1.

P.110.5. Yulou chun: *Sending Spring Off, I Match the Rhymes of Suchuang*

In one night I've slept through spring's three months—
Butterflies in my dream are still afraid of the cold.
At dawn I was startled by the wind scattering the flowers,
Disappointed that fragrant plants so easily disappear.

The Lord of the East again made his soul-searing departure.
In scented lanes I idly seek fruit among the dense greens.
Wordless the cuckoo perches at the tip of a branch,
It should be ashamed of its voice, too eager to hurry spring away.

(XTLS: *Huansha ci*, 3a)

line 5: The Lord of the East is the deity of spring.

P.110.6. Yu meiren

I

By my window the "Rouge" peach is blossoming at its peak, but the "Lady-face" peach has not yet bloomed. I wrote this in jest.

Peeking in the window, reflected on the bamboo by the golden well,
An expanse of red, fragrant shadows,
All wearing rouge on both cheeks,
Has crazed bees and driven butterflies mad for quite a while.

The pale one is determined to hide her charming face,
She has not unveiled her spring colors.
The dawn wind urges her to make herself ready,
(8) But shamed by the other's rich beauty, she hesitates to compete with her bloom.

II

The "Rouge" peach having faded, the "Lady-face" peach began to blossom. I then wrote this.

A lonely branch peeking into the golden well,
Thin, her splendid shadow much reduced.
How often tears of rain have spoiled the rouge!
Unable to bear the windblow, she must now wash off her make-up.

Consorts Yin and Xing, loath to meet, preferred to hide.
Now alone, she shows forth her spring colors.
The jade-like one, hurried by insistent swallows and orioles,
(8) Could only bully the red and force the white to bloom in unison.

(XTLS: *Huansha ci*, 4b–5a)

ii, line 5: Yin and Xing were two consorts favored at the same time by Emperor Wu of the Han; by imperial decree, they were not allowed to meet each other (*Shi ji*, 49/1083–84).

P.110.7. Huan xi sha

The east wind brushing my face, I began to sober up.
I might go toward the pearl curtain to pluck my zither.
Too lazy to fix my green-black hair, it's too light and soft.

Flowing waters do not carry the flute's sorrow,
Scattered flowers vainly join with feelings in dreams.
Making one feel helpless, as the moon hangs brightly aslant.

(XTLS: *Huansha ci*, 6a)

P.110.8. Huan xi sha: *Spring Day*

The painted pavilion in sunset is so difficult to depict:
Willows locked in light mist by the little bridge.
As swallows chatter outside the window, the musk scent dissipates.

The small courtyard deep in spring, one lonely person inside it,
Blossoms scatter on an emerald pond, the water far, far away.
The orioles' cries pierce the dawn, a day for cherishing flowers.

(XTLS: *Huansha ci*, 6a)

P.110.9. Fenghuangtai shang yi chuixiao

After I composed the flute music score, I showed it to Mr. Xinzhai and sent this recitation to thank all my women friends.

With incense heavy after all-night rain,
And curtains rolled up in the peaceful shade,
I happened to compose a music score by the flowers.
At that moment facing the green peaks,
My deep thoughts were hard to express.
The spring chill here and there by the high loft
Was blown below with the sound of the jade flute.
Memories of those years
In the Qin pavilion, distant and dim,
Linger like gossamer.

How enjoyable—
Moonlit nights and mornings in bloom.
I imagined my lyrical companions of the thatched hut
Were playing refined music,
Surprised by the few lone pear blossoms,
And the brimming stream's waters.
Their feelings and regrets of parting
Were all inscribed in
The emerald clouds' pure playing.
Then I was able
To relax and compose a new score,
Leaning on the inviting balcony rail.

(XTLS: *Huansha ci*, 6b–7a)

headnote: Mr. Xinzhai was Ren Zhaolin.

line 9: "The Qin pavilion" is a reference to the legend about Nongyu, on whom see P.26.5 and P.54a.15.

BIOGRAPHICAL NOTE AND TRANSLATION BY GRACE FONG

江珠

P.111. Jiang Zhu (late 18th century)

Jiang Zhu's style name was Bicen and her sobriquet Xiao Weimo (Little Vimalakirti, a name suggesting Buddhist affinities and perhaps alluding to the great Tang poet and painter Wang Wei). She was a member of the Qingxi Poetry Recital Club and published in their collection *Wuzhong shizi shichao*. Little is known about Jiang Zhu aside from the sensibilities and skills shown in her writing. Her poetry is collected in *Xiao Weimo ji* (Poems of Little Vimalakirti; one *juan*) and *Qinglige ji* (Collection from the Tower of Green Goosefoot; two *juan*, one of *shi* and one of *ci*).[1] Many of her *ci* poems are products of poetry-society meetings, written in response to fellow members such as Ren Zhaolin. Their exchanges demonstrate the ability of a poetry society to foster communication between men and women related only by common artistic and intellectual interests.

P.111.1. Man yuan hua

On reading the manuscript poems of Clear Stream Lady, I wrote this playful letter and also sent it to the other lady students.

Hard to stop chanting great lines—
Imperceptibly one's soul melts away.
When, when will you form an Incense Holder Society?
My thoughts, longing for it, dream it is done.
I venture to tell of my hut,
Deftly built of seamed bamboo near cloudy crags,
Its rocks elegant yet unworked,
(8) And in their midst, a lute and books, stylish, dashing.

Spring waters like unstrained wine,
Spring mountains like a painting,
Waiting for the peonies to flower—yes,

These befit a scene from a visit home.
If that painted boat would come—
Grasping a goblet of wine amidst flowers,
With unworldly talk,
I would wait to receive an assigned theme and, competing for victory,
Willingly concede my lesser place.

(XTLS: *Qinglige ci*, 1a)

headnote: Qingxi translates as "clear stream" and was the sobriquet of Zhang Yunzi, wife of Ren Zhaolin and leader of the Qingxi Poetry Recital Club.

line 3: This poem was apparently written before the founding of the poetry society. An incense holder is a common accessory of the sessions of a poetry society; incense sticks were used as timing devices (see P.46.6).

P.111.2. Wang Jiangnan: *Plum Blossoms*

The wind light and chill;
A cold quietness lingering in the thin woods;
Then came lovely lines from you.
Ah, you, truly, your heart is firm and strong,
The clouds press down, one branch lies horizontal.

Clusters of powdery catkins;
Their fragrance envelops the one in mourning clothes.
I remember parting at Ba Bridge in a time of wind and snow,
Flowers against the faint moon, moon against the clouds
Amidst the shadow of poetry, the essence of plum blossoms.

(XTLS: *Qinglige ci*, 1a–b)

This is evidently a reply to a poem that has not survived, making uncertain the significance of plum blossoms and the references in lines 4 and 5.

P.111.3. Fan xiang ling: *Some Thoughts at Spring's End*

Leaves lush, petals frail, lazy butterflies and bees
Chase flowers and linger by catkins, hating to hurry.
All seem to invite a curtain of lovely rain.
Curls of steam from the tea fend off the east wind.

To have unsettled feelings is to be like a pitiable insect,
To vanquish intelligence, become as the idiot and the deaf.

Get drunk from wine and full from food
The better to find one's muddled way back to sweet sleep.

(XTLS: *Qinglige ci*, 1b)

P.III.4. Zhuying yao hong: *Thoughts on a Rainy Night*

Night rain gusting hard,
The last of the lamp drips on, its light small as a bean.
In literature, who grieves over the west wind
In which one cannot bear to look back
And remember the times of evening moons and dawn flowers?
Then, dripping wet and splattering,
Ink sticking to gown and sleeves,
Tipsy talk of swordsmanship
And gossipy chat,
We quibbled over nothing and made it something.

These things are no more.
Recklessly I think of grinding fine and immersing myself in the new,
Where one need not write of resentments or cares.
Fate—who still can know it?
Release that furrowed frown from your brows,
Shake off attachment to this dusty world,
On a prayer mat, meditate collectedly—
A thousand voices before the venerable Buddha.
A single stick of pure incense
To prepare the way for the eradication of perception.

(XTLS: *Qinglige ci*, 1b–2a)

P.III.5. Fenghuangtai shang yi chuixiao: *Again Following the Rhymes of Heart Studio*

Stanza upon stanza in esteemed missives,
Line upon line of dragon droplets
Cause one to write in the air: "Tsk! Tsk!"
Having read the new poems through,
I wish to match their intricate skill.
Trimming close the last of the lamp, listening to rain,

Truly I undertake to be a responsive spirit
As drop by drop
The sound follows my breaking heart
And tears wet the raw silk's red.

In a reverie I rub my tired eyes,
All colors appear as in a haze,
My head is awhirl.
In every poem the Dao is revealed;
What can be added to these ladies' writings?
It gave me a spell of anxious dreams—
He who thinks to evaluate them
vainly studies the art of butchering dragons.
Uselessly I toil
Year after year in my den of paper, painstakingly carving insects.

(XTLS: *Qinglige ci*, 2b–3a)

Heart Studio is Ren Zhaolin's pseudonym. Many of the members of the Qingxi club took pen names with Buddhist overtones, like this one.

line 3: "Write in the air" alludes to the behavior of the defeated and demoted general Yin Hao; see P.109.2.

line 13: Jiang added a note here: "Little Precious Charter Studio [Shen Xiang] asked me to evaluate and rank the writings of the poetry group. Tonight I have just finished reading them."

line 17: An allusion to *Zhuangzi*, chap. 32: "Dwarfy Diffuse learned how to butcher dragons from Scattered Plus. Having depleted the family fortune . . . he perfected his techniques within three years, but there was nowhere for him to use his skill" (*Zhuangzi jishi*, p. 1046; trans. Mair, *Wandering on the Way*, p. 327).

line 19: "Carving insects" was the great *fu*-writer Yang Xiong's dismissive description of the art of his earlier compositions.

P.111.6. Shang xilou: *Peony Matches Heart Studio*

Rain in strands blown east and west
Slowly washes away the make-up.
Tenderly sad, the expanse of red,
Frail, spent branches.

Golden threads raised,
Heavenly incense emitted
To test the clearing of night rains.

Just now the immortal of Boyu Hall
Sends a new poem.

(XTLS: *Qinglige ci*, 4a)

Peony presumably refers to Jiang Zhu herself.

P.111.7. Baizi ling: *A Reply Offered to Heart Studio in Lieu of a Letter*

An esteemed missive infused with spices—
I split it open, read "Wind and Rain Throughout Jiangnan,"
Read and circled the wonderful phrases.
Your words ended, where else may one seek to feel alive?
A shift in key and a change in mode,
The effect new, the principle old,
Your compositions are truly most unusual,
Three stanzas of lovely lyrics—
Taking up the flute, I try to express them.

For a theme, I received "A courtyard of dense shade."
The cries of shrikes sound again,
In a twinkling, the spring light changes.
At day's end, the medicinal burner remains my companion,
On the inkstone, light dust gathers,
Not many exercises are completed.
The sprite of poetry addiction, the screen of wine,
These are the hardest to overcome.
Talking of Zen and chatting of doctrines,
I'm ashamed to earn merit by words.

(XTLS: *Qinglige ci*, 4a–b)

BIOGRAPHICAL NOTE AND TRANSLATION BY SHAN CHOU

楊繼端

P.112. Yang Jiduan (fl. late 18th century)

Yang Jiduan's courtesy name was Guxue. Her poetry collection in three *juan*, simply entitled *Guxue shichao* (Guxue's poems), first published in 1808, was subsequently included in Wanyan Yun Zhu's *Guochao guixiu zhengshi ji* of 1831 (GGZSJ). Yang was born in Suining, Sichuan, a daughter of Yang Jiwu. She married Zhang Wunlai, an official in the provincial government of Zhejiang. She traveled extensively with her husband, and the joys and pains of travel figure often in her poems. Her favored genre was the song-lyric.[1]

Although some of her poems may be described as conventional *guige ci*, or boudoir poetry, there are many that transcend the conventions of this subgenre. The last poem translated here (P.112.5) is particularly striking in its direct personal reference and relative lack of allusions.

P.112.1. Huatang chun: *Awakening in the Morning*

The crying oriole heeds not her parting sorrow,
But implores her to stand by the eastern gate awhile.
Fallen petals fly, mingling with rain,
Red against the bamboo screen.

Tasting the dregs of wine,
She fears the mirror's gaze.
Her longing found voice in last night's dream.
(8) Now the murmurs remain.

(XTLS: *Guxue shiyu*, 1a)

line 2: "Eastern wall" is often used to signify solitary seclusion. It first appears in the *Hou Han shu* account of Wang Jungong.

P.112.2. Shiliuzi ling

Spring is the season
When she, deep in her gloomy chamber, is a traveler.
This melancholy stays.
Falling willow floss is like the sad one.

(XTLS: *Guxue shiyu*, 1b)

P.112.3. Shang qing yuan: *Autumn Night*

Night silent, courtyard empty, the moon turns.
She leans on winding rails,
Touched by silent thoughts.
Geese fill the sky, bent on their way.

Still the broken dream of today
  carries no news of the traveler.
With so many clouds and rivers to course,
  she holds, unsent, her own letter.
Her fine garments wet with tears,
(8) Cold on her face, the western wind.

(XTLS: *Guxue shiyu*, 2b)

P.112.4. Jiang shen zi: *Young Willows*

Tender feelings never broken,
  from year to year,
By the pond,
  over the rails.
Who is it that spins out these green silken threads
  and fashions you into such perfect canopy?
The shadows meander by the Six Bridges,
Ever enhanced by rain
  or even trailing mist.

Slender-waisted dancers that you are,
  you can vie with any fair maid.
Off you send your fragrant floss,
  to the sky of separation,
(8) Thrice up and thrice down
  leaving behind the pendulum of sorrow.
Not just the sole love of the spring wind,
Truly you are graceful,
  inviting all to admire.

(XTLS: *Guxue shiyu*, 5b)

line 4: The Six Bridges (see P.46.2) refers to the celebrated scenery of the West Lake of Hangzhou, where the poet resided for many years. The following two lines make an oblique allusion to Su Shi's (Su Dongpo) famous poem comparing rainy and sunny weather on West Lake to a woman wearing first heavy, then light, makeup.

P.112.5. Jinlü qu: *Remembering My Mother*

Two long years
  separate me from my mother's northern chamber.

But in my dream, our laughter rings together
   as though it were yesterday.
Sad was the day when my dear father passed away,
When the ranges of Shu and Wu split us apart.
The cuckoo, cry after cry, beckons me home.
But I am not a son, so far away I had to go.
Sec the loving crow,
(8) Too late trying to feed her fledgling.
When is the day
That I may serve you, day and night?

I am like the water lily, rootless, floating,
(12) Following him, one outpost to another,
   to the edge of the earth.
Travelers we must be.
Already, half of your daughter's life gone by in sorrow and sickness.
How yet to bear the thought of your whitening hair?
(16) All I can do is to pray silently:
   let there be good health
   let there be good fortune.
By the time I am home again
   even the gates and lanes will have been changed.
Blessed am I,
   that my lovely daughter-in-law is always before me.
As I recall the days gone by,
(20) Tears soak my sleeves.

(XTLS: *Guxue shiyu*, 7b)

BIOGRAPHICAL NOTE AND TRANSLATION BY HU YING

沈善寶

P.113. Shen Shanbao (fl. early 19th century)

Shen Shanbao (courtesy name Xiangpei) was from Qiantang (Hangzhou), Zhejiang. Her father, Shen Xuelin, was an assistant department magistrate, and her mother, Wu Shiren (courtesy name Huansu), published a collection of poetry, *Xiaoyinlou shiwenji* (Collected poems and essays from Flute Prelude Gallery).[1] Shen's father died when she was young, and she was known as much for her devotion to her mother and the education of her younger brothers as for her exceptional intelligence and precocious abilities in painting and poetry. Shen and Wu Zao (P.122) were close friends and careful readers of each other's work who kept up a correspondence in poetry.

Shen wrote a lengthy volume of commentary on women's poetry, *Mingyuan shihua* (Remarks on the poetry of illustrious ladies, 1846). She also published *Hongxuelou shici* (Poems and lyrics from Swan Snow Gallery, 1836), lyrics from which were included in Xu Naichang's *Xiao tan luan shi huike guixiu ci* (XTLS), and a long afterword to her friend Zhang Qieying's *Danjuxuan chugao* (First manuscript from Pale Chrysanthemum Pavilion, 1850).[2] Shen's best-known lyric is probably the *Man jiang hong* she wrote on the occasion of crossing the Yangzi River (P.113.6), a poem that expresses the frustrations specific to the woman of talent by echoing the heroic tone of an earlier *Man jiang hong* piece by the loyal Song general Yue Fei.[3]

P.113.1. Nan lou ling: *Facing Chrysanthemums in Illness*

Lacking strength to redo my make-up—
Streams of tears of pain,
To straighten my hair I would have to trouble my mother,

Whose nurture—spring sunlight to young grass—I have yet to repay.
Taking care of this gaunt form saddens her.

Time races by:
The chrysanthemums by the east fence have yellowed again.
As I think back over my life, it's all a blur.
Twelve balustrades lonely in autumn:
You're the ones who bear up under frost and wind.

(XTLS: *Hongxuelou ci*, 3b–4a)

P.113.2. Yijian mei: *On the Lake on a Summer Day, Remembering My Late Younger Sister Lanxian [Shen Shanfang], Whose Style Name Was Xiang'e*

Once we chased idle gulls while boating on green waves,
Listening first to the songs of the water chestnut pickers,
And then to the songs of the lotus pickers,
The surface of the lake after rain like a newly polished mirror.
Mountains pressed into green coils,
Rushes spread like green silk.

The lofty rhymes of wind rolling through the pines lingering
Like a strummed lute.
Xiang'e is gone.
Everything before my eyes is she:
The willows like her eyebrows,
Her cheeks like new lotus.

(XTLS: *Hongxuelou ci*, 7b–8a)

P.113.3. Yu meiren: *Listening to the Rain on a Winter Night*

Thwack and rustle of falling leaves against the window,
Cold pressing right up to the lamp.
Since I fell ill, I've been fed up with poetry,
Which, in this state, just further slackens my spirits.

Flock after flock of frost geese in flight—what's the hurry?
Inexpressible sorrow?
A spate of sparse rain, a spate of wind.
Do you know there's someone wasting away in this little room?

(XTLS: *Hongxuelou ci*, 13b)

P.113.4. Langtao sha: *Sent to Elder Sister Bushan*

There's no way to smooth my brow.
Autumn is in my heart.
New geese fly up from an islet at dusk
I'd give them a letter for you far away,
But it might be rough going.

The blind rolled up, the moon like a hook
Makes me gaze out
Longing for vast, endless waters.
I figure someone's looking out in longing like this too
From a twelve-story tower.

(XTLS: *Hongxuelou ci*, 9a)

lines 3–5: On geese as bearers of messages, see P.2.1 (Song 5).

P.113.5. Langtao sha: *Going by Boat, an Evening Scene*

Fishermen's flares like two or three stars,
Misty water dark,
A line of geese flies up from a distant sandbar.
What does travailing to the ends of the sky have to do with me?
Or taking after drifting duckweed?

Where is that beautiful singing coming from?
Sounds of heartbreak.
I remember some fine verse about the Xiang River goddesses.
Then, too, by song's end, there was no one around.
Dark peaks by the river.

(XTLS: *Hongxuelou ci*, 12a)

lines 8–10: A reference to Qian Qi's poem on the spirits of the river Xiang, on which see P.74.3.

P.113.6. Man jiang hong: *Crossing the Yangzi River*

Silver waves roll on and on,
But written words cannot release all the hot blood in my heart.
Was it not here,
At Jinshan ringing with wardrums,
That a rouged beauty performed deeds of valor?

Though Su Qin's seals of office will never hang from my waist,
Jiang Yan's brush remains in my bag.
(8) From olden times,
How many heroes have emerged from among the headdresses?
No words speak my despair.

I look toward the Northern Fastness,
(12) Emerald-like in autumn mists;
Point to the Flickering Jade,
Where autumn brightness glares forth.
Grasping the rail I gaze and crane
(16) (Just so, the spittoon was chipped).
A downpour of tears is smothered in the wanderer's traveling robe:
Frost and snow spot my parents' hair, now sparse.
I plead with the azure vault:
(20) To what purpose was I born?
Life wears on.

(Zheng Guangyi, 1699)

lines 4–5: It was at Jinshan (Gold Mountain) that Liang Hongyu, wife of the Song leader Han Shizhong, "beat the wardrums herself." See P.75a.6.

lines 6–7: During the Warring States period, the political advisor Su Qin had at one point the seals of supreme office of six different states hanging from his belt. Shen Shanbao knows that a political career is not open to her; all she can boast is a literary talent, symbolized by the brush of Jiang Yan (444–505), who was known for his powerfully emotive writing. One night, however, Jiang dreamed that the essayist Guo Pu (276–324) came to him and demanded the return of his five-colored writing brush, which he claimed Jiang had possessed for many years. Jiang gave it back and, when he awoke, felt that his ability to write had vanished.

line 9: "Headdresses" is a metonymic designation for women.

lines 11–14: Beigu or Northern Fastness is a mountain rising over the Yangzi near the battle site of Zhenjiang; Fuyu or Flickering Jade is an alternate name for Jinshan. Both would have been visible from Shen's position on the river.

line 16: Shen alludes to the story of the Jin general Wang Dun (courtesy name Chuzhong), who in his forced retirement would drink wine, chant the martial songs of Cao Cao, and beat time on a spittoon with his official baton, leaving the rim of the spittoon entirely chipped away (Liu Yiqing, *Shishuo xinyu*, "Hao shuang," p. 326; trans. Mather, *Shih-shuo Hsin-yü*, p. 302). Wang's chipped spittoon became a byword for the vehement expression of frustration.

BIOGRAPHICAL NOTE AND TRANSLATION OF P.113.1–5 BY CATHY SILBER;
TRANSLATION OF P.113.6 BY REN ZIPANG

孫雲鳳

P.114. Sun Yunfeng (1764–1814)

Sun Yunfeng (style name Biwu) was a prized student of Yuan Mei and one of a trio of sisters who all acquired considerable fame as writers of *shi* and *ci*. The middle sister was named Yunhe (P.115) and the youngest, Yunxian (style name Xianqing).

Natives of Renhe in Zhejiang province, they were the daughters of Surveillance Commissioner Sun Jialuo. With an admiration born of having read widely in Yuan's examination and literary writings, their father actively encouraged his daughters to make acquaintance with Yuan's compositions and eventually with the author himself.[1] When he showed them Yuan's poems bidding farewell to the West Lake of Hangzhou, Yunfeng took the initiative of answering those poems with matching rhyme schemes, declaring in her last poem (see P.114.15) her desire to become Yuan's pupil. Delighted, Yuan duly acknowledged the young woman's talent and good will by thanking her with a regulated verse of eight lines, prefaced by her letter; the entire exchange was recorded in his collected writings of 1789.[2] Eventually, forty of Yunfeng's *shi* poems, four of her poems written in lyric meters (*ci*), and two narratives were included by Yuan in his anthology of women pupils' verses, *Suiyuan nü dizi shixuan*.

In the spring of 1790, Yuan Mei went to West Lake to sweep his ancestors' graves, and he was entertained by Hangzhou's literati, both male and female. Sun Yunfeng and thirteen women writers met Yuan at a lake resort, and they were feted by him in a banquet of two tables. Two years later, Yuan went again on one of his several pleasure trips to Mount Tiantai, and his women pupils again held parties for him at Hangzhou. Both these festive occasions of fine dining, wine, and poetry were recorded by Yunfeng in verse and prose.[3]

P.114.1. Ru meng ling: *Falling Plums*

Rising—too weak to roll up the screens—
At dusk I stand idle by the rails:
A fine rain draws a light chill,
And a gust sends a shower of plums.

Pity!
Pity!
It scatters a yardful of fragrant snow.

(XTLS: *Xiangyun guan ci*, 1/1a)

P.114.2. Die lian hua: *Late Spring*

On pillows of white clouds the sky grows dark;
The spring dream turning hazy
Is mocked by the oriole's cry.
Hairbun aslant, I have no plans at all—
Too worn to burn incense in the urn of gold.

I may have spring but nowhere to tie it down:
I blame the east wind
(8) For blowing it to heaven's edge.
Butterflies powder, unseen, the floss outside.
At night a few drops of flower-crushing rain.

(XTLS: *Xiangyun guan ci*, 1/1a–b)

P.114.3. Su zhongqing

Red-tower dream breaks at dawn oriole's cries;
Cold rises from embroidered drapes.
Second month in the Southland is late spring:
Deep in alleys and lanes
Flower vendors resound.

Thin mosses and lichens
And light willowy mist
(8) Are the purest sadness.
Last night was both wind and rain;
This morning it is Cold Food;
Tomorrow will be Clear-and-Bright.

(XTLS: *Xiangyun guan ci*, 1/1b)

lines 10–11: On the Cold Food (*hanshi jie*) and Clear-Bright (*qingming*) festivals see P.17.4 and P.38.1 (note to line 105).

P.114.4. Huan xi sha: *Jasmine*

Picked by slim hands, she sparsely dots the hair.
Her secret scent will spread from tree to tree,
Her petals sparkling like pearl and like jade.

When one wakes after fresh rain—round fan in hand
And bathes by green casements in cool nightfall,
She slips by verandah's breeze through jade-gauze screens.

(XTLS: *Xiangyun guan ci*, 1/3a–b)

P.114.5. Nan xiangzi: *A Farewell to Younger Sister Xianpin [Sun Yunhe, P.115]*

I can think of no more schemes—
Just parting thoughts and ten thousand strands of tears.
In the yard at nightfall it's about to rain:
  The wind is wild!
  Don't cross the river tomorrow in your boat.

Twelve windows of jade-green gauze
Awhirl with seal-script incense of the urn.
(8) Speaking of old journeys depresses me:
  Hard to forget
  Those heartbreaking spells of moon, flowers, and snow!

(XTLS: *Xiangyun guan ci*, 1/5a)

P.114.6. Yu meiren

Last year swallows left with flowers in their beaks,
For spring could not be detained.
The year before I leaned in the east painted tower,
Wistful at one screen
  Of flying catkins in dusky mist.

This year once again it is creeper time:
The scene is like the one before,
(8) When I stood forever watching homing crows
And hated the unfeeling
  Grass's growth that reached heaven's edge.

(XTLS: *Xiangyun guan ci*, 1/10b–11a)

P.114.7. Langtao sha: *Wind-Blown Fireflies*

Their green shapes riotous on the screens
Like twinkling specks of spring star.
The blue sky liquescent, the moonlight is bright.
When in cool night's deep yard the people rest,
  They're blown to fall on silver screens.

Beyond the rails bamboo sounds are clear;
Half my arm's gossamer light.
(8) On jade steps recall this state of bygone times
When a round fan's soft silk could not hold them down,
  And jasmine hairpins fell aslant.

(XTLS: *Xiangyun guan ci,* 2/1b)

P.114.8. Zhegu tian: *For a Song Girl*

A fine rain wind-blown wets embroidered drapes;
In spring chill you first try on southern silk.
The orioles sing amidst green-willow shades;
The butterflies dream in red-apricot scent.

You think of the past,
Recalling River South—
Slim, darkened brows by silver torch and screen.
(8) Now's the night of idle windows and cold dreams:
A bright moon, unfeeling, falls on painted eaves.

(XTLS: *Xiangyun guan ci,* 2/2a)

line 6: "River South" refers to Jiangnan, the opulent southeast of China.

P.114.9. Pusa man: *The Double Seventh Festival*

Girl friends in season—a court in season, too—
All face the wind to boast of sewing skills.
They bow and the candles flare up,
Their silk gowns' faint fragrance grows.

Human cares flow away with water.
By whom can this sorrow be told?

Cold stirs on painted screens' autumn;
(8) At dusk the moon is a slim hook.

(XTLS: *Xiangyun guan ci*, 2/3a)

On the Double Seventh festival, see P.5.1 and P.19.2.

P.114.10. Man jiang hong: *Inscribing a Painting on "Listening to Rain Under a Mat Canopy" by Great-Uncle Zhuxi*

One boat in the west wind
That blows the dusk rain across clean, white sandbars.
Let's chant and sing in depths of water and cloud
With carefree gulls and egrets.
The sails hoist homing hearts from distant shores,
And oars row a cool dream past autumn reeds—
Their steady squeaks
(8) Hinder sleep till the midnight hour
With parting thoughts.

Fisher fires blaze;
Mat canopies are still.
(12) The peaks veil their green;
The waves store their jade.
Stopping the undertow's flow and ebb
Are sheer cliffs, a thousand feet.
(16) Raindrops make hazy the trees that line the sky,
Their pure sounds piercing the skiff in mist.
This new painting spread out,
I recall at once our descent of Xiang.
(20) So like the past!

(XTLS: *Xiangyun guan ci*, 2/4b)

line 19: The Xiang River is in present-day Hunan province.

P.114.11. Que qiao xian: *The Double Seventh Festival*

Spiders web the house edges;
Cicadas strum the tree tops;
Rain stops and twilight brings a new clearing;
A crescent moon half appears;

On painted screens early autumn
 Has roused a whole spell of coolness.

Vying to tear our drafts of verse
Or to cut up embroidery—
That's not the flavor of the season!
Mixing both powder and rouge
To dye unknown flowers,
We'd beg for Heaven's Grandchild's clever thoughts.

(XTLS: *Xiangyun guan ci*, 2/6a)

line 12: Heaven's Grandchild (Tiansun) is another name for the Weaving Girl.

P.114.12. Ru meng ling: *Drifting Floss*

The whirling catkins, wildly sticky,
By blue casements disturb my thoughts.
Roguish is the east wind
That should blow them away but stops.
 No clues!
 No clues!
For my sake take sorrow away.

(XTLS: *Xiangyun guan ci*, 2/6b)

P.114.13. Huan xi sha: *My Own Inscription for Painted Plums*

Cool stamens fly their scent up the brush's point:
A forecast of spring beneath cold, farmland clouds.
It's hard for east wind even to send one sprig.

Snap with the moon what seems like emptiness or form;
There's no mist or fog—so pull the screens and watch:
By twilight clear shadows will reach the rails.

(XTLS: *Xiangyun guan ci*, 2/7a)

P.114.14. Xi jiang yue: *An Inscription for My Draft of Unpublished Lyrics and a Gift Sent to Younger Sister Xianpin*

Parting thoughts arouse poetic thoughts;
Doleful hearts change to leisured hearts.

"Beauties, fragrant plants"—their meaning's too deep
For the mere bystander to grasp.

Since with the clouds the wild geese parted,
The flowers have shaded the moon a few times.
When will we play the lute that's like the ocean breeze
(8) And face west window's candle light?

(XTLS: *Xiangyun guan ci*, 2/11a–b)

line 3: The phrase "beauties and fragrant plants" (*meiren fangcao*) alludes to the imagery of Qu Yuan's "Li Sao" (see P.37). According to traditional Confucian commentators, these symbolize the king's upright and loyal subjects; see Hawkes, trans., *Songs of the South*, pp. 68–69.

P.114.15. Answering Grand Scribe Suiyuan's Four Poems on "Bidding West Lake Farewell," Using the Original Rhyme Schemes [from a series of four poems]

I

Flosses smacked the screens and brought an end to spring;
The Grand Scribe returned, but he left quickly, too.
Chrysanthemums in hand he was Three Paths' guest;
A friend of gulls, he is now Five Lakes' old man.
Lines in your pockets became treasures all;
I heard your fame though you I did not know.
Amidst the blooms, I thought, you waved and left
(8) To hoist past the sky your sail in high wind.

IV

I miss you more for not seeing you off;
When you return, it will be one year hence—
Your blue-bird boat at dusk in distant streams
Beneath white-gull sky, new rush, and spring rain.
Song pipes, three thousand, belong to Flower Town;
The twelve who attend you are leisured gods.
I wish I were the pupil of your class
(8) Who serves you in all those mountains of fame.

(Yuan Mei, *Suiyuan nü dizi shixuan*, 1/8a)

In antiquity, the title Grand Scribe (*taishi*) referred only to the Grand Astrologer-Historian, but by Qing times, any member of the Hanlin Academy—of which Yuan Mei was one—would be so denominated as a gesture of esteem.

i, line 3: Three Paths is an allusion to Tao Qian's rhapsody "Guiqulai xi ci" (on which see P.58a.7). Sun's reference here, of course, makes a pointed comparison with Yuan, who, like Tao, gained renown from early retirement.

i, line 4: "A friend of gulls" is a recluse—alluding to a parable in the *Liezi* about a man who gained the trust of seagulls by roaming with them every day ("Huang di," *Liezi*, 2/13a). On Five Lakes as a site of carefree wandering, see P.54b.1.

iv, line 5: Flower Town or Flower County (*Hua xian*) refers to the district governed by the poet Pan Yue (247–300), who planted peach and pear trees everywhere when he was magistrate of Heyang. When their flowers bloomed, the area acquired this nickname. Yuan Mei bought his famous Sui Garden, which he filled with an abundance of various flowering plants. These he would decorate with lighted lanterns during garden parties.

P.114.16. Dawn Journey

A fading moon, a morning-frost bell,
A road of yellow leaves and hooves.
At sunrise no one's visible.
A brook murmurs beyond mist-trees.

(*Suiyuan nü dizi shixuan*, 1/6b)

P.114.17. Ancient Feelings

The silver lamp knots double wicks;
The spiders ascend my skirt-sash.
Rise early to wash off tear stains.
Summon mirth to paint my brows long.

(*Suiyuan nü dizi shixuan*, 1/6b)

line 2: Spiders, *xizi*, stand phonetically and pictorially for happiness, *xi*.

P.114.18. After Climbing the Heights, I Wrote This for Lanyou [Sun Yunhe, P.115] and Other Younger Brothers and Sisters

We join to climb the high tower on the ninth,
When all carry dogwood branches, and chrysanthemums bloom.
One lonely sail far off clean, white sandbars;
In cold mist and blank river a goose arrives.

Humans alone grieve autumn's gradual age;
Youths must treasure water that cannot return.
This landscape, though fair, is not quite our home.
(8) I'd write "Climb the Tower" but my gifts are small.

(*Suiyuan nü dizi shixuan*, 1/8a)

line 1: The ninth probably refers to the Double Ninth Day; see P.5.1 and P.11.4.
line 8: On Wang Can's melancholy "Deng lou fu" (Rhyme-prose on ascending the tower), see P.17.2.

P.114.19. Inscribing a Small Portrait of Lady Official Xi Peilan [P.93] Holding Some Flowers

I

I'd attend as pupil your lotus seat
To see for myself how celestial blooms descend.
The poem's realm, known through the realm of Zen,
You hold forth, never making it disperse.

II

A small, natural portrait sketches your form
Of peerless beauty that enraptures all.
One must deride those pupils of West Lake:
In service they can't match the person limned.

(*Suiyuan nü dizi shixuan*, 1/9a)

i, line 1: The lotus seat is the platform from which a Buddhist teacher discourses.

BIOGRAPHICAL NOTE AND TRANSLATION BY ANTHONY C. YU

孫雲鶴

P.115. Sun Yunhe (late 18th–early 19th centuries)

Like all the children of Surveillance Commissioner Sun Jialuo, Sun Yunhe (style names Lanyou and Xianpin) was schooled in the liberal arts at the family home in Hangzhou. An excellent student, in time she won recognition as a talented painter, a poet of distinction, and an able stylist in the complex and intellectually demanding genre of parallel prose. Both she and her older sister

Sun Yunfeng (P.114) eventually became disciples of the poet Yuan Mei, who chose fourteen of Sun Yunhe's *shi* poems and five of her song-lyric verses for inclusion in *Suiyuan nü dizi shixuan*, his anthology of poems by his women students.

Sun Yunhe's name is sometimes linked with that of her older sister, with whom she published a joint collection of song-lyric verse.[1] Later her own song-lyrics were published separately under the title *Tingyu lou ci* (Song-lyrics from Listening to the Rain Studio) in two *juan*. Little information is available on the actual details of her life. It is known, however, that she became the wife of an assistant district magistrate named Jin Wei and that she died at an early age.[2]

Anthologists of classical song-lyric verse have shown little agreement about which poems best represent Sun Yunhe's talents in this genre or how important she is in the tradition. For instance, while she is liberally represented in the two-volume *Quan Qing ci chao* (Ye Gongchuo, ed.) with fourteen selections, other anthologies of this kind tend to accord her less prominence in comparison with other women poets.

P.115.1. Weed Lake

Riverside villages as far as one can see; lonely is the traveler's heart.
Again, a spring breeze brings the cry of the partridge.
Just now, in this glorious season of orioles and flowers,
A single sail crosses Weed Lake in mist and rain.

(Li Heming, *Guixiu shi sanbai shou*, 338)

Weed Lake is located in present-day Anhui province.

P.115.2. The "Precious Sword" Poem

"Precious Sword," handed down to the present:
Trim the lamp and chant its song to a steady beat.
Favors, wrongs, its concerns for a thousand ages;
And thus, a life spent wandering amid lake and sea.
Its aura is colder than autumnal frosts;
Its radiance causes the moon at night to sink from sight.
Following the military life is its chosen desire;
(8) Heroism, its reply to "one who knows himself."

(GGZSJ, 2/9a–10b)

P.115.3. Dian jiang chun: *Grasses*

The glossy rain falling steadily,
Everywhere in Jiangnan the grass is luxuriant.
Gentle is the apricot blossom breeze,
Silently mixing with blue smoke.

When the swallows return,
Don't lean against the tall tower.
In the setting sun,
(8) In this limitless world,
There are the pains of parting, year after year.

(Ye Gongchuo, *Quan Qing ci chao*, 1665–66)

line 6: According to the compilers of *Zhongguo lidai cainü shige jianshang cidian* (Zheng Guangyi, p. 1674), in this line Sun Yunhe succeeded in capturing the meaning of Wang Changling's poem "Boudoir Lament" (see P.93.8).

BIOGRAPHICAL NOTE AND TRANSLATION BY WILLIAM SCHULTZ

P.116. Li Peijin (early 19th century)

Li Peijin (courtesy names Chenlan, Renlan) was from Changzhou in Jiangsu. She was the daughter of Subprefectural Magistrate Li Huguan, the wife of student He Xiang, and a student of Chen Wenshu (1775–1845), a noted patron of women painters and poets. Her four poems entitled "Autumn Geese" were so famous in her lifetime that she became known as the Autumn Geese Poet. She died in her thirties.

Her collection of verse *Shengxiangguan shici* (Poetry and lyrics from Spreading Fragrance Studio), comprising four *juan* equally divided between *shi* and *ci*, was published in 1819; the lyrics also appear in Xu Naichang's collection, *Xiao tan luan shi huike guixiu ci* (XTLS).[1] Her lyrics show the work of a stylist interested in form who frequently experimented with difficult and obscure tune patterns.

P.116.1. Bu suanzi: *Autumn Boudoir*

Waning moonlight crosses the curtain hook.
Autumn dreams as flimsy as flowers.
A puppy in the corner barks at the night,
The Big Dipper aslant in the deep blue sky.

I iron my old silks,
Wrinkled as the space between my eyebrows.
I mark time, minute by minute, all night long,
Facing the lamp's tiny flame.

(XTLS: *Shengxiangguan shici*, 5b)

P.116.2. Lin jiang xian: *Sent with Thoughts of Sisters Xuelan, Ruiyuan, Linfeng, and Wanlan [two verses from a set of twelve]*

II

I remember you standing beneath the crab apple trees,
So graceful and slender and at ease, I loved you;
Like Zhiqiong, you were exquisite and so clever,
Still not very good at playing the strings,
Just having learned to paint your eyebrows.

Cool mists covered the yard, the spring pond dark,
Hidden pockets of new green like clouds.
We noticed the homing swallows catch the slanting light of sunset,
Didn't bother to let down the bead blind.
High winds scattered spring stars.

V

I remember the sound of night rain on lotus in the wind,
You writing on the sly a lyric by the lamp.
The poem just begun, you were afraid of being found out,
And when I came in, pretended you were using the brush
To paint a branch of crab apple blossoms.

A disappointed Cailuan expertly writing out rhymes,
You gave me that square of white silk,
Each tiny character a gem inscribed by your hand.

I'm afraid to open my locked gold box
For I can't bear to see your poem.

(XTLS: *Shengxiangguan shici*, 23a–24a)

The "sisters" are not kin, but members of Li's poetic circle: Linfeng, for example, is the pen name of Xu Tingzhu.

ii, line 3: The reference is to the legend of Xuan Chao's dream of, visitation by, and subsequent love affair with a fairy maiden named Zhiqiong. She was unusually beautiful (although visible to Xuan alone); furthermore she was skilled in poetry and composed annotations to the *Book of Changes* (*Yi jing*). When others became aware of their relationship, she departed back to heaven. See Gan Bao, *Sou shen ji*, pp. 16–19; for an English rendering, see DeWoskin and Crump, trans., *In Search of the Supernatural*, pp. 16–17.

v, line 6: According to the *Xuanhe shupu* (the Northern Song imperial calligraphy collection catalogue), Wu Cailuan was a great Tang dynasty woman calligrapher from Henan who married into a poor family and earned a living writing out copies of the *Tang yun* rhyme dictionary for sale.

P.116.3. Yi ye luo

One of the two clumps of plantains outside the window was withered, then sprouted anew, but after a rain it died, and I wrote this in mourning.

A leaf falls.
Just waking from a dream:
Listening to the rain tonight is not like last night.
Heartless but afraid of evening cold:
An autumn spirit drifting without rest.
Drifting without rest,
The leaves clack-clacking louder than the watchman's rattle.

(XTLS: *Shengxiangguan shici*, 5b)

P.116.4. Ku xiang si: *Love Beans*

Beads of coral stored in a gold box—
What I felt at that moment of parting,
A thousand strands of sorrow.
So it took a few takes to tell
That the east wind had blossomed the plum.
Someone says

Spring, why do you bother?
Spring says
Why do you?

I remember those gentle fingers so often strumming a sad song,
And wanting many a time to send it to the blocked ends of the sky.
I look out the window,
Coax the parrots into talking.
The flowers say
Cuckoos cry rain.
The cuckoos say
Flowers cry rain.

(XTLS: *Shengxiangguan shici*, 7a)

Called *hongdou* (red beans) here, also known as *xiangsi zi* (seeds of longing) in Chinese, and jequirity beans or rosary peas in English, these pea-sized seeds of the woody vine *Abrus precatorius* are coral red (sometimes with black spots) and poisonous. In Chinese literature they are associated with love and longing; they were also used in jewelry and medicine.

P.116.5. Mo yu'r: *I Had No Letter from Linfeng [Xu Tingzhu] for So Long That I Wrote This to Send*

The night window empty, the new year just begun,
The stealthy change of seasons stuns me.
No answer to my letter—
To whose house did it go by mistake?
Spring has come around again but
I don't see
Plum blossoms and blame that lax east wind.
A poet's soul, downcast, scattered.
Now the water clock sways in sorrow.
Willow mists in hazy dreams,
Cold moonlight shines on clear grief.

Even scissors from Bingzhou
Would have trouble cutting through the cocoon around my heart,
Wrapped round and round so utterly with longing.
The lamp shining through the screen washes out the gauze and
Barely sparks a few spring stars.

That longing across the miles:
We shared ten thousand strands.
The willows have greened to the south bank of the river.
I'm sleepless, remembering everything.
The candle's tears have turned to ash,
The wick dead.
Have we really grown apart?

(XTLS: *Shengxiangguan shici*, 23a)

P.116.6. Bin yun song ling: *Written After Getting Linfeng's Letter*

A good wind blows:
Your letter came,
The peach-blossom page no doubt
Soaked with tears when done.
So eloquent the unbounded longing of your reply
That once I finished reading it
I took it from the top again.

The love you sent,
Tears enclosed—
When it has reached the edge of sorrow,
It is beyond what we felt then.
I recognize the Jiangnan red love beans,
Each one plain and clear and
Full of your tears.

(XTLS: *Shengxiangguan shici*, 10b)

P.116.7. Die lian hua: *A Found Poem*

Rippling curtain brushing the floor in this crisp cold:
Still groggy from a noontime nap,
Tea steam curling over the table,
I prod the ashes to stir up longing,
Sort through my brocade bag and burn old drafts.

Slumped against the silver screen in sadness,
I find the state of my heart
Does not improve with time.

A strand of green mountains misted by clouds.
I watch the birds fly home across the setting sun.

(XTLS: *Shengxiangguan shici*, 18b)

P.116.8. Jinlü qu

The afterword I wrote for *Shengxiangguan ci*, which I also sent to Linfeng and Wanlan.

Thinking over everything past
Before the mirror,
Painted eyebrows furrowed—
When were they ever smooth?
My heart and soul thoroughly spent on these one hundred poems—
The cocoon left of the dying silkworm.
You notice, all over the page,
Tear stains still glistening.
Take care. I send you lines of longing.
I'm always thinking of you.
When will we see each other again?
I know both sides
Share this heartbreak.

How I regret, all my three lives, neglecting my writing,
And here now
Remnants of paper, leftover ink,
The same charred inkstone.
Kith and kin far away, you who know me best departed,
I face this overcome with bitter desolation.
Probably this grief is
Unavoidable throughout history.
If the misty waters of my hometown are still intact,
When I go to Jiangnan
I will look for my old friends.
Beyond that
I want nothing else.

(XTLS: *Shengxiangguan shici*, 18b–19a)

P.116.9. Jian zi mulanhua: *Writing My Feelings in Night Rain*

Dusk rain, lamp dark,
Outside the window, plantains tapping dreams gone cold.
The tip, tip, tap, tap
Keeps the sad one from sleep.

Deep into the endless night
One last wisp of incense a scant and swaying shadow.
Old lines chanted low:
(8) If they don't hurt, I don't want to hear them.

(XTLS: *Shengxiangguan shici*, 4b)

BIOGRAPHICAL NOTE AND TRANSLATION BY CATHY SILBER

趙我佩

P.117. Zhao Wopei (fl. early 19th century)

Zhao Wopei (style name Zhunlan) was a native of Hangzhou, the daughter of Zhao Qingxi and the wife of Zhang Shangce. The latter, also a native of Hangzhou, is reported to have obtained the *juren* (provincial graduate) examination degree.

Zhao Wopei favored the song-lyric genre, which accounts for all of the nearly two hundred poems we find in her collected works, the *Bitaoguan ci* (Song-lyrics from the Hall of the Emerald Peach Immortal) in one *juan*. As a song-lyric poet, she employed both the short and long modes in about equal measure. She also adopted themes and imagery common to the early part of that tradition and to writers of her gender; namely, those of seclusion, parting, separation, and longing.

Critical reaction to her poetry has been mixed. The famous poet and critic Chen Tingzhuo (1853–92), for instance, labeled her efforts as a poet undistinguished and her diction commonplace, excepting only the "Spring Grasses" song-lyric (P.117.3), which he regarded as being elegant in its refinement and emotionally moving.[1] Other critics have taken a more generous view of her talents as a poet, however, and the poems that follow are often found in modern anthologies of women's verse.

P.117.1. Qingping yue

I told grief to leave, but it wouldn't go,
And now there's no place to hide it.
Tiny, curving eyebrows like mine can't bear this burden,
So now I display all this bitter loneliness!

Morning after morning, flowers fade in rain and cold,
While the west wind brings sickness to winding corridors.
Already I've grieved over autumn and grieved at parting;
(8) How can I endure another Double Ninth Festival?

(XTLS: *Bitaoguan ci*, 5a)

line 8: On the Double Ninth festival, see P.5.1. and P.11.4.

P.117.2. Pusa man

Last night autumn filtering through gauze curtains
Caused the red flowers to wilt, the solitary lamp to go cold.
As I listlessly wipe away the last traces of make-up,
Shadows of the *wutong* tree follow the moon around the porch.

With worries aplenty, it is easy to get tipsy;
Sadly I wrap a fragrant coverlet about me to sleep.
Who'd have thought that a dream would be hard to gain?
(8) I sober up and again my grief returns.

(XTLS: *Bitaoguan ci*, 6a–b)

P.117.3. Ta suo xing: *Spring Grasses*

Lichen flowers lining the path,
Willow catkins blowing about the garden,
Lonely is the pond in the Qingming rain.
In the west garden, butterflies are loath to part,
As an east wind blows a dream here from who knows where.

Spellbound on another shore,
Waiting in a painted tower,
(8) Three months since our painful parting on the post road.
For years everything was verdant along the old city wall;
Again it is lush and green as we send a prince on his way.

(XTLS: *Bitaoguan ci*, 9a–b)

line 3: On Qingming, see P.38.1 (note to line 105).

P.117.4. Yi Qin e

Anxious is the east wind;
Fading crab apple blossoms the color of rouge.
The color of rouge
Are the fallen petals, all in disarray
Beneath the swing beyond the veranda.

Who, dressed in evening attire, plays the flute in the tower?
Blue and sad at heart; a solitary weeping willow.
Blue and sad at heart am I,
But where's the beautiful one?
Detained far away in the imperial city.

(XTLS: *Bitaoguan ci*, 12a–b)

P.117.5. Bu suanzi

Inner feelings as chaotic as strands of silk;
Tears at parting thicker than wine.
Eyebrows once like vernal hills, cheeks a sunset hue,
Are now wasted away with the spring.

I recall your words at parting:
You'd return after the plum trees bloomed.
Now the winds have changed and the crab apple season is gone;
And so, will you come back or not?

(XTLS: *Bitaoguan ci*, 18a–b)

BIOGRAPHICAL NOTE AND TRANSLATION BY WILLIAM SCHULTZ

梁德繩

P.118. Liang Desheng (1771–1847)

Liang Desheng (style name Chusheng) was from a prominent family of scholar-officials in Qiantang (present-day Hangzhou). Her grandfather was Grand Secretary and her father was junior vice president of the Board of Works. Her husband, Xu Zongyan, was a brilliant scholar and rose to a position in the Board of War. He resigned this office two months after his appointment to devote himself to writing about literature and other scholarly topics. He was also a book collector, and the catalogue of his library has been preserved. Liang Desheng herself was known as a learned poet and published her own collection, called *Guchunxuan ji* (Poems from Ancient-Springtime Studio). She also completed the composition of the *tanci* narrative *Zai sheng yuan* (The destiny of rebirth), a work begun by Chen Duansheng (P.92).[1]

P.118.1. Nan xiangzi: *Sent to My Fourth Son, Shaowu*

Far away you are, blocked by passes and mountains;
My tender heart is churning—hard to go or stay.
In the splendid hall a night banquet is held,
Yet I look on in sorrow,
And the cypress wine, though strong, fails to make me smile.

These words I send: do free up your heart;
When the waters rise in spring, boating is good.
(8) For you, tonight, in the remote serenity of your office,
I pine from afar.
Amidst the sound of firecrackers, another year is gone.

(XTLS: *Guchunxuan ci*, 3b)

line 5: The cypress tree symbolizes longevity; cypress-flavored wine is commonly offered to parents at New Year's.

P.118.2. Huan xi sha: *Sent to My Third Daughter, When She Failed to Come as Expected*

My ailing body, frail and weak, cannot bear my clothes;
For more than ten years now, nothing's been the same.
In dreams, my spirit often roams the old capital city.

My heart suffered many wounds, so I took up Buddhism;
Sick so long, I might as well be a doctor.
My appearance is fading, I fight to hold on,
Awaiting your return.

(XTLS: *Guchunxuan ci*, 4a–b)

P.118.3. Nan xiangzi: *Farewell Feast at the Lantern Festival*

To stay and to part are the same,
Today my feelings are like tumbleweeds.
Forcing my gaze on the lanterns,
I watch them compete in a dance.
Exquisite craft,
Fragrant haze in a misty space,
The lantern halos are red.

(8) Ill and afraid of willow-thread winds;
The farewell song just sung, my mood is lackluster.
My flesh and blood will be in the river country,
A thousand miles away in dreams.
(12) Bleary eyes,
I turn my head; how many ranges of cloudy peaks will separate us now?

(XTLS: *Guchunxuan ci*, 3b)

P.118.4. Yi Jiangnan: *To Be Shown to Pinxiang and Yingqing*

Amidst spring breezes,
We agreed to pour wine into golden goblets.
The green of willows covers the road along the dike,
The red of peach blossoms enters the village on the water.
Where to wash away traces of sorrow?

(XTLS: *Guchunxuan ci*, 4a)

P.118.5. Ru yan fei

"White moon, clear wind, perhaps they hold some meaning;/ Measured in bushels, carried on carts, the books are already nameless." So reads the elegiac couplet my late husband composed for himself. Whenever it happens to be mentioned, sadness strikes my mournful heart, and I can't control my feelings. Jotting down this piece may ease my grief somewhat.

For ten years, a wounded heart—
I still can't bear to recall those days,
Much less speak of them again.

Lightly he said that in life he had nothing superfluous,
Only ten thousand shelves of books in elaborate covers.
Sad that mist locks in the pavilion, the veranda of old;
A touch of heart—it serves as both teacher and father,
Schooling these orphans on nights of white moon and clear wind.
Before the writing is done,
Tears come pouring out.

By now the trees on his grave are almost as thick as my arm—
When will he have his wish of a green case fulfilled,
And smile beneath the Springs?
From time to time his voice and face appear in a dream,
As if he were still in his Five-Three Studio.
What can I do? Falling leaves swish down to startle me.
Even if these orphans can establish themselves,
I fear that mother's curtains may be taken down,
 her spring sunlight may die out.
I prop up my ailing bones,
For what I shoulder is hard to lay down.

(XTLS: *Guchunxuan ci*, 2b)

line 12: On "green case" see P.82.2.

line 13: The Springs are the Yellow or Ninefold Deep Springs; see P.29.9 and P.60.6.

line 18: It was the custom to take down the curtains in a funeral hall when the body was put into the coffin.

BIOGRAPHICAL NOTE AND TRANSLATION BY NANCY J. HODES AND TUNG YUAN-FANG

汪端

P.119. Wang Duan (1793–1838)

Wang Duan was one of the best-known women writers of the Qing dynasty, with many literary connections. Her marriage to Chen Peizhi made her the daughter-in-law of the art patron Chen Wenshu (see P.116), and she was the niece of Liang Desheng (P.118). She published an anthology of Ming poetry, *Ming sanshi jia shixuan* (Selected poems of thirty Ming poets, 1820), which was unusual in that a woman offered her editorial judgments about the works of thirty men. The collection has been praised for the good taste informing its literary judgments. Wang Duan's close connections with her fellow female poets and with female relatives are nevertheless established in the list of proofreaders, all women, including Xi Peilan (P.93).

From 1825 on, Wang Duan's life was marred by tragedies—the death of her husband and the resulting insanity of her only son—which precipitated a turn to Daoism during her final years.[1] Her collected writings were published posthumously under the title *Ziran haoxuezhai ji* (Collected writings from Natural Love-of-Learning Studio, 1839). Wang is also known to have written a narrative (whether novel or *tanci* is unclear) entitled *Yuan Ming yishi* (Forgotten history of the Yuan and Ming), but she burned her draft of this manuscript, and only fragments survive.[2]

P.119.1. Mourning Xiaoqing at Plum Flower Island

Dusk darkens the mountain and lake where she is buried.
The beautiful woman's inborn talent was the source of much sorrow.
"Autumn laments" and "distant flutes" linger in her surviving writing;
"Rain against dark windows" recalls her tears of old.

In springtime by the peaceful pond where she once met her reflection
I stand in the shade of the western hall and vainly invoke her spirit.
Each year women travel here to consecrate the spot with fine wine.
(8) Cold beauty and chilly incense mark the door of your tomb.

(*Ziran haoxuezhai ji*, 4/6a)

On Xiaoqing, see P.104.1; see also Widmer, "Xiaoqing's Literary Legacy."
lines 3–4: These lines cite phrases from letters and poems by Xiaoqing.

P.119.2. At Zhiguo Temple, Mourning at the Tomb of the Ming Woman Yang Yunyou

To what place does your fragrant spirit return in the moonlight?
It is buried in pure earth near the temple door.
The feeling in your poetry is like faraway trees capturing the spring rain.
The essence of your painting is like a clear lake reflecting the evening glow.
Beside your grave mandarin ducks hear Buddhists chanting in Sanskrit.

Before the wind butterflies change into gauze dresses.
I am sorry that you are separated from your dear friend.
(8) Hearing a tune on the *pipa*, I wipe away my own tears.

(*Ziran haoxuezhai ji*, 46a)

Like Xiaoqing, Yang Yunyou had a following in Ming-loyalist circles. Both Xiaoqing's and Yang Yunyou's tombs were restored by Wang Duan's father-in-law, Chen Wenshu.

line 7: Yang Yunyou's friend was a woman named Lin Tiansu.

line 8: The *pipa* is a strummed instrument of Central Asian origin, associated with Wang Zhaojun.

P.119.3. Mourning at Bian Sai's Tomb in the Brocade Forest of the Ming Capital

Fall shadows at the Xiao and Xiang Rivers outline dewy buds.
On the shores of Lake Grieve-Not lies the home of a former beauty.
In the cold, the butterflies flap their silk skirts against the evening moon.
At dusk a crow stands on spring mud to mourn at the fragrant tomb.

With one tune from an icy string I grieve for your rare abilities.
It was writings from the Buddhist sutras that brought you to enlightenment.
Your attendant, coming to present an inkstone, was touched by your brilliant talent.
(8) Conveying regret for a beauty, the frontier bugle weeps.

(*Ziran haoxuezhai ji*, 4/7a)

On Bian Sai, see P.64. Her actual tomb seems to have been in Wuxi, but this poem places it in Nanjing.

P.119.4. On Yuan Shuyun's Posthumous Collection Jianxianglou yigao

The learning of your family was transmitted generation after generation in the house of Xiao Cang,
Yet your life was cut short, leaving only the fragrance of your writing.
Falling flowers are stirred up by the wind, but the strings of the *qin* are cold.
The new moon's light is sinking, and the mirror frame is cold.

I couldn't allow your jade flute to depart with you.
I am certain that the Immortals' Register must have recorded your autumn music.
The Qing and Huai Rivers are covered by clouds and trees, above them the mountain hovers like black eyebrows.
(8) Where exactly were you buried under the setting sun?

(*Ziran haoxuezhai ji*, 4/8a)

Yuan Shu (or Shuyun) was the granddaughter of Yuan Mei. On her published poetry collection, see Hu Wenkai, p. 491.

line 5: On this allusion to Nongyu and her husband the Piper, see P.26.5.

P.119.5. On a Small Portrait of "The Lady of Hedong" [Liu Shi, P.67]

Your rosy face has become ashes, proving the hollowness of life.
You loved to dress like an immortal scholar.
After the war, you and your husband plowed in the field of literature.
Even before your later ordeals, your reputation had spread far afield.
You need not envy Zhang Nong, who received an official title;
You can compete with Ge Nen, who died for a loyalist cause.
You maintained your integrity, putting your husband to shame.
(8) A talented woman facing a tragic choice, you have my sincere sympathy.

(*Ziran haoxuezhai ji*, 7/12b–13a)

Zhang Nong, a woman of the Southern Song, was commended for being a good wife to her loyalist husband. Ge Nen, captured by Qing troops, chose death over dishonor and was followed in death by her lover; for their story, see Yu Huai, *Banqiao zaji*, chap. 2 (p. 7). Liu Shi's husband, Qian Qianyi, was thought to have compromised his integrity by living on into the Qing dynasty and serving its government, hence the barbed compliment of the poem's last couplet.

P.119.6. At Nanping (near West Lake), Mourning by Zhang Huangyan's Grave

At the end of the island, the gibbon's cry is heard from the far-off forest;
At Wengzhou, a martial spirit galvanizes the chill of fall.
A lone minister, you were prepared to eat the foods of a recluse,
Allied with other stalwarts you planned to take to the sea.

You died a martyr at the river as cold waves rose.
Now at your grave beside the lake the dark mist is deep.
Like a green mountain in the setting sun, your writings still survive.
(8) Do they differ from the patriotic diaries of Qu Shisi and Zhang Tongchang?

(*Ziran haoxuezhai ji*, 1/16b)

Zhang Huangyan (1620–64) was one of the last to receive the *juren* degree under the Ming. After the fall of Nanking he formed a volunteer corps to support the loyalist cause, but had to retreat to coastal and island hiding places. In 1651 he joined forces with the admiral Zheng Chenggong (Koxinga; see line 4) and fought along the south China coast and in Yunnan until he was captured and executed by the Qing in 1664 (Hummel, ed., *Eminent Chinese of the Ch'ing Period*, 1: 41–42).

line 8: Both Qu Shisi and Zhang Tongchang were advisors to the doomed court of the last Ming pretender, the Hongli emperor. Their loyalist writings were reprinted in the early nineteenth century.

P.119.7. On a Small Painting of Hibiscus by Sun Yunfeng

Scarlet maple mingles with evening reeds.
Fall colors cover your vignette of the river, which shines with an evening glow.
Hibiscus fails to blossom in the winds of spring.
You need to avoid the extravagant flowers of the world.

(*Ziran haoxuezhai ji*, 1/21a)

Sun Yunfeng (P.114) was one of Wang's good friends.

P.119.8. On Qu Bingyun's Painting of White Lotuses

Beautiful is the one playing with pearls.
Autumn water washes her immortal bones.
You can see her from afar but you cannot know her,
In the silver pond drenched by the cool moon.

(*Ziran haoxuezhai ji*, 1/21a)

P.119.9. Song on an Abandoned Se *Zither*

The king of Qi loved the *yu*, the king of Qin loved the *zheng*.
What person can understand the music of these stringed instruments?
This *se*'s clear tone and remarkable melody have long not been heard.
From its desolate pearl-inlaid bridges fragrant dust arises.

Its twenty-five strings are half destroyed.
A beauty of Handan long ago used it for her lament.
Exiled, she experienced the bright moon of Dongting in the autumn marshes.
(8) Her grieving heart surely aroused the sympathy of the Xiang river spirit.

(*Ziran haoxuezhai ji*, 1/21a)

The *se*, *yu*, and *zheng* are all stringed instruments of the zither type.

line 5: On the original fifty strings of the *se*, see P.72.3. Wang's allusion to this story also recalls Li Shangyin's enigmatic "Brocaded Zither" poem (QTS, 539/6144).

P.119.10. *On a Fall Night Hearing the Sound of Crickets*

Hearing the sound of crickets means it is the cold part of fall.
I casually hang a golden cage near the moonlight.
The *wutong* leaves wither around the well, the mist turns dark.
Bean flowers are scattered around the bamboo fence as the rain abates.

The embroidered palindrome records bygone words of passion.
The new threads that sustain life twist my inexorable sorrow.
With grieving heart, the beauty casts aside the shuttle.
(8) The evening lamp and the rays of the moon fill her small red boudoir.

(*Ziran haoxuezhai ji*, 4/21a)

line 5: On Su Hui's embroidered palindrome, see C.1 and C.4.

P.119.11. *Wu Zao [P.122] Sends Me a Poem, to Which I Now Reply*

Your small calligraphy, precious as pearls, arrived in several lines.
The parting words at the river bridge were hard to forget.
Beside a plum tree, the sound of a bamboo pipe flowed into Dispersed Incense Pavilion,
Below the moon you repaired a flute in Jade Tea Hall.

Flower shadows cover the staircases, while crickets swallow the dew.
Now as sounds of fall reach my pillow, the geese cry frosty tears.
Bridges and pavilions of Hangzhou: I will be late for my date to see you.
(8) I lie here sick, immersed in the steam of brewing tea and dreams of my old home.

(*Ziran haoxuezhai ji*, 5/9b)

line 8: Although originally from Hangzhou, Wang Duan spent much of her married life away from home.

P.119.12. For Wu Guichen [P.106]

In the rainy season of Jiangnan I meet you again.
The Song of West Bamboo reminds me of your last absence.
Accompanied by Green Duckweed, you were full of heroic spirit.
Like a heavenly being, you carried a flowering bough and wore a white silk skirt.

Amidst the fragrance of lotus blossoms you languidly await the moon.
In the shadow of the *wutong* tree you record your homesickness.
Your new collection, which I have here with me, is as fine as Li Qingzhao's.
(8) On a cool night, it complements the natural warmth of my hands.

(*Ziran haoxuezhai ji*, 5/7a)

line 3: "Green Duckweed" was the name of a famous sword of antiquity. Wu's ability as a swordswoman was widely known.
line 7: On Li Qingzhao, see P.17.

BIOGRAPHICAL NOTE AND TRANSLATION BY ELLEN WIDMER

莊盤珠

P.120. Zhuang Panzhu (fl. early 19th century)

Zhuang Lianpei, more commonly known as Zhuang Panzhu, was born into the family of Zhuang Youjun, a resident of Changzhou, Jiangsu province. On reaching maturity, she married Wu Shi (style name Chengzhi), a man of the same city and the recipient of a *juren* examination degree. Zhuang Panzhu is said to have been a precocious child who displayed a strong interest in classical verse from an early age. Tutored at her father's knee, she soon learned to chant from memory many poems of the Han and Tang eras. It is not surprising, therefore, that while still relatively young she turned to the writing of verse in both the classical *shi* and song-lyric forms.

Over the next decade or so (she died in her mid-twenties of tuberculosis), she composed a significant number of poems, many of which are of excellent quality. These poems she subsequently published in several different collections: the *Lianpei shi cao* (A draft collection of Lianpei's poetry), the *Ziwei xuan ji* (The collected works of the Crape-Myrtle Studio), and the *Qiushui xuan ci* (Song lyrics of the Autumn Waters Studio).[1]

The critical reception accorded her poetry has generally been very favorable. A melancholic air, a pervasive note of personal longing, grief, or despair, pervades many of her poems, especially those in song-lyric form, and it has occasioned special praise from more than one critic. Zhuang has also been applauded for her skillful use of certain key terms, such as the word *ying* ("shadow" or "faint image"), which invited comparison with the Song dynasty poet Zhou Bangyan, noted for employing that evocative term three times in one poem.[2]

P.120.1. Sumu zhe: *Willow Catkins*

Branches first stretched forth,
Then catkins took shape.
Having failed to see the blossoms open,
Now I can only watch the petals scattering on the wind:
Swirling about steps, curling around curtains, and when about to settle
They're snatched up by a sudden eddy
And blown away upon the wind.

(8) In rural villages,
At overgrown fords,
Travelers discard the willow branch,
For this has always been heartbreak road.
(12) Though they cling to the last vestiges of spring, spring pays the catkins no heed;
Now buried in the empty pond,
Ruefully they become duckweed beyond number.

(XTLS: *Qiushui xuan ci*, 1a–b)

line 10: On the willow as a symbol of parting, see P.5.1.

line 14: It was popularly believed that after falling in water willow catkins changed into the duckweed plant. The metamorphosis is a common literary trope for melancholy.

P.120.2. Qingping yue: *Listening to a Flute on a Spring Evening*

Like rushing, rippling water:
The pure sounds of a solitary flute on a clear night.
Blowing out the lamp, I again ascend the small tower;
Melancholy is the moon in the willow branches.

Startled from their places on the rafters, swallows
Are compelled to accompany me as I pace back and forth.
If I fail to listen, how can I fall asleep?
(8) But if I do, spring sorrows will surely arise.

(XTLS: *Qiushui xuan ci*, 6a)

P.120.3. Zui hong zhuang: *An Autumn Evening*

Who knows whence these echoes of the laundry stone!
To my heart,
They are of rare purity.
A lone goose calls down the stars from heaven.
Clouds lower darkly,
Rain obscures the view.

I ask autumn if it is willing to pause awhile
(8) And allow the golden willow to flourish anew.
Instead, the west wind simply blows all the harder;
So all is for naught,
Save for a touch of sentiment.

(XTLS: *Qiushui xuan ci*, 6a)

line 1: On the theme of the sound of laundry being beaten clean, see P.4.3.

P.120.4. Ta suo xing: *Presented in Reply to a Poem Elder Brother Sent to Express His Feelings While Pondering Antiquity at Jingkou*

The midday sun hastened westward,
The great river eastward flowed.
Day after day, night after night, we gathered there.
From ancient times, green hills have sat on its flanks—
Unworried, unsmiling, sentinels to the passing years.
At ferry crossings, masts and sails;

On the waves, the tolling of matin bells:
Those following behind press forward on those in front.
Don't toss the words of your poem on the cold waves,
Lest their profound feelings incite the flood dragons to anger.

(XTLS: *Qiushui xuan ci*, 6b)

Jingkou is the city of Zhenjiang, located near the juncture of the Yangzi River and the Grand Canal.

line 5: The sentinels are the mountains Jinshan and Jiaoshan, which lie in the general vicinity of Zhenjiang.

line 10: An allusion to the *Ru Shu ji*, a famous travel diary by the Song dynasty poet Lu You (1125–1210), and to a story recorded there about the Renzong emperor (r. 1023–64), in which, when an example of the emperor's calligraphy was displayed in a temple on Jinshan, violent winds and waves arose on the river below as flood dragons thrashed about in the water (Lu You, *Ru Shu ji*, *juan* 1, in SKQS, 460: 882).

P.120.5. Yiluo jin: *Faded Chrysanthemums*

How like a beautiful lady ground down by disease,
Or a poor scholar,
Shivering in his coarse and tattered clothing,
Fearing the thick frost of dawn, the moon at night,
And, following Double Nine, painfully taking his leave.
Reed flowers and paper walls alone separate the pure and impure.
Monopolizing the autumn scene,
They are heroines among the flowers.
Not yet rid of worldly cares, I find suffering still persists,
For lo, these many seasons, I've worried about the flowers.

(XTLS: *Qiushui xuan ci*, 7a)

line 5: On the Double Ninth, see P.5.1 and P.11.4.

P.120.6. Tan fang xun: *The Cricket*

News of cold weather it brings
To the foot of the wall with the morning dew,
Or to a crevice in the evening mist.
Just as a dream of brocade coverlets is broken,
The flowering beans are agitated by the wind.
A candle guttering in the window, light fades into darkness;

Beyond the windowpane, the white moon shines.
(8) Startled all of a sudden: is it on West Street or North Lane
That someone spins by night?

When will the task be complete?
Strange sounds bring forth long strands;
(12) Slow is the pace, for the silk is rough.
In the silent night, in cold boudoirs,
Faint sounds mix with those of the tailor's ruler and knife.
Who possesses a myriad of strands of entangled sorrow?
(16) Or strives to fashion a grieving heart?
Even if one lacks regrets,
One cannot bear to listen to its song.

(XTLS: *Qiushui xuan ci*, 8b)

The cricket was also known as "Silk-reeling Maid" or "Weaving Maid" because of the resemblance between its chirping and the creaking of wooden silk-reeling wheels. Poem 114 of the *Book of Odes* links the cricket's call to the end of the year and the *carpe diem* theme. In addition, in popular lore the cricket was said to play the role of matchmaker.

P.120.7. Langtao sha: *A Little Song-Lyric Written to Record My Feelings After the Cherry Apple Trees Burst into Bloom Beside Twin Peak Studio*

In a small boudoir, dreams lie broken
As last night's rains taper off.
The storm passing, bees and butterflies gather at the curtain;
Spring ignores the cherry apple trees in the garden,
But I grieve for their blossoms.
Reading my poems, I recall past experiences,
But in the wink of an eye, everything vanishes.
(8) Ill and facing great odds, I struggle to lift my head;
Next year, I know, whether I'm here or not,
The blossoms will grieve for me!

(XTLS: *Qiushui xuan ci*, 18a)

Twin Peak Studio was the name of the Zhuang family study. Chen Xin calls the reader's attention to the broad thematic similarities between this poem and the famous flower burial poem composed by Lin Daiyu, the heroine of the great classical novel *Honglou meng*, and to many other poems of a similar nature from the post-Tang era (*Lidai funü shici xuan zhu*, p. 269).

P.120.8. Tai cheng lu: *Sent to My Husband*

Last night I imagined tonight would bring some rain;
Instead, tonight the haloed moon is perversely bright.
White frost startles the insects,
Wild geese echo the careless breeze,
Too soon rousing personal concerns.
For whom should I feel remorse?
Were I to ask why I'm so thin,
Even Heaven could not reply.
How I wish there was a potion
To cure forever this illness of mine!
Melancholy, I lie down fully clothed;
Head on pillow and just about to doze off,
Suddenly I'm startled into wakefulness.
Dry lotus flowers rustle on the pond,
By the gate, remnant leaves rattle:
How numerous are the sounds of autumn!
With difficulty I repress a smile.
Why this sudden fear that fall has come,
Then rue that it is leaving?
Illness causes time to pass,
And it also tosses people aside.

(XTLS: *Qiushui xuan ci*, 19b–20a)

P.120.9. Liu shao qing: *The Qingming Festival*

The wind and birds cry out.
On taking ill this time,
How unlike last spring.
Too lazy to ply the needle,
I lie down, but it is hard to fall asleep.
Sorrow alone remains.

Happily, beyond the curtains days of dark clouds
Give way to patches of clear blue sky.

Ill-fated are the peach blossoms,
Laden with emotion are the golden willows,
Just as before at Qingming time.

(XTLS: *Qiushui xuan ci*, 23b)

On the Qingming (or Clear-Bright) festival, see P.38.1, note to line 105.

P.120.10. Ta suo xing: *Rising from a Sickbed*

Most dreadful are the dregs of spring,
When fallen petals cluster along pathways.
This year I fell ill before the flowers bloomed.
Don't let fine rains oppress them any more;
Detain spring even a day and the flowers will be pleased.

The breeze stills, the drapes hang motionless,
Swallows nap, and silence pervades the rafters.
(8) The Qingming festival nears, but a chill still persists.
Rising from a sickbed on the veranda, I find the flowers are gone,
And the setting sun illuminating only floating gossamer images.

(XTLS: *Qiushui xuan ci*, 23b)

BIOGRAPHICAL NOTE AND TRANSLATION BY WILLIAM SCHULTZ

顧太清

P.121. Gu Taiqing (1799–ca. 1876)

Gu Taiqing (style name Chun) was the greatest Manchu female poet of the Qing dynasty. In an eventful life she went from rags to riches and back. The granddaughter of a disgraced Manchu prince, Gu took her surname from the bondservant family that raised her. The Manchu prince Yihui (1799–1838) took her in, first as protégée and then as concubine. Yihui's talents as antiquarian, architect, and poet complemented Gu's own artistic bent. She bore Yihui seven children and became the focal point of Beijing's leading women writers' salon. Then Yihui died young; Gu's stepson expelled her and her children from the palace. Gu spent the rest of her life scraping by, raising her children (all married well), and writing when she could.

She left behind a considerable body of work—more than is easily estimated, since printed editions of her *shi* poems (*Tianyouge ji* [Collection from the Tower of Celestial Wandering]) and *ci* lyrics (*Donghai yuge* [Fisherman's songs from the Eastern Sea]) seem incomplete. Suzuki Torao claimed to have seen a seven-*juan* version of *Tianyouge ji* and a six-*juan* version of *Donghai yuge*. If Suzuki's tabulations are accurate, then Gu's complete oeuvre should include 623 *shi* poems and 354 song-lyrics.[1] The editions in common circulation hold significantly fewer poems. The Academia Sinica in Beijing, however, possesses part of a handwritten *Tianyouge ji* edition once owned by Xu Naichang, editor of the comprehensive *Xiao tan luan shi huike guixiu ci* anthology (XTLS); this fragment contains many poems missing from the common Shanghai reprint.

Gu's prose writing, including a sequel to Cao Xueqin's great novel *Hong lou meng* (Dream of the red chamber, ca. 1750; see P.122.17), has only recently come to the attention of scholars.[2]

Gu's lyrics reflect a refined sensibility and aristocratic reserve. She inhabits a familiar world of weeping willows, screens, railings, and curtained windows. Her boudoir and garden settings offer her a springboard to embody things (see "Inscribed on a Fan," P.121.6), to imitate ancient lyricists (see the *Ding fengbo* song-lyric, P.121.7, whose subject shift slyly undermines the voyeurism in her model—the second of the "Nineteen Ancient Poems"), to inscribe paintings, and occasionally to rise above it all with otherworldly remoteness (see her awakening-verse in the *Zhegu tian* lyric, P.121.9, and the homely allegory in her *Xi fen chai* lyric on the barrel-twirl toy, P.121.10). Throughout, aesthetic appreciation is Gu's strongest suit. Although she often depicts hazy, blurry scenes, she manages to balance vividness, minimalism, and obliqueness.

P.121.1. Langtao sha: *Composed at Random*

Human life is an endless struggle—
The post-horse and plow-ox.
On the brows of the Daoist sadness never grows:
Quietly holding a book of immortality, seated by the window,
What else is there to seek?

Prospects disappear far, far away,
Months and years are hard to detain.
(8) In a hundred years' time everyone will be a pat of mud,
So arrange a firm and safe place in your own mind,
And let the boat float with the stream.

(Gu Taiqing, *Donghai yuge*, 1/7b–8a)

P.121.2. Que qiao xian: *After I Dreamed of My Maid Pomegranate*

One year parted by death,
A thousand years of deep sorrow.
I still remember her childish locks when we first met;
In my mind I cannot forget her tiny frame.
Among my maids
This girl was the best.

The past so far from reach,
I cannot bear to look back.
In vain clear tears fall, breaking my heart.
Deep in the night I often dream your soul comes.
But when I wake from the dream,
I cannot remember most of our talk.

(*Donghai yuge*, 1/12b)

P.121.3. Jiang chengzi: *Recording a Dream*

Haze envelops the cold water, moonlight envelops the sand.
Floating on a magic raft,
I visit an immortal's home.
A clear stream all along the way,
The two oars rise and fall, breaking the mist.
Just past the little bridge the scenery changes:
Under the bright moon,
I see blossoming plum trees.

A myriad of blossoming plum trees: their shadows intertwine
To the edge of the hills,
To the edge of the waters.
They fall into the lake's reflected heaven:
Their loveliness certainly worthy of praise.
I wanted to travel all over the sea of fragrant snow—
But startled out of my dream
I blame the cawing crow.

(*Donghai yuge*, 1/28b)

P.121.4. Zhegu tian: *Puppets*

Puppets on the stage, they behave most brashly:
Passing on false stories, they beguile foolish children.
All lies, their tales of the founding of Tang and Song,
Their magic is in their clever transformations of devils and demons.

Riding red leopards,
Attended by striped foxes,
With fancy caps and gowns they put on a mighty pose.
(8) Once they leave the stage and are hung up high, what use are they then?
Carved wood and pulled strings—just a moment's fun.

(*Donghai yuge*, 2; reprinted in *Cixue jikan*, 1.2 [1933], 152–53)

P.121.5. Qiubo mei: *Sitting at Night*

I laugh at my earlier self trying to work up verses:
Old traces hard to find even in dreams.
How many scrolls of poems?
How many sketches for paintings?
How much time has been. . . .

The spittoon shattered from tapping, I scratch my head often,
Rubbing out my old ambitions.
(8) And now all I've succeeded in getting is
A thousand streaks of tears
And a grieving heart.

(*Donghai yuge, juan* 5 [unpaginated]; in *Tianyouge ji*)

line 7: On Wang Dun and his cracked spittoon, see P.113.6.

P.121.6. Zui taoyuan: *Inscribed on a Fan with Ink-Sketched Gardenias, Sent to Yunjiang*

Blossoms plump, leaves big: two or three boughs.
Perfume drifts from a jade-white cup.
A light, gauzy round fan limns icy raiments.
Why bother to put on powder and paint?
After fresh rains,
A fine breeze blows.

Idle stairs in the hour of moonrise.
(8) Cobalt sky like water, shadows slowly furl.
Pure scent, even better in the dark.

(*Donghai yuge*, 1/17b)

Yunjiang was Gu's closest friend.

line 2: Jade-white cup (*yuzhi*) describes the gardenia, names a flower nymph, and puns on "jade-white limbs" (*yuzhi*).

P.121.7. Ding fengbo: *After the Ancient Style*

Tower and terrace blossom-wrapped, cannot see for sure.
Green willows block and screen off a figure in the tower.
Who said it is the held-in sorrows you cannot glimpse?
  One whole swath . . .
Peach blossoms her face in dear, affecting Spring.
Fragrant grasses lush and lovely, the skies far or near.
  So hard to ask . . .
(8) Wherever his horse's hooves go, they always sear a soul.
I've counted every last single flock of homing crows.
  Perverse to add . . .
Dim and dour evening rains—again—as dusk turns dun.

(*Donghai yuge*, 1/11a)

line 5: An allusion to the Tang poet Cui Hu's famous quatrain about returning to a place where once he had met a beauty, only to find her gone: "Last year, on this day, within this very gate, / Her face and peach blossoms shone each other pink. / And now—her face—wherever has it gone? / Peach blossoms as ever smile in springtime wind" (translated by David McCraw).

P.121.8. Zhuying yao hong: *Hearing Eunuch Chen Jinchao of the Pear Garden [the Imperial Troupe] Play the* Qin

A sense of snow hangs heavy,
North winds coldly cuff a courtyard bamboo-clump.
A white-haired eunuch enters, bearing his zither;
Ere he speaks, his brows knit in fret.
He plays through all those old Jasper Pool tunes:
Tones purling, clear waters flow, clouds cascade.
Here on earth, up in heaven,
(8) Well on forty years now—

Hurts the heart, stabs the eye.
I still recall, back at first
Pear Garden's numberless bevy of famous blossoms.
Pipe and song drifting aloft among slate clouds:
We enjoyed all the luck of the sylphs.
Heave a sigh: and now this aging servant
Thanks to milord's grace draws a scanty stipend.
I can't bear to turn back—
Dusky prospects dim and desolate
Crying a song at road's dead-end.

(*Donghai yuge*, 2/14a)

line 2: The first lines of this poem recall an allegorical ode to bamboos Su Shi (Su Dongpo) wrote while jailed by Censorate officials. His first six lines: "Today the wind comes from the south / And blows atumble courtyard bamboos. / Low and high, struck to tonal harmony: / Armor and blades cuffing in profusion. / Desolately sad, sense of wind and snow / That can snap but not disgrace them" (translated by David Mc Craw). Gu's lyric shares Su's rhyme category and his implicit comparison between noble bamboos and a singer out of luck.

line 5: Jasper Pool refers to the Heavenly Court; it introduces the Heaven / imperial court vs. Earth/exile motif that organizes the eunuch's lament.

line 9: Here and elsewhere in this poem Gu paraphrases lines from Li Yu's laments in exile.

line 18: Out of favor at court, the high-minded but frustrated Ruan Ji, one of the Seven Worthies of the Bamboo Grove [see P.10.1], would drive his cart through the wilds till he reached a dead end, then cry bitterly.

P.121.9. Zhegu tian

On a winter's night, I sat listening to my husband discourse on the Way. Before we had noticed the hour, midnight struck. A withered plum tree in a pot emitted sweet scent; I felt an Awakening, and so wrote down this lyric.

Midnight talk on sutras—jade water clock drips slow.
Life's greatest secrets—just where no wonders reside.
Worldly folk, don't cherish the finery of flowery scents:
When flowers smell sweetest, they begin to wither away.
Bees brew up honey; silkworms spin out silk.
When the task gets finished, how could no one realize?

Withering braids have witnessed every Eon of Endless Sands;
North of Snow and South of Scent, I'll seek a dharma guide.

(*Donghai yuge*, 1/21b)

line 5: These lines recall a couplet from Bo Juyi's allegory "Qin chong shi'er zhang" (QTS, 460/5245): "Silkworms age, cocoons finished—not to shelter themselves; / Bees go hungry, honey matures—given to someone else."

line 7: The Buddhist simile for time calls it infinite as "the sands of the Ganges"; the Chinese call Ganges the "Eternal River." "Withering braids / floral garland" (*huaman*: Sanskrit *kusumamala*) denote the flowers decorating Buddhist altar idols and suggest Gu's graying hair and perhaps the withered plum branches as well.

line 8: To Indian Buddhists, "South of Scents [the Malabar Hills] and North of Snows [the Himalayas]" conveyed a world beyond the mundane.

P.121.10. Xi fen chai: *Watching the Children Play with a* Kongzhong *Barrel-Twirl*

Spring's nearly here.
Sunny-sky weather . . .
Sitting idly by, I watch the children at play.
Borrowing high winds.
To drum up inside . . .
Knotting colored yarn as string.
Sawing up bamboo for the barrel.
Kong Kong.
Here in humans' realm.
Observe fool and sage.
Nearly all make vessels to contain a deep intent.
Nature's laws endless.
Matters without cease.
What's full can make sound.
What's empty can receive.
Chong Chong.

(*Donghai yuge*, 1/11a)

The *kongzhong* is a child's noise-making toy of hollow bamboo manipulated by a string. The instrument's name suggests the void (*kong*), a notion on which Gu plays here in Daoistic mode.

line 16: The word *chong* used here invokes chapter 5 of the *Dao de jing*, which may be an onomatopoeia, but its lexical meanings include "a whirling sound; a dashing movement through air; limpid/placid."

P.121.11. Ta suo xing: *On Aging*

My aging world trips tottering;
Lodging cares to painter's silk.
Idly making myself appear as "the bookworm."
These years often sick, old friends estranged;
Confines of living dependent on mountain hare.
Dreams gone, I'm lazy to pursue;
Songs done, I correct myself.
(8) Strike a spittoon broken—hard to express grief.
Sunk in exile, dare I complain to Fair Divinity
That empty fame has been betrayed by my writings?

(*Donghai yuge* 2/15a)

line 4: Gu quotes part of a Meng Haoran couplet usually understood as a lament for rejection: "Without talent, I find myself discarded by the wise ruler; / Often sick, I see my old friends grow distant" (QTS, 160/1651).

line 5: The reference to a brush made from hare need not mean that Gu makes her living (one meaning for "confines of living") from verse. Rather, verse makes a lonely life bearable (and so marks life's acceptable "margins/confines": *shengya*, a term whose dual meaning we might try to capture with the pun "life's selvage").

line 8: An allusion to Wang Dun; see P.113.6.

lines 9–10: The epithet "Fair Divinity" (*lingxiu*, or, as here, *xiuling*) is used in the *Chuci* tradition to refer to gods and goddesses who are the objects of the speaker's erotic pursuit; in the political-allegorical interpretation of the *Chuci* songs, it designates the ruler from whom the speaker is alienated.

P.121.12. Shuang ye fei: *Harmonizing with a Lyric by Zhou Bangyan From His* Pianyu ci *Collection*

Lush, lush the fragrant grass;
Beyond a clump of trees,
The moon has just climbed above the tree top.
A Lover's Bridge, a flowing stream, and mist at dusk;
Just then, the night is cool and people are quiet.
Far off in the sands, autumn crickets twitter until dawn.
Starlets in threes and fives, drifting glowworms tiny.
(8) See the white dew gather across the sky;
How could I bear facing a lone lamp's glow, small as a pea
Casting back its clear shadow at me?

Last night, in a dream, clear and vivid:
Far I followed the wild geese in flight,
But the place, a thousand miles beyond, is hard to reach.
The west wind has blown across more ranges of mountains:
How I grieve over the mood of my bosom friend!
I guess, by the hedge the chrysanthemums have blossomed:
Before the wine goblet, who is singing this melancholy tune?
You should remember where I stand transfixed in love,
Listening to wind, listening to rain,
My pain deepening who knows how much?
(Shen Lidong and Ge Rutong, eds., *Lidai funü shici jianshang cidian*, 465)

Lyrics by Zhou Bangyan, a Northern Song master of "slow tune" compositions, are generally praised for their sonority and for the denseness of their imagery. Here Gu Taiqing—using the same tune title and rhyme words throughout—attempts to outdo the master's poem "Shuang ye fei" (QSC, 2: 605)

line 4: The text reads *duanqiao* ("Broken Bridge"), which refers to one of the scenic sites around West Lake in Hangzhou, said to be the trysting place between the White Snake Girl and her mortal lover Xu Xian.

P.121.13. Zuiweng cao: *Inscription for a Painting by Yunlin Entitled "Zither Swathed in Moonlight by a Lake"*

Far, far away
A distant sky
Limpid waters
Lost in a lakeful of mist
Vast and boundless.
Resplendent is the clear light of the moon;
There's the Fairest One, the flying immortal.
Quietly, without a word,
Tugging at the sleeve, someone plucks the lilting strings.
Shining on hanging willows, the pale moon's shadow moves slant.

How much I esteem your mind that dwells
On flowing streams and towering peaks!
Let me ask: at such moments
Is your heart attuned to the ease of mountains or the stream?
Clouds aimlessly drift in the sky's unlimited space;
The moon glows brighter as thick dew drops gather.

New sounds harmonizing and perfectly matched;
Pure chords ever so gently, gently plucked.
Transcendent music is broadcast all over the world;
The moon bright, the breeze calm, and autumn night chill.

(*Lidai funü shici jianshang cidian*, 1754)

Yunlin is the famous Yuan painter Ni Zan (1301–74). Although scores of his works are extant today, no painting with this title has been identified in published catalogues.

line 20: The reading of this last line as *Yueming fengjing qiuye han* follows most modern scholarly editions. However, a variant of this line is given in some other editions as *Yeshen xiang ai fei shelan* ("The night is advanced and the air is fragrant with a special scent, neither from the orchid nor from the musk").

P.121.14. Langtao sha man: *Having Received No Letter from Yunjiang for a Long Time, I Wrote This, Using the Rhyme-Scheme of Liu Qiqing*

Again I've waited until late winter,
And still no news from my bosom friend.
Now fresh snow has just fallen,
And a few branches of winter plum blossom
Are just starting to bud liquid jade.
Facing Sparse Fragrance and Sylphlike Shadow makes me long for my guest.
Brooding long and hard over the same longing at two places,
I dread that in dreams
Our tracks are never certain,
And each would finally come to grief.

Boundless,
The twining tender feelings,
The excruciating secret grief!
How many times have I spun them out before the palace gate?
In vain the wild geese have waited for long;
Even though it was a short separation,
It pains my soul and body.

Recalling days of long ago,
How, in the Land of Fragrance we lingered over flowers!

Now the onrushing snow and departing catkins
Daily make one feel isolated and alone.
When might it be that we two could trim a candle together by the western window?
There will be thousands upon thousands of words
Rehearsed over and over again.
Yet still I'm sad,
For I can never quite express all our shared memories.

(Su Zhecong, 460–61)

Yunjiang, along with her sister Yunlin, was an intimate friend of Gu's. She has been identified by Huang Shizong as a member of the Xu family and married to Ruan Fu (b. 1802), a son of Ruan Yuan (1764–1849), the great bibliophile and classicist. Liu Qiqing is the Northern Song poet Liu Yong (987–1053), an accomplished writer of "slow-tune" lyrics and especially admired for his depiction of love as experienced by men—that is, from the profligate lover's point of view. Gu's poem closely follows Liu Yong's *Langtaosha man* (QSC, 1: 26–27).

lines 1–2: In the original, the first few lines of this lyric read almost like prose because the poet wants to maintain a true epistolary style.

line 6: "Sparse Fragrance" and "Sylphlike Shadow" are traditional epithets for winter plum blossoms.

line 19: The Land of Fragrance, or the Pure Land, is a Buddhist term in the *Vimalakirti sutra* for the paradise of the West, ruled by Amitabha Buddha. See Soothill and Hodous, eds., *Dictionary of Chinese Buddhist Terms*, pp. 319, 390.

line 21: Gu borrows two famous lines from a poem by Li Shangyin (813?–58) entitled "Yeyu ji bei" (QTS, 539/6151): "When might it be that we together could trim a candle by the western window / And talk about the time when rain at night fell on Ba Mountain?"

P.121.15. Jiang cheng meihua yin: *On a Rainy Day Receiving a Letter from Yunjiang*

Letter from a friend a thousand miles away:
Open it quick!
Open it slow!
What's in this letter?
Is she well or not? My mind is a blank.
Since our parting, cool and hot seasons have come and gone;
But north and south of the River
Arouse in me the grief of separation as I pace to and fro.

To and fro, to and fro, I long for someone far away
At the far end of the world,
Beyond the water's edge.
I dream, I dream;
Yet in my dream I cannot see your hairpin and skirt of those days.
Who would remember the dark clouds?
I stand transfixed waiting, my heart tied in knots.
Next year when you return and see me again
I should not be
My old self at the time of our parting.

(Zhou Daorong et al., eds., *Lidai mingyuan shici xuan*, 422)

P.121.16. Jiang cheng zi: *Fallen Flowers*

Flowers bloom, flowers fall, all in the same year.
I pity the faded reds
And blame the east wind,
They vex me so, these fallen petals aplenty;
Like snow flurries pelting at the curtained window.
To sit watching whirling blossoms—flower-gazing time is past.
Spring again is gone—
Far too hastily!
With whom can I share my grief in pitying the flowers?
Too lazy for my morning make-up,
So overpowering is my sorrow.
When the swallows return,
A crimson shower falling east of my painted chamber.
Lying everywhere, the spring grief cannot be pecked away;
So utterly thoughtless
Are the wandering honeybees.

(Shen Lidong and Ge Rutong, eds., *Lidai funü shici jianshang cidian*, 1176)

BIOGRAPHICAL NOTE AND TRANSLATION OF P.121.6–11 BY DAVID MCCRAW; TRANSLATION OF P.121.1–5 BY GRACE S. FONG; TRANSLATION OF P.121.12–16 BY IRVING YUCHENG LO

吳藻

P.122. Wu Zao (1799–1863)

The fame and achievement of Wu Zao (style name Pinxiang) may be measured by the attention she has received both from poets and editors of her time and from modern critics. Liang Yizhen's pioneering study *Qingdai funü wenxue shi* (Women's literary history of the Qing period), first published in 1927, devoted an entire section to her.[1] Thereafter, Tan Zhengbi featured her in two of his books,[2] and her poems have been repeatedly anthologized and occasionally translated. In 1946, Xie Qiuping brought out *Wu Zao ci*, a substantial edition of her poems written in lyric meters, for which Xie also wrote an informative and discerning critical introduction. Testimonia reveal that she was much acclaimed in her own day as well.[3]

A native of Renhe (now Hangzhou) and born into a merchant household, Wu seems to have married a businessman. From her youth, however, she had devoted herself to literary activities. She achieved early fame with a *zaju* drama titled *Qiaoying* (Proud silhouette) with the alternate title *Yinjiu dusao* (Reading the "Li Sao" while drinking).[4] Contemporaries took this play to be an autobiographical statement, for the heroine, punningly named Xie Xucai (literally, "talented successor to Xie Daoyun" [see C.24]), loved to dress as a male, drink, and read the "Li Sao" with its laments for unrecognized ability. Wei Qiansheng, who wrote a preface to the first volume of Wu's *ci* poems, mentioned that the play's lyrics, set to music by the people of the region, became extremely popular north and south of the Yangtze River.[5]

As a poet distinguished by a comparatively large corpus of poems in lyric meters, Wu's reputation was firmly established by two collections—the *Hualian ci* (Lyrics of the flowered curtain) and the *Xiangnan xuebei ci* (Song-lyrics from South of Fragrance and North of the Snows, 1844).[6] Chen Wenshu, the most celebrated patron of women poets after Yuan Mei, vigorously praised her. Her lyrics were compared to those of Li Qingzhao (P.17) and of the Manchu prince and subtle lyricist Nalan Xingde (1655–85). A poet of extraordinary range in both technique and interests, Wu demonstrated complete mastery of form. Combining the demotic and the literary in her diction in a manner reminiscent of Su Shi and Xin Qiji, Wu's "articulate energy" could by turn be intensely lyrical or grandly heroic, her power enlarged by the subtlest of wit and irony and the most daring of imageries.

In the preface to her last volume of *ci,* Wu mentioned that she had been plagued by worries and misfortunes for over a decade. Having selected for preservation some of her compositions, she would henceforth renounce writing and devote herself to the Dao. "Whether my body reside at Mount Fragrance in the South or Snow Mountain in the North, I shall submit myself to the Pure Land. How many lifetimes of cultivation will I require to reach the state of the plum flowers?"[7]

P.122.1. Ru meng ling: *A Swallow*

A swallow not having left with spring
Flies deep inside embroidered shades,
For hours speaking softly.
Could his wish be to stay with me?
  He waits . . .
  He waits . . .
I answer him smiling, "You may not!"

(Xie Qiuping, ed., *Wu Zao ci,* 24)

P.122.2. Ru meng ling

Whence come these notes of the jade flute
To blow off flying catkins, fallen plums?
Beyond the tower is a red wall
That can't enclose the fading sunlight.
  Spring leaves . . .
  Spring leaves . . .
And grief kills fine flowers of one tree.

(*Wu Zao ci,* 47)

P.122.3. Man jiang hong

  A gate shut in twilight,
A yard full of forlorn flowers, thinning grasses!
The sparse shades rolled up,
  The wind presses the papered window
  As smoke from the jade urn curls out.
A few cries from the sky's edge—migrant geese pass;
Some specks by the forest—homing crows caw.

Still and vacant—
Fallen leaves trembling on empty steps.
Who'd sweep their red?

There's no end to writing
This grief-stricken draft;
There's no end to routing
This idle distress.
I reckon such sad scenes before my eyes
As added matter for verse.
My shadow pities its two slender sleeves.
My sick soul contracted three autumns' age.
Let's round the eaves
To ask in jest the freezing plums:
Spring's too early yet?

(*Wu Zao ci*, 18)

P.122.4. Langtao sha

While water clocks drip on and on,
The cool study is lamp-lit.
By painted screens in autumn chill a single flute plays:
Truly "when the song ends, no one is in sight"
When the moon crosses flower-tips.

From where do evening bells toll?
Their gloom dissolves my soul.
These heartbreaking verses, this pathetic night.
Don't look for old dreams at the pillow's base.
Those dreams, too, are listless.

(*Wu Zao ci*, 17)

line 4: The sentence is a quotation from Qian Qi's poem on the spirits of the river Xiang; see P.74.3.

P.122.5. He huo ling

The bamboo mat cools as if newly washed;
The plantain screen has yet to snare a dream.
I'd sleep, but rise again to neaten my ice-white silk.

Beneath the blue-gauze windows let me
  Mutely pick incense to burn.

My woes I dread telling Heaven;
Most poems I scan when I'm ill.
Once more this night is like the night before:
  The same lamps aglow,
  The same clock dripping on and on,
  The same moment waking from wine
  As the moon climbs the flower-tips.

(*Wu Zao ci*, 25–26)

P.122.6. Mo shang hua

Double doors are all closed!
From what place at heaven's edge
Does one single transverse flute
Just beyond the red wall
Play to make the willows languid?
Nested crows have no care for such woeful scene
Still wearing the hues of twilight.
Again I rise from a tiring sleep.
Having lit incense in the urn,
I stand idle on the jade steps,

Saddened by this year's illness when my dread of heat and cold
Has wronged many a fine day.
Soon it will be the Double Ninth,
But I still fear that rain will not let up.
Flowing time is swift to leave people behind.
Who can see one move on a zither's frets?
Hence I ponder
That of those twenty-five strings
I've now passed the twenty-first.

(*Wu Zao ci*, 26)

line 13: On the Double Ninth, see P.5.1 and P.11.4.
line 18: On "twenty-five strings" and the allusion to Li Shangyin's celebrated "Brocaded Zither" poem, see P.119.9.

P.122.7. Jinlü qu

Since I came from the Blue Lotus Realm,
How many grievous verdicts I have overturned,
And to whom must I answer?
I'd scoop three thousand fathoms of the Milky Way
To wash off just once a girl's familiar form;
Packing up eyeshadows and leftover rouge,
I would not mimic Orchid Terrace's autumnal plaint
But only boast of smashing through the Cosmic Pass.
  Let me draw a long sword
  That leans beyond the sky.

Many are the seas of pleasures in the realm of man!
They all have their bannered arbors and painted walls
Where the double chignons would bow low.
When wine and singing stop, they still must leave
For all things return to a choiceless end.
Ask where are the ruined ashes of yesterday.
Learn of non-negation, the truth of truths,
For even gods are stumped by emptiness.
  This dusty world's affairs,
  Why should they surprise?

(*Wụ Zao ci*, 35)

line 1: The Buddha's eyes are said to resemble the shape of blue lotus leaves or *Utpala.* The Blue Lotus Realm was also a favorite conceit of the Tang poet Li Bo, who often referred to himself as the "banished immortal" from that region.

line 7: The "Orchid Terrace's autumnal plaint" makes two allusions to the early poet Song Yu, on whom see P.54d.3.

lines 9–10: "The sword that leans beyond the sky" is an allusion to the *yitian jian* mentioned in Li Bo's "Dalie fu" (*Li Taibo quanji*, 1/32a).

line 17: Non-negation or *wuwu* is a technical term for the state of ultimate purity in religious Daoism. See Li Shuhuan, *Daojiao da cidian*, p. 433.

P.122.8. Ku xiang si

Having warmed the silver lamp for just a while,
Alone I turn my back
On the screens of gauze.

Why couldn't I sleep these several nights?
It is hard for my mind to shun its grief,
Hard, too, for my brows to shun their grief.
The paper windows—cold as water—
By gusts of wind
Are slotted through.
I've sat till the slender moon is about to drop:
With dreams I should be asleep;
Without dreams I should be asleep.

(*Wu Zao ci*, 35–36)

P.122.9. Zhuan ying ci: *Thinking of My Elder Sister, Chaixiang, on a Moonlit Night*

She leaves,
She leaves—
Not even her shadow can be detained!
At dusk the wind whips up the curtain;
Moonlight again in front of the flowers.
Bright moon,
Bright moon,
Why persist in waning and waxing!

(*Wu Zao ci*, 41)

P.122.10. Dong xian ge: *For the Courtesan Qinglin of Wumen*

Such a bony, slender frame,
Like that of a Jade City divinity's mate!
Smiling we met, quite forgetting how to speak.
You were always picking flowers,
Though your sleeves grew cold from leaning against bamboos;
In that empty valley
I thought I could see your dear, secret thoughts.

While scented lamps cast our shadows low,
We gamed with wine, assessed our poems,
Only to sing at once those heartbreaking lines
of "Recalling the South."
Alike we are—"brushed-eyebrow talents" both—

But I'm so simple and wild
That I'd want to enjoy this beauty's pledge of heart.
Here's a hazy stretch
Of mist and waves across Five Lakes of spring:
Let me buy a red boat, my love, to take you there.

(*Wu Zao ci*, 41–42)

lines 3–7: These lines exploit several rhetorical borrowings from Du Fu's allegorical "Jia ren," on which see P.89.3. Since Du Fu's poem is usually taken to express the complaint of a rejected official, Wu Zao's appropriation of Du Fu's imagery and rhetoric to compliment her courtesan lover is highly subversive.

line 15: There are several sets of Five Lakes (*Wu Hu*) variously located in China. See P.54b.1. On Xi Shi, see C.38.

P.122.11. Langtao sha

When I returned by boat from Wumen, Younger Sister Yunchang did not manage to see me off. I sent this to say farewell.

A pair of oars beating at Hengtang—
What end to this riverscape?
Could green waves match our parting sorrow's length?
I think most of trimming candles the night before
  When by the west window we spoke.

Helpless we shared the farewell cup
As weeping willows swept the earth;
A flute's few wind-blown notes did break our hearts.
Henceforth by heaven's edge in a bright moon night
  Each will nurse her own grief.

(*Wu Zao ci*, 51)

Yunchang was almost certainly not the sister of Wu Zao, who uses the word as a term of endearment.

P.122.12. Yu meiren: *Illness*

Who could flee the small ordeal of flowers strewn?
  Just shut those screens of gauze.
Why do such sickly feelings cling and cling?
From the herbal urn outside the window
  The wind wafts up some strands of smoke.

A fresh chill like water cools the silky drapes:
  I sleep daily with my clothes.
(8) The same sort of autumn, the same listening to rain!
I don't believe that this year's person
  Can be sadder than last year's.

(*Wu Zao ci*, 51)

line 1: "Ordeal of flowers strewn" may be an allusion to the story of the celestial maiden scattering flowers (*tiannü san hua*) in the section on illness in the *Vimalakirtinirdesa sutra*.

P.122.13. Yu meiren

A dark moon at dusk and autumn sounds astir
  Outside a small window;
I listen to wind, to rain, but nothing is distinct
  Except the soughs and sighs
  That have filled my empty yard.

The cold lamp trimmed low, I am too tired to chant;
  This long night should be half gone.
(8) The pond's spring grasses must be murky all;
  I feel instead tonight
  One dream is not as good as none.

(*Wu Zao ci*, 28)

P.122.14. Die lian hua

Old lines and new songs by window's light compare:
In one sort of sorrow
  I can taste two kinds of grief.
Who could end the heartbreaks of former days?
Right now, I fear, they will all begin again.

To peek in the bright mirror I sweep back my hair:
Blue lines the long brows;
(8)   Where is that faintest sign of woe?
Smiling I toss my book as drapes draw themselves wide;
I take my lute to play before the blossoms.

(*Wu Zao ci*, pp. 51–52)

P.122.15. Shuidiao getou: *Swatting at Fireflies*

My hand wielding a white round fan,
I swat at fireflies below the steps.
Tonight the blue sky seems liquid clear,
Specked with two or three autumnal stars.
I circle well-railings to search for them,
But those weaving flower shades
Have made them indistinct.
A few steps tire my phoenix shoes;
With sleeved hands I lean on a rockery.

  Beyond the moonlit fence,
  Beside the misty steps,
  I meet them suddenly.
As I turn to seek them,
Those rascals dart up to perch on my jade hairpin.
Though doors are screened by a layer of bamboo,
And screens shield a whole set of windows,
They still know how to breach the lattice.
  They must have known my wish,
  To come as study lamps.

(*Wu Zao ci*, 52)

P.122.16. Yi Jiangnan: *Eight Poems Composed in Contemplation of Younger Sister Yunchang*

I

  Recalling the South,
I most recall the times of knowing you:
Peach reddened the lagoon in ten thousand spots;
Willows greened Sutai with a thousand strands.
Our meeting was deemed overdue!

II

  Recalling the South,
I most recall our sumptuous feasts:
Jade goblets flew as in the Queen Mother's jasper pool;

Young beauties stood ranked by scholastic norms.
Which one had Li Bo's talents?

III

Recalling the South,
I most recall your splendid gifts:
A spring morning's light chill perfumed the sea of snow;
One small window's flower-sprig unscrolled sidewise.
A born master in verse and paint!

IV

Recalling the South,
I most recall our beds adjoined:
We read songs with curtains warmed by floral air;
In courtyards cooled by moonlight we played the flute.
Our candles were trimmed till dawn.

V

Recalling the South,
I most recall when green shade thickened:
In the east attic we held cups to view jeweled swords;
At the west garden we joined hands to gallop a horse.
We girls could be heroic, too!

VI

Recalling the South,
I most recall our fete to send off spring:
At third month the ford's flowers were white as fog;
From cups of the last round our wine streamed forth.
Even brief breaks were frowned upon.

VII

Recalling the South,
I most recall Jade City's rally:
For singing of snow you should be called Lady Xie;
In buying silk I'd like to embroider Ban Zhao.
Such writing meets were made in Heaven!

VIII

Recalling the South,
I most recall when I tried sailing home:
Your lovely words with fragrance first filled my sleeves,
While wine spots on my light dress never shed their red.
Could I not recall the South!

(*Wu Zao ci*, 57–59)

vii, line 3: Lady Xie is Xie Daoyun, on whom see C.24.

vii, line 4: The Han woman scholar Ban Zhao was also famous for her *Nü jie* (Admonitions for women; see C.2 and C.6), the first work written primarily on the cultivation of women's virtues in personal behavior and family relationships. Wu Zao's line here may reflect the poetic speaker's recollection of paintings and possibly embroidered portraits of this female instructress popular in Ming-Qing times; see Mann, "Grooming a Daughter for Marriage," p. 224 n. 15, and J. Cahill, *Fantastics and Eccentrics*, pp. 33–34.

P.122.17. Ru yan fei: *Reading* Dream of the Red Chamber

Of what use was the wish to patch up the sky
When one's soul could be consumed in red chamber's depths?
Kingfisher-wrapped and perfume-enclosed,
Foolish girl and silly boy, I fear, will never wake up—
Daily, bitterly, sowing their seeds of love.
Which one of them, I ask,
Is the true seed of love?
Stubborn Stone has sentience but a sylph has woe:
Their three lifetimes reap but spun-thread sorrow, waxen tears.
With one stroke thus concludes
The dream of Supreme Void.

Though murmurs fall futile on greenish moss,
They cling and cling like
The jade pin atop her head,
The small phoenix on *wutong*-blossoms.
"Yellow earth," "gauze windows"—these, the words of doom,
Dissolve with pain a beauty's heart.
Where could I mourn
An old grave of buried fragrance?

Flowers fall, flowers bloom, but the person is gone;
 Weeping in the wind of spring,
 I have tears to match the flowers' pain.
 Flowers stand mute
 But my tears flow.

(*Wu Zao ci*, 53–54)

Dream of the Red Chamber is *Hong lou meng*, the great novel begun by Cao Xueqin and completed by Gao E. The novel's first printed edition dates from 1792. For an English translation, see Hawkes and Minford, *The Story of the Stone*.

line 1: The reference is to the protagonist of the *Hong lou meng*, Jia Baoyu, who is the earthly incarnation of a magical stone originally designed to patch up the heavens.

lines 4 and 8: These lines refer to Baoyu's frustrated love for his cousin, Lin Daiyu, who dies young.

lines 16–17: These lines refer to the episode at the beginning of chapter 79 of the novel.

P.122.18. Qingping yue

One yardful of bitter rain
Has sent Autumn on its way home.
Only poetic feelings have nowhere to stay,
Dissolving in gray clouds and red leaves.

At dusk the moon is cold, the smoke grievous;
Bamboo blinds will not descend from their silver hooks.
Tonight my dream follows the wind's passage
And flies, enduring the chill, up Jade Tower.

(*Wu Zao ci*, 17)

P.122.19. Huan xi sha

One scroll of "Li Sao," one of Buddhist script;
Ten years of secrets, ten lived by the lamp.
How many autumn sounds on plaintain leaves?

I'd weep but fail, and thus I force a smile.
Grief I can't shun—so I learn not to feel.
What misleads me is talk of being smart!

(*Wu Zao ci*, 59)

line 1: The word *jing*, translated as "Buddhist script," has the basic sense of a classic. Tone and context make it more likely that a Buddhist sutra, rather than a Confucian classic, is meant here.

P.122.20. Yu meiren

I rose by dawn's window, its blinds just rolled up;
The chill my fingers sheared.
One night of sparse rains and one night of wind
Made countless crab apples
Look so thin in their piteous red.

No doubt because of flowers I have grown ill,
Often too lax to hold a mirror.
The sun is high but still I have not combed my hair:
I hear only swallows
Who stammer out their sorrow for spring.

(*Wu Zao ci*, 21)

P.122.21. Zhu Yingtai jin: *On My Shadow*

Low winding rails,
A deep yard locked:
At night, too tired to comb and tie.
In regret's boundless sea
I feel myself already sunken.
How then to bear this meddling blue lamp
That at dusk's arrival
Will bring on, furthermore, a shadow!

What's most hopeless
Is that though I'm set to love you, dear,
You do not know how to love me.
Why must you attend
My sitting or walking by windows and books?
I know it's hard to dodge or banish you.
Since I can find you any time,
I'll draw the silk drapes and pretend to sleep.

(*Wu Zao ci*, 22–23)

P.122.22. Man jiang hong: *Two Poems on a Lute Formerly in the Possession of Mr. Xie Dieshan*

The lute, named Symbolic Bell, was kept by the family of Classicist Wu Sujiang of Xin'an.

I

A half-partitioned empire,
Not at all the old trade of beauty and song!
I sigh to think of a monastery ruined, rustic—
Where the moon set in sadness.
Where could you see your homeland's beacon smoke?
Who would know you as augur by bannered kiosks?
I recall how in a lone fort
You held back with one hand the Stream of Stars
And showed a heart like steel.

You just finished writing
"With No Home to Leave."
Better an early death
That's true integrity.
On tea-planted slopes thus year after year
Let the cuckoo weep her blood.
Three feet of scorched wood leaves us ancient tunes;
One mound of yellow earth now tops a loyal grave.
I think these grieving strings
Must make gaunt dragons writhe on Lethe's floor
And mossed blossoms heat.

II

Sad notes and plaintive tones
Recount the kalpas that vanquish each age.
I grieve at how life passes then and now swift as lightning,
How man died but lute remained.
Who took it in southland straight through the clouds?
The scepter of West Terrace had broken in vain.
One subject still

Possessed a heart without despair.
His fame would last.

The yaupon drops its leaves,
Its flowers have no recourse;
But burnt-out wood revives,
And Heaven, too, is pleased.
Try strumming it, stroking it again.
It only adds to your grief—
Dirgelike, like weeping heard in mountain mosques;
Dulcet, not less than songs of wind-blown pines.
Thus I mourn Bo Ya
Whose pain and bitterness of old
Only a bosom friend can know.

(*Wu Zao ci*, 19–20)

Xie Dieshan is Xie Fangde (1226–89), a loyalist of the Southern Song. Using the lute as a synecdochic extension of Xie's life, the poems make various allusions to stories of how Xie resisted the Mongol invaders by hiding in monasteries and tea plantations. At one time Xie disguised himself as a marketplace fortune-teller. When finally brought to the Yuan court, he refused to serve and starved himself to death. See *Song shi*, *juan* 425; Huang Zongxi, *Song Yuan xue'an*, 84; H. W. Huber, "Hsieh Fang-te," in Franke, ed., *Sung Biographies*, 1: 403–10.

headnote: Classicist (*mingjing*) was the name of a degree awarded to men nominated by local authorities to participate in the civil service examinations in Tang-Song times. By the Qing, however, it had become only an unofficial, archaic title of students in the National University. See Hucker, *Dictionary of Official Titles*, p. 333.

i, line 11: This is the title of a pentasyllabic poem in the old style on war-ravaged houses and homes by Du Fu (QTS, 217/2284–85).

i, line 16: An allusion to the story of Cai Yong and his scorched-tail lute; see P.85.5.

ii, line 2: On the Buddhist term *kalpa*, see P.45.1.

ii, line 6: An allusion to the story of the eremitic poet, Xie Ao, who mourned the death of the Southern Song loyalist Wen Tianxiang (1236–83) by ascending the West Terrace. Xie wept and sang a song of Chu to try to summon Wen's soul, beating time on a rock with a bamboo scepter (*ruyi*); when he finished, both scepter and rock broke into pieces.

ii, line 10: The yaupon (*dongqing*) is either the *Xylosma racemosum* or the *Ligustrum lucidum*, both evergreen trees. *Dongqingshu* is the name of a drama celebrating the life of Wen Tianxiang by the famous Qing dramatist and poet, Jiang Shiquan (1725–84). After the desecration of the Song imperial tombs by the Mongols in 1278, daring loyalists gathered the scattered bones and planted *dongqing* trees on the site. (For an essay on a related poetry collection, see Chang, "Symbolic and Allegorical Meanings.") Wu's use of the term seems to want to exploit both its literal and literary meanings.

ii, line 18: On the story of Bo Ya and Zhong Ziqi, see P.24.7.

BIOGRAPHICAL NOTE AND TRANSLATION BY ANTHONY C. YU

左錫璇

P.123. Zuo Xixuan (fl. mid–19th century)

Zuo Xixuan (style name Fujiang) was born into a well-placed family. Her grandfather, Zuo Zhongfu of Yanghu, Jiangsu province, once held the rank of Vice Censor-in-Chief. It is not known, however, if her father, Zuo Ang, ever attained an official title or held public office. After winning the *jinshi*, or highest examination degree, in 1847, her husband, Yuan Jimao (style name Hou'an), also a poet, was first appointed to the Hanlin Academy and later to a provincial post. While serving in the Jiangnan area, he was killed when the city of Zhenjiang fell to the rebel Taiping armies during the bloody Taiping Rebellion (1850–64). Thereafter, left to her own resources, Zuo Xixuan led a precarious existence, caring for her young son and seeing to his education.

Zuo Xixuan and her younger sister Xijia were both trained in the traditional arts and letters, and in their mature years both became accomplished poets and painters. As a poet, Xixuan cultivated both the *shi* and song-lyric forms. Her poems were ultimately collected under two titles: *shi* in the *Biwu hongjiao guan shi* (Poems from the *Wutong* Tree and Red Plantain Studio) in three *juan* and her song-lyric verses in the *Biwu hongjiao guan ci* in one *juan*.

Critical response to her poetry has been mixed. The *Qing shi hui*, a major anthology edited by Xu Shichang, accords her a very respectable showing, but other anthologies are less positive about her place in the tradition. Although it must pose some difficult political problems to scholars living in the People's Republic of China because of its bitter attack on the Taiping movement, her "Little New Year's Eve" poem (P.123.1) is still much admired for its moving language and unquenchable spirit.

The poem "A Song of Runzhou" (P.123.2) is no less remarkable. Caustic in its criticism of loyalist military leaders for their ineptitude on the field of battle, it depicts in graphic terms the enormous death and destruction accompanying a failed attack on the city of Runzhou, held by the Taiping armies.

P.123.1. Shuidiao getou: *Little New Year's Eve*

Together or apart, now and in days gone by,
Inseparable are the ties that bind us.
Eastward flowing, flowing, water without end,
When will it again turn westward in its course?
Could I but borrow the three-foot sword of Wu,
In woman's garb bestride a campaign saddle,
I'd cleanse this vast realm of filth.
No matter all the pain in my heart,
I cannot wipe away my pure tears.
As I, now frail of figure,
Idle with a wine cup,
The night lamp goes cold.
No longer knowing what night this is,
Alone and tipsy, I can find no joy.
In life, joy and sorrow cannot be foreseen;
Month follows month, and thus a year goes by
As silently I lean on the balustrade.
At night amid wind and rain in a desolate village,
In dreams I return to Chang'an.

(Su Zhecong, 462–63)

Little New Year's Eve is the eve of the twenty-fourth day of the twelfth lunar month.

lines 1–2: These lines are addressed to the poet's dead husband.

line 5: A reference to the famous curved sword that the swordsmith supposedly tempered with the blood of his own children before he presented it to the king of ancient Wu.

P.123.2. A Song of Runzhou

Our army's ramparts like paper, rebel ramparts of iron;
Though beseiged these ten weeks, the city cannot be taken.
Our imperial armies in turmoil resound like a nighttime tide;
In the mists, myriad tents turn a deathly hue.
Suddenly fiery clouds mount up the nighttime sky
As our officers rush about and our soldiers fall in battle.
In the glare of blood and fire, everything explodes,
Dyeing the moon the color of scarlet roses.

Small skiffs, large barges, all go up in flames;
The river boils like a cauldron at every bend and turn.
Floating corpses clog the surface, damming the river's flow,
Where lurking krakens gorge themselves on human flesh.
Abandoning its weapons, the Zhejiang army is first to flee,
Causing the stalwarts of Chaozhou to cry out in alarm.
It is as if they had set the fields afire,
Smoking out fox and wolf, consuming stag and roe deer.
Anu's decision to attack with fire was bad strategy;
Lacking any plan, our commander willingly accepted defeat.
As twilight advances across half this realm,
Eight thousand individuals shed identical tears.

(Xu Shichang, ed., *Qing shi hui*, 188/49b–50a)

Runzhou is in the vicinity of modern Zhenjiang, Jiangsu province.

lines 5–7: These lines allude to the annihilation of an army sent south on an expedition by King Mu of the ancient Zhou dynasty.

lines 13–14: References to imperial forces.

line 15: An allusion to a failed military strategy of Eastern Jin times.

BIOGRAPHICAL NOTE AND TRANSLATION BY WILLIAM SCHULTZ

P.124. Zong Wan (fl. late 19th century)

Zong Wan left behind fifty-one song lyrics. Yong Zhilian, who wrote the postscript to Zong's *Mengxianglou ci* (Song-lyrics from the Tower of Xiang River Dreams), compared her to the famous Song lyricist Jiang Kui and praised her as the most important woman poet after Xi Peilan (P.93).[1]

P.124.1. Gao yang tai: *Inscription on a Painting Based on Xiaoqing's Line "A slender shadow coming to, and reflected in, spring water's edge"*

One face of sorrow,
Ten hues of sickness—
Is she then truly obsessed?
With effort putting on adornments anew,

She broods in the east wind, silent and alone.
Without feelings, yet filled with regret—who can see her?
Only one pool of spring water in all its clarity.
Cold and desolate—
The receding depths of the courtyard,
The dense shades of the willows.

Heaven fallen into disrepair and earth growing old are but
commonplaces.
I reckon that in the human world
Only this regret is difficult to be made good.
Relentless destiny suffered by a beauty—
In vain did she earn the reputation of unsurpassed talent.
Grief-stricken, I too am schooled in sorrow.
I turn to the painting to make a pact of mutual understanding,
Wishing that from now on
You would pity me,
As I pity you.

(XTLS: *Mengxianglou ci*, 6a)

The line is from a poem attributed to Feng Xiaoqing (see P.104.1): "Freshly adorned I am a match for paintings, / How should I rank in the Zhaoyang Palace? / A slender shadow coming to, and reflected in, spring water's edge: / You should pity me, as I pity you."

line 6: The four characters translated as "without feelings, yet filled with regret" (*wuqing youhan*) echo Su Shi's line on willow catkins (*wuqing yousi*: "Without feelings, yet filled with longing") in a lyric written to the tune *Shuilong yin* (QSC, 1: 277).

lines 9–10: These lines may allude to the first two lines of a lyric written to the tune "Die lian hua" by Ouyang Xiu: "The depths of the courtyard, how deep? / Willows in dense mist" (QSC, 1: 162).

lines 19–20: These lines may refer to Xiaoqing's address to her reflection, quoted above. The proverbial phrase *guying zilian* ("looking at one's shadow filled with tender emotions toward oneself") is often used to describe a woman. In this case Xiaoqing's lines may also be derived from the mirroring motif in *The Peony Pavilion* (see P.72.6), which aroused such an excess of emotion in her: the awakening of the heroine's love and longing begins with the act of looking into the mirror; pining for her dream lover she paints a portrait of herself.

P.124.2. Wang Xiang ren: *Autumn Sentiments*

Slowly the face of autumn darkens and fades,
The spirit of autumn is solitary.
At a moment of faint mist and sparse rain,
When falling leaves hit the window
And a confusion of peaks traps the dream;
The dream falls with the sound of leaves.
An indisposition in three portions—
Two from the effect of wine,
One from melancholy.
I listen to the distant cries of wild geese over the Xiao and Xiang rivers,
Cries that secretly surprise and shatter the soul of autumn.

Idly I go up the high tower to lean against its balustrade,
As autumn wind gracefully disports
The waves of Lake Dongting.
With a sigh my chant comes to "Encountering Sorrow,"
In melancholy I gaze at the coiffures of mist and clouds.
Setting sun at the tip of the trees,
Evening clouds at the edge of the sky—
In all things a mood of loneliness and desolation.
My faraway gaze
Sees not the Goddess of the River Xiang.
To whom can I send the grass by the shore and the orchids on the
  islet?

(XTLS: *Mengxianglou ci*, 3a)

lines 7–9: Possibly modeld on Su Shi's famous lines on willow catkins: "Spring colors in three portions— / Two of dust and earth, / One of flowing water" (QSC, 1: 277).

lines 13–14: The phrase *niaoniao*, here translated as "gracefully disports," and the reference to Lake Dongting echo lines from "Xiang furen," fourth of the *Nine Songs*: "Autumn wind gracefully disports / The waves of Lake Dongting, and leaves flutter down" (*Wen xuan*, 32/22a). The tune title "Wang Xiang ren" and later references to "Encountering Sorrow" ("Li sao" by Qu Yuan; see P.37) and the Goddess of the River Xiang all allude to the *Chuci* (see P.11.16) and thereby evoke a mood of melancholy and longing.

line 22: In the *Chuci*, the shaman-poet often wishes to gather fragrant plants and send them to the deity. In later allegorical interpretations, fragrant plants and orchids are read as symbols of the poet's lofty virtue. The act of sending such plants thus symbolizes the poet's quest for understanding and just appreciation from the ruler.

P.124.3. Hu zhong tian: *Light of Flowers*

In the midst of hundreds of flowers,
I watch spirit and light separating and converging,
Both proud of their brilliance and charm.
Sun-tinted mist enters the east wind, spring wants to smile,
Uncertain traces of aroma are like water.
Spreading radiance in warm places,
Diffusing colors at bright edges,
The air is thicker than intoxication.
I see red becoming verdure,
In a trice neither purple nor green.

I have heard that fragrant dust on silken paths
Is where these winsome spirits hover.
As they dance, the shadow of spring is shattered.
Filigreed carriages aligned reflect each other's glow.
Can human beings really be like flowers?
Intent on swaying the scarlet,
With feeling rippling the emerald—
How can there be understanding for mournful melancholy?
Play not the sweet lute,
For fear that the shadow of colorful clouds may fall in bewilderment.

(XTLS: *Mengxianglou ci*, 4b)

line 2: The phrase "spirit and light separating and converging" (*shenguang lihe*) is used to describe the elusive charm of the goddess of the river Luo in Cao Zhi's "Luo shen fu" (*Wen xuan*, 19/14a).

P.124.4. Xiang yue: *Inscription on a Painting of an Autumn Scene*

Autumn in its aura
Has myriad transformations.
How can human beings depict it?
All the more surprising that a few brush strokes
Should convey its essence and spirit.
Soundless cold moon,

Shadow of frosty mist
Capture the soul of autumn.
The pure scene here—
I think only I can recognize it.

Up above in the tower is a sweep of Xiang bamboo blinds,
Xiang bamboo blinds not rolled up.
Below the pavilion, the white waves of the River Xiang.
The endless cold stream flows away into the distance,
Reversing and soaking the colorless River of Heaven.
Among *wutong* trees,
By the side of the plantains
Are added rocks from the lake.
Close not the green window—
Allow me, flying, to enter it in a dream.

(XTLS: *Mengxianglou ci*, 7a)

line 1: Echoing Song Yu's lament for autumn, on which see P.54d.3.
line 15: The River of Heaven is the Milky Way.

P.124.5. Chai tou feng: *Sacrifice to the God of Earth*

The smoke of incense burners curls,
Scented wind arrives,
A whole street of radiant brocades and embroidery sparkling together.
The beauty is
At the side of the red pavilion.
Colored banners are passing.
Her maid whispers,
"Look! Look! Look!"

The neighbor lady says,
"What a good year!
How numerous the fragrant carriages and jeweled horses!"
The sky is about to darken,
Travelers turn back.
Setting sun in the west,
Patterned blinds idly rolled up—
Gone, gone, gone.

(XTLS: *Mengxianglou ci*, 8a)

P.124.6. Dajiang dongqu: *Feelings on a Sea Voyage*

The waves in the sea are not rising.
Beyond water and sky,
The gaze extends to a vastness without limit.
A human reflection in a hundred thousand acres of glass
Is totally cleansed of the fragrance of rouge and the softness of powder.
Raised sleeves accost the wind,
Flying winecups offer libation to the moon—
All greatly reminiscent of the mood of bearded Su Shi.
With brass lute and iron clappers,
Allow me to pour forth my soaring spirit.

Do not, because of wanderings and uncertain sojourns in another land,
Or because of an old home overgrown with thorns and weeds,
Be filled with longing and dread.
Bending my fingers and counting years beyond fifty,
I should know how ephemeral is floating existence.
Having experienced to the full travails and tribulations,
I should from now on comprehend
The principle of separation and union, sorrow and joy.
Learning in scholarship, learning in swordsmanship—
Fortunately I have sons intent on self-cultivation.

(XTLS: *Mengxianglou ci*, 13a)

Zong's title alludes to the famous song-lyric written to the tune *Niannu jiao*, "Chibi huai gu" (Thinking of the past at Red Cliff), by Su Shi, which begins with the words "The Great River flows eastward" (QSC, 1: 282). Zong Wan is self-consciously dramatizing her elation as a woman writing in the mode of heroic abandon (*haofang*), supposedly the exclusive prerogative of male poets.

lines 7–8: Another allusion to Su's "Red Cliff" lyric: "With a jar of wine I offer libation to the river moon" (QSC, 1:282).

lines 9–10: On the connection of Su Shi with iron clappers, see P.69.4.

P.124.7. Baizi ling

Inscribed on an inkstone rubbing of the calligraphy by Ye Xiaoluan [P.54d] in the family collection of Wang Foyun (sobriquet Mingfu).

Brought from beyond the seas,
It is shared by the inmates of orchid chambers,
The many talents seated at green windows.
The inkstone partakes of the charm of the person's poetic frame,
Polished to delicate perfection and supple turns.
In the interstices of stone marrow,
Among masses of ink clouds,
The brow-moon, arched, curved, appears.
Beside the zither, next to the dressing case,
This makes for much white silk written to shreds.

It cannot be helped—the dream of the dusty world cannot last long,
The night-blooming cereus fades all too easily,
Scattered and lost are the fragments of jade.
I bend my fingers and count the changes of fortune this sheet has experienced
Before being put away in a brocade bag.
Eight years of tactile appreciation,
One voice urging tender care—
Wrists turn in assiduous imitation of its style.
I am ashamed of my unworthy brush
That, favored by a karmic connection, writes this commentary.

(XTLS: *Mengxianglou ci*, 11a)

line 8: Zong made a note here: "It was eight years since Mingfu acquired this inkstone."

P.124.8. Baizi ling

Bandits are still everywhere. I sat in dejection in front of the window and the rain and composed this under the lamplight.

It is already almost the end of winter.
Why then this piping and whistling,

As if autumn is in the making?
Several blasts drift here, slanting, then straight,
Striking in confusion at the lamplight by the small window.
The wind is harsh, the clouds cold,
The sky low, the moon black.
How can one dream the traveler's dream?
Listening to the last of the night watchman's rattle,
I rise again, throw on clothes, and sit in sorrow.

I have seen and heard warfare in my old home,
Wardrums in another land,
Smouldering smoke blocking the way everywhere.
In my uncertain wanderings I am like duckweed drifting on water.
Final years of failure—when my song is finished who will write to its rhyme?
Old age is pressing upon me,
Hunger has driven my children away,
Leaving only me, desolate and bewildered.
I look up to heaven and sigh,
My tears flying and falling with the rain.

(XTLS: *Mengxianglou ci*, 12b–13a)

headnote: "Bandits" refers to partisans and hangers-on of the Taiping rebels.

P.124.9. Gao yang tai: *Remembering Orchids*

Sounds choking on the jade zither,
Dreams returning from distant waters,
In vain did I stand till the setting sun fades away.
Limitless is my longing
As I dwell on misty sleeves and wind-blown skirts.
Wishing to entrust my feelings to spring wind's understanding,
I yet fear that spring wind comes not to the Xiao and Xiang rivers.
Silent, wordless,
One spell of brooding,
One spell of contemplation.

At a quiet window I read through the lines of "Encountering Sorrow."
Turning to traces of fragrance, to write in imitation,

And to paintings, for further pondering.
Bearing deep passion,
The beauty seems to be in the middest.
(16) The blue clouds fly away, autumn leaves no traces.
Again the vague forms of the faint moon and the cool smoke.
Without reprieve, heartbroken:
Who will share this secret burden?
(20) Who will repair this secret woe?

(XTLS: *Mengxianglou ci*, 2b)

line 4: An allusion to lines from Su Shi's "First *fu* on the Red Cliff" (Qian Chibi fu): "Limitless is my longing / As I look for the beauty at the far end of the sky" (*Su Dongpo quanji*, 1: 268). The motif of the quest of the elusive and inaccessible beauty defines the mood of this song-lyric as Zong Wan goes on to refer in later lines to Qu Yuan's "Encountering Sorrow" and "the beauty . . . in the middest."

line 15: An echo of poem 129 from the *Book of Odes*: "Going upstream to follow her— / She seems to be in the middle of the water."

P.124.10. Fenghuangtai shang yi chuixiao: *Inscription on a Painting by Sister Cansheng on "Seeking Poetry in the Moonlit Pavilion"*

One sheet of empty luminescence,
Several layers of colored paints,
Evenly divided by pavilions at water's edge and huts in clouds.
I envy you, wondering how
Your poetic realm could reach such pure sublimity.
Try seeking lines from the painting:
It should be better than playing flute on the terrace.
(8) Where you lean against the balustrade:
Traces of rouge finely nipped,
Hairpin's jade constantly scraping.

Endless long days that cannot be dissipated.
(12) By day in quest of poetry,
In quest until the middle of the night.
Further, *wutong* leaves chanting in the wind:
Leaf by leaf, fluttering and whistling.
(16) Fluttering, falling, some shades of autumnal mood
Together with the shadow of the moon appear as halo on light silk.

Do pass the word:
The night is cold, the dew chilly,
(20) Do not be totally oblivious as you ponder proper poetic expression.

(XTLS: *Mengxianglou ci*, 10a–b)

line 7: An allusion to the story of Nongyu; see P.26.5.

BIOGRAPHICAL NOTE AND TRANSLATION BY WAI-YEE LI

P.125. Qu Huixiang (fl. 1900)

Qu Huixiang was a native of Linhai in Zhejiang province, and the second wife of Wang Yongni. She frequently exchanged poems with her elder sister Chaixiang, another well-known local poet. The poems exchanged by the two sisters were published in 1909 under the title *Tonggen cao*, which means literally "two manuscripts born of the same root."[1]

P.125.1. Langtao sha: *Matching Elder Sister Yun's Rhyme*

The night's quiet, water clocks fade;
I stand mute in the court's shade.
On mossed steps crickets speak their autumn mind.
I'm sad that brushwood still grows as before,
  But the deer dream is hard to find.

A cold dew wets the resting lute
On three paths dim and dark,
(8) Its pure tones played no more before the wind.
Geese drop on flat sand and autumn thoughts go far.
  How much more, henceforth!

(XTLS: *Heqingge shiyu*, 1a)

lines 4–5: On the story of the "deer dream," see P.80.2. Here the point is the impossibility of finding one's way back to the dreamed-of place.

P.125.2. Lin jiang xian

The sound of the courtyard swing has fallen off,
The grass hues rueful by the steps.

What can be done if east wind's about to leave,
And scented showers
Pelt and pelt me from the sprays?

Pensive, I stand awhile beneath the drapes,
Alarmed by the sun dipping west.
(8) To mourn falling blossoms birds vainly call.
I ask the birds calling,
For what reason do you call to me?

(XTLS: *Heqingge shiyu*, 1b)

P.125.3. Bu chan gong: *Inscribing a Painting on "Saying Farewell at a Riverbank"*

The long dike's willow sports a thousand strands:
Why could it not know
How to tie down a boat?
We long had known to meet was at once to part.
This chanced union we now regret.

In the west wind and twilight I wait in vain.
The sky at dusk spreads far,
(8) But where is the person of old?
I'd like to see the lone sail in the clouds,
But, then, my sight by those green hills is blocked.

(XTLS: *Heqingge shiyu*, 2a)

P.125.4. Jin lü qu: *Saying Farewell to My Husband*

The blue grass cloaks south shore;
I look to heaven's edge
At layers of dusky clouds
And hills cluttered past counting.
Mist and waves now more distant everywhere,
Though a dreamer still loses her way.
I only wish that
(8) Our deep love had no hindrance,
Our heartbeats at one like magic beasts'.
Send your letters often and don't delay.

How many woes do I have?
(12) To whom can I confide them?

Green shades come easy while idle lawns age.
Shutting the screens,
In endless memories
(16) I touch the jade lute sadly.
You are ordered, I know, to leave early
For places of miasma and fog;
Their sun's a flame in the sky.
(20) Your fort barred by cold wind and summer rain,
I hope you'll take great care in sleep and food.
On such "Golden Threads"
I send you my thoughts.

(XTLS: *Heqingge shiyu*, 4a–b)

line 23: An allusion to the title of the lyric meter used here, "Golden Threads Song."

P.125.5. Jin lü qu: *Sent to My Husband, Using the Rhyme of the Previous Poem*

The sail sinks toward cloudy shores;
Propped in the tower,
How many times I stare,
Sadly marking the distance.
I'd weave a text to transmit distant thoughts,
Those thousand twists of my mind's way.
I try sending it,
(8) But it's blocked by river waves
And the dangling willows that hinder sight;
And thus the letter often finds delay.
My heart's suppressed dolor
(12) I have yet to confide.

This year in swift flight will soon become old.
Hearing from frosted sky
The crows' calls at midnight,
(16) I tire to touch the jade strings.

The fruit of endless heartache, endless grief:
  A broken soul who's lost in fog,
  Who faces alone secluded window lamps.
Do you think of a plum blossom of home
  Oppressed by frost and snow? Who will care for her?
  Moreover, where's the place
  To post such parting thoughts?

(XTLS: *Heqingge shiyu*, 4b–5a)

P.125.6. Pusa man: *Thinking of "Sworn Sister" Li Chujuan*

Spring wind recalls my holding your slender hand:
By the window we drank the brimming wine.
I dread thinking of such old affairs;
Sad feelings match the length of dreams.
The moon above crab apple blooms
Loves to shine on humans parting.
With this thought I stroll back and forth;
My shoe-prints cover the green moss.

(XTLS: *Heqingge shiyu*, 5b)

P.125.7. Zui hua yin

One leaf, wind-cooled, and the sparse rain has passed,
The gauze curtains pierced by light chill.
I lean on pillows, my dream hard to come—
While crickets chant chirp-chirp,
  How does one flee such times of grief?

The dim, scented lamp sheds a light small as a bean:
The clock I hear to the end.
The moon's cool, the painted screen dark—
And those clinging willows
  Seem to share autumn's thinness, too!

(XTLS: *Heqingge shiyu*, 6b)

P.125.8. Que qiao xian: *On the Double Seventh*

Deep and dark the jade abode;
Sheer and dipping the silver stream;

They fit this young autumn's lovely night
When rosy clouds mark heaven's time to meet.
Is it true that
The bridge is by magpies built?

Wind and mist of a late night,
Melons and fruits of a cold feast,
And a few courtyards where needles are threaded.
The starry stream is too wide for grief to fill.
Regret that loan
Of a hundred thousand in betrothal cash!

(XTLS: *Heqingge shiyu*, 8a)

On the Double Seventh, see P.5.1 and P.19.2.

line 12: It is not known whether this line refers to a particular event. In the context of Double Seventh, it may be a wry comment on the Herd Boy's eternally frustrated courtship of the Weaving Girl.

P.125.9. Wang Jiangnan: *Sitting by a Stream, Facing the Moon*

The moon above the stream
Is like a mirror and a bow,
Viewed sadly from how many painted towers.
How many times can it grow round in a year?
This tranquil light of autumn mist.

(XTLS: *Heqingge shiyu*, 8b)

P.125.10. Wang Jiangnan: *Facing the Mirror*

I

The caltrop glass
Thoughtlessly shows my combing.
I rue a pink face changing easily
And hate the dark hair turning soon to frost.
So, on and on we share our grief.

II

The caltrop glass
Greets me coldly by green windows.
Its gleam clearly tells me that I am thin;

In madness I'd beg you to pity me.
When will the dream form be complete?

(XTLS: *Heqingge shiyu*, 9b)

i, line 1: Ancient mirrors, made of polished bronze, often had a caltrop pattern on their backs, hence the term "caltrop glass."

BIOGRAPHICAL NOTE AND TRANSLATION BY ANTHONY C. YU

秋瑾

P.126. Qiu Jin (1875–1907)

Poet, essayist, feminist, and revolutionary martyr, Qiu Jin left behind 213 *shi* (8 in fragments), 39 *ci*, one incomplete autobiographical *tanci*, and essays, letters, and song-lyrics set to modern, Western-inspired melodies. Her life and poetry can be divided into five periods.

1875–96. Qiu's happy and well-nurtured childhood and adolescence, mostly spent in Shaoxing, Zhejiang province, had three unusual features: her opportunity to peruse stories of knights-errant and woman-warriors, her mastery of equitation and martial arts, and her tolerated eschewing of conventionally conceived womanly accomplishments such as embroidery. Her *shi* and *ci* of this period have as their most frequent themes eulogies of Ming literatae-warriors and Daoist-influenced celebrations of flowers. Optimism and *joie de vivre* inform her poetry of this period.

1896–1903. In 1896, Qiu's parents married her to Wang Zifang, four years her junior and the son of a wealthy pawnbroker of Xiangtan, Hunan. Most of the forty-six *shi* and thirteen *ci* written by Qiu during the six years and more that she and her husband lived in the household of her in-laws are melancholy expressions of disappointment with her misalliance and nostalgia for her own family and friends. A son was born to Qiu and her husband in 1897 and a daughter in 1901.

1903–4. In September 1903, after Wang Zifang had bought a post in the imperial bureaucracy, Qiu and the children joined him in Beijing. Two events soon altered Qiu's life and art: Wang's declared intention of taking in a concubine and Qiu's friendship with members of Beijing's progressive elite. Wang's disloyalty liberated and emboldened Qiu, while her new friends introduced her to patriotic and feminist causes. Her *shi* and *ci* of this period, including the twenty-five dealing with her estrangement from Wang and the twenty-two *zengda* (literally, "presentations and replies" or *vers de société*) addressed to friends and men and women of achievement, are rich in theme, tone, and emotional complexity.

1904–5. In June 1904, having outgrown Beijing and her friends, Qiu left for Japan after arranging for the care of her children. During her roughly eighteen months in Tokyo (early July 1904 to late December 1905, interrupted by a four-month return to China), she studied at Jissen School for Women and participated eagerly in feminist and anti-Manchu activities, eventually attending workshops on bomb-making and joining the Restoration Society (Guangfu hui) and the Revolutionary Alliance (Tongmeng hui). She also edited the *Baihua bao* (Colloquial-language monthly), wrote fourteen *shi*, four *ci*, several patriotic and feminist essays, and three chapters of her autobiographical *tanci*, *Jingwei shi* (Pebbles of the *jingwei* bird).

All her *shi* and *ci* of this period have feminist and patriotic themes, the one often interlaced with the other. Despite incantational evocations of modern Western events and personalities, her mind-set is profoundly traditional-Chinese in its reverence for Han legitimacy and racial ancestors, virulent denigration of the Manchus, and glorification of individual, quasi-solitary heroes, including failed assassins, who affected the course of history through the repercussions of their successful or failed actions. For the first time we see expressions of her own willingness to die for China.

1905–7. This last stage of Qiu's life found her working in Shanghai and Zhejiang as a teacher and a Restoration Society leader responsible for grassroots tasks as well as for planning the armed Zhejiang uprising scheduled for July 19, 1907.

As a teacher she taught Japanese and sciences at Xunxi School for Girls (March to August 1906) and physical education at a Restoration front organization, the Datong Normal School in Shaoxing (January to July 1907), where she shocked the local gentry by going horseback riding in jodhpurs and requiring her students to use real bullets for target practice.

Concurrently she edited and published two issues of *Zhongguo nübao* (Chinese women's monthly), wrote several essays and six proselytising songs of simple lyrics and melodies, and composed another two and a half chapters of her autobiographical *tanci*, thirty-seven *shi*, and two *ci* commemorating the death of her mother, to whom she was deeply attached.

With rare exceptions, her *shi* of this period are either political allegories disguised as nature poems or patriotic and feminist exhortations showing traces of her scorn for politically indifferent fame- and wealth-seeking careerists. As her last *shi* (written after she had learned that the Restoration Society's plot had been exposed; P.126.38) shows, there was great clarity of vision and purpose in her assessment of the revolutionaries' efforts and her own role: she purposefully gives her life to an ostensibly doomed cause because she has the hope that her martyrdom will alter the course of history.

On July 13, 1907, Manchu troops surrounded Datong and captured Qiu. At her interrogation, Qiu steadfastly refused to speak. When a brush was handed to her for a written confession, Qiu wrote her surname, and then—echoes of her despair after each revolutionary debacle—she followed the character with six others: *Qiu yu qiu feng chou sha ren* (Autumn rain and autumn wind, such eviscerating, life-smothering sorrow!).

She was beheaded early in the morning of July 15, roughly four months before her thirty-second birthday.

P.126.1. Xiang jian huan

To read a book, I toss aside my
  embroidery needle.
Laughing, you and I then play critics,
  you challenging my views and I yours,
Unaware that beyond the window,
The vermilion sun has set in the west.

In my light spring gown,
I draw the curtain,
My evening toilette spankingly fresh.
(8) "Treading on the green" tomorrow:
I'll invite my neighbor to join me
  as my female companion.

(Liu Yulai, *Qiu Jin shici zhushi*, 288)

lines 5–7: These three lines contain three syllables each. The published editions misrepresent them as two lines, one of four syllables and one of five.

line 8: "Treading on the green," or *taqing*, was a festival marked by outings to enjoy the spring air and to walk on the newly greened grass.

P.126.2. Plum Blossoms

I

The whole world rushes to praise red and mauve.
Plum blossom's plain-white isn't *à la mode.*
Banished to the earth's ends—
  unappreciated—
Haggard—
  she loses her frost-defying, snow-challenging glow.

II

Her icy beauty defies the aggression of snow and frost.
Refusing to decorate jade palaces, she
  adorns an ancient peak.
Her sublimity lies in her independence.
Wealth and high position are powerless
  to alter
    her heart's
      pristine
        inclination.

(*Qiu Jin shici zhushi*, 121–22)

P.126.3. Pusa man: *Sent to a Woman Friend*

Moonlight in front of the screen,
  radiant, lovely, a sight to be cherished.
More's the pity that the moon shines on our separation,
  our joyous meetings a thing of the past.
My nostalgia: the mist-imbued, river-bank trees,
  stretching far into the distance—
While the river itself rushes on,
  pitiless and uncaring.
Kept apart by a range of mountains and
  vast, unbridgeable space,
Despite our wish, we have no way
  to see each other.
When I write to you, I struggle for words.

(8) My sorrow, like the clepsydra, drips on and on,
never a pause, or an end.

(Qiu Jin shici zhushi, 289)

line 4: Referring, undoubtedly, to the Xiang River (in fact some versions read "the Xiang River" rather than "the river"). It was in part the Xiang that brought Qiu from a happy life with her own family in Shaoxing to an unhappy one with her husband and in-laws in Xiangtan. The Xiang and its tributary Xiao (sometimes abbreviated as "Xiaoxiang") as contributors to her unhappiness form a recurrent leitmotif in Qiu's poems.

P.126.4. *Autumn Rain*

By the western window,
we trim candles and speak of the pool of Ba.
Then the clouds darken, urging us to
write poems in Du Fu's vein.
After you leave, sorrow creeps into my rooms
high up in a tower, and
A chill invades my baldachin as I awake
from my dreams.
Chrysanthemums, in a heavy fog, are losing
their autumn splendor;
Against the diminished rustle of *wutong* leaves,
the clepsydra is dripping the night away.
No noise distresses me as much
as the sound of rain
falling on eaves bells
(8) Xie *niang*'s getting thin:
my waist has shrunk
to nothing at all.

(*Qiu Jin shici zhushi*, 67)

line 1: *Ba chi*, in present-day Sichuan, denoting in Qiu's time and earlier a remote and exotic place. The entire line recasts the conclusion of Li Shangyin's poem, "Yeyu ji bei" (on which see P.121.14).

line 2: For the conceit that darkening clouds and sudden rain urge one to write poetry, see Du Fu, "Pei zhu guigongzi zhangbagou xie ji na liang wanji yu yu" (QTS, 224/2400). The relevant lines read: "The cloud above our heads has darkened. / It must be that the rain is coming / to urge us to write poetry."

line 7: The association of deep sorrow with rain falling on eaves bells is said to have had its origin in the Tang emperor Xuanzong's mourning for Yang Guifei (see P.18.12 and *Minghuang zalu*, cited in Liu Yulai, *Qiu Jin shici zhushi*, p. 68).

line 8: Qiu Jin here uses Xie *niang*, i.e., Xie Daoyun, as a metaphor for herself. On Xie, see C.24.

P.126.5. Remembering the Past at Red Cliff

High, high is the water's power as it rumbles eastward;
Here, I once heard fire was used in attack.
No wonder that when I come to pay homage,
Flowers on the bank, though scorched, are still red.

(Yi Boyin, 6/193)

The title recalls Su Shi's "Thinking of the Past at Red Cliff"; see P.124.9.

line 2: The reference is to a battle between the states of Shu and Wu at Red Cliff during the Three Kingdoms period.

P.126.6. Remembering the Past at Gold Pavilion

At Jizhou, the King of Yan erected a pavilion;
Yet how sad that wealth was employed to attract officials!
So many worthy talents, but such little achievement.
Can yellow gold really attract people from far and wide?

(Qiu Jin, *Qiu Jin ji*, 58)

line 1: On King Zhao of Yan and his awards of money to scholars, see P.66.25.

P.126.7. Notes on a Spring Outing: Four Poems

I

The neighbor girl invited me on a spring outing,
Saying, "Tomorrow's weather will surely be fine."
Dress and accessories that very night I put in order:
Shoes with phoenix heads, a skirt of embroidered silk.

II

Winding path besprinkled with dew, fragrant grasses tender,
Hand in hand, going eastward we crossed a small bridge.
The flowing stream, utterly lacking in feeling,
Failed to carry my sorrows away, only the fallen red petals.

III

Deep in the willows' shade an oriole sang;
Lush and fragrant grasses covered the bank with green.
Laughing, I asked which house had the finest pavilion?
Beaded curtains hung aslant by cherry-apple branches.

IV

My western neighbor also joined us on the spring outing,
And, holding my hand amidst the flowers, said laughingly:
"Yesterday, my dear, you passed the house of Grand Mentor Jia;
Today you ascended the Terrace of King Ding."

(*Qiu Jin ji*, 58)

iv, line 3: Jia Yi, a poet who held the office of Grand Mentor (Taifu) under the Han dynasty, resided in Changsha, Hunan. His residence had apparently become a tourist spot.

iv, line 4: Another tourist spot in Changsha.

P.126.8. The Man of Qi Fears Heaven's Collapse

War flames in the North—when will it all end?
I hear the fighting at sea continues unabated.
Like the girl of Qishi, in vain I worry about my country;
It's hard to trade kerchief and dress for a helmet.

(*Qiu Jin ji*, 60)

In an anecdote now proverbial for the idea of unfounded fears, a man of Qi once worried that the heavens might collapse. The story is used ironically here to refer to Qiu Jin's urgent but seemingly futile concern as a woman for the deplorable state China was in.

line 1: A reference to the Sino-Japanese War of 1894–95, in which the Japanese were victorious and gained control of Korea.

line 3: A girl of the town of Qishi in the state of Lu once sighed, "The King of Lu is old and the prince is too young." A neighboring lady commented, "That is the officials' concern." The girl replied, "No. In the past, a stranger on horseback trampled our farmland, causing us to go hungry all year. If the country of Lu suffers from disaster, the King, the officials, fathers, and sons will all be insulted. Can women alone be spared?" (Liu Xiang, *Gu lienü zhuan*, 3; in SKQS, 448:33.)

P.126.9. Written Impromptu in the Wind and Rain

If often taken ill,
  don't climb the pavilion beyond the flowers;
A siege of wind and rain
  brings a siege of melancholy.
The swallow, carrying mud in its beak, is overburdened with emotions;
Resting in the light of the crescent moon, it twitters softly.

(Yi Boyin, 6/194)

P.126.10. Viewing the Moon

In sorrow, above the curtain, I view the moon's round visage;
Thinking of my parents, I can only shed useless tears.
Though carrying mud in its grief, the swallow cannot fill in the sea;
Nor can I, lacking the ability to smelt stone, mend the heavens.
The Xiang River and northern clouds became tangled in old dreams;
Amid green hills and red trees young cicadas chirp.
Of ten parts melancholy, three parts are hatred;
(8) Reminiscing about the past only brings self-pity.

(Yi Boyin, 6/195)

line 3: On the fabulous *jingwei* bird, to which the swallow is compared, see P.109.9; note the use of *jingwei* in the title of Qiu's autobiographical *tanci*, mentioned in the biographical note.

line 4: On the story of Nü Wa's repairing of the heavens, see P.87.13.vii.

P.126.11. Wutong *Leaves*

When night comes, *wutong* leaves brush the painted balustrade;
In the west wind, already I feel my lined gown is thin.
In utter melancholy, I sit silently by the lamp;
Persistent is my longing, I even sigh in dreams.
Amidst the calling of white geese, autumn thoughts overflow;
By a hedge of yellow flowers, evening melancholy grows.
How sad that in the mirror my face grows ever thinner;
(8) Chanting my poems, I sit until the water clock runs dry.

(*Qiu Jin ji*, 65)

P.126.12. Longing for My Mother

Far removed from my loving mother, meetings are difficult;
Separated on the Xiang River, the wild goose flies alone.
There are ways to mend the sky, but whom can I ask?
Lacking the means of shrinking distances, I can only sigh!
Warding off indolence, I live in melancholy;
How can I watch myself grow thin in the mirror?
Beyond the curtain, the dim yellow moon is like a hook;
(8) Perhaps in the inner chambers she also leans on the balcony.

(Yi Boyin, 6/196)

P.126.13. Sitting Alone on an Autumn Day

Sitting for a moment by the window, I read aloud,
Unfurled bamboo curtains hanging silently, wave-like.
My residence remote, hidden, friends are few;
When boredom overtakes me, emotions are many.
The wall half draped in green moss, cricket cries resound;
The courtyard full of yellow leaves, raindrops provide accompaniment.
Oh, pitiable northland, where the autumn wind comes early;
(8) Already I feel the chill penetrate my green silk sleeves.

(Yi Boyin, 6/197)

P.126.14. The Water Lily

A lady riding the waves of the Luo River,
She faces the wind and opens weary eyes.
Petals, like a proffered jade tumbler,
Roots, the banished jade pavilion of heaven.
In delicate whiteness surpassing the snow,
In light fragrance not yielding to plum blossoms.
From birth I've been addicted to flowers,
(8) Facing the water lily, daily I linger.

(*Qiu Jin ji*, 69)

P.126.15. Notes Recorded Aboard Ship: Two Poems

I

Looking round about, all is shoreless,
Wave after wave: truly a grand prospect!
Like a bird in flight, the ship sails on;
Mountains writhe like poisonous dragons.
Myriad streams remote from tidal sounds;
Endless peaks cluster in cloudy realms.
Boundless, boundless are the misty waters
(8) As thoughts of home press upon my brows.

II

Water and sky of identical hue,
High and lofty rise the lonely peaks.
Looking afar, my aspirations grow;
Leaning against the window, my prospect widens.
Silver billows standing upright like walls,
On the green sea, one is harried by the cold.
The capital very close at hand;
(8) Don't sing "A Song of Hard Journeys."

(Yi Boyin, 6/199)

line 8: "Song of Hard Journeys" is an ancient folk-song. Qiu Jin suggests that, because of modern means of transportation, the song is out of date.

P.126.16. Sending a Letter Home

Sad it is to be parted from my kind mother:
Until now, three months and more.
Your appearance must be the same as before;
Have you been sleeping and eating well of late?
Hating this separation, long I stroke these clothes.
Sad at heart, I can only send you this letter.
Autumn's come, so do take special care,
(8) Guard well against the early night chill.

(Yi Boyin, 6/199)

line 5: That is, clothes made by her mother.

P.126.17. A Japanese, Mr. Ishii, Asks Me to Write a Poem to Match His; I Used the Same Rhyme

Don't say women are dull and unheroic.
I've come east alone, riding the winds
for a thousand leagues.
My poetic imagination ranges far and wide,
as freely as a sailboat on an open sea.
Even before I came, I had dreamt of your islands—
jewels dazzling with moon beams.
But much to my sorrow and shame
although bronze camels are covered
in brambles in my country,
I've done nothing to stem the rot;
I can't even claim the merit
of a sweating horse in combat.
Laden with anguish, grieving over my land,
(8) How can I, a guest in yours, enjoy the spring breeze?

(*Qiu Jin shici zhushi*, 207)

line 4: "Your islands" translates *sandao*, literally "three islands," referring to Honshu, Shikoku, and Kyushu, while omitting Hokkaido—an old-fashioned way of referring to Japan.

line 5: Derelict or resplendent, the condition of bronze camels, symbolic guardians placed before the imperial palace, is traditionally considered to reflect the state of health of the ruling dynasty. But in Qiu's poetry, it reflects instead the state of health of China, comprising its—to her—legitimate residents, the Han people. To Qiu, the Manchu rulers of the Qing dynasty were usurpers; their weakness and degeneracy had brought about the invasion of China by eight foreign powers in 1900 and the subsequent carving out of "spheres of influence," thus causing the bronze camels to be so neglected as to sink in brambles.

P.126.18. Preoccupation (Written While in Japan)

A lusterless sun and a wan moon have cast heaven and earth
in obscurity—
Sinking without help,
more imperiled than anyone else,
are the women of my race.
Searching for a remedy,
I pawned my jewelry, left behind my children,

And sailed across the ocean
  to this foreign land.
Unbinding my feet, I washed away
  a thousand years of poison.
My heart fired with excitement, I awoke
  one hundred slumbering flower-spirits.
But pity my shagreen handkerchief—
(8) Half stained with tears
  and half with blood.

(*Qiu Jin shici zhushi*, 229–30)

line 6: *Huahun* ("flower-spirits"), a metaphor for woman/women.
line 8: A poetic conceit: when one has no more tears, one weeps blood.

P.126.19. A Poem Matching That by the Revered Elder Poet Letian, Celebrating the Painting, "Trying Out One's Horse on a Spring Field" [one of two poems]

In the year *jiachen* [1904], I returned to [visit my mother at] our old home in the south. [While in Hangzhou,] I happened to witness the revered elder poet Letian of Nanhai writing a celebratory poem on the painting, "Trying Out One's Horse on a Spring Field." His verse immediately inspired a multitude of matching poems, exhibiting every kind of excellence and beauty. Unmindful of my own inadequacies, I respectfully wrote two matching poems myself. Since my endeavor was impromptu, I was unable to reproduce the rhyme used in the original.

On the Bai dikes, Su's willows display their
  green silken strands—
It's exactly the season to gallop
  on the field of poetry.
The third month's orioles and blossoms
  weave thousand-mile dreams.
Half a woods of wind and moon
  yield a sackful of poems.
Yuanlong's lake and sea enhance my generous, untrammeled spirit.
Yu Xin's passes and mountains carry my homeward thoughts.
I want to go to Letian's estate, there
  by the main hall—

(8) In the shrine honoring the Water Immortal,
I'll worship my exemplar with burning
petals of incense.

(*Qiu Jin shici zhushi*, 208–19)

Besides the information given here in the title and the headnote, nothing is known about a Letian of Nanhai contemporaneous with Qin. The title of the painting given here is corrected, according to the content of the poems and preface, from that given in the printed editions.

line 1: On the Bai dikes or causeway and Su willows, renowned elements of Hangzhou's landscape, see P.46.2. The willows planted along the bridges built by Su Shi lead Qiu to make a natural association with Su's poem on willow catkins ("Shuilong yin," QSC, 1: 277), which are an image for femininity through a further association with Xie Daoyun (see C.24.1).

line 5: Presumably because of their expansiveness and lack of rigidity, the lake and the sea have long been associated with generosity and untrammeled freedom. The earliest statement making this association and linking it to Yuanlong (Chen Deng, an official-general of the Jian'an period, 196–220) occurs in Chen's biography ("Chen Deng zhuan") in the third-century *San guo zhi*, 7/229: "Chen Yuanlong is a man of the lake and the sea whose generosity and untrammeled spirit never leave him."

line 6: A celebrated Liang dynasty poet and statesman forced by political upheavals to remain in north China while he pined for his native south, Yu Xin (513–81) expressed his nostalgia in his "Ai Jiangnan fu," which bemoans the many passes and mountains that separate him from the sights and splendors of his native region.

line 8: The Water Immortal is the great poet and rejected advisor Qu Yuan, author of the "Li sao." Incense, *banxiang*, can be either compressed in the shape of petals or powdered, resembling melon pulps. Burning such incense in honor of someone implies a strong desire to follow in that person's steps, an implication followed in this translation.

P.126.20 Lamenting Qu Yuan

King Huai of Chu was a weak leader,
Just as if he were deaf and blind.
When slander is rampant, truth is hard to promote;
When worms flourish, trees naturally rot.
A minister's heart may be like a *zhai*,
But bazaar talk thrice-repeated creates a tiger.
Why did the king favor the obsequious,
(8) While the loyal and upright met with obstinacy?
Alas! you orchids of the nine realms,

Demoted to the company of the common grasses.
Though facing the wind, you remained fragrant and beautiful,
And, moreover, were envied by the malodorous weeds.
I sigh deeply for you, Master Qu Yuan;
Why weren't you born in the land of Lu?

(*Qiu Jin ji*, 74)

line 1: King Huai of Chu (r. 328–299 B.C.E) was the ruler who failed to listen to Qu Yuan's advice and later was captured by the enemies of Qin.

line 5: The *zhai*, a fabulous beast, is said to be able to discern good and evil.

line 6: This popular phrase means that slander can be as fierce as a tiger in hurting the person.

line 9: I.e., people of many talents; here the worthy talent is Qu Yuan.

line 14: Lu was the native state of Confucius, where it was said true talent and high principle were appreciated.

P.126.21. *To Wu Zhiying, My Sworn Elder Sister*

Once singing the same tune, we explored heaven's reaches;
When good friends meet, joys are naturally mutual.
Were we not bound in life and death, our pledge would seem
common;
Playing in harmony ocarina and flute, our music is superb.
In noble friendship united, our hearts coincide;
Firm in our aspirations, we join in silent harmony.
Friends by correspondence, intimate like Guan and Bao;
May our mutual love persist and never fail.

(Yi Boyin, 6/200)

line 7: Guan Zhong and Bao Shuya of the ancient Spring and Autumn period were famed for their friendship.

P.126.22. *Inscribed on a Wall in Shenjiang*

Aboard a steamer, once again I return to the south,
Sojourning briefly in Wusong, which I'd rather avoid.
Here horses and carriages stir up the dust and close friends are few;
Here strings are muddled, pipes strident, and correct tones rare.
How often have tears been shed over these troubled times?
Instead, they vie in luxury, compete over dance costumes.

I worry endlessly over the vulgar miasma that fills the eyes,
For daily things worsen as public morals are lacking.

(Yi Boyin, 6/201)

Both Shenjiang and Wusong refer to Shanghai.

P.126.23. A Ballad of the Autumn Wind

An autumn wind rises and all the grasses turn yellow;
It is the nature of the autumn wind to be keen and stern,
For it can cause hosts of flowers to grow sere and wither,
And assist autumn chrythanthemums to shine in the autumn frost.
Autumn chrysanthemums, branch upon branch, all a yellow species;
Storied layers of petals, like surging wind and clouds.
The autumn moon, mirror-like, brightly illuminates the river,
An upwelling of clear waves—how dare they move?
Last night brought autumn's heavy winds and rain:
Autumn frost, autumn dew, all bearing sorrow.
Green, green are the leaves, fearful of being shaken down;
Exotic birds singing sadly circle the tree tops.
From of old, autumn has always been the saddest time;
At Han frontiers and Tang gates, autumnal thoughts arise.
Beyond the frontier in high autumn, the horses now plump,
A general angrily demands his golden yellow armor.
Donning golden armor, he fights the barbarian dogs,
And a million barbarian slaves turn about and flee.
With a hearty laugh, the general calls to his fellow Chinese:
"Let's drink the wine of freedom at Huanglong."

(*Qiu Jin ji*, 81)

line 18: In *Qiu Jin shiji*, this line reads "One million barbarian cavalrymen depart holding their heads."

line 20: The place name Huanglong connotes "enemy base." When the Jürchen grew strong with their main base at Huanglong in the twelfth century, Song generals often vowed to drink a victory toast at Huanglong.

P.126.24. Thoughts

Alas, this vast sacred realm is sinking;
With no means to save it, I live in shame.

Xiang Yu, molding sand, sought to restore vanquished Chu;
Zhang Liang, lacking an ax, planned to attack the tyrant Qin.
When the country is shattered, we realize the abject nature of our
  people;
When the cause is righteous, being a poor sojourner is no handicap.
How hateful that I cannot repay my comrades for all their efforts;
As I hold my sword and sing a sad ballad, tears flow down my cheeks.

(Yi Boyin, 6/202)

line 3: "A handful of sand" refers to an uncohesive mass, usually of relatives or allies. Xiang Yu was the rival of Liu Bang in the fall of the Qin dynasty; see P.28.1.

line 4: Jing Ke was the brave assassin who attempted to kill the tyrannical First Emperor of Qin with a knife and failed. Zhang Liang, a scholar without a weapon, helped Liu Bang to defeat Qin and establish the Han dynasty.

P.126.25. Ta suo xing: *For Tao Di*

Murmuring to my shadow.
Writing "Alas! Alas" in the air.
I act oddly not because I'm drunk or we'll soon part.
I have, instead, a citadel of sorrow
  right smack in my heart.
Separated from friends and kin; all alone;
My sorrow is a secret all my own.

In vain have I had soaring aspirations.
The scope of my life is too narrow, my choices far too few.
Altrustic and generous impulses of a knight errant
  remain unexpressed.
I want to remonstrate with the Heavenly Lord for
  my wretched lot:
A woman, incurring nonetheless,
  envy and hatred as vicious as that
  inflicted on the Poet.

(*Qiu Jin shici zhushi*, 323)

In Liu's and several other editions, Tao Di is mistakenly printed as Tao Qiu. My emendation is based on Guo Changhai and Li Bingbin, *Qiu Jin shiji yanjiu*, pp. 207–8.

line 2: Alluding to the behavior of Yin Hao; see P.109.2.

line 11: The "Poet" is Qu Yuan.

P.126.26. Inscribed on a Photograph of Myself Dressed as a Man

This image I see, so dignified, so grave,
who in fact, could it be?—
Knight-errant bones of an earlier incarnation
trapped, regrettably, in a female body.
Dead and buried is my previous form:
it was nothing but an illusion.
My future vista, on the other hand, promises
possibilities for authenticity.
Too much time has elapsed; still my selves have finally met,
generating naturally a mixture of emotions.
When once again I lament the times,
it will be with unprecedented boldness.
At future meetings with old friends,
(8) They'll be told—
I've swept away all that's trivial,
all that's just
surface dust.

(*Qiu Jin shici zhushi*, 168)

P.126.27. For Aunt Qinwen

It must have been karma that brought us together—
two floating duckweeds side by side by chance.
Instantly, with no reservation, you bestowed upon me
exorbitant affection.
Iris and orchid of similar scent,
we do, each the other, understand.
My hair is artemisia black, yours moxa grey, but
in friendship age doesn't matter.
However joyous and stimulating our conversation,
we can't delay our separation.
Listlessly, with downcast looks,
we communicate our distress in darkest gloom.
My letter, tied to a wild goose's foot
will fly to you on the wind—
(8) Boundless is the longing for a like-minded friend:

it is a sea with no shores that
one can see.

(*Qiu Jin shici zhushi*, 228)

"Aunt Qinwen" would not be a blood relative. In China, "Aunt" is often a respectful and affectionate appellation for a female friend of one's parents' generation. Qiu's exquisite politeness here belies the fact that she was in fact Aunt Qinwen's benefactor, lending the older friend and her husband money soon after she had met them in Shanghai in spring, 1904. No more is known of Qinwen's identity.

line 4: A literal translation of this line would read, "The feeling between us is as strong [deep] as that between *xiao* and *ai*, and we have developed a friendship which takes no account of age." *Ai*, moxa, is a standard metaphor for people in their fifties, when the hair is gray like the downy covering of the leaves of *Artemisia moxa*. *Xiao*, *Artemisia lactiflora*, has dark purple stalks that look black in certain lights. The present translation incorporates the underpinnings of the metaphors.

line 7: On the wild goose as letter carrier, see P.2.1 (Song 5).

P.126.28. Ballad of a Red Hair's Saber

Pure autumn water unblemished by even
the tiniest specks of hair.
From afar, I didn't recognize this pool of light
as the sheen of a saber.
It so terrifies jade dragons that they
cringe and coil in their boxes,
Waiting to fly away to the clouds in a thunderstorm:
They say this saber comes from the Red-Haired People.
It is far deadlier than those of Arabia and Japan.
Barely drawing blood, it can cut asunder bone joints,
(8) Hardly touching the neck before the victim's head rolls.
Unsheath it: heaven will shake, and
The sun, moon, and stars will quickly hide their light.
The sound of a single blow is enough to make the sea jump.
(12) Merely three inches of its tip cause a hell wind to howl.
On earth it slaughters elephant and rhinoceros;
in water it bisects the scaly dragon.
Water sprites and mountain spirits
flee in shocked alarm.
How many have fallen victim to the saber's blade?

Skulls have piled up in mounds, and
    blood has surged in billowing waves.
The ghosts of massacred millions are weeping, while
None alive is safe from the blade's swing.
Even when the saber hangs on the wall in temporary disuse,
Nightly it hisses and hoots like a savage owl.
A martial spirit thirsting for the blood of war,
A wronged soul craving for the relief of wine.
But—
    Red Hair, Red Hair, don't you strut.
I mean to reject your weapon though it is lethal.
Self-strengthening depends on people,
    not on weaponry.
True, you have this sword, but only this sword, so
    why should you swagger, why are you
    so arrogant, so overbearingly proud?

(*Qiu Jin shici zhushi*, 175)

"Red Hair" (*hongmao*) means Westerners, especially the Dutch and the British.

lines 2–3: The trope depicting a sword or a saber as a dragon waiting to fly to the clouds (see poems on pp. 152 and 202 in Liu Yulai, *Qiu Jin shici zhushi*) or as a hissing and hooting bird or animal (see poems on pp. 257, 212, 334 in ibid., and see Guo Changhai and Li Bingbin, *Qiu Jin shiji yanjiu*, p. 297, no. 4) was likewise often used by Tang poets.

P.126.29. Zhegu tian

The motherland almost submerged—I can't suppress my feelings.
When free I seek true friends across the sea.
A gold jug chipped must be repaired;
For my country I dare to be a sacrificial lamb.

Alas! Dangers and obstacles!
I sigh at my floating life.
Across ten thousand *li* of mountains and passes I make the intrepid
    journey.
Don't say that women are not heroic figures—
Night after night my Dragon Spring Sword sings on the wall!

(*Qiu Jin ji*, 107–8)

The Dragon Spring Sword was a famous lost sword associated with the Jin scholar Zhang Hua (232–300).

P.126.30. Man jiang hong

A short stay in the capital,
So soon again the fine Mid-Autumn festival.
There beneath the fence
Yellow flowers are all in bloom,
Their autumn looks seem cleansed.
Fragments of songs all round finally shattered Chu,
Eight years of tastes and flavors: in vain I've longed for Zhe.
(8) How cruel to have been forced to be a lady,
Really, never a shred of mercy!

I cannot get into
The ranks of men.
(12) But my heart burns
More fiercely than a man's.
Let me say that in my life
My spleen has often been roused to fury for others' sake.
(16) What vulgar man could ever know me?
Heroes confront ordeals at the end of the road.
In this dirty world of red dust,
  where can I seek an understanding friend?
My green robe is soaked with tears.

(*Qiu Jin ji*, 97)

line 6: On Liu Bang's stratagem of the "Chu songs," see P.28.1. Qiu Jin may be drawing an analogy for the difficult times faced by China as foreign powers sought to penetrate and subjugate China.

line 7: A reference to Qiu's longing for native Shaoxing. Qiu Jin had been living in Beijing with her husband after her marriage.

P.126.31. Climbing Mount Wu

Aged trees spreading wide turn crimson in the evening glow;
Ancient rock spires rising upward approach heaven's winds.
Vast, vast, the boundless spirit joins river and sea.
Half of the green mountains are to be found in Yue.

(Yi Boyin, 6/204)

Mount Wu or Wu Shan is also called Chenghuang Shan or Xu Shan. It is located southeast of West Lake in Hangzhou.

line 4: Yue is Shaoxing.

P.126.32. *Turning to Wine*

I'd not begrudge a thousand in gold to buy a precious sword;
To exchange a sable robe for wine also befits a hero.
I urge myself, "Treasure dearly your breast of hot blood;
Even if it spills, it will still change into blue waves!"

(Yi Boyin, 6/205)

P.126.33. *A Poem to a Precious Sword*

Precious sword, O, precious sword,
What a shame to use you to settle private scores.
It would be better to cut off the heads of enemies
And be cited in the biographies of heroes.
When a woman is insulted she commits suicide;
But a man willingly becomes an obedient subject.
If a horse-decapitating sword is sold,
Why then should you be sparing of yourself!
The sword of Ganjiang shames that of Moye:
Though dull, it was preserved without harm.
Miserable are females once forced to submit;
Don't put on the manner of a hero!
Although a sacred sword hangs upon the wall,
Its sharp point has surprised the world.
At midnight it emits long whistles,
Sad, sad, like the hooting of owls.

(*Qiu Jin ji*, 91)

line 6: Qiu Jin repeated this theme in her matching scroll entitled "Temple of the Lady Who Moved Stones" and other works.

line 9: Ganjiang and Moye are the names of famous swords of the ancient state of Wu. They are also the names of the couple who crafted the swords for the King of Wu in the sixth century B.C.E. According to legend, Moye, in order to make her husband Ganjiang's project successful, jumped into the smelting cauldron, sacrificing her own life.

P.126.34. Reflection on the Times

When all had failed, they begged the Goddess Nü Wa
—who alone knew how—
to smelt the stones and repair the sky.
I, too, am female, but mortal, and my prime vanishes
as quickly as a galloping white colt
speeding by a crack in the wall.
A catastrophe is pressing on our eye-brows and lashes;
China is being carved up:
a melon being sliced by the sharpest knives.
In vain I shout in alarm,
wasting my larynx on deaf ears.
Yet surely to save our sinking country all must
assume responsibilities.
To take up mine, I became a lone stranger drifting
without a home at the earth's ends.
The more my blood seethes, the more deeply I grieve to
look back on my land.
(8) With sorrow rending my bowels,
I even failed to give fifth-month blossoms
the attention they deserve.

(*Qiu Jin shici zhushi*, 209)

line 1: On Nü Wa's repair of the heavens, see P.87.13.vii.
line 4: For rhyme's sake, Qiu used "teeth" where this translation has "larynx."

P.126.35. Man jiang hong

In this filthy world,
How many men are heroic and wise?
I reckon only among women
Are there paragons.
Liangyu's loyal services drench my lapel in tears.
Yunying's lifelong achievements make blood rush to my heart.
When drunk, I stroke my sword and hum like a dragon:
(8) My voice chokes with grief.

Incessantly I've longed to ignite
The incense of freedom.

When, *when* can we avenge
Our country's humiliation?
My peers, let us
Exert ourselves as of today.
Peace and security for our race is our goal.
The prosperity we seek should exceed our own
  showy jewelry and clothes.
Above all, the three-inch bow-slippers
  have been all too disabling.
They must go.

(*Qiu Jin shici zhushi*, 325)

line 5: Qin Liangyu was a Ming dynasty gentry woman of the Wanli era (1573–1619). An expert in archery, equitation, and literary composition, she was also an excellent military strategist. After her husband, General Ma Qiancheng, died in a campaign against the rebel She Chongming, Qin Liangyu, dressed as a man, replaced her husband and quelled the rebellion. Thereupon she was made a brigadier general and military governor of Bozhou.

line 6: Shen Yunying was a late Ming dynasty gentry woman (fl. ca. 1620). An accomplished archer, equestrienne, and calligrapher, she was also well versed in history and the Classics. When her father, the army captain Shen Zhixu, was killed by the rebel troops of Zhang Xianzhong, Yunying, leading a small detachment of cavalry, went into the rebels' camps and recovered her father's corpse. She was made a major general and the successor to her father as the prefect of Daozhou.

line 17: Worn by women with bound feet, these slippers were so named because they ideally measured three inches in length and the soles curved upward in the shape of a bow. The slippers are here used as a metonym for bound feet.

P.126.36. Man jiang hong: *An Inscription for Zheng Shujin's Painting, "Sailing down the Xiaoxiang on a Lone Sampan, in Light Rain" (For my mother, in memoriam)*

A painting, merely a foot long,
Yet it contains so much sorrow and tears.
It evokes that other time,
  also in a fine, misty rain,
When I, overwhelmed with emotion, sailed away
  from you in a skiff.
You had taught me characters by
  tracing them on the ground with a reed—

as Yongshu's mother had taught him.
But I fell short of Cui Bin, I failed
to escort your carriage through
bustling crowds.
Now gone, your loving radiance will never be seen again.
I mourn; I grieve;
My deepest sorrow begins.

The sound of you giving me lessons
has stopped for ever.
The flow of my grieving tears
will go on, and on, and on.
What remains are my Xiaoxiang verses to you
And your unfulfilled ambitions for me.
Tigerhead's brush, however skillful,
Cannot depict the tangled longing of
a bereaved child
for a departed mother.
I await the day when a portrait
of your virtuous self
adorns Sweet Spring—
Adding luster to recorded history.

(*Qiu Jin shici zhushi*, 310)

Zheng Yuan (style name Shujin), a scholar-painter and native of Changsha, Hunan, passed the *jinshi* examination with the third highest honor of *tanhua* in 1894 and was made a member of the Hanlin Academy. He subsequently served in various posts. After the 1911 revolution, he lived in Beijing and associated with Yuan Shikai. In the late 1890s, Zheng was a friend of Qiu Jin's father in Hunan.

line 5: Qiu's intent here is to show that, like Ouyang Xiu (style name Yongshu, see P.92.1), she was taught characters by her mother. The reed part is purely rhetorical; Qiu grew up in very comfortable circumstances.

line 6: The Tang dynasty statesman Cui Bin (fl.ca. 806–21), even after achieving the high position of Chief Minister of Imperial Sacrifices, escorted his mother's carriage through bustling crowds; see *Xin Tang shu*, 163/5017. Cui's behavior is considered the epitome of filial piety.

line 13: "Tigerhead" was a nickname for the Jin dynasty painter Gu Kaizhi (ca. 346–ca. 407), famous for the realism of his paintings.

line 14: A literal translation of this line would read: "Cannot depict my [Di]-Renjie-coiling-and-tangling longing." Di Renjie (630–700; posthumous title, the

Duke of Liangguo) was a Tang dynasty writer and high official celebrated for his compassion and benevolence. Tradition has it that he was deeply attached to his mother and mourned her death incessantly.

line 18: The Sweet Spring Palace of the Former Han dynasty was adorned with imaginary portraits of deities and portraits of revered worthies in history.

P.126.37. A Matching Poem for the Lady Scholar of Yuxi, Xu Jichen, Using Her Original Rhyme [one of two poems]

An immortal lately flown down from her five-color cloud:
It's a pleasure to meet such a talent as you.
You praise me excessively, making me shrink in embarrassment,
While I know it's difficult to match your
  "Song of a Sunny Spring."
Heroic tasks depend on us to initiate and achieve,
Unshirkable, they're our fated duties to perform.
Wind and clouds will compete fiercely in the twentieth century.
(8) We must awake those deep in boudoir dreams
  With discourses on the sexes' equality.

(*Qiu Jin shici zhushi*, 23; for emendations, see *Qiu Jin ji*, 87)

Jichen is the style name of Xu Zihua (P.127), principal of Xunxi School for Girls in Wuxing, Zhejiang, where Qiu taught from March to August 1906.

line 4: "Songs of Sunny Spring" were songs of such refinement that they were not appreciated by the multitude; see P.4.2 for the source of the allusion.

line 7: "Wind and clouds" mean unpredictable and momentous events.

P.126.38. [Untitled]

In the blink of an eye, the most opportune moment is over.
My bold ambition is not fulfilled, to my bitterest regret.
We dropped our whips into the sea
  to check its ruthless inundation.
We raised our swords to the sky
  to sharpen them on the moon.
No clay to seal up Hangu—
  imperiling armored horses.
Copious tears in Luoyang—
  shed by bronze camels.
Having my flesh reduced to dust,

my bones ground to powder,
such fate is now a banality.
(8) I only hope my sacrifice will help to
preserve our country.

(*Qiu Jin shici zhushi*, 259–60)

This is the last poem written by Qiu, on July 12, 1907, one day before her capture and three days before her execution. Lines 3 through 6 show her lucid awareness of the revolutionaries' lack of wherewithal and hence the impossibility at that time of her own and her colleagues' task to overthrow the Qing dynasty. The poem was written on the cover of a book belonging to her ailing fellow-teacher and revolutionary, Xu Yifei, to whom Qiu paid a final visit on her way back to the Datong Normal School to face the approaching Qing troops.

line 5: Sealing up the Hangu Pass with clay is a metaphor for stationing crack troops around a strategic stronghold (see *Hou Han shu* 13/525). The Hangu Pass is situated in present-day Henan province and was traditionally considered one of the realm's first-line defense posts against foreign invasions.

line 6: Here the bronze camels (see P.126.17) weep because of the setbacks suffered by Qiu and her colleagues, who had sought to supplant the usurping and corrupt Qing government with a legitimate and vital one. Luoyang, the eastern capital of many dynasties, including the Han and the Tang, is often used as the epitome of all dynastic capitals.

BIOGRAPHICAL NOTE AND TRANSLATION OF P.126.1–4, 17–19, 25–28, AND 34–38 BY LI-LI CH'EN; TRANSLATION OF P.126.5–16, 20–24, AND 31–33 BY CHIA-LIN PAO TAO; TRANSLATION OF P.126.29–30 BY GRACE S. FONG.

徐自華

P.127. Xu Zihua (1873–1935)

Xu Zihua (style name Jichen, sobriquet Qianhui) is perhaps best known as friend of the revolutionary martyr Qiu Jin (P.126), but she can stand on her own merits as a classical poet and progressive woman educator. Her life exemplifies the transition from traditional to modern that many gentry-class women of the time experienced.

Xu was born into a literary family in Shimen (present-day Tongxiangxian) in Zhejiang. She exhibited a penchant for learning and poetry from the early age of five. Her parents appear to have been quite liberal: they cultivated her interests and talents as she began studying with her cousins under her maternal uncle Ma Yiqing. Later her maternal grandfather gave her further instruction in poetry, lamenting only that she had not been born a male. In her adolescence her poetic development was further nourished by a close relationship with her cousin Xu Huizhen (style name Lanxiang, 1872–92), who in a short life achieved recognition as a poet. His father, Xu Rongshi, was the younger brother of Xu Zihua's father and in 1887 held the post of magistrate of Shunde in Guangdong for a year. He brought his family with him and invited Xu Zihua's family to join them. Xu Zihua's earliest extant poems date from this sojourn in Guangdong and her intimate friendship with her cousin. More than a decade after Xu Huizhen's death, Xu Zihua wrote a biographical essay on her cousin.

At twenty-one, in 1893, Xu Zihua was married to Mei Yunsheng of Huzhou; they subsequently had a son and a daughter. Her husband died in 1900, and Xu remained a widow for the rest of her life. She dedicated herself to the upbringing of her children and to the education of women in general. Her daughter, however, died in 1907.

Xu was principal of the Xunxi School for Girls in Huzhou when she first met Qiu Jin, who had come to assume a teaching post at the school in 1906. The two women instantly struck up a strong friendship, and Qiu Jin exerted a tremendous influence on Xu's thinking. With similar interests and concerns, they discussed a range of subjects: poetry, education, women's issues, current affairs. Xu was inspired by Qiu Jin's experiences studying abroad in Japan, fighting for women's rights. She encouraged Qiu Jin to found the newspaper *Zhongguo nübao* (Chinese women's monthly). When Qiu Jin was organizing the anti-Manchu uprising of 1907, Xu and her sister sold their jewelry to help. After Qiu Jin was beheaded for her part in this uprising, it was Xu Zihua who dared to come forward and make the wintry journey to collect her coffin for burial by West Lake in Hangzhou.

Xu engaged in further political activities, becoming a prominent member of the activist literary group Nanshe (Southern society) in 1909. After the 1911 revolution, Xu founded the Jingxiong Women's School in Shanghai, calling the school after one of Qiu Jin's style names, which translates as "Hero's Rival." She passed on the management of the school to Qiu Jin's daughter, Wang Canzhi, in 1927. In commemoration of Qiu Jin, Xu also founded the Qiushe (Qiu society) and wrote a number of essays about the life and personality of the martyr, when she was reburied in Hangzhou. Her later poetry is mostly social occasional verse; much of it revolves around people and activities of the Nanshe. Xu died in Hangzhou at the age of sixty-three.

Xu Zihua's talent and early training in writing both prose and poetry gave her a medium in which she expressed her thoughts and feelings, described her travels, her friendships and social activities, and captured changes and events throughout her life. By 1903 she had collected her early poetic works into a manuscript titled *Tingzhulou shigao* (Drafts of poems from the Listening to Bamboo Pavilion), which was never printed. During her life, she apparently printed only one collection of her song-lyrics—the *Chanhui ci* (Song-lyrics repenting intelligence). Her literary production is quite voluminous—close to six hundred pieces in several genres, variously published in journals, newspapers, and magazines of the time, now brought together in *Xu Zihua shiwen ji.*

P.127.1. Inscribed on a Painting of a Beauty Playing the Zither

Trees in the courtyard have formed a green shade,
Silently, she plucks the jade zither.
Even were we to ask for a talented scholar's brush
It would be hard to depict the beauty's heart.
She breaks off the melody "Plum Blossom Prelude";
Her secret feelings are chanted by the catkins.
Who would be my companion during this sojourn?
In the painting I have found my bosom friend.

(*Xu Zihua shiwen ji*, 38)

This and the following two poems are among the earliest verse extant by Xu, written in adolescence during and after her stay with her uncle's family in Guangdong.

P.127.2. New Year's Eve

During our sojourn we're reunited, delighting in family and kin,
The banquet to see the old year off begins amidst sounds of talk and laughter.
Lamps reflect off glass, flowers form buds;
Floating in cups of amber, the wine grows scales.
With the sound of firecrackers we take joy in the passing of the year;
A few dots of cold plum blossom bring the happy news of spring.
Tomorrow I will be a girl of fifteen,
But I am ashamed of having no pepper hymn to offer my parents.

(*Xu Zihua shiwen ji*, 41–42)

line 8: At New Year's the aged received cups of pepper-flavored wine and wishes for long life. A "pepper hymn" would be a song accompanying this custom.

P.127.3. *Returning Home from Lingnan, I Complete Two Regulated Poems [first of two poems]*

Scenery along the Pearl River touches off sorrows of separation
But suddenly our returning oars stirred, we will not be detained.
Though long ago I left West Lake, it encircles the traveler's dream;
Now by chance I came to Lingnan—it opened my eyes to poetry.
Three years of official merits are recorded in verse,
But now an earnest heart longing for home flows with the sea.
Don't tease the young lady for having no high ambitions:
(8) She has traveled beyond seven thousand *li*.

(*Xu Zihua shiwen ji*, 42)

Lingnan is another name for Guangdong.

P.127.4. *Weeping over My Cousin Lanxiang [Xu Huizhen; third of a set of four poems]*

On entering again the empty boudoir, my feelings are many and mixed:
Mirror case and books are lying scattered in disarray.
For Bo Ya's zither there remains in vain the knowing friend's feelings,
By Jiang Gong's coverlet I sigh deeply at our sisterly love.
The portrait cannot capture your image
While my three bad dreams are all too clear.
Heartbroken, I write these rhymes for one who is no more.
(8) How can I bear to hear the night rain on the plantain outside the window?

(*Xu Zihua shiwen ji*, 58)

lines 3–4: On the legendary friends Zhong Ziqi and Bo Ya, see P.24.7. Jiang Gong shared his quilt with his two brothers (*Hou Han shu*, 53).

line 6: Here Xu added the note: "Whenever I dream of teeth falling out it is a bad omen. When I dreamed of this in the autumn of *dinghai* [1887], my younger brother Hong died; then I dreamed it again in the spring of *gengyin* [1890], and my nephew Rong died; in the middle of the first month I suddenly had this dream again and felt quite disturbed. Shortly afterward my cousin passed away."

P.127.5. *With Autumn Wind and Rain Outside the Window, My Small Son Is Sick in Bed; I Write a Poem to Dispel Feelings of Ennui.*

Light vapor from the medicine pot wafting in emerald strands of silk:
It is just the time of wind and rain in early autumn.
I got angry with the foolish maid at the dust on my study's window,
I am weary of the sound of the child crying on the sickbed.
He doesn't yet know where sorrow comes from,
I pity so much that common habits cannot be cured.
By nature I am idiotic: I'm impossible to change,
When I have a moment of stolen leisure, I chant poetry again.

(*Xu Zihua shiwen ji*, 73–74)

P.127.6. *The Tenth of the First Month Is the Anniversary of My Husband's Death; I Wrote This After Weeping*

Three slow years have gone by, my tearful eyes have dried up,
Although alive I seem dead—how much more this hurts me!
Having tasted bitterness deeply, I know the hollowness of human
 affairs,
I envy those sleeping in peace in the world of the dead.
The cuckoo survives, weeping for its millennial pain:
It might change into a crane and return once and for all to the void.
I suppress my grief, supervise the libation and vegetarian offerings,
Then return to teaching the two little orphans at my knees.

(*Xu Zihua shiwen ji*, 84)

line 5: On the legend of the cuckoo, see P.5.1. The crane, in contrast, is popularly associated with longevity and immortality.

P.127.7. *One of My Girlfriends Showed Me the Poems of the* Fragrant Dressing Case*; I Responded with Four Poems in Jest*

IV

That two hooked feet are bewitching is such nonsense:
A beautiful golden lotus left behind at each step!
I hate so much the last ruler of the Southern Tang:
He originated an evil to plague a thousand years.

(*Xu Zihua shiwen ji*, 94)

On the *Fragrant Dressing Case Collection* (*Xianglian ji*) attributed to the late Tang poet Han Wo, see P.76.6. Presumably this is the anthology to which Xu responded, although several poetry collections by women bear the same or similar titles. Xu cites ironically a number of stock metaphors used to describe bound feet. On bound feet as a subject for gentry women's poetry, see Ko, *Teachers of the Inner Chambers*, pp. 166–69.

P.127.8. Two Poems Presented to Woman Scholar Qiu Xuanqing [Qiu Jin]

I

Often I've wondered if she is an immortal fairy on the other side of the clouds,
How fortunate that we now meet with the joy of holding hands.
She harbors ambitions no bearded man can match,
Talent that is even harder to find among women.
To support her motherland she summons those with the same love,
Traveling all through Japan, she invigorates her views.
How many frail women have been lying low for so long,
(8) Relying on you to recover our right to freedom!

II

Long blown about like traces of duckweed, I suddenly met you,
What I see, to my surprise, surpasses even what I had heard.
With noble blessing and marvelous talent you had changed your attire,
With Mulan's high aims you could join the army.
Enlightening the world of women you introduce a novel way,
Organizing for equal rights you are good at bringing groups together.
Laughing at my own impudence, I want to attach myself to your greatness,
(8) I will share equally in all the duties of a citizen!

(*Xu Zihua shiwen ji*, 108)

ii, line 3: The author made a note: "You had changed into man's attire."
ii, line 4: On Mulan, see P.109.1.

P.127.9. Soliciting Shareholding Contributions for Nübao *and Not Meeting with Much Enthusiasm, I Am Moved to Compose Two Poems*

I

To heal our country who will work on a saving cure?
It takes a lot of planning to advocate a newspaper for women.
Extirpating our slave mentality to become a united group,
From now on women should be strong on their own.

II

Bright pearls and kingfisher feathers daily compete for beauty,
Who is willing to be first to give up her wealth for the common good?
I advise all my sisters from the vermilion boudoirs:
When improving your appearance, skimp some money from buying pearls.

(*Xu Zihua shiwen ji*, 116)

P.127.10. Taking an Excursion at West Lake with Xuanqing [Qiu Jin], I Am Moved to Write

Like meteors for the moment we have a spring outing together,
Lake and hills coming into view—how they sadden our spirits.
After death my name will not be known in the highest ranks,
While alive good friends are not too many.
Wanting to ease your accumulated grief, you rely on wine,
Willing to make a sacrifice, do you ever think of yourself?
It pains us to look towards Phoenix Hill
(8) Where the Song imperial tombs are sunk in barbarian dust.

(*Xu Zihua shiwen ji*, 116)

line 5: The author added a note: "You have a capacity for wine."

P.127.11. Mourning the Woman Warrior of Mirror Lake [Qiu Jin; third in a series of twelve]

Your heroic talk full of suppressed anger—how lofty your spirit!
Risking your life, you shed hot blood for compatriots.
Suddenly you were vilified with no light of day,

In the end you became the sacrifice, decapitated on the execution
ground.
You bring utter shame to these officials whose disgrace is plain,
Letting them see there is a great hero among women.
How can your wronged soul consent to be extinguished?
(8) Diving into Qiantang you become its angry billows.

(*Xu Zihua shiwen ji*, 118)

line 8: The Qiantang River near Hangzhou is known for its tidal bores; see P.75b.4. Xu here is alluding to the force of Qiu Jin's spirit as well as her wish to be buried in Hangzhou, which Xu carried out at great risk to herself.

P.127.12. Mourning My Daughter Rong [third in a series of three]

Reading lessons by a bright window or with one lamp at night,
Diligent, fond of learning, when was she ever tired?
By pointing to details on maps, she came to know topography,
By discussing history beside open books, she understood rise and fall.
With the "Rhyme-Prose on the Charming Daughter" finished, grief is
not dispelled,
When the "Epitaph for A-Nu" was completed, its author could hardly
bear his emotions.
Dawn and dusk I face your picture in vain:
(8) There is no response, no matter how hard I knock on the glass.

(*Xu Zihua shiwen ji*, 122)

line 5: A reference to the Jin poet Zuo Si's (d. ca. 306) poem on his little daughter.
line 6: The author made a note: "Tie Wen Gong's daughter A-Nu also died at age twelve."

P.127.13. On the 27th of November, I Crossed the Yangzi During a Snow Storm to Take Care of Xuanqing's [Qiu Jin] Burial; I Was Moved to Write

I

This time I have been delayed by illness from crossing the River,
Wanting to visit your remains, I am undeterred by the cold.
Would I give up this aim because my daughter died?
You spoke for the public good; dare I speak of private feelings?

II

My tears had not yet dried from weeping for my daughter,
When I hurriedly embarked on the journey to seek your coffin.
Since hot-blooded zeal still fills your heart,
I am not afraid of the cold even if I have to face wind and frost.

III

Red clouds closing in on all sides as evening sorrow rises;
A lonely boat in a river full of wind and snow.
How can I bear to walk the road to Shanyin today
Where no one but me comes to bury Autumn?

IV

To bury you I select a piece of land at Xiling.
When I die in the future, who will bury my bones?
This has stirred me to thoughts on life and death,
I hurriedly plan to arrange a tomb in advance.

(*Xu Zihua shiwen ji*, 122)

iii, line 4: Qiu Jin's surname means "autumn."
iv, line 1: At West Lake in Hangzhou.

P.127.14. After the Central Plain Was Recovered [from the Manchus], I Returned to Yue and Mourned Xuanqing [Qiu Jin] [from a series of four poems]

I

Every year in wind and rain I was accustomed to grieving for autumn,
This year the autumn wind scattered all grief away.
A cry from Wuchang summons a chorus from all the world:
At last we have recovered our ancient land.

II

In autumn wind and autumn rain, dust rises from battlefields,
Barbarian dust blown far, evil air swept away.
Such pity that on the day the revolution has succeeded
You are missing from the cavalry ranks by the hills of Wu.

IV

I dread going to West Lake, it brings up my grief—
A scoop of barren earth, ashes after the disaster.
Crossing the river I don't feel the cold in my light fur;
Twice I've come to Shanyin in wind and snow.

(*Xu Zihua shiwen ji*, 139–40)

Written after the 1911 revolution, which defeated the Manchu dynasty and established the Chinese Republic.

i, line 4: The 1911 revolution began with risings in Chengdu and Wuchang.

BIOGRAPHICAL NOTE AND TRANSLATION BY GRACE S. FONG

Part Two CRITICISM

Female Critics and Poets

武则天

C.1. Wu Zetian (624/627–705)

On Wu Zetian, see P.6.

C.1.1. On Su Hui's "Silk-Woven Palindromic Verse"

During the time of Fu Jian [334–94] of the Former Qin, the Regional Inspector of Qinzhou [Gansu province] was Dou Tao from Fufeng [Shaanxi province]. Dou Tao's wife was Su Hui, the third daughter of the magistrate of Chenliu [Henan province], Chen Daozhi of Wugong [Shaanxi province]. Su Hui's style name was Ruolan. She was learned, capable, and bright, and her appearance was refined and lovely. She was humble and reserved, with no interest in pursuing fame. At the age of sixteen she married Dou Tao, who respected her very much. However, Su Hui was a bit quick-tempered and easily hurt by jealous feelings.

Dou Tao's style name was Lianpo. He was the grandson of the General of (2)
the Right, Dou Zizhen, and the second son of Dou Lang. Handsome and well-mannered, Dou Tao was conversant with the histories and classics and talented in both the literary and martial arts. He was held in high regard by his contemporaries, and the ruler, Fu Jian, entrusted him with the most important duties. Tao had held several distinctive positions, all of which he discharged admirably, but during his service as Regional Inspector of Qinzhou, Dou Tao was to be exiled to Dunhuang [Gansu province] for disobeying Fu Jian. It happened, however, that the formidable enemy of the Former Qin
was approaching Xiangyang [Hubei province], and in the face of this press- 669
ing danger, Tao was recalled because of his military talents. He was posted to Xiangyang with the title General for Pacifying the South.

Dou Tao had a favorite concubine named Zhao Yangtai. Marvelous in sing- (3)

ing and dancing, none could compare with her. Dou Tao arranged a separate residence for Yangtai. When Su Hui heard of this, she sought Zhao out and, exceedingly bitter, had her beaten and humiliated. Dou Tao felt very badly about this. Moreover, Yangtai deliberately emphasized Su Hui's shortcomings, mixing flattery with slander. This made Dou Tao even angrier. Su Hui was twenty years old at the time. She was invited to accompany Dou Tao to his new post at Xiangyang, but, still angry, she declined. Accordingly, Dou Tao took Yangtai along with him, and he cut off communication with Su Hui.

(4) Su Hui regretted what she had done and was extremely wounded by what had happened. Because of this she composed a palindromic verse and had it woven in silk, using five beautiful colors that shone radiantly into one's eyes and heart. On a piece of silk a mere eight inches square, she wove more than two hundred poems of more than eight hundred characters. Whether one read vertically or horizontally, in whatever direction, verses would emerge with nothing missing at all. The marvels of her talent and feeling far surpass those of both the past and present. Her embroidery was called the Xuanji Diagram. Most readers, however, were unable to grasp all of the verses. Su Hui laughed at this and said, "As it lingers aimlessly, twisting and turning, it takes on a pattern of its own. No one but my beloved can be sure of comprehending it." She then sent it by messenger to Xiangyang. When Dou Tao looked at the silk with its woven characters, he was deeply touched and amazed by its excellence. He sent Yangtai away to Guanzhong [Shaanxi province] and prepared carriages, attendants, and numerous gifts to invite Su Hui south of the Han River [to Xiangyang]. Their love was deeper than ever before.

(5) Su Hui wrote more than five thousand items of prose and verse in her lifetime, but because of the turmoil at the end of the Sui dynasty, her writings were scattered and can no longer be recovered. Only her silk-woven palindromic verse has been widely transcribed and passed down to the present day. It serves to represent all of the laments of recent generations from the inner chambers and should be taken as a model by all literary scholars. In my leisure time away from handling affairs of state, I concern myself with the texts of antiquity, and by chance I came across this diagram among some fragmentary writings. Thus, I narrate the story of Ruolan's talent and praise Lianpo's regret and self-correction. I compose this record simply for the benefit of future generations. [Dated] the first day of the fifth lunar month, the first year of the Ruyi reign [692], the imperial writing of the Heavenly-Crowned Golden-Wheel Emperor of the Great Zhou.

(*Quan Tang wen*, 97/1257–58)

par. 4, "Xuanji Diagram": See Zhu Shuzhen's "Record on Su Hui's Xuanji Diagram" (C.4.1) for an explanation of how the silk-woven palindromic verse diagram works. The diagram is reproduced as the frontispiece to Su Zhecong's anthology, *Zhongguo lidai funü zuopin xuan*.

par. 4, "a pattern of its own": The Chinese terms used here (*zi cheng wen zhang*) are polysemous and could more inclusively be translated as "of itself, it forms a complete pattern/order/writing/composition."

TRANSLATION BY HUI-SHU LEE

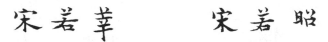

C.2. Song Ruoxin (d. 820?) and Song Ruozhao (d. 825)

Song Ruoxin and Song Ruozhao were two of the five talented sisters who impressed Emperor Dezong (r. 780–804) with their literary refinement. All five became court ladies and were asked to participate in the poetry-composing gatherings of the emperor and his ministers. Of the five sisters, Song Ruoxin was the oldest and Song Ruozhao the second oldest. They are best known for the manual titled *Nü lunyu* (The female analects), said to have been compiled by Ruoxin and annotated by Ruozhao.

When Ruoxin died, she was given the posthumous title of Commandery Mistress of Henei. Ruozhao, the most refined writer among the five sisters, shunned the sexual favors of the emperor and often compared herself to the "lady scholar" Ban Zhao. Her writings include several volumes of poetry and prose. She was appointed Shanggong, in charge of the six branches of the palace household. and retained the position through the succeeding reigns of emperors Xianzong, Muzong, and Jinzong.[1] All the princes and princesses regarded her as their mentor. She was given the posthumous title of Consort of the State of Liang.

Related to the *Analects* of Confucius only by title, the Song sisters' *Female Analects* is divided into chapters describing the various virtues and behaviors required of women. The respect with which the *Nü lunyu* was regarded is indicated by its inclusion in the imperially ordered compilation *Guige nü sishu* (The four books of the inner chambers, for women), which was compiled by a man named Wang Xian in 1580. Also included were Ban Zhao's *Nü jie* (Admonitions for women; see P.60.9), Empress Xu's *Nei xun* (Precepts for the ladies of the palace; see C.6.1), and Lady Liu's *Nü fan jeilü* (Brief notes for female guidance).

C.2.1. *Preface to* Nü lunyu

Cao Dagu remarks: "I am the wife of a virtuous man and the daughter of a distinguished family. I am somewhat in possession of the four virtues and conversant with the Classics. When I lay down my needlework and browse through books in my leisure, I am awestruck by the multitude of women in the old days who exemplified uncompromising chastity and virtues." Thinking it a great pity for women of later generations not to be able to emulate Great Lady-scholar Cao, we have written *The Female Analects*, a book that counsels women in prudence and admonition. If a woman heeds these words, she will be virtuous and wise, and she will not let her predecessors be the only role models for the generations to come.

(Hu Wenkai, 22)

par. 1, "Cao Dagu": The "Great Lady-scholar" Cao refers to Ban Zhao, sister of the historian Ban Gu and wife of Cao Shishu. On Ban and her writings, see P.60.9, P.69.5.

par. 1, "the four virtues": The four virtues refer to the moral standards prescribed for women in traditional Chinese society: proper speech, morality, diligent work, and modest manner. See P.60.9.

BACKGROUND NOTE AND TRANSLATION BY WAN LIU

C.3. Li Qingzhao (1084–ca. 1151)

On Li Qingzhao, see P.17.

C.3.1. *On the Song-Lyric* (Lun ci)

Yuefu ballads and popular song were both well in evidence during the Tang dynasty. They especially flourished during the Kaiyuan [713–41] and Tianbao [742–56] reign-periods. There was a certain Li Balang who was so fine a singer that he dominated the world. Once, when those who had just passed the examination to become *jinshi* [presented scholar] were having a banquet at Qujiang, the top one on the list of successful candidates summoned Li ahead of time. He had him change his clothing and disguise his name; putting an old and tattered cap and clothing on him, he made him look quite run-down. Together they went to the banquet, where the one said, "My cousin would like to sit at the foot of the table." No one paid any attention. When it was time for the wine to be served and for musical entertainment, singers were brought on, headed by Cao Yuanqian and Niannu. Their singing over, the top candidate, pointing at Li, said, "Let's ask my cousin to sing." Everyone laughed, and not a few were annoyed. But having vocalized a few strains, with a single song he had everyone sobbing. People formed a circle around him to pay respects, saying, "It's Li Balang!"

From this time on, the strains of Zheng and Wei [i.e., the corrupting music of states in decline] daily intensified, and licentious mutations [in song] became daily more noisome. Tune-titles of the time included the following: "Pusa man," "Chun guang hao," "Shaji zi" [The cricket], "Genglou zi" [The nighttime water clock], "Huan xi sha, "Meng Jiangnan," and "Yufu," too numerous to enumerate in full. [See Appendix A.] (2)

During the Five Dynasties, a time of strife when the realm was carved up, all culture died out. Only the sovereigns of Jiangnan, surnamed Li [Li Jing and Li Yu], as well as their minister [Feng Yansi], esteemed what was cultured and dignified. As for their poetic lines—"Done playing in a tiny pavilion, the cold of jade pipes" and "[A breeze about to rise] / Blows ripples over a pool of spring water"—even though their diction is unique in the extreme, nonetheless, as it is said, "The tones of a ruined state are filled with lament and brooding." (3)

Coming to our own dynasty, when the rites and music, the civil and military, are all well in place, it took more than a hundred years of careful nurturing before there emerged a Liu Tuntian or a Liu Yong, to transform old songs and fashion new ones. He issued a *Yuezhang ji* [Collection of musical compositions], which gained the widespread approval of the age. Even though his compositions accord with the rules of prosody, their language is lower than dust. (4)

Then Zhang Xian, Song Qi and his brother, Shen Tang, Yuan Jiang, Chao Duanli, and their crowd appeared in succession. Although at times their expression is marvelous, since this occurs only in fragments, overall how can they be counted famous writers? (5)

Coming to Yan Shu, Ouyang Xiu, and Su Shi, even though in learning they were virtual celestials, they composed but minor song-lyrics. These can best be likened to dipping a gourd of water from the great sea. Their compositions are nothing more than *shi* poems made up of lines of uneven length and often do not accord with the rules of prosody. (6)

How is this so? *Shi* poetic writing makes the distinction between level and oblique [*ping/ze*] tones. But in the song-lyric, there is the additional classifi- (7)

cation of the five tones [*yin*], the additional classification of the five sounds [*sheng*], the additional classification of the six pitches [*lü*], and the additional classifications of the clear and the muddy [*qingzhuo*] and the light and the heavy [*qingzhong*].

(8) Furthermore, in recent times the song-tunes titled "Sheng sheng man," "Yuzhong hua," and "Xi qianying" [Rejoicing that the warbler has flown] either use a *pingsheng* rhyme or additionally use a *rusheng* one. "Yulou chun" originally could use a *pingsheng* rhyme, but it can also employ a *shang-* or *qu sheng* or a *rusheng*. A tune to a *zesheng* rhyme can work well with a *shangsheng*, but a *rusheng* would make it unsingable. As for Wang Anshi and Zeng Gong, their writings are like those of the Western Han [i.e., full of difficult characters]; if they manage a minor song-lyric, people are overwhelmed, finding it unreadable.

(9) Song-lyrics form a realm of their own. Those aware of this fact are few. Only when Yan Jidao, Ho Zhu, Qin Guan, and Huang Tingjian emerged on the scene was there recognition of the fact. Yet Yan is sadly lacking in more extended narrative, and Ho has lamentably little classic gravity. As for Qin, he puts great store on the expression of feeling, and gives scant attention to the substantive and real. His writing is like a beautiful woman of poor family—it is not that she is not alluringly beautiful, it is just that in the end she lacks a wealthy, high-born air. Huang, on the other hand, esteems the substantive and real, yet has numerous defects. His writing is like a fine jade with flaws, whose worth is thereby diminished by half.

(Guo Shaoyu and Wang Wensheng, eds., *Zhongguo lidai wenlun xuan*, 2: 350–54)

The text of "Lun ci" on which the present translation is based is the *Tiaoxi yuyin conghua* text (Houji, *juan* 33), as reprinted with added punctuation and notes by Guo Shaoyu and Wang Wensheng. With specific reference to this piece, see also Wixted, "The Poetry of Li Ch'ing-chao," esp. pp. 160–62.

par. 3, "all culture died out": An echo of *Analects* 9.5.

par. 3, "Done playing . . . spring water": Translations from Bryant, *Lyric Poets of the Southern T'ang*, pp. 64 (Li Yu) and 35 (Feng Yansi).

par. 3, "lament and brooding": Li Qingzhao refers here to "Yue ji" (Record of music), *Li ji* (Records of ritual). Translation from Owen, *Readings in Chinese Literary Thought*, p. 52.

par. 6, "a gourd of water from the great sea": In other words, something very simple to do, according to Guo Shaoyu and Wang Wensheng.

par. 7, "level and oblique [*ping/ze*] tones": This distinction is essential for the composition of Recent-Style *shi* poetry (*jinti shi*), namely *jueju* quatrains and *lüshi* regulated verse. The four tones of northern Chinese of the time (*ping*, *shang*, *qu*, and *ru*) were divided into "level" (*ping*) and oblique tones (the other three—*ze*). The "level" tone later split to become the first and second tones of modern Mandarin, *shang* became the modern third tone, *qu* the modern fourth tone, and *rusheng* (*ru*-tone or *ru*-sound) characters came to be distributed among all four modern tones. For discussion of prosody in the poetry of the time, including rhyme and *ping/ze* tones, see Radtke, "The Development of Chinese Versification."

par. 7, "the five tones [*yin*]": The five tones of early Chinese music (*gong, shang, jue, zhi, yu*) "are not to be construed as fixed pitches but are rather a 'movable doh scale [Needham].' When any one of the five was fixed with a keynote, the entire group was fixed with respect to pitch and became a mode-key, i.e., a distinct performance group of five tones" (DeWoskin, *A Song for One or Two*, p. 44).

par. 7, "the five sounds [*sheng*]": Perhaps the five sounds are those identified by Zhang Yan (thirteenth century, using the term, "five tones") as being associated with the lips, teeth, throat, tongue, and nose. The "five sounds" may refer to the "five tones," and vice versa.

par. 7, "the six pitches [*lü*]": See DeWoskin, *A Song for One or Two*, pp. 46–48 and 85.

par. 7, "clear and muddy [*qingzhuo*] . . . light and heavy [*qingzhong*]": "Clear" and "muddy" "are variously explained as 'high' and 'low' when referring to pitch, 'unvoiced' and 'voiced' when referring to speech, and 'pure' and 'resonant' when referring to timbre" (DeWoskin, *A Song for One or Two*, p. 125). "Light" and "heavy" presumably indicate "unstressed" and "stressed."

par. 8, "people are overwhelmed": The phrase *juedao* means to be so overwhelmed that one breaks out in laughter, swoons from grief, or is awestruck with admiration—laughter being the likely implication here.

TRANSLATION BY JOHN TIMOTHY WIXTED

朱淑真

C.4. Zhu Shuzhen (13th century)

This Zhu Shuzhen, who lived in the early thirteenth century, is not to be confused with the twelfth-century poet Zhu Shuzhen (P.18).[1] Her "Xuanji tu ji" (Record on Su Hui's Xuanji diagram) was not included in any of the anthologies of her writings, nor is it recorded in any other early sources. It is only found in Wang Shizhen's (1634–1711) *Chibei outan*. Wang writes that he saw the original manuscript in Zhu's own writing while he was in the capital in the year 1671. The frontispiece title to her scroll read "Xuanji bianhua" (The transformations of the Xuanji diagram). At the end of the scroll were mounted four illustrations by the Ming dynasty artist Qiu Ying (ca. 1494–1552). The text that is translated here omits the beginning narration, which is taken from Wu Zetian's "On Su Hui's 'Silk-Woven Palindromic Verse' " (C.1.1).

C.4.1. Record on Su Hui's Xuanji Diagram

Empress Wu Zetian of the Tang dynasty once inscribed a preface for this Xuanji [palindrome] diagram. However, some of the characters have become corrupted over time and can no longer be read. In the past my father traveled around west Zhejiang on official business. He was fond of collecting elegant objects and was willing to pay a high price for whatever appealed to him. One day, while my father was attending a banquet at a local official's residence, he unexpectedly spotted this diagram on the wall. He managed to purchase it and brought it home to give to me. Thereafter, I found myself studying it constantly. Finally, I awakened to the principle of the diagram. Following the vertical longitudes and horizontal latitudes, I sought the verses, and as I had expected, it read fluently.

(2) The Xuanji functions like the Heavenly Platter itself. While the longitudes and latitudes are the moving tracks of the constellations, in the middle a single "eye" is preserved that serves as the Heavenly Heart [the character *xin*, "heart," in the very center]. This is like the fixed star [Polaris] that does not move. The constellations revolve in their paths, never straying by a single degree, guided by this controlling star that sits in the middle.

(3) The Central Square [of eight characters around the central character *xin*] can be equated with the constellation Grand Palace. When each character is repeated once, a four-character poem emerges. One then goes on to the Second Square, which can be equated with the Purple Palace. Four-character palindromic poems are located here. The four rectangles growing out of the four sides of the Second Square form five-character palindromic poems, while in the four squares off of the corners of the Second Square one finds four-character palindromic poems. In the four rectangles growing out of the four sides of the Third Square are four-character poems, if only the last character of one line is repeated as the first character of the next line. (These lines, however, cannot be read in reverse.) In the four squares adjacent to the corners of the Third Square are three-character palindromic poems. The perimeter of the Third Square and the perimeter of the entire diagram are all seven-character palindromic poems which can be read in different directions following the boundaries. Inscribed on the eighteenth day of the second lunar month, in

the spring of the third year of the Shaoding reign [1230], by the Laywoman who Roosts in the Hidden, Zhu Shuzhen of Qiantang.

(Wang Shizhen, *Chibei outan*, pp. 366–67; Su Zhecong, pp. 61–63)

par. 3, "the constellation Grand Palace": In Chinese this is *Taiwei yuan*, otherwise known as *Taiwei gong*. This constellation is considered the Heavenly Emperor's southern palace in the sky, located on the ecliptic in Virgo and Leo. Zhu Shuzhen also refers to the Purple Tenuity Palace, *Ziwei yuan* or *Ziwei gong*, where the Heavenly Emperor resided. It partly corresponds the western constellations Cassiopeia and Ursa Major. See Schafer, *Pacing the Void*, pp. 47, 52. In her explanation of the Xuanji diagram, Zhu Shuzhen borrows two of the three heavenly *yuan* (walls) of Chinese astronomy to describe two square fields of characters, one surrounding the other, in the diagram.

par. 3, "following the boundaries": In fact, there are various other boundaries around the squares that Zhu Shuzhen delineates, and poems can be read along each of these palindromically.

TRANSLATION BY HUI-SHU LEE

鄭允端

C.5. Zheng Yunduan (ca. 1327–56)

On Zheng Yunduan and her poetry collection *Suyong ji* (Solemn harmonies), see P.24.

C.5.1. Preface to Suyong ji

The Zheng family belongs to an aristocratic clan and has produced generations of Confucian scholars. My father and older brothers are well-known in Wu for having taught the Classics to students in the area. When I was young I inherited this family tradition and was taught how to read. Later, as I turned to studying, I stole snippets of knowledge and thus gained a rough idea of moral principles. I grew up and was married to Shi Boren, of the same prefecture. Boren's family had also been long established as a clan well schooled in the literary arts, and Boren himself was a cultured scholar. Our interests were thus shared. In my free time from the duties as a wife I would play with brush and ink and express my feelings in poetry. In the past I have been critical of the fact that women of recent times who wrote poetry had no thought for expressing inspiring and admonitory ideas. Rather, mostly they would sing noisily of wind and moon, express their deepest emotions with delicate and sentimental words, and linger in their feelings for the moment and place. Wishing to abolish these old habits, to toss aside these common banalities, I composed a number of songs and poems and sealed them in a wicker box to await some skilled master who could correct them before I showed them to many people. I have been ill now for a number of years, and I know that my death is not far off. Fearful that after I die no one will hear my poems, I have transcribed them onto new paper and arranged them to make a volume. It will be kept in the family school to be shown to our descendants. In the past the Mountain Man Tang wrote on his "poetry gourd," "Whoever reads this will know the labors of my heart." I feel the same way. *Bingshen* year of the Zhizheng reign [1356], on the day of the Qingming Festival, written by Zheng Yunduan of Yingyang.

(Hu Wenkai, 75–76)

The title of Zheng's collection derives from poem 24 of the *Book of Odes*: "Shall we not greet with solemn harmony / The chariot of the royal lady Ji?"

par. 1, Tang's poetry gourd: This refers to the Tang dynasty scholar Tang Qiu, who lived on a mountain by the Weijiang River in a remote area of Shu (Sichuan province). He kept his poetry drafts rolled up in a big gourd, which he tossed into the river when he felt that his end was near, saying, "If this writing does not sink, whoever finds it may know the labors of my heart." The gourd floated to Xinqu, where someone who recognized its contents remarked, "This is the gourd of the Mountain Man Tang" (Ji Yougong, *Tang shi jishi*, 50/626).

TRANSLATION BY PETER STURMAN

徐皇后

c.6. Empress Xu (1362–1407)

Empress Xu was the eldest daughter of Xu Da (1332–85), the Duke of Zhongshan, one of the main contributors to the founding of the Ming dynasty. According to her official biography, from the time she was a child she was known as chaste and serene of temperament and broadly learned.[1] The founder of the Ming dynasty, the Hongwu Emperor (r. 1368–98), proposed a marriage between his fourth son, the Prince of Yan (Zhu Li), and Xu Da's daughter, who was then fifteen years old. The Prince of Yan later became the Yongle Emperor (r. 1402–24). As empress, Lady Xu gained a lasting reputation both for feminine virtue and literary talent. Her mother-in-law, Empress Gao (1332–

82), is said to have been deeply fond of her, and Empress Xu returned the favor, respecting Gao as her mentor and crediting her as the primary inspiration behind her writing. After Empress Xu's death at the age of forty-five, Yongle never installed another empress to succeed her. She was given the posthumous title Renxiao (Human-Hearted and Filial).

Besides two prose works, *Nei xun* (Precepts for the ladies of the palace) and *Quanshan shu* (Exhortations for good deeds), a small collection of poetry in one *juan* is recorded for Empress Xu. *Nei xun* (1404) is her best-known work. As she states in her preface, which integrates the titles of her twenty precepts (with the exception of the fifteenth: "Conduct During Sacrifices"), the goal behind the compilation was to provide a written set of guidelines for the ladies of the inner palace. The Wanli Emperor (r. 1572–1620) later ordered the Confucian scholar Wang Xiang to provide notes and commentary to Empress Xu's *Nei xun*. The whole was then published together with three other works by women for women: Ban Zhao's (ca. 49—120) *Nü jie* (Admonitions for women; see 60.9), Song Ruoxin and Song Ruozhao's *Nü lunyu* (The female analects; see C.2), and the *Nü fan jielü* (Brief notes for female guidance) by Wang Xiang's mother, Lady Liu. In emulation of Zhu Xi's basic Confucian syllabus, the *Four Books*, these were given the collective title *Guige nü sishu* (The four books of the inner chambers, for women).[2]

C.6.1. Preface to Nei xun

As a child, I received the teachings of my parents, reciting the standards expressed in poetry and in the Classics as well as learning the skills befitting a woman. Benefiting from the accumulated good deeds of my ancestors, I was chosen to become an imperial consort while still young. I was given the honor of attending to Empress Gao. During this period of attendance, day and night the Empress would instruct all of the women of the imperial family to be ever cautious and vigilant in pursuing the rules of decorum. I humbly respected her as a model of propriety and carefully listened to her words of admonition. I admired her and dared not disobey.

I have reverently served the present emperor for over thirty years, following (2)
Empress Gao's will and applying it to the affairs of governance and education. When I reflect on my position as empress, however, I am ashamed of my insufficient virtue and feel apologetic for my inability to provide a proper model. Nor can I assist the emperor, my husband, in governing the affairs of the inner palace and thus have not fulfilled the teachings of Empress Gao.

(3) Oftentimes I peruse historical biographies in search of wise and chaste women of the past. Even though many were well known for their good and virtuous natures, none ever achieved success without proper education. In ancient times there was always a way to teaching. At the age of eight, young boys began elementary learning [*xiaoxue*]. At the age of ten, young girls began to receive instructions from their mothers. Books for elementary learning were not transmitted to later times. Thus Master Zhu composed and edited one set, providing the means by which young boys could begin their studies. However, there were still no texts for young girls. People simply took as lessons Madame Cao's [Ban Zhao's] "Precepts for Women" [*Nü jie*], which had been included in Fan Ye's *History of the Latter Han*. Madame Cao's text, however, was insufficient because of its brevity and simplicity. As for the so-called "Female Guidance" [*Nü xian*] and "Female Principles" [*Nü ze*], these are little more than titles. Only in recent years have instruction books for young women become popular, but these usually are little more than compilations of phrases regarding the behavior of women taken from the "Lesser Rituals" section of the Rites, the Little Prefaces to the "Zhou nan" and "Shao nan" sections of the *Book of Odes*, and some biographies.

(4) The great teachings of Empress Gao, familiar to my ear and stored in my heart, are far superior to those of the past and sufficient to set as a model for generations to come. Thus, in the winter of the second year of the Yongle reign [1404], I narrate Empress Gao's teachings and compile them under twenty headings to be collectively titled *Precepts for Ladies of the Palace* [*Nei xun*]. These will serve to make her teachings known and to provide instructions to the palace women.

(5) For following the way of a sage and cultivating oneself, nothing is more important than nurturing one's moral character. Accordingly, I list *Moral Character* as the foremost heading and *Self-Cultivation* as the second. They are followed by *Circumspect Speech* and *Discreet Behavior* since these two are most crucial for cultivating oneself. From these we are led to *Diligence* and *Frugality*, and from these to *Vigilance*. Moreover, among the means by which one attains long-term good fortune, none is better than *Accumulation of Good Deeds*. Conversely, for being faultless, nothing is superior to the *Reformation of Bad to Good*. The above are all crucial to one's self-cultivation, and in order to adopt these rules, one must follow the teachings of Empress Gao. Thus *Respecting Sacred Teachings* is the succeeding heading. To go further, one adopts lessons from the ancients. Thus, *Cherishing Virtuous Models* is the next.

Concerning one's superiors, there are the precepts *Attending to One's Parents*, *Serving the Emperor*, and *Attending to One's Parents-in-Law*. These lead to the precepts *Being a Model Mother*, *Harmonizing Relations in the Family*, *Kindness to Youth*, and *Treating One's Subordinates*. Finally, at the end is *Dealing with Maternal Imperial Relatives*.

Because my words and phrases are shallow and coarse, I fail to enhance (6)
the profound meanings. Moreover, the headings are in somewhat unpolished form. The reader of these precepts should not be bound by the words, but rather simply seek their meanings. Then it may be possible to gain some small benefit in the handling of domestic matters.

(Hu Wenkai, 138–40)

par. 3, "Master Zhu": This refers to Zhu Xi's (1130–1200) *Xiaoxue jijie* (preface dated 1175), which served as a textbook for young Chinese boys.

par. 3, "Fan Ye's *History*": See *Hou Han shu*, 84/3377–80.

par. 3, "*Nü xian, Nü ze*": There is no record today of *Nü xian*. *Nü ze* is said to have been composed by Empress Changsun, consort of the Tang dynasty emperor Taizong; see Hu Wenkai, pp. 27–28.

par. 3, Rites, *Book of Odes*: The "Qu li" chapter of the *Li ji* (Records of ritual) is concerned with the proper deportment of inferiors in the presence of superiors. The Little Preface preceding the "Zhou nan" section of the *Book of Odes* contains moral lessons for imperial ladies, and that preceding "Shao nan" discusses the role of aristocratic women.

BACKGROUND NOTE AND TRANSLATION BY HUI-SHU LEE

孟淑卿

C.7. Meng Shuqing (fl. 1476)

On Meng Shuqing, see P.30. Meng was known during her lifetime for her poetry and her astute and outspoken views on literature. Unhappy in her marriage, she earned the disapproval of contemporaries by flouting social conventions and openly receiving guests.[1] Her disapproval, recorded here, of the Song poets Zhu Shuzhen (P.18) and Li Qingzhao (P.17) seems in keeping with her reputation for eccentricity.

C.7.1. Comments on Zhu Shuzhen and Li Qingzhao

Meng Shuqing, a native of Suzhou, was the daughter of Deng, the assistant instructor. She was a skillful poet and called herself "Reclusive Scholar of Mount Jing." Once she said this about Zhu Shuzhen's poetry: "In poetry writing one strives to 'escape from the embryo' and transform the substance. This means that in poetry written by Buddhist monks, the best is that which is free of the aura of burning incense. Face powder is to be handled similarly. Mistress Zhu's poetry is ultimately flawed by vulgarity. She can only be discussed together with Li Yi'an [Li Qingzhao]."

(Chen Jiru, *Taiping qinghua*, 3/53–54, quoted in Wang Xuechu, annot., *Li Qingzhao ji jiaozhu*, p. 321)

BACKGROUND NOTE AND TRANSLATION BY RONALD EGAN

沈宜修

C.8. Shen Yixiu (1590–1635) and Her Husband, Ye Shaoyuan (1589–1649)

On Shen Yixiu, see P.54. Shen (style name Wanjun) compiled a one-*juan* anthology of poems, song-lyrics, rhapsodies, and prose writings by women titled *Yiren si* (Thoughts of one far away). It is included in the *Wumengtang ji* (Collection of the Hall of Noontime Dreams) of her husband Ye Shaoyuan (style name Tianliao), a compilation of the many works written by and addressed to his female relations that he edited from 1632 to 1636.[1]

The title of Shen Yixiu's collection employs a phrase, *yiren* ("that person"), that appears in poems in the *Book of Odes* in the context of a search for a lover or companion; see Ye Shaoyuan's preface (C.8.2) for the specific references. According to subheadings in the *Wumengtang ji* edition, the collection's contents were drawn from a variety of sources: works of eighteen authors from printed editions; nine from unpublished manuscripts; six encountered fortuitously through personal transmission; and eleven found recorded in miscellaneous notes (*biji*) and other scattered texts. In addition, an appendix supplies the works of two authors communicated after death through séances—an unusual method of text-gathering sometimes practiced in the late Ming. The collection of 241 poems was published by Ye Shaoyuan after his wife's death. Both Shen Yixiu and Ye Shaoyuan composed prefaces for the anthology.

C.8.1. *Shen Yixiu's Preface to* Yiren si

Contemporary anthologies of the poetry and prose of famous women are numerous indeed, but the great majority of them are concerned with preserving works of antiquity and do not broaden their purview to include the present. The Grand Historian [Sima Qian, ca. 145–90 B.C.E.] in his biography of Guan [Zhong] and Yan [Ying] says: "Their writings are widely available now, so I shall not discuss them; I shall speak rather of affairs that have become scattered and neglected." I will venture to emulate his intention; thus from those authors who have been recorded in other collections of precious gems I shall not select again. My husband has publicized unknown works that may be deemed of anecdotal interest, and others may also already be in public circulation. However, as the days and months pass, they sink from sight, or mountains and rivers impede their transmission—which is certainly to be sighed over. Now from these slivers of jade that have reached my ears, as well as desultory reading in other books, I have assembled a collection of which I dare not eliminate anything. Only after a far-ranging search can one hope for resplendent comprehensiveness.

(Ye Shaoyun, comp., *Wumengtang ji*, 2, second p. 1; see also Hu Wenkai, 115).

par. 1, Guan Zhong and Yan Ying: Guan Zhong was a famous minister and military strategist to Duke Huan of Qi during the Spring and Autumn period; he died in the forty-first year of the duke's reign, 643 B.C.E. Yan Ying, or Yan Pingzhong, took office in Qi about a century later, in 555 B.C.E., and was the author of the *Yanzi chunqiu* (Master Yang's annals). Their biographies constitute *juan* 62 of Sima Qian's *Shi ji*.

C.8.2. *Ye Shaoyuan's Preface to* Yiren si

The *Book of Odes* says:

Green, green are rushes and reeds,
White dew becomes frost.
He whom I call "that person"
Is by the side of the water.

It also says:

Consider those birds:
They seek the sounds of their companions.
Even more does that person
Not also seek for his companion?

Thus we know that though the Big Dipper lies across the sky from Shen [in Orion], hovering clouds gather together. Fragrant grass follows the same principle [of evoking unswerving fidelity], and thoughts lodged in a secluded cassia can arouse a mutual longing. Over mountains and rivers we return to share the pleasures of wind and moon. With zither, wine goblet, and companions we fully appreciate the mists and clouds. Like-minded friends take deep pleasure in long-lasting intimacy and a far-roving spirit.

(2) I earnestly spread rushes out for old acquaintances. To my astonishment I gained as bosom friend someone in a silk gauze skirt. For after all, just as the birds ardently cry *yingying* in search of the sounds of their companions, should a beautiful woman not also be able to share such affection? Why must her interests be [limited to] hibiscus jackets, coiling bracelets, pomegranate [lips], blackened eyebrows, combs, and hairpins; to the green bamboo mat, piping harmonies on a mouth organ; or to following dance steps in red-lined garments; to the beauties of fragrant ointments and feathery adornments; to shuttle and treadle, weaving thin yellow silk at the loom, in what has been called women's work?

(3) My wife Shen Wanjun was a person of far-reaching emotions and melancholy singularity, of broad-minded nature and unoccupied solitude. In her leisure she chanted "The Mulberries by the Path," and composed poems in imitation of "The Round Fan." She was vexed that though exemplary models were near at hand, recorded standards were far away. Focusing on famous gentry women poets of recent times, she collected some of their works and selected from them the finest lines, setting their clear tones forth for us. They are like colors gleaming from a brocade bag, or fragrance wafting from latticed-silk sleeves. From the Shining Consort on the Tartar frontier one returns to linger on the islet of sweet pollia. The imperial daughter by the waves of the Xiang River is none other than the companion of Divine Balance. Bewitching flowers extend for ten miles and cause orioles to chirp everywhere in springtime trees. Evening birds through layered curtains partially enter dreams under autumn lamplight. But silently combing one's hair before a mirrored dressing case and secret chants before needle and loom frame lack the value of stitched book covers at the market hall, where gold is spent on paper.

(4) Now my wife is gone, but her chapters most certainly remain. These scattered and fragmentary pieces lie desolate in my portfolio. In isolation and neglect, by whom can they be appreciated? They are but scant remnants of an intimate and precious book. Alas, how can I bear them, since they are like a

neighbor's flute? I have transmitted my heart's grief in this funeral inscription so that it can go out to the world of men and offer a refined pleasure within the boudoirs of young women. May it therefore be cut on wooden printing-blocks.

Written in the *bingzi* year of the Chongzhen reign period [1636], on the fifteenth day of the fourth month, by Ye Tianliao (Shaoyuan).

(*Wumengtang ji*, 2, first p. 1.)

par. 1, *Book of Odes*, first quote: Poem 129; cf. Karlgren, *Book of Odes*, pp. 83–84.

par. 1, *Book of Odes*, second quote: Poem 165; cf. Karlgren, *Book of Odes*, pp. 108–9.

par. 1, "clouds gather together": According to the preface to Tao Qian's (365–427) series of poems titled *Ting yun*, the title phrase, which translates as "hovering clouds," evokes thoughts of intimate friends. See Hightower, trans., *The Poetry of T'ao Ch'ien*, p. 11.

par. 1, "fragrant grass": On the associations of fragrant grass (*fang cao*) with virtue and loyalty, see P.54a.2 and P.114.14.

par. 2, "spread rushes out for old acquaintances": The two old friends Wu Ju of Chu and Sheng Zi of Cai spread rushes when they met for a meal on the outskirts of the state of Zheng to discuss the feasibility of Wu's return to Chu after a forced flight from his home; see *Zuo zhuan*, Duke Xiang, year 26. What is translated as "old acquaintances" is literally, "white silk belt" (*gao dai*), referring to a gift presented by the Ducal Son Zha of Wu to Zichan of Zheng, whom the former treated as an old acquaintance upon meeting him; see *Zuo zhuan*, Duke Xiang, year 29.

par. 2, "sound of their companions": See the second quote from the *Book of Odes*, poem 165, above.

par. 3, "Mulberries by the Path": *Mo shang sang*, a well-known *yuefu* (Music Bureau song) that focuses on the stock folk figure of a beautiful young woman named Luofu; see P.76.2.

par. 3, "The Round Fan": A reference to the "Song of Resentment" by Ban *jieyu* (P.1.1).

par. 3, "brocade bag": Like the satchel into which the late Tang poet Li He (791–817) was said to have tossed lines of poetry he had composed while traveling.

par. 3, "Shining Consort": A reference to Wang Zhaojun, on whom see P.58b.9.

par. 3, "sweet pollia": Sweet pollia is plucked on a fragrant islet in the Xiang River by the shaman speaker awaiting a tryst with the coy object of his affections in the poem "The Princess of the Xiang," the third of the "Nine Songs" collected in the *Songs of Chu*.

par. 3, "imperial daughter": This refers to one or both of the two daughters of the legendary king Yao, E Huang and Nü Ying, on whom see P.1.2 and P.37.1.

par. 3, "Divine Balance": In Chinese *Ling jun*, one of the names given to Qu Yuan, on whom see P.54a.16.

par. 4, "neighbor's flute": Music that serves as a painful reminder of the past, as does the flute mentioned in the preface to Ma Rong's (79–166) "Chang di fu," included in the *Wen xuan*, 18/1b.

BACKGROUND NOTE AND TRANSLATION BY PAULINE YU

陸卿子

C.9. Lu Qingzi (fl. 1600)

Lu Qingzi (see P.52 and C.33) composed a preface for Xiang Lanzhen's (P.57) collection of poems titled *Yongxue zhai yigao* (Manuscripts from the Snow-Praising Studio), published early in the seventeenth century.

C.9.1. Preface to Xiang Lanzhen, Yongxue zhai yigao

As women, we need to devote attention to cooking and preparing wines and broths, for these are assuredly our duties. When we have to abstain from our duties because of illness, we emulate the women of ancient times and make poems by following sounds and customs that have been handed down. Poetry is definitely not the calling of men; it is really what belongs by right to us women. I used to regret that there were no accomplished lyrics to transmit our ambitions, and I felt acutely ashamed. But now we have Madame Huang of Jiahe, whose maiden name was Xiang Shu [Lanzhen]. She was an outstanding talent of a famous inner chamber, nourished in a noble family in which the classics and histories are transmitted, one which has made refined writing its business for generations. Dipping her brush in ink, she can compose without pausing for thought. Each time she puts pen to paper, she captures beautiful words in an accomplished style. With graceful ease and fresh beauty, her writing embodies all the marvels, dazzling the reader's eyes and startling the heart. Men of letters cannot achieve this, but you can. To you it is as easy as taking pearls out of a bag. If you haven't retained talents and feelings from former lives, how can this be possible?

(2) Recorded works by women are few and far between; the number of survivals decreases even more the longer they are handed down. And those who sympathize with women's works record, through ignorance, only what is dull among them, so that our works seem to be not much different from chaff in a year of famine—rough and worthless, but still all there is to be gleaned.

In future, those who are moved and inspired by Madame's work will not be limited to the cleverest among the young. Therefore I know that, as jade ringing on metal brings out its sound, we can expect that you will become a great poet of our age of peace. Because you have so kindly treated me as a friend, I have written this as encouragement: please do not be too modest. After I read your *Caiyun cao* (Cloud-tailoring drafts), the surrounding mountains all turned into fine jades and tinkling pendants. The mountain dwellers will not be poor at all! I inscribe these few words at random for the *Yongxue zhai* Collection. (3)

(Hu Wenkai, 176)

TRANSLATION BY GRACE S. FONG

方維儀

C.10. Fang Weiyi (1585–1668)

On Fang Weiyi, see P.55. She wrote this preface for a collection of poems by her sister Fang Mengshi, *Renlan'ge shiji* (Collected poems from the Orchid-Stitching Pavilion).

C.10.1. Preface to Fang Mengshi, Renlan'ge shiji

The poems in *Renlan'ge shiji* are apt to provoke the deepest sadness in the reader. My elder sister has exhausted her heart and will in the face of the many afflictions of her life. For this reason she exerts herself in her devotion to songs and verse.

Alas! My sister is by nature loyal, filial, reverent, and chaste. She has a quick mind and loves learning. So talented is she that she started composing at age nine, emulating [the girl prodigy Xie Daoyun's] snowflake lines. Our late father, Tingwei, was extremely fond of her. He often gazed at her and sighed: "I would love to have a son like her; too bad that she is a girl." At marriageable age, she was wedded to the magistrate Mr. [Zhang] Zhongyang. In serving her in-laws and husband, she devoted herself to the womanly way, winning the praise of elders in both families. Following the official appointments of her husband, she traveled far and wide, trekking through Beijing, Fujian, the land of Chu, Guangdong, Qingquan [Hunan province], and Xun- (2)

yang [Jiangxi province]. She assisted him in his duties, and the two composed poems in matching rhymes to celebrate a relationship of harmony and respect.

(3) Not until she was over twenty did she give birth to a son. All her daughters having died in infancy, she arranged for her husband to take a concubine. While trying to make sure that his line would prosper, she managed to have a son as harbinger of her later fortunes. With frugality she managed the household; with industry she provided for the food and wine. Treating the concubine and maids as if they were her own daughters, she taught them the "Seven Admonitions," the *Odes*, and the *Rituals*. Hence her husband the magistrate greatly benefited from her role as an inner helpmate.

(4) I grieve that my elder sister has met many unexpected misfortunes and is now left to mourning on her own. Although her name is known throughout the world for her talent, and she may be compared to a kindly downward-bending tree, nonetheless her honors have not brought her peace of mind. Despite all the difficulties she has encountered, those above and below alike burdened her with more duties. Who has shown her sympathy? Any other would have shrunk from such worries, yet my elder sister has steadfastly practiced the four teachings. She remained generous and cheerful in the service of her husband. Grayed, lonesome, stricken, and ill, she strikes the *qin* and chants her verse, calling on the brisk wind and the clear moon to bring her relief. As one born of the same womb, I grieve for her while respecting and admiring her. Hence I do not intend to dwell only on how deep her wounds are.

(Hu Wenkai, 83–84)

par. 2, Xie Daoyun's "snowflake lines": See C.24.1.

TRANSLATION BY DOROTHY KO

王微

C.11. Wang Wei (ca. 1600–ca. 1647)

On Wang Wei and her poetry collections *Wanzai pian* (As if I were there) and *Yueguan shi* (Poems from shaded halls), see P.62.

C.11.1. Preface to Wanzai pian

Whenever I need to rest, I steal away to the mountains and streams. I have named my poetry collection *Wanzai* for this reason—not because I dare to compare myself to the *yiren*, the person pursued in the poem from the *Book of Odes*. Alas, how deeply have I felt the vicissitudes of being and non-being, of life and death! All too aware of the frailties of the body, why haven't I thrown away my writing brush, burned my ink slab, and vowed to forsake "cunning words"? Have I not, moreover, let myself take pride and delight in these writings of no greater value than the chirping of cicadas or the murmur of earthworms in their tunnels? "The autumn water swells; the dewy wind waxes"—if there are indeed emotions in these, who can capture them? I have spoken too much; but I did not realize how much I was speaking.

(Hu Wenkai, 88)

par. 1, "*yiren*": On this expression, see c.8.

par. 1, "cunning words": A Buddhist term (*qiyu*), one of the "ten evils" believed to be cause for transmigration.

c.11.2. Preface to Yueguan shi

Not having been born a man, I cannot right all wrong that prevails under heaven; instead I had to work within the confines of one room. During the time left from devotions and reciting sutras, every word and every chant that came upon me, be it in remembrance of flowers in rain or longing for waters and mountains, all arose from mighty gusts of inspiration and did not come to rest until my sentiments had been lodged [in a poem]. I venture to say that in this world of ours, it is through grass that spring may be known and through leaves that autumn may be known; any scenario or color that happens to be is poetry. Can such poetry be expressed in words? Or can it not be expressed in words?

(Hu Wenkai, 88)

TRANSLATION BY DOROTHY KO

c.12. Wu Xiao (mid–17th century)

On Wu Xiao and her poetry collection *Xiaoxue an gao* (Manuscripts from Howling-Snow Studio, 1659), see P.73.

C.12.1. Preface to Xiaoxue an gao

From an early age, I have been unusually devoted to poetry. Learning from Cai Yan's book on the zither and inspired by the pen and ink stone of Lady Zhen (wife of Emperor Wen of Wei), I have read voluminously and taken notes on my readings for over twenty years. On winter nights or summer days, in good states of mind and bad, I have never failed to express my feelings in writing.

(2) In assessing the talent of women writers, I feel that Han Ying's abilities are not up to Zuo Fen's [P.3] and that Xu Shu's writings are inferior to Ban *jieyu*'s [P.1]. Even imagining that I, weak vessel that I am, had been born in an earlier age, it is unlikely that with my many defects I would have helped to transmit the *Rites of Zhou* or completed the *History of the Han*. But as for singing and chanting, I daresay I have some small gift, and in that respect I need not entirely efface myself before the ancients. In recent years I read a book entitled *Records of the Immortals of Yongcheng* and was impressed at how female immortals, garbed in feathers, succeeded in the examinations. I also read a book entitled *True Teachings* and on seeing the part about Consort An of Nine Flower Mountain, whose literary talent was outstanding, I admired her compositions with all my heart. Traveling around the five sacred mountains of China or floating on the three mountains of the boundless sea is not an activity fit for women, but when I look out upon clouds and mists or gaze at the sun and moon, these domains do not seem far away. Accordingly, I have devoted myself to a Daoist style of life, wear simple clothes, and eat vegetarian foods.

(3) At the end of last month, I happened to be straightening out my old writing chest and noticed that my compositions to date had filled it to capacity. Lush gardens full of flowers, evening views from the women's quarters, a day, a night, a word, a laugh—nothing that had ever caught my attention was omitted. I copied everything over and came up with these two volumes of writings. Unlike peaches and plums, people cannot express themselves without words; unlike daylilies and thyme, worldly affairs are never free of troubles. I am overcome with such thoughts as I set down my pen.

(Hu Wenkai, 106)

On the date of *Xiaoxue an gao*, see Sun Dianqi, *Fanshu ouji*, p. 503. Hu Wenkai notes a later collection of works by Wu Xiao published in 1695, but this is certainly a reedition.

par. 1, Lady Zhen: For more on Lady Zhen, see Tan Jiading, *Zhongguo wenxuejia da cidian*, p. 80.

par. 2, Han Ying: By Han Ying is meant Han Lanying; see P.95.1 and C.23.4.

par. 2, Xu Shu: See P.54a.4.

par. 2, *Rites of Zhou* and *History of the Han*: For these signal accomplishments of Mother Wei (also known as Lady Song) and Ban Zhao, see C.47.1, par. 12, and P.69.5.

par. 2, *Records of the Immortals of Yongcheng*: A book about female immortals by Du Guangting of the Tang dynasty.

par. 2, *True Teachings*: By Tao Hongjing, a Daoist recluse of the Liang dynasty.

TRANSLATION BY ELLEN WIDMER

王端淑

C.13. Wang Duanshu (1621–ca. 1706)

On Wang Duanshu and her anthology *Mingyuan shiwei* (MYSW, The longitudinal canon of poetry by women of note, 1667), see P.69.

C.13.1. Preface to Mingyuan shiwei

Someone asked me: "The Canon of Poetry is a classic [*jing*]; why do you take your title from apocryphal and extracanonical works [*wei*]? *The Book of Changes*, the *Records of Ritual*, the *Book of Music*, and the *Spring and Autumn Annals* all have their apocrypha, but why must you allude to a nonexistent 'Apocryphal Canon of Poetry'?"

I answered: "The sun and the moon, the rivers and streams all take their (2) vertical bearings from heaven and their horizontal bearings from earth. Thus the poetry of heaven and earth is made up of a stable and unchanging part—namely the Classics [*jing*]—and of a part in constant motion, which is the *wei*. The *jing* markers, canonical and unalterable, run from north to south, and the transitory markers move from east to west. A wild and uncharted piece of poetry, if it cannot be located on the *wei*, has no place on the *jing* either!"

The *wei* of antiquity were composed in imitation of the Classics, and when (3) the authentic texts themselves had been lost, scholars were able to restore the *jing* by the help of the *wei*. The entire *Book of Odes* has its source in the poem about the "pure and secluded girl"; the *Airs of the States* were chosen from among the songs of "wandering girls." By reading those poems, we learn to distinguish between pure and decadent mores, and vividly to bring to mind whatever is sagely and good. With what purity and sincerity did those "beauties skilled in verse" undertake the moral education of their contemporaries!

I regret that I did not get to know those who lived in ancient times. It par- (4)

ticularly pains me to find that so little of the poetry of the women of the past survives, and that what does remain is the work of so few authors. Having chosen to restrict myself to more recent writers about whom I could speak with certainty, I found none better suited to my task than "women of note."

(5) I wished to make a selection that would be at once comprehensive and exquisite. When I had written notices on the poets and comments to the poems, my anthology was already more than forty chapters long.

(6) The wives of kings, princes, and dukes, along with other palace-dwellers, I put in a Palace Collection.

(7) Those who had lived at the turning of the Yuan and Ming dynasties I put next, in a Preliminary Collection.

(8) Wives of high officials, gentry women, and so on down to the principal wives [*qi*] of upright common people formed my Main Collection.

(9) After them came persons who had turned away from a disorderly life; these I put in an appendix at the end of the Main Collection.

(10) The years preceding the change in government and the early years of our present dynasty were represented in a New Collection.

(11) Songs of the "ambling fox" and "Mulberry and Pu River" sort I relegated to an Intercalary Collection. I put the poems of women who remained in the pleasure districts to the end of their lives in a Collection of Erotic Poetry.

(12) The work of women who, although they are Buddhist nuns, Daoist priestesses, and foreigners, nonetheless harmonize with the *Feng* and *Ya*, went into the Buddhist, Daoist, and Foreign Collections.

(13) Spirits, ghosts, tales of the strange, fictions, jokes, inexplicable events, prognosticators, and recluses entered a Fictive Collection, a Supplementary Collection, and a Collection of Mysteries.

(14) I divided song-lyrics (which are certainly an extension of *shi* poetry, despite their name) and random writings with a poetic flavor among a Song-Lyric Collection, a Collection of Elegances, and a Collection of Scattered Notes.

(15) As for those whose poetry has vanished like smoke and water or those who were skilled calligraphers but have left behind no poetry, wherever I could discover their names I recorded them in a Collection of Remnants and a Pictorial Collection.

(16) Alas, it is only after the intricate labors of our sex—embroidery, the reeling of silk, and all our other tasks—have been completed that we women are able to borrow from the Classics to complete the patterns of our writing. Seated at their looms, women of a hundred households confide their thoughts to scrolls

of paper and answer one another's essays. So it is that in their poetry writing, some take their subject matter from icy silkworm cocoons, while others beg the Weaving Girl for counsel on the night of the Double Seventh; some brighten their faces by washing in the Brocade River, while others shed their guilt by donning the flame-proof robe; some entrust their sincerity to bolts of cloth, while others clothe their feelings in undyed silk; some vie with bamboo chests of black and yellow, while others compete with the beauty of silk-bound books.

So truly can these poems be said to be "of a feather" with the antique *Odes*, (17)
they complement their predecessors and form a classic in their own right—a complementary canon [*wei*] answering to the Six Classics. I invite all under the four heavens to see for themselves.

Carelessly written in the sixth month of the eighteenth year of Shun- (18)
zhi [1661] at the New Yuanyang Retreat by the Mistress of the Grieving-for-Brightness Studio in Shan-yin, Yingranzi Wang Duanshu, also known as Yuying.

(MYSW, 1a–4b)

par. 1, jing/wei: The title of Wang Duanshu's anthology might also translate as "The Extracanonical/Apocryphal Canon of Poetry by Famous Women." Wang plays on the words of the title throughout her preface. The word *jing* in book titles usually means a "classic" (in distinction from lesser books) or an "original text" (as opposed to a commentary or apocryphal imitation), but Wang's preface punningly reawakens its other connotations: "warp" (the vertical strands of a weaving, established on the loom before the horizontal threads of the weft are interposed), "meridian," "longitude," or "vertical bearing" (as opposed to latitudinal or horizontal measurements). *Wei*, the symmetrical counterpart to *jing*, stands for "weft," "latitude," and "horizontal position-marker." In bibliographical parlance, the *wei* are a collection of extracanonical texts, often commentaries to or apocryphal versions of classical texts. In later ages, many of these were considered unreliable, not only philologically but also from the point of view of doctrine.

par. 2, "north to south . . . east to west": "Paths running north and south are called *jing*, paths running east and west are called *wei*" (Jia Gongyan [Tang dynasty], annotation to *Zhou li*, "Kaogong ji: jiang ren"). The association of the north-south axis with permanence and the east-west axis with change is customary (see preceding note). Not only do the sun and the moon seem to move parallel to the equator, but all the major rivers of China flow from west to east.

par. 3, "wandering girls": The first poem of the *Book of Odes*, praises a "pure and secluded girl" and pronounces her "a fit match for our lord." Poem 9 declares that "By the Han river there are wandering girls, but one cannot pursue them"—in which the traditional preface to the poem sees evidence of pure morals and sagely rule.

par. 8, "Main Collection": "Main" also connotes "proper, correct." Here Wang is careful to distinguish between principal or official wives—*qi*—and concubines, or *qie* (see the next "collection" in this list and its note). For her, the difference in marital status takes precedence over inequalities in social position.

par. 9, "turned away from a disorderly life": There was something of a fashion among men in the late Ming dynasty for taking former courtesans, particularly accomplished women able to write and paint, as concubines or even official wives. The courtesan-turned-wife with whom Wang Duanshu is most likely to have been acquainted was Liu Shi (P.67), after 1644 the wife of Qian Qianyi.

par. 11, "Intercalary Collection": In the *Book of Odes*, the "ambling fox" is a motif for the male philanderer (see poem 63). The ancient musical compositions known as "Among the Mulberries" and "On the Banks of the Pu" were bywords for licentiousness. With her part title "Intercalary Collection," Wang may intend a reference to the similarly titled appendix to Qian Qianyi's *Liechao shiji* (LCSJ), completed around 1650 (on which see C.14). Qian contributed a preface (dated 1662) to Wang's anthology.

par. 12, "harmonize with *Feng* and *Ya*": *Feng* is the name of a section of the *Book of Odes* devoted to folk song (invariably interpreted so as to give moral instruction); *Ya* is the name of two sections that mix folk and ceremonial genres. To "harmonize with *Feng* and *Ya*" is to display poetic talent and moral propriety.

par. 16, "answer one another's essays": In the foregoing two sentences, Wang reawakens the dormant metaphor of textile work (a woman's craft) that lies behind the words *jing* and *wei*.

par. 16, "icy silkworm cocoons . . . Double Seventh": "Icy cocoons" (*bing jian*) are the source of a particularly resistant silk fiber used for embroidery. On the Double Seventh festival, see P.5.1 and P.19.2.

par. 16, "Brocade River . . . flame-proof robe": Xue Tao's (P.10) collection was entitled *The Brocade River* (*Jinjiang ji*, from the Jinshui stream in Szechuan province). The original collection has been lost (see Hu Wenkai, pp. 33–37). Buddhist teachers often wore robes made of a cloth called *huo wan*, reputed impervious to flame. The cloth was most easily cleaned by being passed through fire, hence its name, "fire-washed [material]."

par. 16, ". . . bolts of cloth . . . undyed silk": Both these clauses describe the act of writing by reference to the materials on which it is inscribed—materials that, as already observed, are intimately bound up with the traditional daily tasks of women.

par. 16, "bamboo chests": Bamboo chests (*fei*) were used as containers for precious objects.

par. 17, "answering to the Six Classics": As before, Wang observes the parallelism of *wei* and *jing*, to assert that her collection resembles the *Book of Odes*, but also complements it as the "wings" or addenda to the *Book of Changes* round out the meaning of that classic's lapidary core text.

TRANSLATION BY HAUN SAUSSY

柳是

C.14. Liu Shi (1618–64)

On Liu Shi, see P.67. She wrote biographical and critical prefaces on some of the poets included in the anthology *Liechao shiji* (LCSJ, Collection of poetry from the former [Ming] dynasty; ca. 1650) compiled by her husband, Qian Qianyi. The women poets are relegated to a special section, *Runji* (LR, Intercalary collection).

C.14.1. Zhang Hongqiao [P.27]

Zhang Hongqiao was from a good family in Minxian. She lived to the west of the Hongqiao [Red Bridge], and therefore named herself Hongqiao. She was intelligent and excelled at the art of letters. The local magnates competed to get her as a wife, but Hongqiao rejected their approaches and said to her parents, "I will only marry someone with the talent of a Li Bo." Thereupon literary scholars all tried to win her favor with poems in five- or seven-character lines. Wang Gong, a young man in the district, had very high opinions of his own writings; but after glancing at them Hongqiao paid them no more attention.

Wang Cheng of Changle rented a house next door to Hongqiao's. He spied (2)
on her daily and sent her poems. She was offended by his impudence and would not go out her door. [Wang] Cheng went away dejected. Lin Hong of Fuqing was a friend of [Wang] Cheng's. He happened to pass by [Wang] Cheng's house one day, and stayed in a neighboring house to the east. By chance he saw Zhang burning incense in the courtyard, and asked a neighboring woman to deliver a poem for him. As Zhang held up the poem to read, she smiled. She reached for a brush and wrote a poem in response. The neighboring woman congratulated [Lin] Hong as she gave him the poem, saying, "Lady Zhang's table is piled high with poems that people have sent her, but she never once wrote anything in response. Now she has answered your poem; it is a rare honor indeed." [Lin] Hong was overjoyed. He asked the woman to send Zhang his solicitous regards. A month went by and the woman came back with [Zhang] Hongqiao's consent. [Lin] Hong thereupon left home, and set up a separate household for [Zhang] Hongqiao. From then on the two of them grew more and more attached to each other; they composed poems jointly, deliberating the choice of words together.

(3) [One day] [Wang] Cheng, in full dress, paid [Lin] Hong a visit, and requested to see Zhang. But she hid herself away from him. [Wang] Cheng then secretly bribed Zhang's maid to let him peep in on [Lin] Hong and Zhang as they made love. He then wrote two poems entitled "Soft Breast" and "Cloud-like Hair" to tease them. Zhang became all the more furious. [Wang] Cheng knew how she felt, and took [Lin] Hong to go roaming the three mountains with him. After a few days, [Lin] Hong escaped and came home. When he arrived at his house at night, Zhang was leaning against the bridge, waiting. [Lin] Hong composed three quatrains, and Zhang responded from where she was standing.

(4) One year went by. [Lin] Hong was getting ready to go to Jinling. He sang "The Great River Flows East," and could not bear to say farewell. Another year went by. [Lin] Hong sent from Jinling a lyric to the tune *Mo yu'r* and four other quatrains. After [Lin] Hong's departure, Zhang sat alone in her small building, gazing at her own reflection and feeling completely heartbroken. When she received [Lin] Hong's lyric and poems, she missed him so much that she fell ill. A few months later, she died.

(5) When [Lin] Hong came back, he hurried to see Zhang. When he arrived at Hongqiao and learned that Zhang had already died, he broke down and cried as if he no longer wished to live. Just as he was feeling totally lost, he suddenly caught sight of a letter tied to a jade girdle-pendant and hanging from the head of the bed. He opened the letter and found a lyric to the tune *Die lian hua* and seven quatrains. [Lin] Hong was overcome with grief; he composed a lament and offered a libation to Zhang. Wang Gong also wrote a lyric to accompany it.

(6) Ever after, whenever [Lin] Hong passed by the village of Hongqiao, he would feel dejected for days afterward. [Lin] Hong's wife Zhu also wrote poetry. She died at nineteen. In the poems Zhu sent [Lin] Hong, one line runs: "Waiting for the morning watch to go pay respects to the emperor," so it must have been written after Lin Hong became a court official.

(LR, 738–40)

C.14.2. *Woman Lu [Lu Qingzi, P.52], Wife of Zhao Huan'guang*

Woman Lu's given name was Qingzi. She was the daughter of Lu Shidao, Chief Minister of the Imperial Seals Agency in Gusu [Suzhou], and the wife of Zhao Huan'guang of Taichang, whose style name was Fanfu. Fanfu abandoned his home and ancestral graves and retreated together with Qingzi to the distant mountains, where they cleared the undergrowth with their own hands, dredged the mountain springs, and built bridges over the ravines. They marked the way for the waters to go and brought several streams to flow in one channel.

Qingzi was good at poetry. Her poems were widely read at the time; she was very famous. As the wife of a lofty hermit, she was as inaccessible as the partner of an immortal. (2)

Fanfu was a person of little learning, but he loved to write. What he wrote came from his own mind, unaided by any master or disciplined skill. Qingzi was far more learned than he. Her youthful *Yunwoge ji* [Poems from Resting in Clouds Lodge] was a patchwork of clichés, inadequate to refine the nature and emotions. In her last years, she became too famous and was too busy entertaining and socializing. Whenever she exchanged poems with other ladies, she would write something meaningless and inappropriate, laying herself open to the charge of lacking taste. This is particularly true of her two collections *Kaopan* [A recluse's perfect joy] and *Xuan zhi* [The fungus of immortality]. Her rhapsodies and dirges for the dead followed closely the style of the Six Dynasties. The dirge she wrote for her grandmother Lady Bian is elegantly written and highly readable. Her daughter-in-law, Wen Shu, could paint in an original style. Her paintings are considered by master painters to be unique in our time. Their comments can be found in the tomb-inscription I wrote for her. (3)

(LR, 751)

C.14.3. Wang Wei [P.62, C.11], the Daoist of the Straw Coat

[Wang] Wei, style Xiuwei, was a native of Guangling. She lost her father when she was seven years old and was taken to live in the brothel district. She grew up to be exceptionally talented, and traveled in a boat loaded with books on her frequent trips between Suzhou and Kuaiji. Her associates were all high-ranking literary celebrities.

Not long after, she experienced sudden enlightenment and became a Buddhist adept. In cotton robe and with a bamboo staff, she traveled all over the Yangzi River region and the Chu area. She climbed the Dabie Mountain, looked out from the Yellow Crane Pavilion, and scanned the Parrot Isle and many such scenic sites. She visited Mount Xuan, scaled Tianzhu Peak, went upstream on the Yangzi River to Mount Kuang and Mount Lu, visited the thatched hut of Bo Juyi, and had an audience with the Buddhist Master Han- (2)

shan on Mount Wuru. When she returned home, she built herself a tomb at Wulin, and gave herself the sobriquet Daoist of the Straw Coat. She planned to spend the rest of her life at Wulin.

(3) But as it happened, one day when she was walking by Wumen, she was harassed by some hoodlums. She subsequently became the wife of Lord Yingchuan of Huating [Xu Yuqing]. Lord Yingchuan served in the Censorate. During a time of political disorder when the state was in peril, he repeatedly remonstrated with the emperor and was dismissed from office on account of his uncompromising integrity. Xiuwei had a part in all of this. When the political disorder ended, they braved all dangers and endured the vicissitudes of a wandering life, vowing to die together. After three years, she passed away. Lord Yingchuan was grief-stricken.

(4) The Superior Man would say, "Xiuwei is like a lotus with lush green leaves, rising tall out of the mud; she is like the white jade of Kungang, untouched in its luster by searing flame. Such is what I would call a perfect ending. Happy is she."

(5) Xiuwei wrote a *Yueguan shi* [Poems from shaded halls] in several chapters, to which she provided her own Preface, saying, "I was not born a man, hence I was unable to cleanse the world [of evildoers] but had to offer my service to a single person. When I had some spare time from my religious study and services, I wrote poetry. Sometimes, I expressed my feeling through flowers and rain; at other times, I recorded my thoughts through the landscape. When moved, I wrote; as soon as I had given expression to my feelings, I stopped. I presume that in this world of ours, spring brings the grass and fall colors the leaves; of this cycle of natural beauty there is nothing that is not poetry. Can such poetry be expressed in words? or can it not?"

(6) It was Xiuwei's nature to love scenic sites. She wrote several hundred chapters recording famous mountains and waters, accompanied by her own prefaces.

(LR, 760)

C.14.4. *A Young Woman of the Xu Family [Hŏ Kyŏngbŏn, P.43]*

Xu Jingfan [Hŏ Kyŏngbŏn], style Lanxue [Nansŏrhŏn], was a Korean. Her brothers Feng and Jun were both *zhuangyuan* ["Optimi," top-ranked among the *jinshi* degree holders in a given year]. When she was eight years old, she wrote a prose piece called "The Topmost Rafter in the Jade Tower of the Guanghan Palace of the Moon." She was known as being more talented than her two brothers in the art of letters. She was married to a *jinshi* named Jin Chengli, but her husband could not tolerate her ways. After Jin died a martyr for his country [during the Hideyoshi invasion], Xu became a Daoist nun. When the *zhuangyuan* Zhu of Jinling was sent as an ambassador to Korea, he brought back a collection of Xu's writings. Thus her works became widely known in China.

Liu Rushi said: The poems of the young woman Xu are highly ornate (2)
and extremely popular. However, I noticed that the following lines in her "Song of the Roaming Immortal"—"I merely sought the company of the Mao brothers, / and ten thousand years have gone by in the human world"—come from two poems by Cao Tang. "They know how to say farewell but not how to say welcome," from her song-lyric "Willow Branches," is taken from Pei Yue. "The carpets and the screens are newly installed" in her palace poem is taken verbatim from Wang Jian's line. "You once laughed at someone else's entry, and never expected that you yourself would be here today" is a direct copy of Wang Ya's words. "Bundled inside the red silk is the tea from Jianxi, / The maid sealed the bundles and tied colored flowers over them. / After an imperial seal in vermilion ink was pressed onto them, / They were carried by officials of the inner court and bestowed to the leading aristocratic families" combines Wang Zhongchu's stanza beginning "In a case of yellow gold, there lies the red-snow tea" and Wang Qigong's line "Tea for the emperor was presented in a new container from the palace provision bureau." Her "Standing by the screen, now and again [the parrot] tossed her jewel-pinned head, / Chatting casually with the emperor about Longxi," on the other hand, steals Wang Zhongchu's line about the parrot "Repeatedly reminiscing with the emperor about the old days in Longshan." The lines in her poem "Written After Secretary Sun's Beili Poem," "Newly made up she looked into the mirror time and again; / Brooding over last night's dream, she hesitated to go downstairs," is from the brilliant untitled poem by Zhang Guangbi of the Yuan dynasty.

Wu Ziyu said in his *Selection of Korean Poems* that there exist three hun- (3)
dred "Songs of Roaming Immortals." I have acquired eighty-one in his manuscript copies. Most of those in circulation today borrow lines from Tang poets. The "Roaming Immortals" verses written by Ma Haolan of the present dynasty, which can be found in the *Xihu zhiyu*, are also included. The same is true of poems that carry such familiar titles as "At the Frontier," "Willow Branches," "Bamboo Branches." Could it be that the books of Chinese poetry that reached Korea were taken there as exotic curiosities, little known to the

world, and so Korean writers thought they could claim those poems for their own? Literati of our country, easily impressed by whatever is new and strange, noticed only that these poems were written by a foreign woman and in their surprised delight did not bother to inquire into their sources.

(4) Lady Fang of Tongcheng has compiled a history of poetry. In evaluating Xu Yuan's poetry, she dismissed all of the women-of-letters in the Wu area with a single phrase: *haoming wuxue* [avid for fame but lacking learning]. But about this woman Xu's poems, she went on at great length. I cannot understand how she could do it.

(5) My husband asked me to collate and edit "poems from the scented trousseaux." Whenever something caught my attention, I added a collation note. I chose twenty or thirty percent of Xu's poems from the *Selection of Korean Poems*. Where she has borrowed words or lines, I have picked out some typical examples—not all of them, certainly. I leave it to readers to do it more thoroughly.

(LR, 813)

par. 1, "a Korean": In the present section Korean names and institutions are rendered in their Mandarin pronunciations, the better to recall Liu Shi's instinctively sinocentric reading of Hŏ's poetry.

par. 2, Cao Tang: Cao Tang (fl. 860–74) lived as a Daoist and never passed the *jinshi* examination. The lines here quoted occur in his series of ninety-eight "Poems on Roaming Immortals" (see QTS, 641/7347, 7351). The three Mao brothers were famous Han dynasty hermits.

par. 2, Pei Yue: Pei Yue passed the *jinshi* examination in the Tianyou era of the Tang dynasty (904/5). For the line cited here, see QTS, 720/8269.

par. 2, Wang Jian: Wang Jian, style name Zhongchu, passed the *jinshi* examination in the tenth year of the Dali era (776). For the line quoted here, one of his hundred "Palace Poems," see QTS, 302/3442.

par. 2, Wang Ya: Wang Ya passed the *jinshi* examination in the Zhenyuan era (785–805) of the Tang dynasty. For the allusion here, see QTS, 346/3878.

par. 2, "red-snow tea": The allusion is to another one of Wang Jian's palace poems; see QTS, 302/3443.

par. 2, "old days in Longshan": The allusion is to still another of Wang Jian's palace poems; see QTS, 302/3444.

TRANSLATION BY YU-SHIH CHEN

孫惠媛

C.15. Sun Huiyuan (later 17th century)

Sun Huiyuan (courtesy name Jingwan) was the daughter of Sun Zengnan of Xiushui, Zhejiang province. She married Zhuang Guoying, a *juren* degree-holder from Tongchuan, but was widowed early. Her poems were collected in *Chouyu cao* (Draft of overflowing melancholy). A specialist in the *xiaoling* song-lyric form, she joined three other women poets (Gui Shufen, courtesy name Suying; Shen Li, courtesy name Xunzhong; and Shen Zhenyong, courtesy name Qiongshan) in the compilation of *Gujin mingyuan baihua shiyu* (Song-lyrics by one hundred famous ladies of past and present, 1685), divided into four *juan* for the four seasons. She composed this preface.

C.15.1. Preface to Gujin mingyuan baihua shiyu

I occasionally pick up the scribes of rustic solitude. Some gave a particular depth of feeling to the rhymes they have left behind. But none of the ladies who remain in their golden courtyards have yet achieved fame. Anthologies such as *Among the Flowers* [*Huajian ji*] and *The Thatched Hall* [*Caotang ji*] only include one or two poems by such ladies—poems in a few restricted styles and indiscriminately mixed with the writings of men. Often the writers of such verse chose as their subjects "boudoir feelings" and "thoughts of longing"; but how is this different from writing calligraphy while gazing on peonies, or composing songs while pointing to tangles of *miwu* grass? Gui Suying (otherwise known as Mrs. Gao of Cuili), a man's intellect hidden in her matronly headdress, a brilliant mind behind the gauze casement, early took control of Shaojun's elegance, extended the clarity and brilliance of the beautiful Miss Ma. Moved by this talent, her brush has mined out emeralds, her ink stone has stored up crystal; she has edited a history of female poets, now continuing it with a collection of song-lyrics. Divided among the four seasons, these poems include works by a hundred women. The sentences she selects are a word-brocade, a rain of pearls; their carefully arranged wording is a piling-up of agate on a jade terrace. It is fragrant, it is lustrous, it lends itself to humming and chanting; it is, in a word, the perfumed codex of the gauze curtain, the gem-encrusted history of the patterned screen. In her careful selection, Mrs. Gao had the help of two ladies from Wushui and Changxi, both of them known for virtue and talent alike. In beauty and in knowledge, they bear comparison with the legendary women of the past. Does anyone who merely toys with the brush dare to be put next to these models for all womankind? Speaking for myself, I do bemoan those ladies of the red mansions who, despite all their pearl-and-kingfisher ornaments, their fine gauze screens, are lacking in literary accomplishment; and it saddens me that those girls of the green window, who (in the words of the ballad) "weave plain cloth and coarse silk," have no experience of the glories of the writing-brush. Think back on the scenes of incomparable passion by the Chenxiang Pavilion. The kingdom-toppling Yuhuan, knowing that feelings are impermanent, longed to leave behind a record of them, but in the end could only summon the Qinglian Hermit and hold the ink stone while he wrote. Had she been able, like Lady Ban or the Plum-Blossom Consort, to wet her brush and write a Xiang-river song or a slow "Xue'er" tune for musical performance, we would have her own words to know her by, not her silence.

(2) Therefore put this book on your table, look through it while you sit by the window, open the pages so that their perfume may escape. The wind, our elder sister, will not riffle its pages in jealousy. Open the book: its beauty will be revealed, fresh even after a spell of rain. The spring colors of the Shanglin garden do not need to be hung with ribbons; must the pliant branches of the Jingu garden wait for the East Wind's lordly arrival to begin bursting forth in flower? Truly, Mrs. Gao's "flowery scribes" are female scribes, and the rhyming of words is a rhyming of minds. Now that this book has been carved on printing-blocks, those who are of kindred spirit should cut mandarin-duck patterns on their looms and hold this book, like a fragrant rose, in the palms of their hands. We may forgo wealth, but never sully our hearts. And so we shall requite Mrs. Gao's elegant intent. As for talent, I am no match for the Plum-Blossom Consort, and in character I can hardly compare with that "Bamboo Grove spirit," Xie Daoyun. At most, I venture to accompany Mrs. Gao as lowly whip-holder, in which position I am honored to receive the dust that her mighty horses raise in their flight. Blushing for myself, I rejoice in her accomplishment.

(3) Written in the *jiaping* month of the *yichou* year of the Kangxi reign [1685] by Le'an of Tongchuan, the Inner Historian of Tianshui.

(Hu Wenkai, 899–900)

par. 1, "Anthologies . . . *miwu* grass": Sun's view is that the usual poetry about women, narrow as it is in style and subject matter, is so inauthentic as to fall in a different genre entirely from the writing she here introduces. "Boudoir Feelings" and "Longing Thoughts" are stock titles for the kind of poem written (usually by men) about women, frequently with courtesans in mind.

par. 1, Shaojun / Miss Ma: Shaojun is perhaps to be identified with Fu Shaojun, the author of a hundred poems in memory of her husband Shen Cheng (see LCXZ, p. 734). "The beautiful Miss Ma" is doubtless Ma Shouzhen (P.50a), known for her poetry and painting (see LCXZ, pp. 765–66; also C.31).

par. 1, "no experience . . . of the writing-brush": The meaning of the sentence does not strictly require it, but Sun may intend an indirect allusion to the fiction collection *Lü chuang nüshi* (Women scholars of the green gauze window, ca. 1620). On this collection, see Katherine Carlitz, "Desire, Danger, and the Body: Stories of Women's Virtue in Late Ming China," pp. 101–24 of Gilmartin et al., eds., *Engendering China*. On green gauze windows, see P.107.5.

par. 1, "kingdom-toppling Yuhuan . . . Qinglian Hermit": Yuhuan (Jade Bracelet) was an epithet of Yang Guifei, mistress of the Tang emperor Xuanzong (see P.18.12); the Qinglian hermit was Li Bo.

par. 1, "Lady Ban / Plum-Blossom Consort": Ban *jieyu*, P.1. Jiang Caiping, known as the "Plum-Blossom Consort" (Mei Fei) and an accomplished poet, was the imperial concubine eclipsed by Yang Guifei; see P.54a.1.

par. 2, Shanglin and Jingu gardens: On the East Wind and the Shanglin Park, see Wu Zetian, "Proclaiming an Imperial Visit to the Shanglin Park" (P.6.3). The Jin dynasty official Shi Chong (249–300) entertained his literary friends in his luxurious Jingu Garden.

par. 2, Xie Daoyun: "Bamboo Grove spirit" alludes to the frank and open character of Xie Daoyun, as described in a famous story; see C.24.1.

par. 2, "lowly whip-holder": An allusion to *Analects* 7.12.

BACKGROUND NOTE AND TRANSLATION BY HAUN SAUSSY

駱綺蘭

C.16. Luo Qilan (late 18th century)

Luo Qilan was from the vicinity of Mount Juqu in Jiangsu province. A poet and an artist, she is best known for her collection of poems and letters *Tingqiuguan guizhong tongren ji* (An anthology of fellow women writers, from the Listening-to-Autumn Studio, 1797). The "fellow women writers" included Jiang Zhu (P.111) and Bao Zhifen (P.105c).[1]

C.16.1. Preface to Tingqiuguan guizhong tongren ji

It is more difficult for a woman poet to attain to the perfection of her craft than it is for a man. It is also more difficult for her name to become known than that of a male talent. Why is this so?

(2) Confined to their boudoir, Chinese women are extremely limited in experience. They have no friends for discussion whereby to open up their sensibilities, no mountains and rivers to visit and behold whereby to fructify their literary propensity. Unless they have a father or an elder brother to teach them about the origin of different schools of literature or to point out for them what is real and what is specious, they cannot really complete their education. Then, after they are married, when they must take over household chores, serve their husband's siblings, and tend to such trivialities as the supply of salt and rice, they often find no time for poetry.

(3) Men of talent, on the other hand, pass examinations and win honors, vie with one another in the literary world, and see their circle of friends widening by the day. Besides, with high-ranking ministers and celebrated officials of the time following and praising them, their reputation becomes yet more prominent and dazzling. For the talented woman lucky enough to be married to a discerning literary man, the latter—writing paired verses with his spouse—will undoubtedly cherish and circulate her poems so that they will not end in perdition. But a woman married to the wrong fellow, one who does not understand what the humming of verse is about, may find her manuscript used to cover a jar of sour pickles! The transmission of poems by women—how extremely difficult it is!

(4) Moreover, these difficulties show up in different ways. In my case, I learned poetry from my late father and before the age of fifteen understood all the rules of prosody. After I grew up, I was married into the Gong family. When the family's fortunes declined, my husband and I gave up verse-writing and worried about making ends meet. Subsequently, struggling as a widow to keep my family going, I moved from my residence in Yangzhou to Dantu where I rented a house west of the city. It was an old house with just a few rooms, where I gave lessons to my daughter under an autumn lamp, and exerted my brush and ink in lieu of raising silkworms and weaving—the normal sources of income for poor households.

(5) Later, as more and more people sought my paintings or poems, some of those who saw my poems doubted their authenticity, pronouncing that my *Tingqiuxuan gao* [Manuscript from Listening-to-Autumn Studio] consisted only of plagiarized verse. I am by nature uncouth and bold; to say that I cannot write well-crafted poetry is something I can admit to in shame, but to say I am incapable of writing verse is something to which I resolutely object. Now and then I would leave the house and meet with celebrated men of letters

north and south of the Yangzi River, with whom I would compete in poetry contests in order to disprove the unjust charge of plagiarism and to stop the mouths of ignorant people. I became a student of Master Suiyuan, Master Lanquan, and Master Menglou. To all of them I would submit my past work for instruction and from all I would receive words of mild praise. Those who rely on hearsay rather than seeing for themselves might dare to doubt me, but they dared not doubt the words of these three scholars. Thus all the doubters were silenced. But then my conduct became a target of criticism!

People now maintain it is inappropriate for women to write poetry. My (6) friendship with these three scholars is especially condemned as morally opprobrious. But, as I think about it, over half of the three hundred poems in the *Book of Odes* came from the hands of women: "Ge tan" and "Juan er" were written by queens and imperial concubines; "Cai fan" and "Cai pin" were written by women on behalf of court ladies; while "Ji ming" and "Mei dan" were written by wives of officials. If the great sage ever felt rigidly bound by the principle that words spoken inside a chamber must stay indoors, those lyrics would have been excised long ago and become lost. Why then are they still kept in the canon today?

Besides, Masters Suiyuan, Lanquan, and Menglou all belong to the ven- (7) erated generation of elders, and their reputation is the equal of that of those respected members of the Luo Society. Anyone in the empire who knows anything about poetry looks up to them as to Mount Tai or the polar star. A hundred generations hence, I daresay, there will still be those who hear of their talent and look up to them. That I could be nurtured within their circle and receive advice and instruction from them is the blessing of my life. To say that I should not become their disciple and exchange verses with them is to say that women should not pay homage to Mount Tai or look up to the polar star. Anyone who holds such a view should be laughing at himself.

Those who know nothing of others' talent but choose to doubt it are biased; (8) those who know of it but still disparage it are spiteful. Neither bias nor spite is the proper motive of a pure and honest Confucian gentleman. I am already forty-two years old; having recently been studying Buddhist sutras, my mind has turned to the Vacuous and the Void. And I have written a "Guide for Returning to the Dao" [*Gui dao tu*] for my own benefit. Neither praise nor aspersions matter much to me any more. I only regret that in my younger days I was too fond of fame and must inadvertently have made myself a subject of ridicule. But old habits are hard to break. Whenever the cool moonlight filters in through the bamboo curtain or when incense is lit and I sit in silence, I still recall and relish those poems which other women poets far and near sent me in our exchanges from time to time. Each recitation would bring back to me their deep feelings and the goodwill beyond the words, as if I were in their presence.

(9) I have therefore collected and edited these verses and submitted them to a publisher. Let the derisive know that there is no lack of talent among women; it is only that transmission of their work is twice as difficult as it is for men. Those who belittle others henceforth need not overreact because of having seen little! In editing this anthology, I bemoan my fate as being less fortunate than my peers', but also count myself as lucky in gaining fame from my being placed after them.

(10) Written on an autumn day in the *dingsi* year of the Jiaqing reign-period [1797] by the woman-poet of Mount Juqu, Luo Qilan, styled Peixiang.

(Hu Wenkai, 939–40)

par. 4, "under an autumn lamp": "Teaching one's daughters under the autumn lamp" is a familiar theme of genre painting.

par. 5, "poetry contests": Called *fenyun* (assigned rhymes), these contests required participants to write verses on the same subject or with the same rhyme words.

par. 5, "Master Suiyuan, Master Lanquan, and Master Menglou": The poet Yuan Mei (1716–98), the painter Wu Songliang (1766–1834), and the calligrapher and poet Wang Wenzhi (1730–1802), respectively.

par. 6, poems in the *Book of Odes*: "Ge tan," poem 2, traditionally supposed to praise the thrift and obedience of a future queen; "Juan er," poem 3, interpreted as praising the resolve of the queen; "Cai fan," poem 13, thought to commend wives of the nobility for their observance of sacrificial rites; "Cai pin," poem 15, said to extol women of the gentry for holding to the ancestral standards; "Ji ming," poem 96, according to its preface an encomium of those "sagely wives and pure women" who "night and day admonish and perfect" their husbands; "Mei dan," poem 82, said to "mock those who are unable to take delight in virtue"; a dialogue poem, it casts a woman as the more duty-bound speaker.

par. 7, "Luo Society": *Luo she*, a name taken by many renowned literary societies in Chinese history. The name derives from the expression "to chant in the Luoyang scholar's style" (*Luosheng song*), which originates from the way Xie An (320–85) used to chant his verse.

BACKGROUND NOTE AND TRANSLATION BY IRVING YUCHENG LO

蘇畹蘭

C.17. Su Wanlan (19th century)

Su Wanlan, style name Renjiu, sobriquet Xiangyan (Fragrant Cliff), was a native of Renhe in Zhejiang Province. She was the wife of a student named Ni Yiqing. She once edited a work called *Kunwei zhengqilu* (Female constancy: Deeds of righteousness), consisting of records of the extraordinary deeds of women who died in defending their chastity. She also collected poems by famous women of the past, compiling them into her anthology *Guiyin jixiu* (Collection of the finest chants from the women's quarters), and she herself authored *Xiangyan shiwen* (Poems and prose by Fragrant Cliff). Frequently in poor health, she devoted herself to the study of Buddhist sutras.

C.17.1. Preface to Guiyin jixiu

At the time of the Three Dynasties, women were both virtuous and talented. They could wield a brush and wrote with verve, being in full command of literary forms. Their works were well known to the world, and they contributed to the promotion of women's education.

In recent ages, however, few women studied the subject of literature. As a (2) consequence, the subtleties of the "six arts" became lost to women. Every time I opened a volume of the brilliant writings of the past, my thoughts began to soar, and I lamented that we have fallen so far behind the feminine grace of earlier women writers.

Now I have the good fortune to have been born in a time of sagacious and (3) perspicacious government. I have great admiration for the works of past sages. Whenever I obtained a book that I found outstanding, I immediately collated and edited it, making clear notes of what in it most pleases the eye and delights the heart. In a year's time, I was able to discern and correct what was erroneous and obscure also. Thereupon I began to try my hand at writing poems in praise of various objects to express my deep feelings. It took more than ten years for me to gain a fuller understanding of the intricacies of poetry making. By then, I was able to see that people, though physically separated, do not on that account change their feelings, and though the loved ones in their dreams are far away, they nonetheless are united in thoughts and hearts. After that I cultivated the secret teaching of the Daoist school and observed the unusual mysteries of the world. This helped me to combat my worries and gain relief from my illness. It also enabled me to see and think freely, to follow freely my heart's desires, and to enjoy things as I find them in their natural state. Thus inspiration came to me like a multitude of blossoms competing in fragrance, and my brush moved as if aided by gods. I can truly say I was born under a lucky star.

(4) I know that I am foolish and lowly and that it is not suitable for a woman to flaunt her writing. However, every single word in a poem is a waste of time and effort unless it is in keeping with proper standards. Therefore from the depths of my heart, I have offered up what I consider best, inviting constructive criticism and hoping for improvement. I recorded what was originally there under the name of the original author, and also what I edited under my own name. Comparing the one to the other back and forth for diversion is certainly not a high-minded undertaking. Yet when connoisseurs read them, they will surely notice those little deviations from conventional practice and detect from them the underlying intention. Then I will find consolation in the pains I have taken.

(5) I often recall that my family has always been poor and frugal. We never had a meal suitable for welcoming guests, nor did we have any of the scented adornments other women wear. I wrote whenever I had a genuine feeling or thought. Well do I know that I cannot possibly have all the minute details of a thought or a feeling as it comes to me. I then face the wall, so to speak, and start musing. Should the gods give me a clue, then I will be in touch with what has been in my mind and capture therewith what lies in my heart.

(6) I have written the above in the hope that readers will not belittle the anthology, looking upon it as nothing more than a woman toying with her brush and ink.

(Hu Wenkai, 798–99)

BACKGROUND NOTE AND TRANSLATION BY YU-SHIH CHEN

郭漱玉

C.18. Guo Shuyu (19th century)

Guo Shuyu, from Xiangtan in Hunan, was born into an office-holding family and married a government student named Luo Xiangding. Her collection of 120 poems, *Xiuzhuxuan shi* (Poems from Pearl-Embroidering Studio), was published in 1837.[1]

C.18.1. Lunshi bashou *[eight poems on poetry]*

I

Use not *qin* and *zheng* for singing ornate lyrics,
Rely not on wind and rain to lend wings to inspiration.
The one point on which the poet excels others
Is the spontaneous perfection of a "Yellow Court Scripture" first
written.

II

"Yuxi's beaver sacrifice" is no prejudicial judgment,
"Changji's ghostly genius" is yet a superb critical insight.
I love the River Xiang for its good water,
Where waves rise it is absolutely pure.

III

Filigreed pendants and phoenix hairpins vie in elaborate make-up,
Embellished and adorned to a posture of determined abandon.
If the beauty is truly beautiful,
Then disheveled hair and coarse clothes should not matter.

IV

Heaven has let each loom shuttle compete for novelty.
Why then, once brush in hand, the imitation of a frown?
To establish oneself through the schools of Du or Han
Is as laughable as a little maid who apes her mistress.

V

I have blended sauces in the kitchen for six years,
Temperaments inclined toward sourness and saltiness—I have laughed
at their biases.
Of late I grasp and savor the flavor of poetry:
In all manner of elaborate and rare dishes, freshness is most important.

VI

Once the wild swan touches snow it leaves traces.
Willow catkins cannot fly if they are tainted with dust.

By chance facing the caltrop mirror, I intuitively grasp the poetic idea:
It is unmistakably me, yet there is no one.

VII

I pick up needle and thread to pass mornings and evenings:
The brocade of Shu and the silk of Xiang bear much comparison.
As for supreme needlework, one defers to celestial maidens:
In heavenly garments the traces of scissors are totally erased.

VIII

Talents ancient and modern obey one rule:
It is difficult to combine graceful dignity and limpid charm.
Peach blossoms are frivolous, plum blossoms cold,
Claiming all of spring wind are peonies.

(Zhong Huiling, "Qingdai nüshiren yanjiu," 271–72)

i, line 4: "Yellow Court Scripture" is an early masterpiece of calligraphy by the celebrated Wang Xizhi of the Jin dynasty.

ii, line 1: Yuxi is the Tang poet Li Shangyin. "Beaver sacrifice" (*laiji*) refers sarcastically to a densely allusive style such as Li's: the beaver is believed to collect a large number of items of food from various sources and display them.

ii, line 2: Changji is Li He's courtesy name. Some of Li He's poems are marked by a somber and austere mood, and the word *gui* (ghost or spirit) recurs often, hence the epithet "ghostly genius" (*guicai*).

iii, line 4: The nineteenth-century *ci* critic Zhou Ji compares Li Yu's lyrics to "a beauty in coarse clothes, with disheveled hair" (*Jiecun zhai lunci zazhu*, p. 7).

iv, line 2: The famous beauty Xi Shi was known for her special charm as she frowned in pain. The plain Dong Shi was misguided enough to see the frown itself as the source of beauty and imitated it to her great disadvantage.

iv, line 3: A reference to the famous Tang poets Du Fu and Han Yu.

vi, line 1: An allusion to the first half of Su Shi's (Su Dongpo) famous poem "Harmonizing with Ziyou's 'Thoughts of the Past at Shengchi'": "Places reached and passed in a human life—what are they like? / They are like flying swans stepping on snow and mud. / Traces of webs remain by chance on the mud, / But swans flying past no longer ponder east or west" (*Su Dongpo quanji*, 1: 38).

vi, line 3: On the caltrop mirror, see P.125.10.

BACKGROUND NOTE AND TRANSLATION BY WAI-YEE LI

完顏惲珠

C.19. Wanyan Yun Zhu (1771–1833)

Wanyan Yun Zhu (style name Zhenpu, also Xinglian; sobriquet Ronghu daoren) came from Yanghu county in Changzhou prefecture. A descendant of the painter Yun Shouping (1633–90), she showed a special aptitude for painting. Perhaps owing to her grandfather's adoptive tie to a family of Han Chinese who had served the Manchus as bannermen, she was married to Tinglu, a Manchu aristocrat of the Wanyan clan, who died when she was forty-nine. After her husband's death she spent much of her time with one of her three sons, Wanyan Linqing (1791–1846). Linqing left a three-volume illustrated autobiography that includes vignettes describing his companionship with his mother and a drawing of Yun Zhu at work in her Ruby Fragrance studio, editing the anthology *Guochao guixiu zhengshi ji* (Correct beginnings: Poems by the flower of womanhood of our dynasty, 1831) with the help of her granddaughters. Yun Zhu's preface, a powerful assertion of wifely moral and intellectual authority as expressed in poetry and sanctioned by classical studies, is a hallmark of mid-Qing women's writing.[1]

C.19.1. Preface to Guochao guixiu zhengshi ji

Of old when Confucius edited the *Odes*, he did not omit writings from the women's apartments. When later parochial scholars claimed that the tasks of wives and daughters should be limited to taking charge of making wine and drawing water, or sewing clothes and embroidering, they were ignorant of the prescriptions for women's learning that fell under the jurisdiction of the Nine Concubines, as described in the *Zhou li* [Rites of Zhou]. These prescriptions begin with "womanly virtue," followed by "womanly speech." To be sure, "speech" [*yan*] does not refer explicitly to writing, but speech is very close to written words. Given this fact, what harm can there possibly be in a woman learning to write poetry?

But the "Greater Elegantiae" are no longer being composed, and the Way (2)
of poetry has become shallower day by day. One writer may use frivolous or superficial phrases; another may employ excessively artful conventions. At worst, her head may be turned by unrestrained self-indulgence, so that she utterly neglects the dictates of modesty and gentility. The fault here, however, is not that she has learned poetry; the fault is that she has not learned it.

(3) From the time I lost my milk teeth, my father told me that I ought to read books to comprehend their underlying principles, and so he ordered me to study in our family school alongside my two elder brothers. I was tutored in the *Four Books*, the *Classic of Filial Piety*, the *Book of Odes*, and the *Erya* lexicon. When I grew a little older, my father personally instructed me in the ancient and modern styles of poetry, repeatedly stressing the idea that poetry must have a "correct beginning" [*zheng shi*]. At that point, I began learning to compose poems of my own. Since relatively few works from the women's quarters are in circulation, whenever I came upon the collected works of some famous woman poet, I would take a moment when I wasn't embroidering to copy down a verse or two to express my admiration for her.

(4) After I married, I had to manage the "rice and salt," so I set aside my brush and ink stone. As the years passed, I grew absorbed in quiet sitting and meditation, and the only books left on my desk were a few volumes of Song philosophy and the single chapter that makes up the *Leng yan jing* [Surangama sutra].

(5) Then one winter day in the year 1826, my eldest son, Linqing, while on leave from his duties on the Yellow River conservancy, was searching through my old portfolios and found what was left in them, as well as poems that other ladies had written and sent me as gifts, along with many recently obtained collections of poetry. He copied them all into a manuscript. Altogether there were more than three thousand poems. He asked my permission to give them to a woodblock carver so that they could be printed and distributed to a wide audience.

(6) Resuming my customary practice of years past, I read them all through again. Concerned that there were too many poems and undaunted by my own limitations, I made the final selection. I rejected any that did not conform to refined standards. This included all poems depicting sensual images such as rosy clouds, and all poems that conveyed emotion through erotic images, regardless of how well they were written. The poems retained in the present volume are barely one half of the original collection. The final edited version I have entitled *Correct Beginnings*. The genres and their contents vary, but the sentiment and tone of each is correct. Pure beauty, chaste emotion, conjugal harmony, limpid verse—none would shame the Admonitions of the Female Scribe [found in Ban Zhao's *Nü jie*; see P.60.9]; all conform to the standards required of a poet [lit. "one who morally transforms others"].

(7) Written in the ninth year of Daoguang [1829], the second month, by Wanyan Yun Zhu of Changbai, in the Bumei Study at the official headquarters for the Daliang circuit.

(Wanyan Yun Zhu, *Guochao guixiu zhengshi ji*, first preface, 1a–2a)

par. 2, "Greater Elegantiae": A section of the *Book of Odes*, containing poems praising and censuring royal government.

par. 3, "I was tutored in": The *Four Books* (*Si shu*) is a Song-dynasty compilation by Zhu Xi that includes the *Great Learning*, the *Zhong yong* (Doctrine of the mean), the *Analects*, and *Mencius*; it was considered the basic Confucian syllabus. The *Classic of Filial Piety* is the *Xiao jing*. The *Erya* (Approaching correctness) lexicon is an early glossary to the Classics.

par. 3, "correct beginning" [*zheng shi*]: Wanyan's father was alluding to the Great Preface to the *Book of Odes*, which states that the purpose of recording the ancient odes was to show "the way of correct beginning and the foundation of royal transformation." Hence the title of her anthology.

BACKGROUND NOTE AND TRANSLATION BY SUSAN MANN

C.20. Li Shuyi (19th century)

Li Shuyi called herself Female Scholar of the Thirty-Six Cliffs. A native of Xin'an in Anhui province, she was once a maidservant, later becoming concubine to a man named Huang Renlin.

Shuying lou mingshu baiyong (A hundred poems on celebrated ladies from the Tower of Scattered Shade) was printed in 1833 as part of a single volume that also includes *Minghua baiyong* (A hundred poems on celebrated flowers) and *Shuying lou yincao* (Verses from the Tower of Scattered Shade), all composed by Li.[1] Li begins *Shuying lou mingshu baiyong* with the author's preface and ends with three short song-lyrics. A biographical note is provided for each of the one hundred ladies commemorated in the poems.

C.20.1. Preface to Shuying lou mingshu baiyong

It is often said that human beings are filled with emotions while grasses and trees are oblivious of feeling. Where there is feeling, there is also suffering, and yet while people know that emotional beings are liable to suffer, they may not know that even inanimate and unfeeling things are not exempt from suffering. Things suffer because of humans, and human beings suffer because of Heaven. Flowers shed their petals and willows their catkins when the rain drops tears in the howling wind. Such is the suffering of flowers—a suffering that also touches human emotions. Beauty wrinkles with age and history tells of the vicissitudes of fortune. Such is the suffering of human beings—a suffering that also touches the feeling of Heaven. In all these, indeed, are found the innumerable variations of the chaste and the licentious, and the myriad faces of different things; and words can never express them. But after long suffering and deep feeling, flowers may become known for their color and fragrance, and human beings may be famous for their talent and beauty. The power to achieve such reputation is held by flowers and humans, and not to be restricted even by Heaven.

(2) I myself have lived in the midst of emotions, that is, in the midst of suffering. For me it is regrettable that I have learned to read poetry and the Classics, and humiliating to speak of family fortune. For my suffering began when I had to leave my parents at a young age, and it deepened when I lost the protection of kind people; my suffering reached its extreme when I fell into the ranks of servants, and it changed further when I had to endure jealousy from others because of my youthful looks. In delicacy my emotions are not unlike those of the flowers, but it is a delicacy that renders my emotions neither conformable to those of most human beings nor able to escape the feeling of Heaven. Given all this, would it not be commendable then to accept one's sufferings peacefully and to attenuate one's emotions? Why should one need to put them in words? And yet sufferings are more deeply felt the moment one tries to accept them, and emotions are more powerful the moment one attenuates them. Hence the composing of my new poems on the hundred fair ladies that follow my new poems on the hundred flowers. Alas! Before the spring silkworm is old, its lingering tears have combined into threads; though the patterned lute is played to no audience, its rhythmic modulations startle the heart. To me bees and butterflies all sound plaintive, and wherever I turn there is feeling and emotion; but in all the seasonal coming and going of swallows and wild geese, I do not know how many lifetimes will be required for my suffering to reach its end. Should I ask the flowers, they would not understand the cause of my grief; should I ask human beings, they would not get to its source either; not even Heaven would take the responsibility, if I should ask Heaven. Indeed, all this comes from nothing other than the fact that emotion begets suffering!

(3) Composed and inscribed in the autumnal month of the *guisi* year [1833], on the eve when the Twin Stars moved across the Milky Way, by Li Shuyi, Female Scholar of the Thirty-Six Cliffs.

(Hu Wenkai, 335–36)

par. 2, "poetry and the Classics": The idea expressed here is a familiar one, blaming one's own knowledge and sensibility for one's suffering, an idea similar to the well-known biblical expression that "in much wisdom is much grief: and he that increaseth knowledge increaseth sorrow" (Eccles. 1:18).

par. 2, "the spring silkworm . . . the patterned lute": These images are borrowed from two famous poems by the late Tang poet Li Shangyin (813–58): "Wu ti" and "Jin se."

BACKGROUND NOTE AND TRANSLATION BY ZHANG LONGXI

C.21. Mao Guoji (19th century)

Mao Guoji (style name Mengyao, sobriquet Sulan nüshi, or Pure Orchid Female Scribe) came from Changsha in Hunan; she married Yang Xiaobiao of Wuling. Her anthology *Hunan nüshi shichao suojian chuji* (Poetry scripts by the women poets of Hunan province: What I have seen, a first collection, 1834) included the work of seventy writers, with her own *Sulan shiji* (Sulan's collected poems) added on at the end.

C.21.1. Preface to Hunan nüshi shichao suojian chuji

The three hundred poems of the *Book of Odes* were mostly works by women. Although the *Songs of Chu* are not counted among the Classics, many songs and ballads originated in the women's quarters of the southern lake region. Why has the fragrance of the orchids of the Li and Yuan Rivers [in northern Hunan] so rarely been passed on through the jade brushstands of women? Was it perhaps because those exquisite and exotic flowers, budding from the hands of the beauties of the south, bloomed and withered in accord with the seasons? Or was it because no one gathered these poems to present them as gifts to others, thus permitting renowned scholars and poets of the great cities to savor their crisp fragrance?

In recent times, Li Dongyang [style name Xiya] became prominent in Cha- (2)
ling and was definitely an object of admiration in poetic circles. As for other poets, recorded in Tao Zhongdiao's *Shidi* [The zest of poetry] or Liao Dayin's *Chufengbu* [Addenda to the Airs of Chu], there were some whose works were worthy of being passed on and others who are not known to the world. But who will spread the fame of the secluded ladies of remote times or pass on the secret and private writings of the women's quarters? Those poems preserved by Tao Zhongdiao and Liao Dayin were all works by literati scholars who had

their collected works published during their lifetimes. Their poetry was either passed on by their descendants or circulated in their native places; their descendants or local people interested in literature would preserve what is left of their works for posterity.

(3) As for the elegant works of the jade terrace or the lost rhymes of the "Cypress Boat," either they were never printed to begin with or, if printed, the printing blocks did not last for more than a few decades before being broken up and lost amid weeds and ruins. If you asked the descendants [of women poets], their neighbors, or people of the community, none knew of them or were able to recite their poems. As a result, these poetic efforts made by the light of midnight lamps, works that came to fruition with the morning dew, were as if wasted. These lovely orchidlike effusions suffered the same corruption as rotted grass and twigs. How dolorous!

(4) Occasionally I discussed all this with my younger brother, Qingyuan, who shared my feelings. Therefore I searched through Qingyuan's collection of poems. Here I will not record works published before the Ming era; I have selected only works by women poets of Hunan composed in recent times. I have selected, edited, and compiled them hoping to pass them on to future generations. However, since I myself am obliged to live within the women's quarters, I was unable to search for poems in the cities. Also because of my own lack of sophistication and literary training and because of the hardships I experienced, my enterprise was unable to reach all of the chaste and refined ladies of the region. Moreover, in our country learning and culture are widely propagated and reach even to the most remote and distant regions. In the mountains or by the lakesides, women can be found who have mastered the rules of poetry. How could I cast my eyes upon them all? I constantly prodded Qingyuan to search for them, but was able to add only a few dozen more. It is quite difficult to prevent the recent women poets of the Hunan region from being lost to view! This collection is simply "one hair from the hides of nine oxen."

(5) Since this work is being printed, I have given it the title "What I Have Seen: A First Collection" [*Suojian chuji*] and asked Qingyuan to write a short preface to every poet's work, along with some brief and illuminating comments. I hope that women living in the women's quarters of distant places will send me their manuscripts so that I can continue my collection. This is not to say that I am necessarily everyone's kindred spirit, but this is at least a method for us to exchange our feelings and a happy chance for women's literature.

Written in the eleventh month of the fourteenth year of Daoguang [1834] at the Yuyi'an Studio in Changsha by the female scribe Mao Guoji. (6)

(Hu Wenkai, 228–29)

par. 2, "*Shidi* or *Chufengbu*": These are anthologies of local Hunan poets.

par. 3, "jade terrace . . . 'Cypress Boat' ": "Jade terrace" suggests the banquet and palace setting of many of the poems from Xu Ling's anthology *Yutai xinyong* (YTXY). "Bo zhou" (The cypress boat), poem 26 in the *Book of Odes*, was a byword for chaste widowhood.

BACKGROUND NOTE AND TRANSLATION BY MICHAEL F. LESTZ

C.22. Qiu Chan (early 20th century)

Little is known about Qiu Chan other than that she prepared an anthology called *Banyue lou shichao* (Poem-scripts from the Moon-Companion Studio, 1905), to which she wrote this preface.

C.22.1. Preface to Banyue lou shichao

As is always said, "poetry is that which expresses intent." Yet people's intent is not always the same. Much depends on one's situation in life, which then produces a particular way of thinking—this is what the word "intent" means. Thus a particular aspiration engenders a corresponding language; and poetry comes from where such an intent is.

If one is surrounded by such natural beauty as great mountains and vast rivers, one's poetry no doubt centers on such matters as flowers, birds, fish, or insects; if one is serving at the court, one's poetry naturally focuses on such topics as loyalty to the emperor and to the empire; if one is a scholar, then one's poetry of course deals with the art of government and the rise and fall of dynasties; if one's poetry is begotten within the confines of one's boudoir, then it must concern such topics as the spring breeze on the flower or the snow on a moonlit night. That is why it is said that poetry is born of the multitude of feelings, such as happiness, bitterness, sorrow, and joy, as poetry makes manifest each of them. (2)

I have recently read the *Wenhu shichao* and the *Naileng xutan*, and from them I selected some thirty poems by women. These poems were all written (3) by talented women from famous houses of recent times. The topics of their poetry are indeed such matters as personal melancholy and dejection, coupled with exceptional elegance. This is why I am determined to send the poems to the press, regardless of the great cost involved, so that they can be appreciated by kindred spirits. The value of these poems is evident, so that they do not need the wise expert to become known.

(4) Qiu Chan pens this preface in her Moon Companion Studio, one day after the Chongyang festival in the thirty-first year of the reign of Guangxu [1905].

(Hu Wenkai, 947)

par. 1, "poetry is that which expresses intent": The opening statement from the Great Preface to the *Book of Odes*.

TRANSLATED BY HU YING

Male Critics and Poets

鍾 嶸

C.23. Zhong Rong (469–518)

The *Shi pin* (Poetry gradings) of Zhong Rong, an early masterpiece of Chinese criticism, ranks the poets of China and accounts for its rankings with pithy analytical comments. Reproduced here are the statements concerning women poets.[1]

C.23.1. From Shi pin, *Preface A*

The period from Li Ling [d. 74 B.C.E.] to Lady Ban [P.1, ca. 48–ca. 6 B.C.E.] spans roughly a century; but a woman being among their number, there was only one poet for the period.

(Zhong Rong, *Shipin zhu*, 2)

par. 1, "but a woman being among their number": Compare *Analects* 8.20.

C.23.2. From the Shi pin *section on poets of the Upper Grading: On Ban* jieyu *[P.1]*

Lady Ban's poetry derives from that of Li Ling. Her short piece about the round fan [P.1.1] is pristine in language and clever in conception. Her disaffection is deep-seated, expressed in language that is beautiful. She succeeds in capturing a woman's sentiment. From this one fragment, one can appreciate her skill.

(*Shipin zhu*, 12–13

c.23.3. From the Shi pin *section on poets of the Middle Grading: On Qin Jia [fl. 147] and Xu Shu [fl. 147]*

The story of Qin Jia and his wife [Xu Shu] is lamentable; similarly, the language of his poems is sorrowful.

(2) Those who know how to write pentasyllabic verse are few, but they include two women. Xu Shu's poetry on the sorrow of separation is second only to that about the round fan [by Lady Ban].

(*Shipin zhu*, 19)

par. 1: On Xu Shu and her husband, see P.54a.4.

c.23.4. From the Shi pin *section on poets of the Lower Grading: Bao Linghui (P.4) and Han Lanying*

Frequently Linghui's songs and poems quite jut forth, and are pure and well-wrought. Especially successful are her poems in imitation of the ancient style. Only her "Hundred Wishes" is impure. Her brother, Bao Zhao, once responded to Emperor Xiaowu of the Song [r. 454–65]: "Your servant's younger sister is second in ability only to Zuo Fen; your servant's talent does not match that of Zuo Si."

(2) Lanying's poetry is one of fineness and detail and includes quite a few famous pieces. She was also skilled at witty causerie. Emperor Wu of the Qi [r. 483–93] called her "Master Han" and once added: "If you two ladies had been alive during the Han, then Ban *jieyu*'s rhapsody of the jade steps and song of the round fan would lose some of their preeminence!"

(*Shipin zhu*, 49)

par. 1, "poems in imitation of the ancient style": These include poems P.4.1, P.4.2, P.4.4, and P.4.6 in this anthology.

par. 1, "Hundred Wishes": No poem by this name is presently found in Bao's poetic corpus.

par. 1, Zuo Fen and Zuo Si: On this famous sister and brother from the Jin dynasty, see P.3.

par. 2, "rhapsody of the jade steps and song of the round fan": See P.1.2 and P.1.1.

BACKGROUND NOTE AND TRANSLATION BY JOHN TIMOTHY WIXTED

房玄齡

C.24. Fang Xuanling (578–648)

Fang Xuanling was a court historian of the early Tang dynasty and the chief compiler of the *Jin shu* (Official history of the Jin dynasty), covering the years 265–419. The selection below is taken from the chapter of that history devoted to "exemplary women" of the period.

Xie Daoyun (fl. 399), who came from an eminent and powerful family, is celebrated in an earlier work, *Shishuo xinyu* (A new account of tales of the world, by Liu Yiqing), for her literary talent and wit. Daoyun's inclusion in the "Exemplary Women" chapter of the *Jin shu*, however, probably owes as much to her conduct during and after her husband's violent death as it does to her learning.

C.24.1. On Xie Daoyun, from Jin shu

Wang Ningzhi's wife, née Xie, whose polite name was Daoyun, was the daughter of Yi, general of Anxi. Daoyun was intelligent and gifted in speech. Her uncle, [Xie] An, once asked her which lines were the finest in the *Book of Odes*. Daoyun quoted the lines, "I, Jifu, have composed this song of praise / May it be as refreshing as a cool wind. / Zhong Shanfu has constant anxieties / May it soothe his mind." Her uncle said that this showed the deep insight of a person of refinement. Another time, when the family was assembled together, snow suddenly began to fall. Her uncle asked what the snow could be compared to. His nephew, Lang, said, "It is rather like salt thrown into the air." Daoyun said, "It is more like willow catkins lifted by the wind." Xie An was delighted with her response.

Daoyun married Ningzhi, and soon after, when she returned home to visit (2)
her family, she showed herself to be extremely unhappy. Her uncle said, "Master Wang, after all, is Yishao's son. He is not bad. Why do you dislike him?" Daoyun replied, "In this household, I have your noble self and the palace attendant for uncles, and for brothers and cousins I have Feng, Hu, Jie, and Mo. I never thought that between heaven and earth there would be such a man as Master Wang!". . . .

During the crisis caused by Sun En, Daoyun remained unperturbed. Upon (3)
learning that her husband and sons had all been killed by the bandits, Daoyun

ordered her maid-servants to carry her outside in a sedan-chair, the women arming themselves with swords. When the marauding soldiers arrived, she herself killed several of them. . . . Thereafter, she lived as a widow in Kuaiji, maintaining strict and severe discipline throughout her household. . . .

(4) Years before, in the same prefecture there had been another woman of great talent and ability, the younger sister of Zhang Xuan. She had married into the Gu family, and her brother Xuan always praised her, saying that she was Daoyun's match. There was a certain Ji Ni who had spent time in both households and someone asked his opinion. He said, "The spirit and feelings of Lady Wang [Xie Daoyun] are carefree and sunny; she has the manner of the scholars of the Bamboo Grove. The Gu family wife has a mind as pure and bright as jade; she is certainly the flower of the women's quarters."

(5) The poems, rhapsodies, dirges, and eulogies that Daoyun wrote all circulate in the world.

(*Jin shu*, 96/2516–17; Hu Wenkai, 10–11; Liu Yiqing, *Shishuo xinyu [jiao jian]*, 2.71 and 19.26)

par. 1, quote from *Book of Odes*: This is poem 260; the author, Yin Jifu, is said to have written the piece to celebrate and console the Zhou minister Zhong Shanfu on the eve of Shanfu's departure on a royal mission.

par. 1, snow comparisons: Both lines uttered by the cousins rhyme with the last word of their uncle's question. Cf. Mather, trans., *Shih-shuo Hsin-yü*, p. 64 and n. 1.

par. 2, Daoyun on her male relatives: The identification of those named is uncertain; see Mather, trans., *Shih-shuo Hsin-yü*, pp. 354–55.

par. 4, "Bamboo Grove": On the Seven Worthies of the Bamboo Grove, see P.10.1.

par. 5, "circulate in the world": Few of Daoyun's works are known to survive today.

BACKGROUND NOTE AND TRANSLATION BY RONALD EGAN

張說

C.25. Zhang Yue (667–730)

Zhang Yue was a prominent statesman and literatus of the early eighth century. It was probably because of his reputation as a poet and his official position as court historian that he was directed to preface the literary collection of the palace lady Shangguan Wan'er (P.7), *Shangguan Zhaorong wenji* (Shangguan Wan'er's collected works). The preface praises Wan'er for her literary talent and refers as well to her remarkable and controversial career as private secretary and advisor to Empress Wu and Emperor Zhongzong. Several of Wan'er's poems survive, although the literary collection itself, which was a sizable one, does not.

C.25.1. Preface to Shangguan Wan'er, Shangguan Zhaorong wenji

I have heard that among the seven musical notes there is none that is dominant; rather the pitch-pipes are used to combine them all in harmony. Likewise, none of the five colors creates a beautiful pattern by itself; it is when they are interwoven that they make attractive designs. Consequently, when one's mood is laden with pent-up feelings, it is only clever phrases that will be able to express them, and to describe the myriad transformations of forms it is necessary to use skillful writing. That is why the former kings used writing to bring order to heaven and earth, to examine the affairs of men and spirits, to illuminate the void, and to reflect the afterlife. Great indeed is the meaning of phrases used in writing!

Shangguan Wan'er, who bore the title Zhaorong [Lady of Bright Deport- (2)
ment] was the grandchild of Yi, the former vice director of the Secretariat. She was exceptional in virtue and the most talented member of her generation. Her perceptive insight and listening enabled her to probe the mysteries of the world and to reflect its underlying principles. When she opened a scroll, she absorbed everything in it like the ocean, as if she had heard it all before, and when she wrote, her brush moved like flying clouds, as if her reasoning had been organized in advance.

When the Lady of Pei was expecting, she dreamed of a giant who gave her a (3)
huge scale and said, "This will be used to weigh and measure the whole world." Subsequently, Zhaorong was born, and when she was one month old her mother said playfully to her, "Are you the one who is going to weigh and measure the whole world?" The child gurgled in response, "I am." That she should have had the power of speech even at birth shows that she was favored with divine intelligence. When Zhaorong was still in swaddling clothes, she was taken into the apartments of the palace women. Heaven itself was advancing her, so that her family was ruined but she was to support the nation. Her star was rising, so that her inner power was perfected and she was entrusted with office.

After Wu Zetian's Jiushi reign period [700–701] and on through Emperor (4)
Zhongzong's Jinglong period, for more than ten years, the six directions were at peace and free of disturbance. Inside the palace the imperial library was made more grand, and outside a new institute for refined literature was estab-

lished. In the search for outstanding men that was undertaken, no man of talent in the wilds was overlooked. The ranking prefectural officials made rigorous learning their highest priority, while the great ministers felt that a lack of literary talent was a disgrace. Whenever there were imperial outings to palaces and temples, or progresses to rivers and mountains, as white clouds formed, the emperor sang, and when green plumage flew, the ministers rhapsodized. The splendor of these ceremonial songs and eulogies was the equal of the Three Dynasties. It was not just that the sage emperor was fond of literature, but also that others assisted him in lauding it.

(5) In ancient times there was a female historian who recorded good and bad deeds, as there was a woman imperial secretary who decided questions that arose within the palace. Zhaorong combined in herself such excellences for two reigns, and on each day she attended to ten thousand exigencies. No matter escaped her attention, and she responded to each like an echo. During the Han dynasty Consort Ban [Ban *jieyu*, P.1] was acclaimed, while the Jin celebrated Court Lady Zuo [Zuo Fen, P.3]. Although their devotion to the Way of refined literature was similar to Zhaorong's, the assistance she provided to imperial rule was far greater. Yet the record of Zhaorong's deeds is hidden in the upper reaches of Ninefold Heaven, while her body has vanished below the many-layered Springs. Consequently, subsequent generations seldom hear of her fine principles and standards. How shall she be properly esteemed by court women and later scholars?

(6) A great sovereign studies the maps of all the territory within the four seas, and he holds in suspension the lives of his myriad subjects. If he is pleased, people throughout the nine provinces feel as warm as if wrapped in cotton, while if he is angered, blood flows for a thousand miles. If he is at rest, the commoners all live in repose, but if he is restless, the populace becomes worn out. Imagine how difficult it is for his ears to receive advice! To the high-ranking and powerful he must listen with suspicion, while those who are low-ranking and cut off by protocol are kept apart from him. Frivolous advice from intimate attendants will tend to be discounted by him, while officials who are distant and of loyal minds will often seem refractory in what they say. He can listen only to voices of feminine charm and gentility, of nurturing and benevolent hearts. These ladies are oblivious of self-gratification as they stand in the crossroads of the nine virtues, and they infuse their feelings into the garden of the six arts. It was on this account that our emperor's ideas of climbing the Kun Mountains and patrolling the ocean were put aside, his martial

ambition of cutting down the northern barbarians and slashing the southern ones abated, his taste for jade towers and jeweled clothes diminished, and his interest in hunting and revelry discontinued. Instead, all he did was to ensure that the teaching of gentleness and flexibility was spread among all people and that the melodies of odes in the classical style were transmitted to posterity. Were it not that heaven and earth nurtured his concentration, that truth and clarity aided his thought, that the many marvels assisted his perception and the numerous divinities supported his intent by bringing forth treasured men of exceptional virtue and auspicious omens of flourishing rule, what could have brought about such goodness?

The Taiping Princess, protector of the realm, younger sister of Emperor (7)
Daogao, whose talent is weightier than the divinities, used to spend leisure time with Zhaorong behind the eastern walls and feasted together with her on the northern ponds. How quickly she arrived and how abruptly she departed! The things are still intact but the person has disappeared. We grieve over the carved jade flute's remaining words and are saddened by the white fan's empty tunes. The princess broached the matter with the son of heaven, inquiring about precedents in the pepperwood consort's chambers, whereupon a command was issued to the official historians, to write a preface to a new collection from the Orchid Terrace. The several chapters of her verse are contained in what follows.

(*Quan Tang wen*, 225/17b–19a, quoted in Hu Wenkai, 18–19)

par. 4, "at peace and free of disturbance": On the politics of the period and, specifically, Shangguan Wan'er's role in them, see Twitchett and Fairbank, eds., *Cambridge History of China*, vol. 3: *Sui and T'ang China, 589–906*, part I, pp. 322, 325–26, 343. The harsh assessment of Shangguan Wan'er provided there diverges sharply from what Zhang Yue says in this preface.

BACKGROUND NOTE AND TRANSLATION BY RONALD EGAN

歐陽修

C.26. Ouyang Xiu (1007–72)

Ouyang Xiu was the foremost literary figure of his day, known as a poet, a critic, and an arbiter of literary and moral values. His preface to Xie Ximeng's *Cai pin shi* (Gathering duckweed, 1037) was presumably written at the request of Ximeng's elder brother Jingshan, who was Ouyang's friend, not long after

Ximeng had died an early death. In commemorating her poetry, Ouyang also expresses his admiration for the mother who educated her son and daughter so ably. The preface survives because it was included in Ouyang's own works; Xie Ximeng's poetry collection has been lost.

C.26.1. Preface to Xie Ximeng, Cai pin shi

In the seventh year of the Tiansheng period [1029], I traveled to the capital for the first time and made the acquaintance of my friend Xie Jingshan. Jingshan had passed the metropolitan examination in the first rank at a young age and was famous for his skill at writing songs and poetry. Subsequently, somewhere else I came across the tomb inscription that Mr. Song, the current imperial drafter, had written for Jingshan's mother. It said that she had been devoted to learning and had mastered the Classics, noting that she had tutored her son herself. Then I realized that when Jingshan had journeyed several thousand miles outside of his native Ou-Min region, bearing his cultural achievements for all to view, so that he was "purchased as soon as he was put up for sale" and attained great fame in the world, all of this was due to his mother's goodness. This year when I traveled to Xuchang from Yiling, Jingshan showed me some one hundred poems written by his younger sister, Ximeng. Then I realized that this lady had not only shaped Jingshan's fame, she had devoted the remainder of her time to instructing her daughter.

(2) Jingshan studied the literary works of Du Fu and Du Mu, and took pride in the robust power and loftiness of his own style. Ximeng's words are more evocative and profound. She abides by decorum and does not indulge herself. Her poetry has the style of the secluded and virtuous young ladies of ancient times. She is not merely a woman who is able to express herself. Now, Jingshan has circulated among the world's most worthy and eminent men, and so he became famous in his time. Ximeng, however, had the misfortune of being a woman, and there was no one to make her prominent in the world. Long ago, the names of Lady Zhuang of Wei and the wife of Mu of Xu were recorded by Confucius, and their poems were placed among the "Airs of the States." Today, if there were a man of towering stature who could rank contemporaries, leaving a convincing account for posterity, once Ximeng had been acclaimed by him, her name would never perish. I myself have no such ability. What is to be done? What is to be done? Ximeng was married to the metropolitan graduate Chen Anguo and died at the age of twenty-four.

Written on the first day of the eighth month of the fourth year of the Jingyou period [1037] by the magistrate of Yiling County in Xia Prefecture, Ouyang Xiu. (3)

(Ouyang Xiu, *Jushi ji*, 42/59–60, quoted in Hu Wenkai, 66)

Cai pin is also the title of poem 15 of the *Book of Odes*, a description of a model young woman's preparation of foods for the ancestral services.

par. 2, "Lady Zhuang . . . the wife of Mu": Lady Zhuang is the wife of Duke Zhuang of Wei, known as Zhuangjiang; see C.42.1, note to par. 1. The poems attributed to these women are poems 57 and 54 in the "Guo feng" (Airs of the states) section of the *Book of Odes*.

BACKGROUND NOTE AND TRANSLATION BY RONALD EGAN

王灼

C.27. Wang Zhuo (d. 1160)

Wang Zhuo was a native of Shaoshing and the author of a book of *ci* poetry. In his *Biji manzhi* he gives voice to opinions on the craft of *ci* composition; translated here are his comments on Li Qingzhao (P.17).

C.27.1. Comments on the Poet Li Qingzhao, from Biji manzhi

The lay scholar Yi'an [Li Qingzhao] was the daughter of Judicial Commissioner Li Gefei (style name Wenshu) of Jingdong Road and the wife of Zhao Mingcheng (style Defu), the Prefect of Jiankang. Since her youth she had enjoyed the reputation of a poet of such talent and power that she rivaled her predecessors. Even among the gentry, a person like her would be rare. If considered along with the women of the present dynasty, she should rank first in literary accomplishments.

After Zhao died, she remarried a certain person but left him because of (2) litigation. In old age she became a drifter without refuge.

The poems she composed in lyric meters can deftly plumb the depth of (3) human feelings, with diction that is light, skillful, sharp, and fresh, assuming a hundred forms and styles. Even the vulgar and wanton speech of back alleys is freely taken up by her brush. Among literate women from ancient aristocratic households, one has never seen such disdain for decorum.

When the Last Monarch of Chen had his parties, he made the lady scholars (4) and their intimate companions write poems as mutual gifts. Selecting those that were coy and seductive, he would set them to new melodies. However, such poems only used language like

> The jade moon full—night after night;
> Royal trees—fresh—day after day.

(5) Li Kan [fl. 8th century] once castigated the poetry of Yuan Zhen and Bo Juyi, which he considered to be so finely seductive and reckless that people who were not sober and refined would be destroyed thereby. When such writings were disseminated among the populace, the fathers of sons and the mothers of daughters would transmit and teach them from mouth to mouth. All those lascivious words and flirtatious phrases on winter cold and summer heat would penetrate so deeply into human flesh and bone that they could not be removed. Since the collected writings of these two masters still exist, they may be investigated.

(6) In one of the letters Yuan Zhen wrote to Bo Juyi, he declared: "The women of our time darken or lighten their eyes and brows and tie up their hair. The manner in which they tailor their clothing and mix their colors emphasizes the exotic and the seductive. Because of this, I have written over a hundred poems on seductive beauty." These are, however, not recorded in his collected works. What is referred to as "exquisite seductiveness and recklessness," "lascivious words and flirtatious phrases" is limited to such poems as those written by Yuan on "Encountering an Immortal" and Bo on "A Tour of Spring."

(7) The poet Wen Tingyun [ca. 812–70] was fond of composing perverse lyrics and seductive songs. However, even the more extreme examples like

> The nuptial peach's pit is hateful still:
> Its promise within is made to someone else;

or,

> See the red bean encased in a hollow die:
> Such bone-piercing longing could you discern?

were confined only to this sort of language.

(8) The gentry nowadays would like to imitate the coarse, dirty song-lyrics of Cao Zu and the like. Their language is such that not even the lady scholars of the last ruler of Chen and their intimate companions in their meretricious lines, Yuan and Bo in their use of lascivious words and flirtatious speeches, or Wen Tingyun in his production of perverse lyrics and seductive songs, would

dare to try. Where they [i.e., Cao and imitators] sing of the women of the boudoirs, they write in exaggerated fashion without any shame or fear. Such works certainly should not be seen by Li Kan.

(Wang Xuechu, annot., *Li Qingzhao ji jiaozhu*, 319)

par. 1, Jiankang: The name of a county, first established in the Jin period and located south of the present city of Nanjing.

par. 4, "Last Monarch of Chen": Chen Shubao (553–604), the last monarch of the Chen dynasty, is noted for both his poetry and debauchery.

par. 5, Li Kan: A member of the royal household of the Tang, Li was reputed to be a child prodigy who took the *jinshi* degree when he was barely twenty. He was said to have made his own anthology of Tang poetry, selecting only those poems that imitated the style and subject of the ancients. See *Xin Tang shu*, 78/3536.

par. 6, Yuan Zhen's letter to Bo Juyi: Wang is quoting here from the letter, preserved in the *Yuan shi changqing ji*, 30/2a–b.

par. 6, "Yuan on 'Encoutering an Immortal' and Bo on 'A Tour of Spring' ": Yuan Zhen actually wrote a classic *chuanqi* (tale of the marvelous) on the story of Cui Yingying entitled *Huizhenji* (The story of encountering an immortal). The tale, popular in its time, had received further adaptations by later playwrights and became the basis for different dramatic versions of the celebrated *Xixiangji* (Story of the western wing). Yuan might have also written a group of some fifty poems on the theme of liaisons with his several lovers. Bo Juyi's poems mentioned here may have been poems that he wrote in reply to certain poems of Yuan, entitled "Dreaming of a Tour of Spring" (*Meng you chun*). See the discussion of these two groups of poems by Chen Yinke, *Yuan Bai shijian zhenggao*, pp. 81–116.

par. 7, "red bean encased in a hollow die": Red bean has long been a stock symbol for love or yearning. The image is of a filigreed game piece with a rattling dried bean inside it. "Die" (*gu* in archaic pronunciation) is a pun on bone, also *gu*.

par. 8, Cao Zu: An official of the Song period.

TRANSLATED BY ANTHONY C. YU

魏端禮

C.28. Wei Duanli (fl. 1182)

Wei Duanli (style name Zhonggong) was the son of Wei Liangchen (style name Daobi), who had attained the *jinshi* rank in 1121, and later reached high office under Emperor Gaozong (r. 1127–63) of the Southern Song. Because of their father's accomplishments, Wei Duanli and his two brothers were exempted from the examination process before beginning official careers. Wei's collection of the poetry of Zhu Shuzhen (P.18), *Duanchang shi ji* (Poems of heartbreak, 1182), is the earliest evidence of her work. The title slip to a Yuan dynasty edition of Zhu Shuzhen's works notes that Wei Duanli was at one time magistrate of Pingjiang—the present-day city of Suzhou.[1]

C.28.1. Preface to Zhu Shuzhen, Duanchang shi ji

I have heard it said that poetic words and beautiful lines are definitely not a matter for women. However, occasionally there are those whose natural talents are mature and flourishing, and whose native intelligence is concentrated and quick. The words and lines they utter cannot be matched even by exceptional men. Even if it was desired to conceal their names, it would not be possible. For example, Huarui *furen* of Shu [P.15] and Li Yi'an [Li Qingzhao, P.17] from recent times are particularly famous. Each has composed palace lyrics and *yuefu* [*ci*] popular throughout the world, but of their works only one or two command universal praise; how can all be good?

(2) When I traveled to Wulin [Hangzhou], I saw aficionados in the inns frequently circulating and reciting the lyrics of Zhu Shuzhen. Often I would quietly listen to them, and found them fresh and pure, graceful and beautiful, full of longing and emotion, and able to convey the matters of the human mind. How could the common ever attain this? Every poem is "one note, three echoes." When she was young, sadly, her parents lacked discernment. Unable to select a proper partner for her, they gave her in marriage to a common city dweller. Her entire life was spent in melancholy—she could not attain her desires. Therefore in her poetry are many expressions of sadness and lament. Often, facing the wind or the moon, she would be grief-stricken by all that met her eyes. All of this she put in her poetry, in order to express the unsettled spirit in her breast. To the end she had no true friend to understand her, and she died depressed and resentful. From ancient times beauties have often led unlucky lives; is it merely that "beauty is like the flowers and life like the leaves?"

(3) Reading her poetry, thinking of her—such an artistic flair. Matched with a stupid man, she had to endure such a life! At her death, her bones could not be buried beneath the ground and mourned like [those of Wang Zhaojun under] the evergreen mound. Furthermore, her poems were all burned by her parents. Today not one in a hundred of her poems survives—a redoubling of misfortune.

(4) Alas! Because lamenting her loss is insufficient, I take up my brush to write her story in order to give some small solace to her fragrant soul on the lonely

banks of the Nine Springs, which would not be unfitting. As for the complete narration of her life, there is the biography by Wang Tangzuo of Lin'an [Hangzhou]. Here I write only the main points as a preface. I have named the anthology the Poems of Heartbreak. In future, gentlemen who love poetry will realize that my words are not false.

Written this fifteenth day of the second month, in the *renyin* year of the (5)
Chunxi reign period [1182], by the Drunken [ ] Recluse, Wei Zhonggong of Wanling, named Duanli.

(Hu Wenkai, 42–43)

par. 1, "particularly famous": The Zhu Shuzhen entry in Nienhauser, ed., *Indiana Companion to Traditional Chinese Literature* (pp. 334–35) dates Zhu to the Northern Song period based on an unusual reading of this line. The argument is that the words *jin shi*, which in the text modify the name of the Northern Song poet Li Qingzhao and which are translated here as "from recent times," should be read as "near contemporary," thus implying that Li is a closer contemporary to Wei Duanli than is Zhu Shuzhen and that Zhu must be dated to the Northern Song. However, it appears more likely that the words literally mean "recent times," and are included merely to distinguish Li Qingzhao from Lady Huarui, who is generally considered a Tang dynasty writer, although she lived into the early Song period. Wei Duanli's preface does not provide clues to firmly date the life of Zhu Shuzhen.

par. 2, "one note, three echoes": This term of praise refers to the sense of resonance that highly emotional poetry conveys. It derives from the "Ancient Music" (*guyue*) section of the *Lüshi chunqiu*; similar information is found in the *Huainanzi*, and in the "Record of Music" ("Yueji") section of the *Li ji* (Records of ritual). The phrase has its origins in the interpretation of the vibratory response that was noticed when more than one lute was placed in an empty hall; when the string of one lute was plucked, strings tuned to the same note on other lutes would reverberate.

par. 3, Wang Zhaojun: See P.58b.9. Her grave mound was said to be eternally green, in a desertlike frontier landscape.

par. 4, Nine Springs: On the Ninefold Deep Springs, see P.60.6; also known as the Yellow Springs (see P.29.9).

par. 4, Wang Tangzuo: Pan Shoukang identifies Wang Tangzuo as Zhu Shuzhen's second husband, whom she married in 1096. Pan argues that Zhu's first husband, an urban commoner, died in 1091 after ten years of marriage. Wang Tangzuo was of the official class and had a series of government appointments (*Zhu Shuzhen biezhuan tanyuan*, pp. 3–4). Wang Tangzuo's biography of Zhu Shuzhen, mentioned by Wei Duanli, is no longer extant.

par. 5, "Drunken [ ] Recluse": A character is missing in Wei's studio name.

BACKGROUND NOTE AND TRANSLATION BY CHARLES H. EGAN

楊維楨

C.29. Yang Weizhen (1296–1370)

Yang Weizhen was a contemporary of Cao Miaoqing, style name Biyu, sobriquet Xuezhai (Snow Studio), and he wrote the preface to her poetry collection *Xian ge ji* (Songs to string music, 1345). Cao, a native of Qiantang county in Zhejiang province, was skilled in poetry and at playing the lute. Her calligraphy in both running and "grass" styles was accomplished. She served her mother devotedly. Married at the age of thirty, she was a paragon of womanly conduct.

C.29.1. Preface to Cao Miaoqing, Xian ge ji

Of women who read and were able to write, the best known to history is Ban Zhao of the Eastern Han dynasty. In more recent dynasties, for example, Li Qingzhao [P.17] and Zhu Shuzhen [P.18] were famous as writers: their every poem, every essay was of a kind to move the reader. But since they were of limited experience and narrow understanding, of vulgar temperament and custom, they do not meet the standard of proper character. They are in no way comparable to Ban Zhao, whose talent and conduct provided a model for all palace ladies of her time and brought honor to her father and brothers.

(2) When I was living at Qiantang, I heard of a literary lady named Cao Xuezhai, who was praised as clever and talented. She once sent me a number of her own poems and essays through her teacher Qiugong and asked me for an interview. She said: "When I was young, Old Man Guan of the Bookish Studio and Old Man Ban of the Forgiving Studio both granted me an audience, but I have yet to meet you, and I hope that you will give me a word of encouragement."

(3) This year, while I was at Wuxing, Cao Xuezhai, together with her old nurse, came again to visit me at Dongting in Lake Tai. She chanted poetry and played the melodies of the "Guan ju" and "Zhao zhi" to accompany the "White Snow" lyric. I know Xuezhai well as a good and moral person; her literary accomplishment is an extension of her character.

(4) Ah! Isn't there a successor to Ban Zhao after all? I have heard that some of the three hundred poems of the *Book of Odes* were written by women. The lyrics of these poems can all be set to music. Confucius edited them, and they have since become canonical works. In later ages, established writers have not

always been able to reach the same heights. Hence, we cannot disregard literary works simply because they have been written by women.

In the case of Xuezhai, her writings are rooted in her character and informed by her learning. They spring from her inner feelings and are brought into harmony with music. Had she been born in the times of the three hundred *Odes*, her works would certainly have been recorded by the Sage. Therefore, I have edited her writings and selected those poems that follow the tradition of the ancient poets and those lyrics for lute music that express the spirit of heroic and upright personages, to make up her *Xian ge ji*. Future historians may incorporate some of her works into their compilations. (5)

Cut off the excess and fit it to the mean; curtail the deviant and bring it into line with the orthodox. This is exactly what the Kingly Way is all about. Isn't it truly something to celebrate, to have discovered a second woman writer who can stand beside Ban Zhao? (6)

Written on the eleventh month of the fifth year of the Zhizheng era [1345]. (7)

(Hu Wenkai, 71–72)

par. 1, Ban Zhao: See P.60.9 and P.69.5.

par. 3, "Guan ju" / "Zhao zhi": "Guan ju" is poem 1 in the *Book of Odes*; "Zhao zhi" (The early pheasants) is an instrumental melody.

BACKGROUND NOTE AND TRANSLATION BY YU-SHIH CHEN

C.30. Tian Yiheng (16th century)

Tian Yiheng, style name Ziyi, was born in Qiantang. He showed his literary talent at the age of ten by composing a fine poem on the scenery of Caishiji, which he visited while traveling with his father. He held a minor office in Huizhou and then retired to live near the West Lake of Hangzhou, spending his time in wine and poetry. He was held in high regard by his contemporaries and was considered as talented as Yang Shen (1488–1559), the famous man of letters of the Ming dynasty.[1] His poetry and prose writings are collected in twenty-one *juan* as *Tian Ziyi ji*, and a number of his other works are also extant.

Shi nüshi (Women poets, ca. 1570) is one of the earliest efforts to collect poetry by women. In his preface, Tian boldly suggests that literary talent is evenly distributed among women and men and that since official historical records have neglected women's writing, his effort to collect women poets is as significant as the gathering of ancient poetry in the Confucian classic, the *Book of Odes*.

C.30.1. Preface to Shi nüshi

Whether seeking evidence from remote antiquity or examining our own times, one can see that the principles of *qian* [heaven, masculine] and *kun* [earth, feminine], though different, are complementary to one another and that men and women can be equals in rivalry. Although their responsibilities in or outside the household may differ, with each performing the appropriate duties, yet fine speech and moral virtue are cultivated in both sexes, and talents are never bestowed on the one but denied to the other. Those men who have a reputation for literary excellence have indeed acquired it as something additional to their actions; while those women who excel in literary art are truly prominent among themselves. Ever since the Zhou era, there has never been a dearth of literary talent [in either sex], and it is only owing to the lack of effort to collect [the works of women] that there has appeared such an unfortunate imbalance between [men's] fame and [women's] obscurity. Poems of the inner courtyard and the boudoir all took their place in the *Book of Odes*; even words of the vulgar and songs of the licentious were not deleted by the pen Confucius held. For good and evil can be differentiated of themselves, and persuasion and admonition will both be present. Not only do such poems make the influence of kingly virtues manifest, but they are also useful in female education. Their merits being so great, how can one say that they are only of small supplementary benefit?

(2) And yet even our great historian Sima Qian failed to make any record of poetry by women, and what few records were left by historians of later times were sketchy and scattered jottings. Fortunately, however, fiction and unofficial historical annals sometimes give some account, and quite a few poems by women can be found appended to collections of folk songs or anthologies of famous poets. As they may let us catch a glimpse of the configuration of heaven above and the condition of things below, these poems are certainly good enough to exemplify the six principles of the poetic art, even when they may not be considered equal to the best of the *Book of Odes*. Women have even been known to outdo all men at literary parties in which each one is required to compose a line to make a complete poem: where the male poets all put down their writing brushes, women show their capability to reach deeper in

developing the theme. The works of women poets are thus sung by everyone and are able to compete with those of male scholars. I think it is regrettable that we still do not have comprehensive collections of women poets, and I believe that many graceful and fine works yet await our gathering. So I have sought in all possible places for the pure and the unusual. I have tried to give every good thing its due recognition and have not refrained from recording any words, however few and scanty they may be. Augmented with biographical notes at the beginning and supplementary works at the end, the present collection is entitled *Women Poets*. I venture to compare the poems I have collected to those of the "Guo feng" [Airs of the states] section of the *Book of Odes*, and I boast of recording biographical materials that are not even to be found in official records and annals.

The following are principles governing the compilation of this collection. (3)
Though the "Guo feng" section may contain poems by women, it is now difficult to ascertain this. We know the authorship of only seven poems, "Lü yi," "Yan yan," "Ri yue," "Zhong feng," "Bo zhou," "Zai chi," and "He guang," all of them belonging to the airs of the states of Bei, Yong and Wei. As for the other nine poems [that appear to have been composed by women], "Ru fen," "Cao chong," "Hang lu," "Yin qi lei," "Xiao xing," "Jiang you si," "Gu feng," "Zhu gan," and "Bo xi," it is truly regrettable that, owing to the remoteness of their times, we know nothing about their authors. Other attributions of female authorship are all conjectures by Song scholars and not all that reliable, as one can set against them the Little Prefaces and the Han commentaries. Poems written by the literati on behalf of women are easily distinguishable; such are poems like the one on Mulan. I have included one or two of these, but no more. Of poems attributed to female immortals or spirits, some may be authentic, but many of them must be forgeries; I have nonetheless left a few to represent this particular subgenre. For poets from the time of the five emperors to the Qin, because of their great antiquity, everything has been recorded without exception. For those from the Han to the Six Dynasties, I have laid more emphasis on their poetry than on biographical matters. From Tang to the Five Dynasties, my emphasis is on biographical matters rather than the poetry. Those who distinguished themselves during the Song and the Yuan, when poetry was on the decline, are indeed outstanding women. As for our own dynasty, though woman poets are many, it is impossible to gather all their works that are made available, and I have thus recorded only those that I have come to know, leaving the rest to later scholars who will have the interest

and the erudition to compile a sequel to the present collection. As *fu* [rhyme-prose] is a variant of *shi* [poetry], and *diao* [ditty] a variant of *ci* [song-lyric], they are all worthy of inclusion. As women are in a different situation from male scholars, all their writings, even a single word or a single line, ought to be put in the record. And even those whose names are known but whose poems have been lost will appear here for the sake of recording their activities.

(Hu Wenkai, 876–78)

par. 1, "something additional to their actions": An allusion to Confucius's dictum that a young man should first engage in activities to fulfill his appropriate social and moral obligations, and that "if he still has energy left after performing all these deeds, he may then devote it to the learning of literature" (*Analects* 1.6). In Confucius's usage, however, the word *wen* designates "cultivation" through reading and studying rather than "literature" in its later and narrower sense of belles lettres.

par. 3, "authorship of only seven poems": *Book of Odes*, poems 27, 28, 29, 30, 45, 54, 61. The classical Mao annotations to these seven poems ascribe them to various named ladies of noble origin. (Tian's order of enumeration makes it clear that the "Bo zhou" poem referred to here must be poem 45, not the identically titled poem 26.) Nonetheless, such ascriptions were not always taken as self-evident. The Tang commentator Kong Yingda already argued in his exegesis to the poem "Lü yi" that if the poem speaks for a certain woman, it does not follow that the poem must have been composed by that woman herself. By pointing out that the seven poems are all from the states of Bei, Yong, and Wei—that is, not from the leading areas of China represented by the "Zhou nan" or "Shao nan" sections of the anthology—Tian Yiheng means to say that they are in any case not the best of the *Book of Odes*.

par. 3, "the other nine poems": *Book of Odes*, poems 10, 14, 17, 19, 21, 22, 35, 59, 62. Traditional commentators have read the nine poems mentioned here as by or related to women. Out of the nine poems, the first one is from "Zhou nan" and five others are from "Shao nan," which are traditionally held to be the most important sections of the *Book of Odes*.

par. 3, Mulan: On the Song of Mulan, see P.109.1.

BACKGROUND NOTE AND TRANSLATION BY ZHANG LONGXI

C.31. Wang Baigu (1535–1612)

Wang Baigu (given name Zhideng) was a prolific Suzhou man of letters. A recognized leader in *shi* poetry, he also wrote *sanqu* and *chuanqi* drama, along with editing a local gazetteer. He was a patron and lover of the courtesan Ma

Shouzhen (P.50a) and wrote the preface to her collection *Xianglan zi ji* (Collection of Master Orchid-of-the-Xiang-River, 1591).

C.31.1. Preface to Ma Shouzhen, Xianglan zi ji

Moling [Nanjing] is renowned for its beautiful women. In the alleys of the pleasure quarters love is inscribed on peach leaves, willow strands are entangled in sorrow. There are found unruly foibles to dazzle the eyes of Dengtu Zi; unions of cloud and rain to make even the heart of Song Yu flutter. It is indeed the realm of seduction, the home of warmth and softness.

There lives a beauty of unsurpassed talent and charm. Her family name Ma (2)
recalls the priceless stallions on the market of Yan; her given name Xianglan evokes the fragrant grasses gracing the River Xiang. She regards money as dirt —when aiding friends in need she is as generous as Zhu Jia. Yet she considers a promise as weighty as a mountain—in keeping her word she is a female Ji Bu. She unties her jade ornament for none but a Zheng Jiaofu; she throws her shuttle only at a Xie Youyu. Her writings would put Sima Xiangru to shame, but she would not have responded to his seductive playing on the green zither. Her talents would enable her to turn down [the Tang general] Li Jing, and [his lover] Red Feather Duster would have envied her sedentary comforts.

The best talents from the Six Dynasties have enriched her sensitivities; the (3)
luminous three mountains she embodies as her brilliance. She wields a writing instrument made of glittering gems; every word from it moves like wind and cloud. She fingers sheets of paper made of jade leaves; every word she utters is [as serene as] moon dew. She ties the reader's heart in knots when she depicts sorrow in a space as minute as a fly's head. She sends the listener's spirits drifting even as she conceals her emotions deep in a fish's belly. When she expresses her melancholy in five words, they sound like morning orioles circling the valleys. When she voices her loneliness in four rhymes, they resound like silkworms spinning cocoons. Tracing the new sounds of "Midnight," she recreates the old songs of "Garden Blossoms."

I was about to traverse the tidal waves sweeping past Waguan Pavilion, but (4)
the chanting stopped. The trees in front of Zhenglu Pavilion no longer witnessed merry-making as the music fell silent. The Goddess of the River Luo ascended into the fog; she did not hear the "Flying Willow Catkin" song. Empress Zhao sought shelter from the wind; was she skilled in the "Clear Moon" tunes?

[Ma Shouzhen's verse] cannot be said to be soft and languorous, for her (5) range covers that of the "White Snow" songs. Nor can their charm be labeled "feminine," for she possesses the erudition of scholars. Her works have raised the price of paper in the cities; forests were logged [to make printing blocks] without regrets. Under the torsades of the canopy bed, the reader sits up until the late moon peeks in. In front of the jade-mirrored dressing table, the reader recites [her verse] until the morning mist has already descended upon the trees. Who says that only Xue Tao [P.10] from the Brocade City [Chengdu] can claim the title of "Collator"? Nor is Du Wei of Jinchang [Suzhou] the only one who distresses the magistrate so!

(6) Written by Wang Baigu in the year *xinmao* of the Wanli reign [1591].

(Hu Wenkai, 152–53)

par. 1, Dengtu Zi and Song Yu: On the proverbial contrast between the fastidious Song Yu and the lecher Dengtu Zi, see P.11.16.

par. 2, on Ma's names: The family name Ma also means "horse"; Xianglan means "orchid of the Xiang River."

par. 2, Zhu Jia and Ji Bu: Zhu Jia (fl. ca. 200 B.C.E.) was a generous patron of knights-errant in need. One of the knights-errant he saved was Ji Bu, a man so trustworthy that a promise from him was said to be worth a thousand pieces of gold. The comparison of a woman (especially a courtesan) to male knights-errant is a familiar trope.

par. 2, Zheng Jiaofu and Xie Youyu: Legendary characters; on Zheng Jiaofu, see P.74.3. Xie Youyu once attempted to seduce a neighboring girl who was weaving. She responded by throwing the shuttle at him, which broke two of his teeth.

par. 2, Sima Xiangru and Li Jing: The Han writer Sima Xiangru seduced and won Zhuo Wenjun as his wife by playing a love poem on his green zither. Li Jing (571–679) was a Tang general who allegedly eloped with Red Feather Duster (Hongfu), a beautiful maid who gave herself to him upon recognizing his extraordinary talents at first sight.

par. 3, "in a fish's belly": For the association of letters and fish, see P.26.7.

par. 3, "Midnight" and "Garden Blossoms": These are song forms.

par. 4, Waguan Pavilion, Zhenglu Pavilion: Both are in the vicinity of Nanjing.

par. 4, River Luo, willow catkins, Empress Zhao: On the Goddess of the river Luo, see P.124.3. On Xie Daoyun's comparison of snow to willow catkins, later adopted as a kenning for women's verse, see C.24.1. Empress Zhao refers to Zhao Feiyan, on whom see P.1.

par. 5, " 'White Snow' songs . . . erudition of scholars": On the purity and difficulty of the "White Snow" compositions, see P.4.2. In spite of Wang's defense, many critics have considered Ma Shouzhen's works meek, weak, and feminine (cf. Hu Wenkai, p. 152). It is interesting to note, however, that implied in the author's defense is the assumption that a woman who is as educated as a man and who writes like a man is valued more highly than a woman who produces "feminine" works.

par. 5, Du Wei: Du Wei[-niang] was a Tang singing girl whose name became the name of a tune.

BACKGROUND NOTE AND TRANSLATION BY DOROTHY KO

鍾惺

C.32. Zhong Xing (1574–1624)

Zhong Xing, style name Bojing, was a native of Jingling. He was awarded the *jinshi* degree in 1610 and held office in Nanjing and Fujian. A voracious reader and tireless traveler to famous mountains, he left many volumes of writings, and turned to Chan Buddhism in his last years. His *Gu shi gui* (Selection of ancient poetry) and *Tang shi gui* (Selection of Tang poetry) are widely circulated anthologies with influential notes and commentaries. *Mingyuan shigui* (MYSG: Selection of poems by famous ladies, ca. 1600) is, like those collections, also an anthology compiled to advocate the idea of poetry as natural expression unhampered by rules, conventions, and the models of specific schools. Although this anthology is attributed to Zhong, doubts persist about whether he was in fact its editor; see note 3 to P.45.

C.32.1. Preface to Mingyuan shigui

Poetry is the voice of nature. It cannot be achieved by imitation or by following rules. Ever since that song that sings of the climbing of high mountains, the *Book of Odes* sets an example for all those who think of their loved ones; all its words are suitable for singing and recital, and its supreme task is to ensure that gentleness and honesty are achieved. But where can one accomplish this by trying to conform to certain rules? Nowadays, however, those who make poetry talk about laws and rules before ever touching a piece of paper; moreover, they love to assert that this person follows that particular style or this work belongs to that particular school. Thus writers today first think of Cao Zhi, Liu Zhen, Wen Tingyun, or Li Shangyin, and then compose their poems in imitation of such models. The poems of women past and present, however, have always originated from their feelings and are rooted in their own nature; women poets neither imitate models nor know the division of schools; they have neither Nanpi nor Xikun style, but let their sorrow or grace overflow spontaneously. Now a woman is first a little girl who has no sense of gracefulness or awkwardness and knows no deep sorrow, and who wears a dark purple band as the proper headdress. She grows up to have jewels hanging over her head, and her face is soft and moist. Although she sees the woods turning yellow and becoming green again and knows that things in this world are not without alternations of rise and fall, she can turn ice into flowers when she is in a happy mood, or she can change clouds into snow when she feels sad. Whether pure as bathing in green waters or dim as dreaming among flowers, women's thoughts and emotions are suddenly strung together by a single thread, and all their rich exuberance comes naturally. So it is that those who later excel in poetry are those who were incapable of it before [and thus bring fresh perceptions to their work].

(2) The ways to poetry are varied, and I would take that of purity alone. In my foreword to Youxia's *Jian yuan tang ji* [Collection from the Hall of Remote Simplicity] I said that poetry is a pure creature, that its body is fond of leisure but not suited for strenuous work; that its dwelling must be clean and not soiled; that its ambience must be secluded, not crowded and noisy. And to achieve all these, no man can do as well as a woman. Not burdened with the hustle and bustle of business and travel, with nothing but green moss and fragrant trees around her dwelling and no other work than tying curtains and burning incense, a woman is in touch with peace and elegance. Men must travel to all the corners of the earth in order to know the world. When Yu Shiji compiled his *Records of Ten Prefectures*, for example, he had to go and describe mountains and rivers, the various prefectures and counties, cities and their surrounding moats before he could draw maps representing them. But women never have to do that. They have country villages right on their pillows and mountain passes in their dreams, all because they are so pure. Purity begets perceptiveness. Thus Lu Meiniang, at the age of fourteen, could embroider the entire *Spiritual Treasures Sutra* on a piece of silk as small as one square foot, with characters as tiny as millet grains yet clearly discernible. She also used a spool of thread to make a golden canopy under which one could see ten big islands and three small ones, as well as palaces and terraces embellished with figures of dragons and phoenixes. Alas! How far men, with their skillfulness, fall behind women! As for poetry, is that just a matter of counting syllables? But these are not my words: they are Liu Yanhe's, who says that "in four-character lines, which constitute the basic form, elegance and softness are the rudimentary features; and in five-character lines, which have developed from the former, purity and grace are the leading virtues." Writers today trap them-

selves in patterns and rules and pick up nothing but others' leavings; those who wear official hats have lost the way of purity and grace, which is now only to be found among those who wear embellished silk. Alas! What is said of those who lose their simple ways in imitating the art of others is fitting criticism of poetasters today who would not follow nature closely, only to end up getting clumsy in their effort to acquire cleverness. Thus Qinglian would rather admire a girl with unbound feet for her natural beauty lacking all artificial ornament whatsoever. If this is so, is collecting poems by famous ladies not of some benefit? Some may object to the printing of these poems for fear of licentiousness, and some may object that not all these poems have their origin in the Classics; but did not Lady Jiang, wife of Count Zhuang of Wei, and Lady Ban [P.1] all compose poems of rich color and beauty? Because women's poems have not been cited in ancient documents, stored in some mountain treasure house, recorded by royal emissaries as indication of the mores of the time, or preserved in folk songs or tales, it is rather difficult to put them together as a collection. I have only occasionally discussed these poems with a few people who are interested, and so I have decided to ask a printer to give them permanent form.

(Hu Wenkai, 883–84)

par. 1, "song that sings of the climbing of high mountains": The poem referred to is poem 3 of the *Book of Odes*, traditionally interpreted as expressing a queen's concern for the good of the realm.

par. 1, "gentleness and honesty": *Wenrou dunhou* is a phrase attributed to Confucius in the "Jing jie" (Explicating the Classics) chapter of the *Li ji* (Records of ritual), where it describes the ethical influence of poetry.

par. 2, Liu Yanhe: The phrase is quoted from chapter 6, "Ming shi" (Explication of poetry), of Liu Xie's *Wenxin diaolong*; See Shih, trans., *The Literary Mind*, pp. 71–73.

par. 2, Qinglian: A place in Sichuan that is traditionally identified as the birthplace of the Tang poet Li Bo. Two poems by Li Bo are cited here: a poem on "The Feet-Washing Pavilion" ("Xi jiao ting"), a place where "Female woodcutters wash their unbound feet / And travelers put down their baggage in repose," and a poem written for a friend in which occur the lines: "The lotus flower rises above the pure water / In its natural beauty with no embellished ornament" (QTS, 170/1751–52.

par. 2, "Lady Jiang": The wife of Duke Zhuang of Wei, known as Zhuangjiang, is traditionally said to be the author of several poems in the *Book of Odes*; see C.42.1, note to par. 1.

BACKGROUND NOTE AND TRANSLATION BY ZHANG LONGXI

趙宦光

C.33. Zhao Huanguang (d. 1625)

Zhao Huanguang (style name Fanfu) was a native of Wuxian in Jiangsu. He was married to the poet Lu Qingzi (P.52), with whom he took up a life of reclusion and literary pursuits on Cold Mountain. Zhao produced a number of works of scholarship. However, Qian Qianyi, in his anthology of Ming poetry, *Liechao shiji*, was quite disparaging toward Zhao. According to Qian, Zhao was lacking in learning, but being conceited he fabricated writings without being able to follow any classical models. In Qian's opinion, Lu Qingzi far surpassed her husband in learning, though her poetry, too, was not without fault.[1] If the following preface, written by Zhao for Lu Qingzi's collection of poetry *Kaopan ji* (A recluse's perfect joy, 1600), is any indication of his ability to express ideas in prose, one is tempted to agree with Qian's view. The style of the piece is often ornate with imagery and allusions that obscure meaning; the transitions are abrupt and sometimes defy logic; and his attempts to intellectualize tend to obfuscate the subject of his discourse rather than elucidate it, an example being his disquisition on the canonical poetic concepts of *zhi* ("intent") and *wuxie* ("lack of impure thoughts") at the beginning and later in the essay.

C.33.1. Preface to Lu Qingzi, Kaopan ji

Poetry holds no difficulty but the difficulty of intent [*zhi*]. Intent holds no difficulty, but not to be impure is difficult. For when intent lies in high mountains but the tone resembles agitated waters, or when intent lies in flowing waters but the melody is high and lofty, then thought and matter are disconnected and idea and hearing deviate from each other. If the principle of poetry is not established, what basis would we have for collecting folk songs?

(2) When my wife married me at fifteen, her mind was set on learning, and in her studies, she was bent on learning poetry. After more than a decade, we had her *Yunwo gao* [Manuscript of reclining among clouds] printed. But she did not allow it to be shown to others, so it was discarded and not preserved. After my parents passed away, I was debilitated by an illness. My wife daily cared for me with recipes from prescription books and medicinal compresses to help my emaciated form. Only after five to seven years did I show some

sign of recovery. Each day she made obeisance to the Lord of Medicine, praying for wisdom and release from suffering. Rising early to recite her lessons before coming downstairs, she spared no efforts.

When I look back to the past and recall my wife's earliest crafted verses, they seem more unreal than an obscure light, feebler than the fire obtained from drilling stones, and more random and useless than the sound of freely rushing water. Then why do I once again trouble the printer with a second collection? (3)

Thus we know that to pursue learning without application one would not be "without impurity of thought;" however, to pursue no-learning with application would be even further from "not having impurity of thought." Today's truth [*gong an*: kōan] is yesterday's illusory splendor; the non-being of this moment is the being of another moment. Only when we understand this can we speak of "having no impurity of thought." (4)

If I were to discuss my wife's accomplishments in poetry, I would say that in her "imitations of ancient models" [*nigu*] she starts from [the models] of the Western Capital [i.e., the Western Han], selecting her materials from the Six Dynasties. In her five- and seven-character regulated couplets, she has not overstepped the standards set by the Kaiyuan [713–42] and Tianbao [742–56] periods; it goes without saying that she paid no attention to those who came after Changqing [Bo Juyi]. Her quatrains and regulated verse are quite readable. Recently she has begun to tackle the seven-character old style. She says herself that her own writing in some ways resembles the style of the eight masters of the early Tang. Prose essays are not her specialty, but they have been included at the end so that altogether there are six chapters under the title *Kaopan*. As regards this title, she says it is not that she dares to "criticize the times" [in writing these poems], but, like the ancient recluse, she "wakes alone, talks to herself, and does not tell her joy." As for ornate rhyme-prose, we know that it is not orthodox writing, the teaching passed down by the masters. Even Yang Xiong was still able to say this. But from the Jian'an period [196–220], it gradually became popular among the scholar-officials. Who would claim that Qu Yuan, Song Yu, Su Wu, and Li Ling are not writers? Yet they did not become famous men because of their ornate expressions, nor did they take ornate expressions as their hobby. They expressed themselves only because they could not help it. Therefore, of course, they had something to say, unlike women whose conduct is regulated and whose actions follow established patterns. For women, only poetry can express their intent. Poems like the "Ge tan" [poem 2] and "Juan er" [poem 3] of the *Book of Odes* were largely written by (5) women. There is not one dynasty that has lacked the transmission of the way of women's poetry. But meddling Confucian scholars would record poems as though they were sifting gold from sand, in the process mixing up the beautiful and the ugly, the good and the bad. These gentlemen of ignorance—how one is amazed at their interference and their complete abandonment of the distinctions between black and white, superior and inferior! I am afraid that if Ban Zhao were still with us, she would have been laughing for a thousand years at these two beings—summer insects and morning mushrooms.

(6) On the day before New Year's Eve, in the year *gengzi* of Wanli [1600], Zhao Huanguang, the useless husband, wrote this in the Butterflies Bedchamber.

(Hu Wenkai, 168–70)

par. 5, Kaiyuan and Tainbao periods: These two reign periods are considered the High Tang period of poetry.

par. 5, *Kaopan*: The collection is named after poem 56 of the *Book of Odes*. According to the traditional interpretation, the poem "criticizes Duke Zhuang of Wei [r. 756–734 B.C.E.] for being unable to continue the wise rule of his predecessors. He caused the worthy men of his kingdom to withdraw from service and live as recluses" (*Mao shi zhengyi*, in SSJZS, 3: 2/13a.) To guard against the perception that Lu's *Kaopan* collection is inspired by a similar critique, Zhao has her deny it explicitly and quote from the ode's praise of the secluded life.

par. 5, Yang Xiong (53 B.C.E.–18 C.E.): This author of numerous *fu* subsequently repudiated the genre.

par. 5, "summer insects and morning mushrooms": On the lady scholar Ban Zhao, see P.60.9 and P.69.5. In *Zhuangzi*, "summer insects" and "morning mushrooms" exemplify what is short-lived, and here, by extension, the shortsightedness of the scholars whom Zhao Huanguang wishes to attack.

BACKGROUND NOTE AND TRANSLATION BY GRACE S. FONG

花裀上人

C.34. Huayin shangren (early 17th century)

Huayin shangren (the reverent flower-worshipper) is certainly a pseudonym—but of whom is unknown. "Flower-worshipping" would be a recherché way of referring to a visit to the pleasure districts. The anthology by Zhang Mengzheng, *Qinglou yunyu* (Stylish words from the pleasure quarters, 1616) contains poems of 180 writers, principally courtesans.

C.34.1. Preface to Zhang Mengzheng, Qinglou yunyu

Things in this world that people like me find memorable are all distinguished by style [*yun*]. The blue buildings [the pleasure quarters] are a place of style; dwellers in the blue buildings are stylish people. Some may ask: "You call that style? What do those in the brothel themselves have to say? You certainly do not think that they are there to cultivate talent!" In response, one stylish ancient exerted himself to compose *The Classic of Whoring* [*Piao jing*].

Is *The Classic of Whoring* a work of style? Definitely. Some may argue: (2)
"Words composed with a sense of style are subtle and suggestive. There is no style if everything is out in the open. The *Classic of Whoring* does not seem to be very subtle." True enough. But if I use my lack of style to counter what the objector takes to be a lack of style, his discordance will be laid bare, and thereupon I can play gamesomely through it all. With this freedom, could style and rhyme be far away? Thus in my eyes, the brothel and people in the brothel are all most stylish, not to mention their poetry.

Hence the Daoist Adept Mengzheng has compiled this volume under the (3)
title *Stylish Words from the Pleasure Quarters.* Beginning with [a reprint of] *The Classic of Whoring*, he has added poetry, song lyrics, pictures, and evaluative comments that he and Mr. Yuanliang have casually jotted down. The comments are actually commentaries to *The Classic of Whoring.* Mengzheng is indeed the one with style! To those in posterity who are devoted to such a Way, isn't Mengzheng a Master Zhu [Xi]? If students pursuing the way of style honor Mengzheng as Master Zhu, perhaps in the future they will graduate to be erudite scholars and the *Classic of Whoring* will be magnified. Let me turn to the *Classic* and talk stylish words. Written by Huayin shangren at the Green Sky Thatched Hut.

(Hu Wenkai, 892)

par. 1, "style" [*yun*]: *Yun* is an adjective/noun with many meanings. Its primary one is that of rhyme—the recurrence of harmonious sounds. *You yun*, "having rhyme," is a term of aesthetic praise. When used to describe works of literature, it means harmonious and elegant. When used to describe people, it refers to qualities of deportment—elegance, beauty, order. A modern colloquial English equivalent might be "style," as in "having style."

par. 1, "*The Classic of Whoring*": The title of this work, *Piao jing*, is a parody of Confucian Classics, e.g., *Xiao jing* (The classic of filial piety), *Shi jing* (*Book of Odes* or "Classic of Poetry").

par. 2, "discordance will be laid bare": In the original, *buyun*, "without *yun*." In rendering this as "discordance," I refer to the meaning of *yun* that can be understood as "harmony" or "rhyme."

par. 3, "commentaries to *The Classic of Whoring*": Again, in parodic imitation of the text-and-commentary format of the Confucian Classics.

par. 3, "Master Zhu": Zhu Xi (1130–1200) is the famous Song neo-Confucian philosopher, founder of a school whose interpretations of the Classics were the basis of orthodox learning for hundreds of years.

BACKGROUND NOTE AND TRANSLATION BY DOROTHY KO

趙時用

C.35. Zhao Shiyong (early 17th century)

Zhao wrote the preface to Qu Juesheng's anthology *Nü sao* (Poetic elegies by women, 1618).

C.35.1. Preface to Qu Juesheng, Nü sao

Besides the *Book of History* [*Shang shu*], I know by heart the extensive teachings of the *Book of Odes*. The genres of poetry have undergone many changes: from the Airs and Odes to *sao* [elegiac verse modeled after the *Songs of Chu* (Chuci)] and *fu* [rhyme-prose], to four-line poems, to *pailü* (regulated verse sequences), and to song-lyrics. While their subgenres are too many to name one by one, these poems were mostly composed to lament the times, satirize current affairs, voice heartfelt emotions, express feelings, play with the wind and moon, or paint pictures of mountains and streams. Heroes and scholars can recite them from memory. One is all too familiar with [the anthologizing mistakes of] discarding gems with trash or listing details but omitting essentials, and [the examination candidate's shortcut of] reciting summaries. Hence I need not comment on them here.

(2) As for ladies in the inner quarters, they must discipline themselves according to womanly virtue, deportment, word, and looks, as well as cultivating their stillness, quietude, chastity, and serenity. They are not supposed to befriend paper, ink, writing brush, and ink slab. Even when extraordinary literary feats were performed by women, as in the case of Ban Zhao completing the *History of the Former Han*, these authoresses were not properly recognized, not to mention other [lesser writers]. Therefore, although we have biographies of exemplary women and the hundred-*juan Precepts for Women* by the Tang

Empress Wende, both of which are useful in preserving past exemplars for the edification of future generations, no woman has been known especially for her poetry. The works of the occasional women poets are lost or scattered for lack of compilation, although they cannot be said to have completely vanished.

This anthology is like no other: it opens with the Queen Mother of the West, continues with an exhaustive search through the successive generations for choice verse of true emotions, and arranges the results in sections under one cover. Included in this anthology are works of all sorts of women, be they chaste or lewd, transcendent or mortal, barbarian or Chinese, respectable or mean. Their moral character and deeds are not always worth mentioning. (3)

But these poets are all endowed with intelligence and wit, and are capable of turning a phrase with ease. In dispatching emotions, they bare their intimacies without reservation, evoking [the reader's] uncontrollable sympathy. In depicting objects they explore indirect and hidden allegories, making them as plain as a picture in relief. Some poems are vows of unswerving integrity that are in themselves sufficient testimonies; some are admonitions of incorruptible chastity that show the poet's resoluteness. Some poems are detached and nonchalant, yet the reader is pervaded with their rich elegance. Other poems are expressions in the face of scenery, and powerful enough to rend the reader's vitals. Like chirping cicadas or black beetles, the voices of these poems are clear, strong, and brilliant. They are as free and expressive as the notes of the five-tone scale; as crisp and resounding as the percussion of metal and stone. These poems are as good as those crafted by eloquent literati writers. Who can assign them ranks of high and low? (4)

In my spare time I sat up and read the poems in this anthology. It uplifted my spirit and brought a smile to my face. I was so moved that I drafted this colophon: "This publication will stand alongside the *Book of History* in the Hall of Immortality. The editor's intention is none other than this." This compilation is hence entrusted to the woodblock cutters so that it can be made public and available to all. (5)

Composed by Zhao Shiyong of Xin'an, in the year *wuwu* of the Wanli reign [1618]. (6)

(Hu Wenkai, 884–85)

par. 2, "womanly virtue, deportment, word, and looks": It is noteworthy that the virtues listed here depart from the conventional "Four Virtues" in substituting "looks" for "womanly work"; compare the lists at P.60.9 and C.2.1.

par. 2, "biographies of exemplary women . . . *Precepts for Women*": The former refers to the *Lie nü zhuan* (Biographies of women, 79–78 B.C.E) by Liu Xiang. The *Precepts for Women* (*Nü ze*) is a work in ten *juan*, not one hundred (cf. Hu Wenkai, pp. 27–28). Both these works went through many popular and deluxe editions in the late Ming and early Qing.

par. 3, "Queen Mother of the West": On this goddess see P.69.5. Her poetic exchange with King Mu of the Zhou is recorded in the *Mu Tianzi zhuan* (Biography of Mu, Son of Heaven). For a translation of the poems and a discussion of the legend, see S. Cahill, *Transcendence and Divine Passion*, pp. 50–51.

TRANSLATED BY DOROTHY KO

C.36. Zhao Shijie (17th century)

Little is known of Zhao Shijie. He seems to have been engaged to write this preface by the publisher of *Gu jin nü shi* (Female scribes, ancient and modern, 1628), a collection of previously published work issued in a plain edition (eight *juan*) and a more elaborate one (ten *juan*).[1]

C.36.1. Preface to Gu jin nü shi

Confucius surveyed the "Airs of the States" and said: "Poetry can stimulate; it teaches observation, sociability, and the expression of grievances." In collecting and editing those rhymed sayings, he did not reject the songs of the "wandering girls" of the Han and Yangzi Rivers. Who will say that the Three Hundred Odes of the *Book of Odes*, the "Elegantiae" and the rest, can only have been composed by upright sages and scholars?

(2) When one looks back to the beginnings of history—to the days of Fu Xi and the Yellow Emperor—documents are few or none. The scattered writings of the period of Yu and Xia have not been passed down. But the records do speak of Yue's destruction of Wu, how Yiguang and Xiuming were like a pair of phoenixes in the smoke and mist, singing elegant songs in the feasting-halls and performing regrets and complaints in the women's inner quarters. Were they entirely devoid of literary ability? In the days of the Seven Warring States, with battles going on day and night, no time was left for literary composition, but Lady Fan and Zheng Xiu must not have lacked wit and conversational skill. Han E sang but once, yet her sorrows clung to the beams of the inn.

(3) Nonetheless, these women's compositions have all vanished without a trace

—and not only on account of wars or as a result of the fires in the palace of Qin, but also because bamboo codices and lacquered books, while hard to make, were not easy to keep. On the rise of the Han, bamboo gave way to silk, "birds' tracks" writing was replaced by brushstrokes, seal-script was abandoned for the official script, all of which made the preservation of books less uncertain. The song of Xiang Yu of Chu and his concubine Yu could then become famous; and the *History of the Han* records an elegant remonstrance by the Favored Beauty Ban *jieyu* [P.1]. Han Detong spoke up for the Female Scribe Zhao Feiyan and told her story, saving her from oblivion. And Ban Zhao succeeded to the Grand Historian's palace in order to complete the great work of the Western Capital. Who can say that female talent does not deserve to be recorded?

From the Sui and Tang on down to the present day, writings have been inscribed on wood and carved into printing-blocks which, once overspread with ink, carry poems and essays by female talents into every corner of the empire. "Public servants in their light carts" have also selected and recorded their writings. It may be that spiritual beauty on this earth dominates in females and not in males. Why do I speak of them as having "spiritual beauty"? In that phrase, both their writings and their persons are applauded. (4)

The court music of the Han included the "Fangzhong" and "Handbell" songs, composed by Lady Tangshan. And in the Song dynasty there was Lord Kou of Lai who, while posted at the northern gate on a winter's day "so short it was less than a foot long," heard a bewitching woman's singing and was so pleased with it that he gave her a bundle of colored silks, a layer of clothing with which to pass the cold months. (5)

So it is that among female writers, there are those whose floating diction surpasses their substance, those whose delicate artfulness harms simplicity; but there are also those spontaneous talents who can raise a cup and burst into song. One finds the glow of flowers and the rouge of flower stamens; there are those whose graceful tread is like floating; and there are those who sit by the quiet window and listen to the click-clack of the loom, those who write of intricate inner-courtyard sentiments, of orioles on a branch, of lonely dreams beneath a sliver of moon. Their thoughts, concentrated on a single person to the exclusion of all others, impel them to take up the silver tube and write. Such lovely wording, fit to be sung by domestic sing-song girls, is like a single red lotus opening up on green water: a thousand flowers and ten thousand grasses suddenly pale by comparison. One may say: the universe is vast and (6) unfathomable, and the generations of men are enduring; but ladies of exceptional skill, though unknown to fame, march along in an unbroken procession.

(7) In their poetry, contact with external nature induces the release of private feelings. The chill of their fingers and the perfume of their teeth are here transmitted unceasingly by their fragrant throats and castanets of cedar. I do not know the variety of which female talent is capable, nor do I know the many changes it has yet to put itself through. What I have seen is various enough: familiar subjects brought to new conclusions, or old feelings taken to a new depth. These, along with the waxing and waning of literature through dynastic change and the differences of individual talent, are here preserved, in both "the shadow and its original," thanks to animal hair and mulberry leaves [i.e., brush and paper]. At a glance, these women instantly "stimulate, cause one to observe, to feel sociability, and to sympathize with the expression of grievances." They can be taken as testimonials to the "airs and elegancies" of their age. This book is like an immense shop where pearls, ornaments, clothes, and every kind of curiosity are spread out. Open the book: left and right you encounter fresh springs; is it not delightful? There is no need [for women poets] to "carve feathers and tree-leaves" [i.e., become specialist scholars] or to "harness the winds and ride the clouds" [i.e., achieve success in the examinations] in order to create a grand literary purview.

(8) Though these poems may be no more than "whispered conversation between the lamps," "private laughter before the big wine-vessel," "haggard mumblings all alone," "autumn griefs and broken hearts," "lengthy sighs before a landscape" and "short-lived regrets while facing the wind," I have preferred, as a collector, to leave nothing out, so as to make up for centuries of neglect. If you compare my efforts to the devotion of flower arrangers for the single blossom, as recorded in the *Vase Annals*, the two red cheeks that characterize those who often consult the *Annals of Wine*, or the wide learning and happy laughter of those well-read in the *Annals of Humor*, you will find my collection quite unlike those that have gone before. If ever someone comes along to compose the *Vermilion Annals* of women's culture, that writer must attend not only to people's sleeping arrangements but also to the matters of plain and colored silk, the better to renew the yet living sounds of *Sao* and *Ya*. Then everything will be represented, from the deep to the delicate; and that may indeed be called a "history."

(9) Composed and written out by Zhao Shijie of West Lake.

(Hu Wenkai, 888–89)

par. 1, "Poetry can stimulate": *Analects* 17.9.

par. 1, "wandering girls": See *Book of Odes*, poem 9: "The girls by the Han River go wandering, but one cannot pursue them." The Little Preface to this poem states that "The virtue of King Wen [of the Zhou] spread to the southern lands, and his good influence ran as far as the valleys of the Yangzi and Han rivers. None thought of breaking the rules of propriety; one might pursue a woman, but would not obtain her." Confucius was supposed to have compiled the *Book of Odes* as evidence of such acts of moral transformation.

par. 2, "Fu Xi and the Yellow Emperor": The legendary ruler Fu Xi (early third millennium B.C.E.) is supposed to have invented the graphs of the *Yi jing*, the precursors of all later Chinese writing systems. On the Yellow Emperor, see P.76.3; according to legend the emperor's record keeper, Cang Jie, created writing.

par. 2, "period of Yu": Shun, China's last predynastic ruler, gave over the throne to Yu, founder of the Xia dynasty, in 2205 B.C.E., according to the traditional chronology.

par. 2, "Yue's destruction of Wu": For these stories, see the *Zuo zhuan*. Yiguang (also known as Xi Shi; see P.39.2) and Xiuming were a pair of legendary beauties sent by the sovereign of Yue to the court of Wu, where they distracted the ruler of Wu from the proper administration of his state and thus prepared his downfall.

par. 2, Lady Fan and Zheng Xiu: Fan Ji, wife of King Zhuang of Chu, persuaded him to devote less time to hunting and more to the administration of his kingdom. The concubine Zheng Xiu is briefly mentioned in *Shi ji* as having influence over her lord, King Huai of Chu.

par. 2, "Han E sang but once": "When Han E, on her way to Qi, ran short of provisions, she stood at the Yong gate and sang for her supper. After she had left, the echoes wound themselves around the pillars and beams of the inn where she had sung and did not die out for three full days" (*Liezi*, chap. 5).

par. 3, "fires in the palace of Qin": The first emperor of a unified China, Qin Shi Huangdi (r. 246–210 B.C.E.), gathered together all the books in the empire and prohibited their free circulation. In the civil war that followed his death, the imperial libraries were burned.

par. 3, "Xiang Yu of Chu": On Xiang Yu and his consort Yu, see P.28.1.

par. 3, "the great work of the Western Capital": The *History of the Former Han* (*Han shu*), begun by Ban Gu and completed by his sister Ban Zhao.

par. 4, "Public servants in their light carts": According to tradition, these were officials sent out to collect dialect expressions and folk songs as evidence of popular opinion.

par. 4, "spiritual beauty . . . dominates in females": In the original *lingxiu*, "spiritual beauty" or "divine essence." The phrase also occurs in Qu Yuan's "Li sao" as a designation for the ruler.

par. 5, Lady Tangshan: A concubine of Emperor Gaozu of the Han, said to have composed the "Fangzhong" suite of ceremonial songs: see *Han shu* 22, "Li yue zhi."

Zhao innovates by crediting her with the "Handbell Songs" as well. For texts of both sequences, see Lu Qinli, ed., *Xian Qin Han Wei Jin Nanbeichao shi*, pp. 145–47, 155–62.

par. 5, "so short it was less than a foot long": Phrase quoted from Li Bo, "Shu dao nan," QTS, 162/1681.

par. 5, "with which to pass the cold months": This passage represents a somewhat muddled understanding of a story found in Zeng Zao, comp., *Lei shuo*, 52/24a–25a. Kou dreamt of a beautiful woman, and when he encountered the same woman being led about by an old procuress, he bought her for his concubine. While Kou was appointed to guard the Northern Gate, he once was so impressed with a singing-girl's performance that he presented her with a bundle of silks, whereupon his concubine, Qiantao, composed a poem: "For one strain of pure song, a packet of fine silk! / But the beauty seems still unsatisfied. / Who knows how many times the Weaving Girl at her workroom window / Must ply her shuttle for a single piece of cloth?" A short preface to Qiantao's poem in an anthology of women's compositions is likely to have been Zhao's intermediate source.

par. 7, "The chill of their fingers . . . castanets of cedar": Standard allusions for these phrases, as recorded in the *Peiwen yunfu* lexicon, lead into contexts associating females with elegant leisure. "Cold fingers": "When fingers are cold, endurance is easy; / But when eyes grow bleary, it is bitter indeed" (Chen Zao, "Playing Chess with Shi-shi on a Snowy Night"). "Fragrant throats": "When the crimson lips open, breaking through green clouds, / They draw into the fragrant throat delightful red jade" (Cui Jue, "Song of the Beautiful Tea-Drinker"). "Castanets of cedar": "In the painted hall, cedar castanets clap the autumn to bits" (Du Mu) and "Their dance flings forth radiance, captivating the drunken guest; / Now singing with slow voices and cedar castanets, they change to newer songs" (Ouyang Xiu).

par. 8, "*Vase Annals*": The poet and essayist Yuan Hongdao (1568–1610) wrote a treatise on the enjoyment of flowers, entitled *Ping shi* (Vase annals); reprinted in CSJC, vol. 1559.

par. 8, "*Annals of Wine*": *Jiu shi*, by Feng Shihua (Ming dynasty); reprinted in CSJC, vol. 1478.

par. 8, "*Annals of Humor*": *Xie shi*, by Shen Chu (Song dynasty).

par. 8, "*Vermilion Annals*": The term "vermilion scribe" derives from "Jing nü" (poem 42 in the *Book of Odes*). The "vermilion tube" mentioned in that poem, apparently given to the narrator as a love-token by the "quiet girl," was understood by the Han-dynasty annotator Zheng Xuan as the red writing-brush of a female palace official charged with keeping order in the women's quarters and regulating the women's access to the sovereign. Zheng's note, while doubtless a misinterpretation, took on historical authority: from the Tang to the Ming there was indeed an official rank of "vermilion scribe." The phrase allows Zhao to look forward to writers of "vermilion"—that is, women's—history. "Plain and colored silk" are here materials used for writing. *Sao* and *Ya* are two genres of ancient poetry: by the *Sao* is meant a personal song of complaint like those of Qu Yuan, and by the *Ya*, the courtly poetry of the eponymous sections of the *Book of Odes*.

BACKGROUND NOTE AND TRANSLATION BY HAUN SAUSSY

葛徵奇

C.37. Ge Zhengqi (17th century)

Ge Zhengqi wrote the preface to Jiang Yuanzuo's collection *Xu yutai wenyuan* (Garden of writings from the Jade Terrace, second series, 1632).

C.37.1. Preface to Jiang Yuanzuo, Xu yutai wenyuan

While spring orioles do not sing by following scores, they often employ the full range of their weak chirping. In the orchid kingdom many fragrances bloom, serving as a gathering place for the fragrant [ladies]. Casual words dispatched through tiny windows are not meant to be silver and gold; pensive thoughts of the recluse do not dwell on the golden seals and purple insignia [of bureaucratic appointments]. Both the cacophony and silence of birds are [subjects of] literature. Both the laughter and remorse of flowers are to be written about. Fine silks and damasks do not linger on the weaving maid's loom; [ladies with] hearts as fair as orchids vie to spread their lustrous pearls in front of the banquet table.

My friend Jiang Bangyu [Yuanzuo] has so resolved to steal away [from (2)
the world that he would have] dug a hole in his back wall. He turns his back on several generations of illustrious official careers. Instead, he retreats to the mountains, hearing nothing but the chiming of jade from six pine trees. Amidst herb and flower patches, bamboo waves and tea steam, hundreds of friends pass on laudable tales; thousands come with invitations for poetry and drinking games. Every chanted syllable of pearl and jade embraces the [serenity] of the shining moon; every word on the five-tone scale sounds as though it is flying off with the soaring phoenix. [Expressive words on] fragrant, ivory-colored sheath and aged silk form a precious pair; new songs rival the Lantian jade mine in their beauty.

It is not that the luminous force [*qi*] of heaven and earth does not impel (3)
men, but the universe of words is a field that belongs to women. [For Jiang the compiler,] retrieving an inch of [women's writings] from secret scrolls and

torn books is like discovering an inch of priceless jade. He cherishes new utterings gleaned from metaphysical talks and elegant parties like the sweet breath of a new friend. [Before reading them] he wipes his desk with an asbestos cloth until not a grain of dust remains, and he holds his breath at the tip of his tongue, as if afraid of exhaling. Repeatedly he chants the words, until fragrance arises from the depth of his tongue—or does it exude from the words themselves? Then repeatedly he copies the words, until radiance shines through the tip of the writing brush—or does it shine through the paper? When he unrolls these scrolls in front of flowers, the blossoms have their fragrance enhanced; when he ponders on lines in front of the window sill, the snow maiden twists her tongue [in response]. He savors [these writings] with wine in the Su family and drinks into the long night without getting drunk. He reads them by the light filtered from a neighbor's room and sits up until dawn with startled thoughts.

(4) At first [Jiang works as laboriously as] the Weaving Girl toiling over the loom; his movement is constant but his compositions few. Then he gathers eight treasures in a book case and quickly writes several volumes. He does not shrink from the toils of Scholar Xu, hence his works are read in every household. Year after year their impact accumulates, to the satisfaction of the master [compiler]. Those holding office can make their writing brushes sing and their ink dance; they have no trouble finding listeners. Those left in the wilderness [scribble on] broken pebbles and fallen steles, unable to leave behind a legacy. Were it not for the swaying elegance of Jiang Bangyu, the fairies would have averted the wind and halted their steps. But just because of Bangyu's erudite eloquence, even the beautiful one tells her dreams and bares her heart. Therefore no lady writer has her collection overlooked, and no collection has a chapter amiss, lest a fair beauty have a piece unrecorded or a piece contain unrequited regrets.

(5) Even a mansion of gold cannot store all the songs from one era; but a tower of white jade may house all the words and phrases in history. Who withers? Who prospers? Is it the one who sings *wuwu*? Or is it the one who sobs *yuyu*? In a score of thatched huts Jiang hangs up three thousand sandals. Instead of glazed tiles [for decoration] he uses glazed ink slabs and boxes to transfix the minute thoughts of the literati writer. Instead of jade screens, he entices the poet to stay by offering jade brush rests. Reading this volume, I have developed a great admiration for him.

Written by Ge Zhengqi of Dongwu, in a boat on the West Lake, on the Double Seventh Festival in the year *renshen* of the Chongzhen reign [1632]. (6)

(Hu Wenkai, 887–88)

par. 1, "Fine silks and damasks . . . the banquet table": Alternative reading: "Rich youths draped in silk brocades do not figure in the writings of the heavenly weaving girl; ladies with hearts as fair as orchids vie to spread their writings in front of the banquet table." This reading derives from the metaphorical reading of "loom" (*jizhu*), referring to the design and setting of a piece of writing, and of "lustrous pearls," which also refers to well-crafted works of literature.

par. 3, "the snow maiden twists her tongue": Xue'er, a seventh-century concubine, used here to refer generically to singing girls skilled in songs and verse.

par. 3, Su family: Presumably the distinguished Song-dynasty literary family of Su Xun (1009–66), Su Shi (Su Dongpo, 1037–1101), and Su Che (1039–1112).

par. 4, Scholar Xu: The identity of Scholar Xu is not clear. Given the author's emphasis here on the toils and troubles inherent in the writing process, a likely candidate is Xu Shen (30–124), compiler of the monumental philological treatise, *Shuowen jiezi*.

TRANSLATED BY DOROTHY KO

葉紹袁

C.38. Ye Shaoyuan (1589–1649)

Ye Shaoyuan (style name Tianliao) was, like his wife Shen Yixiu (P.54a), a native of Wujiang county in Jiangsu and was born into a family whose sons had become renowned scholar-officials for generations. Because of a prediction shortly after his birth that he would die in childhood and in view of the deaths of four elder brothers in infancy, Ye was given for adoption at the age of four months to Yuan Huang (1533–1606), a close friend of his father, Ye Zhongdi (d. 1599) and a fellow successful *jinshi* examinee of the class of 1587. Raised under another name to protect him from misfortune, Ye returned to his family in 1598—after the force of the prediction was deemed to have been spent—and assumed his given name Shaoyuan ("he who carries on the Yuan tradition"), a tribute to his foster family.

Ye Shaoyuan married Shen Yixiu, who was also a member of a distinguished family of scholar-bureaucrats, in 1605 and spent the next two decades preparing for the civil service examinations. Much of this time he was away from home, leaving Shen Yixiu to raise their four daughters and eight sons. After passing the *jinshi* examination in 1625, Ye embarked on a short-lived official career that essentially ended late in 1630, when he received permission to return home to look after his aging mother.

Of the twelve children of Ye Shaoyuan and Shen Yixiu, the three oldest daughters, Ye Wanwan (P.54b), Ye Xiaowan (P.54c), and Ye Xiaoluan (P.54d), were known as accomplished poets, and the sixth son, Ye Xie (1627–1703), became a noted writer and critic, the author—among other works—of the *Yuan shi* (Origins of poetry). Shen Yixiu had made a point of providing the same systematic classical and literary education to all of her children.

Between 1632 and 1635, Xiaoluan and Wanwan, their mother, and two brothers all died. Ye Shaoyuan spent those grief-ridden years gathering the many works of his immediate female family members and other female relations, along with tributes to them, into a volume titled *Wumengtang ji* (Collection from the Hall of Noontime Dreams). After the death of his wife he did not remarry. He completed an autobiography in 1637 and then took the tonsure in a Buddhist monastery, where he remained until his death. Two collections of his poems have not survived, but, in addition to the *Wumengtang ji*, his autobiography, a supplement to it, a collection of anecdotes he compiled, and his diary are included under the title *Ye Tianliao si zhong* in the *Zhongguo wenxue zhenben congshu* published in 1936.[1]

C.38.1. Preface to Wumengtang ji

There are three ways by which men can achieve immortality: by establishing their virtue, by establishing their deeds, and by establishing their words. Women also have three such methods: virtue, talent, and beauty. These have been respected traditions since antiquity. Certainly, "[she who] resembles Heaven," "the virtuous maid," "[the women by the] Qi River," and "the eminent lady" were not praised because of their alluring beauty alone. But in the *Songs of Chu* it is also said: "Dainty features, elegant bearing grace all the marriage chamber; / Mothlike eyebrows and lustrous eyes that dart out gleams of brightness." It would appear, therefore, that women should exhibit their charms and outshine each other's graces, so that their beauty will be singled out for display, rather than vying in terms of talent or virtue.

(2) However, when [Xun] Fengqian [early third century] grieved over the spirit [of his dead wife], to whom he was devoted with a singularly earnest determi-

nation, later generations of scholars were certain to fault his deluded partiality and criticize his uxoriousness. Therefore they have not spoken about beauty, and songs that are the legacy of "clustered peach trees" and "the hibiscus" are profoundly taboo to the speech of gentry males. Unless a woman is the jade countenance in the imperial quarters, she is not to be distinguished from the rest. Stories are told about Zhaoyang and Huaqing [Springs, where the emperor's] favor allowed [Yang Guifei] to bathe, but supposing that a woman's beauty surpassed that of Yiguang or her charms exceeded those of Zheng Dan, if they were put to song in the manner of [Li] Yannian and vaunted and praised in the women's quarters, this would cause a respectable woman to blush and hide away.

Therefore, since it is forbidden to speak of bewitching appearances, one (3)
leg of the tripod [of the three feminine attributes mentioned above] has been cut off, and thus only the remaining two—talent and virtue—are respected by all today. But although these two attributes have become this respected, still the current consideration of talent is as scant as that of beauty, and it is rarely raised as a topic for discussion. Now why is this so? It is because noble and wealthy women, dressed in intricately woven silks, pearls, and kingfisher plumes, and singing and dancing to whistling pipes, are rather unaccomplished when it comes to [books covered with] light blue and light yellow silk. And the lowborn are busy stitching embroidery and plying the needle on thin fabrics and woven brocades. Furthermore, women have the fragrant sacrificial offerings glistening with starchy rice water to present in person. They do not have the leisure to pore deeply over scrolls. Indeed, how can one speak easily of the talent necessary to read characters written on [paper scented with] the fragrance of red flowers or to append comments on fine powder-white paper?

Since it is not easy to speak of talent and also be forbidden to speak of (4)
beauty, and since gentry scholars also cannot bear to lapse into silence, the women and daughters in their families thus have had no alternative but to find recourse for both of these attributes in virtue. Therefore historians' accounts [written on] green [bamboo slips] of the women's quarters and memorials of women's deeds [written with] the vermilion brush [of the woman historian], such as those of the three Guans of Xiangdong, are too numerous to note. If these assembled accounts of elegant beauties are not rich and pleasing and imbued with deep and unspoken knowledge of individuals in all their multifariousness, then the "crimson tube" will find it difficult to be truthful, and the principles of women's life will be easily disobeyed.

(5) Now the more glorious a name one has, the more laborious must be one's preparation. If one's household is at base wealthy, [a woman] must chant forth "Which [garments] shall I wash?" If her natural appearance dispenses with cosmetics and kohl, then she has long exhibited "nothing imprudent." She takes delight in "picking artemisia" in order to prepare a headdress [to wear] when praying for a child. She laces coils around "hanging branches" like "creepers twined" around them. And she also fosters the virtuous conduct of others by weaving and stitching fabric wrappers for books, respectfully fulfilling the duties necessary to demonstrate filial piety, blending savory flavors for [the sacrificial altars, such as those established by the founder of the Han dynasty at] Fen and Yu, and ministering to the emperor. To maintain the bliss of marital harmony, she gives birth to sons and is a wise mother. She maintains the honorable reputation of the family, displaying goodness and exhibiting subtle virtues. As examples of all of these activities, lavish stories have been told. But has there not also been slander against the virtuous and prudent [woman] of the golden screen, alleging that the hen has crowed the dawn, and the defamation of the admirably virtuous [woman] of the jade canopy [i.e., the Queen Mother of the West] out of sororal jealousy? As I ponder over all the rest that I have heard, how much do I regret to find without basis and not to be believed!

(6) Therefore investigations into virtue lack the solid ground of the evaluation of talent. It is for this reason that when the great sage [Confucius] selected and edited the Three Hundred Poems [of the *Book of Odes*], all of the songs composed by women were included—whether they had to do with "picking thornferns," "plucking plantain," the "flying pheasant," the "flowing stream," or even the "clever youth" or "foolish fellow." If not for the fact that such [female] talent was difficult to find, would he have done it this way?

(7) Nevertheless, how after all has talent been esteemed? I have now and then examined the record from antiquity down through the ages. I shall not of course list all imperial consorts. As for [Cao] Dagu, [Zhuo] Wenjun, Lingxian, and Xu Shu—how could they not have been extolled for the past thousand years and the writings they have handed down not be recorded? However, conjugal bliss may end in tears and lament, and they all suffered an early widowhood. [Bao] Linghui [P.4] was a dazzling beauty but did not find a compassionate mate. Su Hui became a feathered immortal but to the end was a wife repining [the absence of her husband]. What Anren harbored in mourning [his wife's] death was after prolonged thought put to brush and

ink. Yanqing's night under the light of the moon was spent in vain listening to song-lyrics. This being so, if [a woman spends her time] adjusting silk threads and treading the [treadle of the loom], pounding the washstone and plying the shuttle to and fro, with her mind confused by characters in brocade and her eyes blinded by stone inscriptions, she can still have peace, glory, happiness, and wealth and live a long, joyful, and tranquil life. What need has she of brush stand, ink-stone box, tortoise-shell brush, and rue-scented notepaper, unnecessarily subjecting herself to the capricious reversals of the ignorant and small-minded? Thus we know that the flaunting of female talent does not often occur.

My wife Shen Wanjun loved literature from an early age and was thor- (8)
oughly versed in the Airs and Elegantiae [of the *Book of Odes*]. Together with our daughters she would compose pieces on flowers and grasses in ingenious and beautiful ways [literally, "carved the moon and tailored clouds"]. They enjoyed each other's company in such pursuits and were praised widely [for their accomplishments]. However, our eldest daughter Zhaoqi [Wanwan] died of pent-up grief just past the age of twenty, and our younger daughter Qiongzhang [Xiaoluan] died and became an immortal when she was only sixteen. And now Wanjun has also, out of maternal compassion and heartfelt grief, departed forever a life all too brief—like flowing water never to return and clouds of brilliant hues scudding off into the distance. The writings she left remain in her portfolio, manuscript relics over which I grieve in vain: pearls and jade no longer gleam, and agate and jasper have lost their luster. Great indeed are the burdens that talent places upon people! Suppose that Wanjun and our two daughters had not been so talented, or that their talent had not been so highly developed: how could they then have been visited with such misfortune by the great maker or have aroused the envy of celestial powers? If she of the uncivilized hammer-coiled hair could still determine to be the wife of Liang Hong, and if the woman with rudely tangled locks could presume to be part of Wang Ba's household, why could we two not have lived in humble reclusion at Green Gate and grown old in one another's company? But now the zither has been broken and the strings have snapped, the bamboo flute is shattered and the mirror has cracked.

That the misfortunes of the living should have come to this is, alas, to (9)
be lamented! My wife's virtue may not have equaled that of the wise men of old, but in her accomplishments she could stand without shame before any worthy woman. Her looks may have been just about average, but I ventured

to consider her a beautiful spouse. But the snow in front of Xie [Daoyun's] curtain melted away, and the pepper rotted in Lady Liu's small casket. The Court Gentleman would not remarry after his wife died [literally, would not attach another zither string], and Master Huan's [Yi] flute was irreplaceable. Sun Chu's emotional essay lamented in vain the love between husband and wife. Jiang Yan [444–505] had a dream and then shed useless tears over beautiful women. Alas, how sad it is!

(10) Written in the third month of the Chongzhen reign period [1636] by Ye Shaoyuan (Tianliao).

(Ye Shaoyuan, *Wumengtang qianji*, 3–4)

par. 1, "three ways . . . men can achieve immortality": See *Zuo zhuan*, Duke Xiang, year 24.

par. 1, "not praised because of their alluring beauty alone": "She who resembles heaven" is from poem 236 of the *Book of Odes*, which describes the virtues of the mothers of the first Zhou rulers, Kings Wen and Wu; "the virtuous maid" refers to the first poem in the *Book of Odes*, which commentators in the orthodox Mao tradition believed to extol the virtues of the consort of King Wen of Zhou; "[women by the] Qi River" may refer to poem 48 of the *Book of Odes*, which speaks of a rendezvous with three beautiful women on the banks of the Qi; "the eminent lady" alludes to poem 57 of the *Book of Odes*, which describes a stately noblewoman.

par. 1, "in the *Songs of Chu*": From "Zhao hun," *Chuci buzhu*, 9/7b; Hawkes, trans., *Songs of the South*, pp. 223–30.

par. 2, Xun Fengqian: Xun Can, style name Fengqian, was a native of Wei who lived during the Three Kingdoms era. The story of his deep attachment to his wife, the daughter of Cao Hong, is recounted in chapter 35, "Blind Infatuation" (*Huo ni*), of the *Shishuo xinyu*: "Hsun Ts'an [Xun Can] and his wife, Ts'ao P'ei-ts'ui, were extremely devoted to each other. During the winter months his wife became sick and was flushed with fever, whereupon Ts'an went out into the central courtyard, and after he himself had taken a chill, came back and pressed his cold body against hers. His wife died, and a short while afterward Ts'an also died. Because of this he was criticized by the world" (trans. Mather, *Shih-shuo Hsin-yü*, p. 485).

par. 2, "clustered peach trees" and "the hibiscus": From poem 6 of the *Book of Odes*, an epithalamium likening beautiful peach trees to the lovely young bride; and from poem 83 of the *Book of Odes*, where the face of a beautiful woman is compared to the beauty of the hibiscus.

par. 2, "Stories are told . . .": Zhaoyang was the palace where Yang Guifei (see P.18.12) resided; Yiguang was the legendary beauty Xi Shi (see P.39.2 and C.36.1); Zheng Dan, another legendary beauty of Yue, was a contemporary of Xi Shi's; on Li Yannian, see P.8a.2.

par. 4, "the three Guans of Xiangdong": *Xiangdong san Guan* would certainly include Guan Daosheng (P.23). A second famous Guan would be Daosheng's elder sister Guan Gao, who was also a noted calligrapher. See Hu Wenkai, pp. 74–75.

par. 4, "vermilion brush" and "crimson tube": Writing materials in the women's quarters, referring to the Zheng Xuan interpretation of poem 42 in the *Book of Odes*; see C.36.1.

par. 5, "shall I wash?": A reference to poem 2 of the *Book of Odes*.

par. 5, "nothing imprudent": Referring to poem 189 of the *Book of Odes*, which discusses the proper deportment for girls.

par. 5, "picking artemisia": Alluding to poem 13 of the *Book of Odes*.

par. 5, "coils around 'hanging branches' like 'creepers twined' ": Referring to poems 4 and 71 in the *Book of Odes*, both of which speak of the relationship between husband and wife.

par. 5, "the bliss of marital harmony": In the original, *jing qin*, "the peaceful zither," an allusion to poem 82 of the *Book of Odes*.

par. 5, "gives birth to sons and is a wise mother": Like Taisi, the wife of the Zhou king Wen; a reference to poem 240 of the *Book of Odes*.

par. 5, "[woman] of the golden screen": An allusion to a *yuefu* by Emperor Jianwen of the Liang dynasty (r. 550–51), "Du chu chou," in which a woman expresses the fear that the golden screen by which she sits will be deserted next year, that she will have lost favor. See Guo Maoqian, ed., *Yuefu shiji*, 76/1074.

par. 5, "hen has crowed the dawn": See P.1.2.

par. 5, Queen Mother of the West: See P.69.5.

par. 6, "all of the songs composed by women": "Picking thornferns" ("Cai wei") is the title of poem 167 in the *Book of Odes*, traditionally interpreted as a lament of soldiers far from home rather than a composition in a woman's voice; *wei* is most likely an error for *fan*, and the reference should therefore be to "Cai fan," poem 13 (see C.16.1). "Plucking plaintain" refers to poem 8 in the *Book of Odes*, which may have to do with fertility rituals. "Flying pheasant" refers to poem 33 in the *Book of Odes*, a celebration of mates. "Flowing stream" refers to poem 39 of the *Book of Odes*, in which a young bride wishes to return home to mourn her parents but is unable to do so. "Clever youth" and "foolish fellow" are both references to poem 84 in the *Book of Odes*, in which a young girl on a stroll hoping to see her gentleman friend encounters someone else less desirable.

par. 7, [Cao] Dagu: I.e., Ban Zhao, on whom see P.60.9 and P.69.5.

par. 7, [Zhuo] Wenjun: On Zhuo Wenjun and her "Song of White Hair," see P.38.1.

par. 7, Lingxian: Liu Lingxian of the Liang dynasty, younger sister of Liu Xiaochuo and wife of Xu Fei, and renowned, along with her two older sisters, for her literary talent; see Hu Wenkai, pp. 13–14.

par. 7, Xu Shu: Wife of Qin Jia of the Latter Han; see P.54a.4.

par. 7, Su Hui: On Su Hui, see C.1.1, C.4.1.

par. 7, "Anren . . . mourning [his wife's] death": A reference to Pan Yue, on whom see P.10.7.

par. 7, "Yanqing's night": Perhaps Zhang Fu of the Song, whose style name was Yanqing.

par. 8, "grown old in one another's company?": "The wife of Liang Hong" refers to Meng Guang, who with her husband became known during the Eastern Han as a model couple, despite the fact that her coiffure was typical of non-Han peoples like the Man and Yi. "The woman with rudely tangled locks" is the wife of Wang Ba of the Han dynasty; they were both known for their integrity and retired together in protest against the usurpation of Wang Mang (see Wang Ba's biography in *Hou Han shu*, 113). "Reclusion at Green Gate" alludes to Shao Ping, the marquis of Dongling, who after the overthrow of the Qin dynasty by the Han retired outside Qingmen, the east gate of Chang'an, and raised melons that became prized for their delicious flavor.

par. 8, "the bamboo flute is shattered": A precious bamboo flute made by Cai Yong (father of Cai Yan, P.2) and passed down in the family of the great flautist Huan Yi was accidentally broken by a dancing girl, provoking Wang Xizhi's fury. See Liu Yiqing, *Shishuo xinyu* 26.20 (Mather, trans., *Shih-shuo Hsin-yü*, p. 436).

par. 9, "snow in front of Xie [Daoyun's] curtain": On the story of Xie Daoyun's impromptu composition, see C.24.1.

par. 9, "The Court Gentleman would not remarry": This probably refers to Wang Zengru (465–522), who held the office of palace secretary under the Southern Liang. Wang is remembered for a poem lamenting the death of his concubine, ending with the lines: "When a zither string is broken it can still be replaced, / But when one's desire flees it cannot be kept back" (Lu Qinli, ed., *Xian Qin Han Wei Jin Nanbeichao shi*, 21/1768).

par. 9, "Sun Chu's emotional essay": Referring to a composition that Sun Chu of the Jin dynasty wrote following the death of his wife; it was said to have so effectively conveyed the depth of their mutual love that his friend Wang Ji declared the emotion and text inextricably linked. See Sun's biography in *Jin shu*, 56.

par. 9, Jiang Yan: On Jiang Yan and his writing brush, see P.113.6.

BACKGROUND NOTE AND TRANSLATION BY PAULINE YU

陳子龍

C.39. Chen Zilong (1608–47)

The poetic innovator and Ming-loyalist martyr Chen Zilong was a leader of the patriotic Fu she (Restoration Society) in the Jiangnan region. His Yunjian School of Poetry was partially responsible for the revitalization of the song-lyric form in the last years of the Ming. His relationship with Liu Shi (P.67 and see C.14) doubtless provided the occasion for this preface to her collection

Wuyin Cao (Manuscript from the year 1638), in which Chen vigorously advocates Yunjian ideals.

C.39.1. Preface to Liu Shi, Wuyin cao

I have studied poetry of the Han and Wei, the Six Dynasties, the Early Tang, High Tang, and Late Tang. The ways of creating landscape poetry and lofty expressions, and the ways of employing beautiful and flowery words, are indeed infinitely varied according to individual talents. . . . Thus, I can see that in the area of description, no one was as great as Bao Zhao [ca. 414–66] and Xie Lingyun [385–433]. . . . In feeling, none were as profound as Cao Zhi [192–232]. . . . And in literary expression, none were as accomplished as Du Fu [712–70]. As for poets of later generations, they were either lacking in the ability to create refined expressions of emotions or unable to write "poems celebrating objects" [*yongwu*] with profound implications—being largely misled by the principle of descriptive similitude. . . . But now, these poems by Lady Liu: how pure, creative, and far-reaching they are, impressively learned yet subtly uninhibited. . . . Indeed she can rank in the first class of poets. Since my early childhood, I have been fond of writing verse, and have seen numerous changes in the world. I realized that most contemporary works are about trifling experiences, not necessarily containing significant ideas. It was only after [Li Mengyang, 1473–1529] of Beidi established his school of poetry, and after the gentlemen of Jinan attained profundity in literary pursuits that the idea of "gentleness and elegance" [*wenya*] came to be cultivated and poems of lively imagination began to be composed. But still there are few works that are genuinely spontaneous and elegantly beautiful. . . . Finally, in my thinly populated hometown, there emerged several distinguished authors who valued poetry of great eloquence and beauty. Meanwhile Lady Liu came forth from the inner chamber [*qingsuo*], and by sheer chance, her style of poetry turned out to be quite similar to that of our group. Rare, is it not? Rare, is it not?

(Chen Yinke, *Liu Rushi biezhuan*, 1: 111–13)

par. 1, Li Mengyang and "the gentlemen of Jinan": Li Mengyang was one of the Former Seven Masters who dominated the Ming literary scene from 1490 to 1510. The "gentlemen of Jinan" refers symbolically to the Latter Seven Masters, for Li Panlong (1514–70), their chief spokesman, came from Jinan in Shandong province. These Former and Latter Masters were collectively known for their preference for the High Tang style of poetry, but as Andrew Plaks has observed, they "often show a high degree of inconsistency in their theories, especially over the span of their entire careers, and they frequently reverse themselves on key issues" (Plaks, *Four Masterworks of the Ming Novel*, p. 28).

BACKGROUND NOTE AND TRANSLATION BY KANG-I SUN CHANG

丁聖肇

C.40. Ding Shengzhao (1621–1700?)

Ding Shengzhao was the husband of Wang Duanshu (P.69) and wrote the preface for her anthology *Yinhong ji* (Red chantings, ca. 1655).

C.40.1. Preface to Wang Duanshu, Yinhong ji

The *Book of Odes* contains many poems written by women. In the past I have been overwhelmed by certain of these, such as "Male Pheasant" and "Spreading Vines," and also by the writings of Consort Li, which are reflected in the rhythms of the "Song of the Calabash" by Emperor Wu of the Han.

(2) My wife is by nature addicted to literary and historical writings, and she is good at painting and calligraphy. She does not much care for housework, and after she removes her make-up, in the dim light of the lamp, she chants poetry without ceasing. When snow clears over the western hills, when clouds envelop the golden tower, she seizes the moment, writing down her impressions quickly, before words escape her.

(3) We lived in Beijing for several years. Then my father was humiliated by Wei Zhongxian, the dynasty fell, and the emperor suffered his tragic demise at Coal Hill. At that point I took my family south, and my wife wrote more loyalist poetry than ever before. We returned to a humble house in my father's garden, occupying a small chamber known as Jesting Cottage, then moved to a rustic hut near the White Horse Cave for a few years. There she learned an appreciation for nature, which supplemented her more indirect style of observation—through a curtain or via reflections in a mirror. Dressed in coarse clothing and equipped with dusty cooking ware, she let her hair go uncombed until it startled the swallows, but she was peaceful and tranquil, and poems and essays filled her make-up box, the collection being called *Red Chantings*. It fully documents her seventeen years of experience in exile. I have nothing of my own to add, except to say that my wife is my good friend. She and I are

on the wing together, like a pair of wild ducks or geese. My wife's work is an inspiration for me.

Casual remarks by The Free Street Wanderer, Mr. Rui. (4)

(Hu Wenkai, 249)

par. 1, "overwhelmed by certain of these": "Xiong zhi" (Male pheasant) is poem 33 in the *Book of Odes*; "Ge tan" (Spreading vines) is poem 2. Like the work of Consort Li, they are traditionally thought to have been authored by women.

par. 3, "more loyalist poetry than ever before": The wording here recollects the example of the loyal poet-martyr Qu Yuan of Chu.

TRANSLATED BY ELLEN WIDMER

支如璔

C.41. Zhi Ruzeng (late 17th century)

Zhi Ruzeng, otherwise unknown, wrote the preface for the anthology by Zhou Zhibiao, *Nüzhong qi caizi lanke er ji* (Orchid babblings, part two, by seven talented women), which was published in the later seventeenth century.

C.41.1. Preface to Zhou Zhibiao, Nüzhong qi caizi lanke er ji

I read over *Orchid Babblings* and could not help clapping my hands! For the last few centuries, verse composition has followed the course of Princess Shengping's admiration for Li Duan's poetry, or echoed the Tang palace lady Shuangguan Wan'er's [P.7] appreciation of the good and bad points of the new-style verse of Shen Quanqi, and Song Zhiwen: such has been the dominant taste in poetry. But I could not accept this. How is a man of literary gifts to bow his head before a woman's judgments?

I have long dreamt that a gifted critic (if any such were to appear in heaven) (2)
might summon up Xi Shi, Nanwei, Yinji and Lady Xing, Taizhen, Qiaoniang, the Zhao sisters and their ilk. He would luxuriate in their graceful movements and charming airs, their successive expressions of anger and delight. He would command them to write on "parting thoughts," complete the *History of the Former Han*, praise the pepper-flower, sing of willow catkins, weave palindrome poems, set up partitions of red gauze, teach children, and compete *improvviso* with wave-patterned notepaper and round silk fans to decide the merits of "Bamboo Grove mannerisms" and "hidden treasures."

(3) For I, too, would do away once and for all with the humiliation of having palace women of the Tang act as our literary judges. My friend Junjian [Zhou Zhibiao] has the requisite literary gifts to rank the productions of a thousand ages; and as a number of talented women have appeared together in the last few decades, he has had an opportunity of criticizing them. Some time ago he issued a first collection of "Seven Talents." Now he has come forth with a second set of "Seven Talents," entitled, like the first, *Lanke*. The authors are all of a class with Cao Dagu [Ban Zhao] and Xie Daoyun. Are they less outstanding writers than Li Duan, Shen Quanqi, and Song Zhiwen? And lo! The wily Zhou has not only delved into the records of past ages, paying back debts of fame owed to women who have waited for a thousand years and more; he has also satisfied my half a lifetime's unfulfilled wish, and that is why I must applaud this *Lanke ji*.

(4) One may say: "In a woman lack of talent is a virtue." And yet another: "A woman who shows talent cannot live long or happily." If that is really so, and if literary ability is what is meant by "talent," then most women see it as having little importance. In the perfumed quarters, face-paints abound, but not paint for canvas; silver needles may be found, but no jade pipes. "Food, drink, silkworms, and weaving" make up the whole of their lives, as the *Book of Odes* has it. Shall brocade poetry-bags and books bound in figured wrappers be shoved aside as so much useless furniture? Alas! How small-minded a view of women this is! Far better the saying of Chen Zhengjun: "Men are like the sun, and women are like the moon."

(5) I say that women's writings are like the moon, whose splendor lies in its purity. The moon can be full, crescent, waxing, or waning. When it is setting or rising, when it appears only as a thin edge, when it is lost in a haze of clouds, when it is surrounded by comets that dart and dash about it, these are dark days for the moon, no doubt. But just as the moon comes to its "thrice five" and "twice eight," its mid-autumn splendor, so may a woman be fortunate, virtuous, and talented. Her headdress glows with kingfisher feathers, her ornaments are of clinking jade; her exquisite thoughts give forth beauty, and her elegant language is perfumed; pearls of diction fall from her hands. When the full moon is finally revealed in all her crystalline transparency, can one conceive that she is not to be set next to that blazing globe, the sun? Her anxious words and faithful advice; her fixed gaze and pent-up regrets; the separation of phoenix-mates and crane-matches; complaints and griefs of swans, tame and wild; the cricket's clear chirping; blood-washed azaleas—these waning phases

of the moon also have their moments of splendor. In sum, it is all one expanse of moonlight, a luster to be added to the sun's.

Zhou Junjian has carefully shaped and polished his seven treasures. Now he brings them forth in a white-jade tray, so that the world of poetry will now find added to it a land of cool purity, a pond of shadowy moonlight. Yu Chuanzi playing with his shadow—it is for his own pleasure. The moonlight Han Sheng dribbles out from his gourd spoon—you cannot take it in your hands or give it to another. (6)

Anciently there was a certain Mr. Zhou who got together a few hundred bamboo chopsticks, bound them together and said: "This is my ladder for climbing to the moon." And soon he was seen to pull from his breast a moon that shone as brightly as midday. An inspired feat of the spirit—just as is this book of Zhou Junjian's. After reciting the poems of the *Lanke ji*, can anyone hold that literature is not important to women? To pass by their work without giving it a careful reading—is that not to take all this colorful jade and moonlight, this precious "double wheel" and "triple earplug," and throw them out into the dribbling street? The Mr. Zhou of the old story would look on such acts with scorn, while his present-day counterparts would fail to find a hearing. Read the *Lanke* collection, I beg you, and decide for yourselves. (7)

Zhi Ruzeng of Wushui. Written at the Qingtan Tower. (8)

(Hu Wenkai, 845–46)

par. 1, "the dominant taste in poetry": Princess Shengping, daughter of the Tang emperor Daizong, was noted for her patronage of poets; for the story alluded to here, see Xing Wenfang, *Tang caizi zhuan*, 2: 80–81. On Shangguan Wan'er, see P.7 and C.25.1; for the story about her ranking of Shen Quanqi and Song Zhiwen above other court poets, see Zheng Guangyi, p. 294.

par. 2, "summon up Xi Shi . . . and their ilk": On Xi Shi, see P.39.2 and C.36.1; Nanwei lived in the Warring States period. Yinji and Lady Xing are found in *Shi ji*. Yang Guifei (on whom see P.18.12 and P.54a.1) took the name Taizhen [Greatly Transcendent] when in Daoist dress. Qiaoniang, concubine of the last Southern Tang ruler, Li Houzhu, was reputedly the first woman to bind her feet. On Zhao Feiyan, see P.1; Feiyan was eventually elevated to the rank of consort (*hou*).

par. 2, "command them to write . . . teach children": Each of these tasks echoes the subject of a famous piece of women's writing.

par. 2, "Bamboo Grove mannerisms" and "hidden treasures": These phrases allude to the *Shishuo xinyu* anecdote about Xie Daoyun (with her "Bamboo Grove spirit") and the young wife of the Gu family (the "hidden treasure"); see C.24.1.

par. 3, "a first collection of 'Seven Talents' ": The first *Nüzhong caizi lanke ji* seems to date from the late Ming or early Qing. A partial copy survives in the Beijing Metropolitan Library; see Hu Wenkai, p. 844, for bibliographical details.

par. 3, Li Duan, Shen Quanqi, and Song Zhiwen: Poets of the Tang dynasty reputed for their ornate and melodious verse.

par. 4, "Food, drink, silkworms, and weaving": See *Book of Odes*, poem 180, for the original context of this quotation.

par. 5, "like the moon": The extended simile of the following sentences parallels a passage in Feng Menglong's *Zhinang* (1626, 1634): "Some say that 'in a woman, lack of talent is a virtue.' . . . One may compare the sexes to the sun and moon: men are the sun, and women are the moon. When the sun gives off light and the moon borrows it, that is what the ancients had in mind when they glossed *qi* ['wife'] as *qi* ['equal']; when the sun sinks below the horizon and the moon comes out in its place, that is what the ancients had in mind when they glossed *fu* ['wife'] as *fu* ['guide']. Such is the wisdom—the talent—of the sun and moon" (*Zhinang quanji*, p. 504). For the intellectual context of these remarks, see Handlin, "Lü K'un's New Audience."

par. 5, "thrice five" and "twice eight": The moon takes "thrice five days to wax and thrice five to wane again" (*Records of Ritual*, "Li yun"), so that it is full and has not yet begun to decline on the sixteenth day (Bao Zhao: "On the days called Thrice-Five and Twice-Eight"). "Twice-Eight" also refers to the age at which a young girl was considered mature (cf. Li Bo: "red-cheeked and powdered, her years a double-eight").

par. 5, "Her headdress glows . . . pearls of diction fall from her hands": The language of this sentence borrows clichés of literary adulation and makes them into physical attributes of an imagined authoress. Save for "pearls of diction," the prolonged play on words fails to come across in English.

par. 6, "seven treasures": "Seven treasures combined" (*qibao hecheng*) is an epithet of the moon, as is "white-jade tray" below. The "seven treasures" also refers, of course, to the seven women anthologized in Zhou's volume.

par. 6, Yu Chuanzi and Han Sheng: Yu Chuanzi was the nickname of the Tang dynasty poet Lu Tong; for his "Poems on the Lunar Eclipse," see QTS, 387/4364–67, 4383. Han Sheng has not been identified.

TRANSLATED BY HAUN SAUSSY

尤侗

C.42. You Tong (1618–1704)

A well-known literary figure from the Suzhou area, You Tong was a licentiate in his mid-twenties when the Ming dynasty fell. He struggled unhappily for years to advance in the examination system under the Qing dynasty, but achieved official success only after passing the special palace examinations in

1679 at the advanced age of sixty-one, after which he was appointed to the Hanlin Academy to help with the compilation of the *Ming History*. He retired from office in 1683.[1] A prolific writer in many genres during the course of his long life, he enjoyed a high reputation as a man of letters, particularly as a playwright, and moved in top Qing literary circles. His voluminous collected works, *Youtang quanji*, was published during his lifetime and reprinted many times in the next two centuries.

In addition to supplying the following preface to Zhou Ming's anthology of poetry by women, *Linxia cixuan* (Song-lyrics from the lady's Bamboo Grove, 1671), You Tong also contributed a preface to the 1690 anthology of women's poetry *Zhongxiang ci* (Song-lyrics of many perfumes). An ardent subscriber to the cult of sentiment (*qing*), he was fascinated by the paradigm of the talented beauty who dies young and becomes an immortal. His infatuation with Ye Xiaoluan (P.54d), who died when he was fifteen and whom he never met, is richly documented in his poetry. The main female role in his autobiographical Southern Drama of 1655, *Juntian yue* (Celestial court music), is unmistakably modeled on her.[2]

C.42.1. Preface to Zhou Ming, Linxia cixuan

The expression "a lady's writing brush" comes from the three stanzas of "Jing nü." The people of Wei sang of Xuanjiang's cloud-like hair; but though her countenance was indeed fair, she falls short of Zhuangjiang, whose poems "Lü yi" and "Yan yan" arouse sympathy even in our age.

I have amassed a heap of regrets in my life—for instance, I am sorry that (2)
Xi Shi of Zhu, the crowning beauty of her age, left no verse on her travels by land and sea. Even so, ladies who use powder and paint mainly enjoy a life of rich blessings, whereas beauties who wield brush and ink mainly sigh over their poor fate. If the Plum-Blossom Consort, author of "A Peck of Pearls," still had to yield the Emperor's love and favor to the "Plump Maid," Yang Guifei, one may well ask why in the world daughters of commoners would bother to develop their talents.

Xiao Gang used to say: "If you compose in bed looking up at the rafters (3)
[in privacy and isolation], who will transmit your writings a thousand years hence?" The brocade words of a perfumed boudoir are like the secret books we keep under our pillow—occasionally they may circulate, but they are easily lost. If such writings do not find a sympathetic reader who gathers them far and wide, then, like "peach blossoms" and "willow floss," they will be swept

away by the sudden wind, a good half of them falling into the current. How pitiful!

(4) But if these writings are lucky enough to be passed down to the world, then even after the author's rosy cheeks have turned to dust, later generations will still chant her pieces—will imagine how dangling tresses skimmed her brow as she moistened the tip of the brush with her lips and applied the ink—will imagine her anguish and melancholy, as though she were unable to bear the weight of her feelings. So even if we have only fragments of powder and traces of ceruse, bits and pieces of jade, we treasure them ten times more than ordinary writing. These ladies are not like us men, whose beards bristle like halberds, but who toss off feeble attempts at composition just to amuse the common crowd.

(5) My friend Wang Shilu of Xincheng has previously compiled *Ranzhi ji* [The lamp oil collection of women's writings]. His collection was all but finished, with a vast number of chapters, but in the end it was never published. In my humble opinion, [monuments of women's learning] such as Mother Wei's completion of the *Rites of Zhou*, "Honorable Great Aunt" Ban Zhao's treatise in the *History of the Han*, Palace Matron Song's *Analects for Women*, and Nurse Zheng's *Women's Classic of Filial Piety* smack of female pedantry. For a lady writing by a small window [in a private household], poetry is more fitting; the genre of song-lyrics is especially good for setting to music. Liu Yong's line "The lingering moonlight in the morning breeze" calls out for a girl of seventeen or eighteen to sing it slowly to the clapperboard's beat. In the end, even Bearded Su Shi's [martial line] "The great river flows east" cannot equal Wang Zixia singing "Remnants of red after the flowers fade," which makes one heartbroken about fragrant plants at the ends of the earth.

(6) *Song-Lyrics from the Lady's Bamboo Grove* was compiled by Zhou Ming of Suzhou. After gathering his bouquet of fragrant verses, he added further annotation and provided sources. It should leave flowering grasses behind in the dust and make scented orchids cede their ground. Suzhou has long been called a breeding ground for female talent, but the transcendent beauty of Ye Xiaoluan's *Fansheng xiang* is in a class by itself. Even if Li Qingzhao [P.17] were reborn, she would still have to acknowledge Ye as her master; there is no need even to discuss the rest. [In a séance] Ye made this response to [the intermediary spirit] Master Le: "Fashion a cake of tea-leaves into a lady's calligraphy; engrave snow with a young woman's song-lyrics." I would like to borrow these lines to serve as a motto for this collection.

The ninth day of the *xinhai* year of Kangxi's reign [1671], penned by "Hermitage of Regrets" You Tong of Changzhou, in the Shuizai pavilion. (7)

(Hu Wenkai, 895–96)

The title phrase "from the lady's Bamboo Grove" alludes to the appraisal of Xie Daoyun's character in *Shishuo xinyu*: see C.24.1.

par. 1, "Jing nü": On poem 42 from the *Book of Odes* and its use as evidence of early female literacy, see C.36.1, note to par. 8 on *Vermilion Annals*.

par. 1, Xuanjiang: Xuanjiang, a lady of Qi, was brought to the state of Wei as a wife for the heir-apparent, Jizi, but Jizi's father found her so beautiful that he took her for himself (*Zuo zhuan*, in SSJZS, 7/22a–b). In the traditional interpretation, "Junzi jie lao" (To grow old at our lord's side, poem 47 in the *Book of Odes*), which includes the words "Freshly bright is her pheasant robe, the black hair is like a cloud," mixes praise of Xuanjiang's beauty with condemnation of her dissolute behavior.

par. 1, Zhuangjiang's poems: "Lü yi" (The green jacket, poem 27 in the *Book of Odes*) expresses the sorrow of the wife of Duke Zhuang of Wei, known as Zhuangjiang, when her place was taken by a concubine (see Ban *jieyu*'s citation of the poem in P.1.2). "Yan yan" (The swallow, poem 28) is also attributed to Zhuangjiang. It tells of her sorrow at the departure of one of Duke Zhuang's concubines for her native place (*Mao shi zhengyi*, in SSJZS, 2: 1/8a–12a.) Taken as a group, then, the poems attributed to Zhuangjiang of Wei testify to her noble and forbearing character, while the "Junzi jie lao" points to the contrast between Xuanjiang's appearance and behavior.

par. 2, "Plum-Blossom Consort": An allusion to "Mei Fei zhuan" ("The Biography of the Plum-Blossom Consort"), an anonymous story thought to be of Song origin. See Cheng Boquan, ed., *Gudai wenyan duanpian xiaoshuo xuanzhu*, 2: 40–47; and "Meifei zhuan," Lu Xun, ed., *Tang Song chuanqi ji*, pp. 282–86. On the Plum-Blossom consort, see P.54a.1. On the song "A Peck of Pearls," see P.74.4.

par. 3, "peach blossoms" and "willow floss": On Xie Daoyun's willow catkins, see C.24.1. Beautiful women were often likened to peach blossoms, but the phrase "peach blossom" also crops up in both a *yuefu* title, "Taohua xing," associated with Tang palace ladies, and in a *qu* title, "Taohua shui," associated with the expression of private feeling.

par. 5, "Wang Shilu of Xincheng": Wang Shilu (1626–73) was the older brother of the more famous and prolific poet and critic Wang Shizhen. On his important anthology *Ranzhi ji*, see Hu Wenkai, pp. 906–11.

par. 5, "[monuments of women's learning]": On Mother Wei, also known as Lady Song, see C.47.1. All in this list but Mother Wei were included in the prose section of *Ranzhi ji*. See the list of its contents reprinted in Hu Wenkai, pp. 909–10. On Ban Zhao's completion of the *Han shu*, see P.69.5; she added a treatise on astronomy, *Tianwen zhi*. For Song Ruoxin and Song Ruozhao's preface to their *Nü lunyu*, see C.2.1. On the *Nü xiao jing* by a Tang woman née Zheng, see Hu Wenkai, p. 32–33.

par. 5, Liu Yong and Su Shi: On the contrast of Liu Yong and Su Shi, see P.124.6.

par. 6, Ye Xiaoluan: After Xiaoluan's death at age seventeen, her father, Ye Shaoyuan, and others believed she had become an immortal.

par. 6, "Ye made this response": Ye was said to have composed these lines in a séance conducted after her death, through the agency of another spirit, Le An Dashi, a Six Dynasties Buddhist master whose most recent incarnation, a girl named Chen, had died in 1620. See Ye Shaoyuan's account ("Xu yaowen") in *Wumengtang quanji*, 1: 13. The story was widely known and excerpts from it appear in several late seventeenth-century sources.

BACKGROUND NOTE AND TRANSLATION BY JUDITH T. ZEITLIN

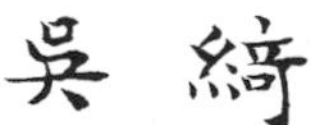

C.43. Wu Qi (1619–94)

Wu Qi was from Yangzhou but moved to Beijing as a senior licentiate in 1654, where he served in minor government posts. His career was assured after the Kangxi Emperor, upon learning of his talents as a playwright, ordered him to compose a play that was performed in the palace. Pleased with the results, the emperor appointed him to the Board of War, and he was promoted to department director of the Board of Works in 1663. He went to serve as a district magistrate in Zhejiang in 1666, but was removed from office on trumped-up charges in 1669.[1] Wu Qi was famed for his song-lyrics and essays in parallel prose as well as his plays. His collected works were published posthumously in 1700 under the title *Linhuitang ji* (Collection from the Hall of the Wild Orchid). He apparently enjoyed a companionate-style marriage with his wife, Huang Zhirou, who was known as a writer of song-lyrics and poetry in her own right.[2]

Xu Shumin's anthology *Zhongxiang ci* (Song-lyrics of many perfumes, 1690), for which Wu Qi wrote this preface, in six *juan*, organizes *ci* by contemporary women in six thematic categories patterned after the educational syllabus of ancient noblemen, as detailed in the *Rites of Zhou* (*Zhou li*).[3]

C.43.1. Preface to Xu Shumin, Zhongxiang ci

In *shi* poetry we require profound meaning, the expression of a valiant man's feelings of indignation; in song-lyrics, we value softness and suppleness, the description of a lovely and enchanting manner. But forced panegyrics to Luofu's charms always involve frivolous diction; and surely no one who today expatiates on Xi Shi's adornments ever gazed upon her.

One seeks a billet-doux to fix a forbidden tryst; missing a secret rendezvous (2)
is natural cause for regret. What better for conveying love than a song-lyric, now passionate, now mild, penned to the tune "Painted Brows"? What better than lines, now long, now short, filled in to the tune "Pounding Silk"?

Where the moon meets the tower, Niannu speaks of her charms; when the (3)
rain pelts the casement, the girl exiled to barbarian lands recites her grievances. But perhaps the shrimp-whisker curtains are too tightly woven, for she refuses to admit she can read; her dragon-clawed hairpin aslant, she is too bashful to praise the act of writing. Ask for a lyric to the tune "White Linen" and she'll suspect you of being a man of sentiment; but inquire about her powder and rouge and she'll lambaste your oafish rudeness.

[During the An Lushan Rebellion (755–57)], dancing beauties and sing- (4)
ing girls sadly sang of chevaux-de-frise; kitchen lasses and scullery maids were ashamed to pass on dharma tunes. Ink traces beside the postal station dissolve in the mountain rain; tear stains on the wall are obscured by clouds over the pass. If one says, "It's none of your business" or "What has this got to do with me?," the result is to neglect this writing [by women] and allow it to perish forever. . . . Therefore sons of the nobility and young men with musical talent bundle up such writings, put them in boxes, and record their myriad stanzas.

[Accompanied by] chattering parrots, she faces a wine shop to tune her (5)
pipes; embroidering ducks and drakes, she inscribes a kerchief at her gauze window. It is after dressing her hair and pulling back the loose strands at her temples that she harmonizes the purple flutes; and it is places where they carve the lintel coverings and make plaster of pepper that are most suitable for playing the red recorder.

Upon noticing that the smoke from the golden lion censer has ceased, she (6)
first realizes the night is long; upon sensing the dew on the jade tree, she is suddenly surprised that autumn is here. Whenever she weaves brocade with the oriole shuttle, her sweet mind follows the flower spirits; as a file of geese breaks through the cold, her lovely dream is often enlaced with the cassia's soul.

Emulating the "Honorable Great Aunt" Ban Zhao merely teaches women (7)
to become teachers, but it is reading the fruits of Xie Daoyun's talents that really takes a man's breath away. Line after line in this collection tinkles like jade, creating a mountain wrought of jade; word after word gives off fragrance, concocting a land of many perfumes. If the [talented] Feng Yan could read this, surely he would stand up and weep in dejection; if the [uxorious] Xun Can looked at this, could it fail to stir his former feelings?

Now I bathe my hands in rose petals and chant the lyrics in this collection. (8)

May the world cover this book in pale green and yellow brocade and treasure it well!

(9) Respectfully written in the "Forest of Letters" on the Festival of Flowers in the *gengwu* year of Kangxi's reign [1690] by an old friend, Wu Qi of Fengnan.

(Hu Wenkai, 899)

par. 1, Luofu and Xi Shi: On Luofu, see P.76.2; on Xi Shi (Yiguang), see P.39.2 and C.36.1.

par. 2, "Painted Brows" and "Pounding Silk": "Painted eyebrows" crops up in two *qu* tune titles ("Huamei shi" and "Huamei er"), but the phrase is also associated with Zhang Chang, fond of painting his wife's eyebrows (see P.22C.1). The phrase "pounding silk" graces a tune title ("Dao lianzi") that could be used for both *ci* and *qu*.

par. 3, "Niannu speaks of her charms": Niannu was a famous court singer of the High Tang period. "Niannu jiao" (The charms of Niannu)" is a well-known *ci* title; see Appendix A.

par. 4, "dharma tunes": The most famous of these tunes (*faqu*) of Central Asian origin was "Rainbow Robes and Feather Skirts" associated with Yang Guifei (see P.18.12 and P.54a.1).

par. 5, "carve the lintel coverings and make plaster of pepper": According to an anecdote in *Shishuo xinyu*, 30.4, the millionaire Shi Cong used costly pepper to plaster his walls; "carving the lintel coverings" (*keta*) probably also suggests luxury and extravagance.

par. 6, "the cassia's soul": This signifies the moon (see P.20.7 and P.26.5), with possible connotations of a high-ranking lover, since "breaking the cassia bough" (punning on the syllable *gui*: "cassia," but also "honor" [see P.11.14]) was a metaphor for success in the examinations.

par. 7, Feng Yan and Xun Can: Feng Yan was a talented writer of the Latter Han who served at court. His description of his sufferings at the hands of his domineering wife is recorded in the annotations to his biography, *Hou Han shu* 28b/1003–4. On Xun Can, see C.38.1.

BACKGROUND NOTE AND TRANSLATION BY JUDITH T. ZEITLIN

陸昶

C.44. Lu Chang (18th century)

Lu Chang's anthology *Lichao mingyuan shici* (Poems of the famous women of past ages, 1773) contains some six hundred *shi* poems and sixty *ci*, ranging from Han to Yuan periods, along with portraits of some "famous women." It was hailed as a worthy successor to the anthologies of Zhong Xing (C.32).[1]

C.44.1. Preface to Lichao mingyuan shici

"Gentleness and simplicity are the teachings of poetry." They are strongly connected with the sentiments and conduct of men. The *Book of Odes* has established for hundreds of generations the greatest examples of poetic teaching. It begins with the [sections] "Zhou nan" and "Shao nan," illustrating the virtue of the queen. The fifteen sections of the *Airs of the States* contain many works by women—for example the poems "Guan ju" [poem 1], "Ge tan" [poem 2], "Juan er" [poem 3], "Fou yi" [poem 8], "Qian shang" [poem 87] and "Man cao" [poem 94]. Virtue and vice are unveiled in order to warn against wrongdoing. Thus the Sage ranked poetry and music highest among the "Three Accomplishments."

Before the Han, the works of women such as Lady Tao's "Huang he" song and the "Cai ge" ode [*Book of Odes*, poem 72] all originated from these very "teachings of poetry." The intent of their words was to give voice to their grief. Later, the style of poetry fell away from that of the ancient songs. As the days of the *Book of Odes* grew more remote, there was a greater tendency to dwell on affection and sentiment. Charm and attractiveness were regarded as fundamental and the style of virtue and reticence became outmoded. Moreover, talented men and learned scholars could not but follow this fashion, absorbed as they were in perfumed dressing cases and jade mirror stands. The abuse of rhyme had descended to its lowest point. When what we call "the teachings of gentleness and simplicity" had decayed and were entirely wasted, who could have pushed back the collapsing waves? (2)

Formerly, when noblemen created anthologies, their intention lay in organizing and recording all the various poems. There was no selectivity in their anthologizing and the poetic climate grew more and more unhealthy. If one wished to find a systematic selection there really were no good editions. I have been dissatisfied with this. (3)

In the era of our present sagely ruler, importance is attached to literature, and even distant nooks of mountain or sea find their way into poetry in this time of glorious poetic teaching. Nevertheless, the subtleties of the Three Hundred Songs might still be obscured among the divers selections. For this reason, disregarding my own vulgarity, I went searching here and there to add the balance to the purport of the *Book of Odes*. (4)

For instance, Lady Ban's song of the fan is steeped in discontent and in loyalty. It carries the import of the "Gu feng" ode. And the poem about Mulan's (5) joining the troops is filled with distress in disorder and emphasizes filial piety, echoing the sound left behind by the "small war-chariot."

(6) Thus, of the works from the Han Dynasty up to the Liao and Yuan, out of every six or seven volumes I have looked through, I have kept two or three [poems]. The works are not numerous and are sufficient for recitation and chanting. One sees virtues and vices presented in them. I have once again explicated the contexts for these poems and perhaps my words may go beyond the trifling to revert to the ultimate goal of "thought without deviance."

(7) As my maternal uncle, Mr. Li Manweng, has long been acquainted with the world of poetry, I consulted him, and he said, "Gentleness is the origin of the *Airs*, and simplicity is the root of the *Odes* and *Hymns*." Perceptive readers should be able to understand this. This composition is published as an aid in ascertaining the lasting poetic teachings of the ages. Thus I have handed it over to the engravers and have written a few words at the beginning of the volume.

(8) Written on the sixteenth of the eighth month of the *guisi* year of the Qianlong reign [1733], at the Plum Cottage of Lu Chang of Suzhou and inscribed in Xupu's Red Tree Poetry Chamber.

(Lu Chang, *Lichao mingyuan shici*, 1a–2b)

par. 1, "Gentleness and simplicity [or honesty] . . .": For this commonplace, see C.32.1, note to par. 1.

par. 2, Tao Ying: On Tao Ying of Lu, see P.26.5.

par. 5, "song of the fan . . . 'Gu feng' ode": On Ban *jieyu* and the song of the fan, see P.1.1. "Gu feng," poem 35 of the *Book of Odes*, expresses the grief of a woman who has been treated poorly by her husband.

par. 5, "Mulan's joining the troops . . . small war-chariot": The argument is that the poem about Mulan (see P.109.1) fittingly echoes poem 128 of the *Book of Odes*, "Xiao rong" (Small war-chariot), which is supposed to have been composed by a woman lamenting her husband's departure for battle.

par. 6, "thought without deviance": This refers to the famous statement by Confucius that all the poems in the *Book of Odes* can be summed up with this phrase (*Analects* 2.2).

TRANSLATED BY MARK A. BORER

袁枚

C.45. Yuan Mei (1716–98)

Yuan Mei was one of the first poets of later imperial China to receive serious attention in the West, an honor due in part to Arthur Waley's inspired biography of him. Best known for his advocacy of the poetics of *xingling* (innate sensibility), Yuan wrote a great deal of poetry and criticism denouncing the imitation of earlier masters and calling for writers to make individual expression their primary concern. Yuan stressed the idea that anyone with heartfelt inspiration could write poetry. In line with this penchant, he sought to teach young women the art of poetry and by 1790 had as many as thirteen female students, among them Xi Peilan (P.93), Dai Lanying (P.95), and Qu Bingyun (P.96). The following epitaph, "Jin Xianxian nüshi mu zhiming" (A tomb inscription for the female scholar Jin Xianxian) was composed for a somewhat less intimate member of his circle, Jin Yi (P.94).[1]

C.45.1. Jin Xianxian nüshi mu zhiming

There was once a woman from Suzhou called Jin Xianxian. Her given name was Yi. She was delicate and fragile from the time she was born, and she had a heavenly endowed countenance. At a very early age she could already read books and distinguish the four tones. She loved to compose poetry and every time she let fall her brush, it was like a fleet horse prancing along unable to stop.

At fifteen she married a young man, Chen Zhushi from Suzhou. On their (2)
wedding night, the newlywed bride, with a sparkle in her eye and an air of seduction, suddenly sent out a maid with perfumed notepaper to request a poem from the bridegroom before he could be admitted to the bridal chamber. Zhushi was pleasantly surprised, for he was well accustomed to writing poetry. He composed a poem and further requested a poem in response from his bride. From that moment on the two were a perfect match.

Alongside the bridal trousseau ink was scattered about. In just a few days (3)
she had transformed the women's chambers into a writing studio. Xianxian served her elders respectfully and was careful not to boast about her literary works. Moreover, she did not neglect any of her household duties.

At this time there were many beautiful women in Suzhou, Shen Sanhua (4)

[Shen Xiang, P.110], Wang Yuzhen [P.100], and Jiang Bizhu [Jiang Zhu, P.111] among them. They all could write poetry and they unanimously chose Xianxian as their "Dean." One day a group of women met at Tiger Hill outside of Suzhou. As the sun was just setting, they sat together beside Sword Pond discussing various stories of the states Wu and Yue in the Spring and Autumn period. Thousands of words flew back and forth in their banter. Some of the officials listening in could not understand the conversation. They were truly "gaping in astonishment." Someone who had seen this gathering sighed and said, "In the *Classic of Mountains and Seas* it is said that when the Emperor sacrifices, one hundred spirits congregate atop the stones of the Imperial Altar. Yesterday when a host of women sat upon the rocks, was that not a truly divine gathering?" Such was the esteem in which these women were held by the villagers.

(5) As for poetry, Xianxian was well read in the masters of the Tang and Song, and was especially fond of my own poetry. When she obtained a copy of my *Xiaocang shanfang shiji* [Lesser Storehouse Mountain Lodge collection], she stole away and read it for four continuous days and nights. Upon finishing it, she sent me a letter and repeatedly asked to become my student. I could sense her determination.

(6) This spring, when I went to pay her a visit, her illness was already quite severe. Someone helped her sit up; she called out, "Teacher!" and bowed twice. After this visit I traveled to Xiling, and at the end of the month when I returned, Xianxian had died. Just before her death she had told Zhushi, "Now that I have seen my teacher, the memory of our meeting will last for a thousand years. But something still distresses me. I have heard that Mr. Yuan has invited thirteen ladies to meet for poetry talks in the Jiang garden. Nine of them have accepted, but I of all people cannot attend and take all the honors. What a disappointment! I still have some doubts about my writing that I had hoped to go over with him, and now I cannot accomplish that either. That is another disappointment. If you wish to make up for these disappointments of mine, then you must see to it that my teacher has pity enough for me to be willing to inscribe my gravestone. Then, although I die, I shall yet live on."

(7) I wept when I heard this. Long ago, Su Dongpo [Su Shi] was exiled to Huizhou although he was already an old man. A daughter of Mr. Wen, the official in charge there, peeked in on his studies, and Dongpo became extraordinarily fond of her. When he returned from his second exile in Hainan, this girl had already passed away. Dongpo could not suppress his emotions and composed

a short song-lyric to mourn her. Although I am not Dongpo, what I have learned from Xianxian is one hundred times what he learned from Miss Wen. How then could I refuse to engrave her tombstone?

Some narrow-minded people say that literature is not appropriate for (8)
women. They must not know that the *dui* trigram of the *Book of Changes* is called the "Younger Daughter," and that the Sage glossed it as "Learning among friends." The *li* trigram is known as the "Middle Daughter" and the Sage glossed this, saying "Brightness illuminates the upright." As for "Ge tan" [poem 2 of the *Book of Odes*] and "Juan er" [poem 3] among the Three Hundred Songs, were they not written by women? The narrow view of those hidebound scholars is mistaken indeed.

I have been around for a long time, and whenever I encounter a woman (9)
with talent, I find her to be ill-fated. Those who have beauty and talent are still more ill-fated, and those who have talent, beauty, and a good match are the most ill-fated of all. In Xianxian were combined these three harbingers of misfortune, and yet I wish she could have lived a long life. My three younger sisters were all talented, and all died young. Among my female students, Xu Wenmu's granddaughter was the most talented, and she also died youngest. The others have suffered either widowhood or poverty. Now Xianxian has died, and thus I know that the heavens are unwilling to grant everlasting harmony to an auspicious pair, whose blessings would otherwise equal those of generals, ministers, or men of high station. This is indeed the unalterable principle of the creator. What more can be said? Of Xianxian's writings there remain the poems in her *Drafts from the Tower of the Slender Reciter* collection.

Died at the age of twenty——— years. Buried at ——— on ———. Her (10)
epitaph reads:

In ancient times when Cang Jie created writing,
He relied on the assistance of Nü Wa;
Today a woman of inspired intellect
Must choose a companion to match her mind.
There is a descendant of the ancient King Jin Tian
Who once divined from the Yellow Emperor:
"The wandering 'marrying maiden'
(8) Shall get in her carriage and travel south."
She lifted up her pure eyes, letting drift her gaze,
Longing for conjugal happiness in the realm of men.

Astride the clouds she descended to earth,
Tying the nuptial sash at Tan village.
She is a fragrance-filled blossom waiting on the wind,
Alive with the brilliant radiance of devotion.
She brought into accord the mysterious rules of prosody,
Like jade chimes, the cry of utmost harmony.
She carved out the feelings in her heart,
Yet again came the stripping away of the hundred wonders.
At the end she sat up slightly but now shall rise no more,
Gone to Nine-Doubt Mountain to visit Ying and Huang.
Walking hand in hand they tarry there,
The spirits in sorrow: how can they not know
The eternity of the Nine Provinces?
And the waves of tears: Alas!
The only glimpse of her is preserved in the bones of her poetry.
Now bunches of *tan*-flowers bloom above her,
Two rows of plants keep vigil at her side.

(Yuan Mei, *Xiaocang shanfang xu wenji*, 32/14b)

par. 4, "they sat together beside Sword Pond": Sword Pond is a site charged with Spring-and-Autumn period associations. In it rest the assassin Juan Ju and the sword with which the First Emperor once attempted to kill a tiger.

par. 4, *Classic of Mountains and Seas*: *Shan hai jing*, a semi-fantastic geographical work sometimes attributed to the legendary sovereign Yu but probably of mixed Warring States and Han authorship.

par. 6, "but I . . . cannot attend and take all the honors": This incident is related in Jin Yi's poem entitled "When the master of the Sui Garden came to Suzhou, he sent out invitations for a gathering of female students. Because I was sick I could not attend. I wrote these two regulated-verse poems to send to my master."

par. 8, *Book of Changes*: See Wilhelm and Baynes, trans., *The I Ching*, pp. 118–21, 223–26, 274.

epitaph, line 7: The "Marrying Maiden," or "Gui mei," is the fifty-fourth hexagram in the *Book of Changes*; see Wilhelm and Baynes, trans., *The I Ching*, pp. 208–11.

line 20: Nine-Doubt Mountain in present-day Hunan province is the burial place of the ancient sage-ruler Shun. On Shun's wives Ying and Huang, see P.1.2, P.37.1.

line 23: Literally, "The one age of the nine provinces," "nine provinces" being an archaic name for China. This is a phrase taken from a letter written by Jin Yi to Yuan Mei. She there describes an ancient gathering of women as "lovely words amongst the lakes and mountains, through ten thousand ages and a thousand autumns, masters of poetic elegance in the one age of the nine provinces."

line 26: The *tan* is a mythical flower that blooms but once every hundred years.

BACKGROUND NOTE AND TRANSLATION BY MARK A. BORER

汪 穀

C.46. Wang Gu (late 18th century)

Wang Gu, a disciple of Yuan Mei was chosen to write the preface to Yuan's anthology *Suiyuan nü dizi shixuan* (Selected poems by the woman disciples of Sui Garden, 1796). Among the poets represented in the work were Xi Peilan (P.93), Jin Yi (P.94), Dai Lanying (P.95), Qu Bingyun (P.96), and Gui Maoyi (P.97).

C.46.1. Preface to Yuan Mei, Suiyuan nü dizi shixuan

The trigram *dui* denotes "the youngest daughter," but the Sage has tied it to the meaning of "the superior man [joining] with his friends for discussion and practice." The trigram *li* represents "the middle daughter," but the Sage has related it to the idea of "doubled clarity, clinging to what is right." The poems "Ge tan" and "Juan er" preside over the beginning of the three hundred poems included in the *Book of Odes*. It is, therefore, most appropriate that women should be able to write poetry.

Since the literary cultivation of our present sagely dynasty is both enlight- (2)
ened and flourishing, its inaugural virtues all auspicious, the illustrious gates and large mansions all bear the influence of "Zhou nan" and "Shao nan." The gentleman of the Sui Garden [Yuan Mei] has been the very fond of refinement and elegance. Now that he has attained greatness of age, he is about to attend an anniversary banquet in the Imperial Palace held for successful *jinshi* candidates. Those lady scholars everywhere who have learned of his reputation honor him as the like of Fu Sheng and Xiahou Sheng. For this reason, in every place he has visited, they bowed to the ground to receive and honor him as their teacher. Our master taught "without discrimination," and t[...] the pages and volumes that had been submitted, he selected a[...] best. After some time, a considerable collection was [...] through Suzhou, he brought it along and asked me to [...]

At first, I declined, saying to him: "This act of yours, [...]

virtue. However, among your contributors are Bizhu and Yizhu, two persons who happen to be my maids. They are young and just beginning to learn their craft. They dare not rank themselves among various noble misses and ladies."

(4) With a smile, our Master replied, "When Duke Huan of Qi and Duke Wen of Jin met with other nobles to forge a grand alliance, were those who attended the meeting only from such large states as Lu and Wei? Did no persons from such petty dependent states as Zhu and Ju come to the meeting holding jade and silk? Why be so narrow-minded?"

(5) Because I could not argue with him, I took the original manuscript and gave it to the printer. Written in the fifth month during the summer of the *bingchen* year of the Jiaqing reign period [1796] by Wang Gu, style name Xinnong.

(Hu Wenkai, 934)

par. 1, "trigram *dui*": See Wilhelm and Baynes, trans., *The I Ching*, p. 223. Wang Gu essentially repeats here Yuan Mei's grave inscription for Jin Yi; see C.45.1. With the "Sage's meaning," Wang is citing one of the commentaries to the *Book of Changes*. See Wilhelm and Baynes, p. 686.

par. 1, "clinging to what is right": Ibid., p. 536.

par. 1, "the beginning of . . . the *Book of Odes*": The poems named are 2 and 3 of the *Book of Odes*, and prominent by their position. Both poems, in the traditional interpretation, express the duties of a queen. Since they seemed to have been written from a woman's point of view, they and other similar compositions in the anthology were regarded by many Qing poets and theorists as evidence for women poets in antiquity.

par. 2, "influence of 'Zhou nan' and 'Shao nan' ": Another reference to the *Book of Odes*. These two sections were said to demonstrate the spread of Zhou culture to the wilder southern regions.

par. 2, "successful *jinshi* candidates": Yuan took the degree in 1738 when he was but twenty-two years old. Since the anniversary banquet would not be held until a Sixty-Year Cycle had been completed in the Chinese calendar, understandably only a few surviving alumni could attend such an event. Yuan made it, and his jubilant anticipation is recorded in a series of nine quatrains preserved in his collected writings. After attending the banquet, Yuan wrote a further ten quatrains to commemorate the occasion. See Yuan Mei, *Xiaocang shanfang shiji*, 37/3a–b, 3b–4a.

par. 2, Fu Sheng and Xiahou Sheng: Fu Sheng was a scholar of the Qin-Han period. When the Qin emperor burned Confucian books, Fu allegedly took volumes of the *Shang shu* and hid them in the walls of buildings; see *Shi ji*, 121, and *Han shu*, 88. Xiahou Sheng was another Han scholar steeped in the Confucian Classics and was noted for living past ninety; see *Han shu*, 75, 88.

par. 2, "without discrimination": In the original, *you jiao wu lei*, "in teaching there is no distinction of categories," said of Confucius in *Analects* 15. 39. The word "categories" has been variously interpreted by traditional commentators as referring to either moral nature (whether it is good or bad) or class (whether it is high or low). Wang's citation here adds the sense of gender.

par. 4, "Duke Huan of Qi and Duke Wen of Jin": The dukes were two of the five powerful chieftains that sought to acquire hegemonic power during the seventh century B.C.E., when the central government of the Zhou was already in decline.

par. 4, Zhu and Ju: Two small feudal states in the modern province of Shandong.

TRANSLATED BY ANTHONY C. YU

C.47. Zhang Xuecheng (1738–1801)

Zhang Xuecheng, philosopher of history, wrote "Fu xue" (Women's learning) to protest the publication in the previous year of Yuan Mei's *Suiyuan nü dizi shixuan*.[1] (For Wang Gu's preface to this anthology, see C.46.1.) It quickly became Zhang's best-known work, catching the attention of contemporaries by using the subject of women writers to sharpen critical debates in eighteenth-century scholarship—arguments about the correct interpretation of classical texts and about the purpose and meaning of writing itself. Salacious as well as erudite, the essay also attracted readers by slandering the controversial poet Yuan Mei as an ignorant minion and benighted intellectual incapable of grasping the true meaning of great classical works. In his essay, Zhang argues that women's classical learning in the past was indeed equal to—and in some cases purer than and superior to—men's, but his main purpose is to show how poorly Yuan Mei understood the historical foundations of women's learning.

Reared as an only son surrounded by sisters, Zhang Xuecheng was educated by his mother and developed close relationships with a few older women. His intimate knowledge of women's lives made him impatient with the narrowly stereotyped ideals of womanhood honored in imperial commendations, standard histories, and local gazetteers. He argued that daughters, as well as sons, transmitted the learning of their own families (*jia xue*). Moreover, at crucial junctures in history, women had been responsible for preserving bodies of knowledge that warfare or death would otherwise have destroyed. Since the historian is a scholar whose "words are everyone's" (*yan gong*), a woman transmitting history is as capable as a man of speaking "public" language. However, she must do so by carefully observing the boundaries of ritual conduct.[2]

C.47.1. *Fu xue*

The *Zhou li* [Rites of Zhou] refers to a Female Libationer and a Female Scribe. During the Han dynasty, the imperial Diary of Work and Rest was composed in the women's apartments. From such evidence we know that women's literary skills had a use in ancient times.

(2) The term "women's learning" appears in the section on the Ministry of State in the *Zhou li*, where women's posts were listed. There it refers to "virtue, speech, comportment, and work," terms which are extremely broad. This definition of women's learning bears no resemblance to the use of the term "learning" in later times, when it has been used to refer to literary arts alone. Thus, for instance, the *Book of Changes* instructs: "Correctness resides in the family alone." The *Zhou li* prescribes as women's work "silkworm raising and hemp." The commentary on the *Spring and Autumn Annals* observes that a wife "offered her services" before the sacrificial altar and "served to her guests the foods that she had prepared." Verses in the "Lesser Elegantiae" section of the *Book of Odes* that speak of toasting and feasting have the same meaning. From such classical sources we know the broad outlines of women's occupations.

(3) The main categories of women's learning were virtue, comportment, speech, and work. Zheng Xuan's commentary on these terms says that "speech" refers to rhetoric. It follows that a woman who was not well versed in classical ritual and accomplished in letters could not be considered learned. Thus we know that in the recitation of poetry and mastery of the rites, the learning of a woman of ancient times was second only to a man's. Although the writings of women who came later have been more inclined toward beauty and ornament, women should know their original heritage.

(4) Women's learning was supervised by the Nine Concubines, and their methods of instruction were extended throughout the royal domain, from the Inner Palace [of the Son of Heaven] to the lands of the feudal lords. Even before the palace women's offices (later designated the Six Managers) came into being, there were precedents for women to follow. An "Instructress," for instance, appears in the poem "Ge tan" the second of the Songs of the States in the *Book of Odes*. The "Nei ze" [Rules for the Inner Household] chapter of the *Records of Ritual* [*Li ji*] describes "women's decorum" taught by a "female instructress."

(5) Perusing the various commentaries on the *Spring and Autumn Annals*, we find that the wives of the various feudal lords and the spouses of the chief officials were able to cite literary texts and tell of the past. Their words and deeds were clear and elegant. For example, Deng Man was able to interpret the omen in the full moon, deriving from it a detailed understanding of Heaven's Way. Mu Jiang was able to realize the import of the phrase "auspicious purity" used in the *Book of Changes*, through her perceptive reading of the milfoil stalk patterns for the first hexagram. The good wife of Earl Mu of Lu is famous for her canonical words and instructions. The spouse of King Xuan of Zhou was granted a nobler title because of her ritual propriety. When the Chief Justice met his end beneath the window, his wife wrote a eulogy to make known his virtue. When Qiliang Zhi died for the kingdom of Qi and his ghost lingered on the battlefield, his widow gently declined to receive condolences sent by a statesman from Qi because it would have been unseemly to do so. As the spring waters gushed slowly forth, the lady of Wei composed a poem lamenting the futility of her plans to return home. While the swallows rose and swooped, Ding Jiang sadly composed a verse sending her daughter-in-law back to the girl's natal family, following the end of the three-year mourning period for her deceased son. Do these classical rituals and standards of conduct, these literary talents and styles, differ in any way from those of the highest-ranking lords and statesmen? As we see, women's behavior originally had no separate or special documentation; women simply appeared in the historical annals wherever they figured in specific events. If these women had appeared in later times, when histories required specialized treatises with a separate category for women's biographies, Liu Xiang's and Fan Ye's collections would include ten times as many women who were as brilliant and distinguished as Ban Zhao and Cai Yan [P.2]. This is how we know that women's learning has been steadily lost with the passing of time. While the Three Dynasties flourished, women studied letters together with men. Such was the ancient precedent; no one saw cause to boast of it or consider it unusual.

Zhang's note [1]: Persons who are not learned have supposed that poems like "Zhen wei" [*Book of Odes*, poem 95] were composed by lovers, and so they claim that young women in ancient times opened their mouths and produced elegant works that were actually superior to those of learned men who came after them. These persons do not understand that there is no possible rationale for this assumption. I shall explain this in some detail below and not tarry over the point here. Suffice it to say that women's learning did exist in ancient times, but it was deployed in the ranks of the noble lords and statesmen, and ordinary women were not party to it.

(6) From the Spring and Autumn period onward, when the roles of official and teacher were no longer one, learning ceased to be the domain of government officers, and writing came to have authors. Men of exceptional talent followed their own proclivities and tastes, and became famous for scholarship.

Zhang's note [2]: I refer here to the schools of philosophy during the Warring States and pre-Qin period, including also the Erudites who specialized in the Classics and the histories during the Western Han period.

Later, as belles lettres emerged, personal talent and beauty of expression were what counted most, and elegance and learning made for renown.

Zhang's note [3]: Here I refer to Western Han writers after the reigns of emperors Yuan and Cheng [i.e., after 48 B.C.E.], and also to the poetry and prose collections of the Eastern Han and later.

The fact that women of extraordinary brilliance and unusual ability, endowed with fine essence, were able to achieve special distinction in fine writing that was recognized in the past and is recognized today, was a consequence of the circumstances of the time, pure and simple.

(7) This was precisely the principle at work when Confucian learning flourished at the Han court, resulting in what Ban Gu called "the route to profit and fortune." That is, what official policy honored was what the wise and talented vied for, so scholars pursued learning just as the farmers tilled their fields. However, a woman's writing was not her vocation. Therefore when a woman excelled, it was the result of her own natural endowment, not because she was competing for literary recognition or seeking fame and notoriety.

Zhang's note [4]: The obsession with fame arose among writers of medieval times and later. Although the ancients were also afflicted with the desire for fame, they did not limit their quest to the realm of belles lettres. The man obsessed by literary fame is despised by those who are knowledgeable. The woman who is stirred by reputation or fame is not acting according to her kind.

(8) The "Songs of the Inner Chamber" composed by the Lady of Tangshan, and the "Rhyme-prose" from the Palace of Unwavering Trust by Ban *jieyu*, were variations—mimetic or ironic—on the forms called *ya* [odes of the court]

and *feng* [songs of the states]. Although they were written in the inner chambers of the palace, these works nonetheless are related to events in the ancient history of our realm and thus were recorded in our historical records. Other writings by women of this period are extremely rare. Those few that have come down to us can be reviewed at a glance by consulting the "Monographs on Literature" in the standard histories.

As for the "Music Bureau" poems [*yuefu*] that were transmitted in oral form (9)
and written verse—such as the story of Hua Mulan going off to war; the tale of the separated couple in "Southeast the Peacock Flies"; the poem "Gathering Mulberry Leaves by the Path" expressing the devotion of a faithful wife; the song "Going Up the Hill to Collect Wild Mushrooms and Grasses," in which a rejected wife offers encouraging words to her former husband; the various poems on the theme of "White Hemp" that were sung for the pleasure of the emperor; the popular "Four Seasons Songs" that describe the longing of lonely women—all of these poems are fragrant and vivid. Their sounds are comfortable and slow, their rhythms gentle and lingering. From the *gu ci* [ancient lyric poems] of the Han dynasty to the *za ni* [miscellaneous imitations] of the Six Dynasties period, all were composed by male poets in the style of Qu Yuan. Though they invoke the passion aroused by thoughts of another person and lodge their sentiments in the voices of young girls, their purpose was actually to criticize [society or government]. That is why these poems are filled with frivolous expressions befitting a dialogue between a man and a woman in love.

> *Zhang's note* [5]: Although poems like "Mulberry on the Path" or "The Gentleman of the Palace Guard" make a pretense of purity and chastity, no secluded woman would chatter and carry on that way! They must have been written in imitation; this is the best conclusion.

As for various verses and miscellanies from the inner apartments, some of (10)
which have come down to us, it makes no difference whether the women who wrote them were pure or dissolute, as long as all the words and phrases they used are restrained and proper. [Zhuo] Wenjun was a profligate woman who ran away and married without the proper ceremonies, yet her "Song of White Hair" only admonished [her husband Sima] Xiangru [and not others]. Cai Yan [P.2] was an unfaithful widow who remarried, yet in writing down the works of her father's library from memory she declined the assistance of the ten officials because she did not wish to seem improper by receiving anything from their hands. As for the others, who were content to remain in the confines of

their families and who followed the norms appropriate to their station and who became known for their purity and chastity—in every case, their writings are serene like still water, wondrous like clear wind. Even though their literary eloquence arose from their own natural endowments, the direction of their thoughts did not stray beyond the confines of their quarters. In all these cases, despite the fact that women's learning was different from what it had been in ancient times, it did not conflict with moral instruction.

(11) The dialogues between men and women in the "Airs of the States" are imitations invented by poets. If we look to confirm this by reference to the writings of Han, Wei, and Six Dynasties poets, it is beyond doubt. Like the male actor who mounts the stage dressed as a pure young girl, [these male poets] cannot capture the refinement and simplicity of the "inner apartments." The ignorant person who does not understand this basic principle wrongly infers that in ancient times even children and women could spontaneously recite original verse, and so argues that women are well suited to writing Airs and Elegantiae. This is tantamount to watching a leading actor mount the stage and enact a historical event from ancient times, and then imagining that the ancients always sang a song before doing anything.

> *Zhang's note* [6]: When an actor impersonates a person in an event from the ancient past, the words of his songs are just like the commentaries and opinions inserted by historians into historical texts. Thus they are words full of meaning, but they surely do not come out of the historical figure's mouth. In the same way, an observer's views will never come out of the person being observed, although the libretto of an opera is designed to erase these distinctions. Thus the gentleman on stage will sometimes appear to engage in praising himself; or the petty man may even humiliate himself. The audience, like the person who reads a history book, will hear both the praise and the blame. The genre is meant to work this way and there is nothing wrong with it. But if those same actual words came out of a gentleman's or a petty man's mouth, they would not make any sense. The words of men and women in the "Airs of the States," and the ancients' imitations of their words, ought to be viewed in precisely this light. If we were to say that these words truly came out of the mouths of real men and women, [we would be wrong, because] the promiscuous among them would never reveal themselves this way, and the chaste among them would never be so indecent.

(12) When long ago the historian Ban Gu died before completing the *Han shu*, the emperor issued an edict summoning his younger sister Ban Zhao to come

in person to the Dongguan Library in the Han Palace [where the Classics and histories were being transcribed] and carry the *Han shu* to completion. Thereafter, the noble lords and ministers all brought her gifts and asked her to be their teacher.

> *Zhang's note* [7]: The great Confucian scholar Ma Yong learned to read the *Han shu* line by line under her tutelage.

Truly this was an extraordinary event without precedent. In this case a specialized school of learning that was cut off had been preserved within a certain family and was never completely preserved in written works. Had it not been for Ban Zhao, there would have been no way to transmit that learning. Or, to take another example, when the Fu Qin rulers first established their educational system and assembled a broad array of Erudites and teachers of the Classics, they discovered that all five Classics were roughly in hand except for the *Zhou li*, which had been lost. The Erudites submitted a memorial stating that one Lady Song, mother of the Chamberlain of Ceremonials, Wei Cheng, came from a family where the *Zhou li* had been transmitted from generation to generation. The emperor issued an edict declaring her home a lecture hall and establishing 120 scholarships. The scholars came and sat on the other side of a curtain to receive instruction from Lady Song, who was ennobled with the honorary title "Master of Illustrious Culture." This too was an extraordinary event with no precedent whatsoever. Once again, at a time when learning flourished in the area "left of the great river" [that is, the eastern coastal region] and the Fu Qin had occupied the Chang'an region, versions of the Classics and lost bodies of learning were fortunately still preserved by a daughter in a family that boasted many generations of learning. Not even the famed noble lords could order this learning to be furthered and disseminated [without Lady Song's voluntary compliance].

These two mothers both carried out men's tasks with a woman's body. To (13)
be sure, transmitting the Classics and recording the histories are properly the domain of heaven-appointed men and the laws of the Way. However, fearing that these bodies of learning might be lost forever, the leaders of that time had no choice but to break from convention and treat women with the ritual respect due a superior. We cannot accuse these women of showing off their illustrious talents or trying to upset the prevailing customs. Similarly, the cases of Xi *furen*, the so-called Wife of the State of Qiao, who pacified the Lingnan frontier; and of the Tang princess of Pingyang who raised an army of seventy thousand to come to her husband's defense and helped found

the Tang dynasty—both, again, were extraordinary events absolutely without precedent. In the former case, a special tent government was created, and the female leader was made an official; in the latter case, at the woman's funeral the emperor ordered a military procession with feather screens, drums and pipes, and an honor guard of warriors and swordsmen. In either of these cases, to say that the Sui and Tang emperors did not act appropriately would be absolutely unacceptable. On the other hand, to insist that all the women of the realm take these two women as their models is not only unacceptable but completely unreasonable.

(14) The people of the Jin period esteemed what we call Daoist studies, the teachings of Lao Zi and Zhuang Zi and of the *Book of Changes* [*Yi jing*]. They indulged their emotions and presented themselves as liberated persons. The men looked upon the six Confucian arts as dregs in a wine glass. Like them, women of the time regarded "pure talk" as elegant and elevated. Consider the story about the wife who concealed herself with a dark veil to help her lord "break the siege" in his negotiations, or the joke about the new wife and her husband's younger brother the military officer. Even though both of the women in these stories adhered to the general principles of chastity, they still flouted the proper order of human relationships. Critics who argue that the destruction of ritual teachings by "pure talk" was the cause of the fragmentation of the country into sixteen kingdoms, as well as the cause of the oppression and degradation of the people, have truly understood the heart of the problem.

(15) Although the great writer Wang Xie Daoyun transgressed the rules of ritual, in her pure conversation and her logical reasoning she showed great intuitive understanding, and in her practice of Confucian manners she simultaneously displayed a thorough mastery of Daoist teachings. If we were to measure her by scholarly standards, she would merely be one of those whom Confucius once referred to as "straying from the middle path" on the "ardent" side.

> *Zhang's note* [8]: In other words, she was closer to being heterodox than to being immoral like a prostitute or an actress.

Not only could she compose five- or seven-word verse; she herself boasted that she surpassed the standards of the Four Womanly Virtues and the Three Followings. But suppose she had written showy, light stuff, or recorded idle conversation over wine, or described extremely fine or delicate things, or sketched and shaded likenesses; suppose she had used make-up to heighten her color, or boasted of her virtues to camouflage and embellish her empty words. Although the people of the Jin dynasty may be called empty and vain, if they had seen anything like that, they would have grabbed their wives and children and run away.

> *Zhang's note* [9]: Which is to say that although Lady Wang Xie [Daoyun] transgressed the rules of propriety, she was still in fact a learned scholar, and therefore the import of what she wrote was profound. It was a far cry from the "talented scholar—beautiful maiden" stuff that is uniformly vulgar and obsessed with fame.

Beginning in Tang-Song times, the only female talent visible in the historical record conveys its lofty respectability through mere short poems about spring love, autumn loneliness, and blooms and grasses in lush profusion and decay. There are notable exceptions, for instance the *Nü lunyu* by Song Shanggong [Song Ruozhao; see C.2], and the *Nü xiaojing* by Lady Zheng. Although these women's intelligence did not save them from a certain dullness and vulgarity, still the general direction of their work was near to refinement and correctness. (16)

> *Zhang's note* [10]: They wished to compose instructions for women, but they did not know enough to study the genre of Cao Dagu's [Ban Zhao's] *Instructions for Women*, instead misguidedly imitating the sagely Classics. We could liken their work to the questions and answers composed in the "Shanglin fu" by Sima Xiangru, which are in fact purely imaginary.

When those of us in the literary world cite their writing, we all acknowledge that their aspirations were praiseworthy.

> *Zhang's note* [11]: All this came about because the women's learning of the ancients ceased to be transmitted; under the circumstances, the best we could expect from women of high purpose was this sort of work.

Similarly, few who came after them were able to match Li Qingzhao's [P.17] notes on epigraphy, or Guan Daosheng's [P.23] pure and subtle calligraphy and painting. Nevertheless, those gems of inscriptions were all collated and collected at Huzhou, and the dazzling calligraphic strokes were a familiar sight only to the Recipient of Edicts. It is unheard-of for a minister's wife to accompany her husband in discussing a letter at the imperial academy, or for a Hanlin wife to debate with the Nine Ministers. (17)

> *Zhang's note* [12]: When Li Qingzhao and Zhao Mingcheng together compiled the *Jinshi lu*, Mingcheng was in the imperial academy at the time, hence this comment.

Although we refer to literary writing as a "public vessel," it is a fact that since ancient times men and women have kept a great distance from one another. How we can distort the strict names and meanings that define our constant moral obligations!

(18) From the Tang-Song period until the Ming, the statutes of the land tolerated female entertainers in the palace. When officials and nobles presented themselves at court, they would always be met with kingfisher sleeves and fragrant incense. When bureaucrats and functionaries organized their documents, they would always see red skirts urging wine upon them. *Wutong* leaves and decorated wells [reminiscent of the lovers Yang Guifei and Emperor Xuanzong] made every courier station redolent of "autumn longings" [i.e., a site for trysting]. Pervaded by the sweet and natural fragrance of beautiful women, the Winding River Pond [where winning examination candidates celebrated their success] symbolized pledges of new love. Official records are full of details about such things. Moreover, under the tyrannical rule of the Ming dynasty, if a degree-holding official lost his post and property, his wife and children were also affected, with the result that many women who were great masters of poetry and ritual sank into the brothels. Those among them who subtly combined sensual beauty with art composed and sang clever verses, drawing scholars to respond in kind. The general themes of their poems were passion and longing, separation and nostalgia. The poems were exchanged as expressions of friendship, but their careful composition conveyed the sentiments of a spouse. There can be no doubt of the range of their emotional expression. When a poem from the women's apartments sounds its bells in the world outside, the Way expressed in the poem is certain to conform to its new environment.

(19) Even when poetry flourished during the three great eras of the Tang, works by women remained rare. If we survey the entire dynasty, we find that the most prolific female writers of poetry were Li Ye [P.9], Xue Tao [P.10], and Yu Xuanji [P.11]; no one else can compare with them. This is clear evidence of two things: that nuns and courtesans were prolific because they frequently exchanged poetry with the literati; and that women from illustrious families governed by ritual considered their writings a warning against inappropriate behavior.

(20) Now the notorious state-toppling courtesans, who constantly interacted with the famous men of their time by exchanging poems and essays, were tantamount to spouses or friends, both in their roles and in their intentions. We may say that their words had a double meaning. They were like the ancient poet who, when he thought of his lord or pined for a friend, adopted the

voice and affected the emotions of love between men and women; or like the poet who, in order to satirize sexual impropriety and immorality, adopted an exaggerated fictional language through which to express himself. Each is a different type of poetry, each following a prescribed narrow path, such that the genre dictates the rhyme and the language, and it is crucial to know the difference among them. Thus the loyal minister or the upright friend will subtly conceal his earnest critique, while in a satire of an odious practice or an attack on perversion one can detect the writer's sorrow beyond the language of the poem. When people stopped writing prefaces to their poems, the strengths and weaknesses of poetry changed; when the original intent of a writer was not clear, the skill or clumsiness of the work was likewise transformed.

> *Zhang's note* [13]: If the "Li sao" is taken literally to be about searching for a woman, then its words make no sense; if the air of the states called "Zhen wei" is taken to be the words of the poet herself, it loses all of its interest. If, on the other hand, we regard these works as allegories, then their import naturally deepens.

So it is that the poems of nameless lovers may very nearly express the principle underlying the Great Ultimate or *yin* and *yang*. If we lodge them in the great expanse between heaven and earth [i.e., if we imbue them with cosmic significance], then "the wise will find wisdom in them, and the humane person will see humanity." The famous courtesans who were skilled poets grasped the ancient meanings in precisely this way, transforming them into concrete expressions of ardent longing between men and women and lodging them in the warm, weighty language of the poet. Thus the words they use are refined and yet informed by a standard, true and yet free of lewdness. They have been transmitted for a thousand years, winning glory as works of grandeur; they cannot be dismissed on account of the person who wrote them.

But to claim a voice is to find one's proper genre, and women are differ- (21)
ent from men. Thus a skillfully composed dirge must await the appropriate funeral of a friend to be chanted, while—conversely—a rowing song may be untrammeled and free, and so it is suitable for a boatwoman to sing. The courtesan who presents a poem to Mr. Li or Mr. Zhang is doing so simply because the situation requires it. But in respectable families, the words spoken in the women's quarters are "not to be heard," so how would it be possible for such a woman to exchange poems with a stranger on the outside?

Although the Office of Entertainment was not instituted by the Former (22)
Kings [i.e., during the ancient Three Dynasties], in fact it evolved out of

ancient precedents. If you are not one of the four great Song Confucian philosophers, what's to prevent "a small deviation from the absolute standards of virtue," as Confucius put it! So it is that meritorious officials who advise on the governance of the country; loyal, upright, pure ministers; cultivated, virtuous Confucians; and even exhalted and reclusive scholars—all from time to time may find an object for their affections. If they describe this in their writings, it will pass through the net of proscribed behavior, and it will not unduly compromise their flourishing virtue.

(23) However, while literary work may model itself after the ancients, institutions must change with the times. In the reign of our present dynasty, instruction through the rites has been pure and strict, and great care has been taken to avoid ambiguity and to clarify the principles of separation [between men and women]. Not since the Three Dynasties has there been a ruling house so reverential toward the rites! Now that female entertainers have been banned from the Palace Precincts and government officials no longer maintain the Office of Entertainment, no one in the empire can use these pretexts for relations between men and women. Corrupt courtesans who circulate among different brothels and prostitutes who buy and sell sex on the street now violate strict laws. They will not be able to pay to escape punishment.

> *Zhang's note* [14]: Office-holders all the way down to licentiates whose conduct is found wanting will never be employed.

Even though an occasional big fish may slip through the net, the law books will never be completely closed. The true gentleman lives in fear of the law, and surely he would never involve himself in such degradation!

(24) Often I see a printed edition of poetry by a famous scholar, and before reading it, I first examine the table of contents, which will contain references to rouge powders and passionate love or allude to exchanges of poetry in the pleasure quarter. This writer calls himself untrammeled and free, claiming that he is just like the ancients. If a man born in this time, a man of the present, can be so ignorant of the official prohibitions, how can he talk about writing? In the rituals of the Duke of Zhou, men and women from the same descent group could not marry. It is utterly preposterous for people born after the Zhou to claim that there is no need for proper separation between men and women, throwing human relationships into confusion as if we were beasts and animals. Can we really maintain that the ancients behaved the same way?

(25) Now talent requires study, and study values intelligence. As Confucius

said, talent undisciplined by study is mere cleverness. A merely clever person who has no intelligence will have no talent, but a person who is merely clever knows no limits. He may call a poem elegant and refined when it is in fact frivolous and shallow.

> *Zhang's note* [15]: "Refined" [*ya*] means correct. It is precisely the opposite of the odious vulgar style [*su*]. What I call vulgar [*su*] is the poetry tainted with a bad air [*feng qi*]. Frivolous poems and vulgar poems are both common [*su*], but even a vulgar poem will do no harm to the moral way or to people's hearts, while common poems that are frivolous represent a crime against elegance and refinement.

He may try to make a reputation out of artificial embellishment and boasting.

> *Zhang's note* [16]: Among the men who quest after fame, there has never yet been one who was not vulgar.

He will show off to his students and make outrageous displays before ladies. The corruption he spreads in human hearts and in ordinary behavior is beyond description. In ancient times frivolous or loose writings were not unknown among the literati, but bragging and boasting by women was unheard-of. Now the person who is in fact worthless but still strives relentlessly for fame, or the person who is not distinguished in his or her own right but instead relies on the assistance of others—a man of high purpose would be ashamed to be classified as either one. When even the breaking of marital bonds, and the rituals that govern giving and receiving between a man and a woman, become the subject of a poet's passionate, florid works and are then couched in various literary idioms and flanked with critical commentaries composed on the basis of bits of rumor from here and there—such works we call "phrases from the mansions of the hairpins." These works were known in former ages. But since the beginning of heaven and earth, what they describe has never been ritually approved behavior for chaste maidens or proper ladies.

The women's learning of ancient times, such as the learning of the Woman (26)
Historian, the Woman Libationer, and the Woman Seer, was often associated with a particular government office, in the same way that men specialize in a particular art in order to hold an official post. But the general learning required of women was encompassed in the phrase "virtue, speech, comportment, and work." Of these four, virtue was elusive and difficult to grasp, and work was crude and easily displayed.

Zhang's note [17]: You had to be as saintly as the mothers of King Wen and King Wu before you could be said to have fully realized "virtue." For "work," silkworm rearing and spinning were widespread in scholarly and commoner households alike.

(27) But most important were the other two aspects of women's general learning, those closest to literary art: speech and comportment. From the smallest household, with its rules for living, to the imperial court and all the high officials, there was not a person who was not schooled in proper ritual comportment. When a court audience was held, when a guest was received, when a funeral took place, when the sacrifices were performed, the empress, the imperial concubines, and the wives of the high officials of different ranks, all had specific duties to perform. If they did not regularly endeavor to practice and prepare for these, how could they have performed so masterfully at the moment when they had to carry them out? The Erudites who discoursed on the Classics in Han times mainly used quotations to talk about the rites. But they also depended on the Minister of Rites Xu Sheng because he was so good at performing them. In this way they achieved the fullest possible realization of dignity and decorum in ritual, which is impossible to acquire merely by reciting and repeating texts. Thus we see that what was called women's comportment had to include actual ritual practice. Even some of the great Confucian scholars of later times have not been able to grasp this.

Zhang's note [18]: We need but read the biography recording the words of Jing Jiang, which so lavishly display the rules of propriety. How can the classical tutors and great Confucians of later times compare with her!

As for women's speech, the most important quality was deferential obedience. In ancient times, words from the women's quarter were not to pass to the outside world. What was called "deferential obedience" was also an essential characteristic of ritually correct literary art. Confucius once said: "The person who has not studied the *Odes* will have nothing to say." This means, of course, that any woman who was accomplished in proper speech—in other words, who could speak with deferential obedience—must have also been well versed in the *Odes*.

Zhang's note [19]: One need only observe the women of the Spring and Autumn period, their deferential obedience gentle yet full of critical moral force.

This makes it clear that as regards women's learning in ancient times, ritual had to be mastered before one could understand poetry.

> *Zhang's note* [20]: Without the *Zhou li* women do not know how to act; without the *Book of Odes* they do not know how to speak.

And there were some women who also excelled in the Six Arts.

> *Zhang's note* [21]: For example, Mu Jiang's discussions of the *Yi jing*.

But in the centuries since then, women's learning has ceased to be transmitted. Some women who are accomplished and elegant and know literature claim, on that basis, to be women who can also do a scholar's work. They wear their virtue like their beauty, on their faces. Such women do not know that women originally had their own learning and that this learning always took the rites as its foundation. Since they have abandoned the instruction basic to their calling and wantonly flung themselves into poetry, the poems they write are not characterized by what the ancients would have called practiced deferential obedience or fine womanly speech. To study how to speak under these conditions is like being a farmer who abandons his fields or an envoy who neglects to take a ceremonial gift when he leaves the country. How can their work be counted seriously as women's learning? It is pathetic! (28)

The women's learning of ancient times always began with the rites and then turned to poetry. The women's learning of today is just the reverse; it uses poetry to destroy the rites. If the rites are cut off, we cannot say anything more about the human heart and mind or about human behavior. Without question it is certain scholars of dubious character who have perpetrated these heretical teachings in order to entice women into following them. Others who truly understand women's learning look on these men as so much excrement. They will never be fooled! (29)

> *Zhang's note* [22]: The wise women of ancient times valued talent. The old saying that "The only good woman is a woman without talent" does not cast aspersions on talent per se. What it means is that a woman who has a little talent but no learning will be pretentious and fame-seeking—unlike village lasses or old peasant women, who would never be laughed at for making fools of themselves.

To dress up a fashionable but middling writer and portray her as the best that the women's quarters can produce, and then to use this as a basis for ranking her poetry is really nothing more than expressing a physical desire for her.

Zhang's note [23]: Here I refer to praise that goes well beyond what a woman writer deserves, and also to the practice of correcting and embellishing her writing.

Where a certain unscrupulous scholar is concerned, there can be no doubt about his motives. Alas! She thinks she has talent and flaunts it; he thinks she is attractive and desires her. The man who pursues her without knowing why is a fool. The man who pursues her while also knowing why is a fool's fool.

(30) The term to use in praising a woman is "serene." To be serene is very near to learning. But the women who are called "talented" today—how they bustle around! What a dreadful noise they make!

(Zhang Xuecheng, *Zhang shi yishu*, 5/30b–38b)

par. 2, *Spring and Autumn Annals*: The *Chunqiu*, a chronicle of the state of Lu between 722 and 468 B.C.E.

par. 3, Zheng Xuan: Zheng Xuan (127–200) was great Han-dynasty scholar and annotator.

par. 5, Deng Man: The wife of the king of Chu, who helped her husband avert disaster as he strategized to invade neighboring states by reading omens in the changing phases of the moon. Her story, which appears in *Zuo zhuan*, Duke Huan, year 11, and Duke Zhuang, years 3 and 4, is retold in Liu Xiang, *Gu lienü zhuan*, 3/1b–2b.

par. 5, Mu Jiang: Daughter of the marquis of Qi, also the wife of Duke Xuan of Lu and mother of Duke Cheng. A skilled reader of the *Book of Changes*, she also had a reputation for promiscuity. See Liu Xiang, *Gu lienü zhuan*, 7/9b–10b.

par. 5, "the good wife of Earl Mu of Lu": The earl's wife, known as Jing Jiang, had a son named Wenbo. After her husband died, she took his place as Wenbo's mentor, teaching him how to build friendships and how to manage political affairs. See Liu Xiang, *Gu lienü zhuan*, 1/9b–13b.

par. 5, "the spouse of King Xuan of Zhou": The lady, daughter of the marquis of Qi, was a paradigm of ritual propriety. She blamed herself when her husband retired too early and rose too late, proclaiming that the fault must be hers for encouraging him to be indolent. She therefore removed her hairpins and earrings, renouncing her title as his consort. The king, moved by her sincerity, restored her title and changed his behavior. See Liu Xiang, *Gu lienü zhuan*, 2/1a–2a.

par. 5, "a eulogy to make known his virtue": Ibid., 2/10b–11b.

par. 5, "unseemly to do so": Ibid., 4/7b–8a.

par. 5, "the lady of Wei": A reference to poem 39 in the *Book of Odes*; see C.38.1, note to par. 6.

par. 5, Ding Jiang: See poem 28 in the *Book of Odes*. See also Liu Xiang, *Gu lienü zhuan*, 1/6b–8b.

par. 5, Liu Xiang and Fan Ye: Liu Xiang edited the *Lie nü zhuan*; Fan Ye was editor of the *Hou Han shu*.

Zhang's note 1: Zhang's own notes expand on his points or provide ampler references. In the original they are, as here, interwoven with the main text and set in smaller-sized characters.

Zhang's note 1, "actually superior to those of learned men who came after them": The polemical reference to Yuan Mei's cult of *xingling* or "innate sensibility" is clear. Statements resembling those attacked by Zhang may be found in Zhong Xing's preface to the anthology *Mingyuan shigui* (C.32.1).

par. 8, Lady of Tangshan: The Lady of Tangshan was a concubine of Emperor Han Gaozu. She composed this song, set to music in the style of the state of Chu favored by the emperor, to celebrate his virtue. See *Han shu*, "Li yue zhi," 22/15a–22a.

par. 8, Lady Ban and her "Rhapsody of Self-Commiseration": See P.1.2.

par. 10, Zhuo Wenjun: On her marriage to Sima Xiangru, see P.38.1, P.79.3, and C.31.1.

par. 12, "the Fu Qin rulers": Also known as the "Former Qin," one of the Sixteen Kingdoms created in successive invasions by Xiongnu and other nomadic peoples from the steppe between 301 and 439. The story of Lady Song, also known as Mother Wei, appears in *Jin shu*, 96/17b–18b.

par. 13, Xi *furen* and the Tang princess of Pingyang: See, respectively, *Sui shu*, 80/5a–9b; and *Xin Tang shu*, 83/1b–2b.

par. 14, "the wife who concealed herself" and "the new wife and her husband's younger brother": The first story, found in the biographies of exemplary women in the *Jin shu* (96/11a–12b), tells how Xie Daoyun shielded herself with a screen to summon her husband's younger brother and advise him in the midst of negotiations in which he was about to be outwitted. In the second, retold in Liu Yiqing, *Shishuo xinyu* 25.8, the wife of Wang Hun tells him, in effect, that she wishes his younger brother had been the father of their son.

par. 15, "the Three Followings": On the Three Followings or Obediences, see P.60.9

Zhang's note 13, "Li sao": On Qu Yuan's famous poem, see P.37 (biographical note).

Zhang's note 18, Jing Jiang: See note to par. 5 above ("the good wife of Earl Mu of Lu"). Here Zhang refers to the fact that even after her son took high office, Jing Jiang continued to spin and weave as before as a caution to her son not to allow his prestigious post to alter his moral upbringing.

BACKGROUND NOTE AND TRANSLATION BY SUSAN MANN

錢三錫

C.48. Qian Sanxi (19th century)

Qian Sanxi (style name Shenfu) came from Kuaiji (Zhejiang province). His anthology of women's poetry, called *Zhuang lou zhaiyan* (Selected beauties from the chambers of adornment, 1833), included 308 poets, with short biographical notices.[1]

C.48.1. Preface to Zhuang lou zhaiyan

In September of 1832, when I failed the provincial exam, we had bitter rains and icy cold wind. The skies did not clear for several days. Since touring the countryside was out of the question, I turned to wine and poetry and gave vent to my inspiration. As for eight-legged essays, I fear them as I do my teachers and keep them tucked away on a shelf; so, instead, I took up some anthologies of ancient and modern poetry. Among them, poems that startle and please, move me to tears or to song, that are enough to drive away nightmares or serve as snacks for wine number more than can be counted on the fingers. Poems by women particularly stand out; those of our present dynasty even more so. Their brocade compositions and pearl-laden works dazzle the eyes and enchant the spirit—almost like climbing Jeweled Mountain and entering the mermaid caverns.

(2) I selected those which had stolen my heart and had them copied out. After two months I had gotten down a few scrolls' worth, quite a few poems altogether. I wished to continue searching for more, but my father, older brother, and friends all advised me not to waste my time, and I could not justify it myself. They said, "Participation in government is not for women, so why draw from the women's quarters to compile a book?" Thus I set the work aside and didn't look at it again. This spring, my friend Yuwen picked up a few pieces and read them. He liked the elegant rhymes of the poems and felt that not many women poets had come to notice except for Yuan Mei's female students; and even amongst those elegantly made-up ladies of talent with refined thoughts and silken voices, not a few had fallen into obscurity.

(3) And so in the end I sent this work to the engravers. I myself am only a rustic with limited knowledge and have not seen a tenth of the women's poetry that has been written during our dynasty. My omissions are many indeed, and

I am greatly dissatisfied with the narrowness of this anthology. Yet, since I did not want to go against my friend's wishes, I agreed to have it published now and must await a selection of greater breadth in the future.

Written in the second month of the *guisi* year of the Daoguang reign [1833] (4)
by Qian Sanxi of Kuaiji.

(Hu Wenkai, 919)

par. 1, "eight-legged essays": A particularly constrained form of prose composition, the standard for late-imperial examination essays.

TRANSLATED BY MARK A. BORER

黃傳驥

C.49. Huang Chuanji (19th century)

Guochao guixiu shi liuxu ji (Willow catkins: A collection of women poets from our Qing era, 1853) was compiled by Huang Zhimo (style name Zhengbo), a native of Yihuang in Jiangxi province. The collection is introduced by the editor's preface and forewords by Zheng Zhiyun, Huang Chuanji, and Caiyun Shanren. It also contains congratulatory inscriptions by Zhang Buqu, Yu Hu, Huang Zhijun, Yu Yuandeng, Huang Tingbi, and Tao Jie. A total of 1,938 authors are represented in the collection, with a further five authors in the supplement and five more in the sequel.

C.49.1. Foreword to Huang Zhimo, Guochao guixiu shi liuxu ji

There is nothing on which the good and animating spirit of the universe does not bestow its favors. Where it is strong, the spirit produces sons of filial piety and ministers of loyal allegiance; where it is graceful, it produces men of letters and ladies with literary talent; where it is congested and pent-up, it solidifies as marvelous treasures; and where it fades out but lingers, it is scattered abroad as fragrant grass and rare flowers. History has continuously glorified devoted sons and loyal ministers and has made them outshine the sun and the moon; even men of letters can find consolation and release in using a piece of writing to win glory in their own day and fame in posterity. But as for talented women: even though many of them are known, no one knows how many more have been buried like hidden treasures and left to decay like weeds and dead twigs. Why is it so? Because women are not valued for their literary talent, and their duties in life are so diverse that they can hardly concentrate on reading the Classics and can hardly spend days choosing the right words for a line of poetry. That should account for the difficulty in compiling a collection of the works of a female poet. Even if the compilation is done, it is not always easy to have it printed: no one cares to pass it on, and the manuscript gets scattered and lost till it is reduced to a pile of waste paper. If it is unknown to her family members, her sons and grandsons, how can it be known to people in other places? And how can one expect to gather such poems from here and there to make a representative collection? That should account for the difficulty especially in compiling and passing on an anthology of poems by women.

(2) My uncle Lisheng, who held an office in the prefecture, is assiduous and inquisitive in his studies, and he is especially keen to illuminate and make known what has been obscure. Whenever he has gathered enough materials, he classifies and edits them, and that is how he compiled the *Xunmintang congshu* [The Hall of Modesty and Intelligence series], which did not cost him much effort beyond putting the contents together and delivering them to a printer. But the reason why it has taken so much time for him to issue this *Liuxu ji* [Willow catkins collection] is that he intended to collect all the works from all sources with no omission. He has in the collection almost two thousand women poets, and he has edited these poems several times. Some of these poets are represented by as few as one or two pieces, but none by more than a few dozen. Since Daoyun's line on the "willow catkins" has always been known and famous, why go to the trouble of making this collection? It is a pity that, though our county of Yihuang has no lack of talented women poets, the works of those in the past are lost and difficult to find, whereas those of more recent poets are hidden in private quarters. Take the example of my aunt Wan Yiren, whose poems written over the years were known only to my cousin Rao Jiexiao, who often composed her own poems in response. And yet Wan cautioned us that we should look after our daily sustenance, because fame in poetry is not a sign of good fortune. Wan's daughter Shengzhi inherited her mother's talent and could not be kept away from writing poetry; and because of that, her mother's talent in poetry was known. When my uncle first compiled the *Liuxu ji*, he did not include Wan's works. I read those works and found them all gentle and peaceful, with nothing deviating from propriety; I urged my uncle to include them in the collection, and finally he did.

(3) Another example would be Lady Ying, a native of Shen'gang, who wrote many elegant and well-constructed works and who was the sister of a cousin

of my deceased first wife Wu Ruren. In childhood the two of them learned to read together, and as grown-ups they lived in the same household, writing poems frequently to one another in mutual encouragement. I was told that Ying was especially learned in ancient books. When Wu and I were married, she often recited her favorite lines from the poems that they had collaborated on. I asked to read her manuscripts, which bore the collective title of *Danwei shicao* [Pale flower verses]. She also showed me letters she had exchanged with Ying, in which they wrote each other poems, and there were several dozen of them. Having read those letters, my impression was that Ying's poems were gentle and graceful, while Wu's were of a soft tone and rich. After only three years of marriage, Wu caught a high fever and died in spite of prescribed medicine. Several years earlier, Ying had married into the Cao family of Fengxin, an old family that had produced many officials at court. But soon the family declined and was reduced to poverty; she lived an extremely simple but noble life, and it was likely that she had long before discarded her writing brush and burned her manuscripts. This seems to confirm Wan Yiren's admonition that fame in poetry is not a sign of good fortune. When my uncle began collecting poems, I wanted to gather Ying's works for him, but I was dismayed to find them all lost. Some ten years ago, I could still recite from memory a number of them, but now I can only remember this last couplet in a seven-character-line poem of the regulated verse form: "I love you for your marvelous talent / And am surprised to find Xiangru incarnate as a woman." This was written as a response to Wu's lines from a poem entitled "Expressing Feelings on a Summer Day": "Quietly facing the garden flowers in lovely summer / I look pale and thin from working too hard over poetry." Yesterday by chance I found several slips of paper in an old bamboo casket. It so happened that in the spring of the year *gengchen* [1820], Wu cut four pieces of paper and attached them to a folded bamboo fan which she sent to her friend with a poem written on it. The paper I found contains Ying's poem in response with some prefatory remarks in parallel prose. The poem itself has been included in the collection, but the prefatory remarks are incomplete. They are, however, as rare and precious as a magic feather of the legendary flying horse and will be cherished by all who chance to see them. Here are her remarks:

> An inch of heart runs across a thousand miles, as my eyes search as far as the remote stars and the Milky Way; a single day feels like three autumns, as my heart breaks to perceive the quick change of light and shadow. Our reunion promised before is difficult to realize, and there is no telling when

> our next meeting will be. Looking back, I recall the days when we put on make-up in front of the same mirror and composed poetry under the same candle light. Together we vied to lavish the highest praise on the fragrant tea, and in literary talent we deemed ourselves no less than Zuo Fen [P.3]. We were proud and competitive then, as I now remember it. My thoughts would not be fully expressed even if I could write them on scrolls made of all the bamboos on the southern mountain, and my feelings could not be emptied even if I could let them flow along the great waves in the eastern sea. Like clouds my sorrows often gather together, and like water my tears are seldom dry. Then came your new and original poems that give expression to every feeling one has in spring and to every sorrow of separation; and there is also the kindness of your gift of a fine jade, delivered on the fine silk of the summer fan . . .

Several hundred more words must have followed these, but it is a shame that I could not find them, however I tried. Before she fell ill, as I recall, my wife had written these lines in reply to one of Ying's poems: "Often ill, I am fit only to wait on the Queen Mother / For at the Jade Lake I'd do nothing but guess rhymed riddles." We little knew then that those words should prove premonitory. The lines I quote here do not represent Ying and Wu at their best, but are merely those that I can still remember. Thus I know that though the good and animating spirit of the universe never grudges its favors to anything, few poems by women have been passed on to the world. I put these on record to show how fortunate are those women poets whose works are now included in this anthology.

(Hu Wenkai, 921–23)

par. 2, "Daoyun's line": On Xie Daoyun's willow catkins metaphor, see C.24.1.

par. 3, "to find Xiangru incarnate as a woman": On the dashing *fu* master Sima Xiangru, see P.8a.1 and P.38.1.

BACKGROUND NOTE AND TRANSLATION BY ZHANG LONGXI

王鵬運

C.50. Wang Pengyun (1848–1904)

Wang Pengyun, style name Youxia, was born in Guangxi. He was a second-degree holder. At court, he was a strong supporter of the Reform Movement headed by Kang Youwei. He was also a member of the Qiangxue hui. He wrote the preface to the 1904 edition of Xu Naichang's anthology *Xiao tan luan shi huike baijia guixiu ci* (XTLS; Song-lyrics of one hundred famous women, 1896/1904).

C.50.1. Preface to Xu Naichang, Xiao tan luan shi huike baijia guixiu ci

The genre of *ci* poetry dawned in the late Tang dynasty and had its high noon in the Song dynasties. At its earliest stage, much of it was couched in the words of young women, in order to portray their sentiments of melancholy and passion. Surely this is because women are particularly well equipped to experience tender feelings and appear as though they cannot withstand such afflictions; therefore their delicate and intertwining emotions easily touch and affect the reader.

Yet as I studied the *ci* collection *Huajian ji* [Among the flowers], I failed (2)
to find a single poem written by a woman. When I turned to the Song collections of women poets, indeed I found the volumes of Li Qingzhao [P.17] and Zhu Shuzhen [P.18]. Yet besides them, all the others are quite fragmentary, with a poem here and there, as though they were broken incense sticks and odd cakes of powder. Then I looked at the *Linxia cixuan* edited by Mr. Zhou from Songling, in which are collections of poems by ladies from four dynasties, plus writings by courtesans, priestesses, and other talents. Yet even there, there are no more than a hundred names or so. Is it really because there are so few talented women poets?

Or is it more because that these women were born and bred in the con- (3)
fines of their boudoirs, and voices from the inner chambers could not reach the outside? Is it also because that they did not have the privilege of traveling to the great mountains, climbing to the top of the well-known pagodas, or having the occasions to expose their talent by engaging in verse exchanges with friends? These must be the reasons that there have been so few poems produced by women and that, among those produced, so few are known in the world far and wide. These must be the reasons that so few people come along to collect and preserve their works, so that they are like the flowers of springtime or seasonal birds, momentarily there to amuse the eyes and the ears. Is this not a regrettable situation?

My esteemed friend Xu Jiyu [Naichang] has always been devoted to writ- (4)
ing song-lyrics. Because works of women's *ci* poetry are particularly known to be easily scattered and lost, he single-mindedly applied himself to the task of

gathering them, so that now he has accumulated the works of over one hundred poets. Lately he has sent some of them to the press so that there are already several volumes out, covering a certain number of poets. In addition, he also followed the format of the *Complete Yuan Poems*: all the poems that do not lend themselves to being assembled as a collection go into a volume together, entitled *Guixiu cixuan* [Collection of lyrics from the women's apartments]. His effort is truly immense.

(5) People who raise their eyebrows at the present-day situation often point to the lack of female moral fortitude as the cause of bad social mores. Alas! It is more the lack of people who applaud and commend their moral behavior.

(6) The writing of song-lyrics is one of the arts of composition. Now that we have the good fortune to have Mr. Xu Jiyu to gather and anthologize it, its glory is properly restored. And if such good examples can be widely emulated, who is to say that the mores extolled in the *Book of Odes* will not prevail today? Were I to ask Mr. Xu about this, he would probably not think my words too far-fetched.

(7) Wang Pengyun pens this preface on the fifteenth day of the second month, in the thirtieth year of the reign of Guangxu [1904].

(Hu Wenkai, 872)

par. 2, "the *Linxia cixuan* edited by Mr. Zhou": For the preface to this collection, see C.42.1.

BACKGROUND NOTE AND TRANSLATION BY HU YING

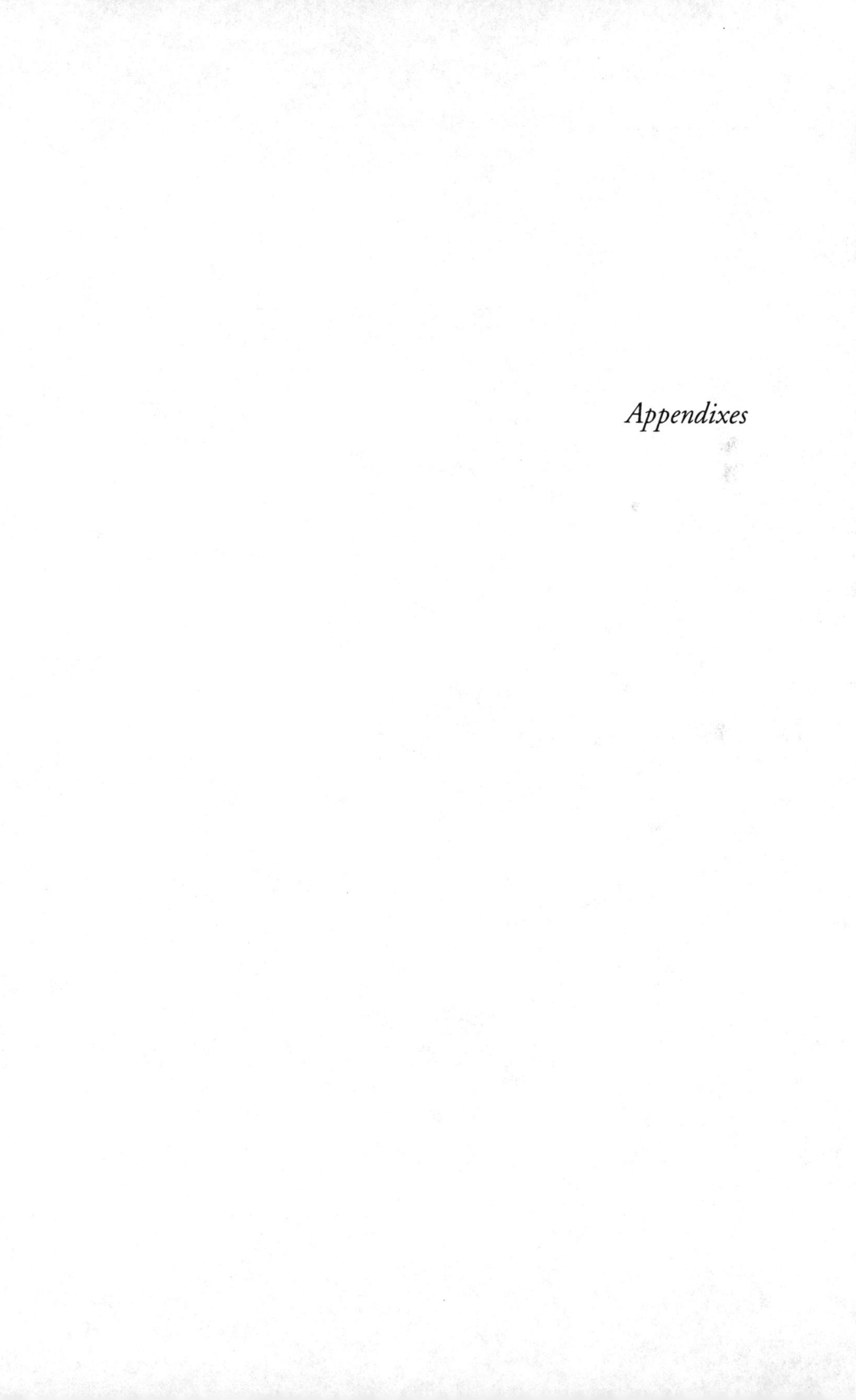

Appendixes

A Note on Song-Lyrics (*ci*, *qu*, *sanqu*), with a Glossary of Tune-Titles

There are two major forms of song-lyric poetry in Chinese, the *ci* and the related *qu* and *sanqu*.

Ci

The poetic genre of *ci* emerged in the High Tang (ca. 713–55). *Ci* were originally lyrics written to popular tunes of the day, hence their name, meaning "words [of a song]." Formally speaking, *ci* distinguish themselves from most Chinese poetic genres in their irregularity and individuality: a *ci* poem contains lines of many differing lengths, and the genre contains hundreds of different poem patterns. The oldest surviving *ci* texts are anonymous songs preserved in Dunhuang manuscripts dating from the eighth century. Early *ci* were, in fact, largely of anonymous authorship and were performed by professional musicians, singing girls, courtesans, and entertainers. The associated music, mostly of Central Asian origin, would have sounded markedly "foreign" to Chinese ears. One center of musical training and production was the Palace Music School, or *jiaofang*. Tune-titles recorded in Cui Lingqin's *Jiaofang ji*, a contemporary account of the training and organization of singers, dancers, and instrumentalists in the employ of the Tang emperor Xuanzong, are accordingly called *jioafang* tunes. This palace style of *ci* underwent numerous transformations after the *jiaofang* was disbanded. In later Tang, the performers became professional entertainers, and literate men became involved in this tradition.

As early as the Northern Song dynasty (ca. 960–1126) the song-lyric genre was appropriated by writers of the literati class as an alternative to the staid and symmetrical *shi* verse form (see Introduction). Since early *ci* were often written by men for performance by women singers, the genre was from the beginning associated with the feminine in language as well as sentiment. Embedded in its form were issues of appropriation of voice and gender. It is not surprising, then, that the song-lyric became an important mode of poetic expression for women writers, who situated their self-presentations within and against the genre's conventional "feminine" language.

Early song-lyric was intimately bound up with music and performance. Though some poets, notably Jiang Kuei (ca. 1155–1221), composed original tunes for their song-lyrics, the usual practice was to set words to existing melodies. Hence the composition of song-lyrics is usually described as a process of *tian ci*, "filling in words"—imitating the metrical pattern of a given tune, syllable for syllable and tone for tone. Over time, however, melodies often became lost or forgotten, and we no longer have the tunes to which the *ci* were set. Nonetheless, *ci* continued to be composed to titles and their patterns of lines and rhymes from the past.

As books of tune-patterns (*ci lü*) and tune-titles (*ci pai*) came to be compiled in the Ming and Qing dynasties, the metrical forms of these songs-without-music became increasingly standardized and rigidly adhered to. The two most important *ci* tune-pattern compilations are the *Yuzhi cipu* (Imperial register of *ci* prosody; hereafter cited simply as *Cipu*), commissioned by the Kangxi emperor and compiled by Wang Yiqing in 1715, which lists 826 tune titles and 2,306 variant forms, and the *Ci lü*, compiled by Wan Shu with a preface dated 1687, which lists 875 basic tune-patterns and 1,496 variant forms. Later editions added new or newly discovered tune-titles to the list, but these two compilations essentially established and codified the core group of *ci* tune-titles.

Ci tunes acquired their names in one of several manners. Some tunes, such as *Sumu zhe* ("Sumu Veil") or *Pusa man* ("Bodhisattva Barbarian"), presumably retain the original titles of the Central Asian musical pieces from which they derive. Other titles bear a relation to the content of the original song and its lyrics, so we assume that early avatars of *Yi Jiangnan* ("Longing for the Southland") were indeed songs nostalgic for the splendors of the region south of the Yangzi River, and that the lyrics of the original *Niannu jiao* ("Charms of Niannu") most likely advertised the seductive powers of that legendary Tang courtesan. A third means by which song-lyric patterns acquired their names is through the association of a particular tune-title with the best-known later *ci* composed to that tune. The tune-pattern *Niannu jiao* is known under a number of variant titles mainly derived from a lyric on that tune by the Song dynasty poet Su Shi (see entry for *Dajiang dongqu* below). Though all these titles refer to the original *Niannu jiao* pattern, later lyricists might have chosen to use the variant titles to evoke passages or sentiments recalled from Su's lyric. Other variant titles (for example, *Jian zi mulanhua* or "Magnolia Blossoms: Shortened") indicate metrical or tonal departures from a known tune.

Adding to the confusion of multiple titles, several variations are recorded for many of the tune-patterns themselves, mostly as a result of creative twists worked on the original form by different poets. In the glossary of tune-titles that follows, the number of variations is listed for each tune, as are some of the variant titles. In the interest of brevity, however, the specifics of the tune-pattern variations are not given here, and usually only those variant titles that cross-reference with some other tune-title are listed; interested readers are encouraged to consult the *Ci lü*, *Cipu*, or other song-lyric prosody books. Anecdotes, legends, and allusions connected with the titles of the tunes are also provided, to give the user of this glossary a sense of how a native reader might perceive a given song-lyric title. However, the tune-titles in themselves for the most part bear no necessary or determining relation to the contents of the lyric, as is indicated by the tendency of later *ci* writers to append an occasional title or short preface to the generic tune-title.

Sanqu *and* Qu

Sanqu, "free aria," a form of dramatic lyric (*qu*), originated in the twelfth century and was at the height of its popularity in the thirteenth and fourteenth centuries. *Qu* is also a performance genre based on melody. As their name betokens, *sanqu* show great formal flexibility: they introduce new rhymes based on the spoken language of their time, and the rules of rhyming in *qu* are more flexible than in *ci* versification. Moreover, the language of *sanqu* tends to be more demotic and to cover a wider range of subject matter (often quite earthy) than that of the *ci*. *Sanqu* tunes are usually categorized as being either "northern" or "southern" *qu*—a distinction arising from stylistic differences in tempo, mood, and form of musical accompaniment. Northern-style *sanqu* were usually accompanied by the *pipa*, a strummed or plucked lutelike instrument, originally imported from the northern steppes. Southern-style *sanqu* were accompanied by the *xiao*, a vertical flute of bamboo, characteristic of southern regions. Some *sanqu* tunes are found in both "northern" and "southern" forms.

Glossary of Tune-Titles

Tune-titles are for *ci* unless otherwise indicated.

Baizi ling, "A Song in One Hundred Characters"
    Also known as *Niannu jiao*, "Charms of Niannu."
Bingtou lian, "Twin-Headed Lotus"
    Sanqu tune.
Bin yun song ling, "Cloud of Tousled Hair"
    Also known as *Sumu zhe*, "Sumu Veil." This variant name derives from a phrase in the Song dynasty poet Zhou Bangyan's *ci* to this tune.
Bu chan gong, "Pacing in the Palace of the Moon"
    Six variations.
Bu suanzi, "Song of Divination"
    Sixteen variations. Also known by six other titles, including *Meifeng bi*, "Azure-Tipped Brows."
Cai sang zi, "Mulberry-Picking Song"
    Tang *jiaofang* tune. Eight variations.
Chai tou feng, "Phoenix on Her Hairpin"
    The title originates with the Song dynasty poet Lu You and derives from an anonymous *ci* line, "Pitifully alone like the lone phoenix on her hairpin."
Chang xiang si, "Endless Longing"
    Nine variations. Also known by eleven other titles.
Chen zui dongfeng, "Deep Drunk in the East Wind"
    Sanqu tune. Exists in both "northern style" and "southern style" variations.
Chengtou yue, "Moon over the City Walls"
    Two variations.
Chongdie jin, "Layers on Layers of Gold"
    More commonly known as *Pusa man*, "Bodhisattva Barbarian," listed among the *jiaofang* compositions. This variant tune-title derives from a well-known Wen Tingyun *ci* composed to the tune *Pusa man*.
Chuanyan yunü, "Divine Maiden Messenger"
    Three variations.
Chun cong tian shang lai, "Spring Descends from the Heavens"
    Four variations.

Chun guang hao, "Spring Splendor"
Nine variations. Known by two other titles.

Dajiang dongqu, "The Great River Runs East"
Also known as *Niannu jiao*, "Charms of Niannu." This version of the title derives from the Song dynasty poet Su Shi's (Su Dongpo) most celebrated lyric to the tune, subtitled "Meditation on the Past at Red Cliff," which was written to commemorate the great battle at Red Cliff between Cao Cao and Zhou Yu of the Three Kingdoms and which opens with the line, "The Great River runs eastward. . . ." Most of the variant names of *Niannu jiao* spring from phrases in this lyric.

Dan huang liu, "Pale Yellow Willow"
Three variations. This is an original tune composed by the Song dynasty lyricist Jiang Kuei. In his preface to the original lyric, Jiang tells of being inspired to write his *ci* tune by the ravishing sight of the pale, graceful willows lining the streets of Hefei in springtime.

Daolian zi, "Silk-Pounding Song"
Five variations. Also known by six other titles. This tune is most often associated with Li Yu, the ill-starred last ruler of the Southern Tang.

Dian jiang chun, "Dabbing the Lips Red"
Five variations. Also known by nine other titles.

Diao qiu huan jiu, "Trading Mink for Wine"
Also known as *He xinlang*, "Congratulating the Bridegroom."

Die lian hua, "Butterflies Lingering over Flowers"
Tang *jiaofang* tune. Three variations. Also known as *Yiluo jin*, "A Basketful of Gold."

Ding fengbo, "Settling Winds and Waves"
Tang *jiaofang* tune. Fifteen variations.

Dong xian ge, "Song of the Cave Immortals"
Tang *jiaofang* tune. Forty-one variations. Also known by three other titles.

Er lang shen, "The Two Male Deities"
Tang *jiaofang* tune. Ten variations.

Fan xiang ling, "Tossing Over Fragrance"
According to *Cipu*, this tune-title originates from the Song poet Su Shi.

Fengguang hao, "Splendid Scenery"
Two variations.

Fenghuangtai shang yi chuixiao, "Flute-Playing Recalled on Phoenix Terrace"

Also known as *Tiao xiao ling*, "Song of Flirtation."

Fengliuzi, "Song of the Gallant"

Nine variations.

Gao yang tai, "High Terrace of Yang"

Three variations. The "High Terrace of Yang" alludes to the celebrated erotic encounter of King Xiang of Chu with the goddess of Wu Mountain, as described in a pair of rhyme-prose compositions (*fu*) attributed to Song Yu (see P.9.2).

Gong zhong tiao xiao, "Palace Flirtation"

Also known as *Tiao xiao ling*, "Song of Flirtation."

Gu luan, "Solitary Luan-bird"

Six variations. The *luan*, or simurgh, is a mythical bird, often used as a symbolic figure of conjugal bliss and paired with the phoenix (see P.18.12).

Gu yan'er, "Solitary Wild Goose"

Also known as *Yujie xing*, "Imperial Avenue Procession."

Haitang chun, "Spring Amidst Flowering Apples"

Three variations. *Cipu* states that this tune derives its title from a verse of the Song lyricist Qin Guan: "I wonder how many of the flowering apples blossomed in the night."

Han gong chun, "Spring in the Palace of Han"

Twelve variations.

Hao shi jin, "A Happy Event Draws Near"

Two variations.

He huo ling, "Fire-Shouting Song"

According to *Cipu*, the earliest known lyric set to this tune is by the Song poet Huang Tingjian.

He xinlang, "Congratulating the Bridegroom"

Fourteen variations. Also frequently known as *He xin liang*, "Welcoming the First of Cool Weather," but also known under other tune titles such as *Diao qiu huan jiu*, "Trading Mink for Wine," *Jinlü qu*, "Song of Golden Threads," and *Ru yan fei*, "Young Swallows in Flight." A great number of these variant title names derive from phrases used in a famous Su Shi lyric composed to this tune, subtitled "Scene from Summer." That *ci* opens: "Young swallows fly into the ornate mansion. Silent, without a soul—passing the day under the shade of the scholar tree, bathing afresh in the evening cool."

Huang ying'er, "Yellow Oriole"

Four variations. Also the title of a *sanqu* tune.

Huan xi sha, "Washing Creek Sands"

Tang *jiaofang* tune. Eight variations. Also known as *Nantang huan xi sha*, "Southern Tang Washing Creek Sands," and some twenty-seven other titles. Unusually among *ci* tune-patterns, *Huan xi sha* features lines having equal numbers of characters (six lines of seven characters each).

Huatang chun, "Spring in the Ornate Chamber"

Seven variations.

Huilanfang yin, "Song of Fragrant Orchids"

This tune-pattern originates with the Song lyricist Zhou Bangyan (*Cipu*).

Hu zhong tian, "Heaven in a Wine Gourd"

Also known as *Niannu jiao*, "Charms of Niannu."

Jiang cheng meihua yin, "River Town / Plum Blossoms Medley"

Eight variations. According to *Cipu*, the title derives from the Tang poet Li Bo's line, "In this river town during the Fifth Month, plum blossoms fall." This tune-pattern is a "medley" because it follows the tune-pattern of *Jiang cheng [zi]*, "River Town," for the first half of the *ci* and the tune-pattern of *Meihua yin*, "Song of Plum Blossoms," for the second half.

Jiang cheng zi, "Song of the River Town"

Six variations. Also known as *Jiang shen zi*, "Song of the River Immortal."

Jiang shen zi, "Song of the River Immortal"

Also known as *Jiang cheng zi*, "Song of the River Town."

Jian zi mulanhua, "Magnolia Blossoms: Shortened"

Three variations. As the title indicates, this is a shortened version of *Mulanhua*, "Magnolia Blossoms." "Jian zi" (literally, "subtracting characters") is a technical term indicating that the original tune-pattern has been shortened by taking out a number of vocalized characters. (This is in contrast to "tousheng" ["swallowing notes"] which would refer to a reduction in notes, so that the lines have been shortened in terms of melody.) In this case, the "jian zi" version has four characters instead of seven in the first and third lines of each stanza.

Jie san cheng, "Relieving Three Hangovers"
Sanqu tune in the "southern" style.

Jinlü qu, "Ballad of the Golden Threads"
This tune-title derives from the Tang woman poet Du Qiuniang's much anthologized poem by the same name. Also known as *He xinliang*, "Congratulating the Bridegroom."

Jiu quan zi, "Fountain of Wine"
Twenty-five variations.

Ku xiang si, "Bitter Longing"
Cipu lists only one lyric by Cheng He as the standard for this tune.

Langtao sha, "Waves Scour the Sands"
Tang *jiaofang* tune. Four variations.

Langtao sha man, "Waves Scour the Sands: Long Form"
Ci lü lists three variations of this tune-pattern; *Cipu* lists four.

Lin jiang xian, "Immortal by the River"
Tang *jiaofang* tune. Fifteen variations.

Liu shao qing, "Willow Twigs Green"
Twelve variations.

Liuzhi, "Willow Branch Verse"
Three variations. Also known as *Zhe yangliu*, "Breaking Off Willow Twigs"; *Yangliu zhi*, "Yang Willow Branches"; or, more simply, *Liu zhi*, "Willow Branch" (although this last title is also used for another tune-pattern as well). According to *Cipu*, this tune is first mentioned in the Tang poet Bo Juyi's lines: "Cease listening to ancient songs and weary tunes, / and listen instead to the new melodies of 'Yang Willow Branch.' "

Mai hua sheng, "Cries of the Flower-Vendors"
Also known as *Lang tao sha man*, "Song of Washing Creek Sands." This variant title is said to derive from a *ci* by Li Qingzhao (P.17).

Man jiang hong, "Red Fills the River"
Sixteen variations. This tune-pattern is most vividly associated with the Song dynasty general and martyr Yue Fei, as well as more generally with the style of "heroic abandon" in *ci* poetry. Yue Fei's martial *Man*

jiang hong, composed after the fall of northern China to invaders, was the model for Shen Shanbao's version (P.113.6).

Man ting fang, "Fragrance Fills the Courtyard"

Seven variations. Also known as *Jiangnan hao*, "Fine Is the Southland."

Man yuan hua, "Flowers Fill the Garden"

The name derives from the Song poet Qin Guan's title to his lyric.

Maoshan feng guren, "Encountering an Old Friend in Mao Mountain"

No variations.

Meifeng bi, "Azure-tipped Brows"

Also known as *Busuan zi*, "Song of Divination."

Meng Jiangnan, "Dreaming of the Southland"

Also known as *Yi Jiangnan*, "Longing for the Southland."

Mo shang hua, "Flowers by the Road"

From *Cipu*: "The people of Qiantang like to sing *Mo shang hua* and *Huanhuan qu*, ballads that recount the long-ago adventures of the kings of Yue and Wu." See *Zui Xi Shi*, below.

Mo yu'r, "Groping for Fish"

Thirteen variations.

Mulanhua, "Magnolia Blossoms"

Six variations. Originally known as *Yulou chun*, "Spring in the Mansion of Jade." Also referred to as *Mulanhua ling*, "Song of Magnolia Blossoms." *Jian zi Mulanhua* derives from this longer form.

Mulanhua man, "Magnolia Blossoms: Longer Form"

Seventeen variations.

Nan gezi, "Southern Song"

Eleven variations. *Cipu* cites *Tang sheng shi*: "*Nan gezi* was a drinking song popular at banquets during the Tang and was eventually set to a short song and dance."

Nan lou ling, "Song of the South Pavilion"

No variations.

Nantang huan xi sha, "Southern Tang Washing Creek Sands"

More commonly known as *Huan xi sha*, "Washing Creek Sands." The title implicitly refers to Li Yu, the tragic last ruler of the Southern Tang, who composed a famous lyric to the tune of *Huan xi sha*.

Nanxiang zi, "Song of the South Country"

Tang *jiaofang* tune. Nine variations.

Niannu jiao, "Charms of Niannu"

Thirteen variations. On its many variant names, see the entry for the tune-title *Dajiang dongqu*, above. Niannu, a famed courtesan of the Tang Tianbao reign, was especially renowned for her singing.

Pusa man, "Bodhisattva Barbarian" or "Bodhisattva Headdress"

Tang *jiaofang* tune. Nine variations. Also known as *Chongdie jin*, "Layer on Layer of Gold," and *Yi luo jin*, "A Basketful of Gold." The rather curious and often misinterpreted name of this tune-pattern refers to a style of coiffure worn by Central Asian dancers. "In the early Dazhong period [847–59], when the barbarian tribes came to pay tribute, their women wore headdresses of golden crowns perched loftily atop their hairbuns, and their bodies were draped in ornamental chains and tassels—they came to be known as the 'Bodhitsattva Barbarian' troops" (Su E, *Duyang zabian*, quoted in *Cipu*). "Ornamental chains and tassels" (*yingluo*) were usually seen adorning the necks of Buddhist statues, but they were also worn as decorative jewelry by non-Han tribes. The striking appearance of these tribute-payers from Central Asia subsequently inspired Tang entertainers to compose new tunes, such as *Pusa man*.

Qingping yue, "Clear and Even Music"

Tang *jiaofang* tune. Five variations. *Qing* and *ping* are two of the three melodies (*diao*) found in ancient musical notations.

Qingyuan, "Green Jade Goblet"

Seventeen variations.

Qinlou yue, "Moon over Qin Pavilion"

Also known as *Yi Qin e*, "Longing for Qin e." The tune and its title are said to derive from an early lyric attributed to Tang poet Li Bo. Qin E or Chang E is the young woman who fled to the moon and who now resides in the moon palace as a goddess, in splendid solitude.

Qinyuan chun, "Spring in the Garden of Qin"

According to *Ci lü*, this tune derives its name from the famed garden of Han dynasty princess Qinshui.

Qiubo mei, "Bewitching Glances"

Also known as *Yan'er mei*, "Seductive Eyes."

Qiu rui xiang, "Fragrant Flower Buds in Autumn"

Two variations.

Que qiao xian, "Immortals on the Magpie Bridge"

Eight variations. The Magpie Bridge is the annual trysting place for the immortal lovers (and heavenly stars) Herd Boy and Weaving Girl, associated with the Double Seventh festival (see P.5.1).

Ru meng ling, "As in a Dream"

Eight variations. According to *Cipu*, the tune was composed by the Later Tang emperor Zhuangzong (r. 923–34), and initially named *Yi xianzi*, "Remembering the Immortal's Figure," but was renamed "As in a Dream" when the original tune-title was deemed too vulgar. The title *Ru meng ling* supposedly derives from the refrain: "ru meng, ru meng" ("as in a dream, as in a dream") in the original lyric by Zhuangzong.

Ru yan fei, "Young Swallows in Flight"

Also known as *He xinlang*, "Congratulating the Bridegroom." See entry for that tune-title.

Ruyi niang, "A Maiden After One's Own Heart"

According to *Yue yuan*, cited in *Cipu*, *Ruyi niang* is an original tune composed by the Empress Wu Zetian (P.6); see also Guo Maoqian, *Yuefü shiji*, 80.1138. "Ruyi" is the second reign name (from 692) of Empress Wu.

Sai Guanyin, "Rivaling the Goddess Guanyin"

Sanqu tune. This tune is classed in the "southern" style.

Shang qing yuan, "Wronged Feelings"

No variations.

Shang xilou, "Ascending West Tower"

No variations.

Shaonian you, "Youthful Roving"

Fifteen variations.

Sheng sheng man, "Note After Note: Long Form"

Seventeen variations. Perhaps the most famous song-lyric composed to this tune is Li Qingzhao's version (see P.17.20).

Sheng zhazi, "Mountain Hawthorn"

Tang *jiaofang* tune. Seven variations.

Shiliuzi ling, "Song in Sixteen Characters"

Two variations.

Shouyang qu

Qu tune.

Shuang ye fei, "Drift of Frosted Leaves"
Seven variations.

Shuidiao getou, "Prelude to the Water Melody"
Nine variations. Also known as *Jiangnan hao*, "Fine Is the Southland." "Water Melody" (*shui diao*) is known as a court performance piece dating back to the Sui dynasty, though this tune-pattern may have nothing to do with the original *shui diao* melody.

Shuilong yin, "The Water Dragon's Chant"
Thirty-one variations. A melody from the southern region of Yue.

Sumu zhe, "Sumu Veil"
Tang *jiaofang* tune. Five variations. The "Sumu veil" was a special type of Central Asian costume worn by dancers while performing the *hunto* military dance. Since the vigorous dance involved much splashing of water, this particular dance costume (primarily the hat) had a protective veil and was furthermore coated in oil to shield the dancer from getting overly wet (see *Cipu*, "Tang sheng shi"). Also known as *Bin yun song ling*, "Cloud of Tousled Hair."

Su zhongqing, "Telling Innermost Feelings"
Tang *jiaofang* tune. Nine variations. According to *Baixiang cipu*, cited in *Cipu*, this tune was composed by Wen Tingyun, and alludes to a line from "Li sao," by Qu Yuan (see P.37).

Taichang yin, "The Master of Ceremonies"
Sanqu tune.

Tai cheng lu, "Tower Wall Road"
No variations.

Tan fang xun, "Searching for Her Traces"
Five variations. Also known by the variant name *Tan fangxin*, "Searching for News of Her."

Tangduo ling, "Tangduo Song"
Three variations. A melody from the Yue region in the southeast.

Tanpo huan xi sha, "Washing Creek Sands: Expanded Version"
Also known simply as *Huan xi sha*, "Washing Creek Sands." "Tanpo" is a technical term referring to the taking of a verse line from the original tune-pattern, then "breaking up" (*po*) the original line and "expanding" (*tan*) it into two shorter lines or a line plus some extra phrasing. In the case of the tune-pattern *Huan xi sha*, the third and

final line of each stanza is "expanded" into two lines, with three extra characters added to the end of the stanza.

Taoyuan yi guren, "In Peach Garden, Remembering Old Friends"
Two variations. Also known as *Zui Taoyuan*, "Drunk in Peach Garden," and *Yu meiren ying*, "Song of the Beautiful Lady Yu."

Ta suo xing, "Treading the Sedge"
Three variations.

Tianxianzi, "The Heavenly Immortal"
Tang *jiaofang* tune. Five variations.

Tiao xiao ling, "Song of Flirtation"
See *Gong zhong tiao xiao*; see also *Fenghuangtai shang yi chuixiao* and *Zhuan ying ci*.

Wang Jiangnan, "Gazing to the South"
Also known as *Yi Jiangnan*, "Longing for the Southland."

Wang Xiang ren, "Looking for the Xiang River Goddesses"
No variations. Yao and Shun were two sage-kings of antiquity. Yao gave his two daughters in marriage to Shun, and on Shun's death, they became the river goddesses of the Xiang.

Wu jiaqi, "Missing the Lucky [Wedding] Day"
According to *Ci lü*, this tune originates with a song-lyric by the Ming poet Yang Zhen.

Wuling chun, "Spring at Wuling"
Three variations.

Xiang jian huan, "Joy at Meeting"
Five variations. Also known as *Shang xilou*, "Ascending West Tower," and *Xilou zi*, "Song of West Tower," from phrases in Li Yu's lyric to this tune.

Xiang yue, "Xiang River Moon"
No variations.

Xian xian yin, "Music for Offerings to the Immortals"
Six variations. The title is sometimes introduced with the words *faqu*, "Buddhist composition."

Xiao chong shan, "Small Piled Mountains"
Six variations.

Xi fen chai, "Regret over the Parted Hairclasp"
No variations.

Xi huanghua man, "Cherishing the Yellow Blossoms: Long Form"
Three variations.

Xi jiang yue, "West River Moon"
Tang *jiaofang* tune. Eight variations.

Xing xiang, "Incense-Offering Song"
Nine variations.

Xi qunyao, "Attached to Her Skirt"
No variations.

Yan'er mei, "Seductive Eyes"
Three variations. Also known as *Qiubo mei*, "Bewitching Glances."

Ye jin men, "Calling on Golden Gates"
Tang *jiaofang* tune. Five variations.

Yi hu zhu, "A Bushel of Pearls"
Four variations. Legend has it that the Tang emperor Xuanzong granted a bushel of pearls to the Plum-Blossom Consort (see P.54a.1), who refused the gift and stated her reasons in a poem by that very title.

Yi Jiangnan, "Longing for the Southland"
Eight variations. Also known as *Meng Jiangnan*, "Dreaming of the Southland"; *Wang Jiangnan*, "Gazing to the South"; *Jiangnan hao*, "Fine Is the Southland"; and so forth. This tune-title is thematic; many of the lyrics written to this tune and its variant titles concern nostalgia for or celebration of the Southland (the region south of the Yangzi River).

Yijian mei, "A Sprig of Plum"
Ten variations.

Yiluo jin, "A Basketful of Gold"
Variant name of *Pusa man*, "Bodhisattva Barbarian."

Yi Qin e, "Longing for Qin e"
Fourteen variations. Also known as *Qinlou yue*, "Moon over Qin Pavilion."

Yi ye luo, "A Single Fallen Leaf"
This is an original tune composed by the Later Tang emperor Zhuangzong, and the title is taken from his opening lines, an allusion to the Han alchemical-philosophical book *Huainanzi*.

Yong yu le, "Joy of Eternal Union"
Eight variations.

Yuan wangsun, "Bitter over the Young Prince"
  Two variations. Also known as *Yi wangsun*, "Longing for the Young Prince."

Yue hua qing, "Clear Light of the Moon"
  Three variations.

Yufu ci, "A Fisherman's Song"
  No variations. Also known as *Yufu*, "The Fisherman."

Yu furong, "Jade Hibiscus"
  Sanqu tune-title. This tune is classed in the "southern" style.

Yu hudie, "Jade Butterflies"
  Eleven variations. The standard for the *xiao ling* (short lyric) version of this tune-pattern is based on Wen Tingyun. The longer version takes a *ci* by Liu Yong for its standard.

Yujie xing, "Imperial Avenue Procession"
  Eight variations. Also known as *Gu yan'er*, "Solitary Wild Goose." In this case, the "xing" character refers to "walk or procession" instead of the more frequent "song."

Yujing qiu, "Autumn in the Jade Capital"

Yulou chun, "Spring in the Mansion of Jade"
  Eight variations. Also known as *Mulanhua ling*, "Song of the Magnolia Blossoms."

Yu meiren, "The Beautiful Lady Yu"
  Nine variations. "The Beautiful Lady Yu" was the concubine of Xiang Yu, who reigned briefly as hegemon of Chu, 206–202 B.C.E., before being defeated by Liu Bang, the founding emperor of the Han.

Yu meiren ying, "Song of the Beautiful Lady Yu"
  Also known as *Taoyuan yi guren*, "In Peach Garden, Remembering Old Friends." "Ying" (shadow) is another term for song.

Yunü yao xian pei, "The Jade Maiden Shakes Her Transcendent Pendants"
  Three variations.

Yuzhong hua, "Flowers in the Rain"
  Fourteen variations.

Zhegui ling, "Song of Breaking Cassia Twigs"
  Sanqu tune. No variations.

Zhegu tian, "Partridge Sky"
  No variations.

Zhuan ying ci, "Song in Response"
Sometimes also known as *Tiao xiao ling*, "Song of Flirtation."

Zhu Yingtai, "Zhu Yingtai"
The star-crossed lovers Zhu Yingtai and Liang Shanbo, after tragic deaths, metamorphosed into butterflies in order to fly away together.

Zhu Yingtai jin, "A Song for Zhu Yingtai"
Nine variations. "Jin" is another term for "song."

Zhuying yao hong, "Candlelight Sways Red"
Four variations.

Zui chun feng, "Drunk in the Spring Wind"
Also known as *Zui hua ying*, "Drunk in the Flowers' Shade."

Zui hong zhuang, "Flushed Red with Wine"
No variations.

Zui hua yin, "Drunk in the Flowers' Shade"
Three variations. Also known as *Zui chun feng*, "Drunk in the Spring Wind."

Zui taoyuan, "Drunk in Peach Garden"
Also known as *Taoyuan yi guren*, "In Peach Garden, Remembering Old Friends."

Zui Xi Shi. "A Drunken Xi Shi"
Sanqu tune. Xi Shi is a legendary beauty. The King of Yue, Gou Jian, as part of his plan for avenging the defeat of his kingdom in 494 B.C.E. by the kingdom of Wu, sent the beautiful Xi Shi as a gift to the King of Wu, hoping to distract him from affairs of state. Yue succeeded in conquering Wu in 473 B.C.E.

Zuiweng cao, "Ballad of the Old Drunkard"
No variations.

Eileen Cheng-yin Chow

A Chronological Chart of Chinese History

The dynasties and governments in boldface are the major ones in Chinese history. The italicized city names are the dynastic or national capitals. These names, like other place-names in the chart, are modern names unless otherwise indicated.

B.C.E. Xia dynasty (unverified), 2205?–1766?

Shang dynasty, 1766?–1122? (last capital at *Yin*, in Hoenan)

1000 **Zhou** dynasty, 1122?–256
Western Zhou era, 1122?–771 (*Xian*, then called *Hao*)
Eastern Zhou era, 770–256 (*Luoyang*, then called *Luo*)
500 Spring and Autumn period, 722–481
Warring States period, 403–221

Qin dynasty, 221–207 (*Xi'an*, then called *Xian-yang*)

200 **Han** (or Former or Western Han) dynasty, 202 B.C.E.–9 C.E. (*Xian*, then called *Changan*)

C.E. Xin dynasty, 9–23 (usurpation of Wang Mang; *Chang'an*)

Latter Han (or Eastern Han) dynasty, 25–220 (*Luoyang*)

200 Three Kingdoms era, 220–80

NORTH	WEST	SOUTH[a]
Wei, 220–66 (*Luoyang*)	Shu Han, 221–63 (*Chengdu*)	Wu, 222–80 (*Nanjing*)

300 **Jin** (or Western Chin) dynasty, 266–316 (*Luoyang* to 311, then *Changan*)

Era of North-South Division, 316–589

SIXTEEN KINGDOMS, 301–439

Based in Shanxi and Shaanxi	*Based in Sichuan*	*Based in Gansu*
Han or Zhao, 304–29 (Xiongnu)	Cheng Han or Shu, 301–47 (Tibetan)	(Former) Liang, 313–76 (Chinese)
Later Zhao, 319–52 (Xiongnu)		Southern Liang, 397–414 (Xianbei)
	Based in Hobei	
(Former) Qin, 352–410 (Tibetan)	(Former) Yan, 348–70	Later Liang, 386–403 (Tibetan)
Later Qin, 384–417 (Tibetan)	Later Yan, 383–409 (Xianbei)	Western Liang, 400–421 (Chinese)
Xia, 407–31 (Xiongnu)	Southern Yan, 398–410 (Xianbei)	Northern Liang, 397–439 (Xiongnu)
Western Qin, 385–431 (Xianbei)	Northern Yan, 409–36 (Chinese)	

NORTHERN AND SOUTHERN DYNASTIES, 317–589

	Northern dynasties, 386–581	*Southern dynasties, 317–589*[a]
	(Northern) Wei, 386–534 (Toba)	Eastern Jin, 317–420 (*Nanjing*)
400	Eastern Wei, 534–50 (Toba)	(Liu) Song, 420–79 (*Nanjing*)
	Western Wei, 534–57 (*Luoyang*)	Southern Qi, 479–502 (*Nanjing*)
	Northern Qi, 550–77 (in northern Henan)	Liang, 502–57 (*Nanjing*)
	Northern Zhou, 557–81 (*Chang'an*)	Chen, 557–89 (*Nanjing*)

600 **Sui** dynasty, 581–618 (*Chang'an*)

Tang dynasty, 618–907 (*Chang'an*)

900 Five Dynasties era, 907–60

NORTH: FIVE DYNASTIES, 907–60	SOUTH: TEN KINGDOMS, 907–79	
Later Liang, 907–23 (*Kaifeng*)	(Former) Shu, 907–25 (in Sichuan)	Southern Tang or Qi, 937–75 (in Nanjing area)
Later Tang, 923–34 (*Luoyang*)	Later Shu, 934–65 (in Sichuan)	Wu-Yūe, 907–78 (in Zhejiang)
Later Jin, 936–47	Nanping or Jingnan, 907–63 (in Hubei)	Min, 907–46 (in Fujian)
Later Han, 947–51 (*Kaifeng*)	Chu, 927–56 (in Hunan)	Southern Han or Yūe, 907–71 (*Canton*)
Later Zhou, 951–60 (*Kaifeng*)	Wu, 902–37 (in Nanjing area)	Northern Han, 951–79 (actually in north, in Shanxi)

1000 **Northern Song** dynasty, 960–1127 (*Kaifeng*)
Northern Conquest dynasties, 916–1234
Liao dynasty, 916–1125 (Qitan; in Inner Mongolia)
1200 Jin dynasty, 1115–1234 (Jurchen; in Manchuria; *Beijing* from 1127)

Southern Song dynasty, 1127–1279 (*Hangzhou*)
Yuan dynasty, 1264–1368 (Mongol; *Beijing*)
1400 **Ming** dynasty, 1368–1644 (*Nanjing* to 1421, then *Beijing*)
Qing dynasty, 1644–1911 (Manchu; *Beijing*)
1900 Republic of China, 1912–49 on mainland, 1949– in Taiwan (*Beijing* to 1927, *Nanjing* to 1949, then *Taipei*)
People's Republic of China, 1949– (*Beijing*)

[a] The Wu dynasty and its successors, the five "Southern Dynasties" (317–589) are collectively known as the "Six Dynasties."

Based on Hucker, *China's Imperial Past*, pp. 434–35.

Notes

Introduction

1. Yang Lun, comp., *Du shi jingjuan* (Shanghai: Guji chubanshe, 1980), 5/230.

2. See Meng Haoran, "Liubie Wang shiyu Wei," QTS, 160/1639.

3. For a fuller account of *ci*, see Chang, *The Evolution of Chinese Tz'u Poetry*, and P. Yu, ed., *Voices of the Song Lyric in China.*

4. The privilege of biography over writings is especially clear in the case of Xie Daoyun. Virtually none of her work survives, but the story of her childhood poetic improvisation becomes a byword for female talent in general.

5. It may be helpful to explain here the conventions of marital status in traditional China. A man had one principal wife (*qi*)—typically chosen for him by his elders with an eye to maintaining or improving the fortunes of his family. Thereafter he might take one or more secondary wives (*qie*, or concubines), ostensibly to provide him male descendants, but generally for purposes of sexual enjoyment and companionship. Concubines did not typically have a claim on the family's finances, although any male children they bore were usually raised as the children of the master and his principal wife.

6. William Butler Yeats, *Four Plays for Dancers*; quoted in Z. Qian, *Orientalism and Modernism*, p. 4.

7. Two valuable studies of the poetics of allusion are Palumbo-Liu, *The Poetics of Appropriation*, and Allen, *In the Voice of Others*. For a broad survey, see Jullien, *La Valeur allusive.*

8. On these developments, see Chang, "A Guide to Ming-Ch'ing Anthologies." Widmer and Chang, *Writing Women in Late Imperial China*, contains several different perspectives on the question.

9. The study of Indian languages by Buddhist devotees caused Chinese writers to notice that their own language employed variations of tone and pitch to differentiate among homophones. Shen Yue (441–513) is usually cited as the first author to classify these variations into four tone-classes and to set down rules for their harmonious disposition in poetry.

P.1. Ban jieyu

1. The most thorough modern study of the poem's attribution was done by Lu Qinli in his "Han shi bielu" (1948). Lu examines the use of the fan image in early Chinese prose and poetry, and he shows that the fan does not become a symbol for abandonment until after the Han dynasty. He concludes that "Song of Resentment" was probably written by a high-class musician of the Cao-Wei court.

2. Although extracts of the "Rhapsody on Pounding Silk" survive in *Yiwen leiju* (85/1456), the earliest complete text is preserved in the *Guwen yuan* (in Sun Xingyan, comp., *Dainan'ge congshu*, 2/1b–3a), which is notorious for its misattributions.

P.2. Cai Yan

1. "Biography of the wife of Dong Si", in *Hou Han shu*, 84/2800–2806.

2. Guo Maoqian, *Yuefu shiji*, 59/860–65.

3. Zhu Xi, *Chuci houyu*, 3/12b–19b. In the twentieth century, the authorship of the three poems attributed to Cai Yan and their historical and artistic relations have been the subject of much scholarly debate. See especially Guo Moruo, ed., *'Hu jia shiba pai' taolunji*; and Frankel, "Cai Yan." For a pictorial version of the legend, see Rorex and Fong, *Eighteen Songs*.

4. On the influence of Cai Yan's "Eighteen Songs of a Nomad Flute" on later Chinese poetry and painting, see Levy, "Transforming Archetypes." For a discussion of Cai Yan's narrative poems, see Levy, *Chinese Narrative Poetry*, esp. chap. 3.

P.3. Zuo Fen

1. *Jin shu*, 31/957–62.

P.4. Bao Linghui

1. Zheng Guangyi, 191–92.

P.6. Wu Zetian

1. Twitchett and Fairbank, *Cambridge History of China*, 3: 244–45. One useful general work is Fitzgerald, *The Empress Wu*.

2. Twitchett and Fairbank, *Cambridge History of China*, 3: 245–332; see also Guisso, *Wu Tse-t'ien*, pp. 8–25.

3. Hu Wenkai, pp. 23–27.

P.10. Xue Tao

1. Modern editions of Xue's poems include Zhang Pengzhou, ed., *Xue Tao shijian*, and Chen Wenhua, ed., *Tang nüshiren ji san zhong*. Jeanne Larsen's English translation, *Brocade River Poems*, contains some three-fourths of the total corpus.

P.15. *Huarui* furen

1. See "Huarui furen gongci kaozheng," in Pu Jiangqing, *Pu Jiangqing wenlu*, pp. 47–101.

P.16. *Lady Wei*

1. Chen Tingzhuo, *Baiyuzhai cihua*, quoted in Zheng Guangyi, p. 722.
2. Hu Wenkai, p. 67.

P.18. *Zhu Shuzhen*

1. On the issues of authenticity surrounding Zhu's writings, see Huang Yanli, *Zhu Shuzhen ji qi zuopin*. On her dates, see Miao Yue, "Lun Zhu Shuzhen shenghuo niandai ji qi 'Duan chang ci,'" pp. 47–77, in Miao Yue and Ye Jiaying, *Cixue gujin tan*; and Pan Shoukang, *Zhu Shuzhen biezhan tanyuan*, pp. 1–10.

P.19. *Yan Rui*

1. Zhou Mi, *Qidong yeyu* 20/7.

P.20. *Empress Yang*

1. A reconstruction of Empress Yang's biography and her role in the development of court-sponsored art during the Southern Song may be found in H. Lee, "The Domain of Empress Yang."
2. *Song shi*, 243/8656.
3. This was combined by Mao Jin of the Ming dynasty with the poems of the Song emperor Weizong to form *Erjia gongci* (Palace lyrics of two poets). On Yang's collection and its history, see H. Lee, "The Domain of Empress Yang," pp. 77–78, as well as Hu Wenkai, pp. 61–63.

P.21. *Wang Qinghui*

1. Li E, *Song shi jishi*, 84/2019.
2. Zhou Mi, *Haoranzhai yatan*, 2/8b; Tao Zongyi, *Chuogeng lu*, 3/38.
3. Wen Tianxiang, *Wenshan xiansheng quanji*, 14/ 498–99; Zhou Mi, *Haoranzhai yatan*, 2/8b–9a; QSC, pp. 3305–6.
4. These farewell poems are in Li E, *Song shi jishi*, 84/2029–32.

P.22. *Yuan Entertainers*

1. These are role-types in drama: the first plays an emperor, the second a seductive or licentious woman, the third a scholar or young student.
2. Xia Tingzhi, *Qinglou ji*, pp. 82–88.
3. *Qinglou ji*, pp. 209–11. Since we know from other sources that "Com-

mander" Ding was married to a geisha, this title probably refers to his position among the clients of the Entertainment Quarter. Another source gives a variant form for the poetry quoted: "Green pines curling and weird—the python grows teeth."

4. *Qinglou ji*, pp. 98–99.

5. Tao Zongyi, *Chuogeng lu*, p. 271. The Min dialect was spoken in the area of Fujian in south China.

6. *Qinglou ji*, pp. 211–15. "Right of the River" refers to modern Jiangxi province. Guanghai is the area of modern Taishan district in Guangdong. Quan Ziren was a Mongol from the Turfan area of Xinjiang. He was demoted from the Censorate after accusing the powerful Wang Jia'nu of ten crimes and was banished to Ganzhou. During the rebellion of 1358, Chen Youliang attacked Ganzhou; surrounded and with no troops or supplies left after a four-month siege, Quan committed suicide.

P.23. *Guan Daosheng*

1. Chen Baozhen, "Guan Daosheng he tade *Zhushi tu*," pp. 51–52. See also Rossabi, "Kuan Tao-sheng."

2. Wu Qizhen, *Shuhua ji*, pp. 626–27.

3. Their marriage was late by standards of the time; evidence suggests that Zhao Mengfu had been married previously. Zhao Mengfu, "Weiguo furen Guanshi muzhiming," in *Songxuezhai ji*, "Waiji," p. 121a; Weng Tongwen, "Wang Meng wei Zhao Mengfu waisun kao."

4. J. Cahill, *Index of Early Chinese Painters*, pp. 293–95. For reproductions of Guan's bamboo paintings and a discussion of her artistic career, see Weidner et al., *Views from Jade Terrace*, pp. 66–70.

5. Zhao Mengfu, "Weiguo furen Guanshi muzhiming," in *Songxuezhai ji*, p. 120; "Zhao gong xingzhuang," p. 120.

6. Tang Shuyu, *Yutai huashi*, 2/130.

7. The painting on which "Xiuzhu fu" was inscribed, as recorded by Hu Jing et al. in *Shiqu baoji sanbian*, p. 3084, is now lost. This rhyme-prose should be attributed to Guan Daosheng because it is consistent with the style and content of her poetry even though it is attributed to her husband in his collected writings, *Songxuezhai ji*.

P.24. *Zheng Yunduan*

1. Zheng Guangyi, p. 1141.

P.25. Wu shi *nü*

1. Zheng Xi (courtesy name Tianqu) was a native of Wenzhou in present-day Zhejiang province, who passed the metropolitan civil service examination and served as vice prefect of Huangyan, also in Zhejiang.

2. It may be that the brief account of her life related by the Ming-dynasty literary scholar Wang Changhui in his anthology is based solely on poetic evidence, since even Wu's given name seems to have been lost to history. See Wang Changhui, *Shihua leibian*, 13/49b–51a.

P.27. Zhang Hongqiao

1. Hu Wenkai, p. 160; LCXZ, pp. 738–39.

P.28. Zhu Jing'an

1. For notes on the publication history of Zhu's work and excerpts from historical reports on her life and reputation, see Hu Wenkai, pp. 94–95.

P.29. Chen Deyi

1. Hu Wenkai, p. 168.

P.30. Meng Shuqing

1. Quoted in LCXZ, p. 741.

2. She made this remark when critiquing the Song dynasty poet Zhu Shuzhen (P.18, and see C.7). See Su Zhecong, p. 286.

P.31. Shen Qionglian

1. See Hu Wenkai, pp. 118–20, which transcribes a section from the Wuchang local gazetteer.

P.33. Zou Saizhen

1. For these titles, see Hucker, *Dictionary of Official Titles*, nos. 457, 3070, 4635.

2. MYSG, 26/5a–b; Hu Wenkai, pp. 189–90.

P.34. Wang Su'e

1. MYSG, 26/9b; Zheng Guangyi, pp. 1280–81.

P.35. Huang E

1. See the biography of Yang Shen by L. Carrington Goodrich and Chaoying Fang, in Goodrich and Fang, *Dictionary of Ming Biography*, pp. 1531–35, and the biography of Huang E by Hok-lam Chan, in ibid., pp. 667–69.

2. For a review of this period and these events in Chinese history, see James Geiss, "The Cheng-te Reign, 1506–1521" and "The Chia-ching Reign, 1522–1566," in Twitchett and Mote, *Cambridge History of China*, vol. 7, *The Ming Dynasty*, pp. 403–510.

3. The Qing period scholar Li Tiaoyuan (1734–1803) reported that at Xindu he once saw a letter written by Yang to Huang, but was unwilling to say that it was genuine. See Wang Wencai, *Yang Shen xuepu*, p. 522.

4. The *sanqu* genre, derived from the song lyrics of the Yuan drama, was prosodically more complex than Song dynasty *ci* lyrics and less elevated in tone than either regulated poetry or *ci*. (See Introduction and Appendix A.) As it developed into an independent poetic genre in Yuan and Ming times, it retained the liveliness of its theatrical origins while at its best also displaying the erudition and literary imagination of its writers. Writers who believe that Huang E wrote many or all of the *sanqu* attributed to her sometimes argue that, precisely because a certain racy style was permitted, she exploited the genre to express her feelings boldly. See for example Gao Meihua, "Yang Sheng'an fufu sanqu yanjiu," pp. 185–92. I am grateful to Professor Kang-i Sun Chang for drawing this study to my attention.

5. Brief recent studies of Yang and Huang are found in Liang Rongruo, *Zhongguo zuojia yu zuopin*, pp. 1–40. Liang accepts all the poems and provides an explanation for their tone. The translations here take as their base text *Yang Shen ciqu ji*, compiled and edited by Wang Wencai. Wang incorporates the critical edition of Yang's poetry prepared by Ren Ne (Ren Erbei), preface dated 1928. For Wang's view that, with very few exceptions, Huang Xiumei's poems are spurious, see Wang Wencai, *Yang Shen shi xuan*, pp. 175–76; *Yang Shen ciqu ji*, pp. 425–29.

P.36. Li Yuying

1. See Su Zhecong, p. 298–99; Zheng Guangyi, p. 1254; and Ann B. Waltner, "Writing Her Way Out of Trouble: Li Yuying in History and Fiction," in Widmer and Chang, *Writing Women in Late Imperial China*.

P.37. Wen shi

1. Xie Wuliang, 3: 2/22–30. Hu Wenkai, pp. 80–81, lists Wen's volume as "not seen"; it seems to have contained some three hundred pieces.

P.38. Wang Jiaoluan

1. MYSG, pp. 1457–65. The Suzhou court would have presided over Wujiang, where Zhou was then living.

P.41. Duan Shuqing

1. See Hu Wenkai, p. 190; Tan Jiading, *Zhongguo wenxuejia da cidian*, p. 1089; *Dangtu xian zhi, juan* 23; *Ming shi zong, juan* 86; *Ming ci zong, juan* 11; MYSG, *juan* 30.

P.42. Dong Shaoyu

1. Hu Wenkai, p. 186.

P.43. Hŏ Kyŏngbŏn

1. Hu Wenkai, pp. 165–66, 433–34.
2. "Famous Figures of the Past in Korea: The Poetess Ho Ran Sol Hon," *The People's Korea*, March 4, 1989, p. 7.
3. P. H. Lee, *Anthology of Korean Literature*, pp. 116–18. See also Xu Bingchang, "Chaoxian chao nü shiren yanjiu," pp. 81–95.

P.44. Yi Sugwŏn

1. See Xu Bingchiang, "Chaoxian chao nü shiren yanjiu," pp. 111–12.

P.45. Bo Shaojun

1. The facts in this biographical sketch are derived from information contained in Bo Shaojun's poems and in a long preface to Shen Cheng's collected works written by a close friend named Zhou Zhong. The preface is dated 1626 and can be found in *Mao Ruchu xiansheng pingxuan Jishan ji*, which presumably was published soon after that year. Bo Shaojun's "Daowang shi" is attached at the end of her husband's collected works. I have seen only a microfilm of this text, but it is identical with the text of the "Daowang shi" contained in the *Mingyuan shigui* (MYSG). For the sake of accessibility, the MYSG is referenced here.
2. In a colophon titled "Ti daowang shi" (On 'Mourning for the dead'), Zhang Sanguang, another friend who was involved in the editing of the couple's works, made these observations concerning the condition of Bo Shaojun's manuscript and the selection of the eighty-one quatrains that we have today. Zhang's colophon can be found in a somewhat fragmented microfilm of an early twentieth-century edition of the couple's collected works held at the University of Michigan Library.
3. This anthology of women's poetry is usually attributed to Zhong Xing (1574–1624), one of the leading theorists of the Jingling School of poetry in the late Ming, but it has been argued that Zhong Xing could not possibly have edited this important anthology. In any case, he could not have chosen Bo Shaojun's poems for inclusion, since he died a whole year before these elegies were even written. A brief and useful discussion of Zhong Xing and his literary theories can

be found in Nienhauser, *Indiana Companion to Traditional Chinese Literature*, pp. 369–70. The editorship of *Mingyuan shigui* has been discussed in *Siku quanshu zongmu tiyao*; see Hu Wenkai, p. 884.

P.46. *Xie Wuniang*

1. Hu Wenkai, pp. 204–5.

P.47. *Jing Pianpian*

1. Su Zhecong, p. 326; Zhang Gongchang, *Zhongguo de jinü yu wenxue*, p. 155.

P.48. *Xue Susu*

1. Tang Shuyu, *Yutai huashi*, p. 223. For examples of Xue's paintings, see Weidner et al., *Views from Jade Terrace*, pp. 82–88.

2. *Jingzhiju shihua*, cited in *Yutai huashi*, p. 222.

3. Hu Yinglin, *Jiayi shengyan*, quoted in *Yutai huashi*, p. 223.

4. Weidner et al., *Views from Jade Terrace*, pp. 84–85. Translation adapted from Lo, "Daughters."

5. Translation adapted from Ecke, "Hsüeh Wu," pp. 202–3.

6. Ecke, "Hsüeh Wu," p. 206. Li Rihua describes the plight of Xue Susu in her last years; see Bian Yongyu, *Shigu tang shuhua huikao*, 223: 60/26a–b.

7. Translation from Ecke, "Hsüeh Wu," p. 206.

P.50. *The "Four Talented Courtesans of Qinhuai"*

1. On Ma Shouzhen, see *Xiang lan zi ji*, reproduced in *Zhong xiang ci*; Hu Wenkai, pp. 152–53. On Zhao Caiji, see Hu Wenkai, pp. 191–92.

2. For examples of Ma's painting, see Weidner et al., *Views from Jade Terrace*, pp. 73–81.

P.51. *Hu Wenru*

1. Hu Wenkai, pp. 126–27. Originally supplied by the military for the use of unmarried officers, "official courtesans" by the Ming period were retained on the public payroll in order to keep members of the bureaucracy from seeking amusement in private brothels.

P.52. *Lu Qingzi*

1. Selections from Lu Qingzi's collections were included in the Ming anthology MYSG; the LR, edited in early Qing; and the early-Qing *Nüzhong qi caizi lanke er ji*, edited by Zhou Zhibiao (on which see C.41). Zhong Xing in MYSG, Wang Shilu in his biographical notes to *Ranzhi ji*, and Zhou Zhibiao give Lu's given name as Fuchang and her courtesy name as Qingzi. An elegy (*lei*) written

by Lu is preserved in Zhao Shijie's seventeenth-century *Gu jin nü shi* (see C.36), 1113b–14b. The principal sources for this biographical note are LCSJ, p. 751; Zhao Fanfu's preface to *Kaopan ji*, quoted in Hu Wenkai, pp. 169–70; and Pan Jiezhi, ed., *Ming shiren xiaozhuan gao*, p. 211.

2. Hu Wenkai, p. 170.

3. Zhang Dafu, seventeenth-century author of *chuanqi*, as quoted in Tan Jiading, ed., *Zhongguo wenxuejia da cidian*, p. 1212.

P.53. Xu Yuan

1. Xu Yuan often spoke in her poetry of her love, or at least intense appreciation, for other women, including courtesans, gentry women friends, and family members (see P.53.13 and P.53.16). Whether this implies a sexual attachment is debatable.

2. "Silk-reeler" (*luowei*) is one name for the cricket, whose chirring resembles the sounds of silk being wound onto wooden reels; it also suggests the indoor labor of women in the autumn and winter months. The details about Xu Yuan related here are taken from Hu Wenkai, pp. 142–43, and Zheng Guangyi, pp. 1306–9.

P.54. Shen Yixiu and Her Daughters

1. For Cao's preface, see Ye Shaoyun, *Wumengtang ji*, 2, first p. 1. And see Ko, *Teachers of the Inner Chambers*, p. 210.

2. Quoted in Hu Wenkai, p. 112.

3. For copies of Xiaoluan's paintings, see Weidner et al., *Views from Jade Terrace*, p. 137.

4. See Ko, *Teachers of the Inner Chambers*, pp. 166–69.

5. See Hu Wenkai, pp. 187–88.

6. Yagisawa Hajime, *Mingdai juzuojia yanjiu*, pp. 475–525.

P.55. Fang Weiyi

1. On Fang Yizhi, see Peterson, *Bitter Gourd*.

2. These works were entitled *Gonggui shishi, Gonggui wenshi*, and *Gonggui shiping* (History of poetry in palace and boudoir; History of prose writing in palace and boudoir; Poetry criticism from palace and boudoir). All are apparently lost; see Hu Wenkai, p. 81.

3. Mengshi returned the compliment, prefacing Weiyi's *Qingfen ge ji*; for the text of Mengshi's preface, see Hu Wenkai, p. 82.

4. On Fang Weiyi's life and works, see Hu Wenkai, pp. 81–83, and Zheng Guangyi, pp. 1357–63.

P.56. Yin Renrong

1. On Yin Renrong's life and works, see Hu Wenkai, p. 79; Su Zhecong, p. 325; and Zheng Guangyi, pp. 1295–96.

P.57. Xiang Lanzhen

1. Hu Wenkai (p. 175) states that Huang Maoxi was a native of Xiushui; Su Zhecong (p. 336) states that Huang was a native of Zuili.

2. Huang Shude's style name was Rouqing; she was the daughter of the scholar Huang Jiedi, the younger sister of Huang Chenghao, and the wife of the literatus Tu Yaosun. See Su Zhecong, p. 336; *Zhou Meicheng ji*, cited in Hu Wenkai, p. 176.

3. See Fang and Goodrich, eds., *Dictionary of Ming Biography*, pp. 534–44, on the members of the Xiang family.

4. Other criticism and biographical information relevant to Xiang Lanzhen are contained in *Zhong xiang ci* and *Gonggui shiji yiwen kaolue*. For extracts, see Hu Wenkai, pp. 175–76.

P.60. Gu Ruopu

1. Hu Wenkai, pp. 206–9; see also Ko, *Teachers of the Inner Chambers*, pp. 236–50.

P.61. Shang Jinglan

1. Zheng Guangyi, pp. 1341–42. On Shang Jinglan's literary career, see Ko, *Teachers of the Inner Chambers*, pp. 226–32.

2. On the activities of Shang Jinglan's husband, see Handlin-Smith, "Gardens in Ch'i Piao-chia's Social World."

3. Qi Biaojia was later canonized with the title *Zhongmin gong* (loyal and indefatigable).

4. Hu Wenkai, p. 936.

5. Hu Wenkai (pp. 155–56) records a Daoguang-period (1821–50) edition of *Jin nang ji*, appended to Qi Biaojia's complete works and followed by writings of other women from the Qi and allied families.

P.62. Wang Wei

1. Wang's works are catalogued in Hu Wenkai, pp. 87–90.

P.63. Ma Ruyu

1. On Ma Ruyu's writings, see Hu Wenkai, p. 158.

P.64. *Bian Sai*

1. The couplet, by Ye Xiang, is cited in Mao Bao's annotations to Chen Weisong, *Furen ji*, 36/2b. Chen Yuanyuan (1623–95), another southern courtesan, became the concubine of the general Wu Sangui. When she was taken prisoner by peasant rebels and held in Beijing, Wu (who had gone over to the Manchu side) is said to have besieged the city for her sake. As evidence of her renown, see Wu Weiye, "Song of Yuanyuan," in Xu Shichang, ed., *Wanqingyi shihui*, 20/577–78.

2. Wu Weiye, "Qin he ganjiu," *Wu Meicun shiji jianzhu*, p. 353.

3. Hu Wenkai, p. 30.

P.65. *Yang Wan*

1. This and the preceding quotation are taken from LCXZ, pp. 773–74.

P.66. *Xu Can*

1. Hu Wenkai, p. 481.

P.67. *Liu Shi*

1. On their relationship, see Chen Yinke, *Liu Rushi biezhuan*, and Chang, *The Late-Ming Poet Ch'en Tzu-lung*.

2. See Hu Wenkai, pp. 430–34, for the bibliography of Liu Shi's many publications. Examples of paintings by Liu Shi and a discussion of her work are included in Weidner et al., *Views from Jade Terrace*, pp. 99–102.

P.68. *Huang Yuanjie*

1. See Zheng Guangyi, pp. 1457–58.

2. On this date, see Hu Wenkai, p. 936.

3. On Huang's painting, see Yu Jianhua, ed., *Zhongguo meishujia renming cidian*, p. 1154.

P.69. *Wang Duanshu*

1. On her birth date, see Wang Duanshu, *Yinhong ji*, "Ying Ranzi xiaoxiang zan": "I was 30 at the beginning of 1651." See also Yu Jianhua, ed., *Zhongguo meishujia renming cidian*, p. 121.

2. The formulation is Dorothy Ko's, *Teachers of the Inner Chambers*, pp. 129–38.

3. Deng Hanyi, ed., *Shiguan chuji*, 12/37a–b. On Wang's social networks, see Ellen Widmer, "Ming Loyalists and the Woman's Voice in Fiction After 'Hong lou meng,'" in Widmer and Chang, eds., *Writing Women in Late Imperial China*, pp. 366–96.

4. The last date mentioned in the collection is 1651, and an edition of Zou Siyi's *Mingyuan shixuan* with preface dated 1655 already refers to Wang's collection.

5. A total of forty-seven members of the Qiu she or Autumn Society, a literary group with Ming loyalist sympathies, sponsored publication of *Yinhong ji*. See Wang Duanshu, *Yinhong ji*, prefaces (excerpted in Hu Wenkai, pp. 248–49). On Zeng Yi, see Yu Jianhua, ed., *Zhongguo meishujia renming cidian*, p. 1079.

6. Hanan, *The Invention of Li Yü*, p. 18.

7. Yu Jianhua, ed., *Zhongguo meishujia renming cidian*, p. 121.

P.70. *Ji Yinghuai*

1. Marked as "not seen" by Hu Wenkai, p. 439.

2. Entry on Ji Yingzhong in Tan Jiading, ed., *Zhongguo wenxuejia da cidian*, 2: 1279.

3. Shi Shuyi, *Qingdai guige shiren zheng lue*, 1/6a.

4. Wang Shizhen, *Yuyang shihua*, cited in GXCC, 1/12a–b.

P.71. *Li Yin*

1. MYSW says she is from Kuaiji (Shaoxing); Deng Hanyi, ed., *Shiguan chuji*, says Hangzhou.

2. See Huang Zongxi, "Li Yin zhuan," in *Nanlei wen'an*, zhuan zhang ji, 1/17a–18a. On Li's reputation in subsequent history, see Ellen Widmer, "Introduction," in Widmer and Chang, eds., *Writing Women in Late Imperial China*, pp. 5–6.

3. See Wang Qi, comp., *Chidu xinyu* [Modern letters] 3, supplement, p. 3a for evidence of a "painting friendship" with a gentry woman named Shen Hui.

4. Yu Jianhua, *Zhongguo meishujia renming cidian*, p. 356. For examples of her paintings, see Weidner et al., *Views from Jade Terrace*, pp. 102–5.

P.72. *Wu Qi*

1. Hu Wenkai, p. 897. See also Zou Siyi, *Shiyuan bamingjia xuan*, 2, preface.

2. Deng Hanyi, ed., *Shiguan chuji*, 12/1a.

P.73. *Wu Xiao*

1. See Yu Jianhua, *Zhongguo meishujia reming cidian*, p. 301.

2. On Feng Ban, see Ling Jingyan and Xie Boyang, eds. *Quan Qing sanqu*, 1/295; see also Tan Zhengbi, *Zhongguo nüxing de wenxue shenghuo*, pp. 325–27. On Yu Huai, see Zhang Huijian, *Ming Qing Jiangsu wenren nianbiao*, p. 741.

3. Sun Dianqi, *Fanshu ouji*, p. 503. Cf. Zhang Huijian, *Ming Qing Jiangsu wenren nianbiao*, p. 902.

P.74. *Wu Shan*

1. See Widmer, "The Epistolary World of Female Talent," pp. 11–12, and Ko, *Teachers of the Inner Chambers*, pp. 284–85.

2. XTLS, 5/3b.

3. Wei Xi, *Wei Shuzi wenji*, 3: 1163.

4. For poems by Wu Shan's daughter Bian Mengyu, see XTLS, 8/10b–12a.

5. XTLS, 5/3a.

6. Widmer, "The Epistolary World of Female Talent," pp. 11–12, 23.

7. XTLS, 5/5a.

8. Wei Xi, *Wei Shuzi wenji*, 3:1164.

P.75. Chai Jingyi and Her Daughter-in-Law Zhu Rouze

1. Shi Shuyi, *Qingdai guige shiren zheng lue*, p. 182.

2. On the Banana Garden Poetry Club, see P.66, P.77, P.78.

3. As cited in *Guochao huashi*, 16/12b. "Distant mountains" is a familiar description of the arc of a pair of beautiful eyebrows. On Chai's career as a painter, see Weidner et al., *Views from Jade Terrace*, pp. 108–9.

4. As cited in Shi Shuyi, *Qingdai guige shiren zheng lue*, pp. 129–30.

5. See *Qingdai guige shiren zheng lue*, p. 182. A slightly different version recounts that the five women poets were together in the same boat, dressed with the same elegant sobriety, and evoking the jealousy of all the other women (Zheng Guangyi, p. 1569).

6. This poem is cited in both *Qingdai guige shiren zheng lue*, p. 182, and *Guochao huashi*, 17/2b.

P.76. Wang Hui

1. Cited in Zheng Guangyi, p. 1577.

2. The source for this information is apparently the *Suzhou fu zhi*, repeated in Zheng Guangyi, p. 1577, as well as in Shi Shuyi, *Qingdai guige shiren zheng lue*, pp. 133–34.

P.77. Lin Yining

1. Principal sources for this biographical note are Hu Wenkai, pp. 396–97 and 542–43; and the biographical note in GGZSJ, 2: 4/1a. An early edition of Lin's *Mozhuang shichao, ciyu, wenchao* is held in the rare book collection of Beijing Library.

2. Among the original members of the Banana Garden Poetry Club were Gu Yurui, Chai Jingyi (P.75a), Zhu Rouze (P.75b), Qian Fenglun (P.78), and Lin Yining. Later Xu Can (P.66), Gu Qiji, and Feng Youling also joined. For a history of the club, see Ko, *Teachers of the Inner Chambers*, pp. 234–50.

3. For a discussion of how the heroine of this play became a romantic cult figure and how the three wives of Wu Wushan were influenced by her, see Zeitlin, "Shared Dreams."

4. Tan Zhengbi, *Zhongguo nüxing de wenxue shenghuo*, p. 360, mentions her authorship of this play but does not cite his source.

5. Hu Wenkai, pp. 542–43.

P.78. Qian Fenglun

1. The main sources for this biographical note are Hu Wenkai, pp. 756–58, which quotes Gu Ruopu's 1680 preface included in the 1702 edition of Qian's *Guxianglou ji*, and GGZSJ, 2: 4/6a. A selection of Qian's poems from her first published collection, *Sanhua tan ji*, was included in the anthology *Jiefang ji*. Qian's *ci* were selected separately in XTLS under the title *Guxiang lou ci*.

2. GGZSJ, 2: 4/6a.

P.79. Chen Susu

1. See Xu Fuming, *Yuan Ming Qing xiqu tansuo*, pp. 213–14; Zhang Huijian, *Ming Qing Jiangsu wenren nianbiao*, p. 924. See also Hu Wenkai, p. 588, and Zhuang Yifu, comp., *Gudian xiqu cunmu huikao*, p. 1175.

P.80. Gu Zhenli

1. Li Jia, *Zuo an cihua*, 2/11a–b, in Tang Guizhang, ed. *Cihua congbian*, 2: 3151. Li Wenyuan was the younger sister of the Vice Minister Li Zhiling. See also Hu Wenkai, p. 804.

2. *Lingfen guan cihua*, 2/11a–b, in Tang Guizhang, ed. *Cihua congbian*, 2: 1957.

3. Feng Jinbo, ed. *Ciyuan cui pian*, 9, in Tang Guizhang, ed. *Cihua congbian*, 2: 1957. See also *Zuo an cihua*, 2, in *Cihua congbian*, 2: 3151.

4. Zhong Xing, ed., *Mingyuan shihua*, 1/20b.

P.81. Wu Xun

1. See Ruan Yuan, comp., *Liangzhe youxuan lu*, 40/43b. The *Meili shiji*, in which these comments originally appeared, is no longer extant. A *Meili ciji* forms part of the *Shijing ge congshu* edited by Feng Dengfu, a classical scholar of the Jiaqing period (1796–1821).

2. Xu Yaoguang, ed., *Jiaxing fu zhi*, 79/2427.

3. Hu Wenkai, p. 311.

P.82. Hou Cheng'en

1. GGZSJ, 8/8a.

2. The title *Songyun xiao cao* echoes the "Li qi" (Ritual shaping) chapter of the *Records of Ritual*: "[The rites] are to man what the outer skin is to the bamboo or what the heartwood is to the pine or cypress. These two types of plants are the most excellent under heaven, for they pass through the four seasons and never

change their branches or drop their leaves. Thus does the sage observe the rites" (*Li ji*, in SSJZS, 23/1a).

3. Shen Shanbao, *Mingyuan shihua*, cited in GXCC, 8/12a. *Xiaoling* (see Introduction) recall the Tang-dynasty origins of the *ci* genre.

P.83. The Sisters Zhang Xueya and Zhang Xuedian

1. GXCC, 1/1a–b. Zhang Xueya is also recorded in Hu Wenkai, p. 528.
2. See Xuedian's record in Hu Wenkai, p. 529.

P.84. Xu Yingyu

1. Shen's preface to her poetry collection appears in Shen Dacheng, *Xuefuzhai ji*, 6/8a–8b. For details on the collection's publication history, see Hu Wenkai, p. 479.
2. For Wang's preface, see Wang Chang, *Chunrongtang ji*, 40/9a–b.
3. See *Jiaochuang zaji*, cited in GXCC, 2/11b. This work may have been the "jottings" of Li Zongchao, a Jiaxing scholar of the Qianlong period (1736–99) whose sobriquet was Jiaochuang (Banana Window).

P.85. Cai Wan

1. A brief biography of Cai is included in the entry for her father in Hummel, ed., *Eminent Chinese of the Ch'ing Period*, 2: 735.
2. Hu Wenkai, p. 731. Shen Deqian (cited in Su Zhecong, p. 405) notes that he was unable to obtain her poetry collection; one *juan* of it is included in GGSC, fascicle 2.

P.86. Ye Hongxiang

1. Hu Wenkai, p. 684.

P.87. He Shuangqing

1. See Grace Fong, "De/Constructing a Feminine Ideal in the Eighteenth Century: *Random Records of West-Green* and the Story of Shuangqing," in Widmer and Chang, eds., *Writing Women in Late Imperial China*, pp. 264–81.
2. The *Lankavatara Sutra* is a basic text of Chan (Zen) Buddhism, which emphasizes the emptiness or illusory nature of all phenomena.

P.88 Xu Yuanduan

1. Hu Wenkai, p. 470; Su Zhecong, pp. 426–27.

P.90. Xu Feiyun

1. See GXCC, 2/15a–b, and Hu Wenkai, pp. 561–62.

P.91. Xu Quan

1. Hu Wenkai, p. 570.

P.92. Chen Duansheng

1. Hu Wenkai, pp. 598–99. Chen's *tanci* has now earned a monograph in English; see Sung, *The Narrative Art of Tsai-sheng-yuan.*

P.93. Xi Peilan

1. Yuan Mei's female students numbered thirteen according to some sources, twenty-eight according to others. The edition of *Suiyuan nü dizi shixuan* prefaced by Wang Gu (1796; see C.46.1) contains selections by nineteen authors. For Yuan Mei's reputation as an iconoclast as the result of his accepting women as students, and some other aspects of Xi Peilan's life, see Lo, "Daughters of the Muses of China."

2. *Yutai xinyong*, edited by Xu Ling (507–83), ushered in a new era of elegant lyric expression. For Xi's comparison, see Xi Peilan, *Changzhen ge ji*, 4/2a.

3. Hu Wenkai, p. 469.

4. On the use of the term *xingling* by late-Qing critics of poetry and Yuan Mei in particular, see J. J. Y. Liu, *Chinese Theories of Literature*, p. 86. "Xing" by itself translates as "inborn nature," and "ling" as "spiritual powers": the compound thus stresses spontaneity of response that cannot be acquired by effort.

5. See Charles Hartman's translation of this poem in Liu and Lo, eds., *Sunflower Splendor*, pp. 175–84.

P.94. Jin Yi

1. Hu Wenkai, pp. 407, 433–34.

P.95. Dai Lanying

1. See *Suiyuan nü dizi shixuan*, 5/8a.

2. See "Ti zhifu Dai Lanying qiudeng kezi tu," in Yuan Mei, *Xiaocang shanfang shiji*, 36/7b–8a.

P.96. Qu Bingyun

1. Hu Wenkai, p. 392.

P.97. Gui Maoyi

1. See Yuan Mei, "Ti Gui Peishan nüshi lan gao miju tu," *Xiaocang shanfang shiji*, 36/25a–b, 37/3b–4a, 8b–9a.

P.98. Zhang Yuzhen

1. See Hu Wenkai, p. 510.

P.99. Shen Ke

1. Hu Wenkai, p. 364.

P.100. Wang Yuzhen

1. *Mingyuan shihua*, 3/27a. This comment is excerpted in GXCC, 10/11a. The entire text of "Ou yin" is printed in GGZSJ, 14/18b–19a.
2. *Lingfen guan cihua*, 2, in Tang Guizhang, ed., *Cihua congbian*, pp. 1527–28.

P.102. Ni Ruixuan

1. On Ni Ruixuan, see the headnote at QSBC, 31/21a, and Shi Shuyi, *Qingdai guige shiren zheng lue*, 2/21a. On Xu Qitai, see Li Huan, comp., *Guochao qixian leizheng*. Xu was a model magistrate who died—penniless—in office; local people held yearly services in his memory.

P.105. The Sisters Bao Zhilan, Bao Zhihui, and Bao Zhifen

1. For a partial family bibliography, see Hu Wenkai, pp. 602, 762, 852.

P.106. Wu Guichen

1. Su Zhecong, p. 438.

P.107. Jiang Renlan

1. See Hu Wenkai, p. 734.

P.108. Shen Xiangyun

1. Hu Wenkai, p. 368.

P.109. Wang Yun

1. Li Tiaoyuan (1734–1803) discusses *Fanhua meng* in his *Yucun shihua*.
2. On Wang's works and their publication history, see Hu Wenkai, pp. 245–46.

P.110. Shen Xiang

1. See Hu Wenkai, pp. 373, 851. On the Qingxi Poetry Recital Club generally, see Zhong Huiling, "Qingdai nüshiren yanjiu," pp. 143–50.

P.111. Jiang Zhu

1. See Hu Wenkai, p. 287.

P.112. *Yang Jiduan*

1. For the scant facts on Yang Jiduan's life, see Shi Shuyi, *Qingdai guige shiren zheng lue*, 6/20, and Hu Wenkai, p. 679.

P.113. *Shen Shanbao*

1. Recorded in Hu Wenkai, p. 301.

2. The preface to Xu Naichang's anthology appears as C.50.1. On Shen Shanbao's publications, see Hu Wenkai, pp. 366–68.

3. Yue Fei's *Man jiang hong* is entitled "Xie huai" (Writing my feelings), QSC, p. 1246; trans. Ebrey, *Chinese Civilization*, pp. 169–70.

P.114. *Sun Yunfeng*

1. See "Shang Suiyuan Xiansheng shu," in Yuan Mei, *Suiyuan xu tongren ji*, 4/7a–b.

2. See "Da Biwu furen," *Xiaocang shanfang shiji*, 32/9a–10b.

3. Ibid., 8a and 9a–b.

P.115. *Sun Yunhe*

1. See the remarks of the famous scholar-official and poet Wang Chang as cited in Shi Shuyi, *Qingdai guige shiren zheng lue*, p. 327, where he characterizes the verses of both sisters as belonging to the Southern Song style.

2. See ibid. for the statement by the mid-Qing scholar Jiang Baoling that Sun Yunhe died before reaching the age of thirty.

P.116. *Li Peijin*

1. See Hu Wenkai, p. 330.

P.117. *Zhao Wopei*

1. Chen Tingzhuo, *Baiyuzhai cihua*, p. 136.

P.118. *Liang Desheng*

1. Hu Wenkai, pp. 544–45.

P.119. *Wang Duan*

1. See Hummel, *Eminent Chinese of the Ch'ing Period*, pp. 839–40.

2. On this work, see Sun Kaidi, *Zhongguo tongsu xiaoshuo shumu*, pp. 216–17.

P.120. *Zhuang Panzhu*

1. See Hu Wenkai, pp. 555–56.

2. See Shi Shuyi, *Qingdai guige shiren zheng lue*, pp. 366–68.

P.121. *Gu Taiqing*

1. Suzuki Torao, *Shina bungaku kenkyū*, pp. 249–66. Suzuki's totals are as follows: 623 *shi*, of which 445 are found in the Shanghai, n.d., four-*juan* edition and 178 in Suzuki's edition; 354 *ci*, of which 212 are found in the Yangzhou, 1941, four-*juan* edition and 142 in Suzuki's edition.

2. On Gu's *Hong lou meng ying* (Shadows of the *Hong lou meng*), see Ellen Widmer, "Fiction and the Woman Writer in Qing China," in Widmer and Chang, eds., *Writing Women in Late Imperial China*, pp. 393–96, and Zhao Botao, " 'Hongloumeng ying' de zuozhe ji qita."

P.122. *Wu Zao*

1. See Liang Yizhen, *Qingdai funü wenxue shi*, pp. 174–77.

2. Tan Zhengbi, *Zhongguo nüxing de wenxue shenguo* and *Nüxing cihua*.

3. See for example Chen Wenshu, *Xiling guiyong, juan* 16; Liang Shaoren, *Liangban qiuyu'an suibi, juan* 2.

4. The text of this play is available in Zheng Zhenduo, comp., *Qingren zaju erji*.

5. Xie Qiuping, ed., *Wu Zao ci*, p. 4.

6. On Wu's bibliography, see also Hu Wenkai, p. 317.

7. Xie Qiuping, ed., *Wu Zao ci*, pp. 8–9. On the sense of the pairing of "fragrance" and "snow," see P.121.8.

P.124. *Zong Wan*

1. Hu Wenkai, p. 391.

P.125. *Qu Huixiang*

1. Hu Wenkai, p. 393.

C.2. *Song Ruoxin and Song Ruozhao*

1. "Shanggong" is the title of Head Matron of one of six major agencies among which palace women were distributed. The Shanggong generally supervised the other five services and directly controlled four subordinate offices: Record Office, Communications Office, Registration Office, Inner Gates Office.

C.4. *Zhu Shuzhen*

1. Wang Shizhen, whose *Chibei outan* is the only source for the present essay, noted that it occurs neither in the earlier Zhu Shuzhen's collected poetry nor in any anthologies of women's poetry. The "zhen" character of the two women's names is, in fact, written differently, but scholars have often confused the identities of the two women. Only in recent times has Hu Jingling clarified the fact that

there were two Zhu Shuzhens ("Dui gudai liangwei nü zuojia shenfen de zhiyi—'Zhu Shuzhen' yu 'Zhu Shuzhen,'" *Zhongyang ribao* [New York], Oct. 8, 1993).

C.6. Empress Xu

1. See *Ming shi*, 113/3505–8.

2. On the bibliographical career of Empress Xu's works, see Hu Wenkai, pp. 138–39, and also Soulliere, "Palace Women in the Ming Dynasty."

C.7. Meng Shuqing

1. See LCXZ, 2: 741.

C.8. Shen Yixiu

1. A punctuated version of *Wumengtang ji* has been included in the *Zhongguo wenxue zhenben congshu*, series 1, no. 49, ed. Hong Jiaqing. For more information on Ye Shaoyuan, see Goodrich and Fang, eds., *Dictionary of Ming Biography*, 2: 1576–79. On Shen Yixiu and her family, see Ko, *Teachers of the Inner Chambers*, pp. 187–218.

C.16. Luo Qilan

1. For an example of Luo's painting, see Weidner et al., *Views from Jade Terrace*, p. 140.

C.18. Guo Shuyu

1. Hu Wenkai, p. 574.

C.19. Wanyan Yun Zhu

1. Information on Wanyan Yun Zhu may be found in the following sources: Shi Shuyi, *Qingdai guige shiren zheng lue*, pp. 383–84 (7/5a–b); Xu Shichang, *Wanqingyi shihui*, 74: 186/14a–b; and Liang Yizhen, *Qingdai funü wenxue shi*, pp. 194–95. See also Hummel, *Eminent Chinese*, 1: 506–7, 2: 960–61.

C.20. Li Shuyi

1. The Tower of Scattered Shade is a name taken from the first two characters of a famous couplet on plum blossoms by Lin Bu (967–1028): "Scattered shade is cast slantingly over a clear and shallow brook; / A hidden fragrance floats at dusk in the moonlit air" (*Quan Song shi*, 106/1218).

C.23. Zhong Rong

1. For background discussion of the *Shi pin*, see Wixted, "The Nature of Evaluation in the *Shih-p'in*."

C.28. Wei Duanli

1. See Pan Shoukang, *Zhu Shuzhen biezhuan tanyuan*, p. 12. Pan's book is the best source for information on Zhu Shuzhen's biography and poetic corpus and offers the tentative life dates of 1063?–1106, based on internal evidence in Zhu's poetry and miscellaneous outside sources (see pp. 1–10).

C.30. Tian Yiheng

1. On Yang Shen and his wife, Huang E, see P.35.

C.33. Zhao Huanguang

1. Quoted in Hu Wenkai, p. 170.

C.36. Zhao Shijie

1. On the anthology's various printings, see Wang Chongmin, *Zhongguo shanbenshu tiyao*, pp. 453–54.

C.38. Ye Shaoyuan

1. This account is based primarily on the entry in Goodrich and Fang, eds., *Dictionary of Ming Biography*, 2: 1576–79.

C.42. You Tong

1. For a biographical sketch, see Hummel, *Eminent Chinese*, 2: 935–36.
2. See Xue Ruolin, *You Tong lun gao*, pp. 162–64; Goyama Kiwamu, "Min-Shi bunjin no okaruto no shumi"; Zeitlin, "Spirit Writing."

C.43. Wu Qi

1. See Hummel, *Eminent Chinese*, 2: 864–65.
2. On Huang Zhirou's writings, see Hu Wenkai, pp. 657–58.
3. Hu Wenkai, p. 898.

C.44. Lu Chang

1. Hu Wenkai, p. 916.

C.45. Yuan Mei

1. See Waley, *Yuan Mei*; Hummel, *Eminent Chinese*, 2: 955–57. On Jin Yi, see Waley, p. 180.

C.47. Zhang Xuecheng

1. On the controversy, see Hu Shi, *Zhang Shizhai xiansheng nianpu*, p. 129; also Chen Dongyuan, *Zhongguo funü shenghuo shi*, pp. 269–70.

2. I acknowledge with thanks the assistance of Yu-yin Cheng and Lynn Struve.

C.48. Qian Sanxi

1. Hu Wenkai, p. 919.

Bibliography

Abbreviations used in this Bibliography are listed on pp. xxiii–xxiv; those given here in brackets indicate that the work is so cited in notes in the text.

Allen, Joseph R. *In the Voice of Others: Chinese Music Bureau Poetry.* Ann Arbor, Mich.: Center for Chinese Studies, 1992.

Analects of Confucius (*Lun yu*), in SSJZS. For an English translation, see D. C. Lau. *Confucius.*

Bian Yongyu 卞永譽. *Shigu tang shuhua huikao* 式古堂書畫彙考. Taipei: Zhongzheng shuju, 1958.

Birrell, Anne, trans. *New Songs from a Jade Terrace: An Anthology of Early Chinese Love Poetry.* Harmondsworth: Penguin, 1986.

Bo Juyi 白居易. *Baixiangshan shiji* 白香山詩集. Taipei: Shijie shuju, 1963.

———. *Bo Juyi ji* 白居易集. Ed. Gu Xuejie 顧學頡. Beijing: Zhonghua shuju, 1979.

Bodde, Derk. *Festivals in Classical China.* Princeton, N.J.: Princeton University Press, 1975.

Book of Documents (*Shang shu*). In SSJZS. For an English translation, see Karlgren, *Book of Documents.*

Book of Odes, see *Mao shi.* For English translations, see Karlgren, *Book of Odes,* and Waley, *Book of Songs.*

Bray, Francesca. *Technology and Gender: Fabrics of Power in Late Traditional China.* Berkeley: University of California Press, 1997.

Bryant, Daniel. *Lyric Poets of the Southern T'ang: Feng Yen-ssu, 903–960, and Li Yü, 937–978.* Vancouver: University of British Columbia Press, 1982.

Cahill, James. *Fantastics and Eccentrics in Chinese Painting.* New York: The Asia Society, 1967.

———. *An Index of Early Chinese Painters and Paintings.* Berkeley: University of California Press, 1980.

Cahill, Suzanne E. *Transcendence and Divine Passion: The Queen Mother of the West in Medieval China.* Stanford, Calif.: Stanford University Press, 1993.

Cai Dianqi 蔡殿齊, ed. *Guochao guige shichao* 國朝閨閣詩鈔 [GGSC]. 1844.

Cao Xueqin 曹雪芹 (supplemented by Gao E 高鶚). *Hong lou meng* 紅樓夢. 3 vols. Beijing: Renmin wenxue chubanshe, 1982. For an English translation, see Hawkes and Minford, *Story of the Stone.*

Chang, Kang-i Sun. *The Evolution of Chinese Tz'u Poetry from Late T'ang to Northern Sung.* Princeton, N.J.: Princeton University Press, 1980.

———. "A Guide to Ming-Ch'ing Anthologies of Female Poetry and Their Selection Strategies." *Gest Library Journal* 5 (1992): 119–60.

———. *The Late-Ming Poet Ch'en Tzu-lung: Crises of Love and Loyalism.* New Haven, Conn.: Yale University Press, 1991.

———. "Symbolic and Allegorical Meanings in the *Yueh-fu pu-t'i* Poem Series." *Harvard Journal of Asiatic Studies* 46 (1986): 353–85.

Chen Baozhen 陳葆真. "Guan Daosheng he tade *Zhushi tu*" 管道昇和她的竹石圖. *National Palace Museum Quarterly* 11, 4 (1977): 51–85.

Chen Dongyuan 陳東原. *Zhongguo funü shenghuo shi* 中國婦女生活史. 1928. Reprint, Taipei: Shangwu, 1977.

Chen Susu 陳素素. *Erfen mingyue ji.* 二分明月集. In Zhu He, *Qinlou yue.*

Chen Tingzhuo 陳廷焯. *Baiyuzhai cihua* 白雨齋詞話. Beijing: Renmin wenxue chubanshe, 1957.

Chen Weisong 陳維崧. *Furen ji* 婦人集. 1645. Reprint, CSJC.

Chen Wenhua 陳文華, ed. *Tang nüshiren ji san zhong* 唐女詩人集三種. Shanghai: Guji, 1984.

Chen Wenshu 陳文述. *Xiling guiyong* 西泠閨詠. In Ding Bing, comp., *Wulin zhanggu congbian.*

Chen Xin 陳新 et al., eds. *Lidai funü shici xuan zhu* 歷代婦女詩詞選注 [Chen Xin]. Beijing: Zhongguo funü chubanshe, 1985.

Chen Yan 陳衍. *Yuan shi ji shi* 元詩紀事. Taipei: Commercial Press, 1968.

Chen Yinke 陳寅恪. *Liu Rushi biezhuan* 柳如是別傳. 3 vols. Shanghai: Guji chubanshe, 1980.

———. *Yuan Bai shijian zhenggao* 元白詩箋証稿. Shanghai: Guji chubanshe, 1978.

Chen Zhi 陳治, ed. *Zhongguo gudai shici diangu cidian* 中國古代詩詞典故辭典. Beijing: Yanshan chubanshe, 1991.

Cheng Boquan 成柏泉, ed. *Gudai wenyan duanpian xiaoshuo xuanzhu* 古代文言短篇小説選注. Shanghai: Guji chubanshe, 1984.

Chiang Chao-shen. "The Identity of Yang Mei-tzu and the Painting of Ma Yuan." *National Palace Museum Bulletin* 2, 2 (1967): 1–15, and 2, 3 (1967): 8–14.

———. [Jiang Zhaoshen 江兆申]. *Shuangxi duhua suibi* 雙溪讀畫隨筆. Taipei: Guoli gugong bowuyuan, 1977.

Chow Tse-tsung, ed. *Wen-lin: Studies in the Chinese Humanities.* Madison: University of Wisconsin Press, 1968.

Choy, Elsie. *Leaves of Prayer: The Life and Poetry of He Shuangqing, a Farmwife in Eighteenth-Century China.* Hong Kong: The Chinese University Press, 1993.

Chuci 楚辭 (Songs of Chu). For an English translation, see Hawkes, *Songs of the South.*

Chuci buzhu 楚辭補注. Comp. Liu Xiang 劉向 and Wang Yi 王逸. Annot. Hong Xingzu 洪興祖. [SBBY.] Hong Kong: Xianggang Zhonghua shuju, 1963.

Chuci jizhu 楚辭集注. Annot. Zhu Xi 朱熹. Zhenjiang: Jiangsu shuju, 1882.

Congshu jicheng 叢書集成 [CSJC]. Comp. Wang Yunwu 王雲五. Shanghai: Shangwu yinshuguan, 1936.

Cui Lingqin 崔令欽. *Jiaofang ji* 教坊記. In Zhang Tinghua, comp., *Xiangyan congshu.*

Dai Xieyuan 戴燮元, ed. *Jingjiang Baoshi sannüshi shichao heke* 京江鮑氏三女史詩鈔合刻. Jiahe, 1882.

Dangtu xian zhi 當塗縣志. 1750. Harvard-Yenching Library copy.

Dao de jing 道德經 (The book of the way and virtue), in [Laozi], *Laozi jiaogu* 老子校詁. For English translations, see Henricks, *Lao-tzu*, and Waley, *The Way and Its Power.*

Daoyuan 道原. *Jingde chuandeng lu* 景德傳燈錄. Kyoto: Chunbun shuppansha, 1976.

Davis, A. R. "The Double Ninth Festival in Chinese Poetry: A Study of Variations upon a Theme." In Chow, ed., *Wen-lin*, 45–65.

Deng Hanyi 鄧漢儀, ed. *Shiguan chuji* 詩觀初集. 1672.

DeWoskin, Kenneth J. *A Song for One or Two: Music and the Concept of Art in Early China.* Ann Arbor: Center for Chinese Studies, University of Michigan, 1982.

DeWoskin, Kenneth J., and J. I. Crump, trans. *In Search of the Supernatural: The Written Record, a Translation of the Sou-Shen Chi.* Stanford, Calif.: Stanford University Press, 1995.

Ding Bing 丁丙, comp., *Wulin zhanggu congbian* 武林掌故叢編. Qiantang, 1886.

Ebrey, Patricia Buckley, ed. *Chinese Civilization: A Sourcebook*, 2d ed. New York: Free Press, 1993.

Ecke, Tseng Yu-ho. "Hsüeh Wu and Her Orchids, in the Collection of the Honolulu Academy of Arts." *Arts Asiatiques* 2, 3 (1955): 197–208.

———. *Poetry on the Wind: The Art of Chinese Folding Fans from the Ming and Ch'ing Dynasties.* Honolulu: Honolulu Academy of Arts, 1981.

Elman, Benjamin A., and Alexander Woodside, eds. *Education and Society in Late Imperial China, 1600–1900.* Berkeley: University of California Press, 1994.

Fang Mengshi 方孟式. *Renlan'ge shiji* 紉蘭閣詩集. 1695.

Feng Menglong 馮夢龍. *Zhinang quanji* 智囊全集. Suzhou: Jiangsu guji chubanshe, 1986.

Feng Shihua 馮時化. *Jiu shi* 酒史. (CSJC.) Shanghai: Shangwu, 1936.

Fitzgerald, Charles Patrick. *The Empress Wu.* Melbourne: F. W. Cheshire/The Australian National University, 1955.

Franke, Herbert, ed. *Sung Biographies.* Wiesbaden: Franz Steiner Verlag, 1976.

Frankel, Hans H. "Cai Yan and the Poems Attributed to Her." *CLEAR (Chinese Literature: Essays, Articles, Reviews)* 5 (1983): 133–56.

Frodsham, J. D., trans. *The Poems of Li Ho (791–817).* Oxford: Clarendon Press, 1970.

Furth, Charlotte. *A Flourishing Yin: Gender in China's Medical History, 960–1670.* Berkeley: University of California Press, 1998.

Gan Bao 干寶. *Sou shen ji* 搜神記. Beijing: Zhonghua shuju, 1979.

Gao Meihua 高美化. "Yang Sheng'an fufu sanqu yanjiu" 揚升庵夫婦散曲研究. Master's thesis, National Cheng-chih University, Taiwan, 1981.

Ge Hong 葛洪. *Shen xian zhuan* 神仙傳. In SKQS.

Gernet, Jacques. *Daily Life in China on the Eve of the Mongol Invasion, 1250–1276.* Stanford, Calif.: Stanford University Press, 1970.

Gilmartin, Christina, Gail Hershatter, Lisa Rofel, and Tyrene White, eds. *Engendering China: Women, Culture, and the State.* Cambridge, Mass.: Harvard University Press, 1994.

Gipoulon, Catherine. *Pierres de l'oiseau Jingwei: Qiu Jin, femme et révolutionnaire en Chine au XIXième siècle.* Paris: Des femmes, 1976.

Goodrich, L. Carrington, and Chaoying Fang, eds. *Dictionary of Ming Biography.* New York: Columbia University Press, 1976.

Goyama Kiwamu 合山究. "Min-Shi bunjin no okaruto no shumi" 明清文人のオカルトの趣味. In Arai Ken 荒井健著, ed., *Chuka bunjin no seikatsu* 中國文人の生活, 492–500. Tokyo: Heibonsha, 1994.

Graham, A. C. *Poems of the Late T'ang.* Harmondsworth: Penguin Books, 1965.

Gu Chun 顧春. *Donghai yuge* 東海漁歌. Hangzhou: Xiling yinshe, 1913.

———. *Donghai yuge.* 6 juan. In *Tianyouge ji* 天遊閣集. Collection of Kyō-u sho-oku, Osaka.

———. *Donghai yuge*, juan 2. Reprinted in *Cixue jikan* 詞學季刊 1, 2 (1933): 152–66.

———. *Gu Taiqing shici* 顧太清詩詞. Changchun: Jilin wenshi chubanshe, 1989.

———. *Tianyouge shiji* 天遊閣詩集. Ed. Xu Naichang 徐乃昌. N.p., 1909.

Gu Ruopu 顧若璞. *Woyuexuan gao* 臥月軒稿. Reprinted in Ding Bing, comp. *Wulin wangzhe yizhu*. Qiantang: Dingshi Jiahuitang, 1899–1900.

Guisso, R. W. L. *Wu Tse-t'ien and the Politics of Legitimation in T'ang China*. Bellingham: Western Washington University Press, 1978.

Guo Changhai 郭長海 and Li Bingbin 李並彬. *Qiu Jin shiji yanjiu* 秋瑾事跡研究. Changchun: Dongbei shifan daxue chubanshe, 1987.

Guo Maoqian 郭茂倩, ed. *Yuefu shiji* 樂府詩集. Beijing: Zhonghua shuju, 1979.

Guo Moruo 郭沫若, ed. *"Hu jia shiba pai" taolunji* 胡笳十八拍討論集. Beijing: Zhonghua shuju, 1959.

Guo Shaoyu 郭紹虞 and Wang Wensheng 王文生, eds. *Zhongguo lidai wenlun xuan* 中國歷代文論選. 4 vols. Shanghai: Guji chubanshe, 1979.

Guo Yanli 郭延禮. *Qiu Jin yanjiu ziliao* 秋瑾研究資料. Jinan: Shandong jiaoyu chubanshe, 1987.

Guochao huashi 國朝畫史. Beijing: Zhonghua shuju, 1923.

Guoyu yinde 國語引得. Ed. Zhang Yiren 張以仁. Taipei: Academia Sinica, 1976.

Guwen yuan 古文苑. In Sun Xingyan, comp., *Dainan'ge congshu*.

Han Ying 韓嬰. *Han shi waizhuan* 韓詩外傳. [CSJC.] Taipei: Shangwu, 1965.

Hanan, Patrick. *The Invention of Li Yü*. Cambridge, Mass.: Harvard University Press, 1988.

Hanazaki Saien 花崎采琰. *Chūgoku no joshijin* 中國の女詩人. Tokyo: Heibonsha, 1986.

Handlin, Joanna F. "Lü K'un's New Audience: The Influence of Women's Literacy on Sixteenth-Century Thought." In Margery Wolf and Roxanne Witke, eds., *Women in Chinese Society*, 13–38. Stanford, Calif.: Stanford University Press, 1975.

Handlin-Smith, Joanna. *Action in Late Ming Thought: The Reorientation of Lü Kun and Other Scholar-Officials*. Berkeley: University of California Press, 1983.

———. "Gardens in Ch'i Piao-chia's Social World: Wealth and Values in Late Ming Kiangnan." *Journal of Asian Studies* 51 (1992): 55–81.

Han shu 漢書. Ban Gu 班固, comp. Beijing: Zhonghua shuju, 1962.

Hawkes, David, trans. *Ch'u Tz'u: The Songs of the South*. Oxford: Clarendon Press, 1959.

———, trans. *The Songs of the South: An Anthology of Ancient Chinese Poems by Qu Yuan and Other Poets*. Harmondsworth: Penguin, 1985.

Hawkes, David, and John Minford, trans. *The Story of the Stone*. 5 vols. Harmondsworth: Penguin, 1976–86.

Hay, John, ed. *Boundaries in China*. London: Reaktion Books, 1994.

Henricks, Robert G., trans. *Lao-tzu: Te-Tao Ching*. New York: Ballantine, 1989.

Hightower, James Robert. *Han Shih Wai Chuan: Han Ying's Illustrations of the Didactic Application of the Classic of Songs*. Cambridge, Mass.: Harvard University Press, 1952.

———. *The Poetry of T'ao Ch'ien*. Oxford: Clarendon Press, 1970.

Holzman, Donald. *Poetry and Politics: The Life and Works of Juan Chi*. Cambridge, Eng.: Cambridge University Press, 1976.

Hongmeige zhuren 紅梅閣主人 and Qinghuilou zhuren 清暉樓主人, eds. *Qingdai guixiu shichao* 清代閨秀詩鈔. Shanghai: Zhonghua xin jiaoyu she, 1922.

Hou Han shu 後漢書. Fan Ye 范曄, comp. Beijing: Zhonghua shuju, 1965.

Hu Jing 胡敬 et al. *Shiqu baoji sanbian* 石渠寶笈三編. Taipei: National Palace Museum, 1969.

Hu Jingling 胡晶玲. "Dui gudai liangwei nü zuojia shenfen de zhiyi—'Zhu Shuzhen' yu 'Zhu Shuzhen.'" 對古代兩位女作家身分的質疑——朱淑真與朱淑貞. *Zhongyang ribao* 中央日報 (New York), October 8, 1993.

Hu P'in-ch'ung. *Li Ch'ing-chao*. New York: Twayne, 1966.

Hu Shi 胡適. *Zhang Shizhai xiansheng nianpu* 章實齋先生年譜. Ed. Yao Mingda. Shanghai: Shangwu, 1931.

Hu Wenkai 胡文楷. *Zhongguo lidai funü zhuzuo kao* 中國歷代婦女著作考 [Hu Wenkai]. Shanghai: Guji, 1985.

Huainan zi 淮南子. (SBBY.)

Huang Shang 黃裳. *Qianchen mengying xinlu* 前塵夢影新錄. Jinan: Qilu chubanshe, 1989.

Huang Shizhong 黃世中. *Gudai shiren qinggan xintai yanjiu* 古代詩人情感心態研究. Wenzhou: Zhejiang daxue chubanshe, 1990.

Huang Yanli 黃嫣梨. *Zhu Shuzhen ji qi zuopin* 朱淑真及其作品. Hong Kong: Sanlian shuju, 1991.

Huang Zongxi 黃宗羲. *Mingru xue an* 明儒學案. Taipei: Shijie shuju, 1965. Partially translated by Julia Ching and Chao-ying Fang, as: Huang Tsung-hsi, *The Records of Ming Scholars*. Honolulu: University of Hawaii Press, 1987.

———. *Nanlei wen'an* 南雷文案. (SBCK.)

———. *Song Yuan xue'an* 宋元學案. (SBBY.)

Huangfu Mi 皇甫謐. *Gao shi zhuan* 高士傳. (SBBY.)

Hucker, Charles O. *China's Imperial Past*. Stanford, Calif.: Stanford University Press, 1975.

———. *A Dictionary of Official Titles in Imperial China*. Stanford, Calif.: Stanford University Press, 1985.

Hummel, Arthur W., ed. *Eminent Chinese of the Ch'ing Period.* 2 vols. Washington, D.C.: Government Printing Office, 1944.

Ji Yougong 計有功. *Tang shi jishi* 唐詩紀事. In Wang Yunwu 王雲五, ed., *Guoxue jiben congshu sibai zhong* 國學基本叢書四百種. Taipei: Shangwu, 1968.

Jiang Minfan 江民繁 and Wang Ruifang 王瑞芳, eds. *Zhongguo lidai cainü xiao zhuan* 中國歷代才女小傳. Zhejiang: Zhejiang wenji chubanshe, 1984.

Jiang Yihan 姜一函. "Zhaoshi yimen hezha yanjiu" 趙氏一門合札研究. *National Palace Museum Quarterly* 11 (1977): 23–50.

Jiang Zhaoshen, *see* Chiang Chao-shen

Jin shu 晉書. Fang Xuanling 房玄齡, comp. Beijing: Zhonghua shuju, 1979.

Jiu Tang shu 舊唐書. Liu Xu 劉昫, comp. Beijing: Zhonghua shuju, 1975.

Jullien, François. *La Valeur allusive.* Paris: Ecole Française d'Extrême-Orient, 1985.

Karlgren, Bernhard, trans. *The Book of Documents.* Stockholm: The Museum of Far Eastern Antiquities, 1950.

———, trans. *The Book of Odes.* Stockholm: The Museum of Far Eastern Antiquities, 1950.

Knechtges, David, trans. *Wen xuan, or Selections of Refined Literature.* 5 vols. Princeton, N.J.: Princeton University Press, 1982–96.

Ko, Dorothy. "Lady-Scholars at the Door: The Practice of Gender Relations in Eighteenth-Century Suzhou." In Hay, ed., *Boundaries in China,* 198–216.

———. *Teachers of the Inner Chambers: Women and Culture in China, 1573–1722.* Stanford, Calif.: Stanford University Press, 1994.

[Laozi]. *Laozi jiaogu* 老子校詁. Ed. and annot. Ma Xulun 馬敘倫. Beijing: Zhonghua shuju, 1974.

Larson, Jeanne, trans. *Brocade River Poems: Selected Works of the Tang Dynasty Courtesan Xue Tao.* Princeton, N.J.: Princeton University Press, 1987.

Lau, D. C., trans. *Confucius: The Analects.* Harmondsworth: Penguin, 1979.

———. *Mencius.* Harmondsworth: Penguin, 1970.

Lee, Hui-shu. "The Domain of Empress Yang (1162–1233): Art, Gender, and Politics at the Late Southern Song Court." Ph.D. diss., Yale University, 1994.

Lee, Peter H. *Anthology of Korean Literature.* Honolulu: University of Hawaii Press, 1990.

Levy, Dore J. *Chinese Narrative Poetry: The Late Han Through T'ang Dynasties.* Durham, N.C.: Duke University Press, 1988.

———. "Transforming Archetypes in Chinese Poetry and Painting: The Case of Ts'ai Yen (Lady Wen-chi)." *Asia Major* 6, 2 (1993): 147–68.

Li Bo 李白 [Li Bai]. *Li Bo quanji* 李白全集. Ed. Wang Qi 王琦. Beijing: Zhonghua shuju, 1977.

Li Chu-tsing et al. *The Chinese Scholar's Studio: Artistic Life in the Late Ming Period.* New York: The Asia Society, 1987.

Li E 李鶚, comp. *Song shi jishi* 宋詩紀事. Shanghai: Guji chubanshe, 1983.

Li Fang 李昉, comp. *Taiping guangji* 太平廣記. Beijing: Zhonghua shuju, 1961.

———. *Taiping yulan* 太平御覽. Beijing: Zhonghua shuju, 1963.

Li Gongzuo 李功佐. *Nanke ji* 南柯記. In Wu Zengqi, ed., *Jiu xiaoshuo.*

Li Heming 李鶴鳴. *Guixiu shi sanbai shou* 閨秀詩三百首. Wuhan: Changjiang, wenyi chubanshe, 1988.

Li Huan 李桓, comp. *Guochao qixian leizheng* 國朝耆獻類徵. Xiangyin, 1884–90.

Li Junzhi 李濬之, ed. *Qing huajia shishi* 清畫家詩史. 1930. Reprint, Beijing: Zhongguo shudian, 1990.

Li Qingzhao 李清照. *Li Qingzhao ji* 李清照集. Shanghai: Zhonghua shuju, 1962.

Li Shuhuan 李叔還. *Daojiao da cidian* 道教大辭典. Taipei: Juliu, 1979.

Li Tiaoyuan 李調元. *Yucun shihua* 雨村詩話. (CSJC.)

Li Yin 李因. *Zhuxiao xuan yin cao* 竹嘯軒吟草. 1643. Copy in Gest Library, Princeton University.

Liang Rongruo 梁容若. *Zhongguo zuojia yu zuopin* 中國作家與作品. Taizhong: Donghai daxue chubanshe, 1971.

Liang Shaoren 梁紹壬. *Liangban qiuyu'an suibi* 兩般秋雨盦隨筆. Shanghai: Saoye shanfang, 1914.

Liang Yizhen 梁乙真. *Qingdai funü wenxue shi* 清代婦女文學史. 1927. Reprint, Taipei: Zhonghua shuju, 1968.

Liezi 列子. Ed. Zhang Zhan 張湛. (SBBY.)

Li ji 禮記 (Book of Rites). In SSJZS.

Lin Dachun 林大椿, ed. *Tang Wudai ci* 唐五代詞. Beijing: Gudai wenxue kanxing she, 1957.

Lin Shuen-fu and Stephen Owen, eds. *The Vitality of the Lyric Voice: Shih Poetry from the Late Han to the T'ang.* Princeton, N.J.: Princeton University Press, 1986.

Ling Jingyan 凌景埏 and Xie Boyang 謝伯陽, eds. *Quan Qing sanqu* 全清散曲. Jinan: Qilu, 1985.

Liu, James J. Y. *The Art of Chinese Poetry.* Chicago: University of Chicago Press, 1962.

———. *Chinese Theories of Literature.* Chicago: University of Chicago Press, 1975.

———. *The Poetry of Li Shang-yin.* Chicago: University of Chicago Press, 1969.

Liu Jingshu 劉敬叔. *Yi yuan* 異苑. (SKQS.)

Liu Kai 柳開. *Lidai jinguo shici xuan* 歷代巾幗詩詞選. Hefei: Anhui wenyi chubanshe, 1986.

Liu Shi 柳是. *Hu shang cao* 湖上草. 1639.

Liu Shi 柳是 and Qian Qianyi 錢謙益, eds. *Liechao shiji: Runji* 列朝詩集閏集 [LR]. In LCSJ.

Liu Wu-chi and Irving Yucheng Lo, eds. *Sunflower Splendor: Three Thousand Years of Chinese Poetry.* New York: Doubleday Anchor, 1975.

Liu Xiang 劉向. *Gu lienü zhuan* 古列女傳. (SKQS.)

———, attr. *Lie xian zhuan* 列仙傳. (CSJC.)

———. *Shuo yuan* 說苑. Taipei: Shijie shuju, 1967.

Liu Xin 劉歆. *Xijing zaji* 西京雜記. (SBCK.)

Liu Yiqing 劉義慶. *Shishuo xinyu* 世說新語. Ed. Xu Zhen'e 徐震堮. Beijing: Zhonghua shuju, 1984.

———. *Youming lu* 幽明錄. Ed. Zheng Wanqing 鄭晚晴. Beijing: Wenhua yishu chubanshe, 1988.

Liu Yulai 劉玉來. *Qiu Jin shici zhushi* 秋瑾詩詞注釋. Yinchuan: Ningxia renmin chubanshe, 1983.

Liu Yunfen 劉雲份, comp. *Cuilou erji* 翠樓二集 [CLEJ]. Ed. Shi Zhicun 施蟄存. In *Zhongguo wenxue zhenben congshu*, series 1, no. 24. Shanghai: Beiye shanfang, 1936.

Lo, Irving Yucheng. "Daughters of the Muses of China." In Marsha Weidner et al., *Views from Jade Terrace*, 41–51.

Loewe, Michael, ed. *Early Chinese Texts: A Bibliographical Guide.* Berkeley, Calif.: Society for the Study of Early China, 1993.

Lu Chang 陸昶. *Lichao mingyuan shici* 歷朝名媛詩詞. 1773.

Lu Qinli 逯欽立. "Han shi bielu" 漢詩別錄 (1948). In *Han Wei Liuchao wenxue lunji* 漢魏六朝文學論集, 22–27. Xi'an: Shaanxi renmin chubanshe, 1984.

———, ed. *Tao Yuanming ji* 陶淵明集. Beijing: Zhonghua shuju, 1979.

———, ed. *Xian Qin Liang Han Jin Nanbeichao shi* 先秦兩漢晉南北朝詩. 3 vols. Beijing: Zhonghua shuju, 1982.

Lu Xun 魯迅, ed. *Tang Song chuanqi ji* 唐宋傳奇集. Hong Kong: Xiuyi chubanshe, 1967.

Lu You 陸游. *Ru Shu ji* 入蜀記. (SKQS.)

Lun yu 論語 (Analects of Confucius). In SSJZS.

Ma, Y. W., and Joseph S. M. Lau, eds. *Traditional Chinese Stories: Themes and Variations.* New York: Columbia University Press, 1978.

Mair, Victor, trans. *Wandering on the Way: Early Taoist Tales and Parables of Chuang Tzu.* New York: Bantam Books, 1994.

Mann, Susan. "The Education of Daughters in the Mid-Ch'ing Period." In Elman and Woodside, eds., *Education and Society in Late Imperial China*, 19–49.

———. "Grooming a Daughter for Marriage: Brides and Wives in the Mid-Ch'ing Period." In Watson and Ebrey, eds., *Marriage and Inequality in Chinese Society*, 204–30.

———. *Precious Records: Women in China's Long Eighteenth Century*. Stanford, Calif.: Stanford University Press, 1997.

———. "Women in the Life and Thought of Zhang Xuecheng." In Philip J. Ivanhoe, ed., *Chinese Language, Thought, and Culture: Nivison and His Critics*, 94–120. Chicago: Open Court Press, 1996.

Mao Jin 毛晉, ed. *Erjia gongci* 二家宮詞. In *Baibu congshu jicheng* 百部叢書集成. Taipei: Yiwen chubanshe, 1964–70.

Mao shi 毛詩 (The Book of Odes according to Master Mao). In SSJZS. For English translations, see Karlgren, *Book of Odes*, and Waley, *Book of Songs*.

Mather, Richard, trans. [Liu Yiqing] *Shih-shuo Hsin-yü: A New Account of Tales of the World*. Minneapolis: University of Minnesota Press, 1976.

Mathieu, Rémi. *Anthologie des mythes et légendes de la Chine ancienne*. Paris: Gallimard, 1989.

McCraw, David R. *Chinese Lyricists of the Seventeenth Century*. Honolulu, Hawaii: University of Hawaii Press, 1990.

Miao Yue 繆鉞 and Ye Jiaying 葉嘉瑩. *Cixue gujin tan* 詞學古今談. Taipei: Wanjuanlou, 1992.

Ming ci zong 明詞綜. Ed. Wang Chang 王昶. Taipei: Taiwan shangwu yinshuguan, 1968.

Ming shi 明史. Comp. Zhang Tingyu 張廷玉. Beijing: Zhonghua shuju, 1974.

Ming shi zong 明詩綜. Ed. Zhu Yizun 朱彝尊. (SKQS.) 2 vols. Reprint, Taipei: Shijie shuju, 1962.

Morohashi Tetsuji 諸橋轍次, chief ed. *Dai kanwa jiten* 大漢和辭典. 13 vols. Tokyo: Taishūan shoten, 1957–60.

Nan shi 南史. Beijing: Zhonghua shuju, 1975.

Nienhauser, William H., Jr., ed. *The Indiana Companion to Traditional Chinese Literature*. Bloomington: Indiana University Press, 1986.

Nivison, David S. *The Life and Thought of Chang Hsüeh-ch'eng (1738–1801)*. Stanford, Calif.: Stanford University Press, 1966.

Nylan, Michael, trans. *The Canon of Supreme Mystery*. Albany: State University of New York Press, 1993.

Owen, Stephen. *Readings in Chinese Literary Thought*. Cambridge, Mass.: Council on East Asian Studies, Harvard University, 1992.

Palumbo-Liu, David. *The Poetics of Appropriation: The Literary Theory and Practice of Huang Tingjian*. Stanford, Calif.: Stanford University Press, 1993.

Pan Jiezhi 潘介祉, ed. *Ming shiren xiaozhuan gao* 明詩人小傳稿. Taipei: Guoli tushuguan, 1986.

Pan Shoukang 潘壽康. *Zhu Shuzhen biezhuan tanyuan* 朱淑真別傳探源. Taipei: Heluo tushu chubanshe, 1980.

Peiwen yunfu 佩文韻府. Shanghai: Shangwu yinshu guan, 1937.

Peterson, Willard. *Bitter Gourd: Fang I-chih and the Impetus for Intellectual Change.* New Haven, Conn.: Yale University Press, 1979.

Plaks, Andrew. *The Four Masterworks of the Ming Novel: Ssu ta ch'i-shu.* Princeton, N.J.: Princeton University Press, 1987.

Powell, William F. *The Record of Tungshan.* Honolulu: The University of Hawaii Press, 1986.

Pu Jiangqing 浦江清. *Pu Jiangqing wenlu* 浦江清文錄. Beijing: Renmin wenxue chubanshe, 1989.

Qian Qianyi 錢謙益, chief ed. *Liechao shiji* 列朝詩集 [LCSJ]. 1652. Reprint, Shanghai: Guogang yinshua suo, 1910.

———. *Liechao shiji xiaozhuan* 列朝詩集小傳 [LCXZ]. 2 vols. Shanghai: Guji chubanshe, 1983.

Qian, Zhaoming. *Orientalism and Modernism: The Legacy of China in Pound and Williams.* Durham, N.C.: Duke University Press, 1995.

Qian Zhonglian 錢仲聯, ed. *Bao Canjun ji zhu* 鮑參軍集注. Shanghai: Guji chubanshe, 1980.

Qian Zhonglian 錢仲聯 and Fan Boqun 范伯群, eds. *Gudai aiqing shi jianshang ji* 古代愛情詩鑒賞集. Nanjing: Jiangsu jiaoyu chubanshe, 1989.

Qian Zhongshu 錢鍾書, ed. *Song shi xuanzhu* 宋詩選注. Hong Kong: Tiandi tushu youxian gongsi, 1990.

Qingdai guige shiren zheng lue, see Shi Shuyi.

Qingshi liezhuan 清史列傳. Shanghai: Zhonghua shuju, 1928.

Qiu Jin 秋瑾. *Qiu Jin ji* 秋瑾集. Zhonghua shuju, 1960.

Qiu Zhao'ao 仇兆鰲, ed. *Du shi xiangzhu* 杜詩詳註. Beijing: Zhonghua shuju, 1979.

Quan Song ci 全宋詞 [QSC]. Ed. Tang Guizhang 唐圭璋. Beijing: Zhonghua shuju, 1965.

Quan Tang shi 全唐詩 [QTS]. Peng Dingqiu 彭定求 et al., eds. Beijing: Zhonghua shuju, 1960.

Quan Tang wen 全唐文. Ed. Dong Gao 董誥. Shanghai: Guji chubanshe, 1990.

Quan Yuan sanqu 全元散曲. 2 vols. Ed. Sui Shusen 隨樹森. Beijing: Zhonghua shuju, 1964.

Radtke, Kurt W. "The Development of Chinese Versification: Studies on the *shih, tz'u,* and *ch'ü* Genres." *Oriens Extremus* 23 (1956): 1–37.

Rexroth, Kenneth, and Ling Chung, trans. *The Orchid Boat: Women Poets of China.* New York: McGraw-Hill, 1972.

Robertson, Maureen. "Voicing the Feminine: Constructions of the Gendered Subject." *Late Imperial China* 13 (1992): 63–110.

Rorex, Robert A., and Wen Fong. *Eighteen Songs of a Nomad Flute: The Story of Lady Wen Chi.* New York: Metropolitan Museum of Art, 1974.

Rossabi, Morris. "Kuan Tao-sheng: Woman Artist in Yuan China." *Bulletin of Sung and Yuan Studies* 21 (1989): 67–84.

Ruan Yuan 阮元, comp. *Liangzhe youxuan lu* 兩浙輶軒錄. Qiantang, 1801.

San guo zhi 三國志. Beijing: Zhonghua, 1975.

Schafer, Edward C. *The Divine Woman.* San Francisco: North Point Press, 1980.

———. *Pacing the Void: T'ang Approaches to the Stars.* Berkeley: University of California Press, 1977.

Shang shu 尚書 (The Book of Documents). In SSJZS. For English translation, see Karlgren, *Book of Documents.*

Shen Chu 沈俶. *Xie shi* 諧史. In Cao Rong 曹溶, ed., *Xuehai leibian* 學海類編. Shanghai: Hanfang lou, 1920.

Shen Dacheng 沈大成. *Xuefuzhai ji* 學福齋集. 1774.

Shen Deqian 沈德潛, ed. *Qingshi biecai ji* 清詩別裁集 [QSBC]. Beijing: Zhonghua shuju, 1975.

Shen Lidong 沈立東 and Ge Rutong 葛汝同, eds. *Lidai funü shici jianshang cidian* 歷代婦女詩詞鑒賞辭典. Beijing: Zhongguo funü chubanshe, 1992.

Shen Qingyai 沈青崖 and Wu Tingxi 吳廷錫, comps. *Xu Shaanxi tongzhi* 續陝西通志. Taipei: Huawen shuju, 1969.

Shen Shanbao 沈善寶. *Danjuxuan chugao xu* 澹菊軒初稿序. In Wang Xiuqin 王秀琴 and Hu Wenkai 胡文楷, eds., *Lidai mingyuan wenyuan jianbian* 歷代名媛文苑簡編. Shanghai: Shangwu, 1947.

———. *Mingyuan shihua* 名媛詩話. 1846. In *Qing shihua fangyi chubian* 清詩話訪佚初編. Taipei: Xinwen feng, 1987.

Shi Shuyi 施淑儀. *Qingdai guige shiren zheng lue* 清代閨閣詩人徵略. 1922. Reprint, Shanghai: Shanghai shudian, 1987.

Shi Zhenlin 史震林. *Xiqing sanji* 西青散記. Beijing: Zhongguo shudian, 1987.

Shih, Vincent Yu-chung, trans. *The Literary Mind and the Carving of Dragons.* Hong Kong: Chinese University Press, 1983.

Shi ji 史記 (Records of the Grand Historian), see Sima Qian.

Shi jing 詩經 (The Book of Odes), see *Mao shi.*

Shisan jing zhushu 十三經注疏 [SSJZS]. Ed. Ruan Yuan 阮元. Canton, 1815; reprint, Taiwan: Dahua, 1987.

Siku quanshu 四庫全書 [SKQS]. Reprinted as *Wenyuan ge Siku quanshu* 文淵閣四庫全書. Taipei: Shangwu, 1986.

Siku quanshu zongmu tiyao 四庫全書總目提要. Chief ed. Ji Yun 紀昀. Reprint, Taipei: Commercial Press, 1983.

Sima Qian 司馬遷. *Shi ji* 史記. Beijing: Zhonghua shuju, 1959.

Sirén, Osvald. *Chinese Painting: Leading Masters and Principles.* New York: Hacker Art Books, 1973.

Song shi 宋史. Beijing: Zhonghua shuju, 1979.

Song shu 宋書. Beijing: Zhonghua shuju, 1974.

Soothill, William Edward, and Lewis Hodous, eds. *A Dictionary of Chinese Buddhist Terms, with Sanskrit and English Equivalents and a Sanskrit-Pali Index.* London: Kegan Paul, 1937.

Soulliere, Ellen Felicia. "Palace Women in the Ming Dynasty, 1368–1644." Ph.D. diss., Princeton University, 1987.

Su Shi 蘇軾. *Su Dongpo quanji* 蘇東坡全集. Taipei: Heluo chubanshe, 1975.

———. *Su Shi shiji* 蘇東坡詩集. Beijing: Zhonghua shuju, 1982.

Su Zhecong 蘇者聰, ed. *Zhongguo lidai funü zuopin xuan* 中國歷代婦女作品選 [Su Zhecong]. Shanghai: Guji, 1987.

Sui shu 隋書. Wei Zheng 魏徵, comp. Beijing: Zhonghua shuju, 1973.

Sun Dianqi 孫殿起. *Fanshu ouji* 販書偶記. Shanghai: Guji, 1982.

Sun Kaidi 孫楷第, ed. *Zhongguo tongsu xiaoshuo shumu* 中國通俗小說書目. Beijing: Zuojia chubanshe, 1957.

Sun Xingyan 孫星衍, comp. *Dainan'ge congshu* 岱南閣叢書. Ca. 1796–1820.

Sun Yuanxiang 孫源湘. *Tianzhen ge ji* 天真閣集. 1829. (Printed with Xi Peilan, *Changzhen ge ji.*)

Sung, Marina H. *The Narrative Art of Tsai-sheng-yuan: A Feminist Vision in Traditional Chinese Society.* Taipei: Chinese Materials Center, 1994.

Suzuki Torao 鈴木虎雄. *Shina bungaku kenkyū* 支那文學研究. Kyoto: Kōbundō shohū 1925.

Tan Jiading 譚嘉定, ed. *Zhongguo wenxuejia da cidian* 中國文學家大辭典. 2 vols. Taipei: Shijie shuju, 1962.

Tan Zhengbi 譚正璧. *Nüxing cihua* 女性詞話. Hong Kong: Baixin tushuwenju, 1958.

———. *Zhongguo nüxing de wenxue shenghuo* 中國女性的文學生活. Shanghai: Guangming, 1935.

Tang Guizhang 唐圭璋. *Cixue luncong* 詞學論叢. Shanghai: Guji chubanshe, 1986.

———, ed. *Cihua congbian* 詞話叢編. Beijing: Zhonghua, 1986.

Tang Shuyu 湯漱玉. *Yutai huashi* 玉台畫史. In *Meishu congshu* 美術叢書. Taipei: Guangwen shuju, n.d.

Tang Xianzu 湯顯祖. *Mudan ting* 牡丹亭. Beijing: Renmin wenxue chubanshe, 1978.

———. *The Peony Pavilion.* Trans. Cyril Birch. Bloomington: Indiana University Press, 1980.

Tao Zongyi 陶宗儀. *Chuogeng lu* 輟耕錄. Beijing: Zhonghua shuju, 1958.

———, comp. *Shuo fu* 説郛. Shanghai: Commercial Press, 1921.

Twitchett, Denis, and John K. Fairbank, general eds. *The Cambridge History of China.* 15 vols. Cambridge: Cambridge University Press, 1978–.

Vanderstappen, Harrie A. "Late Ming Fans." *Honolulu Academy of Arts Journal* 2 (1977): 50.

Waley, Arthur, trans. *The Book of Songs.* New York: Grove Press, 1960.

———. *The Book of Songs.* Edited with additional translations by Joseph Allen. New York: Grove Press, 1996.

———. *Chinese Poems.* London: Allen and Unwin, 1961.

———. *The Poetry and Career of Li Po.* London: Allen and Unwin, 1950.

———. *The Way and Its Power.* London: Allen and Unwin, 1934.

———. *Yuan Mei, Eighteenth-Century Chinese Poet.* London: Allen and Unwin, 1957.

Wan Shu 萬樹. *Ci lü* 詞律. 1687. Reprinted, Shanghai: Shanghai guji chubanshe, 1984.

Wang Chang 王昶. *Chunrongtang ji* 春融堂集. 1808.

Wang Changhui 王昌會. *Shihua leibian* 詩話類編. Taipei: Guangwen, 1973.

Wang Chongmin 王重民. *Zhongguo shanbenshu tiyao* 中國善本書提要. Shanghai: Guji chubanshe, 1983.

Wang Duan 汪端. *Ziran haoxuezhai ji* 自然好學齋集. 1839.

———, comp. *Ming sanshi jia shixuan* 明三十家詩選. 1820.

Wang Duanshu 王端淑. *Yinhong ji* 吟紅集. Ca. 1655. Naikaku bunko copy.

———, ed. *Mingyuan shiwei* 名媛詩緯 [MYSW]. Yale University Library microfilm of 1667 edition.

Wang Qi 汪淇, comp. *Chidu xinyu* 尺牘新語. 2 vols. 1668. Reprint, Taipei: Guangwen, 1996.

Wang Shilu 王士祿. *Ranzhi ji* 然脂集. Preface dated 1672. Partial copy in the Shanghai Municipal Library.

Wang Shizhen 王士禎. *Chibei outan* 池北偶談. Beijing: Zhonghua shuju, 1982.

Wang Shunu 王書奴. *Zhongguo changji shi* 中國娼妓史. Shanghai: Shenghuo Shudian, 1935.

Wang Wencai 王文才. *Yang Shen ciqu ji* 揚慎詞曲集. Chengdu: Sichuan renmin chubanshe, 1984.

———. *Yang Shen shi xuan* 揚慎詩選. Chengdu: Sichuan renmin chubanshe, 1981.

———. *Yang Shen xuepu* 揚慎學譜. Shanghai: Guji chubanshe, 1988.

Wang Xiang 王相, annot. *Guige nü sishu jizhu* 閨閣女四書集注. 1624. Duowentang edition.

Wang Xuechu 王學初, annot. *Li Qingzhao ji jiaozhu* 李清照集校注. Beijing: Renmin wenxue chubanshe, 1979.

Wang Yiqing 王奕清, ed. *Qinding cipu* 欽定詞譜. 1715. Reprint, Taipei: for Wen Ruxian, 1964.

Wanyan Yun Zhu 完顏惲珠, ed. *Guochao guixiu zhengshi ji* 國朝閨秀正始集 [GGZSJ]. 1831.

———. *Guochao guixiu zhengshi xu ji* 國朝閨秀正始續集. 1836.

Watson, Burton. *Chinese Rhyme-Prose.* New York: Columbia University Press, 1971.

———. *The Tso Chuan: Selections from China's Oldest Narrative History.* New York: Columbia University Press, 1989.

Watson, Rubie, and Patricia Buckley Ebrey, eds. *Marriage and Inequality in Chinese Society.* Berkeley: University of California Press, 1991.

Wei Xi 魏禧. *Wei Shuzi wenji* 魏叔子文集. Taipei: Shangwu yinshuguan, 1973.

Weidner, Marsha, ed. *Flowering in the Shadows: Women in the History of Chinese and Japanese Painting.* Honolulu: University of Hawaii Press, 1990.

Weidner, Marsha, Ellen Johnston Laing, Irving Yucheng Lo, Christina Chu, and James Robinson. *Views from Jade Terrace: Chinese Women Artists, 1300–1912.* Indianapolis: Indianapolis Museum of Art; New York: Rizzoli, 1988.

Wen Tianxiang 文天祥. *Wenshan xiansheng quanji* 文山先生全集. (*Guoxue jiben congshu.*) Taipei: Shangwu yinshuguan, 1968.

Wen xuan 文選. Comp. Xiao Tong 蕭統. Beijing: Zhonghua shuju, 1986.

Weng Tongwen 翁同文. "Wang Meng wei Zhao Mengfu waisun kao" 王蒙為趙孟頫外孫考. *Dalu zazhi* 大陸雜志 26 (1963): 30–32.

Wenyuan yinghua 文苑英華. Taipei: Xinwenfeng chubanshe, 1979.

Widmer, Ellen. "The Epistolary World of Female Talent in Seventeenth-Century China." *Late Imperial China* 10 (1989): 1–43.

———. "Xiaoqing's Literary Legacy and the Place of the Woman Writer." *Late Imperial China* 13 (1992): 111–55.

Widmer, Ellen, and Kang-i Sun Chang, eds. *Writing Women in Late Imperial China.* Stanford, Calif.: Stanford University Press, 1997.

Wilhelm, Richard, and Cary F. Baynes, trans. *The I Ching or Book of Changes.* (Bollingen Series XIX.) Princeton, N.J.: Princeton University Press, 1967.

Wixted, John Timothy. "The Nature of Evaluation in the *Shih-p'in* (Gradings of Poets) by Chung Hung (A.D. 469–518)." In Susan Bush and Christian Murck, eds., *Theories of the Arts in China*, 225–64. Princeton, N.J.: Princeton University Press, 1982.

———. "The Poetry of Li Ch'ing-chao: A Woman Author and Women's Authorship." In P. Yu, ed., *Voices of the Song Lyric in China*, 145–68.

Wu Jun 吳均. *Xu Qi xieji* 續齊諧記. In SKQS.

Wu Qizhen 吳其真. *Shuhua ji* 書畫記. Shanghai: Shanghai renmin meishu chubanshe, 1963.

Wu Weiye 吳偉業. *Wu Meicun shiji jianzhu* 吳梅村詩集箋注. 1814. Reprint, Hongkong: Guangzhi, 1975.

Wu Zengqi 吳曾祺, ed. *Jiu xiaoshuo* 舊小說. Shanghai: Shangwu yinshuguan, 1957.

Xi Peilan 席佩蘭. *Changzhen ge ji* 長真閣集. 1829. (Printed with Sun Yuanxiang, *Tianzhen ge ji.*)

Xia Tingzhi 夏庭芝. *Qinglou ji* 青樓集. Beijing: Zhongguo xiju chubanshe, 1990.

Xiangyan congshu 香艷叢書. Ed. Chong tianzi 蟲天子. Shanghai: Guoxue fulun she, 1909–11.

Xianyu Huang 鮮于煌, ed. *Lidai mingyuan shici xuan* 歷代名媛詩詞選. Chongqing: Chongqing chubanshe, 1985.

Xie Qiuping 謝秋萍, ed. *Wu Zao ci* 吳藻詞. Shanghai: Wenli chubanshe, 1946.

Xie Wuliang 謝無量, ed. *Zhongguo funü wenxue shi* 中國婦女文學史 [Xie Wuliang]. 1916. Reprint, Zhongzhou: Guji chubanshe, 1992.

Xin Tang shu 新唐書. Beijing: Zhonghua, 1975.

Xing Wenfang 幸文房. *Tang caizi zhuan* 唐才子傳. Ed. Fu Xuancong 傅璇琮. Peking: Zhonghua shuju, 1987.

Xu Bingchang 徐丙嫦. "Chaoxian chao nü shiren yanjiu" 朝鮮朝女詩人研究. Ph.D. diss., National Taiwan Normal University, 1985.

Xu Fuming 徐扶明. *Yuan Ming Qing xiqu tansuo* 元明清戲曲探索. Hangzhou: Zhejiang guji chubanshe, 1986.

Xu Jian 徐堅, comp. *Chuxue ji* 初學記. Beijing: Zhonghua shuju, 1962.

Xu Ling 徐陵, comp. *Yutai xinyong* 玉臺新詠 [YTXY]. (SBCK.)

———, comp., and Wu Zhaoyi 吳兆宜, annot. *Yutai xinyong jianzhu* 玉臺新詠箋注. Beijing: Zhonghua shuju, 1985.

Xu Naichang 徐乃昌, ed. *Guixiu cichao* 閨秀詞鈔 [GXCC]. Nanking, 1909.

———. *Xiao tan luan shi huike guixiu ci* 小檀欒室彙刻閨秀詞 [XTLS]. 28 vols. Nanking, 1895–96.

Xu Shichang 徐世昌, ed. *Qing shi hui* 清詩匯. Taipei: Shijie shuju, 1982.

———. *Wanqingyi shihui* 晚晴簃詩匯. N.p.: Degeng tang, 1929.

Xu Shumin 徐樹敏 and Qian Yue 錢岳, eds. *Zhongxiang ci* 眾香詞. Shanghai: Dadong shuju, 1934.

Xu Yaoguang 許瑤光, ed. *Jiaxing fu zhi* 嘉興府志. (*Zhongguo fangzhi congshu* 中國方志叢書.) Taipei: Chengwen chubanshe, 1970.

Xu Zihua 徐自華. *Xu Zihua shiwen ji* 徐自華詩文集. Beijing: Zhonghua shuju, 1990.

Xue Ruolin 薛若鄰. *You Tong lun gao* 尤侗論稿. Beijing: Zhongguo xiju chubanshe, 1989.

Yagisawa Hajime 八木澤元. *Mingdai juzuojia yanjiu* 明代劇作家研究. Trans. Luo Jintang. Hong Kong: Longmen, 1966.

Yan Kejun 嚴可均, comp. *Quan shanggu sandai Qin Han Sanguo Liuchao wen* 全上古三代秦漢三國六朝文. Beijing: Zhonghua shuju, 1965.

Yang Bojun 楊伯峻, ed. *Liezi jishi* 列子集釋. Beijing: Zhonghua shuju, 1979.

Yang Lun 楊倫, comp. *Du shi jingquan* 杜詩鏡銓. Shanghai: Guji chubanshe, 1980.

Yang Meizi 楊妹子 (Empress Yang). *Yang taihou gongci* 楊太后宮詞. In Mao Jin, ed., *Erjia gongci*.

Yang Ruicong 楊睿聰, ed. *Mingren jueju xuan* 明人絕句選. Shantou: Tanru shushi, 1936.

Ye Gongchuo 葉恭綽, ed. *Quan Qing ci chao* 全清詞鈔. Taipei: Heluo tushu chubanshe, 1975.

Ye Shaoyuan 葉紹袁, ed. *Wumengtang quanji* 午夢堂全集. 2 vols. 1636. Reprinted as vol. 49 of *Zhongguo wenxue zhenben congshu* 中國文學珍本叢書, series 1. Shanghai: Beiye shanfang, 1935.

Yi Boyin 裔柏蔭. *Lidai nü shici xuan* 歷代女詩詞選 [Yi Boyin]. Taipei: Dangdai tushugongsi, 1971.

Yi jing 易經 (Book of Changes). In SSJZS. For an English translation, see Wilhelm and Baynes.

Yiwen leiju 藝文類聚. Ouyang Xun 歐陽詢, comp. Beijing: Zhonghua shuju, 1965.

Yu Huai 余懷. *Banqiao zaji* 板橋雜記. (CSJC.) Shanghai: Shangwu, 1936.

Yu Jianhua 俞劍華, ed. *Zhongguo meishujia renming cidian* 中國美術家人名詞典. Shanghai: Shanghai renmin meishu chubanshe, 1981.

Yu, Pauline. *The Poetry of Wang Wei.* Bloomington: Indiana University Press, 1980.

———, ed. *Voices of the Song Lyric in China.* Berkeley: University of California Press, 1993.

Yuan Hongdao 袁宏道. *Ping shi* 瓶史. (CSJC.) Shanghai: Shangwu, 1936.

Yuan Hua 袁華. *Gengxuezhai shiji* 耕學齋詩集. Taipei: Shangwu yinshuguan, 1972.

Yuan Mei 袁枚. *Suiyuan sanshiliuzhong* 隨園三十六種. Shanghai: Zhonghua tushuguan, 1913.

———. *Suiyuan nü dizi shixuan* 隨園女弟子詩選. In *Suiyuan sanshiliuzhong.*

———. *Suiyuan xu tongren ji* 隨園續同人集. In *Suiyuan sanshiliuzhong.*

———. *Xiaocang shanfang shiji* 小倉山房詩集. In *Suiyuan sanshiliuzhong.*

———. *Xiaocang shanfang xu wenji* 小倉山房續文集. In *Suiyuan sanshiliuzhong.*

Yuan Zhen 元稹. *Yuan shi changqing ji* 元氏長慶集. (SBCK.) Shanghai: Shangwu, 1928.

Zeitlin, Judith F. "Shared Dreams: The Story of the *Three Wives' Commentary on the Peony Pavilion.*" *HJAS* 54 (1994): 127–79.

———. "Spirit Writing and Performance in the Work of You Tong (1618–1704)." *T'oung Pao* 84 (1998): 101–35.

Zeng Zao 曾慥, comp. *Lei shuo* 類説. Shanghai: Guji chubanshe, 1993.

Zhang Gongchang 張弓長. *Zhongguo de jinü yu wenxue* 中國的妓女與文學. Taipei: Changchunshu shufang, 1975.

Zhang Huijian 張慧劍. *Ming Qing Jiangsu wenren nianbiao* 明清江蘇文人年表. Shanghai: Shanghai guji chubanshe, 1986.

Zhang Pengzhou 張篷舟, ed. *Xue Tao shijian* 薛濤詩箋. Chengdu: Sichuan renmin chubanshe, 1981.

Zhang Xuecheng 章學誠. *Wen shi tongyi* 文史通義. Hong Kong: Taiping shuju, 1964.

———. *Zhang shi yishu* 章氏遺書. N.p.: Jiayetang kan, 1922–23.

Zhao Botao 趙伯陶. "'Hongloumeng ying' de zuozhe ji qita" 紅樓夢影的作者及其他. *Hongloumeng xuekan* 41 (1989): 243–51.

Zhao Chongzuo 趙崇祚, comp. *Hua jian ji* 花間集. Taipei: Jinfeng chubanshe, 1987.

Zhao Mengfu 趙孟頫. *Songxuezhai ji* 松雪齋集. (SBCK.) Shanghai: Shangwu yinshuguan, n.d.

———. *Songxuezhai wenji* 松雪齋文集. (*Lidai huajia shiwenji* 歷代畫家詩文集.) Taipei: Xuesheng, 1970.

Zhao Shijie 趙世杰. *Lidai nüzi shiji* 歷代女子詩集. Taipei: Guangwen shuju, 1972.

Zheng Guangyi 鄭光儀, ed. *Zhongguo lidai cainü shige jianshang cidian* 中國歷代才女詩歌鑒賞辭典 [Zheng Guangyi]. Beijing: Zhongguo gongren chubanshe, 1991.

Zheng Yunduan 鄭允端. *Suyong ji* 肅雝集. In Sun Yuxiu 孫毓修, ed., *Hanfenlou miji* 涵芬樓秘笈. Shanghai: Shangwu yinshuguan, 1921.

Zheng Yunshan 鄭雲山. *Qiu Jin pingzhuan* 秋瑾評傳. Henan: Henan jiaoyu chubanshe, 1986.

Zheng Zhenduo 鄭振鐸, comp. *Qingren zaju erji* 清人雜劇二集. 1934. Reprint, Hong Kong: Longmen shudian, 1964.

Zhong Huiling 鍾慧玲. "Qingdai nüshiren yanjiu" 清代女詩人研究. Ph.D. diss., National Chengchi University, Taiwan, 1981.

Zhong Rong 鍾嶸. *Shipin* 詩品. Annot. Chen Yanjie 陳延傑. Taipei: Taiwan Kaiming shudian, 1958.

Zhong Xing 鍾惺, ed. [attr.]. *Mingyuan shigui* 名媛詩歸 [MYSG]. Ming Wanli period edition.

Zhongwen da cidian 中文大辭典. Yangmingshan, Taiwan: Zhongguo wenhua yanjiu suo, 1962–68.

Zhou Daorong 周道榮, Xu Zhixu 許之栩, and Huang Qizhen 黄奇珍, eds. *Zhongguo lidai nüzi shici xuan* 中國歷代女子詩詞選. Beijing: Xinhua shudian, 1983.

Zhou Ji 周濟. *Jiecun zhai lunci zazhu* 介存齋論詞雜著. Beijing: Renmin wenxue chubanshe, 1984.

Zhou Mi 周密. *Haoranzhai yatan* 浩然齋雅談. (*Juzhenban congshu* 聚珍板叢書.) Taipei: Yiwen yinshuguan, 1969.

———. *Qidong yeyu* 齊東野語. Shanghai: Shangwu, 1920.

Zhou Shouchang 周壽昌. *Gonggui wenxuan* 宮閨文選. Changsha, 1843.

Zhou Zhibiao 周之標. *Nüzhong qi caizi lanke ji* 女中七才子蘭咳集. Suzhou: Baohong tang, preface dated 1650.

Zhu He 朱䳥. *Qinlou yue* 秦樓月. Microfilm of original in *Guoli Beiping tushuguan shanben* series 國立北平圖書館善本, Beijing.

Zhu Xi 朱熹. *Chuci houyu* 楚詞後語. In Zhu Xi, *Chuci jizhu* 楚詞集注. Zhenjiang: Jiangsu shuju, 1882.

Zhuang Yifu 莊一拂, comp. *Gudian xiqu cunmu huikao* 古典戲曲存目彙考. 3 vols. Shanghai: Shanghai guji chubanshe, 1982.

Zhuangzi jishi 莊子集釋. Ed. Guo Qingfan 郭慶藩. Beijing: Zhonghua shuju, 1961.

Zhuo Chengyuan 卓承元, ed. *Zhongguo funü renming cidian* 中國婦女人名詞典. Shijiazhuang: Hebei kexue jishu chubanshe, 1991.

Zou Siyi 鄒斯漪, ed. *Shiyuan bamingjia xuan* 詩媛八名家選. Preface dated 1655. Original in Academy of Sciences Library, Beijing.

Zuo zhuan 左傳 (Zuo Commentary to the Spring-and-Autumn Annals). In SSJZS. For a partial translation, see B. Watson, *The Tso Chuan.*

Index of Names

NOTE: Page numbers for poets and/or critics appearing in **bold** type indicate the main sections containing their poetry and/or criticism.

Library of Congress Cataloging-in-Publication Data

Women writers of traditional china : an anthology of poetry and criticism / edited by Kang-i Sun Chang and Haun Saussy ; Charles Kwong, associate editor ; Anthony C. Yu and Yu-kung Kao, consulting editors.

p. cm.

Includes bibliographical references and index.

ISBN 0-8047-3230-2 (alk. paper). — ISBN 0-8047-3231-0 (pbk. : alk. paper)

1. Chinese poetry—Women authors—History and criticism. 2. Chinese poetry—Women authors—Translations into English. 3. Women and literature—China. I. Chang, Kang-i Sun, 1944- II. Saussy, Haun, 1960- . III. Kwong, Charles Yim-tze, 1958-

PL2278.W65 1999

895.1'10809287—dc21 99-19030

∞ This book is printed on acid-free, archival-quality paper.

Original printing 1999

Last figure below indicates year of this printing:

08 07 06 05 04 03 02 01 00 99

Typeset by Tseng Information Systems, Inc., in 10.5/14 Adobe Garamond.

Designed by Janet Wood.